HARDPRESS.NET
HOME OF HARD-TO-FIND BOOKS

A Foundation and Plain Instruction of the Saving Doctrine of Our Lord Jesus Christ
by Menno Simons

Address:
HardPress
8345 NW 66TH ST #2561
MIAMI FL 33166-2626
USA
Email: info@hardpress.net

A
FOUNDATION
AND
PLAIN INSTRUCTION
OF THE
Sabing Doctrine of Our Lord Jesus Christ,

BRIEFLY COMPILED FROM THE WORD OF GOD.

TRANSLATED FROM THE DUTCH LANGUAGE INTO THE GERMAN,

TOGETHER WITH OTHER

INSTRUCTIVE TREATISES, WRITTEN BY THE AUTHOR OF THIS 'FOUNDATION,' WHICH WERE FORMERLY PUBLISHED SEPARATELY, BUT HERE APPENDED, AND THE WHOLE ARRANGED AS A

COMMON MANUAL.

BY MENNO SIMON.

TO WHICH AN INDEX IS ADDED, IN ORDER THAT ALL THE POINTS, ARTICLES, PASSAGES, AND ADMONITIONS HEREIN CONTAINED, MAY BE READILY FOUND.

For other foundation can no man lay than that is laid, which is Jesus Christ. 1 Cor. iii. 11.

PRINTED IN EUROPE, A. D., 1565.

TRANSLATED INTO THE ENGLISH BY I. DANIEL RUPP,
Author of "Der Maertyr Geschichte," &c., &c.

PUBLISHED BY ELIAS BARR & CO,
No. 6 EAST KING STREET, LANCASTER, PA.
1863.

JOHN HERR'S PREFACE.

BELOVED READER: We live in a period of time, in which many writings are circulated among the people, which, generally are more injurious than beneficial, since the greater part contain not the pure and uncorrupted truth of the gospel, although it is the only rule, in accordance with which every thing should be regulated, written and taught, as St. Paul testifies: Though we, or an angel from heaven, preach any other gospel unto you than that which we have preached unto you, let him be accursed. (Gal. 1.) If its directions were followed, there would not be so many scorners of the christian religion; for, by the pious, virtuous, and godly life of its professors, they would be convinced, that something true and substantial is in its composition; as Paul teaches, that the gospel of Christ is the power of God unto salvation, to every one that believeth. (Rom. 1.) Yea, it is so powerful an operator in all those who truly believe, that their hard hearts become softened, renewed, and enlivened, so that, as they were formerly carnally minded, so they have now become spiritual and heavenly-minded; and as they have been proud, imperious, envious, and implacable against those, who may have aggrieved them, so they are now humble, mild, condescending, patient, peaceable, and forgiving towards their opponents, according to the example of their Lord and Saviour Jesus Christ, and the instructions of his word. But this salutary influence is to be found and perceived in so small a degree among the present christians, that the reverse is much more in vogue, from which circumstance, it, consequently, arises that atheism, the rejection of all revealed religion advances with such rapid strides. For, say its advocates, were the professors of christianity firm believers in the truth of scripture, they would conduct their lives according to its tenor, as Christ and his apostles have inculcated; but since this conformity is but seldom evinced, they conclude it to be the work of man, and a fabric of imposture, and exclaim: Our bonds are in twain and we are free, we will none of us go without his part of our voluptuousness, for this is our portion, &c. Such things do they imagine, and are deceived; for their own wickedness hath blinded them, so that the mysteries of God they know not; neither hope they for the wages of righteousness, nor discern a reward for blameless souls. (Wis. 2.) Oh! how deplorable that so many profess Christ with the lips, but yet by their works deny both him and his doctrine, whence, in the eyes of God, they are not better than the manifest scorner of his word, although comforting themselves, and being comforted by their unregenerated preachers with the belief that they are christians, because they have an outward profession.

The dark vapours of false and perverted doctrine, have so much obscured the clear light of the gospel, that oftimes, sincere souls scarcely know how to distinguish between right and wrong.   For this reason, I and my brethren, out of love to mankind, and particularly to serious minds, have been induced to publish, in the English language, in which they never before appeared, the works of the zealous and heaven-devoted Menno Simon.   And since I sincerely believe, and from the word of God acknowledge, that therein is contained the pure and unadulterated truth, according to the testimony of the Holy Scriptures; and as I myself, by the grace of God, have derived much benefit from the reading of this book, it is my hope, that to those who, in these confused times, when unbelief, universalism, the despising of God and his word, and the denial of our Lord, Jesus Christ, some by their lips and others by their conduct, is so extensively prevalent, impartially read and compare it with the word of God, it may be serviceable for their illumination and the advancement of their salvation.   Yea, dear reader, in the writings of this zealous and godly man, you will find how sincerely and fearlessly he exhibited to every one the powerful and undefiled truth.   He feared neither emperor nor king, neither high nor low, neither pope nor monks, neither life nor death.   He sought the glory of God, and he exerted himself to extricate poor mankind from the darkness of popery and deliver them from all false doctrine.   In zeal for God, and his rightful worship he was not inferior to Josiah, king of Judah.   (2 Kings, 23.)   With the sword of the spirit, which is the word of God, (Eph. 6,) he went forth, breaking down the strange altars, and overthrowing the inventions of papacy with which the ignorant people from time to time were burdened, and the errors, which Luther and other reformers overlooked, he laid aside, namely the human instituted baptism of infants with other erroneous usages.   Thus he again introduced and built up the true and apostolic service of God, so that a large people, as a pure and chaste virgin, were led to Christ, and many erring sheep were gathered together, which formerly were compelled to drink the impure water of false doctrine, which their shepherds defiled; and thus were founded many communities, in many places in Friesland, Holland, Groningen, East Friesland, Brabant, and on the border of the Baltic Sea, and likewise in Germany, in the Palatinate, in Alsace, Bavaria, Suabia, Switzerland, Austria, Moravia, &c.   The word of the Lord spread itself by his instrumentality, so powerfully, in defiance of all the tyranny and persecution of priests and governments, that it was evidently seen, how the strong hand of God, whom he glorified, rescued him from the power of his enemies.   For by a bloody decree issued in 1543, he was declared an outlaw, and a sum of money was offered for his body, at the same time, that it was forbidden under pain of death to harbor him.   Even criminals and murderers, as historians show, were promised the emperor's pardon, in case they would deliver him into prison; so that he was continually in danger of his life.   But he was not discouraged, on the contrary, he untiringly prosecuted the labors which God imposed upon him.   The hand of the Lord conducted him, until, at length, after long combatting, and great victory, he terminated his career at Fresenburg, and died the death of the blessed, January the 31st, in the year 1561, at the age of sixty-six years.   Beloved reader, in our author's writings, you will find, if impartial, with what simplicitly and energy he proclaimed the gospel, in its correct sense and scope ; how he defended Christ the crucified, and his saving doctrine, against false principles and perverted teachers, with whom he dealt sharply and keenly, and represented to them the dreadful judgments of God with which the scriptures threaten all deluding ministers, and which he well perceived would be their lot if they were not converted. Indeed, he might well say with the apostle, he knew none according to the flesh, "he reproved, threatened and exhorted," as Paul teaches, without respect to persons, he, sought not good will or honor among men, but instead his zeal in the Lord's. house was so strong and ardent that every thing besides was deemed of no importance ; he showed every one that there was no other way to happiness, than through self-knowledge and true self-denial and the acceptation of Christ through faith, together with his righteousness, which he merited for us, out of pure love, grace and mercy by his blood and death. He further taught, that whosoever believes this, and experiences this love and elevated grace, in his soul, will, through them be induced to imitate Christ in every thing, and to place himself with childlike obedience, under the guidance of his doctrine and commandments ; but, those, on the contrary, who are not obedient to him in all that he taught, and follow not daily after him, plainly evince, that they, likewise, are not partakers with him— with his cross and death, and have not in possession that righteousness, which is acceptable to God, or if they had received a portion, "they have again lost it by deviating from the holy commandment." Hence, he never flattered such with hopes of peace, nor comforted them with soft pillows ; but, with the force of scripture, spread before them, the eternal doom, and destruction of their miserable souls, so that, they might, possibly, reflect, and be converted ere it would be too late.

Further, it will easily be perceived by all those, into whose hands this book may fall, and who will read it with consideration, that the doctrine which I profess and teach, and that, of this godly reformer, entirely agree. He acknowledges Christ as the only foundation of our salvation ; so likewise do I. He confesses, that he who has thus found Christ, will follow him in all that he has commanded, (Matt. 28) will be of the same mind as he was, (Philip, 2, 1) he will love his enemies, do good to those that hate him, overcoming evil with good, and thus heap coals of fire on their heads. (Matt. 1 ; Rom. 12.) The same do I inculcate, as my writings plainly show. He teaches, that in the kingdom of Christ, and in his church, no other sword is used, than the sword of the spirit, and no other regulation, than the regulation of Christ and his apostles, and that this church can not be kept in a state of purity, without bringing to bear, upon all ungodly scorners, and perverse and apostate members, all apostolic excommunication ; and that, then it is necessary to avoid the intercourse, without respect to persons with them, so as to induce a feeling of shame and self reproach ; all of which he clearly points out in this work, and which I also confess. Menno exhorted all believers, with scripture testimony, to abjure all false doctrine, to refrain from hearing corrupt teachers, to shun them, and separate themselves from them, as Christ's doctrine sets forth, (Matt. 7 ; Jer. 23, 16 ;

John 10; Rom. 16, 17, 18; 1 Tim. 6, 1; 2 Tim. 3, 5; Tit. 3, 10; Rev. 2, 3.) This I also teach, and am fully persuaded, that where these instructions of Christ and his apostles are not heeded, but the faithful after being enlightened, and having perceived the great treachery of the faithless shepherds, yet, to please them, listen to them, there will not long be a communion in spirit, nor a unity of mind. For the leaven of misleading principles, will speedily insinuate itself, and confuse their minds; so that, one will believe one thing, and another something different; as the melancholy evidence of experience indicates amongst all sects. O how did the churches, in our author's time, who were taught and regenerated out of the word of God, and gathered from all sects by him unto one flock, so faithfully adhere to the word of God in this matter! They sacrifice fortune, body, and life, in preference to going into meeting, where the word of God was not proclaimed in its purity; for which reason, also, many thousands had to suffer the most dreadful torture, or were forced to go into miserable banishment.

These people were, by their persecutors, called anabaptists, because they considered no baptism apostolic, except its reception was grounded upon true faith, according to the injunctions of Christ and his apostles. Afterwards, they were named after Menno, as being his fellow believers, Menonites, which name they have ever since borne to the present time; but how far they have deviated, from time to time, from the doctrine of this zealous and godly reformer, their fruits plainly exhibit to every one.

It is, indeed, mournful to contemplate that, so great has been their degeneracy, as to make numbers, teachers not excepted, unwilling to assist in giving these his works to the world; but, at the same time, I am in hopes, that a great proportion are innocent, in this respect, and such are exempted from the charge; and, I have reason to believe that many are kept so much in darkness, that they are unacquainted with the writings of Menno, and imagine, that they are in entire agreement with what he taught, and consequently, they infer, that we have, as is frequently said, originated something new. But I have the pleasing confidence, that when they impartially read this work, which now makes its appearance both in English and German, and properly contemplate it in conjunction with scripture, and compare it with my writings, they will find that we insist on the same principles, and profess the same foundation of faith according to scripture. I must confess, however, that I feel myself far behind him, and, in my own eyes, cannot claim equality with him, since, although, exposed to the most terrifying persecutions, he, without the least concession, indefatigably pursued his vocation. This heavy trial I have never yet experienced, notwithstanding which I feel myself armed with the resolution, if God would allow such to be the case, to remain, with his help steadfast to the end: and this also, must be the mind of all christians. (1 Pet. 4, 1.)

If our author, occasionally, uses severe expressions against the unrighteousness of the world, the misleaders of the people, and blood thirsty priests and governments, it is no more than what Christ, the instructor of all, himself did, (Matt. 23; Luke 11) likewise the apostles: (Acts 8, 20 to 23; chap. 13, 10; Rom. 1; Gal. 1; 2 Pet. 2; James 1; 2 John 1; Rev. 21. 8; Rev. 22, 15; &c. So also did the prophets, and all faithful messengers of God, continually, represent his threatening judgment to the perverse and unregenerated, whence, they, likewise, were encessantly, more or less hated and persecuted by the world.

Oh! all ye, who profess to be peaceable christians, read this book carefully, in which you can perceive, with the direction of scriptures, what properly constitutes a true and pacific christian, and conduct your lives accordingly, showing, in truth, that you are lovers of peace. Take upon you the disposition of the dove, and the innocence of the lamb, and evidence that you are branches in the vine Jesus, and made partakers of his divine nature. Let every one read for himself: For all scripture given by inspiration of God, is profitable for doctrine, for reproof, for correction, for instruction in righteousness; that the man of God may be perfect, thoroughly furnished unto all good works. (2 Tim. 3, 16, 17.)

Let us not any longer, after the fashion of our indolent flesh, say: Yet a little sleep, a little folding of the hands to sleep, &c. (Prov. 24, 31) for the messenger is before our door, calling upon us to give an account of our stewardship. O it is dreadful to fall into the hands of the living God! he is a consuming fire to all who believe not, and whosoever has his name not written in the book of life, will be cast into the lake of fire and brimstone, which is the second death. Therefore, awake every one, and be converted to the Lord, learn of Christ, as the true prophet and teacher, accept his word and follow him, as Menno clearly inculcates, and your soul shall triumph over all that is sin, death, devil and hell, and shall reign with Christ forever and ever, Amen.

But should you despise, for unjust reasons, the doctrine herein set forth, take heed that the judgments of God fall not the more heavily upon you; for our author had, while yet living, many enemies and persecutors on account of what he taught, and so, also, did Christ and his apostles suffer for truth's sake. Yea, my God, work thou, with thy grace, in the hearts of those, who read this book, give them enlightened eyes, and open understandings to perceive thy holy will, and prepare them to do in every thing, as is pleasing in thy sight, in these perverted and confused times, for the glory and honor of thy ever praised name, Amen.

JOHN HERR,
Near Strasburg, Lancaster Co. Pa.

MARCH 25TH, 1835.

TO THE READER.

PIOUS, BELOVED READER: Since I perceive that our work, called, "THE FUNDAMENT OF CHRISTIAN DOCTRINE," which I published a few years ago, has been productive of much good, through the grace of God, to whom be eternal praise and thanks; and God's holy word which was obscured for such a long time, has been again a little explained, through our limited talents; and many well disposed children, requested and entreated me, to revise and correct such parts as were obscured through the negligence of the printer, and which deprived the reader of the sense; I was prevailed on, and did so. In some places I made additions; explained the obscure parts, and corrected those that were defective, and omitted all redundancies; the style, language and form I improved, in order to be better suited to aid the reader, to make known and acceptable, the rejected truth.

Not my reader, that I altered the first ground and contents; by no means! I have not altered, but as appears to me, improved its form, and confirmed it with more power and plainness. Those who fear God may judge. The former, as well as this, is God's word; and all what the first teaches, this teaches also. May the almighty, merciful Father grant his grace, to accompany our little work, that it may produce much fruit in many thousands, Amen.

MENNO SIMON.

NOTE. *The following Preface shows to whom this book is addressed, and was written at the time when the errors of Muntzer yet prevailed.*

PREFACE.

To those in authority and all others, of whatever condition, Menno Simon wishes them the illumination of the spirit, and the pure knowledge of the kingdom of God, of God our heavenly Father, and his son Jesus Christ our Lord, who has loved us and washed us from our sins with his blood. To him be praise, honor, glory, and thanksgiving to eternity, Amen.

Dear Sirs, Friends and Brethren, since we teach from the scriptures, and from experience find, that the prediction of the prophets, Christ and of the apostles, is in full power concerning oppression, misery, want, persecution, danger, anxiety and false doctrine, in this last time, (Matt. 24; Mark 13; Luke 21; 1 Tim. 4; 2 Tim. 3; 2 Pet. 2;

Jude 1.) and this so powerfully, that the gracious Father must shorten these days, otherwise none will be saved. Therefore, we poor miserable men entreat and admonish every one, and that through the mercy of the Lord, that he would for once candidly read our Ground and belief, lay it well to heart and understand it. that you might know what kind of doctrine we inculcate and what faith we maintain, what kind of life we lead, and how we are disposed, on account of which we have to suffer so much,—must endure imprisonment, exile, be robbed, derided, defamed and slain as innocent sheep. In order that you may cordially weep and lament over your former bloody deeds before God, and be more circumspect and watchful and may henceforth be found to be more pious, sincere; yea God-fearing magistracy, (Exod. 18, 23; Deut. 1, 17; 2 Chron. 19; Lev. 19) not to mortify and destroy, but be fathers and guardians of all miserable and wretched; not exterminate, but defend righteousness, not persecutors, but followers of Christ and his word. Therefore, anoint your eyes with eye salve that you may see and know which is the true way of truth and life. (Rev. 3; John 14.) The way which is so strait and is found of few. (Matt. 7.) The truth, which is known to none, but to those who are taught of the spirit of the Lord, illuminated and drawn by the Father. (John 16; Matt. 11.) The life which is to know God the Father as the only true God, and Jesus Christ whom he sent, (John 17,) that you may see him whom you pierced so outrageously, (Acts 1) and that you may with holy Paul fast and weep and humble yourselves before the Lord, (1 Cor. 15; Gal. 1; Eph. 3; Joel 2,) clothe yourselves in sack-cloth; rend your hearts and not your garments, that you may find grace in his sight. For he is long suffering, gracious and merciful and pardons the iniquity of all who sincerely repent and seek his grace, (Mic. 7.) Be no longer like Jeroboam, Ahab and Mannasseh, but like David, Hezekiah and Josiah; that you need not stand confounded in the great dread day of the Lord on account of your entrusted office—in that day which shall burn as an oven; and all who have used violence and did unrighteously upon the earth shall be burnt up as dry straw and stubble. (Mal. 4.)

Therefore, we most humbly entreat you for the sake of Christ's merits, that you would thoroughly ponder and reflect upon our faith, doctrine and undertaking; and not esteem us to be worse than you do thieves and murderers, whom you do not condemn without having perfect knowledge of their case. Our doings are not thievish, nor have we to do with possessions, but with God and his word, our bodies and souls, eternal life or eternal death. Therefore do not look upon the usages and customs of the fathers, nor upon the worldly wise and the learned, for it is hidden from them. (Matt. 11.) They were always those who from the beginning thrust from them the wisdom of God through their own wisdom and have trampled it under foot. For the wisdom of God, which we teach, is a wisdom which none knows, except they who are desirous of living and walking according to the will of God, (1 Cor. 1; John 7.) It is wisdom that is not to be brought from afar and to be taught in colleges. It must come from above and be learned through the Holy Ghost. (John 3.) As Paul says: (Rom. 10.) Say not in thine heart; who shall ascend into heaven? That is to bring Christ down from above: Or, who shall descend into the deep? That is to bring up Christ from the dead. But the word is nigh thee, even in thy mouth, and in thy heart. That is, the word of faith which we preach, namely: That if thou shalt confess with thy mouth the Lord Jesus, and shall believe in thine heart that God hath raised him from the dead, thou shalt be saved; therefore, look to God's word, to the testimony and example of the holy prophets, the Lord Jesus Christ and his apostles. Let these be your doctors, teachers, and not the ambitious feudal preachers of this world, then you will soon perceive, whether we are within or without the truth. May the almighty and eternal God give you such hearts and minds. To him be honor, praise and gratitude, the kingdom, power and majesty for ever, Amen.

Seeing then, beloved, that satan can transform himself into an angel of light, (2 Cor. 11,) and thus sow tares among the Lord's wheat (Matt. 3) such as the *sword*, polygamy, secular kingdom, and kings and the like errors on account of which the innocent have to suffer much; hence we are urged to publish this our faith and doctrine; and we desire for Jesus' sake that we might obtain so much grace, that they would not treat and judge us except according to the word of God as is reasonable and just. But should we not obtain so much grace, we have to commend it unto the Lord, who is the only helper of every one in need. We will, nevertheless, through the grace of God, abide in the word of the Lord; and comfort ourselves with the scriptures, which say: Thus saith the LORD that created thee, O Jacob, and he that formed thee: O Israel; fear not: for I have redeemed thee, I have called thee by my name; thou art mine. When thou passest through the waters, I will be with thee; and through the rivers, they shall not overflow thee; when thou walkest through the fire, thou shalt not be burned; neither shall the flame kindle upon thee; for I am the LORD thy God, the Holy one of Israel, thy Saviour. (Isa. 43.) Again: Fear ye not the reproach of men, neither be ye afraid of their revilings; for the moth shall eat them up like a garment and the worms shall eat them like wool—I, even I, am he that comforteth thee: who art thou that shouldst be afraid of a man that shall die, and the son of man which shall be made as grass? (Isa. 51.) Christ also says: Fear not them which kill the body, but are not able to kill the soul; but rather fear him which is able to destroy both soul and body in hell. Whosoever will confess him before men, him will he also confess before his heavenly Father; but whosoever denies him, him will he also deny before his heavenly Father. (Matt. 10; Luke 12.) With the heart, says Paul, we believe unto righteousness, but with the mouth we make confession unto salvation.

Since then the scriptures urge so much both as to believing and confessing, and comfort us so pleasantly against the raging and raving of men, therefore, do we desire to abide by the scriptures until death. And hereby testify before you in Christ Jesus, that we neither have, nor know of any other Ground, Faith or Doctrine, than what may be plainly read, heard or understood from the word of the Lord, Amen.

MENNO SIMON.

MENNO SIMON'S RENUNCIATION

CHURCH OF ROME.

MY READER—

I write to you the truth in Christ, and lie not. In the year 1524, being then in my twenty-eighth year, I undertook the duties of a priest in my father's village, called Penningum, in Friesland. Two others of similar age to myself, also officiated in the same station. The one was my pastor, and was well learned in part—the other succeeded me—both had read the scriptures partially; but I had not touched them during my life, for I feared, if I should read them, they would mislead me. Behold! such a stupid preacher I was, for nearly two years.

In the first year thereafter a thought occurred to me, as often as I handled the bread and wine in the mass, that they were not the flesh and blood of the Lord. I thought that it was the suggestion of the devil, that he might lead me off from my faith. I confessed it often—sighed and prayed, yet I could not be freed from this thought.

Those two aforementioned young men and myself spent our time daily in playing, drinking, and all manner of frivolous diversion, alas! as it is the fashion and way of such useless people: and when we were to treat a little of scripture, I could not speak a word with them without being scoffed at; for I did not know what I asserted—thus concealed was the word of God to my understanding.

At length I resolved that I would examine the New Testament attentively;—I had not proceeded far therein, ere I discovered that we were deceived. My conscience, which was troubled on account of the sacramental bread, aforementioned, soon obtained relief, without any human aid or advice; though

I was encouraged by Luther in the belief, that human authority cannot bind to eternal death.

Through the illumination and grace of the Lord, I continued daily to examine the scriptures, and was soon considered by some, though undeservedly, as being an Evangelical preacher. Every one sought my company—the world loved me and had my affections, yet it was said that I preached the word of God, and was a clever man.

Afterwards it happened, before I had been aware of the existence of brethren, that a pious, paitient man, named Sicke Snyder, was hanged at Leuewarden for having his baptism renewed. It sounded strange to me, to hear a second baptism spoken of. I examined the scriptures, and meditated on them assiduously and earnestly, but could find nothing in them concerning infant baptism. After I had discovered this, I conversed with my pastor on the subject; and after much discussion, we carried it so far that he had to confess, that infant baptism had no scriptural foundation. Notwithstanding all this, I dared not trust my own understanding, but consulted several ancient authors. They taught me that children were to be washed by baptism from their original sin. I compared this doctrine with the scriptures and found that it made baptism take the place of the blood of Christ.

Afterwards, desiring to know the grounds for infant baptism, I went and consulted Luther. He taught me that children were to be baptized on account of their own faith. 1 perceived that this also was not in accordance with the word of God.

Next I consulted Bucer. He taught that infants were to be baptized—that their baptism would cause those, who had their training, to be more careful in bringing them up in the way of the Lord. I perceived that this doctrine, too, was without foundation.

I then consulted Bulliger. He directed me to the covenant and circumcision. This I found incapable of being substantiated by scripture.

Having thus observed that authors varied greatly among themselves, each following his own opinion, I became convinced that we were deceived in relation to infant baptism.

Shortly after, I went to the village in which I was born, called Witmarsum. Covetousness and a desire to obtain a great name, were the inducements which led me to that place. There I spoke much concerning the scriptures without spirituality or love, even as all hypocrites do. I made disciples of my own stamp, such as vain boasters and light-minded persons, who, alas! like myself, took but little of scriptural instruction to heart. And though I was able now to understand much of the scriptures, yet I wasted that knowledge, through the lusts of my youth, in an impure, sensual, unprofitable life. I sought nothing but gain, ease, favor of men, splendor, reputation and honor, even as they all generally do, who embark in the same course of life.

Thus, my reader, I obtained the knowledge of baptism and the Lord's supper, through the illumination of the Holy Ghost, —through much reading of the scriptures, and meditating upon them, and through the gracious favor and gift of God, but not by means of the service of misleading sects, as it is reported of me. I hope that I write the truth and do not seek vain glory; though some, doubtless, may have contributed to my assistance in the pursuit of truth, yet will I, for this, render thanks to the Lord forever.

Meanwhile it happened before I had resided there one year, that some had almost broke in upon us with baptism, but whence the first beginners were, or where they resided, or who they properly were, is unknown to me; neither have I ever seen them.

Afterwards the sect of Munster made inroads, by whom many pious hearts in our quarter, were led into error. My soul was much troubled, for I perceived, that though they were zealous, they erred in doctrine. I exerted my feeble efforts, as far as I was able, in oppposing them by preaching and exhortations. I conferred twice with one of their leaders, once in private, and again in public; but my admonitions availed nothing, because I did that myself which I well knew was not right.

The report spread far abroad, that I could silence these persons. All looked to me. I saw that I was the leader in this combat—the surety of the impenitent—all depended upon me. This pained my heart; I sighed and prayed: Lord help me least I make myself partaker of other men's sins. My soul was troubled and I reflected, if I should gain the whole world, and live a thousand years, and at last have to endure the wrath of God, what would I have gained?

Afterwards the poor straying flock, who wandered as sheep without a shepherd, after many severe edicts and slaughters, assembled near my place of residence, called Oude Cloistre, and, alas! through the ungodly doctrine of Munster, drew the sword to defend themselves, which the Lord commanded Peter to put up in the sheath.

The blood of the slain, although they were in error, grieved me so sorely that I could not endure it—I could find no rest in my soul. I reflected upon my carnal, sinful life—my hypocritical doctrine and idolatry, in which I continued daily under

2

the appearance of godliness. I perceived that these zealous persons would willingly have resigned their lives and their estates, though they were in error, for the principles which they maintained. I was one of those who had discovered to them some of their abominations, and yet I myself remained satisfied with my unrestrained life, and known defilements. I wished only to live comfortably and without the cross of Christ.

Thus reflecting, my soul was grieved beyond endurance. I meditated with myself—I miserable man? What shall I do? If I continue in this way and live not agreeably to the word of the Lord—if I refuse to exert my limited talents to rebuke, by the aid of the word of God, the learned hypocrisy, the impenitent lives, the perverted baptism, the Lord's Supper, and the false worship of God—If I, through bodily fear, refuse to show them the right foundation of truth, or forbear to use my powers to direct the wandering flock, who would gladly do their duty if they knew it, to the true pasture of Christ—Oh how shall their shed blood rise against me in the judgment of the Almighty, and pronounce sentence against my miserable soul.

My heart trembled in my body. I prayed to God with sighs and tears, that he would give to me, a troubled sinner, the gift of his grace, and create a clean heart within me; that through the merits of the blood of Christ, He would graciously forgive my unclean and unprofitable life, and bestow upon me, wisdom, candor and fortitude, that I might with sincerity, preach his adorable name and holy word, and make manifest his truth to his praise.

I began in the name of the Lord to preach publicly from the pulpit, the word of repentance—to direct the people into the narrow path—and through scripture to reprove all ungodliness and sin—all idolatry and false worship—and to present the truth concerning baptism and the Lord's Supper, according to the doctrine of Christ.

I faithfully warned every one in relation to the abominations and crimes of Munster, concerning *kings, polygamy, wealth, the sword*, &c., till about the period of nine months, when the gracious Lord granted me his fatherly spirit and aid; then I voluntarily renounced all my worldly honor and reputation—my unchristian conduct, masses, infant baptism, and my unprofitable life, and willingly submitted to poverty and distress, and to the yoke of Christ. In my weakness I feared the Lord—I sought out the pious, and though they were few in number, I found some, who were zealous and maintained the truth. I confered with the wicked, and through the word and power of God, reclaimed some from the snares of damnation, and gained them to Christ. The hardened and rebellious, I commended to the Lord. Thus, my reader, the God of mercy, through the benign influence of his grace, exerted upon the heart of me a miserable sinner, produced in me a new mind, humbled me in in his fear, taught me to know myself in part, turned me from the way of death, and called me into the narrow path of life— to the communion of his saints. To him be praise forever more.

About one year thereafter, at which time I exercised myself in writing and in reading the word of God in secret, it happened that six, seven or eight persons came to me, who were of one heart and one soul with myself, in their faith and life, and as far as man can judge, were unblamable, separated from the world and subdued to the cross. They cordially abhorred not only the sect of Munster, but the anathemas and abominations of all other worldly sects. With much solicitude, they kindly requested me to reflect on the sufferings, the oppression and distress of those souls whose spiritual hunger was great, whilst the faithful stewards were few. They desired that the talents which I had unmeritedly received from the Lord, might be applied to advantage.

When I heard this my heart was greatly troubled. Trouble and fear were on every side; for on the one hand I was sensible of my limited talents, my great ignorance, my weak nature, the timidity of my flesh, the unbounded wickedness, perversity and tyranny of the world, the powerful sects, the subtlety of different minds, and the heavy cross that would press me, should I comply with their solicitations. On the other hand, I saw the miserable starving condition of the Christians; for I was aware that they erred as innocent sheep which have no shepherd.

At last, after much prayer, I placed myself and these circumstances before the Lord and his church, in order that we might pray to the Lord for a season, that should it accord with his holy will, he would give me such a mind and heart as would enable me to say with Paul, "Woe is me, if I preach not the Gospel;" for Christ says, "That if two of you shall agree on earth as touching any thing that they shall ask, it shall be done for them of my Father which is in heaven. For where two or three are gathered together in my name, there am I in the midst of them." (Matt. 18.)

Thus, my reader, behold, I was not called to serve among the followers of Munster, nor of any other seditious sect, (as it is falsely reported concerning me,) but I have been called by a people who were ready to receive Christ and his word, led a penitent life in the fear of God, served their neighbors in love, bore the cross, sought the welfare and salvation of all men, loved righteousness and truth, and abhorred wickedness. Thus they manifested that they were not such perverted persons as as they are slanderously reported to have been. But they were true Christians, though unknown to the world; if we otherwise believe that Christ's word is true, and his holy life and example unblameable.

Thus have I, a miserable sinner, been enlightened of the Lord, converted to a new mind, fled from Babel, went into Jerusalem, and finally I have, though unworthy, advanced to this high and arduous station.

When the persons before mentioned, did not desist from their supplications, and my own conscience in some degree made me uneasy, (although in weakness) because I saw the great hunger and need, already named, I surrendered myself, soul and body, to the Lord and committed myself to his grace, and commenced, according to the contents of his holy word, to teach, and to baptize, to labor in the vineyard of the Lord with my limited talents, to build up his holy city and temple, and to repair the dilapidated walls. The great and mighty God has made known the word of true repentance—the word of his grace and power, together with the salutary use of his holy sacraments, through our insignificant service and unlearned writings, together with the service, labor and help of our faithful brethren in many towns and countries. The Lord made the condition of his churches glorious, and accompanied them with such a subduing power that many exalted and proud hearts were not only humbled, the unclean not only purified, the drunkard made sober, the avaricious benevolent, the ferocious mild, and the impious pious; but they also faithfully renounced their possessions and blood, bodies and lives, for the testimony of Jesus, as may daily be seen. These are not the fruits and evidences of false doctrines, where God is not a co-worker. Neither could they endure so long under such grievous misery and oppressive crosses, were it not the power and word of the Almighty which sustains them. Yea, more, the Lord endued them with such grace and wisdom, as Christ has promised to all his children in their trials, so that all the worldly-wise and renowned teachers, together with the blood-guilty daring tyrants, who, O God, boast that they are Christians, were vanquished and abashed by these invincible champions and witnesses of Christ. Those ferocious persons knew of no other weapons or refuge to which to resort than those of banishing, seizing, punishing, burning, murdering, and destroying, even as has always been the custom of the old serpent, from the beginning, and as may be daily witnessed in many places of our Netherlands.

Behold these are our calling, our doctrine and fruits of our practice; on account of which we are so grievously slandered and so malevolently persecuted; whether or not all the prophets, apostles, and faithful servants of God have endured similar sufferings on account of their faithfulness, we willingly leave all the pious to be judges.

But as much as regards my poor, weak and imperfect life, I freely confess that I am a poor wretched sinner, conceived of sinful seed in sin, and sinfully brought brought forth. I can say with David, "That my sins are ever before me. My thoughts, words and actions condemn me." I see with holy Paul, "That nothing good dwells in my flesh." Nevertheless, I must be allowed to boast this much in my weakness, if this wicked desolate world would hear our doctrine (not ours but the doctrine of Christ) with patience and follow it implicitly, in the fear of God, there would soon be another kind of Christianity than is, alas! existing now.

I thank God, who has made me willing with holy Paul, to hate the evil and follow the good; and willingly would I with my own blood, reclaim the wicked world from ungodly works, and gain it to Christ. Through the grace of God, it is all my desire to fear the Lord with all my heart; to love, seek and serve him, to do right before him, and be an unblamable godly Christian.

I hope through the Lord's mercy and assistance, that no one upon earth may have ground to accuse me of leading an avaricious and luxurious life. Money and affluence I have not—I desire them not, although alas, some from a perverted heart, say that I eat more roasted than they do seethed; and drink more wine than they do beer. My Lord and master, Jesus Christ, was also called a winebibber, and a glutton. I trust that through the grace of the Lord, I am innocent in this matter, and stand acquitted before God.

He who purchased me with the blood of his love, and called me who am unworthy to his service, knows me, and knows that I seek not wealth nor luxury nor ease, but only the praise of the Lord, my salvation, and the souls of those on whose account I, with my poor weak wife and children, had to endure for eighteen years, so much affliction and persecution. Every where around me were fears and dangers; yea when the ministers repose on easy beds and downy pillows, we have to conceal ourselves in secret. When they at weddings pipe and beat the tambour and vaunt loudly, we must look out, when the dogs bark, lest the captors be at hand. Whilst they are saluted as doctors, lords and teachers by every one, we have to hear that we are Ana-baptists, hedge preachers, deceivers and heretics, and must be saluted in the name of the devil. In short, whilst they are gloriously rewarded for their services with large in-

2*

comes and easy times, our recompense and portion must be fire, sword and death.

Behold my faithful readers in such fear, poverty, misery and danger of death, have I wretched man, performed to this hour, without change, the service of the Lord, and I hope through his grace to continue therein to his glory, as long as I remain in this earthly tabernacle. What I and my co-workers have sought in performing our arduous duties, is apparent to all the well-disposed, who may readily judge from the works and their fruits.

I will here humbly entreat the reader for Jesus' sake, to accept in love, this my confession in relation to my illumination, conversion and calling, and to meditate thereon. I have made it on account of urgent necessity; because I was slandered by the clergy, and am accused without foundation of truth, of being called and ordained to the service of a seditious and heretical sect. He that feareth God let him read and judge.

MENNO SIMON.

OF THE DAY OF GRACE.

In the first place we teach, (John 3,) what Jesus, the teacher from heaven, the oracle and word of the Most High God, himself, taught, that now is the time of grace, a time to awaken from the sleep of our abominable sins, (Rom. 13,) and obtain an upright, converted, renewed, contrite and repenting heart, and cordially to lament before God, our past profligate and dissolute course of life. And now is the time, in the fear of God, to crucify and mortify our depraved, sinful flesh, temper and nature, and arise with Christ into a new, righteous, and penitent life and conduct. (Eph. 4; Gal. 5; Rom. 6; Mark 1.) The time is fulfilled, and the kingdom of God is at hand: repent ye and believe the Gospel.

The time is fulfilled, that is, the promised day of grace approaches—the time for the appearing of the promised seed, the time of redemption, the time of that offering by which all things were to be reconciled in heaven and upon earth. (Gen. 3; Col. 1; Eph. 1.) The time for the consummation of all the literal and figurative transaction into new, spiritual and abiding truth. The time for which the fathers, Jacob, Moses, Isaiah, David, Daniel, &c., with all the patriarchs and prophets, looked and hoped with many tears. They saw this time, by faith, from afar, and drew their comfort and hopes therefrom. (Heb. 11.) Yea, it was to them such a great and pleasing consolation, that good old Simeon desired life no longer, when he beheld the time and saw the Redemer. He said, Lord, now lettest thou thy servant depart in peace, according to thy word, for mine eyes have seen thy salvation which thou hast prepared before the face of all people.

The time is fulfilled.—The predictions of the prophets and promises of the fathers, are performed.—The sworn oath is accomplished—Israel has obtained its David, its Prince and Chief. He has arisen as a mighty one to prepare his way. (Ps. 2; Isa. 9; Jer. 23, 30, 33; Hos. 3.) His going forth is from the heavens—the Anointed who was the desire of all nations has come, girded with the sword of the spirit and valiant for battle. (Is. 19; Mich. 5; Hag. 2; Is. 24.) He has declared the gospel of the kingdom—the word of his Father. He taught by precept and by the example of his unblemished life. (Mat. 4; John 7, 13, 15.) He has conquered the mighty, and subdued the power of the devil; he bore our sins, abolished death, reconciled the father, and acquired for all the children of God, grace, mercy and eternal life. (Matt. 11; Luke 11; Heb. 2; Isa. 53; 1 Peter 2; 1 Cor. 15; Col. 1.) He has been ordained by his Almighty and eternal Father as an omnipotent King over the holy Mount Zion. He has become the head of the church, a dispenser of the heavenly blessings, yea, he is an Almighty Ruler over all, in heaven and upon earth, Isa. 2; Eph. 2; Heb. 3,) and this is what Christ saith, the time is fulfilled, and the kingdom of God is at hand.

Out of compassion and a sincere heart, I beseech you with the apostle Paul, that you take heed to this day of grace, and be obedient to the word of God, which says: "I have heard thee in an accepted time; and in the day of salvation, have I succoured thee. Behold, now is the accepted time, now is the day of salvation." Let us, with Paul, give no offence to any one, that our ministry be not slandered, but in all things approving ourselves as the ministers of God, in much patience in afflictions, in distresses, in stripes, in imprisonment, in tumults, (understand this in relation to things which befall us,) in labors, in watchings, in fastings; by pureness, by knowledge, by longsuffering, by kindness, by the Holy Ghost, by love unfeigned, by the word of truth, by the power of God, by the armor of righteousness, in the right hand, and in the left by honor and dishonor, by evil report and good report; as deceivers and yet true; as unknown, and yet well known: as dying, and behold, we live; as chastened and not killed; as sorrowful, yet always rejoicing; as poor, yet making many rich; as having nothing and yet possessing all things, (2 Cor. 6, 1, 10.) Oh my beloved sirs, friends and brethren, my mouth is open unto you and my heart is enlarged for your sake. I am much grieved that you are so careless, and pay no attention to these plain, intelligible scriptures—that you wholly contemn the word of the Lord, and suffer the precious time of grace to pass so shamefully away, and regard nothing more than to live according to the lusts of your flesh whilst you bow to dumb idols. Alas! It is the time to awaken. The angel has sworn (Rev. 10) by him that liveth for ever and ever, who created heaven and the things that are therein and the earth, that after this time, there shall be time no more. We know not but that now, the present time, is the last vigil of the year, the last proclamation of the holy gospel, the last invitation to the marriage of the Lamb, which is to be celebrated and promulgated before the great and terrible day of the Lord. Hence we may conclude that the summer will pass away and the winter approach. They, who like the foolish virgins, ·neglect to trim their lamps, will come too late, and knock, and shall be excluded. (Mat. 25.) Therefore, comfort not one another with idle comfort, and vain hope; even as some

do who think that the word should be taught, whilst they reject
the cross. I mean those who know the word of the Lord, but
live not according to it. The Lamb is slain from the foundation of the world, (Rev. 13,) yea, he did not only suffer, in his
body, but he also through the cross and death, entered into that
glory which he had left for our sakes. (Luke 24; John 17;
Phil. 2.) If Christ then had to suffer such anguish, misery and
pain, how can his servants expect peace, whilst they are in the
flesh. If they have called the master of the house Beelzebub,
how much more shall they call those of his household? (Math.
10, 25.) All that would live godly in Christ Jesus, says Paul,
must suffer persecution, (2 Tim. 3.) Ye shall be hated, saith
Christ, by all men for my name's sake. (Matt. 10.)

Banish then all thoughts of delay from your heart, lest ye be
deceived through vain hopes. I knew some who waited for
more propitious days, to serve the Lord, but they did not live
to realize their hopes. Had the apostles and the Fathers thus
delayed, the gospel would, at this day be unknown and the
word of the kingdom would be concealed. Oh, if you, who
boast that you are christians and the children of God, were as
you ought to be, you would say with Paul : Who shall separate
us from the love of God, (Rom. 3.) For the flesh, the devil,
sin, hell and death would all be subdued, there would be no
desire to remain any longer in this depraved, wicked, sanguinary
world. Ye would boast of nothing save the cross of Christ,
(Gal. 6,) and like Paul desire to be delivered from this body
and live with Christ, (Phil. 2.) I cordially desire that you may
awaken without delay; and may the gracious Lord give us
liberty and joy, which we shall thankfully receive at his
gracious hands; but should he withhold his blessings, still his
great name must, and shall be praised eternally. We have all
enjoyed the acceptable time of grace; for now is the day of
salvation. Let us not, like ungrateful, disobedient, bloodthirsty
Jerusalem, reject the divine peace, heavenly grace, but let us
awaken, with sober hearts and hear the inviting voice and rise
now from the slumber of our offensive sins, for the Lord is,at
hand; the night is far spent, the day is at hand; let us, therefore, cast off the works of darkness, and let us put on the armor
of light, let us walk honestly as in the day; not in rioting and
drunkenness, not in chambering and wantonness, not in strife
and envy. But put on the Lord Jesus Christ, and make not
provision for the flesh, to fulfil the lusts thereof. (Rom. 13.)
Let every one be vigilant, for now is the time which the grace
of God has given for repentance. *Ecce, nunc tempus accep-
tum, Ecce, nunc dies salutis*. Behold, now is the accepted
time, behold now is the day of salvation.

OF SINCERE AND TRUE REPENTANCE.

In the second place we exhort you in the language of Christ, repent for the kingdom of heaven is at hand. (Math. 4.) Oh thou faithful word of divine grace and love, thou art read and sung, and preached with the mouth, with life, and death, and proclaimed in different parts of the world, but thy power so few desire; and what is more deplorable, those who receive thee, are made a prey by an ungodly world. Beloved, it will avail us nothing to be called christians and boast of the Lord's blood, merits, grace and gospel, as long as we are not con verted from a sinful life. It is all in vain that we are called christians, or that Christ died, or that we were born in the days of grace, and baptized with water, if we walk not in obedience to all the commandments of God, therefore let us awaken from the slumber of sin. Behold the world lieth in wickedness. All around may be seen sensuality, pride, lying, fraud, avarice, strife, incontinence, murdering, hypocricy, blasphemy, idolatry and false worship. (Ps. 31; Ezek. 22; Mic. 6; Hos. 4; Rom.4.) In short, the efforts of a sinful world are directed against what God commands. Who can relate the alarming condition of the present times. Yet the wicked want to call themselves the holy christian church! Oh no! they who do such things, saith Paul, will not inherit the kingdom of God. (Rom. 1; 1 Cor. 6; Gal. 5; Eph. 5; Rev. 21; John 3.) O ye men, awake from your slumbers, for thus saith the Lord, verily, verily I say unto you except ye be born from above ye shall not see the kingdom of God. Again, verily, verily I say unto you, except ye be born of water and spirit, ye cannot enter into the kingdom of God. Again, verily, verily, I say, except ye repent and become as little children, ye cannot enter into the kingdom of heaven, (Matt. 18.) What does it profit to speak much of Christ and his word, if we do not believe him and obey his command- ments. Again, 1 say, awaken, banish accursed unbelief with all unrighteousness from your hearts; live a pious, penitent life according to the scriptures; for Christ says, except ye repent, ye shall all likewise perish. (Luke 13.) Here do not understand such repentance as is taught by an erring world, which is only an outward appearance, consisting of human righteousness, such as hypocritical fasting, pilgrimage, praying and reading of Pater Nosters and Ave Marias, hearing frequent masses, auricular confessions and the like hypocricy, which Christ and his holy apostles did not teach and command, and, therefore, instead of profiting, it will tend to provoke and excite divine displeasure. Such doctrines are fruitless and unavailing—the commands of men—the enchanted wine of Babylonian whoredom, which those, who have dwelt upon the earth have drunk for so many ages. (Rev. 17.) But we speak of a repentance possessed of power. That which was taught by John, to the Jews—"Bring forth fruits meet for repentance, and think not to say within yourselves we have Abraham for our father, for I say unto you, that God is able of these stones to raise up children unto Abraham. And now also the axe is laid at the root of the trees; therefore, every tree which bringeth not forth good fruit is hewn down and cast into the fire."

Behold, dear reader, the repentance we teach, is to die unto sin, and all ungodly works, and live no longer according to the lusts of the flesh. Do as David did, (2 Kings 12 : 22, 24,) when he was reproved by the prophet on account of his adultery, and for numbering the people : He wept bitterly, called upon God, forsook the evil and did so no more. Peter sinned very grievously but once, and no more. Matthew, when called by the Saviour forsook his former way of life. (Matt. 16.) Zaccheus and the sinful woman did not again return to the sinful works of darkness, (Matt. 9.) Zaccheus made restitution to those whom he had defrauded, and gave one-half of his goods to the poor and distressed, (Luke 10 : 8.) And the woman wept bitterly; she washed the feet of the Lord with her tears, and wiped them with the hair of her head; she anointed him with precious ointment, and sat humbly at his feet to listen to his blessed word. (Luke 7 : 10.) These are the precious fruits of that repentance which is acceptable to the Lord. Therefore, it was said unto David, (2 Kings 12,) that the Lord removed his sins from him. To Peter it was proclaimed that the Lord had arisen from the dead. (Matt. 9, 10.) Matthew was called to be an apostle. Zaccheus was told that he had become a son of Abraham. Magdalena was commended for choosing the better part which would never be taken from her, (Luke 10.) And Christ said to the adultress to depart in peace and sin no more.

Such a repentance we teach and none other. Namely, that no one can count himself pious, and glory in the grace of God, the forgiveness of sin, or the merits of Christ, unless he has truly repented. It is not enough to say, we are Abraham's children, that is, that we profess to be christians and be esteemed as the followers of Christ. But we must do the works of Abraham, that is, we must walk as all the true children of God are commanded to walk. John says, "If we say we have fellowship with him and walk in darkness, we lie, and do not the truth.   But if we walk in the light as he is in the light, we have fellowship one with another : and the blood of Christ, his son, cleanseth us from all sin.   (1 John 1, 6, 8.)   I ask my readers if they ever read in the scriptures that an impenitent, obdurate man who fears not God nor his word, who is earthly, sensual, and devilish, and lives according to his lusts can be a child of God and a joint heir of Christ? you must answer, *no*. But he that with all his heart ceases from evil and learns to do well, to him in the whole scriptures, the grace of the Lord is proclaimed.   Thus the prophet says : wash ye ; make you clean ; put away the evil of your doings from before mine eyes, cease to do evil, learn to do well, seek judgment, relieve the oppressed, judge the fatherless, plead for the widow.   Come now let us reason together, saith the Lord :   Though your sins be as scarlet, they shall be as white as snow ; though they be red like crimson, they shall be as wool, (Isaiah 1.)   And again.   But if the wicked will turn from all his sins that he hath committed, and keep all my statutes and do that which is lawful and right, he shall surely live,—he shall not die.   All his transgressions which he hath committed, they shall not be mentioned unto him.   (Ezek. 1, 8.)   And further, search the whole scriptures, the true instructions and testimonies of the holy prophets, evangelists and apostles ; and you will find it clearly stated how this godly repentance is to be performed in sincerity ; and that without it no one can receive grace, or enter into the kingdom of heaven.   In short, as far as in us lies, we teach repentance from the word of the Lord, in order that ye may destroy those carnal lusts which war against the soul, (1 Pet. 2 ;) crucify the flesh with its lusts and desires, (Gal. 5 ;) refrain from conformity to this world, (Rom. 18 ;) subdue the love of this world and the things therein, (John 1 ;) put off the old man with his deeds, and put on the new, which is renewed in knowledge, after the image of him, that created him, (Col. 5 ;) put off old Adam with his whole nature and deceitful lusts, such as pride, avarice, unchastity, hatred, envyings, gluttony, drinking, idolatry, and that ye put on the new man which after God is created in righteousness and true holiness, whose fruits are faith, love, hope, righteousness, peace, joy in the Holy Ghost.   (Eph. 4 ; Gal. 5 ; 1 Cor. 13 ; Rom. 14.)   In suffering be patient, merciful, compassionate and chaste ; and hate and rebuke all sin.   Entertain a cordial zeal for God and his word. I repeat it again, this repentance must be sincere, fruitful, acceptable to the Lord and according to his word.   He that receives this grace, and retains it to the end, may rejoice and thank God, for the end thereof is eternal life.   But he that rejects it and desires it not, be he warned that the end is eternal woe.

Beloved, do for once lay it to heart, what it is, and what the consequences will be, to wilfully transgress the commands of the Most High. Adam and Eve ate but once of the forbidden fruit, which the Lord had commanded them not to eat, (Gen. 3;) and the earth was cursed. In the sweat of his face, Adam was doomed to eat his bread all the days of his life. Eve and her daughters must bring forth in pain and be in subjection to their husbands. Both were driven from Paradise, and, with all their race, placed under the sentence: Dust thou art and unto dust shalt thou return. There was no forgiveness, no consolation. But the Eternal Word, God's eternal Son, came from the high heavens—assumed human nature, suffered hunger, temptation, misery, the cross and death, for the redemption of man. Oh beloved, if this single transgression was so great before God, what shall become of those who proudly despise the holy word, the covenant, the will and command of the Lord; who do not confess, nor desist from their sins, though they are full of iniquity from the crown of the head to the soles of the feet. Cain was cursed and became a vagrant upon earth, because he so enviously slew his innocent brother Abel. (Gen. 4.) Alas, what will become of those who at the present day without compassion, persecute, plunder, and murder the pious Abelites, who, with warm and sincere hearts, seek Christ and eternal life. The ancient world was drowned in the waters of the flood, because the "sons of God looked upon the daughters of men, that they were fair, and took to themselves wives of all which they choose." And also, because they would not be reproved by the spirit of God, for every imagination and thought of the heart was evil continually. (Gen. 6, 7, 8.) Reflect upon the lusts with which the marriages of the present day are contracted; Yea like horses and mules, without the fear of God. (Job 6.) How the Holy Ghost is reviled, slandered and grieved. and how they all walk in their perverted way which leads to hell. Sodom and Gomorrah with the surrounding cities, were burned up with the fire of the furious wrath of God, and cast into the abyss of hell, on account of their pride, wantonness, cruelty and abominable crimes. (Gen. 18, 19; Ezek. 16.) Alas! what will befall those miserable men in the great and terrible day when the Lord will appear in his glory, those miserable men, whose pride, covetousness, debauchery, pomp, tyranny, blood thirsty, adultery, fornication, papal abominations, no heart can conceive, no tongue can express or describe. (Rom. 1; 1 Tim. 1.)

Koran, Dathan and Abiram, though they were the seed of

Abraham, and some of them born of Levi, yet because they revolted against Moses and Aaron, and entered uncalled into the sacerdotal office, they and all their company, were sunk into the earth alive. (Numb. 16.) Reflect, what will ultimately befall our Korites, or what they have to await, who have never acknowledged God, much less, have been sent by him. Their service and calling are not from God, nor according to his word, but, as the scriptures teach, are from the infernal abyss, and are of the dragon and the beast, (Rev. 9, 13, 17,) who mislead so many miserable souls by their seducing doctrines, Babylonian sorcery, and hypocritical lives, and not only despise, but persecute, crucify and kill Christ—the righteous Moses and Aaron. Moses, the faithful servant of God, could not enter the promised land, only because he was once faint-hearted, and doubted the word of the Lord, (Num. 4;) how much less shall this unbelieving, faithless, perverted, stiff-necked generation, enter the eternal promised land of glory, who not only disbelieve, but despise the word of the Lord—the delightful gospel of Christ. They hate it bitterly and persecute it; trample the blood of Christ under foot, stop their ears against the truth, and refuse to be taught by any means, either by truth or the unblamable lives of the saints, or by the innocent blood of the worthy-witnesses of Jesus, which has been shed, and, in many countries flowed like water.

O ye miserable men, who commit so much evil, and are such loathsome objects before God, take heed, to the word of the Lord. Cleanse yourselves, purify your hands and unbelieving hearts, and do not longer despise God's grace with your vain boastings, and say not, Abraham is your father, (James 4;) or that you are children of God, that Christ died for you; that you trust in his mercy. Trust not to lies, says Jeremiah the prophet. Say not here is the temple of the Lord, the temple of the Lord, the temple of the Lord, for it avails nothing that Christ died, and that we are called by his name, if we do not possess a sincere and powerful faith in Christ Jesus, and exercise unfeigned love and lead an obedient, pious, unblamable life. God's mercy, says the scriptures, is towards his saints, and his care is over his chosen. (Wisd. 4.) The hope of the wicked is in vain, (Wisd. 5.) The eyes of the Lord are upon the righteous, and his ears are open to their cry, (Ps. 33; 1 Pet. 3;) Ye are my friends, saith Christ, if you do whatever I command you, (John 15.) Therefore we pray and exhort you again to reform yourselves. He is the same unchangeable God. (Math. 3; James 1.) He is a strict, jealous, and rigid punisher of all wickedness, yea, a righteous judge of all ungodliness, and every evil work. He visits the iniquities of the fathers upon the children, until the third and fourth generations of them that hate him; on the other hand, he is gracious, kind and merciful unto thousands of them that love him and keep his commandments. (Ex. 30.) Oh reader, reader, beloved reader, it is a fearful thing to fall into the hands of the living God. (Heb. 10.) The time is fulfilled, now is the accepted time—now is the day of salvation. (Mark 2; Cor. 6.) The kingdom of heaven is at hand, would you inherit it and enter into it? You must reform, not only in appearance, as the hypocrites do, but as sincere penitents, with all your heart and with all your powers, and bring forth good fruit. If not, you must be cut off and cast into the fire of fierce wrath. (Matt. 3; Luke 3; John 15.) *Imo, nisi resipuerite, omnes similiter, perilites,* (Luke 13,) (*i. e.*) unless ye repent, ye shall all likewise perish.

OF FAITH.

In the third place, we teach with Christ, and say " Believe the gospel." Mark 1. That gospel is the glad tidings, and promulgation of God's grace to us-ward, and of the forgiveness of our sins through Christ Jesus. Faith receives this gospel through the Holy Ghost, and does not look upon former righteousness or unrighteousness, but the believer hopes, (Rom. 4,) and with the whole heart, depends upon the grace, word and promises of the Lord. He knows that God is true and that his promises are sure, (Ps. 51, 14, 4,) whereby the heart is renewed, converted, justified, made pious, peaceable and joyous. (Rom. 3, 5; Gal. 2.) He is born a child of God, (John 1,) approaches with full confidence to the throne of grace, (Heb. 4,) and thus becomes a joint heir with Christ, a possessor of eternal life. (John 7; Rom. 8; 1 Tim. 1.)

Believers awaken in time. They hear and believe the word of the Lord. They weep over their past unworthy life and conduct. They desire medicine, help, and advice for their sick souls. (Matt. 26.) To such, Christ, who is the comforter of all troubled hearts, says, " Believe the gospel." That is, fear not; rejoice and be comforted; I will not punish you, but will heal you, comfort you, and give you life. (Isai. 41.) A bruised reed I will not break, and smoking flax I will not quench ; but I will bind up that which was broken, and will strengthen that which was weak, I will seek for what was lost. (Ezek. 24; Matt. 11.) For I came not to call the righteous, but sinners to repentance. (Matt. 9; Luke 2; John 1; 1 John 1.) According to the good pleasure of my heavenly Father, I came into the world, and by the power of the Holy Ghost, I became a visible, tangible and dying man ; in all points like unto you, sin excepted. (Heb. 4 ; Luke 2 ; Phil. 2.) I was born of Mary the spotless virgin ; I came down from heaven, proceeded from the mouth of the Most High ; am the first born of every creature ; the first and the last ; the beginning and the end, (Eccle. 24 ; Col. 3 ; Rev. 1, 21 ; I am the Son of the Almighty God ; Matt. 16,) anointed with the Holy Ghost to preach the gospel to the poor, and to bind up the broken hearted, (Isa. 61 ; Luke 4,) to proclaim liberty to the captives ; to give sight to the blind ; to set at liberty the prisoners and to preach the acceptable year of the Lord. Believe the gospel. I am the Lamb that was offered for you all. I take away the sins of the whole world. My Father has made me unto you wisdom, sanctification and redemption, (Exodus, 5 ; 1 Cor. 5 ; John 1 ; 1 Cor. 1 ; Isai. 28 ; Rom. 6, 10 ;) those who believe on me shall not be made ashamed ; yea, all that believe that I am he shall have eternal life. (John 3.) Behold, beloved, all who believe this, are those of whom the scriptures say, to them gave he power to become the sons of God, even to them that believe on his name, which are born, not of blood, nor of the will of the flesh, nor of the will of man, but of God, (John 1, 12, 13.) These are they who are justified by faith and have peace with God, through our Lord Jesus Christ, through whom we have obtained this grace, that we can boast of the hope of the glory of God. (Rom. 5.) And this, as Paul says, is all of grace and love ; for all are sinners and have come short of the glory of God. Being freely justified by grace through the redemption which is in Christ Jesus, who God hath set forth to be a propitiation, through faith in his blood, &c. (Rom. 3.) There is none that can boast of this faith—that he is saved of himself ; for it is the gift of God. (Eph. 2.) All who receive faith from God, receive, as it were, a tree full of all manner of suitable fruit. Happy they who receive this gift of God, for it is more precious than silver or gold, or gems—it is incomparable. He that obtains it, obtains Christ Jesus, forgiveness of sins, a new mind, and eternal life. True faith, which is acceptable to God is not dead. It brings forth fruit, and so manifests its nature. It is even fruitful in charity, it works and wills righteousness ; it mortifies the flesh ; it crucifies lust and sinful desires ; it rejoices in the cross of Christ ; is renewed and regenerated, it quickeneth, it makes holy and joyful in Christ Jesus. Such a faith, we say, is the gift of God, (Rom. 1,) by which according to the scriptures, the righteous are to live, as did Abel, Enoch, Noah, Abraham, Moses, Rahab and all the saints. (Heb. 11.) Every good tree bringeth forth good fruit. (Gal. 3 ; Heb. 10.) And every tree which bringeth not forth good fruit, although in full and verdant foliage, must be accursed and consumed by fire. (Matt. 3, 21 ; Mark 1, 6 ; Luke 3.) And thus, also, a fruitless, powerless faith, such as is possessed by the world, and is not operative in love, be it ever so learned, and wise, and eloquent, and imposing and miraculous, still it is in the sight of God, unclean, dead, and cursed. (Matt. 6 ; 1 Cor. 13 ; James 2.)

Therefore, we exhort you with Christ Jesus, *believe the Gospel ;* that is, believe the joyful news,—the message of divine grace, through Jesus Christ. Leave off sinning, manifest repentance, mourn for your past life, submit to the word and will of the Lord, then you will become joint-heirs and children of the new and heavenly Jerusalem, and be freed from your enemies, hell, the devil, sin and death. Walk according to the spirit and not according to the flesh. (Rom. 8.) *Quid credit filio Dei habet vitam æternam,* i. e. he that believeth on the son of God hath eternal life.

SUPPLICATION TO THE MAGISTRACY.

WE, poor wretched men, forsaken of every human assistance, and all consolations, have, like innocent sheep, without a shepherd, become a prey to the roaring and fierce lions of the forest, and the devouring beasts of the field ; to the world we have become a spectacle and a reproach. (1 Cor. 4.) We have to suffer daily the oppression of lords and nobles, the inhuman reviling and abuse of the learned ; and the lying, scorning and mockery of the common people. We humbly entreat the imperial majesty, kings, lords, princes and officers, every one in his station, of worthiness and highness, by the deep and bloody wounds of our Lord Jesus Christ, that you lay aside all displeasure and bad opinion of us, and reflect with pity on the inhuman and severe trials, misery, wants, crosses, and murderings of your helpless and innocent servants ; for the great Lord before whom we stand, who is the searcher of all hearts, and before whose eyes all things are revealed, (Ps. 7 ; Jer. 17 ; Rom. 8 ; Heb. 4,) knows that we seek nothing else upon this earth, than that we, with a good conscience, may live according to his holy commandments, ordinances, word and will. But there are, alas ! in our day, some evil sects, which will doubtless, be manifested in due time.

Do, therefore, condescend so much as to read our writings

3*

with attention, and with a godfearing and impartial heart, so that you may know us, and cease to deter us from our doctrines, faith and practice, by persecution, poverty, misery and death. Be pleased, therefore, to examine more deeply into the truth—and be no longer guilty of innocent blood.

Show some natural pity—some humanity towards your poor servants. Think not that we, miserable, forlorn men, are wood or stone, but we are descended with you, from one father, Adam, and from one mother Eve, and are created by the same God. We have a common entrance into this world, are clothed with the same nature, which desires rest and peace,—have wives and children as well as you, and are naturally like all other creatures on earth, afraid of death.

Therefore, humble yourselves in the name of Christ, and save your poor souls. Examine our doctrine and instructions, and you will find through the grace of God, that they are the pure, unadulterated doctrines of Christ,—the holy Word, the Word of eternal peace, (Acts 20; Eph. 2,) the Word of eternal truth, the Word of divine grace, the Word of our salvation, (James 1,) the all-conquering Word, against which the gates of hell shall never prevail. (Matt. 16.) It is the two-edged sword which proceeded out of the mouth of the Lord, (Rev. 1,)—the sword of the spirit by which all living upon the earth are to be judged. (Eph. 6.)

Oh ye beloved sirs, put your swords into the sheath; for as true as the Lord lives, you do not fight against flesh and blood, but against him who has eyes like a flame of fire; (Rev. 1;) who dispenses justice, and makes war in righteousness: who is crowned with many crowns, whose name no one knows but himself, who is clothed with a vesture dipped in blood; whose name is called the WORD OF GOD; who rules the nations with a rod of iron; who treads the wine-press of the fierce wrath of Almighty God; who has a name written upon his vesture and on his thigh, THE KING OF KINGS AND LORD OF LORDS. (Rev. 19.)

Oh ye high renowned lords and princes, it is against this Being you are contending and taking such a stand with your counsel and sword. Remember what the great prophet (Zach. 2) said concerning the children of God, who are suffering here: He that toucheth you toucheth the apple of mine eye. It is a dreadful abomination, mad wickedness, and insanity, so miserably to slay, to destroy and exterminate those who with such warm hearts, seek the Lord and eternal life, and who would not molest any one upon earth. The death of the righteous, saith David, (Ps. 16,) is precious in the sight of the Lord. It is Jesus of Nazareth whom ye persecute, (Acts 9,) and not us,

Therefore waken, desist, fear God and his word, for you and we will all be summoned to appear before one Judge, before whom all are on a level—there is no distinction there; neither power, exaltation, fair speeches, nor talents will there avail. Judgment is there passed impartially and without respect to persons—and there the oppressed will have justice done him, and then the murdered Jesus, with all his elect will enter into his promised inheritance—his kingdom and glory, and be beyond the power of death, and the reach of tyrant's cruel hands.   Seeing then, that you deal so unjustly and tyrannically, according to the evil intentions of your wicked hearts, without the sanction of scripture, with the helpless and godly, how can you expect any favor and mercy in the day of the Lord, when we will all have to stand before the impartial judgment seat; where every one will receive according to his deeds. (James 1; Rom. 14; 2 Cor. 5,)

We desire not this favor as the evil doers of this world; for we have not sinned in our doctrine, faith and practice, although we have to suffer so much but we, only with the word of the Lord, as the scriptures direct us, resist anti-christian doctrines, ordinances, and evil courses of life. We resist neither the emperor, nor the king, nor any authority to which they are called of God, but we are ready to obey till death, in all things not contrary to God and his word. (Matt. 17, 22; Rom. 13; Tit. 3; Pet. 1.)   And we very well know what the scriptures teach and command us, concerning this.   But we desire so much mercy as that we may, under your gracious protection, teach, act and serve the Lord, according to the dictates of our consciences, so that to you and many with you, the gospel of Christ may be rightly preached, and the gate of life opened. Alas! had only the learned the word of God, and not we, how gladly would we be taught by them.   But since we have it, and they not, we therefore pray, for Jesus' sake, do not urge us to leave Christ, and join Antichrist! to go from truth to error—from life to certain death. (Wisd. 6.)

Oh, ye high renowned lords and princes, who are appointed by God, to be heads and rulers of the people, consider well and believe the word of the Lord: for if you will not desist from unrighteousness, and fear God and do right, it would be better for you if you had never been born.   The innocent blood of Abel calls unto heaven, (Gen. 4) and will be demanded at your hands at the last day.   Again we say, awake, fear God's word; for God the Lord himself, will rule in heaven, his kingdom, and in the thoughts and consciences of men. (Isa. 14.)   He will permit none to detract from his glory, or attempt to become exalted above him.   Lucifer the fair angel of God, desired to exalt himself to the Most High, but was cast down from heaven into the abyss of hell, and is retained in chains of darkness till the judgment of the last day. (Rev. 12 ; 2 Pet. 2 ; Jude 1.)

Beloved sirs, receive it in love, and be not offended, for the truth must be made known. Your pride has arisen to heaven ; this you will find to be true if you look at Christ, and his word, his example and life. The Almighty and everlasting Father, through his eternal Wisdom, Jesus Christ, has given ordinances, and commands, in his kingdom, which is his church, about doctrines, sacrament, &c. But you, through the counsel and instigation of the learned, have changed these, and resorted to persecution and extermination, by your inhuman mandates, as if the almighty and everlasting Word, were to yield to your authority ; and as if the divine ordinances of the Son of God, might be improved into a more suitable form, and made to answer a better purpose, through the wisdom of men. Oh presumption of presumption ! oh madness of all madness—why exalt thyself, O earth and dust ! Acknowledge Christ Jesus as your chief Lord, who, of God, is made to you a Prince and a Judge. (Eccl. 10.) The heavens are the Lord's, saith David, but the earth he gave to the children of men. (Eph. 1 ; Col. 2.) If any one were to rise up against the earthly emperor or king, and enter upon the kingdom and government, he would not be borne patiently, nor go unpunished ; much less will it be left unpunished, when an army of earthly flesh rises against the emperor and king, Christ Jesus, to dethrone him from the seat of his divine majesty, and to rob him of his sceptre and his crown, as though Christ, the eternal Wisdom of God, were unreasonable and unfit for the heavenly government. Reflect what befel the haughty and proud hearts who were for erecting their seats near the throne of God.

Therefore humble yourselves under the Almighty hand of God, as Peter teaches, (1 Pet. 5) and take the prosperous, great king, Nebuchadnezzar, as an example, (Dan. 3, 4 ;) and observe how grievously he was punished by God, on account of his pride ; and how, after being punished, he turned his heart to wisdom, and feared the Almighty ; he praised his works and adorable name.

Beloved, awaken and mend your ways, for it does not become the creature to rise up against the Creator. Christ will *himself* be the head of his church—the only teacher in his school—the only king who will judge his kingdom—not with the doctrines and commands of men, nor with slaying and murdering, but with his holy spirit, his power, his grace, and his word.

Therefore, we pray you, O you great ones of the earth, whom we, through the mercy of God, acknowledge in all temporal things before our gracious Lord, that you would not grieve the eternal Almighty king, Christ Jesus, who has been ordained by his Father as the only Lord and Saviour of our indigent souls; and that you perform the duties of your office in *temporal* government, to which you have been called. We do with all our hearts, desire to render Cæsar, the things of Cæsar, and to God, the things that are Gods. (Matt. 22.) Be pleased to consider well, this, our doctrine and instruction, concerning baptism, and the Lord's supper, and the shunning of Babylonian deeds; and compare it with the word of the Lord. We hope, through the grace of God, you will find in truth that we believe and teach nothing else, than what the true oracle of the Lord has commanded us, and his holy apostles have testified. To this end, may the great Lord grant you his grace. Amen.

CONCERNING BAPTISM.

Christ, after his resurrection, commanded his apostles saying, Go ye therefore, and teach all nations, baptizing them in the name of the Father, and of the Son, and of the Holy Ghost; teaching them to observe all things whatsoever I have commanded you, and lo, I am with you always, even unto the end of the world. (Matt. 28.) Here we have the Lord's command concerning baptism, when and how it shall be administered after God's ordinance; namely that the gospel must first be preached and then those baptized who believe therein. Christ says, "Go ye into all the world and preach the gospel to every creature. He that believeth and is baptized shall be saved, but he that believeth not, shall be damned." (Mark 16.) Thus hath the Lord commanded and ordered, therefore, let nothing else be taught or practised forever. (1 Cor. 3.) God's word abides forever. (Isa. 40; 1 Pet. 1.) Young children are without understanding and cannot be taught, therefore, no baptism can be administered to them, without perverting the ordinance of the Lord, misusing his high name, and doing violence to his holy word. In the New Testament there are no ceremonies commanded children, for it treats, both in doctrines and sacraments, with those who have ears to hear and hearts to understand. (Matt. 13; Mark 4; Luke 8.)

As Christ commanded, so the holy apostles taught and practised, as may de perceived in many parts of the New Testament. Thus Peter said, Repent and be baptized in the name of Christ for the forgiveness of sins, so shall ye receive the gift of the holy ghost. Again, Philip said to the Eunuch, "If thou believest with all thine heart, thou mayest be baptized." (Acts 8.) Here faith followed not baptism, but baptism followed faith. (Matt. 28 ; Mark 16 ; Eph. 5 ; Heh. 6.)

Thus has Christ commanded baptism, and received it himself, according to the following manner :—when the time had come, and the hour had approached, in which he was to execute his enjoined commission, to preach the word, and make known his Father's holy name, he went to John, to the Jordan and was baptized by him, that he might fulfil all righteousness. He prepared himself to meet temptation, misery, the cross and death. And as a willing, obedient child, he resigned himself to his father's will ; he himself said, that he did not come to do his will, but the will of him that sent Him. (John 6.) He was baptized by John, attested to by the Holy Ghost, and acknowledged by the Father, as a beloved son. (Matt. 3.)

Behold, thus Christ commands, and was himself baptized ; and thus the apostles taught and practised. Who will rise up against the Lord, and say, it shall not be so ? Who will teach and instruct WISDOM ? Who will charge the apostles and evangelists with falsehood ? It would be altogether unbecoming for a child to command and judge his father, or a servant his master , and it is much more improper for the creature to oppose the Creator. But now it is manifest that the world with its unprofitable doctrines and commandments of men— with its anti-christian customs, long-standing usages, its tyrannical, murdering sword, judges over Christ and his word. Christ's truths are esteemed lies ; his wisdom, foolishness ; his light, darkness ; and his gospel, perverted and false. In short, Christ must be silent and suffer.

Now it may probably be said, that a command of this kind was necessary in the beginning of the gospel, for at that time there were no believers whose children might be baptized. But if the parents are believers, their children then are also baptized, even as Abraham, when he believed, circumcised his children. (Gen. 17.) Oh no ! this does not follow. Although Abraham believed God, only one half of his seed was circumcised, namely. the male children, and not the females, though he was the father of the female. as well as the male children : of which, in the replication, by the grace of God, more shall be said.

In the beginning the gospel was to be preached, and faith followed hearing, and baptism followed faith ; this is incontrovertible, for so the scriptures teach. (Rom. 10 ; Mark 16.,

That believers' children should be baptized because Abraham's children were circumcised (Gen. 14,) cannot be supported by scripture; but if it could be established, though it cannot, but few, would then be baptized, for the number of true believers, it is to be lamented, is very small. They are not all christians who are so called. But those only who have the spirit of Christ, are true christians; and I know not where many are to be found. Yea, all who with Abel bring an acceptable offering; those who are born with Isaac of the free woman, and with Jacob, have the birth-right, and have obtained the paternal blessing, must be slain by Cain, mocked by Ishmael, and hated by Esau, (Gen. 25, 27; John 3; Gal. 4.) even as we hear and see on all sides—may God effect a change for the better,

This is the word and will of the Lord, that all who hear and believe, be baptized, (as above stated) in order to profess their faith, and declare that they will henceforth not live according to their own will, but according to the will of God, (2 Cor. 6.) That for the testimony of Jesus they are ready to forsake their lives and property, and to suffer hunger, affliction, persecution, the cross and death; yea, they desire to subdue the flesh with its lusts, and arise with Christ, even as Paul says, know ye that all who are baptized with Christ are baptized unto his death. (Col. 2) We are buried with him, by baptism, into death; that, like as Christ was raised up from the dead, by the power of the father, even so we also should walk in newness of life. (Rom. 6.)

Beloved reader, take heed to the word of the Lord. for this also Paul teaches, (Gal. 1,) who received not his gospel of men, but of the Lord Jesus Christ himself; Even as Christ died and was buried, so also ought we to die unto our sins, and be buried with Christ in baptism; we are not to do this after we have been baptized, but we must commence the work beforehand. For if we have been planted together in the likeness of his death, we shall be also in the likeness of his resurrection: knowing this that our old man is crucified with him, that the body of sin might be destroyed, that henceforth we should not serve sin. For he that is dead, is freed from sin. Now if we be dead with Christ, we believe that we shall also live with him.—Knowing that Christ being raised from the dead, dieth no more; death hath no more dominion over him; for in that he died, he died unto sin once; but in that he liveth, he liveth unto God. (Rom. 6.)

Think not, that by dying unto sin, we teach that christians are to become insensible to sin. By no means; but they die so unto sin as to be no longer under its dominion; thus Paul says; Let not sin reign in your mortal bodies, &c. John says whosoever is born of God, doth not commit sin; for his seed remaineth in him; and he cannot sin because he is born of God. (1 John 3, 5.)

Even so, the death of the Lord would not have profited us, had he not risen from the power of death to the praise of his Father. Neither would it avail us anything to bury our sins in baptism, if we do not arise with Christ Jesus, from the power of sin, unto a new life, to the praise of the Lord. That Christ died, he died once unto sin, says Paul, but that he lives unto God. Likewise, reckon ye also yourselves to be dead indeed unto sin, but alive unto God, through Jesus Christ our Lord. For as ye have yielded your members servants unto uncleanness, and to iniquity, unto iniquity; even so, now yield your members servants unto righteousness and true holiness, and the end is everlasting life. (Rom. 6.)

Here observe, sensible reader; you who desire to know the truth, and seek your soul's salvation, what the great and holy apostle Paul has taught you here. If you believe his word, doctrine and testimony to be true, you will readily perceive, from these instructions, and from many other passages in scripture, that baptism is no more serviceable to children, than circumcision was for the Israelite females. We are no more to baptize children than Israel was to circumcise female children. And it is impossible for little children to die to sin so long as they have not been alive to it; and they cannot rise to a new life, as long as they are not born of God through faith, and by the spirit of God led into righteousness; and therefore beware, for the intent of baptism, is to bury sin and to rise with Christ into a new life, which can, by no means, be the case with young children, therefore look well, into the matter, what the word of the Lord teaches you, on this subject.

Again, Paul calls baptism *the washing of regeneration.* Oh, dear Lord, how lamentably thy holy word is abused. Is it not lamentable, that men are attempting, notwithstanding these plain passages, to maintain infant baptism, and pretend that infants are regenerated thereby, as if regeneration were effected by simple immersion into water. Oh no, regeneration is not a work of such hypocrisy, but is an inward change, which converts a man, by the power of God—the working of faith, from evil to good, from lusts to spirtuality, from unrighteousness to righteousness, out of Adam into Christ; this can by no means take place with little children. The regenerated live by the power of the new principle, they mortify the flesh, with its evil lusts; they put off the old man with his deeds; they avoid every appearance of evil; they are taught, governed and influenced by the Holy Ghost, &c. (Hab. 2; Rom. 1.) This is true regeneration, and its fruits of which the scriptures speak; it comes by faith in the word of God (1 Pet. 1; 1 Cor. 4; James 1,) without which no one can be saved, who has arrived to the years of understanding; for Christ says, verily, verily, I say unto you, except a man be born again he cannot enter into the kingdom of God (John 3.) Yea, it is all in vain, if one were baptized by Peter or Paul, or Christ, himself, if he be not baptized from above with the Holy Ghost and with fire.) (Matt. 3; Luke 3; 2 Cor. 5.) Paul says, in Christ Jesus, neither circumcision nor uncircumcision availeth any thing, but a new creature. All who are thus born of God, are changed and renewed in the inner man —translated from Adam into Christ, and are ready to obey the word of the Lord, and say with holy Paul: Lord what wilt thou that we should do? Such deny themselves with all their minds and hearts—they submit themselves to the word and ordinances of the Lord, without dislike or gain-saying. They suffer themselves to be baptized according to the commands of the Lord. (Matt. 23; Mark 16.) They manifest themselves to be fruitful branches of Christ the vine, and joint heirs of the community of the Lord. (John 15; 1 Cor. 12.) They receive the forgiveness of their sins and the gift of the Holy Ghost. (Acts 2.) They put on Christ, (Gal. 3,) and enter the ark of safety, and are secured from the dreadful flood of wrath which will come upon the world. (1 Pet. 3.) This is not effected by the power of the water or the sign, but by the power of the divine word, received through faith; for where there is no faith, which, through love worketh obedience, (we again speak of those who have arrived at years of understanding,) there is no promise. He that believeth not the son, will not see life, but the wrath of God abideth upon him. (Gal. 5; John 3.)

The Lord commanded Moses, (Ex. 14,) that he should stretch forth his hand with a rod and smite the sea, and the waters would divide. Moses believed the Lord's word; he stretched forth his hand, and smote the sea with his rod, and the waters divided and Israel was redeemed; this was not effected by the rod or the stroke, but the power of divine word, received by Moses through a lively and sincere faith. (Exod. 14.) Had Moses not believed God's word, and through disobedience not smote the water, undoubtedly oppressed Israel would have fared ill. He also received a command in the wilderness, to erect a brazen serpent, so that when Israel looked thereon, they might be healed of the bite of a serpent, (Wisd. 16,) not through the power of the image of the serpent, but by the power of the divine word received by them. (Num. 21.) In the same manner salvation is ascribed to scriptural baptism, (Mark 16,) the forgiveness of sins, (Acts 2,) the putting on of Christ, (Gal. 3,)

4

incorporating into the church, (1 Cor. 12,) not on account of the water, or the administered sign, (else the kingdom of God would depend upon the elements and the signs) but on account of the power and truth of the divine promise, which we receive in obedience through faith. Those who trust to words, elements and works, make with Aaron, a golden calf and suffer the people to commit idolatry and abominations therewith; for, in Christ, faith alone avails which is effectual in love, (Gal. 5,) which is manifested in the new creature, and in the keeping of the commands of God. (1 Cor. 7.)

Ye beloved sirs, friends, and brethern, awaken and delay not, render the Most High his praise and honor, and give ear to his word, for those who maintain that the baptism of ignorant children is a baptism of regeneration, do violence to the word of God; they gainsay the Holy Ghost; they make Christ to falsify, and his holy apostles to be false witnesses, for Christ and his apostles taught that regeneration is wrought through faith and the word of God, (John 1, 3,) which word is not to be taught to those who are *naturally* unable to hear or understand, but to the hearing and rational—this is incontrovertible, (Matt. 13; Mark, 4; Luke 8.)

The Holy apostle Peter explains the same, and says, that baptism saves us, not the putting away of the filth of the flesh, but the answer of a good conscience towards God; (or the covenant of a good conscience towards God) by the resurrection of Jesus Christ, (1 Pet. 3.)

Here Peter teaches us how the inner baptism saves us, by which the inner man is washed, and not the outward baptism by which the flesh is washed; for only this inward baptism, as before said, is of value in the sight of God, while the outward baptism follows only as an evidence of obedience, which is of faith; for could outward baptism save without the inner washing, the whole scriptures which speak of the new man, would be spoken and written to no purpose, the kingdom of heaven would be bound to elemental water; the blood of Christ would be shed in vain, for none who is baptized would be lost. O no, no! Outward baptism profit nothing, as long as we are not inwardly renewed, regenerated, and baptized by God, with the heavenly fire and the Holy Ghost. But if we are baptized with the baptism from above, we will be constrained through the spirit and word of God, by a good conscience, which we have thereby, to cordially believe in the merits of the death of the Lord and in the power and benefits of his resurrection; and henceforth, because we are inwardly cleansed by faith, and endued with spiritual strength, we obediently covenant with the Lord, (through the outward sign of baptism, which is enjoined on all the believers in Christ,) even as the Lord has covenanted with us in his grace, through his word, that we will no longer live according to the evil, unclean lusts of the flesh, but walk according to the witness of a good conscience.

And though these words of Peter are very plain, still the learned are not ashamed to wrest them into a foreign signification, by means of their plausible comments and highly boasted reason. They do this, that they may enjoy the favor of the world; and live at ease, without affliction or persecution. They teach that baptism is a sign of grace, which according to our limited understanding, can in no wise be established. Our sign of grace is Christ Jesus alone, through whom God's abundant love is freely dispensed and declared unto us, (John 3, 4; Rom. 8.) By signs he was gloriously prefigured to the ancient patriarchs, as by the coats of skin, to Adam and Eve; by the rainbow to Noah, (Gen. 3, 9) by circumcision to Abraham; (Gen. 17,) by which sign they were assured of the divine covenant. But we are only assured by God, of divine grace and peace, through one sign, which is Christ; the seal in our conscience is the Holy Ghost, (Eph. 4,) But baptism is a sign of *obedience*, commanded by Christ, by which we testify, when we receive it, that we believe the word of the Lord, that we are sorry for our former life and conduct, (Gal. 4; Rom. 8; Mark 15,) that we desire to rise with Christ in a new life; and that we believe in the redemption from sin through Jesus Christ, (Rom. 6; Col. 2; Acts 2.) Not, my beloved, that we believe in the remission of sins through baptism:—by no means; because, by baptism we cannot obtain faith and repentance, neither do we receive the forgiveness of sins, nor peace, nor liberty of conscience, but we testify thereby, that we have repented, received pardon and faith in Christ, as before said. But with the fathers it was not thus, for they, through the signs, received assurance and comfort, that the promise would be true and sure. We have this assurance in Christ alone, in whom all the figurative signs were completed. We have it in the only true sign, Christ, but the fathers had it in many figurative signs. In short, had we forgiveness of sins and peace of conscience, through outward ceremonies, and elements, then the REALITY would be superceded and its merits made of no effect.

Behold, this is the true basis of baptism which the scriptures maintain, and we teach or practise none other, though all the gates of hell exert themselves and become indignant thereat; for we know it is the revealed word of the Lord, and his divine ordinance, from which we dare not take away, nor add thereto, lest we be found disobedient and false before God, who alone is the Lord and God of our consciences, for the word of the Lord is pure, he is a shield to them who put their trust in him. (Prov. 30, 5.)

Oh God, what are the learned and highly learned masters of this world doing, who are so earnestly engaged in derogating from God's word and wisdom, and ingeniously urging their own vain reason; but they will not prosper; God will not give his honor to another, for he is the Lord, and there is none beside him. (Isa. 42.) Conquering, he will conquer them. He will turn their wisdom to folly and their reason to disgrace, for he knows that the thoughts of the wise are vain. (1 Cor. 3; Ps. 93.)

Luther writes: that children should be baptized on account of their own faith, and adds, "If children had no faith, then their baptism would be blaspheming the sacrament," &c. It appears to me, to be a great error in this learned man, through whose writings at first the Lord effected much good, that he maintained that ignorant, irrational children had faith, while the scriptures teach so plainly, that they know not good from evil, (Deut. 1.) Yea, they cannot discern their right hand from their left, (Jona. 4.) He saith that faith is dormant and concealed in children, till they arrive at the age of understanding. If Luther writes this as his sincere opinion, he writes much in vain concerning faith and its power, but if he writes to please men, may God have mercy upon him, for we know of a truth it is only human reason and the invention of men, but it shall not make void the word and ordinance of the Lord. For we do not read in scripture that the apostles baptized a single *sleeping believer.*—They baptized those who were awake, and not the slumbering. Why then should children be baptized before they awaken from their dormant faith, or even before the possession of such faith is known to them?

Bucer does not thus support the doctrine, but he maintains infant baptism differently, namely: not that children have faith, but that they, by baptism may be added to the church of the Lord, and instructed in his word. He admits that infant baptism is not expressly commanded, and he is correct in this. O Lord! how lamentably they do err, who court the favor and honor of men, and seek not the favor and honor of God. Since infant baptism is not expressly commanded by God, as he acknowledges, it cannot be acceptable to the Lord, *Et per consequence,* i. e. and by consequence, no promise can follow. Therefore, the reader should know, that true christians ought not to be governed in this matter, by the opinions and traditions of men, but by the word and the ordinances of God. For we have but one Lord and master of our conscience, Christ Jesus, whose word, will, command and ordinance, we, as his willing disciples, are implicitly to follow, even as the bride rejoices greatly to hear the bridegroom's voice. (John 3.)

Since we have not a single command in the scriptures, that infants are to be baptized, or that the apostle did practice it; we modestly confess, with a clear conscience, that infant baptism is but human sentiment; a capricious notion; a perversion of the ordinance of Christ; a manifest abomination, standing in the holy place, where it ought properly, not to be. (Matt. 24; Dan. 9.)

Beloved sirs, how little the word of the Lord is regarded, which says: What thing soever I command you, observe to do it: thou shalt not add thereto, nor diminish from it. (Deut. 12.) Did not the Father testify from heaven and declare, This is my beloved son, in whom I am well pleased; him ye shall hear?. (Matt. 3, 17; Mark 9; Matt. 28.) Does not scripture direct us to Christ? Are we not baptized in his name that we should hear his voice; and be obedient to his word? Do you not boast to be the apostolic church? Why do you then depart from Christ and adhere to anti-christ—depart from the apostolic doctrine and usages, and maintain the usages of the learned? Do observe how severely and often God punished the opinions which men held concerning holy works, and divine worship.

Nadab and Abihu died when offering strange fire before the Lord. Saul had mercy on Agag, the king of the Amelekites, and he spared the best sheep and oxen, to sacrifice unto the Lord, contrary to the word of the prophet. That seemingly act of mercy and laudable zeal was punished as the sin of witchcraft and the iniquity of idolatry, because he acted according to his own judgment, and not according to the word of the prophet. He was reproved by the prophet—smitten with a pestilence—his kingdom was taken from him, and given to a more faithful one. (1 Sam. 13.)

Manaseh, the king of the Jews, and others in Israel, made their children pass through fire—they built temples, and reared altars in many groves, cities and countries, with good intentions (2 Kings, 21.) For they were desirous to honor the Almighty thereby, as may be plainly seen from Isa. 36. This glorious and holy choice was so offensive before God, that Jeremiah refused to intercede for the people. Israel was desolated, Jerusalem and the temple burnt; and the people with the holy vessels were carried into a foreign land, (2 Kings, 15; 2 Chron. 36.) Therefore, saith God by the prophet: Obey my voice, and I will be your God, and ye shall be my people; and walk ye in all the ways that I have commanded you, not those of your own choice, that it may be well with you. (Jer. 7.)

What advice then, my beloved friends, in relation to such wilful deceivers, who presumptuously do violence to the word of the Lord, and so shamefully belie the Almighty, the most high-

4*

God, in teaching that their doctrines are in the word of God?
Teaching such things that He never did, or will command.

How awful it is thus to sin against God, to pervert his holy and
precious word! Yea, they will be sorely beaten and severely
punished of the Lord—they will not escape the ire of his wrath,
if they do not repent and reform; for God is an enemy to all
liars. They have neither part nor lot in his kingdom; but
their portion is eternal destruction, in the lake of fire. (2 Thes.
2.; Rev. 21, 22.)

In the second place, it is evident, that infant baptism is an accursed abomination and idolatry; for all those who are baptized
in infancy, are called christians and are accounted partakers of
the Lord's grace, merits, death and blood, and are called his
people (although the whole course of their lives, is heathenish
and dissolute, nay, idle, carousing, drinking, gaming, whoring,
cursing and swearing are their works—they believe that the
water in baptism can make and preserve them christians.) O no!
no! Paul positively declares: He that hath not the spirit of
Christ, is none of his. (Rom. 8.) Yea, the helpless, innocent
children, though baptized with the blood of the Lord, and having
the sure promise of the kingdom of God, if not baptized, by this
baptism, are buried without the grave yard as accursed. What
infamy!—what blindness! We will say nothing of godfathers,
of crossing the children, breathing upon them, sprinkling with
salt water, annointing; and spitting upon them, and that abominable exorcism, all which is nothing else than open blasphemy,
and not commanded by God. What abominable, detestable
idolatry!

In the third place, we are informed by historians, ancient, and
modern, (Matt. 28; Mark 16,) and we also learn from several
decrees, that baptism was changed both as to its mode and time
of administering. (In the beginning of the holy church, persons
were baptized in common water on their first profession, on account of their own faith, agreeable to scripture. Afterwards a
change was made; they were examined seven times before being
baptized—After that, they were baptized at two stated periods,
namely; at Easter and Whitsuntide. Higinius, the tenth pope,
instituted godfathers, in the year A. D. 146. Luther tells us,
that in the year A. D. 407, Pope Innocent confirmed infant
baptism by a decree, and it is to be feared, that it will not be
abrogated but at the expense of much innocent blood, of the
saints of God; even as the prophets, in their days reproved the
accursed abominations and idolatry of the kings, priests and
people, not by admonition only, but also, with their blood, as we
read in sacred and profane history.)

If infant baptism was commanded of God, why did Innocent

add his decree? How can baptism as practised, by the world, be right, since it has been so frequently changed? We entreat you, for Jesus' sake, to reflect, that Christ Jesus, but not the learned, is King and Lord of his community, he rules his church with his sceptre, spirit and word. He is Wisdom, and none can instruct him; he appeared to testify the truth; they that love the truth, hear his voice, (Matt. 11; Eccl. 24, Rom. 11; John 19;) believe his word and not that of the learned; for his word is truth; but the word of the learned, in this respect, is seduction; for Christ commands that believers should be baptized. He has not commanded that children should be baptized. But the learned say: He that has his children not baptized, (and is himself baptized upon his faith, even as Christ commanded) is a fanatic, ana-baptist and heretic.

Now you know the principal reasons why we are opposed both in word and doctrine, to infant baptism, and resist it with all our powers. For we well know, by the grace of God, that there is not one word in the scriptures in its support.—We tell you the truth and lie not. Is there one under the canopy of heaven who can show us, by divine truth, that Jesus Christ, the son of Almighty God, the Eternal Wisdom and Truth, the lawgiver and teacher of the New Testament, has given a single command that children should be baptized; or that his holy apostles ever so taught, or practised. If they did not, why urge us to such a ceremony, by tyranny and punishment? Show it to us in the word of God, and the difficulty is removed. For God, who is omniscient, knows, that in our weakness, we humbly seek to walk according to the divine ordinances, word and will, for which, we miserable men, are shamefully reviled, dispersed, robbed and slain, in many countries, like innocent sheep. But the Lord be eternally praised! We are esteemed as unworthy of heaven or earth, even as Christ said: They shall deliver you up to be afflicted, and shall kill you; ye shall be hated of all nations for my name's sake. (Matt. 24.)

It is our determination, that we will not only have a clear conscience in this matter, but we will, in everything else, to escape the wrath of Almighty God, be not influenced by lords and princes, or be governed by doctors and teachers, neither by the councils of the fathers, and long established customs; for in this matter, nothing contrary to the word of God, neither emperors nor kings, nor doctors, nor licentiates, nor councils nor proscription shall stand. We dare not be bound to any person, power, wisdom and place, but we must be governed alone, by the expressed and positive commands of Christ, and adhere, as said, to the pure doctrines and usages of his holy apostles; for if we do so, we neither deceive any one, nor are we deceived. Alas!

woe to him, woe to him, who departs from this foundation, or is compelled to do so, either through bodily fear or care, or tyranny, or by false doctrine ; and will not testify unto this wicked and sinful generation, both in word and deed, of the word of his Lord. (Matt. 10, 16, 24 ; Mark 8; Luke 9.)

All of you who reject the word of God and persecute his people, take particular notice of this our doctrine, ground and belief concerning baptism, which are in accordance with the instructions and words of Christ, viz. : that we must first hear and believe the word of God, and *then* be baptized; we are not seditious and for war; we do not approve polygamy ; we neither seek nor wait for any kingdom upon earth ; O no ! no ! God be praised, we know what the word of the Lord teaches us on this subject. (Matt. 28 ; Mark 16.) The Lord commanded us to die to sin, to bury them with Christ, and to rise with him into a new life, (Rom. 6 ; Col. 2,) even, as baptism is a figure thereof. That we humbly strive to walk in the covenant of his grace, and his eternal peace, and live upright and humble in Christ Jesus, with an approved conscience before God, (1 Pet. 3.) even as the mouth of the Lord has commanded, as he has testified by his example, as we are taught by the pure doctrines and practices of the apostles.

COUNTER ARGUMENTS WITH THEIR REPLICATIONS.

HAVING briefly noticed the Lord's command and the apostolic doctrine and usages concerning baptism, and its design ; that it is the true, and will be the true baptism to the end of time ; we will, therefore, now call your attention, by the grace of God, to another part of the same subject; and answer some of the arguments which have been adduced by the learned from scripture, in support of their doctrine, whereby they perverted and made void the ordinance of the Lord, and substituted their own.

In the first place, they teach, that we are all sinful, and the children of wrath, born of the sinful seed of Adam, and therefore, say they, children are to be baptized, in order to be purified and washed from original sin, &c.

To which we reply, thus, with the word of the Lord: We believe and confess that we all come from, and are born of unclean sin ; that we through the first Adam, became wholly depraved, and children of death and of hell. (Rom. 5 ; 1 Cor. 15.) Nevertheless, as we fell, and became sinners in Adam, we also confess and believe that we were restored by, grace and justified through Christ, the heavenly Adam; for he appeared upon earth, that in and through him we might have life. Through him we glory to have obtained grace, favor and the forgiveness of our sins with God our heavenly Father; and not through baptism, whether we are children or believers; for if redemption, and the washing away of sins, were through baptism and not by the blood of Christ, alone, then would the sweet smelling sacrifice, which is of eternal worth, have been in vain, and without effect, or, there would be two remedies for our sins? Alas, no! the scriptures speak but of one, which is Christ with his merits, death and blood. (1 Pet. 1; John; Acts 2.) Therefore, he who seeks the remission of his sins through baptism, rejects the blood of the Lord and makes water his idol. Therefore, let every one be careful lest he ascribe the honor and glory due to Christ, to the ceremonies and the elements.

It is true, Peter says: (Acts 2.) Repent and be baptized every one of you in the name of Jesus Christ, for the remission of sins, &c. But this is not to be understood, that we receive the remission of our sins through baptism. O no! for if it be so, then Christ and his merits must fall. We receive the remission of our sins, in baptism, in this manner: The Lord commanded his gospel to be preached to every creature, so that all who believe and are baptized, may be saved. Where there is faith, which is called the gift of God, by Paul, (Eph. 1.) there also are the power and the fruits of faith. Where there is an active, fruitful faith, there also is the promise; but where such a faith does not exist, (we speak of adults,) there also is no promise. For he that hears the word of the Lord, and believes it with all his heart, manifests his fruit, he observes all things the Lord commanded him; for the scriptures teach, the just shall live by faith. (Heb. 1; Rom. 1; Gal. 3; Heb. 10.) Then the remission of his sins is preached to him, as Peter teaches.

Had Noah and Lot not believed the word of the Lord, they would have fared ill. (Gen. 6, 7, 8, 17.) Had Abraham not believed, he would not have obtained such glorious promises: but they believed, and did right, and became heirs of righteousness. (Heb. 11.)

Had Moses and Israel not believed the word of the Lord and been obedient, how could they have been succored in the sea and in the wilderness? But they believed, and according to His promise, were protected by the mighty hand of the Lord. But those who provoked Him, and believed not his gracious word, and the great miracles, fell in the wilderness, and entered not the promised land. (Exod. 16; Num. 11, 14; Ps. 94; Heb. 3, 4.)

There was also reconciliation connected with the sacrifices of the Old Testament, not on account of the worth of the smoking offerings upon the altars; for it was not possible, says Paul, that the blood of bulls and goats should take away sin; (Heb. 10.) Before it was offered, it was all the Lord's, and the cattle upon a thousand hills, were his, says David. (Ps. 49.) But because the righteous believed the word of divine promise as true, and walked in obedience to his command. Thus now is the remission of sins preached through baptism; not on account of the water, or the ceremonies, for Christ is the only source of grace. But, because the righteous receive the promises of the Lord by faith, and obediently follow his word and will.

This direction does not extend to children. For in all the scriptures, there is not a single command given to baptize them. Therefore, it is not required of them as a sign of obedience. Since, then, infant baptism is performed without the command of God, it cannot be a ceremony of God, but a pernicious superstition of men, and evidently idolatry; therefore, the promise of God cannot be connected with such abominations. It seems to me, it is high time to awaken, and to give heed to the scriptures. Sins are not imputed for Christ's sake to infants. Life is promised, not through any one ceremony, but out of pure grace, in the promises of the Lord; as he himself says: Suffer little children to come unto me and forbid them not, for of such is the kingdom of heaven. (Matt. 19; Mark 10; Luke 18.) But concerning baptism he did not command them any thing. According to my opinion, it is a great error, (which some entertain,) that little children were pleasing to Christ on account of circumcision; and that ours on account of baptism, are also pleasing to him. O blasphemy! In every instance, Christ, the only medium of divine grace, must be set aside, and grace be attributed to the rites and elements. Here I would ask all the Pedobaptists, how they are going to prove that these blessed children were all circumcised—and that there were not among them female children? Were they acceptable on account of circumcision, as they pretend, and why not adults, who were circumcised? Although they were circumcised, he commanded that adults should be baptized upon their faith; but concerning children, he did not command that they should at all be baptized. He took them into his arms, laid his hands upon them and blessed them; promised them the kingdom, and dismissed them, but did not baptize them.

Thus did the wisdom of God himself; but the world would be his teacher. Christ does not command that *infants*, but *adults* should be baptized. What is more abominable, if any one is baptized on believing, because the Lord commanded him to do so; and for conscience sake has not his children baptized, because the word of God does not command it, he must, alas, have reproachful epithets applied to him by every one; and in addition, he may expect torture, misery and death. And this persecution is not to be attributed so much to the rulers, as to those who are esteemed learned, for what the rulers do, they do generally by the counsel of the learned. By their fruits, they show who is their father, for they do his works. It seems to me there ever were, and ever will be those, who, with false doctrines and hard hearts, shed the blood of the righteous. (Matt. 23; Rev. 17, 18.) Alas! such persecution is so disgraceful, that it is almost a shame to mention it. Even as the sun shines before all the world, and of these inhuman, learned, against the Lord and his chosen. God grant that these blind, perverted, blood-thirsty teachers, with all their tyranny, may see and become tired of their false doctrine, and their shedding of innocent blood, Amen.

In the second place, they teach that the children of Israel under the Old Testament, were initiated into the church and admitted into God's covenant through circumcision. But now, our children are admitted into church through baptism. In accordance with scripture, we reply, no! For whoever reads the scriptures understandingly, will clearly perceive, that Abraham was in covenant with the Lord, many years before he was circumcised. And that the children were circumcised on the eighth day, although they had been in the covenant before. For it is evident, that we do not become the children of God through any outward rites, but through the paternal and gracious choice, through Christ Jesus. (Eph, 1.) But an outward sign was commanded Abraham as a seal of obedience and faith. And likewise of his seed, that they should circumcise the male children on the eighth day, no sooner nor later, and not the female children. (Gen. 17.) Had the covenant depended upon the sign, and not upon the grace, what would have become of the female children, and the males that died before the seventh day.

Reader, give heed to the word of God. Although the women and female children were not circumcised, they had the promise in common, in the promised seed, the holy land, the kingdom and glory. They were no less the seed of Abraham and in the covenant, and the things signified by the circumcision, than the circumcised men and male children. From which it is evident, that the children of Israel were not in the Lord's covenant, on account of circumcision, as Pedobaptists assert, but through the divine choice of grace.

And even as Abraham and the children of Israel,—the female as well as the male children, were in the covenant through the divine choice, so also are our children in the covenant of God, although not baptized. The word of Paul is incontrovertible: Who has chosen us in him before the foundation of the world, &c., and has ordained us His children by Jesus Christ. (Eph. 1.)

Again. Children are entitled to the kingdom of heaven, and are under the promise of the grace of God, through Christ; as has been said; and therefore we truly believe, that they are blessed, holy and pure, acceptable to God, are under the covenant, and in his church, not by any external sign; for there is not a word in all the scriptures whereby to maintain, that children were admitted into the covenant, and incorporated with the church. Besides, it is very evident that they cannot be taught or admonished by word, or sacrament, long as they are without understanding.

Therefore, are the signs not to be used for any other purpose than they were designed and commanded by the Lord. Since Christ has ordained and commanded to baptize believers; and not said a word of infant baptism; we believe and teach that the baptism of believers is of the word of God, and infant baptism of the dragon and the beast.

All the rites ordained of God, both of the Old and New Testament, are ordained to exercise our faith and to show our obedience. Therefore, we are not to use them in such a way, and change them as we think proper; but, we must use them as the Lord himself, has ordained and commanded, if we would escape being punished by the fierce wrath of God, as were Nadab and Abihu. (Lev. 10.)

Since Christ has commanded that believers should be baptized, and not infants, and the holy apostles taught thus, in accordance with the instructions and commands of Christ, as may be seen in many places of the New Testament, all reasonable-minded men must admit, that infant baptism, although held by nearly the whole world, and maintained by tyranny, is nothing less than a ceremony of anti-christ, open blasphemy, an enchanting sin, a molten calf, yea abomination and idolatry.

We also know how they apply circumcision figuratively to allude to baptism, and adduce the saying of Paul, in proof thereof, (Col. 2, 11,) namely: In whom also ye are circumcised with the circumcision made without hands, &c. He that will attempt to prove, by this passage, that infant baptism is right, does violence to holy Paul, and perverts his testimony. (For he does not teach that eternal circumcision is a figure of baptism, (Gen. 18; Jos. 5,) but alludes to inward circumcision, (Rom. 2; Phil. 3; Coll. 2.) For even as actual circumcision of the foreskin was performed with a knife of stone, so also must our inbred and Adamic nature be cut off with that spiritual knife of stone, done without hands. The stone is Christ. (1 Cor. 10.) The knife is the word of God. (Heb. 4; Eph. 6.) It is with this circumcision that believers not children, are circumcised, as Paul evidently intends to teach by this scripture: Ye are circumcised with the circumcision made without hands, in putting off the body of the sins of the flesh by the circumcision of Christ, buried with him in baptism, wherein also ye are risen with him through the faith of the operation of God. It appears to me, that these words plainly show that Paul spoke not in relation to the baptism of children; but in regard to inner circumcision of the believers. Read also what we said above (Rom. 6.)

In the third place, they say, that children are regenerated, put on Christ, and receive the Holy Ghost, in baptism.

To which we reply: To be regenerated, to put on Christ, and to receive the Holy Ghost, are one and the same thing; and according to its power, inseparable. Have you the one, you have the other also. But that does not at all concern children; for regeneration takes place through faith, through the word of God, and is a change of heart, or of the inward man, as above said. To put on Christ, is to be transplanted, into Christ, and to be like-minded with him. To receive the Holy Ghost, is to be a partaker of his gifts and power, to be taught, assured and influenced by him, as the scriptures teach. This cannot take place with children; for they have no ears to hear the word of the Lord, and no understanding to comprehend it. Faith is by the hearing, of the word.

Here it may be asked, whether God is not powerful enough to work faith in children; because John the baptist, yet unborn, leapt in his mother's womb for joy. (Luke 1.)

We reply to this, that we are not speaking of the POWER of God; he made aged and barren Sarah fruitful, (Gen. 18, 21,) and caused Balaam's ass to speak. (Num. 22.) But it does not follow that all old, barren women will become fruitful, and that all asses are to speak. Therefore, he does not ALL he could do; but we speak of the scriptures, what they teach and command us concerning this matter.

Because little children do not understand, therefore, they cannot believe, and because they do not believe, they cannot be born again. Reason teaches us that they cannot understand the word of God. That they do not believe and are not regenerated, is evident from their actions. Be they baptized or not, their inbred nature is from their youth prone to evil. (Gen. 6, 8.) They know no difference between Christ and Satan; between good and evil; between life and death. (Deut. 1; Jonah 4.) Whereby then shall we know their faith, regeneration, or that

5

they possess Christ and his Spirit? The regenerating word must first be heard and believed with a sincere heart, before regeneration, the putting on of Christ and the influences of the Holy Ghost, follow.

Behold, thus we are taught by the word of the Lord. He that does, therefore, not desire the palatable bread of the divine word, upon which our souls have to live, may satisfy himself with husks,—we cannot forbid him. (Deut. 8; Matt. 4; Luke 15.) I trust that the gracious Father will protect and preserve us, out of his great mercy, from their anti-christian doctrines and Pharisaic leaven.

In the fourth place, they say: that although children are not so washed from original sin in baptism, that there are no remains of it, still for the sake of baptism these shall not be imputed to them as sin.

To which we reply: Thus to teach and believe, is open blasphemy against Christ and his blood. I have proved more than once by the word of the Lord, that Christ is the only remedy for our sins, and that there is forever none other. (Isa. 43, 53; Matt. 1, 20, 26; Mark 14; Luke 2, 22, 24; John, 1, 3; Acts, 4, 10; Gal. 1, 2; Eph. 1, 2, 5; Col. 1, 2; 1 Tim. 1, 2; Tit. 2, 3; Heb. 1, 2, 3, 4, 5, 6, 7, 8, 9, 10, 13; 1 Pet. 1, 2, 3, 4; 1 John 1, 2, 3, 4, 5; Rev. 1.) If men will not believe the word of God, there is no help for them. But the way or manner in which believers receive the remission of sins, in baptism, is fully explained above, and he that reads it understandingly, will give the Lord Jesus the praise due him, and not ascribe the remission of his sins to rites and elements.

In the fifth place, they say, that Christ has cleansed and sanctified his church with the washing of water. (Eph. 5,) Children, (say they,) belong, to the church, therefore, they must be cleansed with the washing of water by the word.

To which we reply, Paul does not speak of children, but of those who hear and believe the word of the Lord, and thus by faith, their hearts are sanctified and cleansed. (Acts 15.) For such are cleansed by the washing of water, as the mouth of the Lord has commanded.

Since children have not this pure, sanctifying faith, nor the means thereto, (Rom. 10,) namely, the understanding, and are not commanded in scripture to be baptized; how can they then be cleansed with water by the word, having no faith in the word, and no washing of water by the word? Therefore, all pedo-baptists should know, that their infant baptism does neither cleanse nor sanctify, but that it is idolatry *in toto*, without promise—pernicious, and contrary to the word of the Lord.

We have before shown, that the remission of sins, or reconciliation was connected with and consequent upon the Jewish offerings, if performed according to the instructions of Moses. But when not thus performed, they did not obtain reconciliation, but made themselves the more guilty, as Saul, Uzziah, Nadab, Abihu and others. (1 Sam. 15 ; 2 Chron. 26 ; Lev. 20.) In like manner is the church sanctified and cleansed, with the washing of water, by the word, if it is done in every respect according to the instruction of the word. But if not, a man is not cleansed, but sins much more.

And although children have neither faith nor baptism, no one has a right to believe, that they will therefore be damned! O no! they are blessed ; for they have the Lord's own promise of the kingdom of God ; not through any elements, ceremonies and external rites, but they are saved only by grace, through Jesus Christ. (Matt. 19; Mark 10; Luke 18.) And therefore, we do truly believe, that they are in a state of grace, acceptable to God, pure, holy, heirs of God and of eternal life. For on account of this promise, all sincere, christian believers, may assuredly comfort themselves and rejoice in the salvation of their children.

In the sixth place, they say, that children are to be baptized on account of the promise made them, as above stated ; although Christ did not baptize the children brought to him, or had them baptized ; but they say, that he had infant baptism, taught and practised after his death.

To which we reply : This is a false doctrine, and has not the word of God to sanction it ; yea, it cannot be supported by a single word in the scriptures. We rejoice with all our heart, that they have this promise ; the scriptures, however, do not teach that they should, therefore, be baptized. And that they were not baptized before Christ's death, gives us greater assurance still, that they were not baptized after his death ; for we certainly know, that he taught no other word, no other doctrine, no other baptism, nor did he give another spirit, or another promise, nor had he instructed others to teach differently, after his death, than before that event. That he commanded his holy apostles, after his ascension, to teach and practise infant baptism, can never be proved by the word of the Lord.

O flesh, flesh! thou art not ashamed to charge lies upon Jesus Christ and his apostles, and to practise infant baptism under the semblance of the divine word, as if the Lord had taught it, though he never did. How much you are like those who say : Thus saith the Lord, Lord, albeit, I have not spoken it, saith the Lord. (Jer. 23 ; Exod. 13.)

As often as the question is put to us, why shall children not be baptized. since they belong to the church of God, and are partakers of his grace, covenant and promise ?

We answer : Because the Lord neither taught nor commanded it.

In the seventh place they say : The scriptures inform us, that the apostles baptized whole families, from which we may readily conclude, that there were infants among them.

To which, in the first place, we reply, that they acknowledge by their own argument, which they base upon uncertain *conjectures*, that there is not a word in the scriptures, which teaches this doctrine.

In the second place, we answer, that in things of such importance, we dare not build upon uncertain suppositions, but upon the sure word, which is a lamp to our feet and a light to our path.   (Ps. 119.)

We answer in the third place, that four families are mentioned in the scriptures, as having been baptized ; namely, Corneilus's, the jailor's, Lydia's and Stephanas's, (Acts 10, 16 ; 1 Cor. 16.)   And the scriptures plainly show that these four families were all believers, namely, the family of Cornelius, the jailor's, and that of Stephanas. But, touching the family of Lydia, although the scriptures say nothing definitely concerning it, the reader should know that it is not usual in scripture, nor the common custom of the world, to call the family by the woman's name, as long as the husband is living.   Since then, Luke mentions the family by the name of the woman, reason teaches us, that Lydia was at that time either a widow or a virgin.   Of the difficulty to determine whether there were children in her house, we shall let the pious reader judge.

We answer in the fourth place, that the word *household*, or houses, does not include the minor children as mentioned in the scripture : for Paul says : That the idle talkers subvert whole *houses*.   And that a little child cannot be subverted by any false doctrine, is incontrovertibly true.   Therefore, by the word *house* or *houses*, no others can be understood, than *those* who have ears to hear, and hearts to understand.

In the last place, they appeal to Origen and Augustine, and say, that these assert, that they have received infant baptism from the apostles.

To which we answer, and ask : Can Origen and Augustine, prove this by the scriptures ?   Have they done so ?—we desire to know ; if not, then must we hear and believe Christ and his apostles, and not Augustine and Origen.

That this is not the case may readily be seen from Cyprian ; because he left infant baptism at liberty, if the preachers of Nordlingen, for many years past, have rightly informed me in the history of their church, and not deceived me with the meaning of the word *Libertum.* Cyprian also was a Greek, as well as Origen, and lived twenty-five years after him. If then infant baptism was the doctrine of the apostles and practised by them, as Origen and Augustine assert, it must first be proved by the scriptures, and then Cyprian must not have sinned a little, to leave the observance of the doctrines and usages of the apostles at *liberty.* For any thing that is apostolic, dare not be changed by any man. The word of Paul is indisputable; if an angel were to come from heaven to preach another gospel unto you, than that which he had preached unto you, let him be accursed. Else we would be constrained to acknowledge, that the twelve apostles with their doctrine, were not the twelve foundations and twelve gates of the new Jerusalem.

If infant baptism is apostolic, why does Tertullian write and say, "They who are baptized, confess for a considerable time in the church, before the bishop, that they renounce the devil, his pomp and angels," &c.

Revanus annotates on this passage and says : That it was the custom of old, that the adults,—the grown persons, be baptized in the bath of regeneration.

That infant baptism was not apostolic, may be seen from the insipid remarks of Athanasius, as Rufinus plainly shows ; see *Eus.* 10 *Libro Eec. His. Cap.* 14.

And, remember how the early writers contended about infant baptism. Had it been apostolic, and found in the gospel, why would they have thus wrangled.

Read also Erasmus Rottered, *in sua concion., in his public orations,* Sebastus Frank's Chronicle. Ulrich Zuingle in his book of Articles, Martin Cellarius, *de immensis operi, Dei, concerning the immense works of God,* there you will find, that infant baptism is not the doctrine and the usuages of the apostles.

Behold, beloved reader, I admonish and advise you, if you seek God with all your heart, and do not wish to be deceived; depend not upon men and their doctrine, no matter how old, how *holy* and *excellent* soever they may be called; for one divine, ancient or modern, is against another; but put your trust in Christ and his word. Depend upon the sure instruction and usages of his holy apostles, and you will through the grace of God, be perfectly safe from all false doctrines and power of the devil; and you can walk with a pious mind before God. (Matt. 17.)

AN ADMONITION
ADDRESSED TO THE SCORNERS OF THE WORD AND BAPTISM.

WE well know, beloved reader, that there are many unprofitable talkers, who teach from the letters of the scriptures, that little children should not be baptized, but only christian believers; nevertheless they say: Why my dear sir, what can water avail us? We have been once baptized in the name of God. Had we only the new life, it would suffice. O, dear Lord! thus is thy precious word every where esteemed of this vicious world, as fables of Æsop; as if omnipotent majesty, the eternal wisdom and truth had taught and commanded some things to no purpose. No, my good reader, no, his name, is the governing Lord; his word is his will; his command is eternal life, (John 11.) All things which he has taught and commanded us, he will undoubtedly have us to observe: if we do not, woe to us! Christ says: He that hath my commandments, and keepeth them, he it is that loveth me. (John 15.) My counsel, says the prophet, will stand, and my will shall be done. Therefore, O creature, do no longer fight against God. Give ear to him and obey his voice, for it is his divine counsel, word and will. Who are you, that you would contend with God? Christ's sheep hear his voice. (John 10). True christians believe and obey. Are you sincere christians, born of God? Then why do you dread baptism; which is among the least that God commanded you? it has always been a weighty command, to love your enemy; to do good to those who hate you; to pray in spirit and in truth, for those who persecute you; (Matt. 5) to crucify your wicked and ungodly flesh, with its lusts and desires; (Rom. 12.; Gal 5) to subdue your arbitrary arrogance; your avariciousness; your offensive unchastity; your bloody hatred; your banqueting, eating and drinking to excess; to renounce your accursed idolatry; to desist from your envious revilings; to curb your slanderous tongue; to govern your heart, and flesh; to love and serve with all your heart, your Lord and God, your Creator and Redeemer; and in all things to submit to his holy word, and to love and serve your neighbor sincerely, with all your powers; (Deut. 6, 10; Matt. 22; Gal. 5) with all your possessions, with your counsel, with your labor, yea, if required, your death and blood, (Eph. 4,) to suffer misery and disdain for the Lord's word; with a sincere heart to bear the oppressive cross of Christ; (1 John 3) and to confess Christ

Jesus, before lords and princes—in prison and bonds—in life and death.

We think that these, and the like commands, were more powerful and weightier to perverse flesh, which is so naturally prone to follow its own way, than to have a hand full of water applied. And a sincere christian must at all times be ready to do all this; if not, he is not born of God : for the regenerated are of one mind with Christ Jesus.

All who have been translated from Adam into Christ, and become partakers of the divine nature, through the grace of God, and are baptized of God, with the spirit and fire of heavenly love, will not contend with and speak so deridingly of the Lord, and say : My dear sir, what can water avail ? But they say with trembling Paul ; Lord what wilt Thou have me to do ? (Acts 9.) And with the penitents on the day of Pentecost : Men and brethren, what shall we do ? (Acts 2.) They will renounce their own wisdom ; and willingly obey the word of the Lord; for they are influenced by his spirit; and through faith, willingly do all things commanded them.

But as long as their minds are not renewed, and they are not of the same mind with Christ, (Phil. 1,) and are not washed in the inner man, with clean water, from the living fountain of God ; they may well say ; What can water avail us ? (John 7 ; Heb. 10.) For as long as they are earthly and sensually minded, the whole ocean would not cleanse them.

My faithful reader, think not that we put great stress upon the elements and rites. I tell you the truth in Christ, and lie not. If any one were to come to me, even the emperor or the king, and would desire to be baptized, still walking in the unclean, ungodly lusts of the flesh, and were he not unblameable, penitent and regenerated, I would sooner die by the grace of God, than to baptize such an impenitent and sensual man. For where there is no renewing, regenerating faith, leading to obedience, there baptism should not be administered. Even as Philip said to the Eunuch; If thou believest with all thy heart, then mayest thou be baptized. (Acts 8.) But nevertheless, you ought to know, should the person to be baptized, come with a hypocritical heart, under semblance of faith, that his hypocrisy would not be imputed to the baptizer as a sin, but to the dissembler ; for no man knows the heart of man, save the spirit of man which is in him. (1 Cor. 2.)

It appears to me, that you might readily conclude that we desire no other water, than that which the Lord commands. For since we believe, that Christ is the true Messiah, to whom the law and the prophets directed, whom all the righteous patriarchs and prophets desired, that he came from heaven and testified the truth, and that his command is eternal life, we must, therefore, hear his voice and obey his word; if not, we actually show that we do not believe, but that we reject his counsel and word, and are ungrateful towards him, for his love.

I know well, that many of you will say: We were once baptized in the name of God, and with that we are satisfied. To which we reply: If you fear God with all your heart, and acknowledge that his word and ordinances are just and good, you must be judges yourselves whether you are baptized in the name, or against the name of God. It is true that the adorable, high name of God was pronounced over you, but not otherwise than it is pronounced over church-bells, chapels, altars, consecrated water, tapers and palms. All anti-christian idolatry and abominations, are performed under the semblance of the divine name; although they are not done by virtue *of* but *against* his name, (Exod. 20,) for they are done contrary to his word and will.

My beloved reader, reflect well upon these words, and judge them by the word of the Lord, and you will find that your baptism is instituted and invented of men, without the command of God, and must be accursed of God, who will himself rule and govern his church. (Gal. 1.) Would you rejoice in the promise and be partakers of the church of Christ, you must believe the word of the Lord, be obedient to, and follow his counsel, will and ordinances. But if you refuse, and follow your own, and not the Lord's counsel and will; you cannot comfort yourselves with any scriptural promise. For he that believeth not, says Christ, is already condemned. (John 3.)

Therefore, do no longer comfort yourselves with such vain comfort, and say, we have been once baptized. You are still unbelievers, rebellious and unclean. Your whole life is earthly and sensual, and your baptism is anti-christian, and is without the sanction of the word of God. Therefore, awaken, repent, believe in Christ, seek, fear and love God with all your heart, then the word of the Lord and his unction, will teach you what is proper for you to do in this matter. And say not, as some do, I will renounce the church and idolatry; I will serve my neighbor, &c.; but I do not wish to be baptized.

O you blind men! Do you think that the Lord is pleased with your staying away from the church, or with your alms, or any thing of the kind, if you reject his counsel and word? No! no!! He desires your obedience, but no sacrifice, (1 Sam. 15.) He desires the whole heart, the entire man. With him, neither church nor alms will avail, neither words nor deeds, as long as you are unrenewed. For in Christ Jesus, says Paul, neither circumcision, nor uncircumcision availeth anything, but faith which worketh by love, (Gal. 5) and a new creature, (Gal. 6) and the keeping of the commandments of God, (1 Cor. 7.)

And whosoever is renewed in Christ and born of God, he liveth no more, as Paul says: but Christ lives in him, (Gal. 1.) In all his ways he conforms to the word of the Lord, for the powerful, active faith constrains him to all obedience, and to every good work. But where this new principle is not, there fair words may indeed be, but in truth, nothing else than unbelief, disobedience, presumption, and perverseness.

I hereby entreat and admonish you, beloved reader, not to be so obstinate against the Lord, and say: what can water avail us? But do reflect that Christ Jesus himself was baptized, (Matt. 3) though he was without sin, and in his mouth guile was not found; (1 Cor. 1,) yea, righteousness himself, the way, the truth, and life, (John 4.) Say then, what could water avail Christ, who was all in all things? The disciples at Ephesus were re-baptized of Paul, because they knew nothing of the Holy Ghost, although they were baptized with the baptism of John, (Acts 19.) If Christ himself was baptized, who was without sin, (Matt. 11) and others were re-baptized of Paul, who were baptized with the baptism of John, which was also from heaven? Why do you then despise the Lord's baptism, you miserable, poor sinners, who were baptized without knowledge and faith, with the baptism of the dragon and the beast?

Cyprian, the martyr, with his council, in Africa, resolved that those who were baptized of heretics, should be re-baptized with the christian baptism, and they, therefore, maintained that heretical baptism could not be the baptism of Christ. Reflect a little, kind reader, who they were that baptized you; of whom they were sent; what kind of faith they had; what kind of lives they led; with what doctrine and usages you were baptized. If you will seriously reflect thereon, I hope by the grace of God, if you desire the true peace and liberty of conscience, you will soon be aware that you never knew either the external or internal baptism, much less received it.

Behold, beloved reader, here you have the true foundation and scriptural instructions of the baptism of Christ, and an explanation of the baptism of Antichrist.

Pray the Lord, the Most High, for a sound and clear understanding, that you may know the right and blessed truth, might believe and in the fear of the Lord, faithfully observe all things. Quit all useless disputing and gainsaying; for whosoever will dispute and gainsay with the determination to remain in the broad way, will ruin his soul, and will never walk honestly, and with a good conscience before God; and he will always find occasion to dispute and wrangle.

. Therefore, do examine, believe, and obey the word of God, with a sincere and devout heart, and be not deceived by fair speeches under disguise, and you will certainly obtain the sure ground of the saving truth, and the consoling promise of grace. The Lord Jesus grant, and give you his grace thereto, Amen.

THE LORD'S HOLY SUPPER.

You know, beloved sirs, friends and brethren, that every where much is written, preached and said concerning the Lord's supper. But with what knowledge, in what manner, with what faith, love, peace, and unity, they celebrate it, is evident. It is true, the Lord commanded, in the New Testament, the breaking of bread, or the last supper, but not to be celebrated as you do. Your Lord's supper is common to all, no matter who they are; the avaricious, the proud, the gay, drunkards, wranglers, idolators, debauchees, whoremongers, and rogues, celebrate with you. It is also used in an abominable, offensive, pompous, hypocritical and idolatrous manner; and besides, it is dispensed by such ministers, who, in truth, seek but the world, honor, ease, to serve their flesh and body, alas! as may be seen in many places.

Since so many of you are so zealous about the Lord's supper, but not according to the scripture, as you shall hear; for your table is more the devil's table than the Lord's, (1 Cor. 20.) I would, for Jesus' sake, that you would in the true fear of God, reflect and enquire whom, why and wherefore, the Lord instituted, ordained and left, this his supper, in the church, so that it may prove to you a living and an effecting sign; that it might be impressed upon, and bring to your mind the Lord's abundant kindness, the peace, the love, and union of his church, the communion of his flesh and blood; and that you may die to unrighteousness, and every other ungodly work; to live to righteousness and godliness: and renounce the devil's table; and that you may sit down at the Lord's table in the church of Christ, with true faith, and unfeigned love, as pious, penitent and regenerated.

Thus saith Paul: I have received of the Lord, that which also I delivered unto you, that the Lord Jesus, the same night in which he was betrayed, took bread, and when he had given thanks, he brake it and said: Take, eat, this is my body, which is broken for you, this do in remembrance of me. After the same manner, he took the cup, when he had supped, saying, this cup is the New Testament in my blood, this do ye as oft as ye drink it in remembrance of me. (1 Cor. 11.)

Here you have Paul's explanation of the words of the Lord's Supper, instituted by Jesus Christ, (Matt. 26; Mark 14; Luke 22;) concerning which words, the learned taught and disputed much; and alas, some of them, through their idolatrous misunderstanding, if we may call it such, and not pride, disputed at the expense of much innocent blood; and what holy Paul says, (Rom. 1.) concerning them is fulfilled. Professing themselves to be wise, they become fools. For they disputed most about the sign, which avails little, but they touched not the thing signified which avails much. In my opinion, they are indifferent what the qualification of the guests or communicants should be in order to sit with Christ at his table, to celebrate this holy sacrament.

There is not a single word in the scriptures, that should give cause for dispute concerning the visible and tangible sign: The spiritual judge all things spiritually. (1 Cor. 2.) For whatever that may be in the substance, it can be handled, seen and tasted. But it is more important for us to perform as much as we can, in our weakness, what is signified—the thing which is set forth to all true and Christian believers.

On this account, we will not trouble the well meaning and pious reader, with jarring, fruitless disputing, as the learned do; but we only desire, by the help and grace of the Lord, by the power of the divine word, to point out to you, for whom, and why Jesus left and ordained this supper, so that we do not prefer the visible sign to the reality of the thing signified, and depart from the truth to images.

To come to a right and profitable understanding of the Lord's Supper, what it is, why, and wherefore it was enjoined, four things in particular must be observed.

In the first place, we must take heed that we do not as some who make the visible, perishable bread and wine, the Lord's real flesh and blood; to believe this, is contrary to nature, reason and scripture; yea, it is open blasphemy of the Son of God, abomination and idolatry. But as Israel had to hold the passover annually, according to the command of Moses, to commemorate that the Almighty God, the God of Abraham, of Isaac and Jacob, did signally deliver them in *passing* over, and sparing their first born, when he slew the first born of the Egyptians; and by his strong hand and outstretched arm, gloriously redeemed, and rescued them from the iron furnace of Egypt and the dread tyranny and dominion of Pharoah, according to the word of his promise, (Exod. 15,) and hence the *paschal lamb* is called the *Lord's passah*, that is, *passover*, (Exod. 12.) The sign for the reality, for the *lamb* was not the *passover* (leap over) although so called, but it only typified the *passover*, as said. So in the Eucharist, the *bread* is called the *body*, and the *wine* the *blood* of the Lord. (Mark 16 ; Luke 24 ; Acts 1 ; Rom. 8 ; Eph. 4 ; 2 Pet. 3.) I say the sign is put for the *reality*, the thing signified or typified, not that it actually is the real flesh and blood of Christ; for with that he ascended into heaven, and sitteth at the right hand of his father, immortal, and unchangeable, in eternal majesty and glory ; but it is a memorial and type that Jesus Christ the Son of God has redeemed us from the power of the devil, from the dominion of hell and eternal death, by offering up an immaculate sacrifice, —his innocent flesh and blood, and has triumphantly led us into the kingdom of his grace, (Heb. 10,) as he himself says ; (Luke 22.) This do in remembrance of me.

In the second place, it is to be observed, that there is no greater evidence of love, than that one suffers death for another, as Christ says : Greater love hath no man than this, that a man lay down his life for his friends. Since this holy sign is only a memorial of the Lord's death, and since death is the greatest evidence of love, as said, we are therefore, reminded, when we are at the Lord's table, to eat his bread and to drink his cup, that we not only show forth and remember his death, but also all the glorious fruits of divine love, manifested towards us, in Christ; namely, that God, in the beginning, made man after his image—placed him in Paradise, and made all creatures subject to him, (Gen. 1, 2.)

And when he was beguiled of the serpent, he was comforted with the promise of a coming Conqueror and Saviour, Jesus Christ. That God sent Moses and the prophets, who sedulously practised the law, and directed to the promised Christ and his kingdom. That Christ Jesus, according to the promise of the Scriptures, finally appeared in this world,— a true man, born of the Virgin Mary, (Matt. 1, 2 ; Luke 1 ; John 1.) That in much misery, affliction and labor, he preached the saving and gracious word to the house of Israel—sought the lost sheep, and brought them to their true Shepherd. (Matt. 18 ; Luke 15.) Who has pacified and reconciled us before the Father, through his painful death and precious blood, (Eph. 2 ; Col. 1, 2,) as he himself says ; For God so loved the world that he gave his only begotten Son, that whosoever believeth in him should not perish but have everlasting life. (John 3.)

Oh ! the great, wonderful unsearchable and incomprehensible love of God, He did not send into this unfriendly world an angel, a patriarch, or a prophet, but his eternal ALMIGHTY WORD, his ETERNAL WISDOM, the brightness of his glory, in the form of sinful flesh, (Rom. 8,) and made him to be sin for us, who knew no sin ; that we might be made the righteousness of God in him. (2 Cor. 5.)

My good reader, do not understand this as if Christ had been a sinner. Far from it. The scriptures acquit him of all sin. He was the spotless lamb. He knew not sin, neither was guile found in his mouth. But Paul calls him *sin*, according to the Hebrew manner of expression; that is an offering for sin as the prophet says: He was wounded for our transgressions, he was bruised for our iniquities; the chastisement of our peace was upon him; and with his stripes were we healed, (Isa. 53.)

Beloved, worthy reader, all those who believe with their whole hearts in this glorious love of God, this abundant, great blessing of grace in Christ Jesus, manifested toward us, they are more and more renewed through such a faith; their hearts are filled with joy and exultation; they will break forth with joyful heart, in all manner of thanksgiving—they praise and commend God with all their heart, because they know, and believe with joyful heart, in the spirit; that the Father loved us so, that He gave us poor, wretched sinners, his own and Eternal Son, with his merits, as a gift and eternal ransom as Paul says: The kindness and love of God our Saviour toward man appeared, not by works of righteousness, which we have done, but according to his mercy he saved us, by the washing of regeneration, and renewing of the Holy Ghost; which he shed on us abundantly, through Jesus Christ our Saviour: That being justified by his grace, we should be made heirs according to the hope of eternal life. (Tit. 3.)

Here it is proper to observe: How the righteous died for the unrighteous, when we were yet sinners and enemies. (Rom. 5.) How the spotless lamb was prepared for us, in the fire of affliction—suffered upon the cross, and was offered an eternal propitiation for our sins. He, the creator of all things was bruised for our sakes, (Ex. 12; Heb. 1; John 1; Col. 1; Ps. 45.) And he, the most High, who was above all the children of men, &c., became as the most unworthy, and was counted with evil doers, (Isa. 53.) The innocent bore the sins of the whole world, and blotted out all our transgression, by the price of his crimson blood; as the scriptures declare: I restored that which I took not away. (Ps. 69.) In short, that Jesus Christ through His obedience, delivered Adam and all his seed from the consequences of disobedience, and by his painful death, again restored life. (Rom. 5.)

The apostle Paul, who knew this great and glorious work of divine love, broke forth and said, (Rom. 8:) Who will separate us from the love of God? Shall tribulation or distress, or persecution, or famine, or nakedness, or peril, or sword, as it is written. (Ps. 43.) For thy sake we are killed all the day long; we are accounted as sheep for the slaughter. Nay, in all

6

these things we are more than conquerors through him that loved us.   For I am persuaded, that neither death, nor life, nor angels, nor principalities, nor powers, nor things present, nor things to come, nor height, nor depth, nor any other creature, shall be able to separate us from the love of God, which is in Christ Jesus our Lord.

And this is what John says : Let us love him for he first loved us. (1 John 4.)   For nature teaches us to love those, who love us.   And this is the first fruit of the holy sacrament, if rightly celebrated.

In the third place, we have to observe : That christain union, love and peace are presented to us, and we are reminded of them, by the Lord's supper ; after which all true christians will have to strive with all their heart.   For we being many, (says Paul) are one bread, and one body :   For we are all partakers of that one bread.

Like as natural bread is made of many grains, broken and kneaded together, and baked by the heat of fire ; also is the church of Christ made up of many true believers, broken in their hearts, by the hammer of divine word, and are baptized by the Holy Ghost, and with the fire of pure love, into one body. (1 Cor. 12.)   And as the natural body is in harmony and peace with all its members, and as each member discharges its duty to promote the good of the whole body ; thus it also becomes the true and living members of the body of Christ, to be in harmony, of one heart, one mind and one soul.   Not quarrelsome and unpeaceable, not spiteful and envious, not wrathful and hateful, not malicious, not obstinate or rancorous, one toward another, not like the ambitious, covetous of honor, or the haughty of this world ; but in all things, one toward another, be long suffering, friendly, peaceable, ever ready to serve his neighbor in true christian love, in all things possible ; by exhortation ; by reproof, by comforting, by assisting, by counselling, with deed and with good, yea, in labor, with body and life. (Eph. 4.)   Ready to forgive one another, as Christ forgave us, and served us by his word, with his life and death. As Paul says :   Put on, therefore, as the elect of God, holy and beloved, bowels of mercies, kindness, humbleness of mind, meekness, long suffering : forbearing one another, and forgiving one another, if any man have a quarrel against any :   Even as Christ forgave you, so also do ye.   And above all things, put on charity, which is the bond of perfectness : and let the peace of God rule in your hearts, to which also ye are called into one body ; and be thankful. (Col. 3.)

And again ; as in the natural body, the more honorable members, such as the eye, the ear, the mouth do not proscribe the less honorable, and they also do not envy the more honorable ; but every member in its place, is peaceable, and contributes to the good of the whole body, whether it is honorable or feeble ; and thus in the church of the Lord God gave, says Paul, some apostles, some prophets ; some evangelists ; some teachers. Let every one be mindful that he boasts not of the things he has, for it is all the grace of God. Let every one attend to his duty, to the perfecting of the saints, for the work of the ministry, for the edifying of the body of Christ : till all come in the unity of faith, and the knowledge of the son of God. into a perfect man, unto the measure of the stature of the fullness of Christ. (Eph. 4.)

This is also set forth in the holy supper ; but how the world, calling themselves christians, live up to this, is shown by their fruits and actions.

In the fourth place, we have to observe : That the holy supper is the communion of the body and blood of Christ ; as Paul says : The cup of blessing which we bless, is it not the communion of the blood of Christ ? The bread which we break, is it not the communion of the body of Christ ? (1 Cor. 10.)

Since then it is a communion, as said, I would fraternally exhort all of you ; that you would earnestly examine yourselves, whether you have been made partakers of Christ ? (Heb. 3.) Whether you are flesh of his flesh, and bone of his bone ? (Eph. 5.) Whether you are in Christ, and Christ in you ? For all who would worthily eat of this bread, and drink of this cup, must be changed and renewed in the inner and outer man through the power of the divine word and the operation of faith ; (John 3 ; 2 Pet. 1.) and be of a new mind, as new creatures born of God, and translated from Adam into Christ ; be of a christian disposition, long suffering, peaceable, merciful, affectionate, and truly humble, and be obedient to the word of the Lord. The proud, ambitious, selfish and sensual heart must be circumcised. (Col. 2.) The evil eye must be plucked out, (Matt. 18.) the ear that delights to hear evil, must be closed ; the unprofitable, backbiting tongue must be bridled ; the unclean, bloody hand must be cleansed ; the unclean, unchaste flesh must be corrected, &c. (Isa. 2.) They must lead a crusade against the world, flesh and the devil ; their loins must be girt about with truth ; having on the breast-plate of righteousness ; their feet shod with the preparation of the gospel of peace ; they must be armed with the shield of faith ; with the helmet of salvation, and the sword of the spirit. (Eph. 6 ; 1 Thess. 5.) They must be led by the spirit of God, to become the sons of God ; and strive with all their powers, that they may be like-minded with Christ Jesus. (Phil. 2 ; Rom. 8.) When he insti-

tuted and celebrated it with his beloved disciples ; he said : With
desire I have desired to eat this passover with you before I
suffer. And then he took the cup and gave thanks and said :
This is my body which is given for you. Likewise also the wine.
This is the cup of the New Testament in my blood, &c. This do
in remembrance of me. (Matt. 22 ; Mark 14 ; Luke 22 ; 1 Cor.
11.) As if he had said : Behold, dear children, so far has that
love which I have had for you and the whole human family, and
shall ever have for you, constrained me, that I left the glory of
my Father, came into this world of affliction, and am as a poor,
miserable servant, to serve you, (John 3, 1 ; John 4 ; Rom. 8 ;
Phil. 1.) for I beheld that you all belonged to satan, and there
was none to redeem you, (Heb. 2.) and that you had all gone
astray, like erring sheep, and there was none who cared for you.
That you were a prey to devouring wolves, and there was none
to ransom you. (Isa. 53 ; Exod. 34 ; Matt. 18 ; Luke 15.) That
you were wounded with death, and there was none that could
heal you. (Luke 10 ; Exod. 16.) Therefore, did I come from
heaven, and became a poor, weak and dying man, in all things
like unto you, sin excepted. (John 1 ; Heb. 4.) In my great
love I zealously sought you, and I found you helpless, loathsome
and miserable, yea half dead, (Exod. 16,) the services of my love
I have so cordially manifested toward you ; your sores I bound
up ; your blood I wiped off ; I poured wine and oil into your
putrid wounds, (Luke 10,) set you free from the jaws of the
bears and lions of the pit ; I laid you upon my shoulders, and
led you into the tabernacles of peace ; (2 Kings 17 ; Ezra 1 ;)
your nakedness I covered ; had compassion on you in your
misery ; I fulfilled the law for you ; (Matt. 5 ; Rom. 8 ;) your sins
I took away ; I proclaimed to you the peace, the grace and favor
of my Father ; I made known to you his good will ; I pointed
out the way of truth ; and I have powerfully testified to you,
by my unheard-of signs and great miracles, that I am the true
Messiah, the promised Prince and Saviour. (Isa. 53 ; 1 Pet. 2 ;
Gen. 49 ; Job. 17 ; John 3.)

Beloved, children, so long as I have been with you, taught
my Father's word, admonished, reproved and comforted in his
name ; but now my hour is at hand ; this night I shall be
betrayed. All what the prophet said of me, has come to an
end. (Matt. 26 ; Luke 22.) But, since I can serve you no longer,
with my doctrine and life, I will, at last, serve you with my
painful sufferings.

And this is the reason why I called you to this supper, so that
I might institute a memorial in the use of bread and wine, and
that you might occasionally come together after my death, and
commemorate the gracious favors of my ardent love, so abun-

dantly manifested to you-ward; and especially, that I loved you so dearly, that I offered my body for you; and shed my blood for you. Greater love hath no man than this, that a man lay down his life for his friends. (1 Cor. 11; John 15.) I have by my death obtained for you everlasting reconciliation, grace, mercy, favor and peace with my Father, as I told you, namely: Even as the Son of man came not to be ministered unto, but to minister, and to give his life a ransom for many. (Matt. 20.)

Beloved reader, take notice of the word of the Lord and the institution. For where this holy supper is celebrated with such faith, love, devotion, peace, harmony, and so much cordiality, there Jesus Christ is present with his grace, spirit, and promise, and with the merits of his sufferings, misery, flesh, blood, cross and death; as he himself says: Where two or three are gathered together in my name, there am I in the midst of them. (Matt. 18.) But where the knowledge of Christ, active faith, new life, christian love, peace and harmony do not exist, there is not the Lord's supper, but a despising of the blood and death of Christ, a consolation of the impenitent, a seducing hypocrisy, and open blasphemy and idolatry. As, alas! we know and see by the world.

O! delightful assembly and christian banquet, called and ordained of the Lord himself, where there are no sensual pleasures, to gratify the flesh, but where are set forth, the glorious, holy mysteries by visible signs, under bread and wine—those mysteries are set forth, sought for, and desired by all true christian believers. (Matt. 26; Mark 14; Luke 22.)

O! delightful assembly and christian banquet, where no unseasonable, slanderous mockery, and trivial songs are sung; but there obtain the devout, christian life, peace, and harmony among all the brethren; besides the joyful word of divine grace, his gracious kindness, favor, love, service, tears, prayers, cross and death, with delightful praises of divine thanksgiving in devout joy, are all set forth, and exhibited to all.

O! delightful assembly and christian banquet; to which the impenitent and proud despisers, according to scripture are not invited; such as whores, and whore-mongers, rogues, adulterers, debauchees, the giddy, robbers, liars, defrauders, tyrants, bloodshedders, idolators, slanderers, &c., for such are not the people of the Lord.

But these are the people of Christ, who are invited, the true christians, who are born of God, who have subdued their sins and walk with Christ in newness of life, who crucify their flesh, are influenced by the Holy Ghost, who believe God with all their heart, seek, fear, and love him, and in their weakness gladly serve him, and are obedient unto him;—such are members of the body of Christ; flesh of his flesh; and bone of his bone. (Eph. 5.)

O! delightful assembly, and christian banquet; when there is not excess of eating and drinking, nor the ungodly frivolity of piping and drumming is heard; but there the troubled consciences are satisfied with the heavenly bread of the divine word, and with the wine of the Holy Ghost, joyful souls, singing and making melody in their hearts to the Lord.

Awaken, O you, who sit in darkness and walk in the region and shadow of death. Awaken, I say, and observe that the supper which you have, to the present held, is not the supper of Christ, but of antichrist; not the table of the Lord; but the table of the devil. For it is generally dispensed only by open deceivers, and worshippers of idols; and received by a people that is as yet quite dissolute, sensual, disbelievers, of the word of God and obstinate thereto. And moreover, they believe it to be the real body and blood of the Lord, and celebrate it with such unbecoming, heathenish pomp and splendor. O! abominable idolatry!!

Beloved reader, I bear witness to the truth in Christ and lie not; I tell you that the holy supper of Christ is not to be dispensed by a deceiver, nor to be received by an impenitent and obstinate sinner. Nor does it require such a gorgeous and splendid array to celebrate it; as the world is wont to celebrate it. Neither golden vessels, nor hypocritical semblance of confessions, absolution, bowing, and smiting upon the breast, &c., but it must be celebrated with a broken heart, and humble mind;—with unfeigned, ardent love, with peace and joy in the Holy Ghost. Again, I say, awaken, and reflect upon what I write. God's word and his work are no dead letter; it is not buffoonry. Nor is it the sounding of many bells and organs, and singing; but it is a heavenly power and a living, moving, of the Holy Ghost, which warms the heart and mind of the believers; pervades, comforts, anoints, and enlivens them; makes them joyful and happy in God. For this is the true nature and power of the Lord's word, if it be rightly preached, and of his holy sacraments, if rightly used.

It is, therefore, high time, to take heed to the word of the Lord. For all who are earthly and sensually minded, are not born of God and his word, are obstinately averse to the Lord's word; love not their neighbors, nor are ready to help them; all these are not the community of God, therefore they cannot be part of his body or guests at his table. For Paul says: To be carnally minded, is death, (Rom. 8; John 3.) Christ says: Those who are not born from above, cannot see the kingdom of God. And Samuel says: Disobedience is as iniquity and idolatry. (1 Sam. 15, 23.) John says: He that loveth not his brother, (neighbor) abideth in death. Again, He that loveth not, knows not God, for God is love. In short, without love, all preaching, all faith, baptizing, celebrating the Lord's supper, and prophecying, are vain, profit nothing. (1 Cor. 13.)

We do, therefore, admonish all those desiring to celebrate this supper, that they might rightly learn to know what the true supper is,—what it signifies—how it is to be used, and who are to celebrate it. And then also to examine themselves well, as Paul teaches, before they eat of this bread and drink of this cup; that they do not comfort themselves with the visible sign, and err in regard to the reality, represented by these signs; for they who know not Christ and his righteousness, believe not him and his word, and walk not according thereto; but according to the superstitious doctrines and commands of men, though they sit down at the Lord's table, they eat and drink damnation to themselves.

All who have received the word of the Lord through faith, and acknowledged it to be true, and have again transgressed it, and have not continued to walk in the truth, but are walking again in the broad way, have returned to the love of the world, and are rejecting Christ and his word, and depending upon the seducing doctrines, the interpretations and promises of the learned, such have no part at the Lord's table, for they are without God; as John says: Whosoever transgresseth, and abideth not in the doctrine of Christ, hath not God. (2 John I.)

All who walk in their heart's pride, and despise their poor distressed neighbor, and know not that they themselves are poor mortals, seed of Adam, and food for worms, and a wilted flower, yea dust and earth, whether they are emperor, king, rich, or learned, &c. and sit down at the Lord's table with a proud heart; eat and drink damnation of themselves.

All who boast of the Lord's spirit, name, covenant, word, knowledge, merits, grace, blood and death, and yet reject his holy counsel, doctrine, command, ordinance and his unblamable example, or reject and grieve his holy Spirit. hate, defraud and belie their neighbor, and sit down at the Lord's table; eat and drink damnation to themselves.

All who love houses, lands, friends, children, honor, ease of flesh, voluptuousness, and this life, more than they do Christ and his word, though attending the Lord's table, eat and drink damnation to themselves. Christ says: He that loveth any thing more than me, is not worthy of me and cannot be my disciple, (Matt. 10; Luke 14.)

And this is the sum of the whole matter, that all those who would sit down at the Lord's table, with the disciples and guests of Christ, whether rich or poor, high or low, must be sound in faith, unblamable in conduct and life. None are excepted, neither emperor nor king, nor prince nor earl, knight nor nobleman. Yea, as long as they err in doctrine and faith, and are in their lives sensual and blamable, they are by no means to be suffered to commune with the pious and penitent, to appear at the holy supper; for they are not in Christ, but must remain without, till they sincerely repent and are converted to Christ, walk in the ways of the Lord, and be of one spirit and one faith with Christ and his church. For the Lord's supper is a communion of the flesh and blood of Christ, which is not to be given to the ungodly and obdurate as a pledge of reconciliation, but to the sincere, penitent, christian believers.

If any one has a good appearance before men, and is inwardly proud, avaricious, sensual and without the spirit of God, he is not judged of the church, but of the Lord himself, the searcher and trier of men's hearts, and reins, as the scripture says. (Ps. 7; Jer. 17; Rom. 8; Rev. 2.) We do, therefore, admonish all those who would go to the Lord's table; to examine themselves before they approach; for all who eat unworthily of this bread, and drink of this wine, eat and drink damnation to themselves. (1 Cor. 11.)

Thus, beloved, does the holy supper instruct and admonish us: first; the bread, as the body of Christ, which he offered for us, and the cup, the blood of Christ which he shed in great love, for the remission of our sins. (Matt. 26; Mark 14; Luke 22.) In the second place, we are admonished to union, love and peace, which must be among all true christians, according to the spirit, doctrine and example of Christ; for Paul says: For we being many are one bread; and one body, &c. (1 Cor. 10.) In the third place, we are admonished to true regeneration, to all righteousness, thanksgiving, peace and joy in the Holy Ghost, to a pious and unblamable life. For it is a communion of the blood and body of Christ, of which no one is a partaker, nor can be, unless, he is born of God, dead unto sin, an humble, peaceable, pious christian, one who is in Christ, and Christ in in him; flesh of his flesh, and bone of his bone: This is to be a true partaker of the body and blood of Christ; as Paul says: For we are made partakers of Christ, if we hold the beginning of our confidence steadfast unto the end. (John 3; Eph. 5; Heb. 3.)

Behold, beloved readers, here you have the true instructions concerning the Lord's holy supper, with its significations, fruit, power, nature, and the guests, as the mouth of the Lord and the holy apostles have left it and taught us. The usages and ordinances which belong to the church of God, are to be observed and kept with knowledge, faith, love, union, peace and piety.

Here compare the supper of the world with *this*, and you will know the true one; what an abomination the Antichrist has made of it, and what enchantments he practised by it, and how we poor sinners, with all our forefathers, have offered incense, as idolatrous Israel of old, for hundreds of years, unto the brazen serpent, (2 Kings 8; Exod. 32,) and danced before the golden calf. (2 Chron. 12.) O! my faithful reader, fear God, with all your heart, examine the scriptures, and believe the truth.

OF THE CORRUPTION OF THE HOLY SUPPER.

THE scriptures teach that we have no other offering for sin than the body of the Lord, (Isa. 53; Matt. 20, 26; Rom. 3; Heb. 9, 10,) as before said. But because the enemies of Christ, have possessed the cathedral for so many years, and according to scripture, have altered the laws of the Most High, and have instead thereof, erected their abomination of desolation, (Deut. 7,) and have altered and corrupted the holy supper with their councils, power and false doctrine, till, alas! it retains but the shadow, and the mere name, and they did this to destroy and corrupt the true, eternal offering of Christ, which only avails with God, and changed it into a daily offering for sin, as we may plainly read in the canons of the mass; which undoubtedly is an abomination of abominations; for thereby, Jesus Christ with his all-sufficient, eternal offering, is abolished and made of none effect though he is the propitiation and mediation of the New Testament. He is thrust from his throne of majesty; his merits, cross, blood, and death rejected: yea, all the types and shadows of Moses, all predictions of the prophets; the promise of angels, and the whole New Testament, are thereby denied, for they all harmoniously point to the one and eternal offering of Christ; in opposition to, and instead of it, they ordained an unholy, blind, seductive and sensual idolatry, with a piece of bread! Beloved reader, here put no other construction upon these words; what I write is the truth.

It has come so far with this ungodly seducing corruption, that they have arrogated to themselves all power in heaven above, upon earth, and in hell below; they therefore break the bread into *three* pieces. With the *first*, they reconcile God; with the *second*, they intercede for the world; and with the *third*, as they pretend, they pray for the souls in purgatory.

Through this accursed infamy they rose so high in honor,

that they are above all the potentates of earth, (Acts 17,) whom they made their own servants. By their hypocritical service and enchanting idolatry, they hold in possession, money, goods, gold, silver, land, rents, cloisters, cities, principalities and the dominions of this world, because every one loved this splendid service as holy and divine, honored and feared their exalted and pompous names as the messengers of God!!

By this ingenious and subtle magic, the Roman Antichrist has gained such respect and authority, that even the imperial majesty, the highest soverignty on earth, whom we are commanded of God to respect and obey, had to humble himself and kiss his feet; yea, what is still worse, Frederick Barbarossa, a prudent man, an emperor of renown, could not be reconciled with Pope Alexander III. until he humbled himself at Venice, before the church, and suffered the Pope to tread upon him with his feet!

Behold, thus *Antichrist* has enchanted the whole world with his offering. The gracious Father be eternally praised, that he has, through his paternal grace delivered us, his poor children, from this enchanting offering, and given us to know the only and eternal offering of his son, Jesus Christ, who, according to the order of Melchisedek, is ordained an eternal high priest over the house of God; who, in the days of his flesh, offered up prayers and supplications with strong crying and tears, unto him that was able to save from death, and was heard, because he honored God. (Heb. 5, 7, 9, 10.) This one, I say, offered an acceptable offering, a sweet smelling sacrifice, of eternal worth, whereby he appeases the Father's wrath, reconciles the human race, opened heaven, and closed hell; and made peace between heaven and earth; and sits now, and henceforth, at the right hand of his Father, till his enemies be made his footstool, (Col. 1; Ps. 109,) yea, with this one offering, he has perfected forever all those who are sanctified. This cannot be gainsayed, whether by emperor or king, doctor or teacher, angel or devil. This word stands firmly and immovable. He has with one offering, I say with *one* offering, perfected for ever those who are sanctified. (Heb. 10.)

O, my beloved reader! I mean all those who are without the spirit of Christ and his word, take heed what the word of the Lord teaches you, and observe the true doctrine of Christ, the true sacraments, the true teachers, the true church and the true christian life, so that you may once learn to know what kind of pastors feed you; what kind of baptism and supper you practice; by what kind of offering you are reconciled; what kind of lives you lead, and of whose body you are members.

O how long, says Solomon, will you simple ones love simplicity? And you scorners delight in scorning? How long will you remain prisoners of sin? How long will you remain in the communion of the devil, and suffer yourselves to be dragged down to the abyss of hell by the cords of unbelief? Awake, and ransom your poor souls! Come out from among them! Avoid every appearance of evil; (Isa. 52; 2 Cor. 6; Rev. 18; 1 Thess. 5;) believe in Christ Jesus; repent and lead an unblamable life; follow Christ with a sincere heart; enter into the house and covenant of his everlasting peace, into the communion of his flesh and blood. Take upon you his easy yoke and you will find rest for your souls, (Matt. 11,) and you may then of a truth say, that you are christians; that you have obtained the remission of your sins, by the grace of God, through the merits of Christ; and that you are joint heirs of the eternal kingdom. May God grant his grace to you all. Amen.

In the second place, they made the bread, in the holy supper, into the real flesh, and the wine into the real blood of Christ, and understood the words of Christ literally: Take, eat, this is my body, &c., and did not observe that Christ (John 6) does fully instruct us, how we are to eat his flesh and drink his blood, and says, that it would profit nothing really to eat his flesh, and to drink his blood, for this could not be done, because he was about ascending to heaven where he was before; we are therefore not literally to understand this eating of his flesh, and drinking of his blood; but spiritually, as he himself says: The words that I speak unto you, they are spirit, and they are life. All those who thus understand this from the scriptures, are called and accursed as heretics and profaners of the sacrament, and suffer for it by water, fire and the sword.

O dear Lord! is this not an ungodly error, and great blindness, to teach and to believe; that a piece of bread, and a drink of wine should be changed into the real and essential flesh and blood of the son of God, whereby we may be delivered from hell, the devil, sin and death, and are made children of grace? O, horrible heresy!

O you poor, miserable, blind people, believe the words of Christ, when he says: It is the spirit that quickeneth; the flesh profiteth nothing: the words that I speak unto you, they are spirit, and they are life; believe that he ascended up to heaven and is at the right hand of his Father, (Mark 16; Luke 24; Rom. 8,) therefore he cannot be eaten nor confined in the body by any one, nor is he to be placed upon any altar, nor can he be consumed by fire or worms, as it is evidently the case with the visible bread and wine. (Col. 2.)

But where the Lord's church, the beloved disciples of Christ, who have met in his name, celebrate the holy supper in true faith, love and obedience, there the outward perishable man eats perishable bread and wine ; and the inner, the imperishable man of the heart, spiritually eats the imperishable flesh and blood of Christ, which can neither be eaten nor destroyed, as above said ; like is profited by like ; this is incontrovertible. The visible man is nourished upon visible food, and the invisible man is fed upon invisible bread, as we may plainly learn from the mouth of the Lord. (John 6.)

Therefore, all who are in Christ and with believing, penitent hearts, know and rely upon the pure offering of the body and blood of Christ, that it is the only sacrifice and ablution for their sins, the only and eternal medium of grace, eat the true flesh and drink the true blood of Christ, not with their mouths, but *spiritually*, by faith, as said before.

The reader may readily observe from these words, that the bread is no flesh, and that the wine is no blood ; for were they flesh and blood, as the idolators pretend and teach the poor people, one of two consequences must follow : either the perishable bread and wine are changed into the imperishable and heavenly Son of God ; or the Son of God must be changed into bread and wine. This is incontrovertible.

O dear Lord ! they are more ignorant than the heathens ever were ; true, the heathens worshipped sun, moon and stars, which have their influence upon things below. They worshipped the ox, the dragon, serpents, fire, and other creatures, some of which had living breath within them. They also worshipped images of wood, stone, gold and silver, made by skilful workmen, who cast, carved and decorated them in the likeness of man. But those who are called by the name of Christ, pray to, worship and adore a piece of bread and a mouthful of wine, as the real flesh and blood of Christ, who came from heaven for our salvation,—and was made an offering upon the cross for our sins. O intolerable abomination and infamy ! that the praise of God, the glory of Jesus Christ is converted and changed into such a feeble idol, which can neither speak, hear nor see ; neither can stand nor walk, which worms eat and fire consumes ; and must be locked up, preserved, assisted, and carried about by the hands of men, like the idols at Babylon, of which Baruch writes.

O my faithful reader, rightly learn to know Christ Jesus. He is not like the fabulous Proteus but he is now the everlasting, almighty Son of the eternal, omnipotent God, and not a perishable creature, bread and wine. Oh no ! he is unchangeable through all eternity. Neither can he be confined in any house, church nor chamber, in silver nor golden vessels ; for, according to his eternal divine being, heaven is his throne and the earth his footstool, and according to his holy humanity, he ascended into heaven and sits at the right hand of his Father. (Isa. 66; Acts 6, 17; Mark 16; Acts 1; Rom. 8.) He is the eternal and almighty power, brightness, word, truth, wisdom and image of God. (Heb. 1; Matt. 28; Eph. 1; Phil. 2.) He has all power in heaven above and on earth below, all things are under him; every knee has to bow, and every tongue to confess to him, that he is the Lord, to the honor and glory of his Father, (Matt. 26; Rev. 1.) and he will not appear again in the flesh, but he will come in the clouds of heaven, to judge the goats and sheep. (Matt. 25.)

Therefore I say again: That he cannot be eaten, nor can he be digested in the body of man. Augustine well knew this; when he says: Why do you make ready to eat? only believe, and you have eaten him.

Beloved reader, we well know, that Augustine did not write this of the natural eating of the holy supper; but of the spiritual eating, which is by faith; and with that view, we adduced it, so that the godfearing reader might see the difference between outward and inward eating, and not mistake the one for the other; for the external use of the sign is nothing but a false appearance and hypocrisy, if the thing which is invisibly represented, is not connected with it. That this is the case with infant baptism and the world's supper, may be readily proved from the scriptures; but where the mystery is connected with the sign, for which purpose it is ordained, there is the baptism of Christ, and his supper, as the scriptures teach. But this is hidden from the world. They know that the scriptures teach a supper, but what it actually is, what it prefigures and who are to enjoy it, they know not. The Babylonian whore has so completely deceived and bewitched them in this matter. (Rev. 17.)

The holy supper, as taught by Christ and his apostles, reproves all idolatry; foreign mediums of reconciliation; hatred, discord and unrighteousness; for it directs alone to the one offering of Christ which was made by his flesh and blood, once for all, as related; it represents christian peace, harmony, brotherly love, and a pious, unblamable life, as already said. For that reason they are forsaking the Lord's word and ordinances, and have turned away from the Creator to the creature, and from the true reality, to the perishable signs;—yea, they call the disgraceful mass, the sacrifice of the Lord; and the bread and wine his real flesh and blood; for this is the custom and manner of the ungodly, because they know not the true God,—God of heaven and earth, and hate the true service, and are inimicable thereto, believe not his holy and worthy word;

7

in God's stead they have a visible and tangible creature; and a service of their own choice. So did Israel with the golden calves, with Baal and Moloch; and Antioch with his Maosim, (god of forces,) (Exod. 31; 1 King 12; Jer. 7, 5; Deut. 20; Sam. 12,) the Babylonians with their Belus; the Egyptians with their Isis; &c. From this source, all disgraceful idolatry, which is practiced with this abomination, such as carrying about the bread, exalting it, praying thereto, offering of incense on every occasion to pay it divine honor and divine service. Concerning which there is not a letter in all the scriptures. Yea, alas! many esteem it so highly, that they say this is the same one who reconciled us upon the cross. Even as Israel said to the calf: These be thy gods, O Israel, which have brought thee up out of the land of Egypt. (Exod. 32.)

Beside this, the use of the cup is withheld from the people in the Roman church. If it were the Lord's supper, as they pretend, they would, in every respect, use it according to the ordinance of the Lord. But this custom shows that it is not the supper of Christ, but a deluding seduction of anti-christ.

Therefore, be wise and sober, you who name yourselves after the name of Christ. Spew out the wine which you have drunk of Babylonian whoredom. (Rev. 17.) You have danced and burned incense long enough to the golden calf. Give the Almighty the praises and honor due him; lest it happen to you as it did to faithless, disobedient and idolatrous Israel. (1 Cor. 10.) Although the Lord God graciously redeemed them from the power and tyranny of Pharoah, yet they had to suffer punishment on account of their unfaithfulness and obstinacy, and were destroyed in the wilderness. (Exod. 14.) And so it is also in vain that we are redeemed by the blood of the Lord from the dominion and power of the devil, if we do not repent, but remain idolators, and believe not in Jesus, and are not obedient nor live according to his word in our weakness. (Ps. 94; Heb. 3, 4.)

In the third place they teach; that this bread is dispensed for the remission of sins. My faithful reader, take notice of what I write. Where Jesus Christ and his word and spirit, are not known and acknowledged, there is nothing but unbelief, idolatry, error, and an uncertain wavering conscience, as may be seen.

All seek some remedy for their sins, but the true remedy, Christ, they do not acknowledge; hence they have contrived so many remedies, that we can neither describe nor relate them all; such as absolution, holy water, fastings, confessions, masses, pilgrimages, infant baptism, bread and wine, &c., &c.

I know not to whom to compare this race, other than to a

sick and wounded person, who has entrusted himself under the care of an unskilful physician, who can give him no suitable medicines, and apply no healing plasters ; he spends his money in vain ; he suffers pain and affliction: and is getting worse instead of better. A skilful, experienced and philanthropic physician is recommended, who would visit him without money and without price, bind up his wounds, and would gladly cure him ; but the sick man will not receive such a well-disposed physician ! Who then could feel for such a man, because he would rather perish than get well ?

So it is with this perverse race. They feel and are sensible, at times, that they are failing and sick, but they seek medicine and counsel of those who sicken them still more with their poison ; and are not healed of their wounds and cured of their disease. (Matt. 9.) They refuse the skilful, the heavenly chirurgen and physician, Jesus Christ, recommended by all the patriarchs, prophets, apostles and by angels, yea, appointed of the Father himself—him they will not have who would willingly visit all so deadly wounded ; he offers his services without money and without price ; he has a well scented, healing salve, good to heal our wounds,—it is his powerful word, to instruct ; and his crimson blood, to reconcile, as was said. (Matt. 11 ; John 7 ; Luke 10.) But they desire him not ; they turn away, and persecute him with all manner of false doctrine, with contumely, with lies, betrayings, mutiny, and murder; as has been fully shown. (Luke 19.) O dear Lord ! counsel thou with this disobedient, perverse and blind people ?

My worthy reader, we testify the truth in Christ; beware, believe, obey, hope and seek, where and what you desire ; we are assured that you will find no other remedy to all eternity, for your sins, in the word of God, which can stand before God, than the one we pointed out to you, Jesus Christ; else the scriptures must be false.

Thus says Isaiah : I, even I, am he that blotteth out thy transgressions for mine own sake, and will not remember thy sins.

He was wounded for our transgressions. (Isa. 53.) The angel said to Joseph : Thou shalt call him Jesus, for he shall save his people from their sins. (Matt. 1.)

This is my blood of the New Testament, which is shed for many, for the remission of sins. (Matt. 26.)

Lo this is the lamb of God which taketh away the sins of the whole world. (John 1.)

For he made him to be sin for us, who knew no sin, that we might be made the righteousness of God in him. (2 Cor. 5.)

Who, his own self bore our sins in his own body on the tree. (1 Pet. 2.)

The blood of his own son, Jesus Christ cleanses us from all sin. (1 John 1.)

He loved us, and washed us from our sins in his blood. (Acts 1.)

My good readers, look well to yourselves, and do not deceive yourselves; if there were any other remedy for sin, as related, we might then with propriety say, that these and other passages, have not rightly directed us; and holy Paul, also erred not a little, when he says: For there is one God, and one Mediator between God and man, the man Christ Jesus, who gave himself a ransom for all, to be testified in due time. (1 Tim. 2.)

All those, however holy they may appear, who seek for another remedy for their sins, instead of the remedy provided by God, deny the Lord's death, which he died for us, and his innocent blood which he shed for us; and they are those of whom the Lord complains and says, through his prophet Jeremiah: For my people have committed twofold evils, they have forsaken me, the fountain of living waters, and have hewn them out cisterns, that can hold no water.

And all false doctrine goes to deny the true throne of grace, Jesus Christ, who alone is our righteousness, acceptable to God; and all the erectings of strange Baals, who are worshipped and honored in Christ's stead, do so likewise.

Behold, beloved sirs, friends and brethren, here you have the salutary truth and the only ground of the Lord's supper, plainly and briefly set before you, what it is, for whom it is ordained, and what it teaches, and represents to us with its mysteries and significations.

And you have also a view of the anti-christian supper, with its dreadful abominations, whereby the Lord's supper is destroyed, and the kingdom of anti-christ is fortified, and is placed in the stead of God's throne, whereby, alas! tens of thousands of poor souls were and are yet daily deceived. On account of which so many pious are so slanderously spoken of and reproached by the learned, and so dreadfully murdered and slain in some cities, because they renounced this abominable idolatry.

Place these two beside each other—weigh them well by the spirit, word and ordinances of the Lord, and you will find, if you do at all believe that the word of God is true, to what an abominable pitch idolatry has risen, and that we have according to our feeble abilities, plainly explained to you the immovable foundation of truth out of the word of God.

Praise the Most High, all of you who fear the Lord, that he has manifested his unbounded love and grace to us-ward, poor sinners, in this dreadful time of unbelief; that he let shine out darkness, the clear light of the holy gospel, which was concealed for several centuries in this dark Egypt, under the clouds of the anti-christian abominations. (2 Cor. 4.)

Therefore, let us be vigilant thereto, and diligently walk therein, so that thick darkness may not again cover us, as the prophet says. (Jer. 13.)

O my dear reader, rightly learn to know Jesus Christ, who ordained this holy supper and breaking of bread for his disciples and all christians. Believe the glorious and unspeakable gifts of his grace. Fear, love, honor and serve him; walk in godly union, in love and peace with your neighbor, even as this supper, with its representation, testifies and admonishes; die to your wicked flesh, crucify its unclean lusts; in all things submit to the spirit of the Lord, and his word; imitate his example, and your supper will redound to the praise of the Lord, and it will be a blessing to your souls to eternal life.

OF SHUNNING BABYLON.

WE further teach and admonish from the word of God, that all true children of God, who are regenerated from the incorruptible living seed of the divine word, who have separated themselves, according to the scriptures, from the idolatrous race, and yielded to the yoke and cross of Christ, and who are able to judge between true and false doctrines—between Christ and anti-christ, must shun, according to scripture, all seducing and idolatrous preachers with their doctrines, sacraments and worship, (Jer. 23; Matt. 7, 15, 16; John 10; Rom. 16.) They must avoid all, of every sect, creed and name, who are not found in the pure doctrine of Christ, and in the scriptural usage of his sacraments. (1 Tim. 6; 2 Tim. 2, 3; Tit. 3; 2 John 1;) because they have neither calling, doctrine, nor life, according to the word of God, but are sent by anti-christ, and ordained in his employment and service. And

Because they not only fail to observe the pure doctrine of Christ, and to conform to the established usages of the apostolic church, in relation to the holy sacraments, but to vain confusion, they add (as has been stated) abominable and open idolatry.

Because they have deceitfully mingled the light froth of man's doctrine, with the fair, precious gold of the divine word, and the pure wine, with the unclean waters of their foolish wisdom. (Isa. 1 ; 2 Chron. 25, 26.)

Because they so shamefully censure, and would willingly root

7*

out and destroy the holy city of God, the city of righteousness and eternal peace ; the lovely Jerusalem with its sacred temple, the house of prayer, and rule therein with their spiritual mart, Pharasaic commands, and enchanting traffic. (Isa. 56; Jer. 7; Matt. 21; Mark 11; Luke 19; John 2; 2 Pet. 2.)

Because they, like Belshazzar, in their Babylonian idolatries, so miserably misuse and degrade the precious vessels and utensils of the Lord——the precious souls whom he has consecrated with his crimson blood, (1 Pet. 1) and by whom the *true* service of the Lord should be performed. (Rev. 1 ; Dan. 5.)

Because, like Herod, they mock Christ, the eternal Wisdom of God, as a fool arrayed in a fool's garment ; and his holy apostles, the witnesses of eternal truth, they regard as useless talkers and liars, and thrust them out with scorn. (Luke 27.)

In short, they preach and lay before the poor people lies for truth ; darkness for light ; death for life ; and Anti-christ for Christ.

Therefore it is unfit that the bride of Christ, who stands prepared to hear only the bridegroom's voice—the dear children of God who have their feet washed and their garments cleansed in the blood of the Lamb, (John 3, 13; Rev. 7.) who are established upon the immoveable foundations of the apostles and prophets, upon the precious corner stone, Christ Jesus, (Eph. 2,) should again hear the strange voice and doctrines of anti-christ, and again defile their garments, (John 10,) and in faith, doctrines, worship, and life accord with anti-christ. They who do so, (if they repent not) are condemned by the scriptures and adjudged to death, (2 Pet. 2 ; Rom. 1 ; 1 Cor. 6 ; Gal. 3 ; Rev. 21, 22.)

This we teach according to our limited talents, with all earnestness, not out of contempt, (as the Lord knows,) nor yet out of obstinancy, caprice, or party stubbornness, as the world ascribes to us. Oh no ! God preserve all his own from party spirit. But we so preach out of the pure fear of the Lord and the great distress and burthen of our consciences. God's pressing word, and love for your poor souls, urge us, (Gal. 5,) as may, through the grace of God, be seen with clearness hereafter.

OF THE SENDING OF PREACHERS.

ACCORDING to the scriptures, the sending of true preachers was performed in two ways : some were called by God alone, without any human instrumentality, as was the case with the **prophets and apostles.** Others were called through the medium of the pious, as may be seen from Acts 1, 14; 1 Tim. 3; Tit. 1. We hope no one will be so ignorant (who is otherwise of a candid and rational mind,) but that he will know that the whole scriptures, both of the Old and New Testaments, were written for our instruction, admonition and correction; and that they are the true sceptre and rule by which the Lord's kingdom, house, church and congregation must be governed and adjusted, (Rom, 15; 1 Cor. 10; 2 Tim. 3; Ps. 44; Heb. 1; Rev. 21.) Every thing, whether it be doctrines, sacraments, worship or conduct, which should be measured by this infallible rule, and divine justifying sceptre, without any respect to persons, if not so measured and adjusted, will be destroyed and brought to nothing. Therefore would we, your willing servants and associates, of like mortal nature with you, each one in the office and station to which he is called, humbly admonish you, in all love, that you would reflect on the salvation of your immortal souls, and would rightly examine the *sending* or *calling*, the doctrine and lives of the bishops, pastors and preachers of your churches. Examine them by the aid of the spirit of the Lord and by the doctrines and customs of the apostles, because you have persecuted and destroyed so many pious, godly christians, by the idols' houses of the ungodly, which are supported by the bloody havoc-cries of the learned. Yea, we doubt not, but that if you follow our advice with a sincere heart, you will soon perceive, that we, miserable men, do nothing more in this matter, than God's own word teaches and enjoins; and that your preachers are not the servants of Christ, but hirelings, hypocrites, deceivers and mockers, concerning whom the scriptures warn us, on every side, and represent them under many evil names. (John 10; Matt. 29; 2 Pet. 3; Jude 6.)

Candid reader! let this be to you a true and unwavering rule: All who rightly preach Christ and his word, and thereby bring forth obedient children to the Lord, (Rom. 10,) such must have been called through one of the aforementioned means. They must have been brought into the vineyard of the Lord, through unfeigned love of God and man—through the power of the Holy Ghost. They must improve the talent of grace which they have received from God, (Matt. 9; Luke 10.) They must rebuke sin, and teach faith and righteousness, without any respect to persons, (Matt. 25; Luke 19,) they must set forth the Lord's word and praise: they must perform correctly the work and service of the Lord and bring the gathered sheaves into his barn and acquired wealth into his treasury. Such a shepherd was the faithful Moses; for when the Lord informed him that Israel had made a molten calf, he hastened from the mountains, and when he heard the tumult and saw the multitude sporting, and dancing, a provoked zeal burned in his heart, so that he cast down and brake the stone tables which the Lord had written with his own finger.   He cared neither for life nor death, but rushed forth among the idolatrous people, and rebuked them by word and by sword, because they gave to a molten creature the honor of Almighty God, who with such love gloriously effected their deliverance from Egypt. (Exod. 32.)

When Zacharias, the son of Barachias, a man full of the Holy Ghost, saw the false worship of the people, he hazarded his life, and stood forth for the honor of the Lord.   He rebuked his brethren—erring Israel, and said :   Why transgress ye the commandment of the Lord that ye cannot prosper. (2 Chron. 24.)

Also the worthy prophet, Jeremiah, was burthened with suffering and cares. He was much troubled on account of his faithful services, and had determined in his heart to prophecy no more in the Lord ; but when he saw the people were ungodly nor acted nor spoke aright, he said, God's word was in my heart as a burning fire shut up in my bones, and I was weary with forbearing and I could not stay. (Jer. 20.)

Again, also holy Paul says : (1 Cor. 9.)   Wo is unto me, if I preach not the gospel ; For if I do this thing willingly, I have a reward ; but if against my will, a dispensation of the gospel is committed unto me.

Behold, my good reader, all, who by such a power are touched in their hearts, who are moved by the Holy Ghost, who are pressed by love to God and man, and urged by the Lord himself, or by his spotless christian church, are rightly called to the service of the Lord—to instruct, admonish, threaten, correct and comfort the house of God, the church of Christ, with sound doctrine and an unblamable life ; to set forth and administer the Lord's holy baptism and supper, in a right manner ; to repel diligently, with God's word, all deluding and false teachers to exclude all evil members from the communion of the godly, &c. To such, the word of Christ, is, I send you as my father has sent me ; (John 20 ;) without such a sending, no one can ever rightly preach the gospel, as Paul says :   How can they preach except they be sent. (Rom. 10.)

Yes, it was with this sending and calling that all prophets, apostles and servants of God came forth.   They sought not their own honor, as the preachers of this world do ; but like Aaron, they were called by God, or, as has been said, by the spotless church.   They were brought by the spirit of God, with pious hearts, into his service ; they had always esteemed themselves unfit to serve the people of God, or stand forth in such a high and responsible station. (Heb. 5 ; Acts 1, 14 ; 1 Tim. 3 ; Tit. 1.)

When Moses was called of the Lord, that he might lead out the people, he refused from his heart—he excused himself and declined, because he was of a slow tongue; he desired not the office to which the Lord had chosen him—yea, he resisted so long that the Lord was angry. (Exod. 4.)

Isaiah was confounded because he was to preach the word of the Lord. He lamented that he was of unclean lips till the angel purged them with a coal from off the holy altar. (Isa. 6.)

Jeremiah was called and prepared from his birth by God, to be a prophet; he said: Ah Lord God! I am not fit to preach, for I am but a child. (Jer. 1.)

Peter was asked by the Lord three times, if he loved him, before he gave him charge of his sheep. (John 21.)

Paul was called from heaven, and appointed by the Lord himself in the service of the Gospel; for the Lord chose him as suitable for the ministry. (1 Tim. 1; Acts 9; Gal. 1.) Matthias was chosen through the zealous prayers of the church, and the lots of the apostles, to be an apostle in Juda's stead. (Acts 1.)

All who are not sent by God, nor by an unblamable church, conformably to the regulations of Christ and the apostles are not called, (as above said.) Such are not called by the Holy Ghost, by the sincere love of God and their brethren, and with correct knowledge and zeal for the divine word, but they enter upon it with a temporal, sensual life, seeking man's favor, praise, money and profit. They will never gather fruit in the vineyard of the Lord, though they may be learned in language, eloquent and esteemed as great and excellent men, But all that they attempt is lost labor. They will rise early, and go out long, but their calling is powerless, their service is vain, their labor without fruit, yea, it is nothing but seeding by the way, and beating against the wind; for no one can serve in this high and holy office, conformably to God's will, except those whom the Lord of the vineyard has made worthy and fit, by the spirit of his grace.

Since then, this sending is the true sending and calling, which is taught in the scriptures, (as has been observed,) we faithfully counsel the reader, that in the pure fear of God, he would mark what kind of people their teachers are; how, of whom, in what way, and to what they are called. For it is manifest that some of them are useless, haughty, lustful men; some are avaricious, usurers, liars, deceivers, idolators, &c., concerning whom it stands written: If they repent not, they shall not inherit the kingdom of God. (Rom. 1; 1 Cor. 6; Gal. 5; Eph 5.) Some also, are idle profligates, young and haughty, wholly unlearned in the scriptures; and were anointed by anti-christ, when they obtain a little knowledge of the Latin tongue, like as if the qualifications for the ministry and for the care of our souls, were not to be founded upon godliness and the gifts of grace, but upon language! Oh no, my reader, no, their foundation must be sought for more deeply.

Besides, this, those so chosen, desire nothing but an indolent, carnal life and filthy lucre and benefices, which heretofore antichrist and his servants have collected together and multiplied by means of sorcery, theft and robbery.

They are only called by carnal love, favor and faction : one has a son, another a brother, a third a friend, a fourth is made willing by money and gifts.

They are also with a similar spirit installed and established in their office ; to wit : With eating, drinking gormandizing and luxury ; with pompous greeting choir letters, appellations, presentations, investitures, and such like antichristian titles. But by whom are they thus called? By the church? No. Christ's church knows no such callings, customs, practices and teachers, but they are called by the assemblies of the impenitent, the haughty, avaricious and unchaste, by gamblers, drunkards and idolators, who neither know God nor his word, but who abuse, persecute and hate all christian truth and walk after the lusts of the flesh.

Again, to what are they called? That they may genuinely preach the word of God? That they may go before the poor people, with doctrines and conduct consistent with the commands of scripture? O no: but that they may teach the doctrines and commandments of men : that they may withstand the holy truth, and betray the pious and godly, who refrain from the broadway, into the hands of the blood-thirsty.

But, beloved reader, why shall I much lament ; it is yet much worse than can be written. One blind man calls another ; one idolator another; one ungodly man, another. It is, as the prophet said, deceivers, liars, drunkards, and gluttons are good prophets for this people. (Mich. 2.)

O sensual preacher! You who with Korah, Dathan, and Abiram, (Num. 16) ran uncalled—particularly you who know that your calling and conduct are not of the word and spirit of God, judge your hearts by the word of the Lord, fear his rigid punishment and severe sentence, and reflect how the aforementioned persons, for the same reason, were fearfully destroyed by the Lord before all Israel. (Num. 16.)

It suits perverted fleshly ease to live in voluptuousness here upon earth, with fattened bodies—with gloves on the hands, with ostentatious show—to be greeted by men as doctor, lord and

and master. (Luke 16.) But when the messenger of death shall knock at the door of your souls and say, "give an account," you will no longer remain as stewards and hirelings. When you must appear before the throne of the eternal Majesty, (Rom. 14,) and the poor miserable souls which you have misled with your false and deceiving doctrine, idolatries, sorceries, and ungodly wanton lives, shall be required at your hands. O where then shall you conceal yourselves from the wrath of God? Then shall ye cry, O ye mountains fall upon us, and ye hills cover us. (Rev. 16.) O then you will know what kind of calling ye had; what kind of life you led, that ye served no other God than your belly, the devil, and your selfish evil flesh, (Phil. 3; Jer. 14, 27, 29; Ezek. 34,) that you ran unsent and came uncalled, that you sought nothing but the milk, wool and flesh of the sheep, (Matt. 15) and that one blind man has led another, till both have fallen into the abyss of the eternal wrath of Almighty God—into the torments of hell. (Luke 6.)

O precious souls! waken up and fear God, for the hour draws near that this your momentary laugh will be changed into an eternal wail, (James 5,) these short lived joys to eternal pain, and this easy carnal life to death and endless wo. Jude says: Wo to them! for they have gone in the way of Cain, and ran greedily after the error of Balaam for reward, and perished in the gainsaying of Core. Again, to them is reserved the blackness of darkness. (2 Pet. 2; Jude 1)

Behold, beloved sirs, friends and brethren, we openly declare, that the sending and calling of your preachers are neither of God nor his word, but are from anti-christ, the dragon and the beast. (Rev. 13.) That they are not called to preach the word of the Lord, by the spirit of God, and the church, but they are called and urged by their lusts with the priests of Jeroboam, to worship the golden calf. (1 Chron. 12.) They enter not in by the right door, therefore, we testify from the scriptures that they are thieves and robbers. (John 10.)

Since then, we have been saved out of the mouths of the lions and bears of the pit, (Heb. 13; 1 Kings 17) and out of the snares of concealed thieves and robbers, through the great Shepherd of the Sheep—the High Priest of our souls, Christ Jesus, and are now upon the chosen and fruitful mountain of Israel, (Ezek. 34) and the green luxuriant pastures of the holy word (the Lord be eternally thanked) our hungering consciences have been fed with the food of eternal life, it must ever be a condemnable folly to forsake such a true shepherd, and such precious pastures, and again enter upon the barren and waste heaths, under the false shepherd who do nothing else but rob and deprive God of his glory, and ruin and murder our poor miserable souls. (John 10.)

This I have said particularly in relation to the *Popish Priests:* But what is the calling and sending of the Lutherans and Zuinglians. By what spirit are they moved? what do they seek? and what fruits of repentance do they show by their doctrines and sacraments? We willingly leave all the godly to judge.

OF THE DOCTRINE OF THE PREACHERS.

As I have presented to the reader, the first part in relation to the sending and calling of a true preacher, according to the word of God,—I will now, through the grace of God, present in like manner the second part, relating the doctrine; for there is but little difference between their calling and their doctrine—as the calling is, even so, most commonly, is the doctrine.

Where God's spirit urges or moves to preach, there will the word be genuinely taught in the power of God, and upright children of the spirit will thereby be born. But where flesh and blood calls, there will a fleshly doctrine be taught and carnal disciples will be made, for that, like produces is like, incontrovertible. I deem it unnecessary here to prove this with much scripture, for actions bear testimony.

The scriptures show plainly how a rightly called preacher of God's word is to genuinely teach that word without perverting glosses,—without any mingling of leaven; as Peter says: If any man speak, let him speak as the oracles of God. (1 Peter 4.) They are the children of the Holy Ghost who speak the word of the Spirit, as Christ said: For it is not ye that speak, but the Spirit of your Father which speaketh in you. (Matt. 10.) For he whom God hath sent speaketh the words of God. (John 3.) It is the highest and heaviest command enjoined by Christ to preach the word salutarily and unblamably. He said: Go in all the world and preach the gospel to every creature. (Mark 16.)

The Gospel, the unmingled words of God, preached in the power of the spirit, is the only right, true seed, out of which believers, obedient children of God, are born.

Therefore may nothing else be preached in Christ's kingdom and house—the church, except her king and husband's own commands and words, according to which she and all her servants must conform.

The same command and word (I say) all Christ's true messengers preached, as he spoke: *Preach the gospel,* (Mark 16) and teach them to observe all things whatsoever I have commanded you. (Matt. 28.)

My faithful reader, observe, all the true servants of God, both of the Old and New Testament, they taught nothing but God's word, as may be seen and read in many places in the scriptures.

Moses is found faithful of God in all his house. He regulated and taught nothing which God had not before commanded him. (Heb. 3 ; Num. 12.)

Isaiah, and all the other prophets, testified in many places what kind of doctrine they taught, and from whom they had received it. They said : Thus saith the Lord your god, who brought you out of the land of Egypt : Thus spake the Lord of Hosts : Again the mouth of the Lord has spoken it. (Isa. 40, 42 ; Jer. 9, 11 ; Ezek. 4, 7.) Paul dare not speak of any thing which Christ had not wrought through him. (Rom. 15.) Yea, Christ himself did not teach *his* word, but the word of his father, (John 7,) as he said, my doctrine is not mine, but is of him who sent me : All that I have heard of my Father, that have I declared unto you. (John 15.) Since then the true messengers of God, taught nothing but the Lord's word, which is the only doctrine from which our souls can obtain eternal life, as the Lord said. (Deut. 6 ; Matt. 4 ; Luke 4.) So it is easily here to mark and to judge what kind of teachers they are who direct the poor uncultivated people to legends, histories and fables ; to holydays, images, tapers and palms ; to confessions, pilgrimages, masses and matins ; who teach of purgatory, vigils, times, bulls, offerings, and satisfactions for souls and sins, who also make a piece of bread and a drink of wine, to be the essential body and blood of Christ. Who teach and say that when they have but spoken these words, "*Hoc est corpus meum*," (*this is my body*) the Lord, willing or not willing, must descend into their idolatrous hands, even though the Heavens should rend assunder, and the earth crumble down ! O blasphemy !

O dear Lord ! my heart trembles in my body that I must relate and mention such terible abominations. But because the simple plain people, who cannot guard themselves against these deceivers, are born with blind eyes and the hands and feet of their conscience bound, by these useless men, down to eternal death, and the gulf of hell ; so that I cannot remain silent, but must disclose this, through undissembled love to God and your souls. Who knows but that God may give grace that you may be prevailed upon to hear, your eyes opened to see, and your hearts to understand,—that you may be freed from the snares of the devil, whereby you are taken. (2 Tim. 1.)

Yes, my dear reader, they have made lords, princes, and the world drunk by their cup, (Rev. 17,) and have completely be-

witched them, so that all who turn from their shame, and would
not pervert the honor of their Savior, by a piece of bread—all
who shun false teachers, and desire the salutary administration
of the Lord's supper, as above said, will be upbraided by all
men, as profaners of the holy sacrament, and as degraded, cursed
heretics, they must suffer and take to flight.

O blind leader! you, who throughout your life have not rightly
understood one sentence of the Lord's word, nor have received
one ray from his spirit, but have trodden the kingdom of God
with your feet, and have thrust it from you with your horns.
(Ezek. 34.)   How truly are you associates of those of whom it
stands written, that they say : We have made a covenant with
death, and with hell we are at agreement; when the overflowing scourge shall pass through, it shall not come unto us; for
we have lies for our refuge, and under falsehood have we hidden
ourselves : (Isa. 28) again ; Wo unto them who call evil good,
and good evil ; that put light for darkness, and darkness for
light. (Isa. 5.) Wo unto you, for ye shut up the kingdom of
Heaven unto men, said Christ, (Matt. 23,) and make the poor
souls to err from the way. Yet again : Wo unto you ! (Deut. 24.)

However, I am not much astonished that such persons teach
such shameful doctrine, since they have known neither Christ
nor his word, but they hold and teach all things as they were
taught from youth up, out of the old usages, and the papistical
laws.   But that which grieves me most, is, that those also who
now are aware in part of the hidden whoredom of the Babylonian
woman, and have put from them some of her abominations, yet
cling to human sophistry, so that they cannot be moved nor
taught, either with the powerful word of God, or with the unblamable lives, the candid professions, or the innocent blood of
so many godly saints. Nevertheless, some of you, have, at times,
to yield to the truth with stopped mouths and subdued hearts,
but still ye cease not to upraid and defame, with envious tongues
and slanderous lips, the bright, clear truth of Christ, and the
pious children of God, before your fleshly, blind churches which
are of like calling with yourselves.   This also your writers do
as may be seen and heard every where.   Besides, I fear that
they are not less guilty than the papists in moving the lords,
princes and ruling powers, by commissions, complaints, outcries
and writings, to persecute the Lamb of God, and his chosen,
(Rev. 17) and to uproar, when their deceiving leaven, particularly the calf worship of their infant baptism, and their
unfounded supper, is rejected. Let each one behold for himself
and learn to know them rightly.   I know of a truth that they
are without the spirit, the sending, or the word of Christ; for I
am sensible how malicious they are for most part against all

who are rightly led—who fear the Lord from the heart and would gladly become christians. In their doctrines and deeds they seek, not less than the papists, for human friendship, honor, or pride, rest, handsome houses, and an easy licentious life.

O my beloved reader, these are not the teachers who lead many to righteousness, and who shall shine as the light of heaven, and as the stars now and in eternity. (Dan. 12.) For I know not where a single congregation shall be found which they have led with their doctrines and conduct to repenting lives, and to the worship of God. Their great clamor is against the pope and his cardinals, bishops, priests and monks. All must be upbraided by them, as profaners of the sacraments, anabaptists, fanatics, and heretics, who through the word of God, reprove their deceiving doctrines, idolatrous sacraments, idle lives, and who would gladly see the best of their poor souls.

Yea, when they can find but one, (though cut off) who was *before* united with the pople of God, but who has now fallen into some vice, they judge and sentence *all* the godly by this *one;* "Behold!" say they, "what manner of people they are." They seek nothing so much as to find cause of censure; therefore, they look upon Judas, but not upon Peter, Andrew and John. But they do not regard what manner of people they are themselves; and what kind of disciples they have.

Besides, their coveteous, haughty, proud, drunken, impure and impenitent church, preachers and boasts, nothing but pure grace, favor, mercy, and love of God. They observe not that the whole scriptures testify that such shall not inherit the kingdom of God. They strengthen also the hands of the wicked, so that no man repents himself of his wickedness, as the prophet lamented.

O ye useless unprofitable teachers, who think that you bear the vessels of the Lord—these my words are to you! Why do you declaim so much of faith and love, whose fruit you so greatly hate and dislike. (Jer. 25.) Have you the sincere and unfeigned fear and love of God? So let them appear and be made manifest through your words. (James 2.) Say, beloved preachers! Where is your christian humility, your godly, christian zeal, pleasure, peace and joy in Christ Jesus?

Where is your mercy which you shew? Where are the naked whom you have clothed, the hungry whom you have fed, and the needy whom you have entertained? (Matt. 25.) Where is the lost whom you have again sought, the wounded whom you have bound up, and the sick whom you have healed? (Ezek. 34.) Where is your unblamable, pious life which is from God? That which you preach, perform and do, is for the most part idle hypocrisy.

Some of you approve in some degree, a godly, christian life, preach also much of Christ, of his merits, spirit, and grace, and are yourselves, manifestly those who lead a gross, sensual life, who crucify Christ anew, and grieve his spirit and dispise his grace, as may be seen.

O preachers, preachers ! how aptly has the Holy Ghost likened you to dry wells and empty clouds from which no water can be obtained, and to fruitless trees from which no fruit can be taken. (2 Pet. 2.)   I know not to what you may be more suitably compared, than to a woman who lives in all manner of shame and wantonness, and yet talks much about modesty, decency and virtue ; should not her words be regarded as mockery ?   Might it not be said, why do you talk of modesty and chastity, since you, yourself are full of all manner of immodesty and shame.

We are well aware that you have in part demolished the little gods of Babylon, such as the Roman indulgences, the invocations of departed saints, unclean purification, abstaining from meats, and the like idolatry and other superstitions but the horrible blasphemy and abominations are still retained ; such as accursed unbelief, the headstrong obstinacy, the earthly mind, the unscriptural infant baptism, the idolatrous supper, and the impenitent old life which is of the flesh.

Therefore, we testify with the truth and declare that you are not ambassadors of God nor teachers of Christ.   For it is plain that you reject the word and ordinances of the Lord, and run of yourselves, (Jer. 8, 23 ; John 10 ; Ezek. 34,) and have pastured yourselves under the name and appearance of the evangelical shepherds of the Lord, and have led to destruction so many hundred thousand souls, through your wanton doctrine, idolatrous sacraments and carnal lives.

But the teachers who are sent of God, and who have been rightly called, teach God's word genuinely, they abide in its holy ordinances, live (after their weakness) unblamably, for they are born of God, and are taught and moved by his holy spirit, they seek neither gold, nor possessions, neither an easy life nor earthly applause—they wait upon their enjoined duties with all earnestness—they fear God from the heart, seek their neighbour with fidelity ; they are armed with the weapons of righteousness, on the right hand and on the left. (Acts 3 ; 1 Thes. 2 ; Gal. 1.)   They deal without respect to persons. (2 Cor. 6.) The powerful, sharp sword of the divine word cuts out of their mouth (Luke 12) ; it is a shining lantern in their hands ; they are taught in righteousness, are full of all spiritual wisdom ; (Jer. 15) they divide the good from the evil ; the holy from the unholy, and the clean from the unclean.   In short, they shine in doctrine and conduct, even as from the beginning till the present time, it has been written and remarked of all true prophets, apostles and servants of God. (Matt. 5)

O dear Lord, how lovely are those pastors and teachers who seek nothing else but to extend the kingdom of God ; who preach rightly the word of repentance and grace, that they may win many souls ; and for this end, they expose their name, reputation, houses, property, persons and lives.

These are they, who, with Christ, the chief shepherd, gather together and feed his lambs; but the others are those who scatter and destroy them. They are prophets,—but not of God— they preach, but not out of the Lord's mouth. They strengthen the hands of the ungodly. They destroy the souls who should have eternal life, and encourage those who must forever die ; and this they do for handfuls of barley and pieces of bread. (Jer. 23 ; Ezek. 13.) They preach to the people peace when there is no peace. Therefore, shall they stand in shame, who follow such abominations, though they yet are not ashamed and yet forbear to blush. (Jer. 8.)

Behold, dear reader, since they so shamefully deprive Christ of his honor and gain, and scatter his sheep, (John 10,) and, with the sword of their deceiving doctrines, destroy the poor souls who are so greatly loved by the Lord—whom he so earnestly seeks for, and whom he so dearly purchased. And since they so enviously war against the word and ordinances of the Lord, we say and teach with Christ : Let them alone, they be blind, leaders of the blind. (Matt. 15.) Guard yourselves against such false prophets ; for though they come in the appearance of sheep, they are nevertheless, inwardly ravening wolves. They are the strangers whose voice Christ's sheep know not. (Matt. 7 ; John 10.) They are those of whom Paul warns us and says : Now I beseech you, brethren, mark them which cause divisions and offences, contrary to the doctrine which you have learned, and avoid them ; for they are such as serve not our Lord Jesus Christ, but their own belly and by good words and fair speeches, deceive the heart of the simple. (Rom. 16.)

Again : John says, whoever transgresseth and abideth not in the doctrine of Christ, hath not God. If there come any unto you, and bring not this doctrine, receive him not into your house, neither bid him God speed : For he that biddeth him God speed, is partaker of his evil deeds. (2 John 1.)

The word of God abundantly warns us that, we leave such and beware of them. Shun their voice and retreat from them, and that we should not take them into our houses, (as has been said.) If we are Christ's sheep and the children of the Holy Spirit ; so must we even hear Christ's voice, and follow after and obey the monitions of the Holy Ghost. Reflect how sincerely holy Paul admonished the Philippians, that they should guard themselves from the evil doer and the concision. He taught the true servants of God that they should shun those, who failed no further (as it appears) than only, that they out of zeal without knowledge, held fast to circumcision, which they had received from their fathers, and would not admit that it should be abolished through Christ. How much more earnestly it becomes us to beware of them, who have deceived the whole world, who upbraid and persecute the godly and fight against truth; of all false teachers and blasphemers of God, who urge, set up, and permit idolatrous and abominable doctrine,

---

OF THE CONDUCT OF PREACHERS.

As you have just heard the ground of the *calling* and *doctrines* of the preachers, we will proceed, and through the grace of God point out by the scriptures how the *true* apostles, bishops, teachers and pastors, in the church of Christ, should conduct themselves in their deportment and lives; for it is not enough that a man appears to speak much of the word of the Lord, but what he says must also be maintained by a devout and unblamable conduct, as the scriptures teach.

Thus says Paul : But I keep under my body, and bring it into subjection ; lest that by any means, when I have preached to others, I myself should be a cast-away. (1 Cor. 9.) If it becomes the hearers and disciples to lead an unblamable life, how much more does it become teachers, because they rule the hearers and are their overseers. (Eph. 3 ; Phil. 2.) As Paul says : Remember them who have the rule over you, who have spoken unto you the word of God, whose faith follow, considering the end of their conversation. (Heb. 13.)

He also admonishes Timothy thereto, and says : Let no man despise thy youth, but be thou an example of the believers, in word, in conversation, in charity, in spirit, in faith, in purity. (1 Tim 4.) But in all things shewing thyself a pattern of good works; in doctrine, shewing uncorruptness, gravity, sincerity, &c. (Tit. 2.) For it is undoubtedly proper, if any one teaches and reproves others, that he first himself be rightly taught and unblamable, as Paul teaches : If a man desire the office of a bishop he desireth a good work. A bishop then must be blameless, the husband of one wife, vigilant, sober, of good behavior, given to hospitality, apt to teach ; not given to wine, not greedy of filthy lucre ; but patient, not a brawler, not covetous ; one that ruleth well his own house, having his children in subjection with all gravity : for if a man know not how to rule his own house, how shall he take care of the church of God ? Not a novice, lest being lifted up with pride, he fall into the condemnation of the devil. Moreover, he must have a good report of them who are without ; lest he fall into reproach and the snare of the devil, he must be sober, just, holy, temperate ; holding fast the faithful word, as he has been taught, that he may be able by sound doctrine, both to exhort and to convince the gainsayers ; even so must their wives be grave, not slanderers, sober, faithful in all things. (I Tim. 3 ; Tit. 1.)

Behold dear reader, it is requisite that every preacher and teacher, who would rightly govern and rule in the church of God be thus qualified ; for if any one were to reprove and teach others, and is himself not blameless and is ignorant ; he will justly have to hear : Why do you teach others and teach not yourself first ! Thou teachest a man should not steal, and thou dost steal. Thou sayest a man should not commit adultery, and thou dost. Thou abhorrest idols, yet thou committest sacrilege. Thou boastest of the law of God ; and dishonorest God by breaking the law ! (Rom. 2.)

All those thus called, who are in doctrine sound, and unblamable in life, may teach, exhort, reprove, root up, and build up in the name of the Lord ; their labors will not be fruitless, as may be seen, in the case of Moses, Samuel, Elias, Elisha, Isaiah, Jeremiah, Peter Paul, John, and with all the true prophets, apostles and servants of God, who preached the word unblamably in the power of the spirit.

Their doctrine cuts like a sharp edged sword, for it has power, it is fruitful, has spirit and energy, as the prophet says : For as the rain cometh down, and the snow from heaven, and returneth not thither, but watereth the earth, and maketh it bring forth and bud, that it may give seed to the sower, and bread to the eater, so shall my word be, that goeth out of my mouth : it shall not return unto me void, but it shall accomplish that which I please, and it shall prosper in the thing where I sent it. (Isa. 55.)

Yea, all those who enter the vineyard of the Lord being so sent, called, with such a spirit, with such a doctrine and life, as said ; are the shepherds of whom it is written : And I will give you pastors according to mine heart, which shall feed you with knowledge and understanding. (Jer. 3.)

They are the teachers who turn many to righteousness ; and they shall shine as the brightness of the firmament, as the stars forever. (Dan. 12.)

They are the spiritual streams, and the rivers of the paradise of Christ, which issue from the fountains of the paradise of God, to irrigate and fertilize the whole country. (Gen. 2.)

They are the spiritual posts and pillars in the court of the tabernacle with hangings of fine twined white silk. (Ex. 27.)

They are three score valiant men, of the valiant of Israel, who are around Solomon's bed; they all hold swords; being expert in war: every man with his sword upon his thigh, because of fear in the night. (Cant. 3.)

They are the seven horns or trumpets, of the golden years, before whose sounds, (their teaching and preaching,) the walls of Jericho fall, that is, all false doctrine, all powers and dominions raised up against the true Joshua, Jesus Christ, and his people, are brought low. (Josh. 6.)

They are the beautiful messengers of peace, who preach the gospel of peace, mercy and grace, and bring glad tidings of good things, to us, poor, miserable, troubled sinners. (Isaiah. 52; Rom. 10.)

They are seven mighty mountains, whereupon grow roses and lilies, whose sweet scent refreshes with joy all who fear the Lord. (2 Ez. 2.)

They are the splendid crown of twelve stars of the woman big, and in travail. (Rev. 12.)

They are the walls of the new and heavenly Jerusalem, based upon the twelve foundations, that is upon the ground and doctrine of the twelve apostle. (Rev. 2.)

See, worthy reader, with such and similar glorious images and parables, are all the pious pastors and teachers honored in the scriptures, whom the Holy Ghost has ordained as bishops and overseers in his church, congregation and house.

These may say with holy Paul: Follow us as we are the followers of Christ for our exhortation was not of deceit, nor of uncleanness, nor in guile, but as we were allowed of God to be put in trust with the gospel, even so we speak; not as pleasing men, but God, who trieth our hearts; for neither at any time, used we flattering words, as you know, nor a cloak of covetousness; God is witness. Nor of men sought we glory. (Thess. 2.)

I repeat it: These are they who gather with Christ what has been scattered, bind up the wounded, and heal the sick, (Ezek. 34,) for they are influenced by the spirit of the Lord and urged by unfeigned love. (Luke 11.) They are vigilant, and are assiduous in the discharge of entrusted duties. They fight daily with the weapon of obedience. (Jer. 1.) They tear down and break and destroy all that which is against the word of God, not by external power, with sword and spear, but by the preaching of the holy word, in power and spirit—with the word of the Lord. They till, sow, water and plant, (Cor. 3; John 4.) They cut down what is ripe. They gather their grain and sheaves, and carry them into the Lord's barn, and their fruits will abide unto eternal life. (John 15.)

Since the scriptures require such teachers, as said, it is then indispensable, that we weigh the conduct of your preachers in the balance, and determine their actions before your eyes, by the plummet of the divine word, that you may discover how much they are wanting of the pattern of the true bishops, preachers and pastors, spoken of by Paul to Timothy and Titus, in all their lives and actions; and that they are the very reverse, who, without spirit, word, work or truth, but in semblance only, are so called of the world.

It is manifest, beloved reader, that they changed the meek office of a true bishop, preacher and pastor, which is an office of christian service, and if rightly attended to, is an office full of trouble, care, reproach, misery, tribulation, cross and affliction, into ungodly gorgeousness and princely glory, so that they are greatly respected and feared, of those whose names are not written in heaven, because they appear in such splendid robes and are dressed in such shining garbs, (Rev. 13, 17,) and are called by pompous names, and use in their services, ointments, palms, caps, togas, unclean purifications, and have cloisters, chapels, bells, organs, music, masses, offerings, &c. of which there is not a word to be found in scriptures. By their splendid trappings, we know and see the covered, slily, croaching wolf, the earthly, sensual mind, the antichristian seductions and bloody abominations; for they seek nothing but the the favour of men, honor, splendor, venery, idleness, self, gold, silver, gluttony, &c., and suffer themselves to be called spiritual doctors, teachers, lords, abbots, guardians, fathers and priors.

Alas! how vastly they do differ from the prophets and apostles in their office, services, examples, usages, lives, and in all they did—who entered the vineyard of the Lord without purse, without money, or much clothing, (Matt. 10; Luke 10,) who were made a spectacle to the whole world; and for Christ's sake were killed all the day long, and accounted as sheep for the slaughter: (1 Cor. 4; Rom. 8,) as may be seen from the scriptures.

But these have their chests and coffers full, they are waxed rich through the abundance of the Babylonian sorcery.) Rev. 18.) In all things they are blamable, violating female chastity, which is carried on to such an unblushing degree, that it cannot be expressed; they are full of inordinate desires, unchaste, unmerciful, malicious, scorners, unfriendly, unrighteous, liars, drunkards. All their tables are full of vomit and filthiness, as Isaiah, the prophet says, (Isa. 28.) Their hearts are full of

avarice, and malicious towards those who will not contribute to
their support.   They even prepare war against them, as Micah
teaches.   They are full of adultery. (Mich. 3 ; 2 Pet. 2.)   They
sit with harlots in their houses.   They beget children illegiti-
mately.   They are unbelievers, they are refractory ; proud,
ambitious.   Obey not the word of the Lord ; are bound with
the cords of the devil, and there are many who have not known
the truth, (2 Tim. 2.) they are a scandal and disgrace to the
world.   Their dreadful, abominable fruits make this manifest
to all.   They fight against Christ and his word.   They hate all
the pious.   They speak reproachfully of all those who seek,
love and fear the Lord with all their hearts.   In short, it is not
possible to relate all their abominable crimes, their lewdness,
their ungodly deeds, their private and public vices, infamy and
abominations.

O dear Lord ! how much more are they the reverse of the
upright and true bishops, overseers and pastors, although they
boast that they can bring Christ from heaven, reconcile God,
forgive sins, and that they are the true pillars, the heads and
eyes of the church.

And although I have written this especially of the Roman
priests, the reader should know, that I cannot acquit those in
any wise, who boast of the word, if they seek, in the common
walks of their lives, unlawful gain, and practise idolatry with
infant baptism and the Lord's supper, and hate the pious,
oppress, backbite and slander them, and differ little from the
church of Rome, except in a few idolatrous abuses of the bread,
which are not found with them.

Therefore, I fear all, who preach for money, and flatter
the world, are the spiritual sorcerers of Egypt, (Ex. 7, 8 ;
2 Tim. 3) priests of the groves, (1 Chron. 12) servants of Baal,
and prophets of Jezabel, (1 Chron. 18) destroyers of the Lord's
vineyard, (Jer. 12) defilers of the land, (Jer. 23) blind watchmen and dumb dogs, (Isa. 56) spoilers of the good pastures,
they trouble the waters and make foul the rivers, (Ezek. 34)
devourers of souls, (Ezek. 22) false prophets and ravening
wolves, (Matt. 7) devourers of widows' houses, (Matt. 23)
thieves and murderers, (John 10) enemies of the cross of
Christ, whose end is destruction, whose God is their belly, and
whose glory is in their shame, who mind earthly things,
(Phil. 3) false teachers, founders of sects, cursed children,
wandering stars, withered trees, without fruit, twice dead,
plucked up by the roots ; foaming out their own shame, to
whom is reserved the blackness of darkness forever, (2 Pet. 2 ;
Jude 1) anti-christs, (1 John 2) locusts that rose from the bottomless pit, came to hurt those who have not the seal of God

in their foreheads, (Rev. 9.) In short, if they will not repent, they are already condemned according to the scriptures, (Matt. 15, 23; Luke 11; Phil. 3; 2 Tim. 3; Tit. 3; 2 Pet. 2; Jude 1; Rev. 21, 22.)

Not that I would judge any one, my good reader, I well know that it is written: Judge not that ye be not judged; condemn not and ye shall not be condemned; (Luke 6) but they are judged of him, who say: The word that I have spoken, the same shall judge him in the last day. (John 12.)

Who do such and the like things, says Paul, shall not inherit the kingdom of God, (Rom. 1; 1 Cor. 6; Gal. 5; Eph. 5.) But if any one do the works whereof Paul speaks, he is not judged of me, nor of any other man, but by the word of the Lord. We do therefore entreat you to measure the conduct of your preachers with the scriptures, and you will find, by whom they are judged.

O miserable preachers, whose blindness we may well lament; how much better would it be for you never to have been born. For if you have finished your short, perishable, voluptuous and idle life; and have not repented, as above stated, your portion will be God's eternal wrath, punishment and judgment in the torments, the pains and burnings of hell; woe and death shall be your end, as the scriptures threaten, (Matt. 15, 23; Luke 11; 2 Tim. 3; Phil. 3; Tit. 3.)

The reason is, because you reject Christ, and despise his word, which is everlasting food for the soul, upon which we must eternally subsist. (2 Pet. 2; 2 John 1; Jude 1; Rev. 21, 22.) And despise his word because it reproves your vain and frivolous conduct, showing that you are indeed sensual; of the world, and of the devil, as is evident; and that you so miserably deceive poor souls; and so cruelly hate, belie, reproach and betray all those who sincerely seek their souls' salvation; take their property, deprive them of honor, and life, who in great love admonish, by the word of God, your deceiving teachers, and reprove their ungodly deeds with all discretion. (Deut. 8; Matt. 4; Luke 4.)

O Balaam, Balaam, how long will you so unmercifully kick and cuff the poor ass which has to suffer all the opprobium, scorn and disgrace, for the sake of his master's testimony? And never kindly listen how he answers you in a human voice, and reproves your great folly and error? That he is driven by an angel with a naked sword, namely, by the spirit and word of the Lord, that he can longer carry (endure) you in your ungodly deeds. (Lev. 22.)

Well now! seed of Cain, Korah and Balaam, prepare for defence; lie, cheat, censure, blaspheme, hate, root up, disgrace and murder as much as in you lies; allege all the councils, authors, and learned teachers who have been for centuries; appeal to all the lords and princes, emperors, kings and the mighty of the earth. (Jer. 51.)   Use all the power, art and cunning that you can command, it avails you nothing: the Lamb will conquer and gain the victory, the people of God will triumph, not with tangible weapons, but in patience with the spirit and word of God.   Jerusalem and the temple must be built up, although the Azotes and Sanabalats may attempt to hinder it, not with inanimate stores, which are now tread upon in every street with your unclean feet, (Rev. 17; 1 Ex. 2; 1 Pet. 2; Tim. 1; Neh. 4) and although all the gates of hell may resist, Babel must be destroyed and laid waste.   The ten kings *will* and *must* perform their services. (Rev. 17.)   You will gnaw your tongues for pain, bitterly cry and weep on account of the torments of Babel, and say: Alas! alas! that great city, that was clothed in fine linen, and purple, and scarlet, and decked with gold, and precious stones, and pearls! For in one hour so great riches is come to nought; for her sins rose up to heaven, and the Lord remembered her wickedness. (Rev. 18.)

The gospel *will* and *must* be heard; lies must be exposed, and your blind folly made known to all men. (Matt. 14; 2 Tim. 3,)

And although I and my brethren may be called off by death before this takes place, yet it will undoubtedly happen at the appointed time, which the Holy Ghost so plainly foretold and taught through the worthy disciple, John.

O stiffnecked, evil generation, how long will you resist the Holy Ghost?   How long will you revile the truth, and prefer lies?   How long will you be guilty of innocent blood?   Reform your wicked lives, fear God with all your hearts, treat us according to the word of God, so that the gospel may be rightly preached, and be maintained by a pious and blameless life. Alas! were you to do so, no innocent blood would be shed, and the truth would be made known.

But we are afraid it will be as the prophet said: The wicked shall do wickedly, and none of the wicked shall understand; but the wise shall understand. (Dan. 12.)   For it is the custom of all the sects, who are out of Christ and his word, to defend their foundations, faith and actions with the sword.   The Romans, the Arians, the Circumcellions, the Lutherans, the Zuinglians, and the Munsterites, are our witnesses; but Christ's people suffer and forbear.

Is it not a grievous error, that these poor people want to be Christians, and be guilty of such abominable things, as exterminating, robbing, apprehending, burning, murdering, &c., under pretence, as if the kingdom of Christ, the glory of the Lord, the word and truth of God, were to be defended and maintained with such horrible disgrace ?

Alas, no ! you miserable men, no ! All who are moved by the spirit of Christ know of no sword but the word of the Lord; their weapons are powerful prayer, a long-suffering and patient heart, strong, unfeigned faith, living hope, and an unblamable life, (Ezra. 13; Eph. 6; Heb. 4,) whereby the gospel of the kingdom, the word of peace, is to be promulgated, and to be defended against the gates of hell.

Beloved reader, see, if you have the fear of God, then learn rightly to know your bishops, prophets, pastors and teachers, and remember what is written : Come out from among them, and be ye separate, saith the Lord, and touch not the unclean thing; and I will receive you, and I will be a Father unto you, and ye shall be my sons and daughters, saith the Lord God Almighty. (2 Cor. 6.) And again : Come out of her, my people, that ye be not partakers of her sins, and that ye receive not her plagues. (Rev 18.) Reflect that the mouth of the Lord said : Beware of false prophets, which come to you in sheep's clothing, but inwardly they are ravening wolves : ye shall know them by their fruits. Do men gather grapes of thorns, or figs of thistles? (Matt. 7.) They are the salt which has lost its savor, and is henceforth good for nothing, but to be cast out and to be trodden under foot of men, as the Lord says. (Matt. 5.)

In short, they are those of whom Paul warned and said : This know also, that in the last days perilous times shall come; for there shall be men, lovers of their ownselves, covetous, boasters, proud, blasphemers, disobedient to parents, unthankful, unholy, without natural affection, truce-breakers, false accusers, incontinent, fierce, despisers of those that are good, traitors, heady, high-minded, lovers of pleasure more than lovers of God; having a form of godliness, but denying the power thereof; from such turn away. (2 Tim. 3.)

Again, thus you see that your preachers are such persons as described, and that the scriptures abundantly admonish and command that we shall forsake them, fear them, avoid and flee from them, &c.(Matt 7 ; 1 Thes. 5 ; John 10.) And this is the reason why we openly teach *not* to hear their seducing doctrines, *not* to use their sacraments, and to have nothing to do with their false worship.

Rather say : What godliness can Israel bring from Assyria, Egypt, from Babylon.

How can the true service be found with the priests of Baal ? How can you be taught in divine things to righteousness, of those who are ignorant thereof themselves ?

9

How can you learn Christ from anti-christ; and the word of God from false prophets?

How can you be blessed by the cursed, and be rightly led by the blind?

How will you draw water from dry fountains, and gather fruit from withered trees? (2 Pet. 2.)

How can you be partakers of the Lord's table and of the table of devils?

How can you drink both of the Lord's cup and the devil's cup, and be in the communion of Christ and of anti-christ?

You cannot serve two masters who are opposed to each other; you must love the one and hate the other, or else you will hold to the one and despise the other. (Matt. 6) You must be for Christ or against him, you will gather with him, or destroy in opposition to him.

Since we, by the grace of God, so plainly see how your preachers are sent, see their doctrine and lives, how they go without being called, falsify the word of God, lead a wanton, sensual life, deceive the poor people; and we being so abundantly admonished by the scriptures, that we should forsake, avoid and flee such preachers, because they are so diametrically opposed to Christ and his word, and we desire to be obedient to the voice of our shepherd in this matter as it becomes all the pious of Christ, (John 10,) for the kingdom is promised to the obedient, as the scriptures say: Not every one that saith, Lord, Lord, shall enter into the kingdom of heaven; but they that doth the will of my Father. (Matt. 7.)

And we also, agreeably to the contents of God's word, departed from their doctrine, sacraments and service, and this we testify both by word and deed, with possessions and blood before lords and princes, in cities and in the country, before you, and the world as an admonition, doctrine and instruction, so that you all, both teachers and hearers, might awaken, to reflect on the truth, repent and come out from the kingdom and fellowship of anti-christ, and enter the kingdom and communion of Christ; and thus extricate your poor souls from the snares of unbelief, that you may be rescued, preserved and eternally saved.

For we will sooner endure, in our mortal bodies, misery, poverty, tribulation, hunger, thirst, heat, cold, bonds and death, and adhere to the Lord's word, than lead secure easy lives with the world, and for the sake of a short and temporal life, ruin our souls.

We think with holy Peter, (Acts 15, 6,) that we should rather obey God than man; and with virtuous Susan, it is better to fall into the hands of man, than into the hands of God. (Dan. 13.) All who fear the Lord may read and judge.

COUNTER ARGUMENTS

OF BABYLON AND OF ITS BUILDERS, WITH THEIR REPLICATIONS.

BELOVED reader, although we have clearly shown you the difference between true and false preachers, and why we will not hear them, we do, therefore, hope that the god-fearing, who acknowledge the word of the Lord to be true, might fully comprehend this GROUND AND TRUTH; still we find some among those preachers, who partly know that their cause cannot stand the test of the scripture.

Nevertheless, not being born of God, neither fearing him and seeking unlawful gain, the world and ease, they have wrested a variety of scripture passages, by which they persuade the simple, those who dread the cross of Christ, that it is lawful to hear their doctrine and attend upon their church services, and this they do in order to live at ease and enjoy good times.

In the first place, they say, that Christ said: The Scribes and Pharisees sit in Moses' seat: all, therefore, whatsoever they bid you observe, that observe and do; but do not ye after their works, (Matt. 23.) From which they conclude, that, as the Scribes and Pharisees were sitting in the seat of Moses, and mingling leaven with the unleavened lump, of which Christ warned his disciples, because Christ said: all therefore whatsoever they bid you observe, that observe and do, they also now sit in Christ's seat, although they are in their doctrine and lives not upright and free from guilt; that therefore we are to hear them, so far as they preach the word of God, but not to do after their works. (Matt. 16; Mark 8; Luke 12.)

To which we reply, first, and ask them whether they and the Pharisees are one or not? If they answer yes! they must then be their own judges, and decide that they are of those who crucified Christ, stoned Stephen, beat the apostles, persecuted the saints, and they are of those who are threatened with eternal woe, (Matt. 28; Mark 15; Luke 23; John 19; Acts 5, 7; Matt. 2, 3,) they may well then be afraid and fear the Lord and his judgments. If they answer, no! then they can prove nothing with this passage.

Secondly, we reply: If they adduce this passage, *quasi argumentum assimili*, i. e. as it were an argument of similitude, and remark that to sit in Moses' seat, is to rightly preach and attend to Moses' law with its ceremonies. This did the Scribes and Pharisees, they left the law and ceremonies entire and altered nothing therein, although they practised some superstition with it, as may be seen from Matt. 15, 23.   For had they altered the law and ceremony, they would not have been sitting in Moses' seat.

But even as the Scribes and Pharisees did sit in Moses' seat, these will then also have to show that they sit in Christ's seat, that is, they must prove that they preach Christ's gospel, baptism, supper, separation ; preach and practice all things correctly, or the *argumentum assimili* cannot stand.   If this is the case, we may then ask counsel of the scriptures ; why they suffer the traditions of men to be added thereto ? and why retain them ? But we well know that the scriptures are silent on this subject.

Thirdly, we reply : So long as the Scribes and Pharisees were sitting in Moses' seat, and practised the ceremonies and taught the law which pointed to Christ, as before related ; so long did Christ direct his disciples and the people, at that time, to them ; for the law was not fully accomplished ; the perfect sacrifice, which was to abolish all typical sacrifices, was not yet offered ; the veil of the temple was not yet rent, the figures and shadows were not yet changed into the new and abiding reality.   But after it was all accomplished according to the scriptures, and all things made new in Christ, (John 19 ; 2 Cor. 5,) he did not then send out the Scribes and Pharisees, with Moses' law, but sent out his disciples with his own doctrine ; and said : Go into all the world and preach the gospel to every creature, (Mark 16,) and teach them to observe all things I command you. (Matt. 28.)

Since then all things are new in and through Christ ; and as the people of Moses were directed to his preachers, by Christ before his death, to those who sat in Moses' seat and rightly taught the law, practised the ceremonies ; in like manner, now, in the new Testament, are we, after the death of Christ, directed to those preachers who sit in Christ's seat, teaching his words unblamably, and using his sacraments as the scriptures teach. (1 Tim. 1.)

But the scriptures abundantly warn us of those who adulterate Christ's doctrine, misuse his sacraments, seduce the people, lead dissolute and wanton lives; such we are to flee, avoid and abandon, not to admit them into our houses, for they sit in anti-christ's, not in Christ's seat, as said, (Matt. 7 ; John 10 ; Rom. 16 ; 2 Tim. 6 ; 2 John 1.)

Secondly ; they adduce what Paul says : Quench not the spirit ; despise not prophecying ; prove all things ; hold fast that which is good. (1 Thes. 5.)

I answer, Paul himself explains, according to our opinion, of what spirit and prophesy he thus spake in. (1 Cor. 4.) For if it were the opinion of the apostle that we should repair to houses where this open seduction and idolatry are carried on, and there try their spirit and prove their doctrines, Paul would then have contradicted himself, when he says, that we shall separate and flee from them; for we know of a certainty that they do corrupt the word and sacraments of the Lord, and seek nothing but a good living, and are without the spirit and doctrine of Christ.

O no; Paul did not write this of such preachers as the Scribes and Pharisees were, neither of the idolatrous priests of Egypt and Babylon; but he said this touching the prophets, pastors and teachers in the Church of Christ, that we are not to quench their spirit, but prove their doctrine, and hold fast to that which is good. And if they taught any thing not in accordance with the scriptures and the true faith, to avoid it. (Rom. 4.) If any man prophesy, let him prophesy according to the proportion of faith, (Rom. 12,) and this is to what John exhorts his disciples: Beloved, believe not every spirit, but try the spirits, whether they are of God. (1 John 4.) And this passage: Avoid the appearance of all manner of evil, may be understood as not properly referring to what is just mentioned.

My good reader, we have proved your preachers so well, both as to their spirit and doctrine, that we may with a clear conscience say, that they are not of God and his word, but of the bottomless pit, of the dragon and of the beast. (Rev. 9.) Say, dear reader, how shall we acknowledge those as teachers who so wantonly fight against the word of God? What fellowship has light with darkness? What communion has Christ with Belial? (1 Cor. 6.) The greater part of what they teach is delusion and hypocrisy. My reader, do not pervert these words, for what I write is the truth, and I can prove it to the whole world, from their doctrines, lives and sacraments.

Thirdly, they ask: Why will we not hear them; for the wise men of the East gave heed to what Herod said?

Answer. To adduce this passage seems to me to be so puerile, that it is by no means worthy of reply. For Herod did nothing else than by the instruction of the scribes, point out to the wise men the town in which the king of the Jews was to be born, and he did it with a blood-thirsty heart, as the following act shows: He sent them to Bethlehem and said: Go and search diligently for the young child, and when you have found him, bring me word again, that I may come and worship him also.

Herod was afraid when he heard that the Jews had a king born, lest he might lose his glory and kingdom; he therefore spoke out of pure hypocrisy and slyness, with the wise men, in order that he might destroy the child, for he was desirous of his death. But when he saw that he failed in his hypocrisy, he was very much enraged, and showed his fierce, tyrannical, ungodly

9*

disposition; he sent forth and slew all the children that were in Bethlehem, and in all the coasts thereof, from two years old and under; as may be seen from Matt. 2.

O my good reader, how justly they do appeal to this hypocritical, lying, ambitious and tyrannic Herod; for the greater part of them are of the same spirit and disposition. They are so much pained that Christ is born again through his word. They are like hypocritical Herod; they lie and say, that they are sincere; but they fear their unlawful gain, their rich and lazy life, lest Christ should rule, as Herod feared, lest he should lose his kingdom. And they are ready to destroy the pious, as Herod was determined upon the blood of Christ, as you have heard.

Since then they are such manifest, hypocritical liars, and so earthly-minded, some of whom also are lurking for blood, as may be seen openly in such places; and in this respect we will take the wise men as an example; who being privately exhorted from heaven not to return to Herod again, (Matt. 2,) and by the grace of God take sure heed to the Lord's inspirating counsel, doctrine and exhortation, and turn to those who recommend Christ to us in power, and according to the spirit, rightly teach and exhibit the truth.

Fourthly, some of them say: Although the devil should preach the word of God, why should we not hear him?

In the first place I reply to these vain, slanderous calumniators, that it would be well for them to learn to rightly distinguish between the spirit and disposition of the devil, and the spirit and nature of Christ, before they would utter such unseasonable, blasphemous words before the poor people.

The devil was a liar from the beginning, and will undoubtedly always be. (John 8.) Since then he is a liar, and lying his nature, disposition and work, as the Lord says, how can he then rightly teach and preach the word of God, which is truth, and diametrically opposed to his lying disposition and nature, and though he did rightly teach the truth, and give Christ his praise, still he does so with a false heart: for he is a devil and the truth is not in him.

He confessed Christ, rightly and according to the contents of his word, when he said: Thou art Christ, the holy one of God: thou art Christ, the Son of God. However, Christ wanted not his confession, but reproved him and said: Hold your peace, and come out of him, (Luke 4,) for his confession was made with a diabolical heart, as said.

Secondly, I say: If any one would hear the voice of the devil, he need not go far; alas! he can hear him every where. All who speak lies, speak of the devil. (John 8.) In the beginning he spoke through the serpent: in Israel through the false prophets, and now through *his* preachers, in order to deceive the people of the world, and divert them from the truth, that they never can be saved.

Since then, that he was from the beginning, a lying spirit, an adversary of God, a falsifier of the scriptures, and a murderer of souls, and will eternally be such, who can neither teach nor endure any thing good, because he is by nature unclean, a liar, and a deceiver, always the enemy of God, we will therefore stop our ears through grace, and not hear such blasphemous speaking; turn our backs upon the devil, with all his lying preachers, as the scriptures teach; and we will sincerely believe the scriptures, which direct us to Christ to hear him. (Deut. 18; Matt. 17; Mark 9.) And Christ directs us to his disciples, and they direct us to such teachers who are blameless in doctrine and life, as related. (Matt. 10; 1 Tim. 3; Tit. 1.) May the merciful and gracious Lord eternally preserve all the pious hearts against this Herodian generation, and against the devil's preachers. Amen.

Fifthly, some also say: That we may hear them, if we suffer ourselves not to be deceived by them.

I answer, the reader should observe how the people of God ever were, from the days of Abraham, separated from the world; and especially since the days of Moses, they have had their own particular preachers, teachers, ceremonies, ordinances and services, as may be abundantly read and seen in all the books of Moses.

Secondly, that Israel was commanded by God, that if a false prophet were to rise up among them, and though he were to do wonders and signs, he should die. (Deut. 13, 18.)

Thirdly, Israel was not allowed to teach or to receive any doctrine or worship from any strange nations circumjacent to them, but to keep closely to the law and testimonies. (Isa. 8.)

Fourthly, where there arose some ungodly kings, such as Jeroboam, Ahab, Mannassah and many others, who loved their own righteousness and idolatry more than the word and right worship of the Lord; and when the false prophets multiplied, who turned the people from the Lord and his law, then also did the Lord raise up true prophets such as Isaiah, Jeremiah, &c., to reprove the disobedient, idolatrous kings and false prophets, warned the people faithfully of them, and said: Hearken not unto the words of the prophets that prophesy unto you; they make you vain; they speak a vision of their own hearts, and not out of the mouth of the Lord. (Jer. 23. These prophets all gloriously pointed to Christ, to his kingdom and reign.

Fifthly. That Christ did, as well as Moses, ordain and

appoint in his kingdom, community, or church, prophets, preachers, teachers, ceremonies and ordinances, which are to be observed by all true christians for ever, (Matt. 18 ; Mark 16.)

Sixthly. The holy apostles teach us abundantly, that we are to separate ourselves from those in doctrine and in worship, be they baptized or not, if they agree not with the spirit, doctrine, regulations and examples of Christ. Matt. 15 ; John 10 ; Rom. 16, 3 ; 1 Tim. 6 ; 2 Tim. 2, 3 ; Tit. 3 ; 2 John 1 ; Tit. 6 ; 2 Tim. 2 ; 1 John 1.)

Seventhly. That the whole world with their spirit, doctrine, sacrament, worship and conduct, are far from Christ's spirit, word, sacrament, worship and example ; and, alas ! are nothing but a new Sodom, Egypt and Babel. (Rev. 11, 17.) .

Eighthly. That all those who acknowledge God's word, and are partakers of his spirit, are called on to let their lights shine out of darkness and give light to the world, that they reprove all ungodliness by word, deed, life and death, confess the Lord's holy name, word and will, and confirm it by a pious and unblamable life, according to the scriptures. (Matt. 5 ; Phil. 2 ; Eph. 5 ; 1 Pet. 2.)

Ninthly. That it were better to have a mill-stone hanged to one's neck, and to be cast into the depth of the sea, than to offend one of these little ones, who believe in Christ. (Matt. 18.)

Tenthly. That we reflect well, why or for what reason we are not to hear such preachers. If we do hear them, and desire to be taught of them, then seek we the truth among lies, and life among the dead. But if we will not be taught of them, but use our liberty, as they call it, we must then confess that such hearing is no hearing, but trifling and hypocrisy, by which we despise Christ's spirit, doctrine, regulations, counsel, admonition, community and church ; and encourage anti-christ's seducing abominations, idolatry and kingdom ; and conform to the world in all appearance of evil, act the hypocrite, grieve and vex many a pious child of God, cause strife among the pious, and esteem lightly the innocent blood which is shed in many places on this account.

Behold, my readers, all who fear the Lord, and rightly examine and judge *these ten articles*, by the spirit and word of the Lord, will not halt here, but will faithfully take heed to the counsel and admonition of the Holy Ghost; reprove the world both by works and doctrine, flee all appearance of evil and walk unblamably in the house of the Lord.

But touching the false worship, the light-minded comfort one another, and say : children may be baptized ; for the child is clean ; the water is clean ; to wash and to bathe is also clean, &c. We may also receive the supper of the Lord at the hands of these preachers, although it is in idolatrous houses ; christians have no idols any more, they only use bread and wine as such, which is pure to the pure ; (2 Cor. 8) for Paul says : To the pure all things are pure. And they appeal to the case of Naaman, the Captain of the king of Assyria ; and to the house of Rinmon, (Rom. 14 ; Tit. 1 ; 2 Chron. 5) and say : We care not for the idolatry of the priests, but we worship Him who made heaven and earth, &c.

I answer : Can a single passage be adduced from the scriptures, that uncleanness, sin, falsifying the ordinances of God, idolatry, disobedience to the word, and hypocrisy are all pure to the pure, that is, to the true believers ; then we might consider a little on it. But we know certainly, that not a single passage can be advanced.

O my reader, had the men of God thus understood the scriptures, as these poor people do, the three valiant young men would have by no means suffered themselves to be cast into the fiery furnace. (Dan. 3 ; 2 Macc. 6, 7.) The upright Eleazer, pious Susan ; the mother with her seven sons, the holy prophets, apostles and pious witnesses of God, would have saved their lives, would have escaped the cruel tortures and pains, and said : To the pure all things are pure, we will cheerfully comply.

O no, my good reader, no : the clean are not to touch the unclean. Touch not, says the spirit of God through Isaiah and Paul, the unclean thing, that is, what the scriptures forbid. (Isa. 52 ; 2 Cor. 6.) He that washed himself, after the touching of a dead body, if he touch it again, what availeth his washing ? Is it not folly for any man to wash his clothes, and afterwards tread them into the mire again ? (Eccl. 34.) The scriptures plainly teach : That the just shall live by faith ; and that a good tree brings forth good fruit. (Heb. 1 ; Rom. 1 ; Gal. 3 ; Heb. 10.) And we certainly know that an humble, lowly-minded soul will never magnificently array itself, dressed in gold, pearls or other costly apparel, (Matt. 7, 12,) and that those who fear the Lord, will be honest, chaste, sober ; they will not drink with dishonorable women, sing and dance with them ; for the knowledge, fear and love of God and his word forbid them ; and should one do so, we would know that his light is darkness, and his conduct not agreeable to the scriptures. And so it does also illy become those who boast of the word, and would reprove seduction, the idolatry and abominations of preachers by the scriptures, and yet associates with them in their false service, doctrine and sacraments, words without actions profit nothing. (Matt. 23 ; Rom. 1.) Have no fellowship with the unfruitful works of darkness, but rather reprove them. (Eph. 5.)

It is true, that to the pure all things are pure, which are not contrary to the spirit and word of God. For none are called pure in the scriptures, except those who conform to the spirit and word of the Lord. All who agree with the word, to them all lawful, pure things, are pure, such as eating, dringing, clothing, houses, manors, land, gold, silver, wives, children, goods, food, to wake, to sleep, to speak, to be silent, and all things which God has given us as necessaries; because they are pure, they will also use all lawful, pure things purely; namely, in the fear of God, with thanksgiving and moderation, to the praise of God and to the service of their fellow man; for which end, these things were given by God, to the use of men.

But all things prohibited of God, such as hypocrisy, unfruitful works, conformity to the world, living in affluence and splendor, living in idolatry, are by all means, impure to the pure, to the willing obedient children of God; and the pure can never use things impurely through all eternity, according to the will of. God; for the spirit of God and his word forbid them.

Adam was allowed of God to eat of all the vegetables and fruits of the earth, for his subsistence, except of the tree of knowledge of good and evil; for if he would eat thereof, he was to die. (Gen. 3.) All the fruits and creatures allowed of God, were pure to pure Adam, but one tree was impure to him through the command of God; he eat thereof, and with all his seed he fell under the power of death.

And even as all things are pure to the pure, and are for the good of the pious, so also to the impure all things are impure, and encourage the evil one to do wickedness; because they are impure they use all the creatures of God impurely. They eat and drink with excess; they dress gorgeously; and indulge in lewdness; they raise their children to idleness; they avariciously hoard gold, silver, houses and lands, (Tit. 1) and there is nothing they use purely according to the will of God; for they are impure, sensual, disobedient to the word, and are earthly-minded, as the scriptures say.

Further; it is also an abominable calumny and slanderous seduction, what some pretend and say; outward idolatry cannot defile and make impure, if not sanctioned by the heart.

My good reader, if that were true all the passages would have been spoken to no purpose, which say; neither be ye idolators as were some of them—have no fellowship with the unfruitful works of darkness; avoid all appearance of evil, &c., (1 Cor. 10; Eph. 5; 1 Thes. 5;) then would also the offence of the cross have been ended. No, no, it becomes a true christian to be wholly pious, to glorify God, both in body and spirit. (1 Cor. 6.)

Aaron, a high priest called of God, a type of the Lord Jesus, when he was constrained of the people to make gods for them which should go before them, he was overcome through the weakness of the flesh, that he yielded to the idolators, and made them a golden calf. Aaron did not worship it, in his heart; for he well knew it was not God, who led them through the red sea, but that it was a creature made of gold. Nevertheless this guilt was charged to Aaron, for Moses said: What did this people unto thee that thou didst bring so great a sin upon them? (Exod. 32,) yea, the Lord would have destroyed him had not Moses interceded for him. (Deut. 9.)

We would, that all founders of sects and erring spirits, whose rejection of the cross, ease, sensual minds and hypocrisy, is cloaked under the semblance of the word of God, would reflect well upon the history of Aaron; I trust they would no longer conceal their nudity and disgrace with fig-leaves; but would clothe themselves with the true coat of skins, with Jesus, Christ made of God; (Gen. 3,) for they comfort and encourage the poor, rude people in their idolatry and faith, by their ungodly dealings, which they call liberty, grieve the pious unto death, discourage and offend the poor, wavering souls of whom it is written: But whoso shall offend one of these little ones, which believe in me, it were better for him, that a mill-stone were hanged about his neck, and that he were drowned in the depth of the sea. (Matt. 18.)

What christian liberty is, and how it is to be used according to the will of God, is fully explained in Rom. 14; 1 Cor. 6, 8, 10.

Say, beloved, how can we count that as belonging to christian liberty, which is so openly committed against so many passages in the scriptures against brotherly and universal love, and contrary to all the examples of so many saints, as said?

O, were they pure of heart, who introduce such subtle arguments, and would they but love Christ supremely over every thing, how soon they would then know that that which they maintain is contrary to the spirit and word of God. But I fear they are those concerning whom it is written: There is a generation that are pure in their own eyes, and yet are not washed from their filthiness. (Prov. 30.)

Touching Naaman, we have to notice attentively the following passages.

First, that Naaman was neither a Jew, nor a proselyte, but a foreigner, who was not included in the doctrine, ceremonies, ordinances and righteousness of Israel, although he would no longer serve idols, and would serve and offer to God, he was not circumcised.

Secondly: that he was the servant of his master, upon whom the king depended; and therefore had to attend to the service of his master when the king worshipped in the house of Rimmon, Naaman would worship none other than the true God who had cleansed him.

Thirdly : That we cannot conclude with certainty from the answer of the prophet, how far he did, or did not comply.

Fourthly ; That the house of Rimmon, and the service thereof, and our temple with its services, are not the same ; for in the house of Rimmon the name of God, the laws, the ordinances and ceremonies, were not abused, for they were not known there. But what abuses, disgrace, scoffings, abomination and blasphemy, are carried on in our temples under the name of Christ, all rational men may determine by the scriptures.

But if any one says : Why do you concern yourselves about the doings of the priests ? Worship God as Naaman did, &c., this sounds to us thus : "Behold your pious father will be very slanderously mocked, insulted, reviled and much abused ; let such things not move you, or confound you, but be unconcerned and contented. Submit quietly, but in your heart honor your father, &c." Say, beloved, what rational and upright child could see his father thus treated, and say nothing, and submit quietly ?

Since then, we see with unclouded eyes, how miserably they treat our eternal Father, who loved us so greatly, in their houses of abomination ; and how they behave towards his son, Jesus Christ, who bought us with such a precious price. Again. How they quench his Holy Spirit, hate his will, his word, and abuse his sacraments, reject his ordinances and commands, revile and reproach his children, deceive poor souls, rob Christ of his own, and his glory ; and with all this, we are to unite with such open enemies of God !—to act the hypocrite with them, to listen to their ungodly seductions and abominations !— if we should, we would be very ungrateful children, and without love. This is incontrovertibly true.

No ! Such is not the way of pious christians ; but as Christ defends his church, is not ashamed of her, and enlightens her by his Holy Spirit and word, comforts her in all her distresses, strengthens her in sufferings and endows her with power and wisdom, before lords and princes, wise and learned, and before the whole world, that all have to be silent and ashamed in presence of a poor, humble christian ; and in the day of judgment acknowledge her before his Father, (Matt. 10 ; Luke 12,) and will bestow her the eternal kingdom ; and so do the spirit and love of Christ also demand of us, that we confess before men his divine honor, word, and ordinances ; and besides, we are to testify it by our works, possessions, blood, life and death, and not clandestinely frequent such houses of abomination, where his great and adorable name is so miserably dishonored and slandered ; and where we hear not the truth, nor learn any piety.

For it is nothing but hypocrisy which they teach ; although they do disguise it with the word of the Lord, (Jer. 8) as may be evidently observed by their works.

They all, teachers and hearers, run, says the prophet, like a frantic heifer (Hos. 4)—they all hate reproof and instruction, and live imprudently according to their own lusts. (Ezek. 11.) They desire not God's word, therefore. I fear the scourge is ready, and the avenging sword of the Lord is drawn ; that soon one ungodly man will eat another, so that many of them be eaten up, for this foolish people desire to be beaten. (Hos. 4.)

Fifthly. We have to observe, that in the New Testament we are only directed to the spirit, word, counsel, admonition and usages of Christ : what he allows us we may do, but what he forbids we dare not do ; it become all true Christians to conform thereto, and not according to such doubtful histories and obscure passages, from which we can draw no sure ground, and which teach the very reverse of what the Lord's apostles publicly taught.

Here I would faithfully admonish the sincere reader, that he would not suffer himself to be deceived with such words; but at all times to keep to and abide in the unchangeable and sure ground, (1 Cor. 3) which the faithful witnesses of Christ, the holy apostles left to us, which they taught us plainly in their writings ; for the deceivers seek but to confound the wavering, and to be free from the cross of Christ.

But, say they : We esteem it to be better, though we do so sometimes, so that we may administer to our wives and children, and serve the poor, than that we wholly abandon the preachers, and thereby make all our possessions a prey. (Deut. 6 ; Matt. 22.)

To which we reply, in the first place : The first command teaches, thou shalt love the Lord thy God with all thy heart, with all thy soul, and with all thy strength. Where the name of the Lord is profaned, and where his word is violated, there it behooves you to reprove such things with an unblamable life, and by the word of God, and to defend the praises of God, as as much as in you is ; and reflect upon what the Lord says : Whosoever loves father, mother, brother, sister, wife, children, possessions and life more than me, cannot be my disciple. (Matt. 10 ; Luke 2, 14,)

Secondly. That all who believe, that God made heaven and earth, and sustained Israel for forty days with bread from heaven, and water from the rock, sent Elias his necessary food by a raven, (Gen. 1 ; Lev. 16, 17 ; Deut. 8, 16 ; 1 Kings 17) who gives the birds in the air, the fishes in the water, and the reptiles upon earth, all their food ; those will not doubt the goodness, power and promise of their Lord Jesus Christ, who says : First seek the kingdom of heaven and his righteousness, and all other things shall be added unto you, (Matt. 6) for if the countenance of his grace is in this matter over those who reject him, how much more over those who fear him and keep his commandments.

Thirdly. That the Almighty. bountiful God, God Shaddai, who is all-sufficient to support the poor and needy without any idolatry, hypocrisy and service of the devil; because he has no delight in such offerings and gifts of unrighteousness; as the prophet says: Behold, to obey is better than sacrifice, and to hearken, than the fat of rams; for rebellion is as the sin of witchcraft, and stubbornness is as iniquity and idolatry. (1 Sam. 15.)

All, therefore, who say that they do this on account of their wife and children, and for the poor's sake, they ought to know that they love their wife and children more than God, and lessen the arm and power of God, (Eccl. 35) and lie unto the Lord; hence their indolence, and thus they avoid the cross, and cloak their unbelief, their earthly mind and hypocrisy under such a pretext. Let every one take heed to himself and fear God, who has eyes like flaming fire, which penetrate heaven and earth, and cannot be blinded by fair words. (Acts 5; Rev. 1.)

Again: They further pretend that Paul purified himself according to the Jews' custom, (Acts 16) and Timothy was circumcised. This is quite different, for these were things which God had commanded, although they ended in Christ. The reason why Paul consented thereto was, that he might preach the word with more freedom to the Jews, as he says: Unto the Jews I became a Jew, that I might gain the Jews; to them that are under the law, that I might gain them that are under the law. (1 Cor. 9.)

And since these works originated not with anti-christ, but from God, with which Paul would not offend the weak Jews; as explained: How can we then show by them, that we are at liberty to hear false preaching, receive the baptism and enjoy the supper of anti-christ; and to take part with the world in open idolatry and blasphemy? Though this be not done with the heart, it is at least in appearance. Or we must consider the works of the law, which were of God, to be as unclean and ungodly as the works and abominations of darkness, which are of the devil; and to esteem the avoiding of the cross of Christ as the laudable zeal of Paul, when he would teach the Jews the gospel of Christ!

O my faithful reader, if you would not lose your poor soul, do not then dishonor Christ, do rightly, seek his praise, obey his spirit, doctrine, counsel, admonition and example, and you will never be made ashamed; you will soon discover that Paul's purification, and Timothy's circumcision, are vastly different from the doings, works, abominations, idolatry and blasphemy of anti-christ, which have been practised from time to time, in the name of Christ, even to the present day. May the gracious, merciful God grant that you may all come to the knowledge, and walk in his truth, Amen.

Lastly. They say: That we are yet prisoners in Babel, and that we may therefore do in semblance the works of Babel; and allege Baruch's sayings: Ye shall see in Babylon gods of silver, and of gold, and of wood, borne upon shoulders, which cause the heathens to fear: beware, therefore, that ye in no wise be like to strangers, neither be ye afraid of them, when ye see the multitude before them and behind them, worshipping them: but say in your hearts, O Lord, we must worship thee. (Bar. 6.)

Answer. Here we have first to observe, what is shown by the Babylonian captivity; for when the Israelites did not serve God aright, in their own country, they were scattered according to the prediction of Moses, by the righteous and gracious judgment of God, among the heathen nations, and were led captive under the dominion of Babylon. (Deut. 4, 28.) So it is with those who boast themselves as being the spiritual Israel; because they became unfaithful to the Lord, and rejected his word, and turned their ears to preachers of lies, the Babylonian king, anti-christ, has taken advantage of them and deprived them of the true doctrine, ceremonies and services, and led them captive under his dominion, and has bound them miserably with the cords of error and idolatrous abominations.

But all those who are again enlightened by the spirit and word of the Lord, and born of God, and die unto the old man, sin; forsake all human misleadings, and rightly use the Lord's holy sacraments, ordinances and divine services, they are freed from spiritual Babylon, that is, from sin, hell, death, devil, from the doctrines and commands of men, and from all idolatry, abominations and crimes, as Paul says: There is, therefore, now no condemnation to them who are in Christ Jesus, who walk not after the flesh, but after the spirit; for the law of the spirit of life in Christ Jesus, hath made me free from the law of sin and death. (Rom. 8.)

All, then, who say that they are yet captives of Babylon, testify that they have not been set at liberty by the Cyrus, Jesus Christ, from their sins, and not come from Chaldea to Jerusalem. (2 Cor. 3; 1 Ezra 1.)

Secondly: That Israel is not commanded here to conform themselves to the gentiles; but when they saw them carry their idols, (even as we may see on the days of papistical processions and abominations, although we are not in their temple,) then they should worship God only, and give him the honor ; for if God had commanded them to conform in all things to the Babylonian idolatry, and only to serve the Lord with their heart secretly, then Schadrach, Meshach and Abednego acted foolishly to refuse worshipping the great golden idol, on account of which they hazarded their lives. (Dan. 3.) O no ! the miraculous work, shown of God to them, testifies that they acted rightly. All, then, I say, who teach that true believers are not released from Babylon, do thereby deny the merits. death and blood of Christ, and faith with its power, and the Holy Ghost with his liberty, and despise wholly the innocent blood of the free witnesses of the free children of God, which is shed so abundantly.

Let every one see well to it what he believes and learns ; for I fear that both the bloodshedder and the despiser are alike guilty. My good reader, examine the scriptures well, and you will find, that to the free children of God here upon earth, there is no liberty promised as to the flesh, as Christ says : Ye shall be hated of all men for my name's sake. (Matt. 24.) Again : He that would follow me, let him deny himself, and take up his cross and follow me. (Matt. 16.) Again : All who will kill you, think they do God service. (John 16.) All who would live godly in Christ Jesus, says Paul, must suffer persecution. (2 Tim. 3.) And through much tribulation we must enter into the kingdom of God. (Acts 14.) For the liberty of the spirit is to be maintained with much misery, tribulation, persecutions, bonds, fear and death. The servant is not greater than his lord, and the disciple is not greater than his master ; but it is enough that he be like his lord and master. (Matt 10 ; John 13, 15.)

Behold, beloved sirs, friends and brethren, here you have the leading parts and chief articles of a CHRISTIAN GROUND AND FOUNDATION, with a plain instruction and exposition of the antichristian abominations and Babylonian acts, whereby the true apostolic foundation, for a long time, was corrupted and razed to the ground ; and we have contrasted light and darkness, truth and falsehood, that the whole truth by our seeking, doctrine and belief, undertaking and weak attempts, may be made manifest.

And 1 hope by the grace of God, that you will readily receive it, if you are at all honestly disposed, read it with a sincere heart, fear God, and acknowledge Christ as the true head ; and see that we are grounded upon the eternal corner stone, that we walk in the right way, although in weakness, and hold the plain truth, (Isa. 28 ; Eph. 2 ; Ps. 117 ; 2 Pet. 2 ; Matt. 21 ; Luke 20 ;

Acts 4,) and that there is no other ground or way, and truth to be found in the scriptures, that can stand before God, other than this, which we have pointed out, and which we on every occasion maintain and defend in so much tribulation.

And I have served you all with this small gift, as I received it from my God. I gladly would that I could serve you longer with great and abundant grace, to the praise of the Lord. Therefore, have I renounced praise, honor, ease, and forsaken all, and willingly submitted to the pressing cross of my Lord Jesus Christ, which oftimes assails my weak flesh. I seek neither gold nor silver, (the Lord knows this,) but am ready, with faithful Moses, to suffer affliction with the people of God, rather than to enjoy the pleasures of sin for a season; and I esteem the reproach of Christ greater riches than all the treasures in Egypt, for I know what the scriptures have promised us, (2 Thes. 2; Heb. 11,) and this is my only joy and heart's desire, that I may extend the borders of the kingdom of God, publish the truth, reprove sin, teach righteousness, feed the hungry with the word of the Lord, lead the stray sheep into the right path, and win many souls to the Lord through his spirit, power and grace, and so act in my weakness, as he taught me who purchased me, a miserable sinner, with his crimson blood, and gave me this mind, by the gospel of his grace, namely, Jesus Christ, to him be praise and glory, and the eternal kingdom, Amen.

A CHRISTIAN AND
AFFECTIONATE EXHORTATION TO ALL IN AUTHORITY.

Also to the learned, to the common people, to sects and to the bride of Christ, that is not a little scorched by the heat of the sun every where.

WE showed you in the preface, faithful reader, why or wherefore we published these our writings, to wit: on account of the abominable deceiving, and the manifold dangers at this time, when are to be found so many schisms, communities, churches and sects, who are all called after the name of the Lord; such as *Romans* or *papists*, *Lutherans*, *Zuinglians*, erring sects, and the christians who are upbraided as ana-baptists. Even as in former times among the Jews, were the Chasidim, Zadikin, Essenes, Saducees, Pharisees, &c., which sacred and profane history mention. Each boasts to be the Church of Christ, and

10*

to have the Lord's word, although the greater part of them not only live inconsistently with the spirit, word and example of Christ, but they very enviously upbraid and slander, and are inimically opposed to it; and it is just as it was in the beginning, that the pious every where have to suffer much from the impious; as Abel had to suffer of Cain; Isaac of Ishmael; Jacob of Esau, &c., although created by the same God, having one common origin, boast all of one Christ; and in the day of Judgment, find the same judge. Anti-christ rules through hypocrisy and lies, with power and sword; but Christ reigns patiently, with his word and spirit. He uses neither sword nor sabre. O man! man! Look upon the irrational creatures, and learn wisdom, (1 Cor. 12.) Roaring lions, frightful bears, and all devouring wolves agree among themselves with their respective species; but you, poor, helpless worms—you, who are created after God's own image, and are called rational beings, without tusks, claws and horns, born into this world feeble, senseless, speechless and powerless, yea, neither able to stand nor walk, and have to depend entirely upon maternal aid, which teaches you that you are to be peaceable and not contentious; but when you attain your understandings and manhood, then you are so very restless, tyrannical, revengeful, blood-thirsty and unmerciful, so much so that it cannot be fully conceived, related or described. Your open works bear testimony to this, still you boast yourselves to be christians. O no! my faithful reader, no! Christ teaches: "My peace I give you; my peace I leave you." (John 16.) Paul says: Let the peace of God rule in your hearts, to which also ye are called in one body, and be ye thankful. Col. 3.) Again: The Son of man has not come to destroy, but to make alive. (Matt. 18; Luke 9.)

Since there are so many of you who treat the children of God so inhumanly, as we see, we have compiled summarily our *acts, ground, faith and doctrine*, from the word of God, and have published it; so that every slanderous reviler, foul-mouthed speaker and bloody persecutor, may out of it learn what our undertaking, seeking and doings properly are, and upon what ground the city of God must be built, and which of all the aforementioned congregations or communities is the lawful and true church of Christ. Even as there was but one Adam and Eve; one Noah and one ark, (Gen. 3.) One Isaac and one Rebecca, (Gen. 7,) so there is but one community of Christ, which is the body, the city, the temple, the house and bride of Christ, having but one gospel, one faith, one baptism, one supper, and one service; walking in the same way and leading a pious, unblamable life, as the scriptures teach.

All who have not the pure, unadulterated word of God, the

true, active faith, with the Lord's holy baptism and supper, in power and spirit, and walk the broad road of the flesh, are not the community and church of Christ. Here neither name nor boasting prevails; we must be in Christ, and Christ in us; we must be moved by his spirit, and in every respect abide in his holy word, else we have no God. (2 John 1.)

Israel was not saved, though of the seed of Abraham, because they walked not in the way of Abraham. (John 8; Rom. 9.) Much less we, though we are called after the name of Christ, if we seek not his promise with all our souls, and not cordially hear and follow, and be obedient to his holy will. (1 John 2.)

Since it is well known to all the pious, that we and our forefathers, for many hundred years, were under the heavy burden and in the service of Egypt, (Exod. 10,) deceived by the false prophets, never heard the book of the law, the holy city, and temple lay waste, and were under the tyranny and dominion of Babylon, (2 Chron. 22, 25,) as heard above. The merciful Father had compassion on the pressing misery and tribulation of his people, and raised up to us the true Moses, Zerubbabel, Christ Jesus, through his word and spirit; now then, it becomes you, O you high renowned lords and princes, since you and we boast of the same Christ, gospel, redemption and kingdom, that you no longer obstruct by your mandates and powers, the journeying of the people of God to the eternal promised land; but you should favor them more, and prosper their journey by your gracious permission; that you may hear and read with the venerable and pious Josiah, with a broken, meek heart, in the true fear of God, the lost book of the law of Christ, which was lost for a long time. Rend not your garments but your hearts; for you are not only led off from the true path, but you are so much bewitched by the man of sin, (2 Thess. 2,) that you persecute the innocent, pious hearts, who injure neither you nor any one upon earth even the beast.

That you would, with king Cyrus, release the poor captive children from the land of Chaldea, who cry and weep at the rivers of Babylon, (Ps. 136,) that they may again possess the spiritual land of Caanan, and build up the spiritual Jerusalem, the altar and the temple in their ancient city, (Jer. 30,) and establish the spiritual priesthood, and practice the spiritual offering and divine service according to the instructions of God's word, that they may no longer hear and observe the Babylonian laws, namely, men's commandments; but Israel's law, God's word and righteousness. Although some of you, (alas how few!) are so far taught, through God's grace and word, as I trust, that you know, that neither usages nor councils, neither learning nor acuteness, nor subtlety, nor sword, nor mandate, can bend or break the word of the Most High, the word of truth, the word of the heavenly witness, the gospel of the kingdom, for other foundation cannot be laid to all eternity, than that which is laid, which is Christ Jesus. (1 Cor. 3.)

Therefore, wisdom cries : Turn at my reproof; behold I will pour out my spirit upon you, I will make known my words unto you. (Prov. 1.)

Love, righteousness ye rulers of the land. (Wis. 1.)

Be wise, now, therefore, O ye kings ; be instructed, ye judges of the earth, serve the Lord with fear, and rejoice with trembling, (Ps. 2;) for the king that honors wisdom shall rule forever. (Wis. 6.)

Do, therefore, with a meek heart, and in the fear of God, examine these our faithful instructions, and judge by Christ's own spirit and word, as much as in you is ; compare it with the doctrine and lives of the apostles, with the piety, love, usages, doings, misery, cross and sufferings of the primitive church ; I hope, by the grace of God, you may plainly comprehend that our doctrine is the infallible doctrine and ground of the scriptures. Read these our FUNDAMENTALS, together with other books, appended to this, viz : *the book concerning faith and its power ; concerning regeneration or the new creature ; of the cross, sufferings and persecution of the saints ; of excommunication, ban or exclusion, with other tracts, published from time to time,* you will then find, by the grace of God, that this doctrine is the unadulterated gospel, which the Lord taught by his own mouth, and which his holy apostles preached through the whole world, and by the power of the spirit testified thereto with life and death. Ours is no new doctrine, as the preachers without truth, pretend and persuade you ; but it is the old doctrine, which was preached and practised in the church, fifteen hundred years ago, whereby the church was, is, and shall be borne, till the end. (1 Cor. 4 ; Gal. 4 ; 1 Pet. 1 ; James 1.)

O you high-renowned lords and princes, turn to the truth of God, and receive reproof, correction and wisdom; for through wisdom kings reign, and princes decree justice, (Prov. 8,) and do observe how far your spirit, faith and lives differ from the Lord's spirit, word and life.

Think you, dear sirs, that you are born to live only in great splendor, wantonness, gluttony and revelling, and lead a vain, sensual life ; that you are to follow on in your wantonness and pernicious lusts, as it pleases you, and be christians? O no, whosoever has not the spirit of Christ, is none of his. (Romans 8.)

Solomon says : As a roaring lion, and a raging bear ; so is a wicked ruler over the poor people. The prince that wanteth understanding is also a great oppressor. The poet also well knew this, when he says : *Quic quid delirant reges, plectantur Achivi;* i. e. The mischief which kings do, the common people have to pay or atone for; but a wise king disperseth the ungodly. (Prov. 28.)

Therefore, beloved sirs, see well to it ; this is that to which you are called, namely : that you are to chastise and punish, in the true fear of God, with all equitable and just discretion, the open evil doers ; such as theives, murderers, buggerers, sodomites, adulterers, debauchers, menslayers, the violent, fornicators, sorcerers, robbers, &c., that you give each his portion, execute judgment and righteousness, and deliver the spoiled out of the hand of the oppressor, (Isa. 22 ;) that you are to prevent, by proper means, understand without tyranny and bloodshed, open deceivers, who so miserably lead poor, helpless souls, by hundreds of thousands into destruction, be they priests, monks, preachers, baptized or unbaptized ; so that they will no longer derogate from the almighty majesty of God, our only and eternal Saviour, Christ Jesus, the Holy Ghost, together with the word of grace ; nor introduce those ridiculous abuses and idolatry, under semblance of truth, as it happens from time to time, till now ; and thus you may, with all love and zeal, enlarge the borders of the kingdom of God without violence, blood or sword ; assist it by your gracious permission, wise counsel ; and with a pious, unblamable life defend it.

Behold, beloved lords, this is your calling and your incumbent duty, (Exod. 18, 23 ; Lev. 19 ; Deut. 17 ; 2 Chron. 19 ; Rom. 13 ; Tit. 13 ; 1 Pet. 2 ;) and not domineer so maliciously over God's children and his word : as alas, many of you evidently do, and is customary.

Such rulers were Moses, Joshua, David, Hezekiah, Josaphat, Josias, Zerubbabel, &c., they faithfully discharged their enjoined duties ; conformed to the word of God, protected their subjects with solicitous concern, obeyed the Lord's commands, abolished the false prophets and the priests of Baal, with their altars, groves and idolatry, and faithfully kept their people and country, to observe the ordinances of the Lord, his laws and divine service as commanded by Moses ; for they feared God, and had the book of the law to which they conformed, and by which they judged the people : and always remembered the Lord their God, who set them over his people as potentates and rulers. (Deut. 17.)

They feared God with all their hearts, praised his name, and humbled themselves with all their strength, as David did, when he was girded with a linen ephod, and danced before the ark of the Lord, yea that he was even despised of his wife Michal ; but he said: I will play before the Lord, who chose me, and I will be yet more vile than this, in my own sight.   (2 Sam. 6.)

O you high-renowned, noble lords, do believe Christ's word, fear God's wrath, love righteousness, do justice to widows and orphans, judge rightly between man and man, fear no man's highness; despise no man's business, hate all avarice, chastise with discretion, suffer God's word to be taught in liberty, prevent none to walk in the ways of truth; yield to his sceptre who called you to this high charge, and your throne shall stand fast. (Prov. 19; Wis. 6.)

Now as the sceptre of Christ is an upright sceptre, (Heb. 1) and teaches, judges and corrects every one, without respect to person, I, a poor and unlearned being must lay aside my diffidence, and grow bold in love, whereby I would desire to save your poor souls, and with Samuel reprove Saul, with Abdia reprimand Jeroboam, with Elias chide Ahab, with Isaiah reprehend Hezekiah, with Nathan and Gad rebuke David of their misdeeds and transgressions, (4 Sam. 15; 1 Kings 13, 17, 18; Isa. 38; 2 Sam. 12, 24) and thus proclaim my Lord's spirit, word and will, who knows but there might be some one that will regard the fidelity and love of his poor minister, hear his well-meaning voice and christian exhortation, and depart from an ungodly and evil way: thus some of the aforementioned kings heard the reproving word of the mouths of the prophets with fear, and reformed, and meekly received the word.

And were it even so, that my faithful service and love, should be rewarded with death, as I have reason to suspect it may happen, because haughty and proud flesh is unwillingly reproved, but uses at all time its evil nature, however, nothing worse can happen me, than did the pious Isaiah of Manassah; Zachariah of Joaz; Urias of Jachin, Abimelech and other priests of Saul; (Chron. 24; 1 Samuel 22) John of Herod; Christ of Pilate and of the Scribes; and as it happened to all the apostles and pious witnesses of the whole world.   (Matt. 7, 24, 26; Mark 15; Luke 23; John 10.)

I do not esteem my life to be better and dearer than the beloved men of God did theirs.   I can only be deprived of perishable and mortal flesh, which must once die, and return to dust.   Should I even attain to the age of Methuselah, not a hair can fall from my head without the will of my heavenly father, (Gen. 5, 3; Matt. 10,) if I lose my life for the sake of Christ and his testimony, and on account my sincere love for my neighbor, I certainly know, that I will save it in life eternal, (Mark 8; Matt. 16,) therefore, I cannot conceal the truth; but I must testify and reveal it in the true fear of God, to my beloved lords.

Beloved, noble lords, do learn to rightly know yourselves, whence you are, what you are, and what you will be. All of you, one as well as another, be he emperor, or king, are from the same seed that we poor and unregarded are, and you came into this world as we, and you are no more than vapor, frail flesh, a withering flower, dust and ashes, as we all are. (James 4; Isa. 4; 2 Pet. 1; Gen. 3; Sirach 10.) To-day you are kings and triumph in great and high houses, to-morrow you are laid low, and must be food for serpents and worms.

O Sirs, my beloved sirs, humble yourselves, righteous is he who will examine your case, and mighty is he, who will pass judgment upon you; his name is the RULING LORD; he is the almighty, the holy, the terrible, the high adorable and omnipotent God, who created heaven and earth, and who has in the hands of his strength all majesty, power and dominion. Learn to know him; learn to fear him. Awaken, look out, the time is not far off, when you will hear: *Give an account of your stewardship, for you may no longer be steward.* (Luke 16.)

Do, therefore, not hear those who seek fat prebends and a lazy life, they deceive you, they teach you according to the lust of your hearts; they flatter you for the sake of unlawful gain, they preach to you wanton deception according to their own opinion, and not out of the mouth of the Lord, they fatten their bodies, and have fine days, from the fatness of your poor souls, (beloved sirs, understand rightly what I mean,) although they boast much of the gospel; hear them, who are not like the wind-shaken reed, (Matt. 11,) those, who with John and Elias, are not so much frightened by the wilderness of misery, who suffer daily for the truth's sake, love gold and wood alike, who esteem all things alike, both praise and reproach, riches, and poverty, life and death, who seek only the honor of Christ, and the salvation of their beloved brethren, (Rom. 5; 1 Cor. 15,) and preach nothing but the pure, unmixed word of God, and seal it, with spirit, power and work, as it is commanded of Christ, and as it is proclaimed and taught through the whole world by his holy apostles.

I repeat it, hearken not, follow not, and believe not the multitude of the learned, who suffer themselves to be called doctors, lords and masters, for they are sensual and bloodthirsty, (Phil. 3; 1 Cor. 4;) but seek and follow those who are the spectacle, filth of the earth, curse and offscouring, there you will find Christ's spirit, truth, power, works and life. And you will soon find, by the grace of God, that you are from Christ, with your doctrine, spirit, faith, baptism, life, church and all your doing, from Christ's spirit, doctrine, command, prohibition, ordinances and usages.

Say, O you kings and rulers of the land : Where is your faith and love, with their pious nature ? Where is the fear of your God ? Your lamp and light ? And your unablamable, godly life, which is out of God ? Is it not all world and sensuality which you seek and follow ? We find, generally, in your houses and courts, nothing but extravagant pomp, and gorgeousness, pride, presumptuousness of heart, insatiable avarice, hatred, envy, backbiting, betraying, whoredom, debauchery, gaming, eating, drinking, dancing, swearing, stabbing, housebreaking, &c. This is your lordly custom and court conduct during the whole course of your lives ; and you never once reflect on the misery, tribulation, humility, love and righteousness in which the Lord of lords, and King of kings, lived before you, what he taught the children of men, and what pattern or example he left them : the affliction and misery of the wretched reach not your ears ; the sweat of the poor we find in your houses, and the innocent blood in your hands ; you receive gifts and presents to pervert judgment, and you take counsel together against the Lord and his anointed. (Ps. 2.) The prophets of Jezabel, and the priests of Baal, sensualists and flatterers, are much respected with you, they set upon soft cushions, and live well. But those who with Micha, (1 Chron. 18,) preach to you adversity and truth, must expect imprisonment and bonds, and death, and are deserving of all disgrace ; yea, it has come so far (God better it,) that where four or five, ten or twenty have met in the name of the Lord, to speak of the word of the Lord, and to do his work, in whose midst Christ is, (Matt. 18,) who fear the Lord with all their heart, and lead an unblamable life before all the world ; but if they be apprehended, and complaint brought against them, they must then be devoured of fire, or be destroyed by the sword, or sink into the depths of the waters.

But they who have met in the name of Baal, a meeting of all manner of mischief, who exceed Sodom and Gomorrah far in wickedness, where all manner of inhuman things are carried on between man and man ; and between woman and woman ; as it is in Spain, in Italy, and in the cloisters, &c. Public brothel-houses, theatres, fencing-schools, and the accursed drunken taverns, where many live in open disgrace, and act so shamefully against God's word. Such live in all unmolestedness and at peace.

I mention not the public assemblies of all manner of idolatry, where the most high, blessed and precious name of God is so miserably blasphemed, the blood of Christ despised, the Holy Ghost grieved, and the truth digraced, and lies commended, poor souls deceived, and the blind, ignorant people are not only directed to the holy water, bread, wine and the mass, but also to the dumb idols, of wood and stone, as, alas! it may be so extensively witnessed.

O my beloved lords, what are you doing? Where is the sword of righteousness which was given to you, of which you boast? You have to acknowledge that you leave it in the scabbard, and in its stead you have drawn the sword of unrighteousness. Yes, beloved sirs, things are so, (God better it,) that the prophets cry and call with propriety: Thy princes are rebellious, and companions of thieves; every one loveth gifts, and followeth after rewards; they judge not the fatherless, neither does the cause of the widow come unto them: therefore saith the Lord of hosts, the mighty one of Israel, Ah! I will ease me of mine adversaries, and avenge me of mine enemies. (Isa. 1.)

Behold, the princes of Israel, every one is wise in thee to their power to shed blood. In thee have they set light by father and mother, in the midst of thee they have dealt by oppression with the stranger; in thee they have vexed the fatherless and widow; they are like the devouring wolves to shed blood and destroy souls for their avarice sake; behold, therefore, says the Lord, I have smitten my hand at thy dishonest gain which thou hast made, and at thy blood which hath been shed in the midst of thee. (Ezek. 22.)

Woe to them that devise iniquity and work evil upon their beds! when the morning is light, they practice it, because it is in the power of their hand. And they covet fields, and take them by violence; and houses, and take them away: so they oppress a man and his house, even a man and his heritage. Therefore, thus saith the Lord: Behold against this family do I devise an evil, from which ye shall not remove your necks; neither shall ye go haughtily; for this time is evil. (Micha 2.)

Hear, O heads of Jacob, and ye princes of the house of Israel; is it not for you to know judgment who hate the good and love the evil? You pluck off their skin from off them, and their flesh from off their bones; who also eat the flesh of my people, and flay their skins from off them, and you break their bones and chop them in pieces, as for the pot, and as flesh within the caldron. Therefore, when you shall call unto the Lord, he will not hear, he will even hide his face at that time, as you have behaved yourselves ill. (Micha 3.)

Wo to her that is filthy and polluted to the oppressing city! she obeyed not the voice; she received not correction; she trusted not in the Lord: she drew not near to God. Her princes within her are roaring lions; her judges are evening wolves; they gnaw not the bones till the morrow, her prophets are light and treacherous persons; her priests have polluted the sanctuary, they have done violence to the law, the just Lord is in the midst thereof; he will do no iniquity: every morning doth he bring his judgment to light, he faileth not; but the unjust knoweth no shame. I have cut off the nations; their towers are desolate: I laid their streets to waste, that none passeth by. (Zeph. 3; Hos. 3.)

There are but few of you, I fear there is scarcely one, who seeks the Lord with all their heart, fears, loves, and serves him; therefore, will also the fury of God be poured out upon you like water, and the sword of his wrath will come upon you, as may be seen daily in many places; God better it.

To you, says the wise man, power is given of the Lord, and sovereignty from the Highest, who shall try your works and search out your counsel: because being ministers of his kingdom, ye have not judged aright nor kept the law, nor walked after the counsel of God; horribly and speedily shall he come upon you; for a sharp judgment shall be to them that are in high places. For mercy will soon pardon the meanest: but mighty men shall be mightily tormented. For he who is Lord over all shall fear no man's person, neither shall he stand in awe of any man's greatness: for he hath made the small and great, and careth for all alike. But a sore trial shall come upon the mighty. (Wis. 6.)

Therefore, beloved lords, take heed that you rightly execute your responsible and dangerous office according to the will of God; since, many of you, I fear, until now, alas! thought very little on it, and hence it is that anti-christ rises up with his wickedness, and Christ is rejected with his righteousness; lay to heart what is written: Keep thee far from a false matter; and the innocent and righteous slay thou not; for I will not justify the wicked, says the Lord. (Exod. 22.)

Here I well know that we have to hear of Munster, of kings, of dominions, of polygamy, of sword, of theft, of murder and the like abominations and disgrace, which, you always assert, result from baptism; and under this pretext you reprove every thing the mouth of the Lord commanded, and what the holy apostles taught and practised, and instead, thereof, you bring forth seditious sects and factions, who sanction the call of the learned and blood-shedding.

No, my beloved sirs, it will not acquit you in the day of the righteousness of God. I tell you the truth in Christ; notice the rightly baptized disciples of Christ, (Luke 22) who are baptized inwardly with spirit and fire, and externally with water, (Matt. 10) baptized according to the word of God; they know of no weapons other than patience, hope, quiet, (Isa. 30) and God's word, these, says Paul, are the weapons of our warfare, and are not carnal but mighty through God to the pulling down of strong holds; casting down imaginations, and every high thing that exalteth itself against the knowledge of God, and bringeth into captivity every thought to the obedience of Christ. (2 Cor, 10.) Our weapons are not weapons with which cities and countries are desolated; walls and gates broken down and human blood shed in torrents like water, but they are weapons with which the spiritual kingdom of the devil is destroyed, and the ungodly passions are annihilated, and the flinty hearts are broken, that have never been sprinkled with the heavenly dew of the holy word. We own no other weapons besides, the Lord knows it, and should we be torn into a thousand pieces; and although as many false witnesses were to rise up against us, as there are spears of grass in the fields, and as numerous as the grains of sand of the sea shore.

Once more: Christ is our fortress; patience our defence; the word of God our sword; and our victory is a candid, firm unfeigned faith in Jesus Christ. We let those take spears and swords, who, alas, regard human blood and swine's blood alike. He that is wise let him judge what I mean. (Luke 11; Heb. 4; Eph. 6; 1 John 5.)

We do acknowledge, beloved sirs, that some of the false prophets were baptized externally in appearance, with us, with the same baptism; even as thieves, murderers, highway robbers, sorcerers and the like, were baptized with you; but they were not of us; for had they been of us, as John says, they would no doubt have continued with us.

Christ says: False prophets and false christ's will arise, and do great signs and wonders, and if it were possible, would deceive the very elect. Behold, I have told you before. (Matt. 24.)

His warning of Christ was not given to the ungodly, obdurate despisers for they are already entangled in the snares of unrighteousness, but is given to the contrite of heart and to the willing souls, so that they might learn to know the spiritual, and suffer themselves not to be led into error; for the devil, says Peter, goes about, seeking the righteous, as a roaring lion seeking whom he may devour. (1 Pet, 5.)

The craftiness and artifice of the devil, who assumes the appearance of an angel of light, are not known by some, therefore, have so many stumbled and erred, and were alas, led into crooked paths by the deceivers: (Rev. 2; 2 Cor. 11) but this was not through baptism; for the elementary water can neither teach, nor pervert, but it was done through false prophets, of which, I say, we have been so faithfully warned by the Lords' own mouth.

Beloved sirs, fear God, judge rightly; the truth of God can never be changed into seduction and error, through the lies of the devil. But the word of our God shall stand forever. (Isa. 40; 1 Pet. 1.)

Should the devout angels be unjustly judged, for the sake of Lucifer's arrogance and be punished with his punishment: or should all the apostles be traitors, for Judas' sake? By no means. Every one shall bear his own burden. The son shall not bear the iniquity of the father, neither shall the father bear the iniquity of the son. The soul that sinneth *it* shall die. (Ezek. 18.)

Should we reproach the doctrine of Christ and his apostles, because the father of lies has resuscitated, in the name of Christ, the practice of circumcision as essential to *salvation*. That the dead will not rise in the day of judgment? (1 Cor. 16.)

That Philetus and Hymenius asserted that the resurrection of the dead has already taken place? (2 Tim. 2.) That some pretended that the great day of the Lord was at hand? (2 Th. 2.)

How could the apostle help it, that the Nicolatians had their wives common, as Eusebias relates?

That the Ebionites denied the deity of Christ, and taught that Christ began only to exist in Mary.

And that the Corinthians maintained, that the world was created by angels; that Christ was no more than a mere man, and had not yet risen, but is to rise with us in future, and that he would reign one thousand years in the flesh with his saints?

All these sects arose in the days of the apostles, nevertheless the gospel of Christ remained the true gospel, the doctrines of the apostles the true doctrine.

The scriptures say that we are to flee and avoid such leaders of sects and heretics; and we hope to obey willingly the injunction all the days of our lives. (Rom. 16; 2 Tim. 2; Tit. 3; 2 John 1.)

Therefore, my beloved sirs, do pass an impartial and rational judgment in this matter, as before God, who will judge you in the great day; this we ask of you for Jesus' sake; for we seek nothing else upon earth, (the Lord knows,) than the true ground of the truth, the praise of Christ, the obedience of his word, and that with a good conscience, as we testify to the whole world, with our writings, word, possessions, blood, life and death.

We also write the truth in Christ and lie not, that we acknowledge spiritually no king, neither in heaven above nor upon earth beneath, than the only, eternal and true king spiritual David, Christ Jesus, who is Lord of lords, King of kings. (Ps. 2, 47; Isa. 33; Jer. 53; Zach. 9; Matt. 21; John 12; 1 Cor. 2; Heb. 7; Rev. 17, 19.)

And if there is one who will declare himself king in the kingdom and dominion of Christ, as did John von Leyden, of

Munster, he shall not go unpunished with Adonai, (1 King 1,) for the true Solomon, Christ Jesus himself, must possess the kingdom, and sit eternally upon the throne of David. (1 Sam. 7; 1 King 8; Ps. 89; Isa. 9; Luke 1.)

But, according to the flesh, we teach and exhort to be obedient to the emperor, king, lords and princes, yea, to all in power, in all their transactions and civil regulations, so far as they are not contrary to the word of God. (Matt. 17, 22; Rom. 13; 1 Tim. 2; Tit. 3; 1 Pet. 2.)

We teach and confess that we know of no sword, nor commotion in Christ's kingdom or church, other than the sharp sword of the spirit, God's word (as is abundantly shown in our writings,) which is sharper and more piercing than any two-edged sword, and it proceeds from the mouth of the Lord, (Rev. 1, 2, 19,) whereby we make the father mutinous against the son, and the son against the father, the mother against the daughter, and the daughter against the mother, and daughter-in-law against the mother-in-law. (Matt. 10.) But the sword of worldly policy we leave it to those to whom is committed. (Rom. 13; 1 Pet. 2.) Let every one be careful and not take the sword, lest he shall perish with the sword. (Gen. 9; Matt. 26.)

We acknowledge, teach, and approve *of no other* matrimony than that one, which Christ and his apostles publicly and plainly taught in the New Testament, namely, one man and one woman, (Matt. 19; Mark 10; Eph. 5,) and that they may not be divorced except in case of adultery, (Matt. 5; Mark 10,) for the two are one flesh, (Gen. 2; Mark 19; Matt. 10; Eph. 5;) and if the unbelieving depart, a sister or brother is not under bondage in that case. (1 Cor. 7.)

We acknowledge, teach and seek no kingdom other than the kingdom of Christ, which shall and are for ever, in which there are no pomp, splendor, gold, silver, meat and drink, but righteousness, peace and joy in the Holy Ghost; (Rom. 14,) for we confess with Christ, that our kingdom is not of this world, we brought nothing into this world, therefore, it is evident we can not take any thing out of it, as the scriptures say. (James 1; 1 Tim. 6.)

We know of no murdering, much less do we teach or permit it; for we truly believe that a murderer has neither lot nor part in the kingdom of heaven. (Rom. 1; Gal. 5; John 3; Rev. 21, 22.) O beloved sirs, how should we desire the blood of any man, since we have to die *daily* for man's sake? And the Lord who created us knows that we seek nothing, but that we might instruct, and be a pattern to, all the world, with our doctrine, life, blood and death, that they might reflect, observe, awaken,

11*

repent and be saved, for this is the nature of pure love to pray for persecutors, to render good for evil, to love the enemy, to heap coals of fire upon the head; and let him avenge who judges rightly. (Deut. 32; Prov. 25; Heb. 10; Rom. 12; Matt. 5; 1 Cor. 13.)

We know of no theft, much less do we teach or permit it, but we are ready before God and man, with all our hearts, to communicate our own possessions, and all we have, however little it may be, and in addition thereto our sweat and labor, to meet the necessities of the poor, as the Lord's spirit and word, and true brotherly love teach us, (Deut. 15; Isa. 58; Job 4; Matt. 5; Luke 6; Rom, 12; Gal. 6; Eph. 4; Col. 3; Heb. 13; 2 Pet. 1: 2 John 3, 4, 5,) and we well know that theft is expressly forbidden in the scriptures, (Exod. 20; Deut. 5; Rom. 13; Eph. 4;) and that theft is to be punished by death according to the laws of the land, and with eternal death according to the word of God, if not repented of. (1 Cor. 6.)

The almighty merciful Lord will undoubtedly keep and preserve, by his paternal grace, spirit and power, inoffensive to the end of the world, all the pious and god-fearing who acknowledge him, and are sincere, from all such terrible errors and ungodly abominations.

And should it be the case, that one of those be found among us who use violence, (which is quite unknown to me,) and would do that which is from the devil, my beloved sirs, know you that such an one was not of us from the beginning, and will eternally be not of us, except he be thoroughly converted, repent sincerely, and become one with the spirit, doctrine and example of Christ, as the scriptures teach. May the gracious Lord grant that they may awaken, overcome their drowsiness, learn to know their works, see their nakedness, and be extricated from the snares of the devil, by which the poor miserable people are so lamentably led captive at his will.

Therefore, beloved lords, beware that you be not in your belief, like the abandoned and senseless in judgment, who persist without any knowledge of the matter, in their own opinion and wantonness, like irrational creatures, upbraid the good, and praise the evil, persecute and condemn what they understand not. Again, I say, be not like those blood-thirsty, raging and malicious men; but do examine the scriptures with quaking, (1 King 3,) pray with Solomon, for wisdom, look to the spirit, word, doings and example of Christ, and pass an impartial righteous sentence, according to the truth, as it is enjoined upon, and commanded to all the princes and judges in the scriptures, as is heard. (Exod. 13, 23; Deut. 4, 17: 2 Chron. 19; Jer. 22; Rom. 13.)

O beloved sirs, do take heed. If our faith, doctrine, sacraments, transactions and doings are not of God, as we are every where slandered, then are we the most miserable of all men upon earth; if whilst we are to be every one's deceiver, heretic, ana-baptist, knave, footstool and prey; and have to endure the stocks, gallows, wheels, sword, fire, water, and all manner of misery; and our poor souls must nevertheless be the property of· the devil, and brands of hell, although in our weakness we so cordially seek the Lord, and are so sincere, as may be seen. O no! my beloved sirs, no; the spirit, doctrine and life of Christ will not deceive us; for his word is truth, and his commands eternal life. (John 17; John 13) God's promises stand sure and immovable; and they will not fail to be pious. (2 Tim. 2.)

Therefore, we pray and admonish you, yea, we counsel and desire you that you would contrast our seeking with your seeking; our spirit with your spirit; our doctrine with the doctrine of the learned; our conduct with your conduct; our poverty with your riches; our rejection and reproach with your seeking of honor; our affliction and. tribulation with your voluptuousness and luxurious living; our patience with your tyranny; our hard bonds and reproachful death, with your ungracious raging, unmerciful implacableness. I speak of the guilty, if you should then find that your doctrine, faith, life, seeking and doings are more in accordance with the spirit, word and life of the Lord, and are better than ours, then instruct us with a paternal spirit, we will willing hear it, and be obedient, for we do desire to obey the truth till death.

But if you can not reprove us by the scriptures, and see that ours is the better, it would then be heathenish, ungodly and tyrannical, to force us out of life unto death, thrust us from heaven into hell, this you have to acknowledge and confess. But, I am afraid, so much discretion will not be manifested to us-ward as that the matter be weighed in the balance of the holy word, and determined by the plummet of Christ. But the priest's upbraiding, betraying and rising up, and your unmerciful edicts must be our books, and your avengers, beadles, imprisonment, rack, wafer, stocks, fire and sword, O God, must be our instructions, which we, grieved ˌchildren have to hear in many places, and finally have to pay them with our possession and blood. But how this agrees with Christ's spirit, doctrine and life, and with Christian discretion, my beloved sirs, may reflect a little more upon. We well know that all bloody preachers who teach and advise such things, and all the rulers who practise and uphold the same, are not the disciples of Christ; the hour in which you have to render accounts, when you have to depart this life, will teach you this truth. It can never be, says Cyprian, that such lion-like fury and lupine ferocity should dwell in the heart of a Christian. O how good it would be for some of you—yea, how good it would be if you had never been born; for there are so many of you who neither regard law nor gospel, heaven nor hell, God nor devil; but the the evil flesh will follow its propensity.

Think you, beloved sirs, that the Almighty God and Lord, who holds the heavens and the earth in the hollow of his hand, who slays and makes alive, (Isa. 40; 1 Sam. 2) the ruling Lord over all, who upholds all by the word of his power—who creates and destroys, (Heb. 2) the consuming fire, before whose presence the hills melted like wax, (Ps. 97; Wis. 6) that he will yield and give away to sensual minds and earthly hearts? No! before him the great and small are alike; the rich and the poor; the strong and the weak; the learned and unlearned; the wise and the foolish, are all alike. He is no respector of persons, (Deut. 10; 2 Chron. 19) all who fear him not, and conform not to his counsel, doctrine, spirit and example, be he emperor or king, doctor or licentiate, he must suffer eternal punishment and be under his judgment and fury. (Rom. 2; Gal. 2.)

Beloved sirs, fear God, do right, learn wisdom and truth, cleanse your hands, which are wet and imbrued in innocent blood, and reflect how the righteous God will punish in due time, all unrighteousness, malice and violence; and how severely he ever did, and will avenge and require the innocent blood, torture and death of his saints, of those blood-thirsty tyrants.

The blood-thirsty Cain had to be an accursed vagabond and exile in the land all the days of his life, because he so miserably murdered his innocent brother Abel. (Gen. 4.)

The unmerciful arrogant murderer, Pharoah, with his whole host, was destroyed in the Red sea, by the righteous judgment of God, (Exod. 14,) on account of his tyranny and cruelty, which he exercised towards the children of Jacob, God's people. (Exod. 1, 5.)

Joas was slain by his own servants to avenge the innocent blood of Zachariah, whom he slew between the temple and the altar. (2 Kings 12; 2 Chron. 24.)

Mannassah was led captive on account of his great abomination and idolatry which he practiced; and on account of the innocent blood with which he filled Jerusalem. (2 Kings 21; 2 Chron. 33.)

Ahab was shot through with an arrow, and his blood was licked up by the dogs at the waters of Samaria, (1 Kings 21,) and his wife Jezebel was thrust out of the window, and was trodden under foot of horses, and her flesh was eaten of dogs, (2 Kings 9,) to punish her for her ungodly deed and the blood of Naboth, according to the word of the Lord, which he spake by Elijah, the Tishbite. (1 King 21.)

Senacherib had to leave Jerusalem with disgrace, on account of his slanderously pompous words, by which he blasphemed the Most High. The angel of the Lord slew, in one night, one hundred and eighty-five thousand men, in his camp, and he was thrust through with the sword of his own children, in the temple of his idol, Nisroch. (Isa. 36, 37 ; 2 Kings 10.)

Nebbuchadnezzar, for his pride's sake, was rejected of the people, for the space of seven times, was made like the irrational creatures, he ate grass like oxen, his body was wet with the dew of heaven, till his hairs were grown like eagle's feathers, and his nails like bird's claws. (Dan. 4.)

Belshazzar caroused with his mighty men, princes, wives and concubines ; they were merry, drank out of the holy vessels which Nebbuchadnezzar, his father, had plundered out of the temple at Jerusalem ; and being in full glee, and praising their gods and idols of silver, iron and earth, the impenitent and obdurate tyrant was punished of God without mercy, that he at even, was deprived of his dominion and nation, body and life. (Dan. 5.)

Antiochus, the Great, a king and prince of all wickedness, a tyrant of tyrants was punished of God with such a plague, that worms crept from his bowels when yet alive, and pieces of flesh fell from his body, and the stench was so intolerable, that no one could endure it, yea, he himself could not abide his own smell. God's righteous fury laid hold upon this ungodly, miscreant, and he had thus, under unheard of pain and sufferings, to end his proud, blood-thirsty, unrighteous life, and depart this world. (2 Macc. 9.)

Herod, dressed in his royal attire and decorated, sat upon his throne, through the flattering applause of his people, on account of his eloquence and wisdom, exalted himself against God, in his heart, and in that very hour he was smitten of the angel of the Lord, and was eaten of worms. (Acts 12) and, according to Eusebius's writings, departed this life in such a way that all the proud, haughty tyrants may look at themselves in Herod's case, as in a mirror, and fear.

In short, as it happened to Pilate, Nero, Domitian, Maximinius, Diocletian, and generally all malicious, blood-thirsty tyrants, and what kind of a death they generally died, who rose up against Christ and his saints, may be read both in sacred and profane history.

What kind of death and with what conscience some of these blood-thirsty of our day, departed this life, I will not notice for certain reasons; yet I will say so much, that neither emperor nor edicts, upon which they relied all the days of their lives, could quiet them in the hour of their death, but ofttimes were very much concerned, with a sighing heart, and with lamentations, painfully bewailed the innocent blood, which they shed in the emperor's name, and said: O we poor miserable men, what shall we now do?

O God what counsel? Beloved sirs, what counsel? How will your poor souls fare, in the day, in which the heavens shall pass away with a great noise and the elements shall melt with fervent heat? (2 Pet. 3) the earth also, and the works that are therein shall be burnt up? when we have all to appear before the judgment seat, and stand before the impartial judge? when every one shall receive according to his works? (Rom. 2, 14; 2 Cor. 5,) he that keepeth Israel shall neither slumber nor sleep, (Ps. 121.) For yet a little while, and he that shall come will come, and will not tarry, (Heb. 10.)

Therefore, desist from touching the apple of the Lord's eye; for he that touches his saints, touches the apple of his eye, (Zach. 2.) Shudder and be afraid for your own souls, which have to suffer death eternally in the torments of hell, if you do not turn with all your heart to the Lord, and no longer shed the blood of the innocent; for the daily call to him; How long, O Lord, holy and true, dost thou not judge and avenge our blood on them that dwell upon the earth? (Rev. 6,) they call, I say, and their cries are entered into the ears of the Lord of Sabaoth, (James 5,) avenging he will avenge, and the blood of his servants he will require at your hands.

Do not excuse yourselves, you beloved sirs, and judges, and say, that you are the servants of the emperor; this will not acquit you in the day of vengeance. It availed Pilate nothing that he crucified Christ in the name of the emperor, for, instead of serving the emperor, as he thought, to retain his life; honor, and glory, he thereby only incurred the displeasure of the emperor, and lost all, and slew himself with his own hand, according to historians, as a warning to others. Then serve the emperor in imperial things, so far as the scriptures allow them, and are not contrary to God and his word; and serve God in divine things; then you may comfort yourselves with his grace.

Do not interfere with the right and kingdom of Christ; for he alone is the ruler of the conscience, and beside him there is none other, (Isa. 45,) let him be your emperor, and his holy word your edict, in this matter; and you will soon be satiated with raging and murder, if not, then you are the judges of whom it is written in Micah: They all lie in wait for blood; they hunt every man his brother with a net. That they may do evil with both hands earnestly, the prince asketh, and the judge asketh for a reward; and the great man he uttereth his mischievous desire: so they wrap it up. The best of them is a brier; the most upright is sharper than a thorn hedge; the day of thy watchmen and thy visitation cometh; now shall be their perplexity, (Micha. 7.)

Therefore, fight no longer against the lamb and his chosen, it will be hard for you to kick against the pricks. (Acts 9.)

But you will, with all scoffers, say in your hearts: when is the promise of his coming? (2 Pet. 3.) O beloved sirs, do pay attention, we have known so many who made as ostentatious display as you, in silk and velvet, with gold and silver, and sat in exalted seats, and passed sentence upon innocent blood, but now they are no more; we enquire for their places, and they are not to be found.

The day will usher in as lightning, and the hour shall come upon them like a tempest; beware and reform. We see the tree bud, that the summer is nigh at hand, and our Redeemer is hastening, who redeems all the troubled souls from their afflictions, and he will recompence all proud scoffers according to their demerits. (Luke 21.)

Yea, the day is coming, and is not far off, when the righteous shall stand in great boldness before the face of such as have afflicted him, and made no account of his labors; when they see it, they shall be troubled with terrible fear, and shall be amazed at the strangeness of his salvation, so far beyond all they looked for—and they repenting and groaning for anguish of spirit shall say within themselves: This was he, whom we had sometime in derision, and a proverb of reproach; we fools accounted his life as madness, and his end as without honor; how is he numbered among the children of God, and his lot is among the saints! Therefore, have we erred from the way of truth, and the light of righteousness hath not shined unto us, and the sun of righteousness arose not upon us. We wearied ourselves in the way of wickedness and destruction; yea, we have gone through deserts, where there lay no way; but as for the way of the Lord, we have not known it, what hath pride profited us? or what good hath riches with our vaunting brought us? All those things are passed away like a shadow, and as a post that hasteth by. (Wis. 5.).

Then will the righteous intolerable judgment pass upon all who know not God, and that obey not the gospel of our Lord Jesus Christ, who shall be punished with everlasting destruction from the presence of the Lord and from the glory of his power, when he shall come to be glorified in his saints, and to be adored by all them that believe, (Thes. 1,) the wicked will hear: *Depart from me ye cursed, into the fire prepared for the devil and his angels.* (Matt. 25.)

Then shall your laughing be changed into weeping, your joy into sorrow, your sumptuous lives into death, your sensual pleasures into eternal woe, your pride into dust and worms, your power into suffering, your pomp into stench, and your malicious, cruel and unmerciful tyranny be retributed with unquenchable hell-fire. (Luke 6 ; James 5.)

My beloved sirs, with him nothing will be concealed and forgotten. He is the judge that searches the hearts and tries the reins, who penetrates the heights of heaven and the depth of the abyss, and the length of the earth, (Ps. 7 ; Jer. 17 ; Rom. 8,) who will not only judge and punish evil works, and every idle word, but also every unclean, sensual thought. (2 Cor. 5 ; Matt. 12 ; Isa. 66.)

O dear Lord ! O Lord of lords ! where then will be the emperor and his edicts—the false prophets, and their deceiving doctrine ? Then they will howl and weep, and cry in anguish of soul : O ye mountains fall upon us, ye rocks hide us from the presence of him that sitteth upon the throne, and from the wrath of the Lamb. Then, there you will see, that it was nought but lies and wind with which you comforted yourselves, as said. (Acts 6 ; Ps. 94 ; Heb. 3, 4, 10.)

Beloved lords, awaken ! It is yet to-day : do not boast yourselves, because you are of royal family, and are called gracious lords, for it is but smoke, dust and pride ; but boast and rejoice when you are born of God, when you become a chosen generation, a royal priesthood, a holy nation, a peculiar people ; that you should show forth the praises of him who called you out of darkness into his marvellous light. (1 Pet. 2.)

Boast not that you are mighty upon earth, and have great power, but boast that you rule your land in the true fear of God, with virtue, wisdom and righteousness, to the praise of the Lord.

Boast not that you can conquer and subdue lords, princes, cities and countries ; but boast if you subdue your earthly mind and can overcome sensual temptations by the power of faith, and die to ungodliness, and thus triumph through Christ, and be taken in the kingdom of glory, with all the pious soldiers of God, and that you may receive the promised crown at the hand of the Lord, then you will not only be needy and perishable lords and kings, according to the flesh, but eternal, spiritual kings, such as the prince, and the prince of kings, loves and washed them from sin by his blood, and made them kings and priests to God and his Father. (Rev. 1 ; 1 Pet. 2.) Such reign and conquer with all the children of God, the world, flesh, blood, sin, death, devil, false doctrine, and the infernal gates ; they rejoice not because their names are enrolled in the register of the kings of this world; but they rejoice when their names are written in the book of life, in heaven. (Luke 10.)

O you high-renowned lords and princes, O that you would in all love and meekness receive this simple, plain, true instruction of your poor servant, and not despise it, whereby I have so fully, and with a good heart, admonished all your worthy highnesses.

Look not upon my small person or to my little understanding, but look to Christ's spirit, word and example, which I have recommended and taught in sincerity of heart to you and to all men, according to my weak abilities.

Do heartily repent, so that you may stand before God; wail and weep with David; put on sackcloth and ashes, (2 Sam. 12; Ps. 51,) humble yourselves with the king of Ninevah; confess your faults with Manassah, (Jonah 3; 2 Chron. 33;) die unto your ambitious flesh and pride; fear the Lord, your God, with all your powers; deal honestly in the things entrusted and commanded you; seek the kingdom and country that will endure forever; and reflect that you, however highly esteemed, are only pilgrims upon earth and sojourners and strangers, as well as all other men, (Heb. 11,) even as we have abundantly heard and perceived.

Obey, believe, fear, love, serve and follow your Lord and Savior, Jesus Christ, for he it is before whom every knee shall bow: he is God's eternal word, wisdom, truth and Son, (John 1. Rev. 19; Phil. 2; Luke 11; John 14.) Seek his honor and praise in all your thoughts, words and actions, and you shall reign in eternity. (Wis. 6.)

APPEAL TO THE LEARNED.

Herewith I will leave all the lords and princes, with all the magistracy and rulers, and those sent by them, in the hands of the Lords and address myself to you, O you learned, you, who think that you have the keys of heaven, (Luke 11; Rom. 2,) and are the eyes and the light of the people. I will speak with you, as with those whose salvation I seek with all my heart, because I see with open eyes, that both you and your disciples run voluntarily into the eternal destruction of your souls, and nevertheless boast yourselves nothing less than that you are the sent teachers, and your church is the church of Christ; and would have you all, one with another, Romans, Lutherans and Zuinglians, admonished faithfully and in brotherly love, concerning the following articles:

12

That you would notice, in the first place, that your ministry and services are not of God and his word, but are from the bottomless pit, (Rev. 9,) for it is evident that you blaspheme and persecute Christ's word, ordinances and commands, and teach and enforce anti-christ's word, ordinances and commands; that you profane God's temple, you build up and honor temples of stone, break the living images in which the spirit of God dwells, and make and dress up images of gold, silver and wood: that you hate a pious, blameless life, and you encourage and defend by your dissolute examples, a disorderly, frantic life of the flesh. Say, my beloved sirs, where is there a single letter in the scriptures concerning all your doings and divine services, such as of masses, infant baptism, auricular confession, &c? Is not, in truth, the greater part of what you do and transact, all deception, hypocrisy, blasphemy, abomination and idolatry? Whence are your offices and services, and of whom are they? I advise you, in true love, that you would reflect, with the scriptures, in the true fear of God, upon these things.

Secondly. Do reflect what is required of you in this your service and office. You and I, heretofore, stood in the same call, office and service; I candidly confess that in all my studies, from my youth on, in preaching and singing, I sought only a vain, lazy, good living, praise and favor of men, yea, gluttony, till the gracious and great Lord bestowed me the gift of his spirit, and opened my understanding, that I acknowledged with the preacher Solomon, that all my seeking, life and doings were vanity, and that the end thereof was certain death and hell.

But that you continue so to seek is too palpable to be denied. For if there were no prebends and cloisters, but few preachers, priests and monks would be found. This I certainly know. But as long as those exist, the world shall never be in want of deceivers and hypocrites.

Say, beloved, what else is your whole seeking and doing, than world, carnality, gluttony, and a voluptuous life? Who can scrutinize and fully describe your earthly mind and sensual life? Some of you make an ostentatious display in ermine, in silk and velvet, others live in full revelry, others are avaricious and hoard up, some deflower virgins and maids, others defile and pollute their neighbor's bed, others chastity is like that of Sodoms, all your doctrine is deceiving, your sacraments are enchanting, your piety is principally ungodliness, and your divine service is an open abomination and idolatry; some of you neither fear God nor the devil; God's name you blaspheme, his holy word you falsify, his children and servants you persecute, and, in reliance upon his grace, you do all manner of evil; if you can only lead a life free from care, and enjoy fine times, then all is well done. Say, beloved, is it not so? Worthy men, is it not so? This is your chief seeking and striving, among great and small —this you must acknowledge and confess; for the fruit is manifest to all the world, and it cannot be any longer concealed.

O men! do beware! If any one could enter into life, on this broad way which you teach, and in which you walk, and keep his soul in God, who would not lament and say, that the prophets, the apostles, and all the witnesses of God, and also Christ Jesus himself, did not act wisely and prudently, and that they have not done rightly towards us, that they passed their lives with so much anguish, suffering, tribulation and pain in this grievous vale of tears, and directed us, miserable, weak children into such a way.

O no, my beloved, no; truth will eternally be truth; if you are not converted to a better and christian mind, (John 3; Rom. 8; Luke 11;) if you die not to your deceiving, and also to your vain flesh and avaricious life, repent, and become in your dispositions like innocent little children, you cannot enter the kingdom of heaven: For to be carnally minded, says Paul, is death. (Rom. 8.)

Teach, call, hope, boast in any way you choose, if you think to be saved, you must walk in the ways of the Lord, hear his word, and be obedient thereto; for nothing avails in heaven and upon earth, whereby you can be saved, neither baptism nor the Lord's supper, neither eloquence nor erudition, neither councils nor long standing usages, neither emperors nor edicts, neither Christ with his grace, merits, blood and death, if we are not born of God, (understand it right, those who have ears to hear, and minds to understand,) believe his word with all the heart, walk in the light, do right. as John says: This, then, is the message which we have heard of him, and declare unto you, that God is light, and in him is no darkness at all: if we say that we have fellowship with him, and walk in darkness, we lie, and do not the truth: but if we walk in the light, as he is in the light, we have fellowship one with another, and the blood of Jesus Christ, his Son, cleanseth us from all sin. (1 John 1.)

O transgressors, transgressors, examine your hearts, give heed to my words and learn wisdom, you who live in voluptuousness and sit at ease, who say in your hearts: It is we, besides us there is none other; what we command must and shall be heard, and what we speak must be valid upon earth; we cannot go astray in the scriptures, and in counsel we cannot err, and we can teach nothing unlawful. Ah! alas! your great boasting, your wisdom deceives you; return, your path is slippery, and your way leads to the abyss of hell.

Worthy men, do learn to know what God's own and eternal

Son, Christ Jesus, sought upon earth, what he taught, and what pattern he left you; his seeking was his father's praise, and the salvation of our poor souls: his doctrine was his father's word, and his precedence a sure way to the kingdom of God. Who being in the form of God, says Paul, thought it not robbery to be equal with God, but he made himself of no reputation, and took upon him the form of a servant, and was made in the likeness of men, came poor and miserable into this grievous world; he had no room in the inn when he was born; (Luke 9,) he had not a pillow in the days of his ministry wheron to lay his head; nor in his death had he wherewith to quench his thirst, (Matt. 27,) although it is he through whom the almighty, all-bountiful Father grants to all his created beings, residence, clothing, meat and drink, as Paul says: For ye knew the grace of our Lord Jesus Christ, that though he was rich, yet for your sakes be became poor, that ye through his poverty might become rich. (2 Cor. 8.)

If you have any fear of God, and would not lead your own and the souls of your poor people wilfully to death, then contrast your seeking with Christ's, your doctrine with the doctrine of Christ, your spirit with Christ's spirit, and your life with the life of Christ, then you will and can truly find whether you are in or out of Christ, who is your God, what Lord you serve, and of whose spirit and kingdom you are.

Thirdly. Observe what fruits and usefulness your office and services bring forth; for what is your doctrine other than a useless, feeble sowing in the wind, which has neither spirit nor power; your sacraments are encouragement to the impenitent, and your lives are examples of wickedness. Where are the avaricious whom you have meliorated—the drunkards you made temperate—the polluted you have made pure—the haughty whom you have humbled? How will you teach others and you, yourselves, are untaught, and beget Christ an acceptable church, (James 2,) and you, yourselves, are yet anti-christ's servants, and the children of Belial? You must confess, therefore, and your disciples, both high and low, men and women, are all dead bodies, and have not God's spirit; for with you we do not find contrite hearts, true knowledge of Christ, true love, an earnest desire after the kingdom of God, dying to earthly things, true humility, righteousness, friendliness, mercy, chastity, obedience, wisdom, truth and peace; but by all means, hatred, envy, obdurate, malicious, furious hearts, an aversion and despising of the divine word, lust and love of this world, haughtiness, pride, pomp, lies, knavery, disgrace, adultery, whoredom, robbery, burning, slaying, cursing, swearing, and all manner of malice.

Behold, you withered trees, (Jude 1,) and careless shepherds, these are the fruits you bring forth and bear, and the sheep you pasture, these are the churches and disciples you comfort with the Lord's blood, preach to them grace and peace, and to whom you dispense baptism and the Lord's supper. If I write not the truth, reprove me.

O beloved sirs, so entirely have you lost every christian virtue, understanding, and light, and the scriptures, and held captive in ungodliness under the power of hell, the poor, ignorant people—whole kingdoms, cities and countries, yea, the whole wide world, and that O God! for such small hire, namely, for hands full of barley and pieces of bread, as the prophet says. O! that these things were not true; clear is sunshine, but clearer is the truth which I write.

And this is not enough for you, O you men, that you so miserably deceive the poor wretched souls, and besides this, you also rebuke, defame, belie, and betray all those who seek and fear God with all their hearts and rebuke all unrighteousness with doctrine and life, and so willingly walk in Christ. You deprive them of their possessions and lives that you may enjoy great honor among the people, and be not evil spoken of in your doings, that you be not hindered in your ungodly and unlawful gain, be at ease to the end of your days.

O how rightly you are depicted by the wisdom of God, which says: Wo unto you, scribes and pharisees, hypocrites, for ye shut up the kingdom of heaven against men : for ye neither go in yourselves, (take notice,) neither suffer ye them that are entering to go in.

What I think, I write, and dissemble not. I fear, worthy sirs, that there are many of you so ungodly, and are so far bent upon unlawful gain, indolent life, and the praise of men, that you would rather see all the god-fearing put to the stake, than lose a guilder of your rents, or to hear a harsh word from the magistracy, for truth's sake.

O you, with wanton looks, when will you be ashamed ? Yon diamonds ! when will you be softened, and you Moors, when will you be washed white ? I think never more; for how can you do any thing good, because you have learned evil, and are used to it from your infancy ? (Jer. 3 ; Zach 7 ; John 13.)

Alas ! my soul must for your sake, be grieved and has painfully to lament that you err so lamentably, and besides, cover all your disgrace under Christ's word and name, and do not observe, O you men, that you, together with all the false prophets, are promised in the scriptures, and threatened by the spirit of the Lord, every where with nothing but punishment, wrath, damnation and blackness of darkness, the flaming lake and eternal gnashing of teeth, weeping, wailing and death.

The hour is near at hand when we shall and must hear : give an account, &c. (Rom. 1 ; 1 Cor. 6 ; Gal. 5 ; 2 Pet. 2 ; Jude 1 ; Rev. 21, 22 ; Luke 26.) Alas, would it then be due to us, when the day is at hand, to walk a thousand years on burning coals and in red hot gauntlets, (flames,) then we might even rejoice and be of good cheer; but now it is hidden from your eyes, through your haughtiness, avarice and momentary luxury. (Luke 19.)

Perhaps I should be smitten on the cheek by some of you, and with Micah must hear of Zedekiah. Which way went the spirit of the Lord from me to speak unto thee ? (2 Chron. 18.) O my beloved, fear God and understand the truth. You direct the poor dissolute souls to the subtlety and philosophy of the learned, to the many councils, to customs and usages of long standing, to imperial edicts, to the doctrines and commandments of men, which are nothing but quicksands, which cannot save the house from the tempest, (Matt. 7,) but I do not so, I direct you to Moses, (Deut. 18,) add to the prophets, with the apostles, angels, and the Father himself, to Christ Jesus, to whom all the emperors, kings, councils, usages and the learned, have to yield; for his word is truth, and his commands are eternal life. To him every knee shall bow, of things in heaven and things in earth, and things under the earth; all who reject him, reject the Father that sent him, (Isa. 6, 7 ; Jer. 35 ; Luke 1 ; Matt. 17 ; John 7, 12 ; Phil. 2.)

This I teach you, I direct you to his spirit, word, life, command, prohibition, ordinances and usages, as to a sure and immovable foundation, laid in Zion, to a plain and safe way, prepared of God, who, according to all his sure promises, will lead all the truly penitent and Christian believers into eternal life.

Beloved men, do observe there, were four hundred false prophets in the days of Ahab, king of Israel, who unanimously prophecied prosperity and felicity, that he should go out and meet his enemies, for God would give the king's enemies into his hands; but there was but one Micha, spoke the truth and predicted adversity in the name of the Lord. (2 Chron. 18.)

And there were also four hundred and fifty prophets of Baal, and there were four hundred prophets of the groves which ate at Jazabel's table; but there was only one Elijah, a man of God, and a prophet of the Lord, who was zealous for the law of his God, and defended the praise of God. (1 Kings 18.)

Joas, with all the princes, priests and common people, all were unanimous in their groves and their false worship, which they had chosen after the death of Jehoida, the high priest, and there was but one Zacharias, who reproved the ungodly abominations, and threatened them with wrath and punishment of his God. (2 Chron. 24.)

Even as those renowned and worthy men of God, though they were few at all times, reproved, with pure, divine ardor, in the power of the spirit, and faithfully admonished by the law of God with their great and glorious talents, all the disobedient and idolatrous kings, princes, priests and the common people, without respect to persons; and on account thereof suffered misery, tribulation, bonds and death, as we may abundantly read and see in the scriptures and histories; I do also here, with my small talents, for similar views and reasons, openly testify, because I see with my eyes, that you all hypocritically flatter lords and princes, soothe the world; and, alas, that will, with his Lord's word, attack the ungodly life, reprove the wickedness of men; and therefore, as the aforementioned had to do, have not to bear and endure a little, although I mean it well, and have such a true ground.

O worthy men, deliberate, reflect on the matter. Consider the end—contemplate the consequence. You trust to the invention of men; but we put our trust in God's word and truth, you seek the world, we seek heaven; you place your affections upon the present, we upon the future; you depend upon the emperor and temporal powers; we depend on Christ and his promises, till we all shall appear before him, who will come in the clouds of heaven, to requite all flesh; then you will see what you sought, what office you conducted, what fruits you brought forth, for what hire you served, whose word you preached, whose council you rejected, and whom, O men, you so enviously stabbed.

Hereby I will commit you to the Lord, you learned and preachers; and entreat for God's sake, (to the good of all your souls,) that you accept this my faithful warning with gratitude and love, written to you, in sincere and Christian love, (intention,) read it with an understanding heart, reflect upon it, and examine it with fear and trembling. I certainly know that you will find nothing in it but a kindness, love, zeal, and a sure foundation of eternal and invincible truth.

And though some of you may think that I reprove too severely, you ought to know that I have not done so without the instruction, counsel and doctrine of the holy prophets, Christ and the apostles. I have given no name without the word of God. He that is innocent, thank God and rejoice; but he that is guilty, is not reproved by me, but by God's spirit and word.

O, my well-wishing friends, fear God and his judgment; reform your earthly sensual life, abandon all your deceptions, blindness, seducements and abominations, in which you have hitherto been involved; with all your powers seek the right truth; pray to God for wisdom; warn every one; deal and act unblamably; then you will not be of that number of shepherds called by such dreadful names in the scriptures, and you will not be partakers of that displeasure, punishment and wrath, but you will inherit grace, mercy and life, as the prophet says: But if the wicked will turn from all his sins that he hath committed and keep all my statutes, and do that which is lawful and right, he shall surely live, he shall not die. (Ezek. 18.) The gracious and merciful Lord, grant you all his grace, knowledge, spirit, wisdom, light and truth, that you may cordially awaken, repent, and be eternally saved, Amen.

APPEAL TO THE COMMON PEOPLE.

Give ear, you people, and take it to heart, you who trust in lies, and boast you are Christians; tear your bands asunder, and suffer yourselves to be led no longer as asses bound and under a heavy burden of sin, by these aforementioned drivers, for they deceive you; they preach to you according to their own opinion, and not out of the mouth of the Lord; they comfort you in your wicked ways; they call and cry only mercy and peace, though it is displeasure and judgment, as the prophet says. The priests and prophets teach falsely, and comfort my people in their calamity, that they shall esteem it lightly, saying, peace, peace, when there is no peace; (Jer. 6,) they are the blind leaders, who lead you and themselves right into the pit, (Matt. 15,) and the blind watchmen who watch not over the city of God. (Ezek. 33.) Thieves and murderers, who slay your poor souls with the sword of their false doctrine, and steal from you the Lord's word and kingdom (John 10); greedy shepherds who seek your wool, milk and flesh, and not your souls. (Ezek 34.) In short, they are those who wholly desolate the kingdom of Christ, and promulgate in high honor the kingdom of anti-christ through the whole world, and who always comfort and defend you poor children in your dissolute abominations and in obdurate, blind life, so that, alas! there is none who is cordially converted to the Lord laments his sins, and says: What do I?

O, worthy children and brethren, my heart in my body quakes and fears, when I reflect that such a numberless class of men are born in vain and to no purpose; who will have eternally to endure the wrath and judgment of the Lord, if they repent not, and shall never find grace.

Beloved children, take heed, for thus Christ Jesus teaches

you : I tell you of a truth, except ye be converted and become like little children, ye shall not enter into the kingdom of heaven. (Matt. 18.) O, dear Lord, this is spoken by God's eternal truth, which cannot lie, (Heb. 8) and how ungodly you ignorant people live, and how far you are from the innocence of children, your fruits testify and show; for you despise God and his word; you hate all righteousness and truth, (Tit. 1), many of you live as the irrational creatures, others litigate, quarrel, curse and swear, are covetous, hoard up, practise usury, lie, cheat, injure and defraud each other; fidelity and piety scarcely exist among you, but perfidy and knavery prevails generally—eating to excess, drinking and gambling are pastime with you; to pollute women and defile virgins is called courting and loving. To take the advantage of, and to defraud one another, is called understanding and wisdom; you are valiant at beer and mighty at wine, (Isa. 5 ; Rom. 3); unrighteousness and destruction are in all your ways, the poor and weak you oppress, and you revile the afflicted, the god-fearing and pious; to do evil you think and practise, you are without understanding, says the prophet, (Hos. 4) as a frantic heifer. Pomp and pride you call the fashion and custom of the country, you lie in wait for blood, you hunt every man his brother with a net, says the prophet, (Mich. 7,) your faith is hypocrisy, your divine service idolatry, your whole life is world and flesh, as may be seen, and then you say, he that walks in simplicity, walks right, as if ignorance, blindness and despising of the truth, of godliness, were a pious life. Dear children, be ashamed of your offensive wantonness and accursed folly.

Do you suppose that Christ is a liar, and his word a fable ? O no! his sentence stands immovable, and shall never be altered; if you live in pride, avarice, voluptuousness, unchastity and in sensual lusts, believe not Christ and his word, and continue to be earthly-minded, and are not born of God, you must die eternally, or the spirit of God is not true, but is false. (John 3 ; Rom. 8 ; 1 Cor. 5 ; Gal. 5 ; Eph 5 ; Rev. 21, 22.)

Say, beloved, why do you extol the apostles and prophets and consider their doctrine heresy, and their lives madness ? And why do you suffer yourselves to be called christians, and hate and are opposed to Christ's word and example ?

Say you, we are without understanding, untaught, and know not the scriptures ? (Deut. 10 ; Matt. 22 ; Mark 12 ; Rom. 13 ; Gal. 5.) I then again reply, the word is plain and needs no comment, namely : Thou shall love the Lord thy God with all thy heart, with all thy soul, with all thy strength, (Deut. 6,) and thy neighbor as thyself. (Num. 19.) Again, you shall give bread to the hungry and entertain the needy. (Isa. 58.)

If you live according to the flesh, you shall die; for, to be carnally minded is death (Rom. 8); avaricious, drunkards and the proud, shall not inherit the kingdom of God. (1 Cor. 6.)

God will judge adulterers and fornicators, (Heb. 13,) and many like pasages. All who do not understand such passages, we must confess and acknowledge, are more like irrational creatures than men, more like blocks than christians.

O my chidren, my beloved children, do not deceive your own souls; seek wisdom and understanding, even as you do your daily food, that you may find great riches; for the kingdom of heaven suffers violence. (Matt. 11.) Strive, says Christ, to enter in at the strait gate (Luke 13); pray and you shall receive; seek and you shall find; knock and it shall be opened to you. (Matt. 7.) The almighty great God is not satisfied with a bare name, (John 3, 7, 14, 15; Matt. 5,) but he desires a true, sincere faith, unfeigned, ardent love, a new, converted and changed heart, true humility, mercy, chastity, patience, righteousness and peace; he desires the whole man, heart, professions and actions, who delights in the word of the Lord, speaks the truth from the heart, crucifies his flesh, and will give his goods and blood for the word of the Lord, if it be required. (Ps 1. 15; Gal. 5; Matt. 10, 16; Luke 14.)

Behold, dear children, this is the way in which we all have to walk, if we would be saved; therefore, awaken and learn wisdom. Hear the inviting voice of God, open unto him, and meet him that he complain not of you, as he did formerly through his prophets, of obdurate and stiff-necked Judea and Jerusalem: I have nourished, says he, and brought up children, and they have rebelled against me; the ox knoweth his owner, and the ass his master's crib: but Isreal doth not know, my people doth not consider. Ah, sinful nation, a people laden with iniquity, a seed of evil-doers, children that are corrupters! They have forsaken the Lord, they have provoked the Holy One of Israel unto anger, they have gone away backward. (Isa. 1.)

Jeremiah says: Every one turn to his course, as the horse rusheth into the battle; yea, the stork in the heaven knoweth her appointed times; and the turtle and the crane, and the swallow observeth the time of their coming: but my people know not the judgment of the Lord. (Jer. 8.)

Remember, dear children, how greatly Jesus Christ took to heart the obstinacy and blindness of the Jews; when he said: Jerusalem, Jerusalem, how often would I have gathered thy children together, even as a hen gathereth her chickens, and ye would not, (Matt. 23,) he wept and said: If thou hadst known, even thou, at least in this thy day, the things which belong unto thy peace, but now they are hidden from thine eyes. (Luke 19.)

. Wherefore ; lay aside all filthiness and superfluity of naughtiness, and receive with meekness the ingrafted word, which is able to save your souls. (James 1.) Seek God with a full heart, repent sincerely, cleanse yourselves inwardly before the Lord, let go world, flesh, false doctrine, and every thing contrary to God's honor, will and word, hear, believe and follow the only and true shepherd of your souls, Jesus Christ, who sought you in such great love, and purchased you with such a precious price, then you may of a truth boast that you are God's people and church. To him, the Lord and Savior Jesus Christ, be praise and the eternal kingdom, Amen.

APPEAL TO CORRUPT SECTS.

CHRIST said : False christs and false prophets shall arise, and shall show signs and wonders, to seduce, if it were possible, even the elect. But take ye heed, behold I have told you all things. (Matt. 7; Mark 13.) O, you backsliding, erring children! if you had taken to heart the faithful warning of our Lord and Saviour Jesus Christ—if you had acknowledged his spirit, doctrine and holy life as perfect, and had received him for a true prophet, (as promised in the scriptures) and for the true and living Son of God, never would you have suffered yourselves to be misled so far from Him, nor would you have given place to such abominable errors. But now, some of you, O Lord! are so far gone and bewitched, that I fear you will never come to Christ, the true Shepherd, for the abominable, ungodly works, (which are not only contrary to Christ's spirit, word and will, but also against all honest modesty, nature and reason,) you maintain as right and good, and, with a dark perverted understanding, defend the scriptures.

Is it not a grievous error, that you suffer yourselves to be so miserably bewitched, and so lamentably mislead from one unclean sect to another, first to that of Munster, next to Battenberg, now Davidists; from Belzebub to Lucifer, and from Belial to Behemoth? Ever learning, but never able to come to the knowledge of the truth: You suffer yourselves to be led about by every wind of doctrine. You choose out a way for yourselves, as do also the priests and monks: you hold not to the head from which all the body, by joints and bands having nourishment administered, and knit together, increaseth with the increase of God. (Col. 2.)

Such, I fear, shall lead to the punishment of your sins ; for, by your earthly, fleshy mind, you have thrust from you the pure knowledge of Christ, and hated his cross; and in pride, haughtiness, eating, drinking, dissimulation and false worship, you conform to this arrogant, unprofitable, idle, ungodly world, (which you should teach by a godly, humble walk,) in opposing all the admonitions of scripture, and the infallible example of Christ and his saints.

O, you backsliding children! reflect how grievously you disgrace the holy Moses, who teaches and speaks to you out of the mouth of God. He says: I will raise them up a prophet from among their brethren, like unto thee, and will put my words in his mouth; and he shall speak unto them all that I shall command him. And it shall come to pass, that whosoever will not hearken unto my words which he shall speak in my name, I will require it of him. (Deut. 18.) This is repeated by Peter and Stephen in Acts 3, 7.

What do you do with all the great prophets of God, as David, Isaiah, Jeremiah and Ezekiel, who, in so many places, with such plain words, through the inspiration of the Holy Spirit, direct us to Christ and his word? (Ps. 2, 22; Isa. 7, 9, 28, 35, 40; Jer. 23, 30, 33; Ezek. 34.) They must either testify to lies, or your prophets must be deceivers and false teachers—this is indisputable.

Did not holy Paul say: But though we, or an angel from heaven, preach unto you any other gospel than that which we have preached, let him be accursed or anathematized? You must be aware, and admit that your prophets with their kings, dominions, polygamy, sword, &c., agree not with the doctrine of Paul and the apostles; it therefore follows that they, with their doctrine and conduct, are cursed and anathematized. (Gal. 1.)

Say, my beloved, what do you do with the revealed and infallible word and testimony of the Almighty Father, which he himself of his Son has testified, and said: This is my beloved Son, in whom I am well pleased, hear ye him? (Matt. 17.) *Him shall you hear;* but since you reject his spirit, word and example, you follow and bear those who, with their spirit, doctrine and conduct, are from the bottomless pit—yea, manifestly anti-christs and false prophets.

Know you not, that the Son of God has himself commanded us that we should observe all that he has enjoined, and that he will be with us until the end of the world? (Matt. 28.)

Will you then say, that Christ's and the apostle's doctrine was imperfect, and that your teachers bring forth the perfect instruction? I answer, that to teach and believe this, is the most horrible blasphemy, the most mocking perversity, that can be uttered against the Most High; for you thereby declare that Christ is not the true Son of God, the perfect teacher, and the true image of righteousness. You deny the whole scripture, you reject the testimony of Moses and all the prophets, who directed to the only and true Christ, as has been shown; you disparage the Father's word, and reject Christ Jesus, with his spirit, word, kingdom and spiritual government, and raise your hearts and hopes upon lying, mortal flesh, and upon earthly, sensual things, which, as the scriptures teach, must be dispersed like dust before winds. Examine the scriptures in the fear of the Lord, and reflect, if such is not a gross blasphemy against the Almighty?

Say, you deceived children, where is there a syllable in the whole doctrine of Christ and the apostles, (according to which spirit, doctrine, conduct and usage all scripture must be understood,) by which you can prove and establish one of all your erring articles?

Would you then appeal to the literal understanding and transactions of Moses and the prophets, so must you also become Jews, receive circumcision, literally possess the land of Canaan, again erect the Jewish kingdom, and build the city and temple, and after the law, offer sacrifices, and attend to the worship of God, and declare that Christ, the promised Saviour, has not yet come, who has changed the liberal and figurative ceremonies into new, spiritual and abiding substances.

You miserable, erring sheep, (John 19,) observe, I have before remarked to the magistrates, that the kingdom of Christ is not of this visible, perishing world, but that it is an eternal, spiritual and abiding kingdom, (Luke 1; Heb. 1;) Where there are no eating and drinking, but righteousness, peace and joy in the Holy Ghost. (Rom. 14; Isa. 6; Dan. 7.) There no king reigns, but the true king of Zion, Christ Jesus. (Ps. 2.) He is the king of righteousness, (Jer. 23, 33,) the king of peace, (Heb. 7,) the king of kings, (Rev. 1, 17, 19,) who has all power in heaven above, and on earth beneath; (Matt. 28,) before whom every knee shall bow, and every tongue confess. (Phil. 2.) The true king David in spirit, (Ezek. 34, 37,) who, through his righteousness, merits and crimson blood, has ransomed the sheep from the mouths of the lions and bears of the pit, and has slain the terrible Goliah, and obtained for the spiritual Israel of God eternal welfare and peace. Neither the king nor his servants bears any sword but the sword of the spirit—the word, of God, which cuts asunder the spirit, body and soul. With this he brings forth, builds, extends and governs his kingdom, guards and defends it under the pressing cross, in all trials and temptations, from all the gates of hell, onsets and powers, (Matt. 16; Eph. 6; Rev. 12, 19; Heb. 4; Mark 16; 1 Cor. 4; 1 Pet.;

13

James 1,) and not with iron or steel, as the rude, vindictive world does; for his kingdom and dominion are spirit, and not letter, as has been shown.

Again, under this kingdom, and under this king, no other wedlock must be tolerated, except between *one* man and *one* woman, as God had in the beginning established in the union of Adam and Eve; and Christ has further said, that these two are one flesh, and that they may not separate themselves, except on account of adultery. (Matt. 5, 19; Mark 10; Luke 16; 1 Cor. 7; Eph. 5; 1 Tim. 3; Tit. 1.)

This is not a kingdom in which we make a display with gold, silver, pearls, silk, velvet and costly pride. And your teachers also acquit and teach you with this deception, to wit: that you are guiltless, if you do not desire these things in your hearts! Thus might satan approve his haughtiness, and make pure and good the desire of his eyes. But this is the kingdom of all humility: wherein (I say) not the outward adorning of the body, but the inward adorning of the soul, zeal, sincerity, a broken heart, and contrite spirit, are sought and desired. (Matt. 22; Rev. 19.)

Here is known no lying, eating, drinking, or hypocrisy; here none conforms himself to a drunken, luxurious, idle and idolatrous world, nor lays from him the cross of Christ, as you do, but all are upright and godly in heart and deed. (Matt. 5.) They speak the truth from the heart. (Ps. 15; Col. 3; Eph. 5.) They lead a circumspect, temperate life, (Tit. 2; 1 Pet. 5,) they shun all idolatry and false doctrine from within and without; they avoid all appearance of evil, (Matt. 7, 15, 16; John 10; Rom. 16; 1 Tim. 6; 2 Tim. 3; Tit. 3; 2 John 1; Thes. 5;) they perform the true worship of the heart; (Rom. 12; Heb. 12; James 1;) they abide firmly in Christ's word and ordinances; (Matt. 28; John 8; 2 John 1;) they lead an unblamable life before the whole world, (Matt. 5; Phil. 1, 2;) they testify of Jesus Christ with the mouth, with works, with possessions and with blood, as the divine honor requires it. (Matt. 10; Mark 8, Luke 14.)

Here that confession is unknown to which some of you pretend—Here we confess only to the true God before whom we have sinned, and to our neighbor against whom we have trespassed, (Wis. 23; Matt. 17; Col. 3; Eph. 4; James 5.)

Here modesty, rectitude, and honesty are taught and practised, but not immodesty, disgrace and uncleanness. I think you understand well what I mean.

In short, here the spirit, word, will, commands, prohibitions, ordinances, customs, and examples of Christ are taught. The whole scriptures direct to these, and not to the opinions of men who invented words, enchanting appearances, pompous speeches, dreams, visions, lying wonders, of which God's spirit in the holy scriptures, warn and dissuade us on all sides, (Matt. 24; Mark 13; 2 Cor. 11.)

Dear children, reform yourselves. Every one who teaches you otherwise, than is testified by the word of the Lord, even though he were one who could dry up the bottom of the sea, and hurl the stars down from heaven, let him be abandoned, and let his doctrine be regarded as deceiving and erroneous, for, to all eternity there may no other foundation be laid, than that which is laid, Christ Jesus. (1 Cor. 3.) He is the corner stone and foundation in Zion, (Gal. 1,) on whom all the building fitly framed together (according to his will, spirit and word,) groweth into a holy temple unto the Lord, (Eph. 2.)

O ye backsliding children, hear God's word and make haste, for your way is in darkness, and your path leads to death. Embrace the truth and learn wisdom, for your comforters have destroyed you and rendered uneven the way in which you must go. (Isa. 3.) Munster and Amsterdam may well be to you an eternal warning and example. When a prophet, (said Moses) speaks in the name of the Lord, if the thing follow not, nor come to pass, that is the thing which the Lord hath not spoken. (Deut. 1.)

O dear Lord! How many innocent hearts have they ruined —how many poor souls have they deceived— what gross shame have they cast upon the word of the Lord; what great abominations have they committed under the appearance of good— and how have they made the poor blind magistrates, who are destitute of a correct understanding of the holy scriptures, to be guilty of innocent blood.

I believe it is time you should see and learn to know your faithless, lying and deceiving prophets. They are the Foxes which destroy the Lord's vineyard. (Cant. 2.) These are the thieves and murderers of your souls (John 10,) false prophets who deny the Lord that bought them, (2 Pet. 2; Jude,) and have directed you, poor erring sheep, by their own lying visions, and dreams and thoughts of their hearts, and have led you against all the scriptures upon a false and loose ground.

How like you are to those, of whom it stands recorded by Eusebius, that they walked according to their lusts, as the prophets foretold; they denied Paul and the New Testament, and carried about them a book, of which they boasted, that it had fallen from heaven, and had come down to them as a present!!

Also, by you, O ye insane (bear with me for it is the truth which I write) the prophets are read according to the understanding of the Jews. You say the doctrine of Christ and the apostles is at the present time fulfilled; and pretend that there is now another dispensation, &c., and observe not that you thereby, deny the son of 'God, and gainsay the whole scriptures : you comfort yourselves with mere lies, as also did disobedient Israel in their time.

Oh dear Lord! how long shall these sore plagues endure? How long shall the Lord's name through you be blasphemed, and his holy word through you be disgraced? Is it not a grievous error—a man phrenzy, that Christ, the Son of the living God (who brought in eternal righteousness, and has reconciled heaven and earth by the blood of his cross) with his word of truth, and with the counsels of eternal life, is rejected from your hearts, which he so dearly bought, and which should, so properly be the dwelling place of Christ; and an arm of sinful flesh, and mortal man descended from Adam, full of all unrighteousness, haughty speeches, lies and open deception is received by you and adopted in stead :

Oh dear children! what do you do? are you so bewitched that you have lost all honesty, reason and scripture, and are become wholly blind? May God be merciful to you. Observe that a letter of the law of Moses could not be changed till the new Moses, Christ Jesus, came, who was promised through the law and the prophets. If then the letter of the law was so strong, effective and firm, and in its time unchangeable, although given only through a servant, and sealed by a perishable blood, &c. (Exod. 24.) How much more powerful, effectual, firm and imperishable is the free law of the spirit, which was given through the Son himself, and confirmed by the blood of the eternal covenant.

They who taught any thing contrary to Moses' doctrine, were false prophets, for nothing was to be taken from, nor added thereto, but all appeals were to the law and the testimony, (Deut. 4, 12; Isa. 8;) so all the prophets of the present day, are false who teach contrary to the spirit, word, commands, prohibitions, ordinances and example of Christ, even though such should exhibit themselves in appearance, as holier than John, more zealous than Elias, and more miraculous than Moses.

They persuade you that the apostle's doctrine is imperfect. (2 Cor. 13,) and that *they* now teach the perfect thing! This is a deception of deceptions, (as above said,) for thereby the creature is honored more than the Creator. Paul does not refer to any better doctrine or *perfection* other than that which is shewn by the doctrine of the apostles, which will abide in everlasting clearness, according to God's infallible word, and which we shall receive in the resurrection of the righteous, when all doctrine shall receive an end. This is true, otherwise Paul is at variance with himself, and the true reality is not to be found in Christ.

Will you say, then, with the Scribes and Jews, that Elias is to come before the great and terrible day, and so wait for something new?

I answer with Christ's own words, that all the prophets and the law prophesied till John, and if ye will receive it, this is the Elias which was to come, (Matt 11, 17.)

Again: Even though Elias himself were to come, he dare not teach any thing against the foundation and doctrine of Christ and the apostles, but he must, if he would preach aright, teach and preach conformably to the same, for, by the spirit, word, actions and example of Christ, all must be judged, and receive the last sentence, otherwise the whole scriptures are false.

Therefore, it will follow, that we have no Elias more to wait for, since John was he who was to come; or if he should come he must teach us nothing but the foundation, doctrine, and word of Christ, according to the scriptures; for Christ is the man who sits upon David's throne, and shall reign forever in Jacob's kingdom, house and congregation. (Luke 1.)

I would have you all sincerely admonished that you would rightly weigh and prove all spirit, doctrine, faith and conduct, with the spirit, conduct and doctrine of Christ, and that ye be prudent. All spirits which therewith accord, are from God, but those which are contrary, are from him who has turned Adam and his race aside from God, and from the beginning has lead them by lies onward to death.

If you will not hear, but will ever turn your ears to lies, and believe the deceiving creature more than the infallible Creator, if you set your feet upon slippery places; if you neither fear nor regard scripture, admonitions nor the arm and power of God, but reject and set aside all as idle and useless, and suffer yourselves always to be comforted with falsehoods, visions, dreams, splendid delusions and false interpretations and to continue on the broad way, then will the righteous Lord send to you mockers and deceivers, and by his righteous judgment suffer you to be led from one ungodly course to another, as may already be seen. (2 Tim. 4; 2 Thes. 2.)

You shall be satiated with lies, vanity, folly and hypocrisy. You will reap the fruits of your wantonness, and at last, with all false prophets and lying wonder workers, you shall hear the words: Depart from me all ye workers of iniquity, for I know you not. (Matt. 7.)

Be ye then eternally warned and admonished of God. Look for yourselves—the day approaches, repent, reform, God's word is true. Is there any one among you who fears God, let him reflect on what I here write;—search the scriptures and believe the truth, for God hates all liars. (Ps. 5.) Eternal wo and gnashing of teeth will be the hypocrite's portion and reward; whosoever transgresses, and abides not in the doctrine of Christ, is without God. (2 John 1.)

O ye miserable, bewitched children! turn again. If ye knew what it was to forsake the living fountain of Christ, and dig for yourselves dry wells which can neither yield nor hold water, (Jer. 2,) how soon would you turn you back on the false prophets and their hypocritical lives, and surrender yourselves to the true shepherd of your souls, Christ Jesus, and follow after his service, teaching, warnings, ordinances and holy example : (although in weakness,) but enchanting blindness has alas! darkened your understanding. The dear, merciful Lord, be pleased to grant, you all, one another, with eyes to see and hearts to understand—this we heartily wish you. Amen.

TO THE BRIDE, KINGDOM, STATE, AND
CHURCH OF THE LORD, GRACE AND PEACE.

Thus spake the Bridegroom, Christ Jesus, through Solomon, to the church : Rise up, my love, my fair one, and come away, for the winter is past, the rain over and gone, the flowers appear on the earth; the time of the singing of birds is come, and the voice of the turtle dove is heard in our land : the fig tree putteth forth her green figs, and the vines with the tender grape give a good smell. Arise, my love, my fair one, and come away. (Cant. 2.)

Chosen, true children, you who with me are called to like grace, inheritance and kingdom, and are named after the Lord's name, hear the voice of Christ, your king; hear the voice of your bridegroom, ah, thou bride of God,—thou friend of the Lord, arise, and adorn thyself, to honor thy king and bridegroom. Though thou art pure, purify thyself yet more, though thou art holy, hallow thyself yet more, and though thou art right, rectify thyself yet more, (Rev. 21,) adorn thyself with the white silken robe of righteousness, hang about thy neck the golden chain of all piety, gird thyself with the fair girdle of brotherly love, put on the wedding ring of true faith; gird thyself with the precious fair gold of the divine word. Adorn thyself with the pearls of all modesty, wash thyself with the clear waters of grace, and anoint thyself with the oil of the

Holy Ghost. Wash thy feet in the clear limped river of Almighty God; let your whole body be pure and clear, for thy friend hates all wrinkles and spots; so will he have pleasure in the beauty and will praise, and say: how fair are thy breasts, my sister, my spouse, thy breasts are lovelier than wine, and the smell of thine ointment than all spices. Thy lips, O my spouse, drop as the honey-comb: honey and milk are under thy tongue. (Cant. 4.)

Rejoice. O thou bride of the Lord! for your beloved is fairer than all the children of men, the chief among ten thousand, his head is as the most fine gold, his locks are bushy and as black as a raven. His eyes are as the eyes of doves, by the rivers of water, washed with milk and fitly set. His cheeks are as a bed of spices, as sweet as flowers: His lips, like lilies, dropping sweet smelling myrrh. His hands are as gold rings set with the beryl; his belly is as bright ivory, overlaid with sapphires. His legs are as pillars of marble, set upon fine gold. His countenance is as Lebanon, excellent as the cedars; his mouth is sweet, yea, he is altogether lovely. (Cant. 5.) Cry out and say, hearken, O daughter, and consider and incline thine ear—forget thine own people, and thy father's house, so shall the king greatly desire thy beauty. (Ps. 45.)

Draw near, O thou queen, O thou well-prepared and fairest of all women, (Est. 2,) bow thy neck with Esther, under his powerful sceptre; hear his word and fear his judgment—acknowledge his great love, for he has greatly humbled himself towards us. Thy birth and thy nativity were of the land of Canaan, thy father was an Amorite, and thy mother was a Hitite. As for thy nativity, in the day thou wast born, thy navel was not cut, neither wast thou washed in water to supple thee; thou wast not salt at all, nor swaddled at all, no eye pitied thee—Thou wast polluted in thy blood as the prophet lamented. (Ezek. 16.) But he has pitied thee, promised thee life, nourished thee and clothed thy shame, purified thee from thy uncleanness, wiped off thy blood, anointed thee with balsam, clothed thee with spiritual clothes; he has adorned thee with bracelets, ear-rings, and a beautiful crown, and has taken thee for his bride, and made an everlasting covenant with thee; he has fed thee with oil, honey and wheaten bread,—he has led thee to the chamber of his love, and kissed thee with the mouth of his peace.

How lovely and gracious a bridegroom and king is he, who has chosen his miserable, impure, unesteemed, yea, unchaste servant, to such an exalted station, and has called her to be such a glorious queen, and has spared no labor, pains nor costs, till he has made her the fairest, purest, most worthy and precious among women.

Arise, make haste, adorn and dress yourselves, extol and praise him who has created you, and called you to such a high honor through the word of his grace.

The winter is past—the rain is over and gone, the flowers appear on the earth, and the voice of the turtle dove is heard,—there is nothing more which can harm or hinder, for hell, sin, the devil, death, the world, flesh, fire and sword are already overcome by all God's children, through Christ! All they know is Christ Jesus, their seeking is the pure apostolic doctrine and the pious, unblamable life, which is from God.

Praise be to the Most High, who has silenced the falsehoods, for the truth sounds in every street. Anti-christ sinks to shame, and Christ rises to honor, yea, the unfruitful, cold winter has disappeared, and the fruitful pleasant spring has come, the lovely fair flowers shoot forth and vegetate, in every place; the voice of the turtle dove is heard. (Cant. 2.) The wholesome holy word, the word of repentance, the word of grace and eternal peace, is testified with word, writings, life and death, in many countries.

The fig tree putteth forth her green fig, and the vine with the tender grape, gives a good smell; arise, my love, my fair one, and come away. (Cant. 2.) Faith assumes verdure, love blooms, the sun softens, and the truth is published and testified which remained fruitless for so many years; yet you must for a short time bear the heat of the sun, so know you yet well that the kingdom of glory, in eternal joy, is promised and prepared for you.

Rejoice and watch; thou art black but comely, thou art as the tents of Kedar, as the curtains of Solomon. Awake, O north wind, and come thou south wind, blow upon my garden, that the spices thereof may flow out. (Cant. 4.) Fear not, little flock, for it is the Father's good pleasure to give you the kingdom, (Luke 12,) not the perishing kingdom of Assyria, Media, Macedonia, (Dan. 7,) nor of Rome, but the kingdom of the saints, the kingdom of the great king, the kingdom of David, (Luke 1,) the kingdom of grace and eternal peace, which shall never more perish, but shall abide and stand forever, therefore, hear him and be obedient, that you be not thrust out with the haughty, disobedient Vashti, (Est. 12,) but with the pious Esther live in endless glory, before the true Ahasuerus, Christ, and abide with him forever.

Arise, thou daughter of Zion, and observe what is promised thee, O Jerusalem, although thou, as a comfortless one, sittest for a while, and must bear all manner of storms and hail, but your helper will arrive in time, who brings forth thy righteousness as the morning, and is thy shelter from the wind and storm.

For He who has loved thee has said : Behold, I will lay thy stones with fair colors, and lay thy foundations with sapphires, and I will make thy windows of agates and thy gates of carbuncles and all thy borders of pleasant stones, and all thy children shall be taught of the Lord ; and great shall be the peace of thy children. In righteousness shalt thou be established ; thou shalt be far from oppression. (Isa. 54.)

Behold, thy wall stands firmly upon twelve foundations, thy gates are of pearls, the city is of pure gold, the river of living waters, proceeding from the throne of God and the lamb, is in the midst of your way, and the tree of life is on either side, and its leaves serves to heal the nation. Happy and holy is he who has part in this city.

Therefore, so purify yourselves, (Deut. 10,) you who seek the Lord, circumcise the foreskin of your hearts, for the holy city may be inhabited by no uncircumcised person, the golden streets are trodden by no unclean feet ; the unclean drink not of the pure waters, the fruit of life shall never be eaten by any of the ungodly, but without are dogs, and sorcerers, and whoremongers, and idolators and whosoever loveth or maketh a lie. (Rev. 22.)

Be ye all minded like Christ Jesus. Be earnest to hold the union of the spirit through the covenant of peace, (Rom. 5 ; Eph. 4,) ye are all one temple, house, city, mountain, body and church in Christ Jesus.

" Place your candle upon a candlestick, build your city upon a high mountain, live unblamably, (Matt. 5 ; Phil. 1, 2 ; Deut. 10 ; Col. 3 ;) behave in all things consistent with Christianity, fear God in all your ways, praise him in all your works ; great is the grace which has appeared. (Rom. 16 ; 1 Tim. 6 ; 2 John 1.) Prove yourselves in all things, as those who are born of God ; shun all false doctrine ; repay not evil with evil, but return the evil with good ; pray without ceasing ; (Rom. 12 ; 2 Thess. 5 ; Luke 21 ;) in patience possess your souls, judge all your thoughts, after Christ's thoughts, your words after Christ's words, and your lives after Christ's life, so shall you in eternity never more be deceived."

Walk worthily after the calling whereby ye are called. (Eph. 4.) Let the tyrannical, blaspheming, upbraiding and fierce hate the Lord and his word, they persecute not you, but Christ Jesus, to whom they are inimical, (Rev. 9,) they will be judged in their time, and (if they do not repent,) will be repaid again in their own bosoms.

Strive and wrestle valiantly, in order that the crown be not taken from you. Fly to the Mountain of the covert of Christ Jesus.—Gird yourselves with the weapons of righteousness, declare God's word with freedom, neither shrink nor give way. God is your conductor—be faithful unto death, so shall you inherit the crown of life. (Rev. 3; Eph. 6; 2 Thess. 5; Matt. 10; Mark 8; Rom. 10; Rev. 2, 3.)

Whosoever overcomes, will be clothed with white clothing, and his name shall not be erased from the book of life. Although we appear to the unwise, to die and depart from the right way, our souls are, nevertheless, in hope and peace. (Wis. 3.)

It is a faithful saying, (with Paul,) for if we be dead with Christ, we shall also live with him. If we suffer, we shall also reign with him. If we deny him, he will also deny us. (2 Tim. 2.) Therefore, so fear your God from the heart, watch and pray and commend to him your affairs, as Jeremiah did. (Jer. 11.) He has chosen you to be his loving bride, children, and members, and called you to the kingdom of his grace, and the inheritance of his glory, and has bought you with the immaculate blood of Christ Jesus.

Peace be with you, the spirit, power and grace of our Lord Jesus Christ, be with all my fellow laborers, believers, brethren and sisters, till eternal life. Amen.

CONCLUSION OR CLOSE OF THIS BOOK.

BEHOLD, dear sirs, friends and brethren, here we have briefly pointed out and declared upon what grounds and scriptures we stand built,—what we seek and have in view, and how we rebuke, with the Lord's word, all abominable sects and ungodliness of the whole world, both with the greatest and the smallest, without any respect of persons, and we point out to every one, the wholesome, pure truth. This the godly may judge. But this I have not done in order that the cross of Christ may be avoided —in no wise,—for I know and am persuaded, that the lamb with the wolf, the dove with the kite, and Christ with Belial can never be at peace, the truth must be hated; and were it so, that Christ himself should speak from heaven, still would neither scripture nor godliness, neither Christ nor apostle, neither prophet nor saints, neither lives nor property, be regarded by men. All those, who rebuke, in pure, upright zeal, the haughty, avaricious, proud, idolatrous, bloodthirsty world, and who seek their happiness and eternal welfare, must suffer and be oppressed.

You must, (said Christ,) be hated of all men for my name's sake, (Matt. 10, 24,) through much tribulation must you enter into the kingdom of God.   Christ himself so suffered and then entered into his glory. (Acts 14; Luke 24.)

Therefore, have I done this, that the precious, pure truth, might be revealed—that here and there some might be won—that the right way might be pointed out to the blind—the hungry fed with the word of God—the erring directed to Christ, the shepherd—the ignorant taught—Christ's kingdom extended, and his holy name magnified and praised : this, together with our innocence, shall be a witness on the day of judgment to all blood-thirsty tyrants, and all deceivers, false prophets, and all hardened and impenitent, that to them the truth had been testified.   But will ye not hear—then be your sins upon you : I have declared unto you according to my small gifts, God's spirit, word foundation, ordinance and will,—and have pointed out to you righteousness.   Whoever has ears to hear, let him hear, and whoever has an understanding, let him understand. (Rev. 2.)

I testify my Saviour openly : I acknowledge him, and dissemble not.   If you repent not and be not born of God, in your spirit, belief, life and worship, and become not one with Christ, so is the sentence of your condemnation on your poor souls already finished and prepared.

All, who teach you otherwise than we have here taught and testified to you, from the scriptures, betray you : This is the narrow way through which we all must walk, and must enter the strait gate, if we would be happy.   Here is expected neither emperor nor king, neither duke nor count, neither knight nor nobleman, neither doctor nor licentiate, neither rich nor poor, neither husband nor wife.   Whoever boasts that he is a christian, the same must walk as Christ walked. (1 John 2.)   Whoever has not the spirit of Christ is none of his. (Rom. 8.)   Whoever transgresses and abides not in the doctrine of Christ, hath not God. (2 John 1.)   Whoever sins, is from the devil. (1 John 3.)   Here will neither baptism nor Lord's supper avail.   These and other scriptures stand immoveable, and judge all those who live out of Christ's spirit and word, and whose thoughts are upon earthly and fleshy things, they shall never be overthrown nor weakened, by angel nor devil.

Will you say, with refractory Israel, we will not hear the word which you have preached to us in the name of the Lord, but we will do as our forefathers, our kings and princes have done from former years till the present time.   So I answer with holy Jeremiah and say : Although you have pleasure in lies, and do such abominations, so hath the Lord taken your wickedness to heart. (Jer. 44.)   And has sent you one hard punishment after another, as hunger, pestilence, storms, grief, misery and the consuming, devouring sword, that your land is turned to a waste—to amazement and a curse, as one evidently and palpaly may see in many places, because you perform strange worship, despise the Lord, your God, cast his word aside, spill innocent blood, walk according to your wantonness, sin against God, and walk not according to his law, ordinance and commands, as the mouth of the Lord has commanded you.

Again, as the unprofitable and rebellious world are warned and rebuked against their will, the prophets (Jer. 30, 36,) and the true servants of God, are judged and destroyed by the princes and magistracy, as seditious mutinists, and are persecuted by the priests and common people, as deceivers and heretics. (Jer. 39.) Therefore, our expectation is both to teach and to suffer. We judge rightly, that it will not happen better to us than it did to them, but we say with Ezekiel: That when this shall come to pass, then shall you find that the undissembled, pure word of the Lord, had been taught to you. (Ezek. 33.)

The merciful, gracious father, through his loving Son, Christ Jesus, our Lord, grant to you all, the gift and grace of his Holy Spirit, that you may hear and read these our christian labors and service of true love, with such hearts, that you may follow after the pure, undissembled truth, and be eternally happy. Amen.

Dear, worthy lords, grant to your poor servants, that we may fear the Lord from the heart, and preach God's word and do aright This we pray you for Jesus' sake. O Lord! Father of all grace, open the eyes of the blind, that they may see thy way, word, truth and will, and walk therein with faithful hearts, Amen, amen, Lord Jesus.

OF

THE TRUE

CHRISTIAN FAITH,

WHICH CONVERTS, CHANGES, RENEWS,
MAKES PIOUS, UPRIGHT, PEACEABLE, JOYFUL AND BLESSED
THE HUMAN HEART;

WITH ITS PROPERTIES, NATURE, OPERATION AND POWERS.

CAREFULLY RE-EXAMINED AND PRESENTED MORE FORMALLY IN
THE YEAR 1556.

By MENNO SIMON.

He that believeth in me (said Christ) though he were dead, yet shall he live, And
whosoever liveth and believeth in me shall never die.—JOHN 11.
For other foundation can no man lay than that it is laid, which is Jesus Christ.—
1 COR. 3.

PHILADELPHIA:

KING & BAIRD, PRINTERS, No. 607 SANSOM STREET.

1863.

OF THE TRUE CHRISTIAN FAITH.

We wish all the chosen children of God, our beloved brethren and sisters in Christ, an increase of faith, grace, peace and spiritual joy, perfect righteousness and eternal life, all which is of God, our heavenly Father, through Jesus Christ, his only begotten Son, our Lord, who loved us, and washed us from our sins in his blood :—to him be praise, honor, glory, the kingdom, power and majesty, from eternity to eternity. Amen.

CHOSEN, beloved children, brothers and sisters in Christ Jesus, although, O God! we are so violently prevented by the irrational blind world from preaching the true gospel of our Lord and Saviour Jesus Christ to every one verbally; and the revengeful, bloodthirsty, encouraged by your useless, wicked priests and preachers, are so imprudently against Christ and his word; for they (the poor children) seek and love rather more the dross than the gold, the chaff rather than the wheat, and lies rather than truth, and darkness rather than light. Nevertheless, God's eternal, invincible truth, which always triumphs in the true children of God, through the Holy Ghost, will be crowned, notwithstanding it has been so miserably stung in the heel by the conquered serpent and his seed, such as the proud despisers, liars and bloodshedders, and that they with much difficulty can be in obedience to their Lord Jesus Christ. Notwithstanding they do behave abominably, the envious bloody seed of the serpent, with bruised head, must lie powerless and be under their feet, as those who are wholly overcome by the power and spirit, with the gospel truth, in Christ Jesus.

Since, then, this old crooked serpent, which was from the beginning opposed to God in pride, and was an arrogant and fierce murderer, is put under the feet of Christ and his church, and has endured and seen his lying seed destroyed and trampled under feet, through the revealed truth, therefore, does he gnash his teeth in furious rage, and breathe out his accursed, infernal breath of heresy through his prophets and preachers. He casts out of his mouth the terrible streams of tyranny through the rulers and powerful of the earth, after the glorious church, (woman) big with the word of the Lord, with a view to exterminate and destroy her seed. But God be eternally praised, who has protected her against the red dragon, and has prepared her a place in the wilderness. (Rev. 12.)

Since, then, for reasons assigned, I cannot teach publicly, nevertheless, I will serve you by writing, as long as the Lord will permit me. I will serve you with my small talents, which the gracious Father granted me through his Son, Christ Jesus, out of the abundant treasury of his heavenly riches. I say, with Paul: Not with the wisdom of man, not with words of wisdom, to serve you, for I possess and know them not. I let those seek them who are eager after them. My boasting is with Paul; only to know Christ, and him crucified; for, to know him is eternal life. (John 17.) Therefore, God cannot endow us with better wisdom than with this, although it is foolishness to the world; for truth is more precious than gold and silver; than all pearls and precious stones; there is nothing under heaven to be compared to her, her ways are ways of pleasantness, and all her paths are peace; she is a tree of life to them that lay hold opon her; and happy is every one that retaineth her. (Prov. 3.)

Yes, beloved brothers, every one who is thus rightly taught in this wisdom, for she is above the wisdom of the saints, he may glory, by the grace given him, over all graduated doctors, theologists, jurists, orators and poets, and though he could neither write nor speak, and were he the most helpless upon earth. But all those who are not instructed in this wisdom from God, though they were as glorious as Solomon, as victorious as Alexander, as rich as Crœsus, as strong as Hercules, as learned as Plato, as subtle as Aristotle, as eloquent as Demosthenes and Cicero, and as well skilled in languages as Mithridates; yea, be so greatly experienced that his like were not to be found from the beginning, nevertheless, he is a fool in the eyes of the Lord; this must be confessed and acknowledged.

With this wisdom, I say so much as the gracious Father, the Giver of every perfect gift, has given me through his Son, Jesus Christ, I desire to serve not only our brothers and sisters, but the whole world, with all my heart, that all the hungry and thirsty souls may be clothed from above, and be satisfied with this celestial wisdom, who desire to live according to the will of the Lord—those souls which he created to his honor, and purchased with the blood of his Son—that they may learn to know God through his Son and word, in spirit, who says: Let not the wise man glory in his wisdom, neither let the mighty man glory in his might, let not the rich man glory in his riches; but let him that glorieth, glory in this, that he understandeth and knoweth me, that I am the Lord, who exercises loving kindness, judgment and righteousness, in the earth; for in these things I delight, saith the Lord. (Jer. 9.)

O, dear children, you who are born of the word of the Lord

through the spirit, reflect rightly on these things in your hearts, how incomprehensibly great the heavenly bounty and grace are, which have appeared to us, and have been given us of the Father, that he bestowed graciously upon us, grievous sinners, in our most abominable blindness, this glorious and divine gift of his wisdom. Yea, when we knew neither God nor Christ, were strangers to the life out of God, children of wrath and of eternal death, knew not the word of peace, and strayed like sheep who knew of no shepherd. (Eph. 24; Matt. 9; Mark 6.) That he so graciously bestowed us this great treasure, the true knowledge of the kingdom of God. (Matt. 23.) The treasure which lie buried in the field, he discovered to us by his spirit, and made known to us the mystery of his good will, and the true regenerating signification of his holy gospel, which cannot be taught in colleges—cannot be purchased—is not to be brought from foreign lands—nor can it be merited by any thing. That he has opened to us with the key of his word and spirit, the saving truth, and has closed it to all emperors, kings, lords, princes, the wise and the learned—before the whole world. (Exod. 30; Rom. 10.) That he redeemed us from the power of darkness, and, according to his will and good pleasure, led us into the kingdom of his dear Son; yea, that he made us kings and priests, that we are to be a chosen and holy people—a people to serve him in love, and to be his own, (Col. 1; Num. 19,) that we are to publish his power and virtue, because he called us out of darkness to his marvellous light, as Peter says: O great grace and love!

Most beloved brothers, always rejoice in the Lord. Again, I say, with Paul, (Phil. 4,) rejoice, that the great emperor, Jesus Christ, who has all power in heaven and upon earth, (Matt. 28) that he has manifested such grace towards you, that he has called you to such high honor, you who were the reproach and disgrace of the whole world, that he has made you kings and priests. (Rev. 1, 5.) Kings, say I, who have been anointed with the oil of grace, through the Holy Ghost, crowned with the crown of honor, clothed with the garment of righteousness, and governed by Christ, your emperor; not with the weapons of death, such as fire-arms, spears, swords, horses, riders and servants, as the kings of this world do, but by the invincible and eternal sceptre of the power of God, namely, with the sharp sword of the holy word, which will triumphantly prevail by virtue of your faith, over gold, silver, cities, countries, lords, princes, flesh, blood, flags, banishment, swords, staves, water, fire, hunger, thirst, nakedness, hell, sin, law, fear, devil and death—you will be perfect in life and death, and secure from all your enemies, both visible and invisible, who would deprive and rob you of the promised kingdom, through the instigation of the old serpent. The spiritual king's dominion and government are spiritual, therefore, they cannot be deadly hurt or conquered by tyranny, false doctrine, or evil lusts; for they can do all things through Christ, (Phil. 4,) who strengthens them, who also is their helper and redeemer, whose shield and sword is their glory. (Deut. 33.)

You are also priests ordained of God, not with the oil of Aaron and his sons, (Num. 28, 29, 30,) nor with the perishable blood of oxen and sheep; nor with the splendid garments of gold, silk and precious stones, as the law required; but anointed with the Holy Ghost, with the blood of Christ, and clothed with the garment or righteousness, ordained and called of God, not to slay the creatures daily, and offer them upon altars, in temples, as Moses commanded the priests in the law, (Exod. 29; Num. 28,) but you are to slay living men, with the sword of the divine word, understand *spiritually*, together with your own refractory flesh and blood, that is, that you teach and reprove them, and yourselves, with the spirit and word of the Lord, that you and they die to your unrighteousness and evil lusts, destroy them, and thus offer in your spiritual temple or house, not made with hands upon the only and eternal altar of our reconciliation, Jesus Christ, (Heb. 9, 13.)

Besides, you are not such priests, who of their own righteousness offer up bread and wine for the sins and transgressions of the common people, and for the souls of the deceased, neither are you to sing nor read mass, nor worship the golden, silver, wooden and stone images, nor serve nor burn incense to them as the poor ignorant priests of the world do; but you are holy priests, who purify and sanctify your own bodies daily, and in time of need voluntarily offer them up as a sweet smelling sacrifice, for the truth's sake, together with your ardent prayers and joyful thanksgiving, out of a believing, converted, pure heart; for such offerings are well pleasing to the Lord. (Ps. 51; Heb. 13.)

Would to God, that all who are called priests, were changed into such priests. ah! how much innocent blood would be spared, how gloriously the truth would be spread, and what a fine Christian world this would be!

Say, beloved brothers: who can fully comprehend *this* grace, or relate these benefits? Again, I say, we all like sheep had gone astray, we turned every one to his own way, we were as sheep without a shepherd, we walked according to the lusts of our evil flesh, even as they all do, who know not the way of the Father; we were unbelievers in divine things, blind and without understanding, full of bruises and putrifying sores from the sole of the foot to the head, (Isa. 53 ; 1 Pet. 2 ; Eph. 2 ; Tit. 3 ; Isa. 1,) and by nature children of wrath like others. (Eph. 2.) But the Lord be blessed, now we are washed, now we are sanctified, now we are justified in the name of our Lord Jesus Christ, and through the spirit of our God ; (1 Cor. 6,) in short, we are converted to the true shepherd and preserver of our souls, Jesus Christ, (1 Pet. 2,) who pastures us now in the rich pastures of his truth, Ezek. 34,) feeds us with the bread of his word, Matt. 4 ; John 6,) sustains us by the tree of life. (Prov. 5,) and refreshes us with the water of his spirit. (John 7.) Again, I say, who can comprehend and relate this grace ?

Besides this, when we were yet ungodly and enemies, he did not punish us as he did the angels which sinned, (2 Pet. 2 ; Jude 1,) nor like the first depraved world, (Gen. 6, 7, 8,) nor like Sodom and Gomorrah, (Gen. 19 ; Ezek. 16,) nor like those who worshipped the calf, (Exod. 32,) nor like those in the day of provocation, (Num. 21,) nor like the seditious and adulterers, (Num. 16, 25,) nor like those in the wilderness, who acted contrary to his will and word, (1 Cor. 10,) for he destroyed all of them ; but he saved us through his great mercy, led us by his right hand, and drew us by his goodness, renewed us by his word, and begat us by the Holy Ghost. and enlightened us by the clear light of his truth ; that we by his grace renounced the world, flesh, devil and all manner of evil, willingly entered upon the path of peace and submitted to the easy yoke of his gospel. It appears to me, this may properly be called grace.

Most beloved children, take heed. Since then, the gracious Father dealt so marvellously with us according to his great mercy, and manifested his love toward us without our merits, it is right, natural and becoming that we also love, fear and praise such a benevolent Lord and merciful Father, with all our powers ; and serve him, and be obedient to him in all our weakness.

Since then, I say, he has manifested, toward us afflicted sinners, such unspeakable love and grace, as said ; which love and grace cannot be rightly seen and understood, with the blind eyes and the ignorant reason of the flesh, but must be seen and understood with the inward eyes of the mind, and through the unction of the Holy Ghost ; that is, with a sincere, sure, immoveable, confident, vigorous, unfeigned and pure faith, such as the scriptures teach.

Seeing then, that this must be done with unfeigned faith, as related, and which is plainly found in the word of the Lord, as is set forth in true Christianity, such as regeneration, or a new creature, true repentance, dying to sin, a new life, righteousness, obedience, salvation and eternal life, in a sincere, active faith, as mentioned and set forth in all the scriptures, (John 1, 17; Mark 16; Rom. 3, 4, 5; Gal. 3, 5; Heb. 11.) And as may be read and seen in many other passages, I have resolved by the grace of God, thoroughly to instruct all the lovers of eternal truth, with the divine testimony out of the word of the Lord, which is the right faith, acceptable to God, and has the promise in the scriptures; namely, which has energy, power, and effect, agreeing with the gospel of Christ and the doctrines of the apostles. In order that all those who see, read or hear our writings, may thoroughly and understandingly know that the faith of this world is vain and dead, and is eternally cursed of God, for its fruits are vain hypocrisy, commands of men, idolatry and false service. It regenerates none, it is earthly and sensually-minded, hating and persecuting the truth, for this faith knows neither Christ nor his word as may be evidently seen through the whole world. God knows of no other faith than that which has power and fruit, regenerates the heart, converts and renews, as the scriptures say: The just shall live by faith, (Heb. 10; Hab. 2; Rom. 1; Gal. 3.)

It is all in vain to boast of faith where the godly, new fruits and works of faith are not. (James 4.)

I, therefore, exhort all my god-fearing readers in the Lord, and entreat all, that they would take those things to heart, for our holy and christian faith is not a dead and cold speculation, as the world thinks, nor is it only eloquent boasting, as we find it among the great and tolerated sects; but it is an active gift and grace of God, a heavenly living motion in a melted, open heart and conscience, firmly believes and lays hold upon, and acknowledges the whole word of God, (the threatening law, as well as the consoling gospel,) to be right and true, whereby the heart is moved and penetrated through the Holy Ghost with a peculiar regenerative, renewing, vivifying power, and it first produces the fear of God, for it knows the Lord's judgment and wrath over all transgressions and sins which are committed against his will and word; he dreads and fears, and is astonished before God, and therefore, he dares not do any thing, counsel or consent to, other than he knows to be right by the spirit through the word: he dares not do that which God hates, and forbids in his word.

This faith produces the love of God whereby we love him; for we are assured by the holy scriptures, if rightly understood in spirit, of the unsearchably great riches of grace with which the merciful and gracious Father has endowed us through his Son Jesus Christ; and therefore does he love his kind God, being awakened through the manifested bounties of the aforesaid grace, and he is thus voluntarily urged through the operating power of his love, (resulting from such a true faith,) to the obedience of all the commands of God, even as Christ says : If any man love me, he will keep my commandments, (John 14.)

Behold, this is the faith of which we have to treat in the following writings. For it is the only faith which has the promise in scripture, of salvation and eternal life, through Christ, God's only and first begotten Son. To him be praise, honor and glory, from eternity to eternity, Amen.

We find that if any one wishes to build a good house, or high and permanent tower, that first a solid foundation is laid, so that it will sustain the heavy superstructure, that the work began at such great expense, does not fall into ruins. And, thus it must be with true christians ; they must also lay a certain and true foundation in their hearts, that they may stand in building up their faith, against all the raging tempests, rains and floods, (Matt. 7,) which will not try them a little, so that they may stand immoveable, that they may, by the help of the Lord, successfully accomplish the work and building which they have begun, so that they do not with everlasting shame, and to the injury of their souls, depart from the true path, (Luke 14.) For if any man draw back, says Paul, the Lord shall have no pleasure in him, (Heb. 10.)

Faithful brethren, take heed to his precious and only well adapted corner-stone, ground and foundation in Zion, prepared for us by the Father, upon which we have to build the edifice of our faith, upon Jesus Christ, (Isa. 28 ; Rom. 9, 10 ; 1 Cor. 3 ; Eph. 2 ; 1. Pet. 2.) All who are founded upon this ground, will not be consumed by the fire of tribulation ; for they are living stones in the temple of the Lord, they are like gold, silver and precious stones, (1 Cor. 3,) and cannot eternally be prevailed against by the gates of hell, such as false doctrine, flesh, blood, world, sin, devil, water, fire, sword, or by any other means, if ever so sorely tried ; for they are founded upon Christ, confirmed in the faith and assured in the word through the Holy Ghost that they are not to be turned away from the pure and wholesome doctrine of Christ by all the furious and bloody Neros under the heavens, with all their cruel tyranny, they are not to be diverted from an unblamable and pious life, which is of God, as we have seen in many places for more than twenty years past ; for they are as immoveable as Mount Zion, as firm pillars, brave soldiers, and as pious, valiant witnesses of Christ, have fought till death, and do daily fight for the word and truth of the Lord, God be eternally praised. I speak of those who have the spirit and word of the Lord.

Yes, that stone lies firm in their hearts, and is so sealed by faith in them, that in their greatest need they regard neither father nor mother, wife nor child, money nor possessions, life nor death : for they are so constrained by veneration of God in their hearts, because Christ says : He that confesses me not before men, I will not confess him before my Father ; but he that confesses me, him will I again confess, &c. (Matt. 10 ; Mark 8 ; Luke 12 ;) that they are not allowed to speak a false word, even to escape the hands of the blood-thirsty and the dangers of death ; as may be seen.

But, I fear greatly, and indeed it is to be found so, that the greater part calling these innocent lambs accursed heretics, catch them as rats, banish and deprive them of life and possessions ; they are not ashamed, nor afraid of God, who hates all lies, (Ps. 5 ; Rev. 21, 22 :) for the sake of a stiver, to use yea for nay, and nay for yea, boast themselves christians, and are called after his name. If they are such liars and so unfaithful in small things, what will they do in greater things, if life and blood be required, may be readily imagined.

O reader, do reflect. If the old crooked serpent, with all his deception, falsehood and lies, lived in the christian hearts, as is the case with their persecutors, their goods would not be plundered, and their blood would not be shed. And they would not only conceal the truth, but they would with all the children of the devil hate and oppose it. All who are born of the truth, hate lies. Again, all who are born of lies, hate the truth. If they hate the truth, how can they speak it ? Especially when life and possessions are at stake. If our rulers and judges wish to be assured of this difference, let them call some of their evil doers before the judgment seat, who are guilty of death, and examine them in relation to things whereof they are accused, (but without punishing them,) what does it avail, though they would freely confess their guilt, for which they are to die, as these innocent children do in their faith ? Yea, what is more, let your most high renowned monks, in their profession, caps, &c., your most accomplished priests in their terms and masses, be as severely tested as you do these, in their faith ; then we will see what will become of all their professions, caps, terms and masses. But the common proverb is : The wolf escapes, but the lamb has to suffer.

Since then, I say, all those who are born of the truth, and have Christ and his truth dwelling in their hearts, in such we find nothing but the simple, plain truth of Christ, by which they are born unto righteousness, are converted and changed in heart, and it is equally evident, by their pious and unblamable life, that your lying, adultrous, lewd, idolatrous, drunken priests and monks belie them and persecute them before the whole world— (those who openly rob God of his glory, and maliciously murder those whom Christ purchased with his precious blood,) and betray them, to bring them into the stocks, and to the stake ; and this they do for no other reason, only because that the believers, through the revealed truth, with faith in their hearts, are urged by the spirit and fear of the Lord, to renounce their leaven, vain, false doctrine and idolatrous sacraments, and with all their hearts, to live according to the will of God. O Lord! thus they live and deal with those who seek and fear Thee with all their hearts.

Say, beloved lords, when shall this cruel, disgraceful murdering, bloody seed, be prevented by you from continuing in their Judas like conduct? When will you turn your backs to their deceiving lies, and turn your faces to Christ? When shall your deadly and avenging sword be wiped from its blood and again be put into the sheath? When will you hear and fear God, more than you do lords and princes? When shall the abominations of anti-christ be rooted out of your heart, and instead thereof, plant the doctrine of Christ therein? When will you be satisfied with pious and unblamable lives, and be satiated with the blood of innocent saints? When shall Christ Jesus, with his word, spirit and life, through faith, be conceived in you, and in deed be born in you? I fear *never*. For you are earthly and sensually minded, the eyes of your understanding are darkened, that you desire the world rather than heaven ; lies rather than truth ; sin rather than righteousness ; the honor and praise of man rather than the honor and praise of God.

Yes, beloved lords, why say much? With you it is the same as with the priests and preachers, who, through the instruction of scripture, know the truth in part ; but since they love their cross-fleeing body more than God, they preach only so far as the mandates and resolutions of the princes permit and suffer, so that they do not incur the displeasure of the world, and be deprived of their worldly honor, and their easy life. It is the same case with you, my dear lords. Though many of you know that the teaching, ceremonies, divine service and life of your priests and preachers are untrue, deceiving, idolatrous, false and carnal, and that ours are the doctrine and ceremonies of the Lord, according to scripture. But, in order to retain the friendship of the emperor and your incomes, (I mean you who are guilty of blood,) sooner will Christ Jesus, with his innocent lambs, without any mercy, (if the mandates be enforced,) have to endure cruelty and shame, as the ring-leaders, knaves and rogues, be taken by you, exiled, robbed and slain. And then you say : The emperor's mandates, and not we, judge you.

Beloved lords beware ; the hour is fast approaching, that the almighty, the great, and terrible God, the impartial, righteous judge, will judge and sentence all our doings; then you will see too late, whom you have persecuted and stabbed. Therefore, awaken in time, fear God and repent, while it is yet called to-day. (Rev. 1.)

I entreat you, my reader, be not displeased that I have digressed so far; for it was not without cause. But now, we will continue in the name of the Lord, in the thing we have undertaken, and treat and teach as much of it, as the merciful Father will grant us grace and aid thereto, that we may rightly show to all the godfearing, who seek the truth, the difference between faith and unbelief, the fruits of faith and of unbelief, and that they may grow up in the true christian faith, until the gracious Father, out of his abundance of glory, make them strong in the inner man, by power, through the spirit, and till Christ dwell in their hearts, through faith, that they may be rooted and grounded in love, may be able to comprehend, with all saints, what is the breadth and length and depth and height, and to know the love of Christ, which passes knowledge, and be filled with all the fullness of God. (Eph. 3.) And besides, that they may know that it is all hatred and lying which the scribes teach and cast up, touching our faith concerning the sword, sedition, polygamy, &c. I speak of that, which I and my beloved brothers preach and teach, verbally or by writing, publicly or privately, to all the well disposed.

Cordially beloved brothers, if we can rightly see with spiritual eyes, into the impure, abominable doctrine and faith, with all the abominable unbelief and blind evil life, resulting from such abominable doctrine of those, whose boast themselves christians, then we may with propriety be astonished at the great blindness and grievous error; yea, be grieved to death. No matter how cruel and rude so ever, it must be called the holy christian faith, O God!

THE PAPISTIC BELIEF.

It is true, that papists teach and believe, that Jesus Christ is the Son of God, that he offered up his flesh, and shed his blood for us, but with this *difference*, if we would enjoy it, and be partakers thereof, we have to adhere to the pope and his church, and be obedient, hear mass, receive the holy water, perform pilgrimages, call upon the mother of the Lord, and the departed saints, to confess at least twice a year, receive papistic absolution, have children baptized, commemorate the holy days.

The priests have to vow chastity; the bread in the mass, must be called the flesh, and the wine, the blood of Christ. Besides all their other idolatry and abominations, which are daily practiced by them.

And all this is called, by the ignorant, the most holy christian faith, and the institution of the holy christian church. Although it is nothing but mere human opinion, self-chosen righteousness, deceiving hypocrisy, manifest deceiving of the soul, ungodly, indecent bodily nourishment and gain of lazy priests, an accursed idolatry, an incensing of God, a disgraceful blasphemy, an unworthy despising of the blood of Christ, a self-devised undertaking, a disobedient contumacy to the divine word. In short, a false, offensive divine service and open idolatry, of which Jesus Christ (to whom the Father points us) has not left or commanded us a single letter of all these things. (Matt. 17; Mark 19.)

And it does not suffice that they practice such abominations; but they not only also despise as useless all true fruits of faith, (commanded of God himself,) the sincere and pure love and fear of God, the love and service of our neighbor, the true sacraments and divine service, &c., but also revile it as heretical, exterminate and persecute. I think this may properly be called a sect.

OF THE LUTHERAN BELIEF.

THE Lutherans teach and believe, that we are alone saved by faith, without any works. They insist upon it so inflexibly, as if works were not at all necessary; yea, that *faith* is of such a property and nature that no work can be suffered or allowed beside it. And, therefore, had the highly important and zealous epistle of James, (because he reproves such a frivolous, vain doctrine and faith) to be esteemed and considered as straw. O presumption! Is the doctrine straw, then must also the chosen apostle, the faithful servant and witness of Christ, who wrote and taught, have been a man of straw—this is as clear as the meridian sun. For the doctrine shows how the man was. (Mark 12; Luke 7.)

Let every one take heed, how, and what he teaches; for with this rude doctrine they have led the rude and ignorant, great and small, citizens and the common people, into such a fruitless wild life, and have left them so much liberty, that we would scarcely find such an ungodly and abominable life among the Turks and Tartars, as we see among them. Their open deeds bear testimony; for the luxurious eating and drinking; the superfluity and wantonness, whoring, lying, cheating, cursing, swearing by the wounds of the Lord, sacraments and sufferings, shedding of blood, striking and quarrelling, &c., which obtain among many of them, and, alas, have neither measure nor end. Both the teachers and hearers are the same in many carnal things, as may be seen. For what I well know, that I write, and what I myself have heard and seen, I testify, and I know that I testify the truth.

If any one can simply say with them : Ah ! what dishonest knaves and villains are these desperate priests and monks, they wish them the venereal or some other disease. The ungodly pope with his shorn crew, say they, have deceived us long enough with purgatory, confession and fasting. We now eat as we have hunger; fish or flesh, as we desire; For every creature of God is good, says Paul, and is not to be rejected. But what follows they do not want to understand or know; namely, to the believing, who know the truth and enjoy it with thanksgiving. They further say : How shamefully they deceived us poor people, that they have robbed us of the blood of the Lord, and directed us to their mummery and to their enchanting works. But God be praised, we now know that all our works avail nothing, for Christ's blood and death alone must blot out, and pay for our sins. Begin to sing a *psalm: Der Strick ist entzwey und wir seynd frey*, &c., i. e. The cord is cut asunder and we are at liberty. At the same time drunk, full to overflowing of strong drink. Any one who can but read this *distich*, if he live ever so carnally, is a good evangelical man, and a suitable brother. And should some one come, who would in true and sincere love, admonish or reprove them, and direct them to Jesus Christ, to his doctrine, sacraments and unblamable example, and show that it does not become a christian to carouse and drink, and to revile and curse, &c., he must from that hour hear, that he is a legalist, (*Werkheiliger*) one that would take heaven by storm, or a factionist, a fanatic or hypocrite, a defamer of the sacrament, or an ana-baptist.

Behold ! thus God, the righteous Lord, suffers these to err and go astray in their hearts, who rely upon the precious death and the most holy flesh and blood of our Lord Jesus Christ, the Son of God, together with his saving and reverent word, in their sensual lusts and wantonness, and make it an occasion of their unclean and sinful flesh. It appears to me this may also truly be called, a tolerated, large and great sect.

OF THE ENGLISH, ZUINGLIAN, OR CALVINISTIC BELIEF.

THE English, or Zuinglians believe and confess that there are two sons in Christ Jesus, the one is God's son, without mother, and *impassive;* and the other is the son of Mary, or the son of man, without father, and *passive.* And in this *passive* son of Mary, the *impassive* Son of God dwelt; so that the son of Mary, who was crucified, and died for us, was not the son of God. This was acknowledged by one of their principal teachers, called Martin Micron, also by one Harman Von Ronsen, (if I recollect his name rightly,) before me, two or three times in a large assembly, in the year 1554.

Further, the said Micron, when I questioned him in relation to the *aura seminis* of the woman, concerning which we had not a few words, acknowledged and said: I have to confess that a woman has no seminal functions but an afflux of catamenial fluid to the uterus. See, before God, it is the truth that I write! He also wrote in a book, printed in England—these are his words—touching the coagulating of the fluids in her uterus. If the fluids thus changed, as the book says, and as he confesses, that a woman has only catamenial fluids in the uterus, as said; therefore, it is evident, that they believe (if they agree with him) that their Saviour is not God's first and only begotten son, but the mere result of a vitiated state of the uterine fluids.

John a Lasco also writes, that Christ partook of no other flesh than that which was subject to sin and death, in order that he might be tempted. He states in the same book: If he is holy, why was he sentenced in the Father's judgment, for the sake of sin? This I cannot otherwise understand, before God, than that he believes, that the man Christ Jesus, was a sinful Christ and guilty of death. Read his defence made against me, of the Incarnation; there you will find his ground.

O God, watch over all true hearts, that they may never believe such intolerably great abominations. It makes me shudder, and I am astonished in my heart, yea, I am ashamed in my soul, that I must make mention thereof; for it is too offensive. But since they defame and slander us daily before all men, both verbally and by writing, what a very detestable ground and doctrine we have of Christ, (since we confess, with the scripture, that he was the first and only begotten son of God who died for us,) and they present these abominable things to the poor simple people, as said, and deceive them so miserably thereby; for this reason, am I constrained in my conscience, (to the honor of God, and to warn all the godfearing,) that I had to notice this here, to present it to the reader, whose mind is held captive by them, to reflect upon ; for I know not how we could believe more cruelly and abominably of Christ, teach, feel, think or speak of, than to say : It was not the Son of God who died for us, but it was the result of a vitiated catemenial fluid,—a man that had to die for sin, &c.

And though they would gainsay and deny this, and say that I wrote this gratuitously concerning them, it is true, this happened repeatedly, and before many pious hearts ; they may deny it, but it will be found true in the day of the righteous judgment, before the eyes of the Eternal and great majesty, as I have written it. O abominable sect !

OF TRUE CHRISTIAN BELIEF.

WE teach and believe, and this by virtue and power of the whole scriptures : That the whole Christ Jesus from above and below, inwardly and outwardly, visibly and invisibly, is God's first and only begotten Son, the incomprehensible, eternal Word, by which all things are created. (John 1.) The first born of every creature, (Col. 1.) Became a true man in Mary, the immaculate virgin, through the almighty, eternal Father, eternal spirit and power, beyond the comprehension and knowledge of all men. (John 1.) Sent and given unto us out of pure mercy and grace, from the Father. (John 3.) The express image of the invisible God. (Col. 1.) And the brightness of his glory. (Heb. 1.) We teach and believe that the first and only begotten Son of God, Jesus Christ, is our only and eternal Messiah, prophet, teacher and high priest. (Deut. 18 ; Heb. 5, 10.) Who has fulfilled the required and commanded law for all his believers, (inasmuch as they could not fulfil it on account of the weakness of their flesh.) Who taught us his Father's good will and pleasure, and went before us as an unblamable pattern, and freely offered himself upon the cross for our sins, as a sweet-smelling sacrifice to the Father. (Rom. 8 ; Col. 2 ; Eph. 2 ; Matt. 12 ; John 13 ; Eph. 5.) Through whom we all, (who believe this cordially,) have received the forgiveness of our sins, grace, favor, mercy, liberty, joy, life eternal, a reconciled Father and free access to God, in the spirit. (Eph. 2.) And this all through his merits, righteousness, intercession and blood, and not through our own works. Behold this is the true summary of our belief concerning Christ, our Saviour, the Son of God.

All who believe this, in their hearts, as certain and true, and are assured, through the word of God, in their hearts and spirit, are inwardly changed, receive the fear and love of God, and bring forth out of their faith, righteousness, fruit, power, an unblamable life and a new principle, as Paul says: With the heart we believe unto righteousness. (Rom. 10.) Through faith, says Peter. God purifies our hearts. (Acts 15.) And thus follow the fruits of righteousness out of an upright, unfeigned, pious, Christian faith. Observe this well.

For all those who believe the righteous judgment of God and his eternal wrath over all sin and wickedness, and do not doubt at all, look at the fallen angels, (2 Pet. 2 ; Jude 1,) they look at the first, depraved world, (Gen. 6, 7, 8,) at Sodom and Gomorrah, (Gen. 19,) and upon disobedient, refractory Israel, (Heb. 3,) they take particular notice how God humbled his innocent Son, who knew of no sin, and in whose mouth guile was not found, how he was humbled, made the most miserable among men for the sake of our sins. (Isa. 53.) Yea, that he was so beaten and tortured, that, while extended on the cross, he innocently complained to his Father : My God, my God, why hast thou forsaken me ? (Matt. 27,)

All, we say, who truly believe this, in their hearts, certainly will flee from all unrighteousness, as they would from the fangs of a serpent; they turn away from all sins, and dread them more than a burning fire or a piercing sword, for their whole mind and conscience testify to them, that if they premeditately sin against God's law and word, and do not receive Christ in a pure and good conscience, live according to the flesh, despise the inviting voice of God, that they will fall under the dreadful, eternal sentence and wrath of God. (Heb. 10.)

This the pious and aged Eleazar believed, (2 Macc. 6,) and the god-fearing, virtuous mother, with her seven sons, (2 Macc. 7.) The three faithful young men in the fiery furnace, and beloved Daniel, (Dan. 3, 6,) and the fair, virtuous Susan, the honorable pattern of all pious women. (Dan. 13.) And would, therefore, rather endure for a season the ire and fury of tyrants than sin, and thus bring upon themselves the eternal anger and wrath of God. The righteous, say the scriptures, live by faith. (Heb. 2 ; Rom. 1 ; Gal. 3 ; Heb. 10.) For the true evangelical faith, which makes the heart sincere and pious before God, moves, changes, urges and constrains a man so, that he will always hate the evil, and willingly do the things which are right and just. Yea, even as it is not necessarry to admonish or warn a man of understanding not to cut his own throat, or to drink poison, or to thrust himself from a high tower, or to run into deep water ; for he knows well, if he did so, that he would

15*

not escape death. So it is also unnecessary that we should admonish, or warn those, who cordially believe that the wages of sin is death, that drunkards, liars, fornicators, adulterers, the avaricious, idolators, blasphemers of God, envious blood-shedders, perjurers, thieves, and the like sinners, shall not inherit the kingdom of Christ—that they shall not get drunk, shall not commit fornication, &c. (Rom. 6.) For the divine fear, which is of such a faith, warns, reproves, urges and deters them so, that they will never more consent to such sensual, ungodly works, much less do them. For their faith, I say, is sealed of the spirit through the word, teaches them that the end thereof is death. (Rom. 1, 6; 1 Cor. 6; Gal. 5; Eph. 5; Rev. 21, 22.)

We must thus believe with the heart, as Paul says, (Rom. 10,) that is: we must so adhere to the word to receive and impress it upon our hearts, that we never turn or be diverted from it, but that faith be more and more rooted in our hearts, so that, through the virtue thereof, we may fear God with all our powers, and do sincere penance. For cordial, unfeigned fears drives out sin, and it is impossible to be justified without the fear of God. (Prov. 2.)

Here observe, what an excellent, pleasing fruit of faith, the fear of the Lord is, for it is the only power which expels the sins of believers, buries, slays, destroys and makes sin nought, this is the first part of true repentance, as we are taught and admonished by the baptism of believers. (Rom. 6; Col. 2.) The fear of the LORD (says David) is the beginning of wisdom; a good understanding have all they that do his commandments: his praise endureth for ever. (Ps. 111.)

Further: All who comprehend and understand with a sincere, unwavering, believing heart, God's great solicitude and ardent care for us, (here I speak of him according to the manner of man) and his unbounded great kindness, mercy and love, as paternally manifested toward us through Christ Jesus, how that he did not spare his only Son (by whom he created the heavens and the earth, the seas and the fullness thereof,) his incomprehensible, eternal Word, power and wisdom, but that he, for our sakes, gave him over, humbled him, let him endure hunger, thirst, was derided, taken, mocked, spit upon his holy face, was scourged, crowned with a crown of thorns, condemned, crucified and slain, that we, through his sickness and stripes, might be healed, through his poverty might become rich, (1 Pet. 2; 2 Cor. 8,) that we might, through his being despised, obtain glory; through his cursing, obtain blessing; through his punishment, receive grace; through his blood, the remission of sin; through his offering, be reconciled, and through his death might obtain eternal life. He also created every living creature for our use, and made them subject to us. He serves and provides us with winter and summer, heat and cold, with night and day, with rain and dearth; he sent to us his holy apostles with his holy word, endowed us with his spirit, enlightens, governs, admonishes, reproves and comforts us; he has given us shelter, and food to supply our wants, and, in the midst of a perverted lion-like generation, he kept and preserved us by his grace, &c. I say, again, he believes this with all his heart, apprehends and lays hold of, he can never be prevented neither by angel nor devil, neither by life nor death; but he must love this gracious Father, from his inmost heart, who has manifested so great love and mercy towards us grievous sinners; yea, praise, honor and be grateful to him—serve, and be obedient to him, all the days of his life.

For this is the greatest delight and joy of believers, that they in their weakness may walk and live according to the will and word of the Lord, and where unfeigned the love of God obtains, there, without fail, must also be the voluntary, ready service of that love, namely, the keeping of his commands. (John 14; 1 John 5; 2 John 1.) Solomon says: They that put their trust in him shall understand the truth, and such as will be faithful in love shall abide in him. (Wis. 3.) And this is what Paul says: That in Christ neither circumcision nor uncircumcision availeth, but faith, which worketh by love. (Gal. 5.)

That love is of an effective power and nature, can be very plainly seen in natural love; for we need not admonish rational parents, to provide their children with the necessary food and clothing, but natural love will admonish them thereto. And thus with man and wife, who cordially love each other with conjugal love, they think it no displeasure kindly to love each other and be fellow helpers, as it becomes them, being one flesh. (Eph. 5.) And so are also the nature and property of holy, divine love, for all those who by faith are one with the Father and his Son, Christ Jesus, in love and spirit, through the true and genuine knowledge of the aforementioned favor, need not to be admonished that they should serve the Lord, seek the kingdom of God, use baptism and the Lord's supper, according to the ordinance of the scriptures, should constrain heart and tongue, to reflect upon the law and will of God with all earnestness, hear Christ and follow him, and that they should not love gold and silver, money and possessions, wife and children, life and death more than Christ and his word. For the effectual nature of the ardent love of God, which is of a pure heart, good conscience, unfeigned faith urges and constrains, moves and operates so much in their hearts, that they stand prepared with body and soul, possession and blood, to do what he commanded them, and not do that which he prohibited; as we may see (God be praised) in great plainness and power, and hear daily of many pious hearts.

And it is hereby evident, if we would love God and walk in obedience to his commands, we should then believe, have a special regard to his favors, and with the heart adhere closely to the word of his promise, as said; for that love which is sincere, is a very precious fruit, it is a branch and plant of faith from which the other part of true repentance flows, namely, the unblamable new life, represented to us by baptism, as related above, of the fear of the Lord: "Without which love, all eloquence, all tongues, all knowledge and understanding, all boastings of faith, learning, miracles, prophesying, alms, persecution, cross and suffering, are vain before God; yea, dead and without fruit, (1 Cor. 13.")

Every one that loveth is born of God, and knoweth God: and God is love, (1 John 4,) and such a one does all things honestly to the word of the Lord, for love is the fulfilling of the law, (Rom. 13,) the obedience to his commands, (John 14; 1 John 5,) the bond of perfection and peace, (Col. 3; Eph. 4.) prefigured by the splendid girdle of Aaron and his sons, (Exod. 18.)

Love, says Solomon, is strong as death; jealousy is cruel as the grave; the coals thereof are coals of fire, which have a most vehement flame, many waters cannot quench love, (Cant. 8,) yea, so firm and strong and ardent is love that it surpasses every thing, conquers and consumes what is opposed to Christ and his word, be it world or flesh, tyrant or devil, sin or death, or whatever we may think of or name; and this is all through the power and spirit of Jesus Christ of whom it originates. (Rom. 8.)

Moses preceded with fear, then Christ with love. First the terrific land, and afterwards the consoling gospel; first wrath in the feelings of our consciences, afterwards grace; first uneasiness of pain, then peace; first tribulation, then joy. In short, first the letter which killeth, then the spirit which quickens. (2 Cor. 3.)

Behold, my reader, such a faith as mentioned, is the true christian faith, which praises, honors, magnifies and extols God the Father and his Son Jesus Christ, through filial fear and fruitful love, for by it we know the Father's good will towards us through Christ; by it, I say, we know that all the promises to the fathers, the waiting of the patriarchs, the whole figurative law, and all the predictions of the prophets, are fulfilled *in* Christ, *with* Christ, and *through* Christ, (Rom. 10.) That, Christ is our king, prince, Lord, Messiah, the promised David, (Jer. 23

33; Ezek. 34; Gen. 49,) the Lion of the tribe of Judah, (Rev. 5,) the mighty God, the everlasting Father, the prince of peace, (Isa. 9,) God's almighty, incomprehensible, eternal word and wisdom, (John 1; 1 Cor. 1,) the first born of every creature, (Col. 1,) the light of the world, (John 3, 8, 12,) the Sun of righteousness, (Wis. 5,) the true vine, (John 15,) the well of life, (John 7; Rev. 22,) the true door and shepherd of the sheep, (John 10,) the true foundation, (1 Cor. 3,) and the precious corner-stone in Zion, (Isa. 28; Rom. 19; 1 Pet. 2,) the right way, the truth and life, (John 14,) the promised prophet, (Deut. 18; Acts 3, 7,) our master and teacher, (John 3, 13,) our Redeemer; (Matt. 10; Col. 1,) Saviour; (Luke 2; Tit. 2, 3,) Friend and bridegroom; (Cant. 1, 2, 3, 4; John 3.) In short, our only and eternal mediator, advocate, high-priest, propitiator and intercessor, (1 Tim. 2; 1 John 2; Heb. 5, 6, 7, 8, 9, 10, 13,) yea, our head and brother, (Eph. 1; Col. 1; Matt. 12; Heb. 2, &c.) And since we know all this by faith, therefore, I say, we also observe his word rightly, hear his voice, and implicitly follow his example, counsel, and depart from ungodliness:—the heart is changed, the mind is renewed, and with Moses we rely upon the future promises, as though they were in sight, and patiently wait for them with pious Abraham, till he with all the chosen shall in reality inherit them. For faith, says Paul, is the substance of things hoped for, the evidence of things not seen, (Heb. 11.) He says, further: But hope that is seen is not hope, (Rom. 8.) God (says Christ himself) is a spirit, (John 4;) his word and grace are spiritual; the promise of the New Testament is spiritual; his kingdom and government are spiritual; and thus we have to believe all things through a pure, sincere and sure faith, with a candid heart and judge and see with spiritual eyes; but we may well say with Paul: For all men have not faith. (2 Thess. 3.)

Therefore, all those who stop their ears to the threatening and slaying law, and will not fear God, and also reject and desire not the gracious gospel of Christ, shut their eyes to the light of righteousness, and will neither see nor walk the true way, harden their hearts, and will not acknowledge the just judgment of God's wrath and displeasure, his mercy and favor and his unbounded grace, they are unbelievers; for they reject Christ Jesus, run haughtily, yea presumptuously, into perverse ways; they choose to themselves a righteousness and means of salvation contrary to the word of God; the wisdom of the Lord they esteem foolishness; his truth as lies; his gospel as delusion; the virtuous, christian life as madness; and the true use of his sacraments, as heresy, open idolatry, commands of men, superstition and abominable lies, are their consolation and most reasonable service; their belly is their God: they love the world more than heaven;

all their delight is in covetousness, avarice, pride and pomp, in gold and silver, in money and possessions; in buying and selling, they cheat and deal treacherously; their common life is drinking, gambling, cursing, swearing, hatred, strife and fighting, they follow the flesh in its lusts; they defame and seek the calamity of their neighbor, his dishonor, disgrace and shame. In short, they say, with the fool, in their hearts: There is no God. (Ps. 13; Ezra 18.)

Although they boast of God with the mouth, praise his name with their lips, bow their bodily knees, saying, that they are redeemed with Christ's death and blood, it is nevertheless vain hypocrisy; for they do it only from habit, and feignedly, and not inwardly, through faith, in power and truth. They are those of whom it is written: They profess that they know God; but in works they deny him; being abominable and disobedient, and to every good work reprobate. (Tit. 1.) And this, because they do not believe Christ and his word, (their end is death,) as he says: He that believeth not shall be damned, yea, is already condemned. (Mark 16.)

It is true what Paul says: That it is impossible to please God without faith, for he that comes to God, must believe that he is, and that he is a rewarder of them that diligently seek him. (Heb. 11.) O for an open heart! For profound understanding! Yea, if we rightly examine these words, we have reason to be astonished at Paul's wisdom and understanding. For if we do rightly reflect upon the matter, we have to confess before the Lord, (who tries our reins and hearts,) that we never believed it with the heart, that God is, and hence, we led a vain ungodly life. For it cannot be otherwise; if any one believes with all his heart, that God is, he will also believe that his word is true, that the wages of sin is death, that all things are open to his eyes, and that there is nothing concealed before him. (Rom. 8; Heb. 4.) That we must give an account of all our thoughts, words and deeds, before his judgment seat in the day of his coming. (Isa. 66; Matt. 12; Rom, 2; 2 Cor. 5.) Believing all this, we then begin to be astonished before such an omniscient and righteous Judge, yea to fear and tremble greatly.

In the second place, I say: All who believe with the heart, that God is, they also believe that he is true, and therefore, none can be saved contrary to his word; for he is the God of truth, and in him there are no lies. His uttered word abides, it can neither be bent nor broken; those who thus believe, begin to fear his righteous judgment; they cast behind them all their false patchwork, all false promises, all the bolsters and cushions of the false prophets, and the seek the Lord who bought them. They are abased in their own eyes; for the heart is humbled.

They sigh and weep, pray and lament, knock and call at the throne of grace, till they are heard and encouraged by the word of his peace, comforted with the promise of his grace, and anointed with the Holy Ghost.

In the third place, I say : All who believe that God is, also believe that he is gracious and merciful, that he bestowed and sent us his Son, and that he taught us the right way, fulfilled the law for us, reconciled us to the Father, and redeemed us by his blood and bitter death ; has conquered hell, the devil, sin and death, and obtained for us grace, favor, mercy, and eternal life, &c. And therefore, the drooping hearts are again revived (which saw through the threatening law, nothing but the wrath of God and eternal death.) They become candid, peaceable, and joyful in the Holy Ghost, are of a joyful disposition, and are thus made to belong to their head and Saviour, are united and made one with Him, ingrafted through the spirit of God and pure and unfeigned love, that they are of one heart, one soul and spirit with him ; think, speak and live in their weakness as he has taught and commanded them in his word. They renounce and avoid all false doctrine, all unbelief, all false sacraments, all idolatry; put off the spotted garment of sin, which is the evil perverted life, and is of the flesh. They seek the doctrines and sacraments commanded them of Christ ; that divine service which is taught in the scriptures, and that pious and unblamable life which is from God. For by faith they are changed in the inner man, converted and renewed, because they have a sealed, and assured conscience, which bears witness to them that God is, that he is righteous and true, gracious and of abundant mercy. And therefore they desire, to do and act, so that they do nothing but what they know through the word, that Christ taught and left them, through his holy apostles and prophets.

Behold, my brethren, here you have now the true properties and nature of a true christian faith, and what a great mystery, signification, power and spirit are contained summarily in these words : *He must believe that God is;* (Heb. 11,) he that believeth on him has eternal life; (John 3,) he that believeth and is baptized shall be saved; (Mark 16 ;) whosoever believeth on him shall not be ashamed, (Rom. 10,) and the like passages. For it will always be the case where there is a true, sincere, christian faith, there also will be a dying to sin, a new creature, true repentance, a sincere, regenerated and unblamable christian. One does no longer live according to the lusts of sin, but according to the will of him who purchased us with his blood, drew us by his spirit and regenerated us by his word, namely, Christ Jesus.

But where there is only nominal faith and no righteousness, change, or new and penitent life, there is nothing but unbelief, hypocrisy and lies. No matter how much we may speak, or dispute about the scriptures. This rule will abide, and can never be broken : *If ye live after the flesh, ye shall die.* (Rom. 8.) All, therefore, who live in pomp and wantonness, in excessive eating and drinking, adultery, fornication, avarice, hatred, envy, lasciviousness, defrauding and such sins ;—all who defame the Lord's holy and high name, word and will, and also his community, slander and traduce their neighbor ; deprive him of his honor, name, welfare, body and goods ; who curse and swear by the Lord's sufferings, wounds, sacraments, cross and death, &c. *All* who do so are unbelieving heathens, and not believing christians. This is as plain as daylight, for their fruits testify before the whole world, that they are not the true olive tree and vine from which we may pluck or gather the true, ripe fruits ; for, that they comfort themselves with the doctrines and commands of men, use a strange baptism, Lord's supper and divine service, which Christ has not taught; seek the remission of sins by foreign means ; such as holy waters, masses, auricular confession, pilgrimage, &c. ; walk in a perverted, crooked path ; believe not Christ and his word, all must confess who have only natural discernment and understanding. But all who confess and acknowledge Christ to be the son of God, and his word as the truth, that his commands are eternal life, seek no other word, sacraments, or means of reconciliation, nor another way of life than that which Christ, God's only Son, presented and taught them by the word of his truth.

And hence it is evident, where sincere and true faith obtains, which avails before God, which is a gift of God, and comes from hearing the holy word, through the blossoming tree of life, full of all manner of precious fruits of righteousness, such as fear and love of God, mercy, friendship, chastity, temperance, humility, candor, truth, peace and joy in the Holy Ghost, &c. (Rom. 3 ; Gal. 3 ; Eph. 2 ; Rom. 10.) For where there is a sincere, evangelical, pious faith, there also are the sincere, gospel fruits of an evangelical nature.

I say gospel fruit, for the strange fruit, such as infant baptism, masses, matins, vespers, caps, palms, chapels, altars, bells, &c., know not the gospel, for they are neither commanded of God, nor of Jesus Christ, his Son, nor by the holy apostles and prophets, therefore, are they abominations and not believing fruits, even as the golden calves were with Israel, (1 Kings 15,) the worship of Baal, the high places, altars and churches, and the crime of making their children to pass through the fire. (Jer. 7, 11.)

The true evangelical faith looks upon, and has respect to, the doctrine, ceremonies, commands, prohibitions, and unblamable examples of Christ alone, and strives to conform thereto with all its powers even as fire in its nature can produce nothing but combustion and flame; the sun, nothing but light and heat; the water causes moisture, and a good tree brings good fruit, after its natural properties; and thus evangelical faith produces true evangelical fruit, (again I say,) and that after its true, good, evangelical nature: Yea, even as an honest, virtuous bride, by virtue, and the nature of natural love, is ever ready to hear and follow the voice of her bridegroom; and from a sincere, pious disposition, favor and love which she has for, and towards him, will ever so conduct herself, before her most faithful friend and beloved husband, whom she respects and loves with all her heart, for his sake voluntarily endures what ever may befall her; even also it is with a sincere, regenerated believer, who has been joined to Christ, by grace through faith; he has become one with Christ through this ardent love, that he is ever prepared, in his love and will, to endure all things for Jesus's holy name's sake, in evil as well as in good report. Eager to endure all things that may befall him at any time, be it joy or tribulation, satiation or hunger, refreshing or thirst, honor or dishonor, in good or bad report, in prison or at liberty, in exile or at home, an easy or a hard life, death or life. Such a soul partakes of her bridegroom's nature and disposition, is pious in heart and thought; true in words and well seasoned; all her ways are righteousness, devoutness; wise as the serpent, as harmless as the dove; a genuinely pious disposition, fidelity, zeal, peace, fervent prayer, an unblamable conduct, a sincere, pure, brotherly love, and a voluntary obedience to Christ and his holy word; for, I say, the righteous live by faith, (Heb. 2; Rom. 1; Gal. 3; Heb. 10,) as we shall be shown plainly by the grace of God, by the following examples, recorded in the holy scriptures.

OF NOAH'S FAITH.

The holy scriptures testify concerning Noah, the son of Lamech, that he found grace before the Lord, because he was a righteous, godly man, unwavering and perfect in his generation, (Gen. 6.) Peter calls him a preacher of righteousness, (2 Pet. 2.) High and glorious is the testimony, which is given in the scriptures concerning this man.

When all the world was depraved before God, and the face of all the earth was full of wickedness, the sons of God looked upon the daughters of men that they were fair, they took them wives of all whom they choose, and would not suffer themselves to be reproved by the spirit of God; then spake the Lord: I will yet give them the space of a hundred and twenty years;—he also gave Noah a command, that he should make a ship or ark, by which he and his house might be saved from the coming flood, for God the Lord, was about to destroy the whole world with water. Noah believed the Lord's word with all his heart, and kept it in his mind, as if he saw it before him with his eyes. He commenced building as he had been commanded, for he believed with his whole heart, that the threatened punishment would come. And when the appointed year was completed, and the disobedient wicked world repented not, the Lord's word must be accomplished. Noah went into the ark with all clean and unclean creatures as the Lord commanded him. On the same day he entered the ark the foundation of the great deep, and the firmament of heaven were opened, and it rained forty days and forty nights till all the high mountains upon the face of the whole earth, were covered fifteen cubits high with water, and all creatures upon the earth that had in them the breath of life, as men, birds, beasts and worms were destroyed. Noah and his family, together with the animals which were with him in the ark, were preserved in the ark by the power and grace of the Almighty, in whom Noah trusted with all his heart. (1 Pet. 3.)

Through faith (saith Paul) Noah honored God, and prepared the ark for the salvation of his house, according to the divine command which were not yet seen, through which he condemned the world, and became an inheriter of the righteousness which is by faith: (Heb. 11.)

Oh! lovely example, O glorious pattern of a sure and firm faith. For, as he believed his God, so was he upright and unwavering. He believed the threatened punishment firmly, as if he saw it before his eyes, and therefore he laboured so many years, and, through the eternal spirit of Christ, he warned the unbelieving, disobedient spirits, or men led captive by sin, to repent and reform, He feared his Lord's word and doubted not that it would happen as the Lord hath spoken. He well knew that the Lord's word was powerful, as the prophet said: O Lord, by speaking didst thou in the beginning address the creation: Let there be heaven and earth—thy word is an all powerful work. (2 Ezra. 6.)

And when he had preached and built forty, eighty or a hundred years, (the scriptures do not say how long he built and taught,) he did not become weak in faith by long delay, for he well knew that the punishment of God would come upon the impenitent and unconverted, and that he, and his would be preserved through the mercy and grace of him who promised for he is the God of truth, and no lie is found in him. (Tit. 1; Heb. 6.)

The Lord God warned the pious Noah, and said : The end of all flesh is come before me, for the earth is full of violence, and behold, I will destroy it with the earth. (Gen. 6.) So also hath he through his own blessed son, through his holy prophets and apostles, with his word or truth, warned us and said : If you repent not, be not born of God, believe not in Christ, walk not in his commandments, reform not your wicked lives, but serve strange Gods, be haughty, proud, ambitious, lustful, blood-thirsty malicious, unjust, idle, earthly, fleshly, and devilish, you shall die in your sins, (1 John 7,) and shall not enter into the kingdom of heaven, (John 3,) shall be condemned, (Mark 16,) shall be cast into the fiery pool (Rev. 21,) must inherit eternal wo and pain, with all the accursed, and with devils, (Matt, 15 ; 2 Thes. 1,) and have no part nor communion in the kingdom of Christ, to all eternity. (1 Cor. 6.)

My readers, if we, with the upright and godly Noah, take heed to the warnings of Christ and his holy spirit and believe with the whole heart—believe God's word to be true and immutable—that the threatened punishment will come in its time, even though it be delayed a thousand years. I advise that every one watch, for all who die in their sins, receive their punishment, for, the time of grace is then expired. We should undoubtedly threaten the impenitent and unconverted with sore wrath, which will be eternal in its duration. We should fear and tremble from our inmost souls, and pray our God for grace. We should clothe ourselves in sackcloth and mourning garments. We should truly repent, reform the wicked life, follow after righteousness, (1 Pet. 3) and with our new and spiritual Noah, Christ Jesus, enter into the new and spiritual ark, which is his church ; and that we be careful at all times which is his church ; that the fearful flood of the coming wrath of God, overtake us not, with all unbelievers and impenitent, who know neither God nor Christ, neither spirit nor word, as it happened to the old world, (Gen. 7, 8,) yea we should watch and wait from the heart upon the coming of the Lord, and give heed to the time of grace, preserve our wedding garment, and have oil in our lamps, we should see that our house be not cast down, and we with the unclad guest, be cast forth from the Lord's wedding, into utter darkness (Matt. 22) and abide eternally out of doors.

But if we believe not the threatening punishment, wrath and judgment of the Lord, and have little regard to the commands of the scriptures, and say with the mockers: Where is the promise of his coming ? all things abide as they were from the beginning, since the fathers fell asleep, (2 Pet. 2,) it will, I fear, happen with us as it did with the unbelievers and disobedient who were overtaken with sudden destruction in the time of Noah and Lot. (Gen. 7, 8, 19,) as one may plainly see and read concerning the coming of the Lord in Matthew 24, and Luke 17.

Again, if we believe not, neither regard the threatened judgment and wrath of the Lord, it will follow that we will lead a profligate life—do all that our wicked flesh desires, eat, drink, build, sow, reap and marry without any fear or care, and will avariciously hoard up gold, silver, and say haughtily in our heart there is peace and joy, till swift destruction shall overtake us, (2 Thes. 2.) Let every one look well and watch. The messenger, with his peremptory summons is already at the door, who will say "Render an account," thou mayest continue steward no longer. (Luke 16.) But could we with the righteous, unwavering and pious Noah, believe the coming eternal wrath, and the promises through Christ, to all true children of God, we would, undoubtedly, not be found so attentive, drowsy and polluted, but would, with full earnestness without delay, rise from our abominable sin and grievous errors, and would shun wickedness as we would a hungry roaring Lion or a blood-thirsty enemy, we we should also watch with open eyes, lest the master of the house overtake us when we sleep and regard him not. And that he may not give our portion and lot, among the hypocrites, let us not strike our fellow servants, and eat and drink with the gormandizer. (Matt. 24.) Concerning this watching, read (Matt. 24, 25; Mark 13; Luke 12: 1 Thes. 5; 1 Pet. 3; Rev. 3.)

ABRAHAM'S FAITH AND OBEDIENCE.

Abraham the high-renowned patriarch, who had not his equal in honor, as Sirach writes. (Sirach 24.) For he believed God and trusted upon his word with the whole heart, and thus manifested obedience and power as the result of his faith, for as the Lord commanded him and said : "Get thee out of thine own country, and from thy kindred, and from thy father's house into a land that I will shew thee, and I will make thee a great nation, and I will bless thee, and make thy name great, and thou shalt be a blessing : and I will bless them that bless thee, and curse him that curseth thee, and in thee shall all families of the earth be blessed. (Gen. 12.) And when he heard the command, he believed his God and consulted not the ease of his body nor his natural reason, but renounced both, and did not strive nor dispute with God, in whom he trusted and by whose command he went forth ; he did not desire to know before hand into what land he should go. He believed his God with his whole heart, he was obedient and went forth at that hour, together with his wife not knowing where he should go.   He reposed firmly and surely upon the promise of God, who, would not deceive nor betray him, for he well knew that he was a God who was true and firm in all his words and that he would bring him into such a country as he had promised him.

Behold, how upright and perfect, how plain, obedient, and full of confidence is the christian faith, as may be seen in this patriarch.   Compare your faith and its fruits with Abraham's faith and its fruits, and I presume you will find that you have never yet become his faithful seed and children; for, it is manifest that you are stubborn, unbelieving, and disobedient, and so fleshly and earthly minded that you would not give a cottage, a bed, a cow or a horse, nor would endure a hard word for the sake of the word of the Lord, and his testimony; much less would you forsake father or mother, or the land of your birth, for the sake of your faith, and like Abraham, travel with wife and children to a foreign and unknown land.   Cursed unbelief keeps off the whole world from the truth; for, many of you says: We well know that you have the truth, but what dose it avail? We are poor and full of years, we cannot longer labor or earn; we have a house full of children and cannot earn our bread in other lands; we fear, also, that the Lord may not have such a care for us as he had for Abraham; others say we have much wealth—we are yet young in years, and may live long; father and mother hinder us.   The wife says: My husband opposes me—the husband says: My wife is against me, and the like unbelieving fleshly excuses and cares.   They never take to heart, nor understand, that Christ has richly promised you, that if you abide by his word, you shall receive all necessaries, as food, clothing, and shelter. (Matt. 6, 19; Mark 10; Luke 12.) I have been young but now I am old, (said David,) yet have I never seen the righteous man forsaken, nor his seed begging their bread. (Ps. 35.)

Faithful reader, observe, if we had a firm faith and a sure confidence, like as this godly man, and dare trust from the heart upon the living God, O how little should we trouble ourselves with such heathenish cares, concerning food, clothing, eating, drinking, &c.; for we well know, that Christ, God's only Son, has promised that if we seek the kingdom of heaven, and his righteousness, and turn our hearts to some honest labor, he will not forsake us to all eternity, but will supply us our necessities, (Matt. 6) for he cares for us. (1 Pet. 5.)

Observe further: When a message came to Abraham, that Lot, his brother's son, was taken to Sodom by Chederlaomar, the king of Elam, and his confederate kings, Abraham rose up

16*

with three hundred and eighteen of his servants and followed after the aforementioned kings; he overtook them in the night and slew them and re-took all their goods, together with Lot, the prisoners and their wives. (Gen. 14.)

Here the faithful patriarch manifested his love, the result of faith, and feared not the power of the four kings. He trusted in the living God, he sought not his own safety, nor the safety of his servants, but willingly risked all, in order that he might rescue his oppressed kinsman from the hands of his enemies. All spiritual children of Abraham should, after his example, love their brethren who are born of the incorruptible seed of the holy divine word, and not only assist them with money and goods, but also, when necessity requires, they should, in an *evangelical* manner, yield life itself for their sakes. (1 John 3.) I say in an *evangelical* manner, because aid with the sword, in the New Testament, is forbidden to all true christians. True believers must suffer patiently, and not fight and strive with swords and carnal weapons. If we desire, by the help of the spirit and word of the Lord, to save and gain our neighbor's soul, we would not close the door upon him when persecuted for the sake of the Lord's word, but we would receive him into our houses, and in his trouble we should give him our bread, assistance, comfort and aid. In such a case, it becomes us to risk our lives for our brethren, though we must be rewarded with death. This example we have of Christ, who for our sakes, did not spare himself, but willingly yielded his life, that we through him, might live. (Matt. 20, 26; John 10, 3; Pet. 2, 4; 1 John 4.)

In the third place, observe, that Abraham was promised that his seed should be numerous as the stars of heaven—that they should be strangers in another land that was not theirs, and they should be oppressed and compelled to serve four hundred years, &c. (Gen. 15.) When this promise was made he believed; he believed this, I say, and his belief was reckoned to him for righteousness. He waited with patience, and it was fulfilled in its time. (Heb. 6,) he murmured not, nor disputed with God, because his seed should suffer so greatly for so many years. An admonition to all true christians that they should cleave to the Lord's word, with all the heart, and should hold firmly to his promise; for God cannot forget or break his word; heaven and earth may pass away, but his word shall stand and abide eternally. All who trust there shall be reckoned as righteous. Faith was counted to Abraham. (Luke 21; Rom. 4; Gal. 3.) Through faith he saw the promise from afar; he saw it, (I say,) and comforted himself therewith. (Heb. 11.) In like manner also with us, the promise of the future, eternal life, is made in and through Christ, and we are informed that for his name's sake, we must suffer from this perverted and wicked generation. (John 3.) This promise will also, doubtless, be fulfilled in proper time, to all who trust therein, though long and sore they be oppressed by the evil Egyptian race. (Matt. 5.) For, although the children of Abraham were grieved with much sorrow and pain for some hundreds of years, yet did the Lord lead them forth victoriously, and gave them the land of promise. And thus it will be with us if we doubt not the promises, but receive them with a firm faith, as did Abraham, and through faith walk in all the commandments of God, possess our souls in patience and honor, fear, love, thank and serve the Lord. (Luke 21, 22; Exod. 12, 5.) How lamentably soever, we are here persecuted, oppressed, smitten, robbed and murdered by the hellish Pharaoh, and his fierce, unmerciful servants, or burned at the stake, or drowned in the water, yet shall the day of our salvation arrive, and all our tears shall be wiped from our eyes, and we shall be arrayed in the white silken garments of righteousness, and with Abraham, Isaac and Jacob, follow the Lamb and sit down in the kingdom of God and possess the precious, pleasant land of eternal peace. (Rev. 21; Rev. 6, 7, 19; Matt. 8; Luke 13.) Praise God, ye who suffer for Christ's sake and raise your heads, for the time is near when you shall hear: Come ye blessed of my father, and ye shall be eternally blessed. (Matt. 25.)

In the fourth place, observe, that Abraham received a command from God that he, and also his male children of eight days old, should be circumcised, with all his servants, those who who were born in his house, and those who were bought, and this should be a covenant sign between God and him. (Gen. 17.) He was not disobedient to or yet displeased with God, he did not complain nor murmur against him on account of the pain he should suffer in his old age, by obeying this command, nor because such a ceremony, from its very nature, must be thought disgraceful; and one, too, by which he could neither praise God nor serve his neighbor, but he heard and believed the Lord's word, and humbly and submissively followed it without delay. He well knew, that unless he would believe the word of God, he could obtain no grace, no blessing, no promise: For the obedient obtain the promise, (Lev. 26; Deut. 27, 28; Jer. 11; Matt. 7; John 15; 1 Cor. 7.)

The simple, plain submission and willing obedience of Abraham's faith, are made manifest by its fruits. For if he had followed flesh or blood, and reasoned with himself, he would, undoubtedly, not have so obeyed, but he would have entered into argument with God, and said: No, Lord, it shall not be so, for this sign will profit me nothing, for Thou art not praised thereby nor my neighbor served. All the heathens who know not thy great name will mock and scoff at it as foolishness, from the very nature of the ceremony. O no! He spake not against the Lord, but he believed and acted, and it was reckoned to him for righteousness, and he was called a friend of God. (James 2.)

This is for encouragement to the godly to believe the Lord's word, even though it may appear heretical and mockery. They willingly follow it. They strive and dispute not with the Lord, because he so commanded; but it is enough (I say) that they know that he has commanded and in what manner he has commanded.

Again, it shames all haughty despisers and unbelieving mockers, who so presumptuously open their mouths against Christ, and say: What can baptism profit us, or why does God demand water? It is enough, if we are inwardly godly men, regard the commands of love, and lead a godly, virtuous life, and such like hypocritical words, and these poor miserable hypocrites know not when the inward man, (of which they boast,) has become upright and godly by faith in the Lord's grace, word and spirit. No one must depart a hair's breadth from the word of the Lord, let it be what it will.

It is so manifest that the Lord Jesus has commanded water baptism, upon the profession of our faith, (Matt. 28; Mark 16,) be received it himself. (Matt. 3,) the holy apostles did not teach nor practise otherwise, (Acts 2, 8, 10, 16, 19,) their signification and effect were not otherwise, and so many glorious promises depend thereon as may plainly be seen and read, (Mark 16; Acts 2; Rom. 6; Cor. 12; Gal. 3; Eph. 5; Tit. 3; 1 Pet. 3,) not on account of the eternal rite, (understand me well,) but Christ and his word are received through faith. Say, beloved, how shall one obtain the accompanying promise if he does not do what is commanded? But what does it avail all who believe not the Lord's word, who would rather have money, goods, body and life, than Christ; they are earthly-minded, they strive against Christ, break the scriptures and say: What can water benefit us? But if they believed the word of the Lord from the heart, as did Abraham, and were new and changed men in Christ Jesus—through the power of the same faith, they would love their enemies, do good for evil, pray for those by whom they are persecuted, be ready to forsake possessions and all that they have and are, for the glory of the Lord, and for the necessary service of their neighbor. They would not reject the cross of the Lord, but flesh and blood would be mortified; they would fear God and his judgments, and love him, they would not murmur and dispute, but stand prepared, like Abraham, to shew their faith by its fruits; they would receive the commanded baptism, surrender themselves to all obedience, and according to their weakness, walk as the Lord commands all true Christians.

Since they believe not Christ and his word, they neither fear nor love him; hence it follows, that they reject, upbraid and blaspheme his holy doctrine, spirit, &c., as deceiving heresy, they esteem his obedience as an abomination. O reader, beware! God, the Lord, is a God who will adhere to his word; he brought calamity upon Adam, Eve and their posterity on account of the forbidden fruit. (Gen. 3.) Uzzah, for a small transgression, was punished with death. (2 Sam. 6.) The faithful Moses, on account of one transgression, was not permitted to enter the promised land. (Deut. 34.) Whoever received not the bloody sign of circumsision, was to be cut off from among the people. (Gen. 17.) Therefore, it must be plainly understood, that his word and will must be obeyed, otherwise there is no salvation, for he is the God who has made heaven and earth and the fullness thereof; the almighty and terrible God, who lives forever in his majesty and glory—the Lord and Ruler over all. Wo to him who speaks against him and despises his word and will. The works of such an one testify that he believes not on Christ, and whosoever believeth not, (as Christ himself declares,) is condemned already. (John 3.) Therefore, it is all in vain to excuse, or seek for evasion. Whoever is so unbelieving and stubborn that he will refuse God a handful of water, will not obey the command to love enemies, to mortify the flesh, to serve neighbors, and to take up the christian cross. I will commit this to the serious reader for reflection, in the fear of God.

I know for certain, that all your disputation, excuse and covering, are nothing but fig leaves, and your life is nothing but hypocrisy.

Observe, when the Lord had promised to Abraham, that at the end of the year he would return, and that Sarah, his wife, would have a son, whom he should call Isaac, and that he would make his eternal covenant with him and his seed after him, (Gen. 17, 18;) though he was near a hundred years old, and Sarah ninety, nevertheless, he doubted not. He did not think upon, or regard his own frailty and the barrenness of Sarah, but, firm and strong in faith, he trusted upon the promise of his God, and praised him for his grace. He knew that God was able to do what he promised. (Rom. 4.) Therefore, from this same Abraham, descended as many as the sands of the sea shore or the stars of the sky. (Heb. 11.)

Behold, most beloved, how an upright christian faith regards God as almighty and true, it knows that he can and will do all that he promised, and therefore, Abraham looked not upon the frailty and age of himself and Sarah. He doubted not the promised words, but believed without wavering, for he knew well, that the same God who created heaven and earth, (John 1,) who stretched the heavens abroad, and to the raging sea set an established bound, whose word sustains the earth in the midst of the water, who rules all with the word of his strength, and gives life to the dead, (Jer. 5 ; 2 Pet. 3,) could undoubtedly, when he chose, render that fruitful, which before was barren. (Heb. 1 ; Rom. 4.)

Since then, (I say) such a promise was made him by God, he doubted not, but hoped for that, which in nature, was not to be expected. Through faith in God, he received that which was promised to him : That the aged and barren Sarah should have a son. (Gen. 21 ; Heb. 11.) And thus it is spiritually with us—if we believe, with the whole heart. the promised word of grace, (which is the gospel of peace,) whereby the redemption from our sins, through the blood of the Lord, is made known ; so will also our dead conscience flourish and live ; we shall receive the spiritual Isaac, Christ Jesus, with the eternal blessing, and bring forth fruit. Christ has said : My mother and my brethren are those, who hear God's word and will, and do accordingly, (Luke 8 ; Matt. 12 ; Mark 3;) but whosoever believeth not, receives not Christ, but the wrath of God abides upon him. (John 3.)

Observe further, how severely the Lord tried the faith of Abraham, when he said : Take thy only son, Isaac, whom thou lovest, and go into the land of Moriah, and offer him there as a burnt offering upon the mountain which I will shew thee. Abraham heard the word of the Lord and was obedient. He took his son with him and went to the place, which the Lord had commanded him ; and when he came there, Isaac said : Father, behold here is fire and wood, but where is the lamb that shall be offered ? Abraham answered his son, and said : My son, the Lord will provide a lamb for the offering. (Gen. 22.)

O my most beloved, do reflect ! Observe the conduct and conversation of Abraham and his son. I suppose reason will tell you how full of trouble and grief the mind of the father was on account of his beloved son, for Abraham was flesh and blood as we are. That son, who was born to him in his old age, through the promise and gift of God—his only son born of a free woman—the desire, the joy and the peace of his heart—the staff of his age, through whom he received the comforting promise, must be slain and burned with fire.

How hard and sorely he was tried, yet did he not oppose God with a single word, nor contend and say : Why has thou given me a son since he must die ? Neither did he reprove the

Lord, by saying, that he had falsified his promise, for, it was through Isaac that the promise was made. But he confided in his God with his whole heart; he laid aside all reasoning and followed not sense nor flesh. He spared not his beloved son for the Lord's sake. He loved his God far above his child, and therefore, he refused not to offer him willingly as a burnt offering to Him from whom he received him. He bound him and lifted him upon the wood, and raised his hand and knife to slay him—he believed that God could again recall him from the dead. He was about to obey the command which he had received, when an angel spake from Heaven, saying: Lay not thy hand upon the lad, neither do thou any thing to him, for now I know that thou fearest God; seeing that thou has not withheld thy son, thy only son from me. (Gen. 22.) And thus the obedient, faithful Abraham received his son as a type of the resurrection. (Heb. 11.) The word of James is true: Abraham believed God, and it was reckoned to him for righteousness, and he is called the friend of God. (James 2.)

Beloved children, we must always stand confounded before God, when we compare our little faith and its fruit with the faith of Abraham. He refused not to travel in an unknown country, as soon as he was commanded. (Gen. 12.) He was a man full of peace, and sought not his own interest. (Gen. 13.) He released Lot out of the hands of his enemies. (Gen. 14.) He believed the promise concerning the promised land and seed. He murmured not on account of the long time nor of the oppression of his seed. (Gen. 15.) He suffered himself to be circumcised in advanced age. (Gen. 17.) He believed the Lord's promise concerning Isaac, and taught all his servants and children, that they should follow the way of the Lord, and do that which was right. (Gen. 18.) He was willing to offer Isaac as the Lord had commanded him. (Gen. 22.) This may truly be called faith.

So entirely was this pious man dead to himself, that he denied all his lusts, his will and mind, and loved his God alone. He trusted, feared, served and honored his God, with all his soul and heart, and walked according to his commandments, as is evidenced by his works. But what kind of faith our false-famed christians possess, who suffer themselves to think that they are the children of Abraham, I will let their fruits be the judge; for they covet and hoard, curse and swear, lie and cheat; they are proud and haughty; they eat and drink, are incontinent and fierce, they rob and pillage, are full of all idolatry and wickedness. Those who have a little light refuse to remove from one village to another, for the sake of the Lord's word and truth; they seek their own interests and esteem brotherly love but lightly, they are earthly minded; the Lord's promise and good-ness they regard not; they fear not his coming judgment, and punishment; they love the creature more than the Creator; His name be blessed forever.

In short, I know not what it is, in which they do not serve themselves and act contrary to the command of God. They boast notwithstanding, that they are the children of Abraham, and have his promise. Ah no! my friends, your prophets deceive you, and your false hopes delude you; as true as the Lord lives, if you believe not his word, from the whole heart, nor through the power of the same faith, walk in his ways—bring not forth the christian fruits of righteousness, nor follow the footsteps of this pious patriarch: you are not his seed and children, neither have you his faith nor his promise. But all who receive Christ in their hearts, through faith, and adhere to his word, are the children of Abraham, and fellow heirs of his promise, (Gal. 3,) for they are reckoned his seed. (Rom. 9.)

OF MOSES' FAITH AND FIDELITY.

Moses, a servant and messenger of God, was also found faithful, vigorous, living and active in his faith. He was called of the Lord, that he should lead Israel out of Egypt. Moses did not exalt himself to the high station of a prince and leader, but he humbled himself before God with all his heart; he said: Send, Lord whom thou wilt send, but what am I, that I should go to Pharoah and lead forth Israel? Beside, had I not a slow tongue from the time that thou spakest to thy servant. (Exod. 3, 4.) He refused so long, that the Lord was angry. With fear and trembling, he at last took upon himself the commanded duty, and surrendered himself to his God, in whom he trusted.

He went willingly before the fierce Pharoah, and shewed great wonders and power before him and all his servants. (Exod. 5, 7, 8, 9, 10.) He ransomed the people, through God's out-stretched arm and strong hand. (Exod. 14.) He divided the Red Sea and passed with Israel, unharmed, through the deep. (Exod. 32, 34.) He received the tables of stone on which were written the Lord's commands. (Gal. 3.) He caused bread to rain from heaven, and water to flow from the flinty rock. (Exod. 16, 17.) He prepared the tents and the ark of the testimony, as he was directed upon the mountain. He ordained the figurative priesthood, with all the duties, offerings, sanctifications, apparel, &c., according to the Lord's command. (Exod. 25, 30.)

He went with the people—pitched the tents, and took them up again at the command of the Lord. (Num. 9.) He gave them the Lord's statutes and laws. He stood as a faithful mediator between God and the people, when they had sinned, and he turned the wrath from Israel. He published idolatry, whoredom and stubbornness. He slew Sihon, king of the Amorites, and Og, king of Basham. The Lord was with him in all his works and ways. (Num. 9, 25, 16, 21; Exod. 23; Deut. 3.)

Through faith, says Paul, he refused to be called the son of Pharaoh's daughter, and chose rather to endure affliction with the people of God, than the pleasures of sin for a season. Esteeming the reproach of Christ greater 'riches than the treasure of Egypt, for he had respect unto the recompense of the reward; by faith he forsook Egypt, not fearing the wrath of the king: for he endured, as seeing him who is invisible. Through faith he kept the passover, and the sprinking of blood, lest he that destroyed the first born should touch them. (Exod. 12; Heb. 11.)

Good reader, regard the word of the Lord, for when we look upon such holy examples and contrast them with the insupportable pride, haughtiness, avarice, idolatry, disobedience and unfaithfulness of the Prince of the world, and with the hardened, mad unbelief of the common people, we shall know that they are far from the obedience and active faith of Moses. Yea, they are unbelieving heathens, and not Christians.

Moses *believed* his God, he *acted* rightly in all his transactions. He was kind, and was solicitous for the welfare of the people under his care. He was the meekest of mem. (Num. 12.) He served neither for gift nor reward—but obeyed the Lord's word—was faithful in all his house, (Heb. 3,) and faithfully prosecuted his duties in the fear of the Lord. He faithfully commanded out of the mouth of God, and in upright love faithfully admonished the people, that they and their descendants, from generation to generation, should hear and be obedient to the voice of the Lord God of their father's, and should follow no other customs, commandments, righteousness or worship, than he had taught or commanded them, till the new prophet— the teacher of righteousness, the blessed seed of Abraham— Christ Jesus should come. (Deut. 18.)

But if we go to our rulers, princes, lords, bishops, priests, monks, and all of those who boast of the name and faith of Christ, and if we measure their faith and obedience with the Lord's word, and should find any who seek Christ from the heart, fear, love, believe and trust him; who teach the ordinances, commands, sacraments and true worship of God, I fear

17

their number would be few. And though some there are, yet, alas! they must be a prey to the bloodthirsty.

I testify to you the truth, in Christ, and lie not. All who hear not Christ's voice, believe not his holy word, follow not his pure unblamable life, from the whole heart, in all humility, patience, meekness, obedience and love; they have not Moses operating, and living faith, but are after the contents of his doctrines already judged. (Deut. 18.) O, dear reader, beware! neither name nor force will avail you, but energy and action, if you would become happy, and not be condemned.

THE FAITH OF CALEB AND JOSHUA.

Joshua and Caleb, through faith, passed over Jordan and entered the promised land. For when Moses sent out the twelve spies to view and explore the country, he said: Get you up this way southward, and go up into the mountain, and see the land what it is, and the people who dwell therein, whether they be strong or weak, few or many; and what the land is that they dwell in, whether it be good or bad, and what cities they be that they dwell in, whether in tents or in strong holds. And what the land is, whether it be fat or lean, whether there be wood therein or not: and be ye of good courage, and bring of the fruit of the land. Now the time was the time of first-ripe grapes.

They went up and viewed the land, even as Moses had commanded them by the mouth of the Lord, and after forty days they came to Moses and Aaron, and to the whole congregation in the wilderness of Paran to Hadesh, carrying with them grapes, pomegranates and figs, saying: We came into the land whither thou sentest us, and surely it floweth with milk and honey, and this is the fruit of it. Moreover, we saw the children of Anak there.

And Caleb stilled the people before Moses, and said: Let us go up at once and possess it; for we are well able to overcome it. But the men that went up with him said, we be not able to go up against the people, for they are stronger than we. And they brought up an evil report of the land which they had searched unto the children of Israel, saying: The land through which we have gone to search it, is the land that eateth up the inhabitants thereof, and all the people that we saw in it are men of great stature; and there we saw the giants, the sons of Anah, who came of the giants; and we were in our own sight as grasshoppers, and so we were in their sight. (Num. 13.)

And all the congregation lifted up their voice and cried; and the people wept that night, and all the children of Israel murmured against Moses and against Aaron, saying : Would to God that we had died in the land of Egypt, or would to God that we had died in the wilderness, and wherefore hath the Lord brought us to this land, to fall by the sword, that our wives and our children should be a prey. Would it not be better for us to return to Egypt? And they said one to another : Let us make a captain, and let us return to Egypt. Then Moses and Aaron fell on their faces before all the assembly of the congregations of Israel. And Joshua and Caleb rent their clothes, and spake unto all the congregation of Israel, saying, the land which we passed through to search it, is an exceeding good land. If the Lord delight in us, then he will bring us into this land and give it us ; a land which floweth with milk and honey. Only rebel ye not against the Lord, neither fear ye the people of the land, for they are bread to us : their defence is departed from them, and the Lord is with us : fear them not. But all the congregation bade stone them with stones. (Num. 14.)

Behold, dear reader, it is because these two faithful men believed the word and promise of God, with all their hearts, they trusted firmly in his almighty power, paternal mercy and great works, as if they had already obtained them. They saw the heinous unbelief and heard the bitter murmuring of their brethren, that they thereby detracted from the almighty Majesty, as if he were not able to fulfil his promises unto them, and that he had deceived them by his enticing words, therefore, they were very sorrowful and sad, and rent their clothes, as has been said. And therefore they were the only two persons of six hundred thousand, that came with Moses out of Egpyt, who entered into the promised land. All the rest died in the wilderness during the time of forty years, and they did not reach the promised land, because they did not believe on the almighty and powerful God, the God of their fathers, of Abraham, Isaac and Jacob, who, with such unheard-of signs and wonders, led them forth through the Red Sea, and so graciously upheld and guarded them in the wilderness.

Thus, alas, it is with some at the present day. They have spied the pleasant land—have seen and tasted its precious fruits. They have been enlightened by the word of the Lord, and have tasted of the heavenly gifts, have partaken of the Holy Ghost, have tasted of the sweet word of God, and the power of the world to come, (Heb. 6,) they have beheld the grace of the Lord, but since they consult not God, but their own sinful, disobedient, evil flesh, they seek their own, and bear not willingly the cross of the Lord. They behold with carnal eyes that so many powerful tyrants and fenced cities are arrayed against them—that they have to pass a howling wilderness, and must ascend many high mountains;—that they must surrender reputation, possessions, relations, body and life, as a prey. Hence they murmur against Moses and Aaron, and seek to stone Joshua and Caleb.   They give to their poor teachers and leaders, (who with true love direct to Christ's word and examples, and preach the pure truth,) such intolerable suffering.   They backbite and defame them beyond measure, and chose to themselves a false teacher, who, with fair words and under the appearance of good, shall lead them back to Egypt.   They prefer temporal to eternal things, they fear perishing man more than the immortal, eternal God, the Lord and Creator of the world. With unbelieving Israel, they say in their hearts : We are not strong enough to go up against this great and strong people, and are not able to obey and follow Christ's doctrine and ordinances and example : for the world is against us, all lords and princes persecute us, the preachers and priests upbraid and defame us, and we must become a by-word and a derision to all the world.   We are much too weak to bear such great misery. Thus you think and err, for your unbelieving, fleshly hearts have so blinded you, that you know not God's righteous judgment, you hope not that a holy life shall be rewarded, you esteem not the honor of an unblamable soul. (Sap. 2.)

Dear reader, take warning, for as true as the Lord lives, all those who cast aside the word of the Lord, and trust not on God, who are earthly and fleshly minded, who fear those whom they ought not to fear, and fear not those whom they should fear, who think more of the perishable creature as possessions, relatives, body and life, than of the everlasting God and his eternal kingdom, and have a greater desire to enjoy in peace, for a season, the dark Egypt of this ungodly world, than to inherit the pleasant fruitful land, with endless peace with God,—such shall all fall in the wilderness, and, unless they repent, shall never enter into his rest.   (Heb. 3, 4.)

But those who, with Caleb and Joshua, hold firmly to the word of the Lord, and believe on Christ, as the scriptures direct, are firmly assured in their heart by the Holy Ghost, that God will not fail in a single word, but will accomplish in its time, all that he has promised.   He will not suffer them to be prevailed against by the gate of hell, nor to be deceived by the subtle lies and philosophy of the learned, nor to be alarmed by the tyranny of the blood-thirsty, nor to be overcome by fleshly lusts, nor to be bewitched by the fair appearance of false prophets; they walk humbly in their King's highway, they follow Christ, their shepherd and leader.   They judge their ways by his spirit, word, and unblamable example, they turn not aside, either to the right hand or the left.   They, with all saints and believers, take possession of the promised land—the eternal rest and peace —God's eternal kingdom and glory, and will forever inherit the grace of Christ, as Joshua and Caleb possessed the figurative land through faith, and with their children inherit it. O children believe! All things, saith Christ, are possible to those who believe. (Mark 9.)

OF THE BELIEF OF THE PIOUS JOSIAH.

Josiah, an illustrious and pious king in all his works, did that which was pleasing to the Lord, and walked in all the ways of his father David and departed not therefrom either to the right hand or to the left.   And when he was yet a child he began to seek the God of David his father.   And in the eighteenth year of his age he sent Shaphan to Hilkiah the high priest that money might be given to those who worked at the house of the Lord. And Hilkiah said to Shaphan : I have found the book of the Law in the house of the Lord, and Hilkiah gave the book to Shaphan and he brought it to the king.   And when the king heard the words of the law, he rent his clothes, as one who feared his God. He believed the Lord's word and feared the coming wrath which he threatened in the book which was found.   He then commanded Hilkiah, Ahakim, Achbor, and Shaphan saying: Go and inquire of the Lord for me, and for the people, and for all Judah, concerning the words of this book that is found, for great is the wrath of the Lord that is kindled against us, because our Fathers have not hearkened unto the words of this book, to do according to all that is written concerning us.

So they went to Huldah a prophetess, the wife of Shallum and asked her as Josiah had commanded them ; the woman answered them, thus saith the Lord God of Israel, tell the man who hath sent you unto me ; Thus saith the Lord, behold I will bring evil upon the place, and upon the inhabitants thereof even all the words of the book which the king of Judah hath read, because they have forsaken me, and have burned incense to other gods, that they might provoke me to anger, with all the works of their hands, therefore, my wrath shall be kindled against this place and shall not be quenched.   But to the king of Judah, which sent you to enquire of the Lord, thus shall ye say to him.   Thus saith the Lord God of Israel, as touching the words which thou hast heard, because thine heart was tender, and thou hast humbled thyself before the Lord, when thou heardest what I spake against this place and against the inhabitants thereof, that they should become a desolation and a curse, and hast rent thy clothes and wept before me, I also have heard thee, saith the Lord.   Behold, therefore, I will gather thee to thy fathers, and thou shalt be gathered into thy grave in peace, and thine eyes shall not see all the evil which I will bring upon this place, and they brought the king word again.

When now the king heard these words, he sent and gathered unto him all the elders of Judah and Jerusalem.   And the king went up into the house of the Lord, and all the men of Judah and all the inhabitants of Jerusalem with him, and the priests and all the prophets and the people both great and small, and he read in their ears all the words of the book of the covenant, which was found in the house of the Lord.   And the king stood by a pillar, and made a covenant before the Lord to walk after the Lord and to keep his commandments, and his testimonies, and his statutes with all their heart, and all their soul to perform the words of the covenant that were written in this book. And all the people stood to the covenant.   And he caused all to serve the Lord, and they departed not from him as long as Josiah lived.

Here, dear reader, observe what kind of faith and fruits were possessed by Josiah.   He heard and believed the word of the Lord.   He rent his clothes, enquired of the Lord and renewed the covenant because he heard what God had commanded in the same book.   That they should not do according to their own thoughts, and that they should not follow after strange Gods, nor the abominations of the Canaanites and the other heathens which were dispersed before them, but they should serve the Lord alone and cleave to him, and keep his commands as he directed them.   He was strong in the Lord, resolved in a manly spirit, and acted valiantly in all his doings, for he believed and trusted God with all his strength : and with earnest zeal, he tore down all that his forefathers, and former kings out of their own imaginings and choice had brought in and established as holy service.

He burnt all the vessels of Baal and tore down all the groves, high places and altars, in the land of Judea and Samaria.   He prepared Tophet, which is in the valley of the children of Hinnom.   He destroyed the horses of the sun, and burned the chariots of the sun with fire. (Jer. 7.)   He broke down the altar of Bethel and offered the idolatrous priests and the dead bones thereupon, as the man of God had spoken aforetime (1 Kings, 23.)   He destroyed all that was opposed to the law of God.   He kept the passover of the Lord as it was written in the book of the covenant, in such a glorious manner as no judge or king had kept it before. He also destroyed all sooth-sayers and wizards, images and idolatry with all abomination, which existed in Judah or Jerusalem, in order that they might adopt the words which were written in the book of the law that Hilkiah, the High priest had found in the house of the Lord: and like unto him there was no king that turned to the Lord with all his heart and all his soul, and with all his might, according to the law of Moses; neither after him arose there any like him. (2 Kings 22, 23; 2 Chron. 34, 35.)

Hear now, O ye great princes and kings, and all those who suffer themselves to think that they are faithful Lords and christian princes, to you is my admonition! Have you any fear of God? any love to Christ or his blessed word? or is there yet any sincerity of nature with you, who have understanding? Then know that you are not gods from heaven; but poor dying men of Adam's impure, guilty race. Humble yourselves under the powerful and almighty hand of God, and compare Josiah with his faith and works with your faith and works, in order which you may learn to know how far you are from the spirit and word of Christ, and that you bear nothing else than a mere, idle, vain, empty name.

Whilst Josiah was yet a child, and young in years, he feared God, and manifested a mature mind and understanding in all his works; but you, my dear Lords, fear neither God nor the devil; cursed unbelief is your mother and unrighteousness your sister. In divine things you are blind, deaf, mute; yea, during your whole life, you are as destitute of understanding as children.

Josiah was eight years old when he was made king, and in the eighth year of his reign, he began to seek the God of David his father; but you, from your youth follow nothing but pride, haughtiness of heart, wantonness and sport, you seek to enlarge your kingdom, to increase your treasures, to cause wars and uproars and to oppress the poor and miserable. One seeks to glory over another and as much as in you is, to live in all liberty of the flesh full of all lust. The open deed testifies that I write the truth.

Josiah began in the twelfth year of his reign to purify Judah and Jerusalem from the high places, groves, idolatry and molten images, (2 Chron. 34,) but you build them in every city, village, street and alley—upon every high mountain and in every deep valley, and whoever would admonish you with the spirit and word of Christ, he must be a heretic and must tread the press of affliction.

Joseph was solicitous for the house of the Lord, and appointed and paid artificers to labor thereat. But you break down, and, by your vindictive mandates, tyranny and the sword, oppose the house and dwelling of the Christ, which is his church, which he has sanctified by his spirit, cleansed by his blood, and adorned by his father's word, ordinances and sacraments. You prevent it from being rebuilt in its apostolic clearness, and from becoming perfect in its doctrines, sacraments and conduct, according to the command of Christ and his holy word.

Josiah expelled all soothsayers and wizards. He offered the idolatrous priests upon their idolatrous altars, and burned the dead bones, &c., but the bones of the man of God from Judah, and of the prophets of Samaria, he burned not. But you sustain and cherish as shepherds of Christ and keepers of your souls, false prophets and deceiving priests; the greater part of whom are open drunkards, libertines and idolators, full of all unrighteousness, covetous in heart, whose belly is their god, dumb dogs, who dishonor God, destroy poor miserable souls, and are blind watchmen as shepherds of the flocks of Christ. You have them in preference in your courts and give them the highest seats at your tables   (2 Pet. 2; Phil. 3; Isa. 56; John 10.) They are honored with high names and great titles—they are greeted by every one as doctors, lords and masters. You present them splendid dwellings, great rents and possessions, and say: They who serve the gospel must live of the gospel; although they do nothing but place soft pillows and cushions under you, and preach according to the itching of your ears. But the true, pious teachers and servants of Christ, who cordially seek your salvation and that of the whole world—who direct to Christ—who rightly use his sacraments and ordinances —who desire to lead you and all men on the right way—and who walk unblamably, they must without mercy or decency be persecuted by you, sentenced to fire and water, and must bear mockery and shame before all the world.

Josiah made a covenant with the Lord, and with the elders, priests, prophets and people, that they should serve the Lord as long as they lived, &c. But you have made your covenant with anti-christ and with all your preachers, priests, monks, judges and rulers, that the perverted, broad way should be pursued, the doctrines and institutions of men should be taught, followed and observed, instead of the true service of God; to Christ's people, doctrine, commands, spirit, supper, life and separation, you give no place, and whoever acts or speaks contrary to your abominations, must lose his possessions or his life.

Josiah heard the word of the Lord and became contrite in heart. He rent his clothes and wept before the Lord; he feared the coming wrath, because they and their forefathers had rejected the word of God. But you, O my dear lords, are so hardened and blind through cursed unbelief, so bound by your sins and fleshly lusts, and so bewitched by false prophets, that we cannot prevail on you to repent, by the threatening law of God, nor by his fierce wrath, and terrible judgment, by the devouring flames of hell and eternal death, nor by the peaceful gospel, the precious blood of Christ, the pious unblamable life of the saints, who with the simple *yea* and *nay*, are daily slaughtered, like innocent sheep, on account of their faith and righteousness. It is time that you awake, and behold how you and we with our forefathers, so abundantly merited God's righteous punishment and wrath, on account of our sins. May the merciful Lord grant to you eyes that you may see,

Josiah turned to the Lord with his whole heart, soul and might, but you dare proudly disregard the God who has created you, deny the Lord who has purchased you, and turn yourselves to dumb idols, to wood, stone, gold and silver—to water, bread and wine—to the unprofitable doctrines and commandments of men, yea, to open abominations and idolatry, not observing that it stands written: Idolators shall have their part in the lake which burns with fire and brimstone. (Rev. 21.)

Behold, dear sirs, the above is true. I can prove it by your pride, whoredom, fleshly life, and by the ruins of burnt countries and cities, the great number of churches, cloisters, priests and monks and the matins, vespers, and other false worship.

Besides, when we, on account of our sins, are visited with pestilence, famine, war, and other dangerous evils and plagues, your only remedies, to appease the wrath of God, and quench the burning fire of his anger, are masses, processions (as they are called) dead bones, images, crosses, banners. They, the papists, I mean, bear these strange abominations, and follow after them with uncovered heads, folded hands, and burning candles, &c. Therefore, you turn not aside the fierce wrath, but augment it more and more, for the Lord will not give his divine honor to works of man's choice nor to any creature, neither does he accept any such masses, processions, crosses, images and abominations, nor regards them in his mind, as the prophet said. (Jer. 7.)

Beloved sirs, repent. The statute book of Christ is entirely lost to you. Christ and his truth, sacraments, spirit and life, you have never known nor possessed in the least degree. You serve strange gods—you listen to, follow and use anti-christ's doctrine, sacraments, ordinances and commands, you lead an unclean, ungodly and sensual life. O sirs, take warning! your sins have arisen to heaven. (Rev. 18.)

And although it is so little regarded by you, (God grant it

may be otherwise) yet this book of Christ has been found again by some. The pure unadulterated truth has come to light, through the pure unmingled gospel, and is daily read in your ears, and explained before your eyes with a godly, virtuous life, with an open confession, and, above all, with much of the property and blood of the saints, still your hearts continue stony and hard; you cannot be moved nor turned either by grace or wrath, by adversity or prosperity, as we have said. Behold thus has the blindness of Sodom, the darkness of Egypt, the hardening of Pharoah, through the righteous judgment of God, come upon our kings, princes, lords and rulers.

Dear sirs, awake! and make haste, the trumpet is sounded, prepare yourselves: your mortal sickness and cankering wounds are shown to you. I counsel you to suffer yourself to be helped, you possess neither Christ nor his word. Your controversy is against the Lamb and his chosen. (Rev. 17.) Your way is in darkness, and leads to the abyss of hell. The wrath of the Lord has gone forth over you and your land, for you live more carnally and evil than can be imagined or described.

O my dear sirs! reform, repent so that you may stand before God, cleanse your hands and hearts before the Lord; change your pride, into humility, and your mirth, and joy into sorrow; rend your hardened hearts, and your garments, (James 4; Joel 2,) hear and seek Christ, and not anti-christ; implicitly obey Christ's spirit, doctrine, commands and infalible example, and not the vain doctrines and commandments of men, for they corrupt and profit not.

Put away from among you, all offence, abominations and idolatry, masses, altars, infant baptism, the idolatrous bread, or supper, (I mean such as used by the world) images, confessions, the wanton sodomy, unchastity of the papistic priests and monks; destroy and root up all accursed heathen disgrace; such as brothels, every species of gambling, open houses of drunkenness, together with idolatrous temples, high places, groves, churches and cloisters, which were so numerously built contrary to the scriptures by our forefather, through blindness and ignorance.

We call on all, poor deceiving teachers and false sects, great and small, who are against Christ's spirit, ordinances, word and life sincerely to repent, and help us to resist, not by power, tyranny or sword; as, alas! it is the custom with you, but by the spirit of Christ, with doctrine, exhortation and the like virtuous services and mild means, so that they may turn from evil, hear Christ and follow him only,

Permit all faithful messengers and servants of God to preach Christ, to use his sacraments and ordinances according to the scriptures: lead a penitent and unblamable life, and gather Christ a glorious community through the spirit and grace of God, according to the scriptures. (1 Cor. 11.)

Again I say, reform, you have erred and mocked God too long, and prayed too long to anti-christ, and walked too long in the perverse and hard way of death. Awaken! it is high time, the true law, Christ's saving, pure gospel is found, which was covered for so many centuries by the abominations of anti-christ.

Hear and read attentively, believe and observe it faithfully; it is the word of the Lord God, which Jesus Christ the almighty Father's first and only begotten, brought from heaven and taught us. Bow to his righteous sceptre, fear, love, serve, honor and follow him with all your heart, with all your soul and with all your powers, as did the pious Josias. For the Lord our God, is Lord of lords, and God of gods, mighty, terrible, neither, honoring nor fearing any one. (Deut. 10)

Yes, beloved sirs, can you thus convert yourselves with all your hearts? can you change your hearts? can you humble yourselves before God? deny yourselves? seek and follow Christ and his righteousness? renounce the world and flesh with all its lusts, (Wis. 6 ; Acts 10 ; Rom. 10 ; Gal. 2 ; Eph. 6 ; Col. 3 ; James 2,) as you have heard ? Then you will become, true, spiritual kings, priests, and mighty; you will possess your souls in peace, gain the victory and conquest over all the deadly enemies of your souls ; you will live in grace, and die in grace ; and you may in truth be called christian kings and believing princes. The testimony of Peter to all christians, I say to all christians, is : Ye are a chosen generation, a holy nation, a peculiar people. (1 Pet. 2.)

But if you refuse this and remain what you are now, preferring perishing, temporal pleasures and joys, to the imperishable, eternal joy and glory ; I would then that you would reflect upon what Sirach says : Why are earth and ashes proud ? He that is to-day a king, to-morrow shall die. (Sir. 10.) Yea, what are they all who are of Adam, dust and ashes, a passing wind, a vapor, poor, miserable, mortal flesh, food for worms, yea men, and not God. O, Sirs, take warning, awake and reform yourselves! God is Lord, who will judge you. Once more, take warning.

Behold, my kind reader, here you have before you a few examples of true faith, as Noah and Abraham, before the giving of the law, and Moses, Joshua, Caleb and Josiah, under the law, whereby you may learn, how a true christian faith abounds in all manner of fruits and virtues ; what the true faith always was, as may be seen in Abel, Enoch, Isaac, Jacob, Joseph,

Jephtha, Baruch, Gideon, Sampson, Rahab, Samuel, David, Ezekiel, Elias, Helias and others. Now, I will by the grace of God, present you with a few examples from the New Testament, whereby you may very clearly learn what an indiscribably great power, fruit, life and energy, a true evangelical christian faith in its true nature always includes. So that you will not, through a false notion, conform to this ignorant, unbelieving world, who boast and pretend that their fruitless, dead opinion and historical knowledge of Christ, is a sincere, evangelical faith.

OF THE CENTURION'S FAITH OF CAPERNAUM.

It so happened at the time when the Lord Jesus entered Capernaum, that a Centurion's servant lay sick, whom he loved much. When he heard that Jesus was there, he had the consent of some of the elders of the Jews, and sent them with a request to Jesus, that he would come to him and restore his sick servant, and Jesus went with them. And not being far from the Centurion's house, he sent some of his friends to him, who said : Lord trouble not thyself; for I am not worthy that thou shouldst enter under my roof, (here notice his humility,) and I did not think myself worthy personally to call and see thee ; but speak the word, and my child shall be healed. He acknowledged that all must bow to Christ and his word. I also am a man set under authority, having under me soldiers, and I say unto one : Go, and he goeth ; and to another come, and he cometh ; and to my servant do this, and he doeth it. As if he would say to Christ : Behold, Lord, I am but a man, and have to serve the councils at Rome, nevertheless, I have so much power over my servants, that they must obey what I command them ; but thou, Lord, art such a Lord that all the mighty have to bow to thee, all that is in heaven above and on earth beneath, must yield to thee. If thou but command sickness and death, they will have to obey thee, and leave my child. And again, if thou command health and life, they will have to return again. Therefore, it is not necessary that thou shouldst come into thy unworthy servant's house ; Lord, only speak the word, and my child will again be restored. When Jesus had heard these words, he was quite astonished, and said to the people that followed : Verily, I say unto you, I have not found so great faith, no, not in Israel. (Matt. 8 ; Luke 7 ; John 4.)

Behold, faithful reader, here you have the centurion as a living example, by which you may learn how a true christian faith humbles itself before God, and doubts not the power of God, and how kindly and graciously he deals with his poor servants, be they male or female. He was moved with compassion towards his poor servant, and had great concern for him, that he spared no pains to trouble the elders of the Jews to send to Christ and entreat him to come and heal his sick servant. This is to the disgrace of all false christians, and especially to many rich, some of whom are more severe on, and have less feeling for, the servants and hirelings, than they have for their domestic animals; for as soon as the servants sicken a little, so that they cannot perform all manner of drudgery, they are unmercifully turned out of doors, and sent to this, or that tavern, or to their parents and friends, who scarce have bread to satisfy their wants. Others again, have to get a substitute in their place, while sick, and pay him out of their own earned pittance. And if they even do fulfil their engagements with hard and severe labor, still, some of these unmerciful, blood-thirsty, treat these innocent ones, (who have to watch when they sleep, labor when they rest, run when they command, stand when they sit,) in such a manner, as to take the greater portion of their earnings, or scandalize them; now, say they, a spoon is lost; anon, a dish is broken; in short, they always speak evil of them and can never be pleased. Yea, if some of them could feed them upon water or straw, and pay them with the whip and chaff, even as they do their laboring oxen and horses, if they were not afraid and ashamed of men, they would not be ashamed before God, alas, whom they know not. O wo, unto such heathen tyranny and unmerciful cruelty!

The centurion calls his servant *his child*, by which he manifests his paternal love and humility towards his poor servant. Though he was lord, and held in high honor, nevertheless, he did not exalt himself above his poor servant, well knowing, that one God had created them, that they were born of one seed, and had one origin. But what conduct such heathen christians do manifest towards their oppressed servants, their actions, alas, openly show!

How lamentably some of the poor children are despised by them. How many disgraceful words have they to hear, and how many sore stripes to endure. Their cursed swearing and threatning and rash words, continue from morning till night. Some of them make their girls prostitutes and sluts; yea, why speak more, they esteem their servants as filth—as nothing—and even so do some of them, especially the rich, esteem these poor children. Ah! reader, it is all much worse than I can describe it; it is indeed time that they would look into these things, and reflect more deeply upon love.

18

The centurion humbled himself before the Lord with all his heart, esteeming himself not worthy that He should come under his roof. But our haughty, proud heathens strut about with puffed up hearts and extended necks, high-minded, idle, and daring; one boasts of his family, another of his wealth, a third of his wisdom, a fourth of his skill and beauty, &c., and the innocent and meek Christ, who says: Learn of me; for I am meek and lowly in heart, (Matt. 11;) of whose name, word, death and blood they falsely boast, they hear and know not.

The centurion believed, that Christ was mighty and able to do all by his word what he desired to do; but this miserably benighted people esteem it no more than they do Lucian and Æsopian fables. Hence it is, that they lead such an impenitent and carnal life, and use such idolatrous sacraments and false worship, and have departed so far from the true King's highway, still they would be the true apostolic church and the believing community of Christ; but even as Christ testified and said of the centurion; that he found not such faith in Israel; so we might, on the other hand, testify and say of this people, that such a heedless, revengeful, haughty, proud and unmerciful unbelief is unknown among the heathens, and is not to be found with them, who never heard of the word of Christ. Behold, thus does the righteous Lord let those err and fall into blindness of heart, who so little regard his most holy word, and hate and thrust from them his grace, goodness, spirit, knowledge and faith.

But it is not so with you, my most beloved, take this sincere and pious centurion as an example, imitate him in his faith, love, humility and virtues, and be as solicitous for your servants, as he was for his, teach, admonish and reprove them kindly, as oft as they do err; set them an unblamable example, in all righteousness and piety; and have compassion with their severe labor; comfort them in their poverty; comfort, and grieve them not, supply them with their necessary wants, food and their earned hire, and do not curtail them; protect them in all honorable things; contend not with them without cause, lest they become timid; do not drive them away from you, but let them unmolestedly serve out their time as agreed lest the name of the Lord be blasphemed; be at all times friendly towards them, and if they are weak and sick, assist and minister to them; get others to serve in their place, without detriment to them; till the Lord take them hence, or restore them to health; sympathize with, and be merciful towards them, assist them in all their need; lift not your hearts above them, do not despise them, for they are your brethren according to the flesh. In short, be you so minded in love towards them as Christ was towards you. Remember, that we also have a Lord in heaven, before whose judgment-seat we must appear and render an account of all our works. (Eph. 6; Col. 3; Rom. 2, 14; 2 Cor. 5.)

But if they are wanton and obstinate, and will not hear nor follow your admonition and counsel, would rule and not serve; waste their time and not labor industriously; are unfaithful, resist and murmur; ruin your house and children, are roguish, &c.; *then* agree with them and bring the matter, touching their wages, before two or three witnesses, so that the blame may not rest upon you, and the word of the Lord be not evil spoken of. In such case then, let them be dismissed, that your good conscience be not disturbed on their account, and your house and children be depraved. Yea, my brethren, you should do to your poor hirelings, even as you desire that it should be done to you, being called with them. This the law and the prophets teach. (Matt. 7.)

OF THE FAITH OF ZACCHEUS THE PUBLICAN.

It happened, says Luke, that Jesus passed through Jericho; and behold, there was a man, called Zaccheus, chief among the publicans, (or public sinners,) and he was sick, and he sought to see Jesus, who he was, but could not for the press, because he was little of stature; and he ran before, and climbed up into a sycamore tree, or as some say, upon a wild olive tree, to see him; for he was to pass that way—and when Jesus came to the place, he looked up, and saw him, and said to him: Zaccheus, make haste, and come down; for to-day I must abide at thy house. And he made haste, and came down, and received him joyfully, and said to him: Behold, Lord, the half of my goods I give to the poor; and if I have taken any thing from any man by false accusation, I restore him four fold. Jesus said to him: This day is salvation come to this house, for as much as he is also a son of Abraham. (Luke 19.)

Paul says: For whatsoever things were written afore time were written for our instruction; (Rom. 15,) and though we know Zaccheus's faith, fruit, mercy, love and true conversion, it avails us nothing, if we do not practise and come up to his faith, with its contrite, pious fruits. I, therefore, entreat all my readers, who live openly in sin; all the wealthy, avaricious, all unrighteous merchants and grocers, all financiers and bankers, all who love money; judges, lawyers and advocates, all preachers, priests and monks, all drunkards, hosts and guests, together with all those who deal in unlawful gain. I entreat all by the love of our Lord and Saviour, Jesus Christ, that they would take notice of, with an understanding heart, this history and narrative touching Zaccheus, in order that they may learn therefrom, that they do not yet possess the right, true faith and that christianity, which avails with God; and that they have nothing but a fruitless, vain boasting of Christ and of faith.

Zaccheus was chief of the publicans, and he received Christ joyfully in his house and heart. He believed and was renewed; he reformed his life, and departed from his former evil ways. But it is clearer than day-light that our open transgressors do not reform their old ungodly life, and hence they desire not Christ and his faith of which they boast.

Zaccheus was rich, and one half of his wealth he gave to the poor. But our rich people seek more and more, how they may increase their money and possessions, build their houses splendidly, and add farm to farm. They do not defend the cause of the poor and needy—they are unmerciful, proud, avaricious and wanton; do not remember what is written concerning them. Go to now, ye rich men, weep and howl for your miseries that shall come upon you; your riches are corrupted, and your garments are moth-eaten; your gold and silver are cankered, and the rust of them shall be a witness against you, and shall eat your flesh as it were fire. (James 5.) Neither do you reflect on what David says: I have seen the wicked in great power, and spreading himself like the green bay-tree; yet he passed away, and lo, he was not: Yea, I sought him, but he could not be found. (Ps. 37.) Ah! what a hard saying which the Lord uttered: Wo unto you that are rich, for ye have received your consolation. (Luke 6.) It is easier, says he, for a camel to pass through the eye of a needle, than for a rich man to enter into the kingdom of God. (Matt. 19; Mark 10.)

Zaccheus said to the Lord: if I have taken any thing from any man by false accusation, I restore it to him four fold. But our miserably avaricious never desist defrauding their neighbor. For the whole world, both man and woman, are greedy after unlawful gain, that it cannot be fully thought of, related or described.

Lords and princes daily invent new sins and practices, that they may increase their dominions, interests, tolls and rents. They impose upon and exact, hoard up and seize without bounds or mercy; they draw the very marrow from the bones of the poor, and show by their actions, that they are companions of those of whom it is written: Thy princes are rebellious, and companions of thieves, &c. (Isa. 1.) O that he knew Christ, would repent, cease to do evil, and would reflect more on love.

Judges, lawyers and advocates also seek all artifice and advantage to entrap; for they all serve for gifts and money, with few exceptions; for if they did not expect profit or gain, I am persuaded that burgomasters and judges would be few in the whole empire. For the sake of gain, they sit and judge, and they often encourage causes for the sake of a fee. Some of them pervert law and right for a gift's sake, and do not reflect what Jehoshaphat said to the judges: Take heed what ye do; for ye judge not for man, but for the Lord, who is with you in judgment; wherefore now let the fear of the Lord be upon you; take heed and do it; for there is no iniquity with the LORD our God, nor respect of persons, nor taking of gifts. (2 Chron. 19)

Captains, riders, servants and such like bloody men, are ready to serve for gain's sake, swear that they will destroy cities and countries, take citizens and inhabitants, kill them and take their possessions from them, although they never harmed them, nor gave them provocation. O God! what execrated, ungodly abominations and traffic. And still it must be said, that they protect the country and people, and that they assist in administering justice!

Priests, monks and preachers are equally bent upon unlawful gain. They are not shocked to make, alas, God's only and first begotten Son, his eternal Wisdom, the one and only foundation of heaven and earth, Jesus Christ, with his holy apostles, to be open false witnesses, heretics, and deceivers; for Christ says: *He that believeth and is baptized, shall be saved.* (Luke 16.) But they say: *He that believeth and is baptized, is a heretic, and shall be damned.* Christ says: *But if thou wilt enter into life, keep the commandments.* (Matt. 19.) But they say: *None can keep God's commandments.*

Paul says, (Rom. 8,) If ye live according to the flesh ye shall die. Again: neither the unrighteous, nor the covetous, nor drunkards, nor revilers, nor fornicators, proud, avaricious, the unchaste and the like, shall not inherit the kingdom of God. (1 Cor. 6.) But they say: We are poor sinners—who can always live as the scriptures teach? Christ died for sinners, and the like consolations, whereby they deny Christ and his word, and thus they encourage the whole world, rich and poor, great and small, in their hardened and wicked life, that there are, alas, few who truly repent; or seek after God: they preach what the ignorant blind world desires, that they may quietly enjoy Balaam's reward, in cloisters, that they may lead an epicurian life without care, and they, poor creatures, know not that they are those of whom it is written: Wo unto them! for they have gone in the way of Cain, and ran greedily after the error of Balaam for reward, and perished in the gainsaying of Core, (Jude 1,) accursed people. (2 Pet. 2.) O God that they would beware!

The unrighteous merchants and grocers, I say the unrighteous, for I do not mean those who are righteous and pious, together with all those who are avaricious, and bent upon accursed gain, so that they exclude God from their hearts; for if they buy any thing, they say it is worth but little, but when they have it praise and recommend it as the best article. Thus defame what they should praise, and praise what they should with propriety esteem not at all. Lying and swearing, using many vain words, adulterate their goods, in order that they may defraud the people. Sell, lend and trust to the needy, with great gain and usury. Never reflecting, that it is written: If thou sell aught to thy neighbor, or buyest aught of thy neighbor's hand, ye shall not oppress one another. (Lev. 25.)

I would that they might more seriously lay to heart Sirach's doctrine: A merchant shall hardly keep himself from doing wrong: and a huckster shall not be freed from sin: for many have sinned for a small matter: and he that seeketh for abundance will turn his eyes away; as a nail sticketh fast between the joinings of the stones, so doth sin stick close between selling and buying. Unless a man hold himself diligently in the fear of the Lord, his house shall soon be overthrown. (Ecc. 26, 27.)

This I write as a warning to the god-fearing merchants and grocers, so that they will not imitate the ungodly, lest they be overcome by avarice, but be circumspect in dealing and beware of dangers.

Some are made thieves, some murderers and robbers, others jugglers, necromancers, some are whoremongers, others gamblers, others are betrayers, others become executioners and tormentors, and also some persecutors and slayers of the pious, &c. And, I say, all do this for accursed gain's sake. Whereby they openly testify, because they walk in such a way and are so bent upon unlawful gain, that they are of the devil and not of God, that they have not the faith and word of Christ, but in every respect inimical and opposed thereto.

Yes, kind reader, the whole world is contaminated and involved with this accursed avarice, fraud, false practices and unbecoming gain, with this false traffic and merchandise, with this finance usury and self-interest, that I scarcely know how it could be worse; nevertheless, all the priests and preachers are called good christians, and it is said that they get their bread honestly, and do justice to all.

Ah! my reader, how far all this is from Zaccheus's faith, disposition and converted life! For if they had the mind, faith and power of Zaccheus, (which we must have, would we ever be saved,) it is my opinion there would be few lords and princes in their great power and splendid living, there would be few riders and servants engaged in deeds of blood, there would be few judges, lawyers and advocates in their court-houses and offices, few rich would use their riches unlawfully, few merchants and grocers engaged in their usury and dangerous business, and but few preachers, priests and monks in their larders, easy life and cloisters. There would soon be a different state of things; because it cannot be, but that the righteous live by faith. (Hab. 2: Rom. 1; Gal. 3; Heb. 10.) Yea, they would with joyful heart, say with Zaccheus: *The poor we willingly serve with our goods, and if we have defrauded any one, we will gladly satisfy him.*

For all who, like Zaccheus, rightly receive Jesus Christ in the house of their consciences, rightly receive the word of Christ as he did, and be also truly born through the word, are rightly influenced by the spirit of Christ, are of the same mind with Christ, and therefore, it is impossible that they could defraud any one even of a farthing; so that we see that the disposition of all true believers is to injure none on earth; but, as much as in them is, they assist all; will defraud none, but do justice to all, &c., even as Paul says: Let him that stole, steal no more; but rather let him labor, working with his hands the thing which is good; that he may have to give to him that needeth. (Eph. 4.)

But why say much? For my part I do not know where to find the mighty, the rich—in what courts we can find judges, lawyers and advocates—and in what cities and countries, merchants and and grocers—or what cloisters and churches we can look for preachers, priests and monks—who rightly believe and follow Christ; who, being regenerated, penitent and pious, desist from all improper practices, fraud, over-reaching and unlawful gain, and say with Zaccheus: Those whom we defrauded we will repay four-fold. The prophet complains that every one from the least even unto the greatest, is given to covetousness. (Jer. 8.)

Since then they are determined upon the accursed, abominable avarice, and deal so roughly and diametrically contrary to love, and none any where repent, hence, it is also evident that they are not in the church and community of Christ; for Christ's church and community are called his body and bride. If the church be his body, she must then be flesh of his flesh, and bone of his bone; and if she be his bride, she must be of his generation, be righteous, holy, meek, chaste, true, lovely, merciful; yea, hear and be obedient to his voice. (John 3; 1 Cor. 2; Eph. 1; Rev. 19; Eph. 5.) And therefore, Christ cannot admit of any other members in his church but these who are of one heart, spirit and soul with him, partakers of his spirit, who are dead to all unrighteousness, bury the old evil life of sin, walk by faith, unblamably in love, receive the truth joyfully, heartily to serve their neighbor, as did this believing, regenerated and renewed Zaccheus.

He desired to see Christ, and received him with joy; he believed his word, and abandoned his ungodly life; he ministered to the poor, and reconciled those whom he had defrauded. In short, he proved himself to be a pious, sincere, regenerated child of God in all his actions; and therefore he heard the peaceable word of divine grace: *This day is salvation come to this house, forasmuch as he also is a son of Abraham.* (Luke 19.)

Behold, worthy reader, those who are such believing, penitent and renewed Zaccheuses, thus walking in love, belong to the Lord's community and body, as Christ himself says: Hereby men shall know that you are my disciples, if ye love one another. (John 13.) They are the living stones of the Lord's temple, (John 13; 1 Pet. 2,) and the true citizens of Jerusalem; in which neither dogs nor sorcerers, nor whoremongers, nor murderers, nor idolators, nor whosoever loveth and maketh a lie, have part. (Rev. 22.) Yea, as long as Zaccheus was such a one, he was without; for such, says Paul, have neither lot nor part in the kingdom of God and of Christ. (1 Cor. 6.)

But as soon as he believed the word of the Lord, through faith repented, and turned himself to love, from that hour he was entitled to citizenship, of Christ himself, the path of life was opened to him, peace declared, salvation bestowed, and was acknowledged and received as a joint-heir of grace, and a child of God, as the Lord says: *This day is salvation come to this house, &c.* For as Christ is holy, so must also his children, brethren, members, community and bride be holy; (1 Pet. 1,) for as it is written: Be ye holy, for I am holy. (Lev. 11, 19.)

OF THE FAITH OF THE THIEF AND MURDERER.

THE evangelists teach that there were two malefactors crucified with Christ; the one on the right, and the other on his left. And one of them reviled him and said: If thou art the Christ, save thyself and us; but the other reproved him and said: Dost thou not fear God, seeing thou art in the same condemnation? and we, indeed, justly, for we receive the due reward of our deeds; but this man hath done nothing amiss. And he said unto Jesus, Lord, remember me when thou comest into thy kingdom. And Jesus said unto him verily this day thou shalt be with me in Paradise. (Luke 23.)

Good reader, observe particularly what I say. When we critically view the confession of this evil doer, we are astonished at the great power, the good nature, the abundance of fruit, spiritual vision, energetic love and the free confession of his faith. It is evident that he had been an abandoned vagrant—an ungodly reprobate, who neither knew nor feared God, but maliciously committed all manner of sins, robbed his neighbor of his goods and shed his blood. For Matthew and Mark call him a murderer, and Luke calls him a malefactor. This appears to be the case as he testifies himself, how that he had to die for crimes which he had committed.

Notwithstanding all this, as soon as this malefactor, extended on the cross between Jerusalem and Mount Calvary, heard in his last distress, the word of God from the mouth of the Lord; it wrought in him so powerfully, that his heart within him was touched and changed, which led him to seek, from that moment, the salvation of his fellow-men and rebuked his reviling companion, saying: Fearest thou not God,? He confessed his own sins and his maliciousness, saying: We are receiving according to our merits and works; and he acknowledged the condemned Jesus (who was cursed to die on the cross as one of the most abandoned malefactors, by the chief priests, pharisees and scribes, and denied of the people and condemned to death), to be innocent, righteous, pure and without sin, saying: This one has done no evil. Besides this, he also sought grace and mercy of him, although it appeared to human understanding that he was denied all mercy, and every favor both by God and men. For he was at this time the most rejected and despised of all men, as the prophet laments, (Isa. 53,) and the thief applied to none other, in heaven or upon earth, than to this poor, despised, accursed and crucified Jesus; in full confidence drawing near to him, as the throne of divine grace: that he might obtain the remission of his sins, saying: Lord remember me when thou comest in thy kingdom.

I think, this may justly be called, a true christian faith, and a truly worthy fruit of penitence and repentance; and it was nothing else to the Lord, but a refreshing of his panting soul, as a molifying of his deep wounds, as a consolation of his sore distress, and as a comfort in his painful sufferings and cruel death, so that he in the same hour, heard the consoling, joyful word of divine grace and eternal peace, from Jesus, namely: Fear not, all thy sins which thou didst commit in thy ignorance are all covered, they shall never more be remembered, either by me or my Father. I pledge my innocent blood as an earnest;—therefore, be of good cheer, what thou didst desire, thou hast already obtained: *To-day shalt thou be with me in Paradise.*

Behold my reader, here you have, in the thief mentioned, a fair example of a sincere christian faith, with its properties, power and fruits. With this same thief many vain despisers comfort and flatter themselves in their sinful and impenitent lives, think and say to themselves: God is merciful; he knows that we are the children of Adam, and cannot live as the scriptures require, still we hope by his grace to be saved as the thief was. And these poor creatures know not, that the thief, will be a sore condemnation to them; because they hear the word of the Lord so often, and believe it not, nor are they obedient. Ah! reader! do not thus trifle and mock God; I fear many will fail in their hopes in this matter.

Again, I say, that all wilful despisers, who thus say and thus think, in their hearts, must be eternally convicted by this thief and shall stand confounded. For as soon as he heard the gospel of grace, he received it in a pure conscience, through faith, and became penitent, regenerated and pious. And these hear it from year to year, see daily so many fair fruits, and that it is so gloriously testified by possessions and blood; nevertheless, they remain unbelievers and are hardened in sin; for they reject the inviting grace, they resist the operating spirit, they contemn the preached word, they trample under foot the proffered gift. Say! where is the scriptures, whereby we may comfort such unreasonable, shameful scorners or promise and proclaim to them the grace and peace of the Lord?

For I fear, they are the sterile, unfruitful earth, of which Paul speaks, which drinketh in the rain of the holy divine word, that cometh oft upon it, and, nevertheless, bears only thorns and briers, are rejected and nigh unto cursing, who is to be burned. (Heb. 6.) They are those of whom wisdom complains and says: How long, ye simple ones, will ye love simplicity? and ye scorners delight in your scorning and fools hate knowledge? Because I have called, and ye refused; I have stretched out my hand and no man regarded; but ye have set at naught all my counsel, and would none of my reproof: I, also, will laugh at your calamity; I will mock when fear cometh and when distress and anguish come upon you, then ye shall call upon me, but I will not answer. (Prov. 1.) But because they do not look for light, he will turn it into the shadow of death, and make it gross darkness. (Jer. 13.)

The thief believed as soon as he heard. O! that they would do so; and think upon what David said: To-day, if ye will hear his voice, harden not your hearts as in the day of provocation. (Ps. 94; Heb. 3.)

The thief, I say, heard but *once* and *believed*, and these hear it so often; still they believe not. He heard and was changed;

but these hear and continue the same—they harden their hearts the longer the more.

The thief reproved his reviling companion, and admonished him, that he should fear God; but these blaspheme and revile all the faithful who do so; and love those who hate the truth.

The thief unreservedly confessed his sins and wickedness, without fear; but these, no matter howsoever avaricious, drunken, proud, unchaste, unclean, envious and idolatrous, they are, do not confess their transgressions and sins, and when they are called to repent and to reform, they say : Yea, what have we done?

The thief acknowledged that Christ's kingdom was not earthly, for he said : *when thou comest in thy kingdom;* but these have all their pleasures in gold and silver, in eating and drinking, in splendor and wantonness, and in the perishable, visible riches of the world ; do not regard the invisible, eternal riches, which Christ out of grace, has bestowed upon all his believers, and merited them by the shedding of his precious blood.

The thief, confessed the poor, condemned, crucified Jesus before all the rulers, priests, Pharisees and before the people, and acknowledge him as his Saviour and Lord ; but these, alas ! deny his almighty Majesty, his heavenly origin and glory, and do not regard his wisdom, spirit, word, ordinances, command, sacraments and promises, although he has seated himself as a triumphant and conquering prince, at the right hand of the Father, and has received all might and power, both in heaven and upon earth, in eternal glory of the Father. (Heb. 1, 8, 10 ; Eph. 1 ; Matt. 28.)

The thief sought mercy, favor and the forgiveness of his sins, of Christ ; and these seek it of their preachers, priests and monks, through masses, confessions, absolution, bread and wine, holy water and the like superstitions and abominations.

The thief heard, because he believed on Christ, the pleasing words : *To-day thou shalt be with me in Paradise :* but these must hear, because they believe not on Christ, the dreadful, intolerable and awful sentence : *Depart from me ye cursed into everlasting fire.* (Matt. 25.) For their faith was unlike, unlike will also be their reward. Let all mockers take this to heart.

And thus, finally, (take notice) will this penitent sinner rise up against them (who have comforted themselves with him in their sins,) and criminate and condemn them before the face of his Majesty. For they having so often heard the sweet melody of the divine word, and never were grateful—nor ever learned nor believed it with open and renewed hearts; but the thief, I say, heard it but once, and immediately believed. Ah! dear children, beware and seek Christ while he may be found and call on him while he is yet near, lest his anger go forth, and the fire of his fierce wrath consume you.

Think you, O perverted scorners! that you can receive or reject faith, repentance, sorrow for sin, and the grace of God, at pleasure? O no! Holy Paul says: And even as they did not like to retain God in their knowledge, God gave them over to a reprobate mind. (Rom. 1.) All proud scorners shall be sentenced and condemned. Children beware.

Notice this parable: There is a very rich potentate, emperor or king, whom I, through great ignorance, hated all my days; he had compassion upon me, because I am such a poor man, he, through his faithful servants, tendered me not only his great favor and friendship, but also a sum of gold, many precious stones and gems, and all this out of love and compassion; and I am so ungrateful, that I will not only not give meat and drink to the faithful servants of this kind prince, who loves me dearly, for these great favors; but I turn them with ignominy and disgrace, out of doors, throw them with mud and stones, put them into prison and bonds, deprive them of property and life, take the proffered gifts and cast them from me and trample them under foot, &c., and inform the prince: That I do not now desire his favors, but if he will, in the course of one or ten years offer them again, then I will perhaps, think upon it, and receive them and tender my thanks for the favors. Now, I will allow you all to judge me—whether it would be right that such a prince should again offer his favor, since I treated him and his servants so perfidiously? But whether he should not much more turn his favor into displeasure, his love into wrath, toward me, for my presumptuous tyranny, haughty rejection of his favors, and severely punish me? I think, you would award me his punishment and not his grace.

Thus it is with you, O you scorners! The merciful Lord, whose kingdom and grace are immense, has graciously pitied us in these abominable, last days, and had compassion on our great blindness and deadly poverty, (although we hated his holy will from our infancy,) and through his faithful servants freely gave us his beloved Son with his holy word, spirit, merits, ordinances and example—tendered us his grace, peace and eternal life, together with the remission of our sins—he dug about us and fostered us, barren trees, for three long years. (Luke 13.) He calls and teaches daily, through his chosen, who willingly sacrifice possession and life as a testimony; he puts at variance the father against the son, and the son against the father; the mother against the daughter, and the daughter against the mother; and the members of the family against one another; one friend against another, &c. (Matt. 10.) Some he suffers to driven about in strange countries, in tribulation, in sorrow, in misery, in fear, in want and in vexation, in deserts and in mountains, and in dens and in caves of the earth. (Heb. 11.) He gives signs in the sun, and in the moon, and at the stars and upon the earth, earthquakes, war, pestilence, new diseases, famine, and unheard of wonders upon earth, (Luke 21,) that as a hen gathers her chickens, he would gather us under the wings of his love. (Matt. 24.) And as a faithful shepherd of his sheep, would bring us to the right fold of his grace, (Matt. 23; John 10;) bring us into the chamber of his covenant, and kiss us with the lips of his peace, wash us from all our uncleanness, and made us his bride, (Cant. 1,) redeem us from the dominion of hell and death, and lead us into the kingdom of heaven, and of eternal life. In short, that he release us from the power of darkness and the devil, and receive us and make us holy as his chosen children and heirs. (Eph. 1; Col. 1.)

But, alas, in relation to you, it is altogether vain; for (as already said) his proffered grace and word you contemn and reject, you persecute and kill his faithful servants and ministers; you defame and blaspheme the unblamable, pious life, together with the confession of the saints; you scoff at his great signs, wonders and reproofs, and your faces are like those of the lecherous, and your hearts as diamonds; you are neither ashamed, nor will you be converted; you say with perverted scorners: Depart from us, for we desire not the knowledge of thy ways. What is the Almighty, that we should serve him? and what profit should we have, if we pray to him? (Jer. 2; Zach. 7; Job 21.)

Since, then, you are so ungrateful, and prove yourselves to be altogether vain and insulting against God, who manifested so great mercy towards us, that you wholly reject his paternal admonitions, reprovings, doctrine and commands. Obedience to his holy word, the innocent blood of his saints, with all his great powers and miracles, you esteem as idle deception and heresy; you regard not the time of grace; Christ Jesus, with his holy spirit, gospel, new birth, faith, sacrament, death and blood, with all his other spiritual riches and heavenly gifts, and you trample them so unworthily under foot, and the almighty, immortal, one and eternal God; you neither fear nor seek, love, honor, praise nor serve him; still you hope to be saved with the thief.

So I do warn you in true love, while it is yet time. Your hope will fail you, for when you think to find him, he will then hide himself from you; he will turn his fierce countenance

19

upon you, as the scriptures say : Then shall they call upon me, but I will not answer; they shall seek me early, but they shall not find me. (Prov. 1.)

I therefore entreat and exhort my readers in general : Hear while you have ears, and see while you have eyes; understand while you have hearts; awaken and watch while you have time and space, lest your ears, eyes and hearts, and opportunities be taken from you, and you become deaf, blind, impenitent, hardened and perverted.

Friends, beware! now it is to-day, yesterday is past, and to-morrow is not promised us. Short is the time; behold, the judge is at the door, therefore delay not, to turn to the Lord, and defer it not from one day to another. (1 Cor. 7; James 5.) For his wrath will soon overtake you. (Sirach 8.) Late repentance, says Augustine, is seldom true; but if true, it never is too late. Repent while you enjoy health, says he, that you may be certain.

Therefore, do as did the thief or murderer, for, as soon as he heard, he believed. Do you also thus hear, and thus believe, for the eyes of the Lord are upon the faithful. (Jer. 5.) Those who are hungering and thirsting after righteousness, shall be filled; those who seek, shall find; those who desire, shall receive; those who knock, to them it shall be opened. (Matt. 5.) But if you refuse, when he seeks you, to give you his grace, he will, then, also refuse when you seek him, and would fain obtain his grace. Whosoever despises me, says the Lord, him will I again despise. (1 Sam. 2.)

Therefore, I say, seek while it is day, that thou may find; ask, that you may receive : hear, that you may believe; believe, that you may do; and do, that you may live; for, from hearing, faith comes; out of faith, doctrine; on obedience, the fulfilment of the promise depends. (Rom. 10; Gal. 5; Matt. 7; John 15; James 2; 1 Cor. 7.)

For this reason all things are imputed to faith in the scriptures; such as true repentance, the new birth, sanctification of the heart; the righteousness which avails before God; the blessing. (John 1; Acts 2, 15; Rom. 3, 5, 10; Gal. 3; Mark 16; John 3.) For faith is the source and cause of all good, as is fully related.

Seeing, then, that this is the true ground of the scriptures, as we have briefly explained, you will then have to confess that all wilful scorners are put to shame in their doings, by the thief, and that he will be their accuser in the day of the Lord, as the Lord says of the Ninevites, and of the Queen of the South. (Matt. 12; Luke 11.)

But all who hear and believe the word of Christ, and are

turned by the power of faith with all their hearts to Christ, acknowledge Christ openly, by an unblamable life, before all the world, confidently seek his grace and mercy, &c., to them he is a glorious comforter, a precious balm and liniment in their troubled and wounded consciences, by which they may see and know God's unbounded favor, mercy and love towards all truly penitent sinners, if they have sinned ever so long and heinously, that they by faith may satisfy their souls with him, and not doubt the grace of God on account of their sinful lives in which they ever walked; for the Lord did not withhold his grace, nor did he say: No, thief, your sins are too great and numerous, and you also sinned too long. But as soon as he saw his new heart, and heard him confessing, he bestowed his grace upon the poor, distressed sinner, and forgave him all his sins, and said: *To-day thou shalt be with me in Paradise; for he that believeth on me has eternal life.* (John 3, 6, 7, 11.) The propet also says: If the righteous turn from his unrighteousness and does righteousness, I will not remember his unrighteousness which he did.

OF THE FAITH OF THE SINFUL WOMAN.

LUKE says: That there was a Pharisee, who invited Christ to eat with him, and he went into his house, and sat down to meat; behold, a woman of the city, who was a sinner, brought an alabaster box of ointment, and stood at his feet, behind him, weeping, and began to wash his feet with tears, and did wipe them with the hairs of her head, and kissed his feet, and anointed them with the ointment. (Luke 7.)

Here we again learn to know, in the case of this sinner, what kind of a heart and disposition, fruit and life, a sincere, true Christian faith produces. She was possessed of seven devils, (if she was the woman called Mary Magdalene, whom the evangelists mention), for she is called a sinner in the scriptures, (Matt. 26; Mark 14; Luke 8, 10,) so long as the Lord had not called her out of darkness into light, from lies unto truth. (John 12.) But as soon as she heard his word, she with eagerness received in a sincere and renewed heart, by which she (who was a great sinner) became a penitent and pious woman. Her unrighteous, sensual heart was so warmed and touched, that her eyes streamed with tears, that she wet the Lord's feet therewith. Her hair she used as a towel to wipe his feet; her avarice was quelled; she anointed his head and feet with precious ointment, which might have been sold for three hundred pence; her proud heart was humbled; she did not seek the highest seat at the table, but she sat mournfully at the feet of the Lord, and heard his blessed word.

When the Pharisee saw this, he murmured; Christ said to him: Simon, seest thou this woman? I entered into thy house, thou givest me no water for my feet; but she hath washed my feet with tears, and wiped them with the hairs of her head. Thou gavest me no kiss, but this woman, since I came in, hath not ceased to kiss my feet. My head with oil thou didst not anoint; but this woman has anointed my feet with ointment. Wherefore I say unto thee, her sins, which are many, are forgiven; for she loved much: but he to whom little is forgiven loveth little. And he said unto the woman: Thy sins are forgiven; thy faith hath saved thee; go in peace. (Luke 7.)

Behold reader, take notice; all the haughty, proud, avaricious, and sensual, who boast themselves christians and are not (for they show by their whole conduct that they hate Christ) are in their actions, reproved and made ashamed by this sinner. For when she believed her proud and haughty heart was humbled, made contrite, and was changed. And they say, they believe, although they practice all manner of wantonness—in their accursed pride and gorgeous trappings, and soft, flippant dresses and tinsel gewgaws, they strut about, without bounds or reason; not regarding what the enlightened apostles, Paul and Peter, say, who forbade christian women to dress with outward adornings; how much less should men dress so foolishly, who are examples to, and the head of women—nevertheless, they want still to be called the community of Christ.

Every one makes an ostentatious display; yea, sometimes goes beyond his ability to pay. One is desirous to excel another in foppery, or at least to equal him. And does not reflect that it is written: Love not the world, neither the things that are in the world. If any man love the world, the love of the Father is not in him. For all that is in the world, the lust of the flesh, and the lust of the eyes, and the pride of life is not of the Father, but is of the world; and the world passeth away, and the lust thereof; but he that doeth the will of God abideth for ever. (1 John 2.)

Again, I say, this sinful woman believed, and from that moment she was freed from disgraceful sins. For the unclean devil was cast out, as it is heard. But what abominable, disgraceful, unchastity, adultery and fornication obtain among many men and women, (who boast that they believe) in many cities and countries, is best known to him before whose eyes all things are open; and, alas, not wholly concealed before men. For it is manifest that the world is full of lasciviousness, adulterers, and fornicators, sodomites and buggerers, bastards and illegitimate children. And, alas, it has come so far, that they live at peace and liberty, and not thinking, that God commanded through Moses, that both the adulterer and adulteress should be stoned to death, (Lev. 20; Deut. 22,) that there should be neither whores nor whoremongers in Israel, and the illegitimate children even to the tenth generation were not to be admitted into the congregation of the Lord. (Lev. 23.) And further: It was the express command and law that if any one in Israel had sexual intercourse with a virgin, who was not betrothed or engaged, he had to marry her, if her father consented, and was not to put her away all his days, because he humbled her. (Exod. 22; Lev. 22.)

Ah! reader, reflect upon these things, what the last command contains. They all boast, however lascivious, that they are spiritual Israelites, that they have the truth, and are baptized in the name of Christ, still they are not ashamed to make their weak sisters, who are in connexion with them, and are of one faith, one baptism, of one supper and attend the same religious services, to be poor, helpless and disgraceful strumpets, contrary to all scripture and christian love, and although God's word commanded, if they have lain with them, that they should marry them and never forsake them. If they would think more profoundly upon these things, many of the females would not be disgraced, whereas so many a child has been unmercifully disgraced, and so many young girls have been defloured, and deprived of their virgin honor.

I write you the truth in Christ, if you are, or would be a christian, and have seduced but one poor child with your subtle attempts and pretences, (and if you would not lose your soul) you will have to marry her and not forsake her, nor cast her from you; for you have humbled her, as heard. Behold, this is the Lord's own word and law. All, therefore, who knowingly despise this law of God, and reject the disgraced and marry another, will have to confess before God that the *first one* is his wife, and not the *last one*. O, you violators of female chastity, reflect upon these things and learn wisdom.

Would you say that this command has reference only to Israel and not to the christian, I would then ask you in the first place: Whether you consider yourself to be a christian or not? If you say *no*, do then all you can, and look for the judgment threatened to all out of Christ. But if you say *yes*, then the matter is already decided, that she must be your wife. For a christian must not live with a sister, in such a manner as to make her a prostitute. O no! the scriptures teach, that christians are members of Christ, and not whores and profligates. I hope this blunt language will be understood.

19*

In the second place : which of the two people should be the more holy and virtuous, the literal or the spiritual ? Do you say the literal, then you have exalted Moses with his people and service, above Christ, which thing is evidently opposed to all scripture. (Matt. 5 ; 2 Cor. 3 ; Heb. 3, 8, 10.) But if you say the spiritual, then the matter is again decided, that she must be your wife ; then the literal must not make his sister to be a prostitute, much less the spiritual, which is the Lord's own body, brother, sister, generation and bride.

In the third place, I ask, whether the command : Thou shalt love thy neighbor as thyself, is not given to the christians as well as to Israel ? If you say *no* you have denied the whole New Testament, which teaches and earnestly insists upon the love of our neighbor. But if you say *yes*, then I say for the third time, that she must be your wife. Because you did, contrary to this command, so abominably disgrace and humble her, therefore, do the scriptures teach that you are to restore her to honor, and that you shall take her to be your wife. Let every one see to it, the commands of love will ever remain. Blessed are they who take heed to them and observe them in fear.

In the fourth place : I ask, whether there is a single one, who with impunity can transgress and break God's command ? If you say *yes*, then you deny the sciptures, which teach, that we shall walk in the ways of the Lord and keep his commandments. But if you say *no*, then I tell you the fourth time, that she is, and must be your wife ; for it is the command of God, firmly based upon love : That if you have lain with a virgin, that you marry her and never forsake her, as heard.

Behold, my reader, here you are more than plainly taught what the word of the Lord teaches in regard to this matter. And if you continue so ungodly as to transgress the command of the Lord by disgracing one, and marrying another, you may read the consequences in Rom. 1 ; 1 Cor. 6 ; Gal. 5 ; Eph. 5 ; Rev. 21, 22 ; unless you sincerely repent.

This I by no means, write to encourage him to leave his wife he married and take to wife the virgin he humbled before, for I have no doubts, the gracious Father will in mercy overlook the errors of those, who had erroneous views of the subject, and henceforth fear the Lord and do right, but I write this, that every one should guard himself against such disgrace, more profoundly to reflect upon the command of the Lord and of love, and observe how Christ is so wholly neglected of the world ; for, alas, they generally, are influenced by their accursed lusts, whether they are lords, princes, priests, monks, noble or ignoble, citizens and peasants, (with few exceptions)—they are so much inflamed, that they follow this unbecoming, devilish disgrace of accursed lechery, like the dog pursues the hare. They are, says Jeremiah, (Jer. 5) as fed horses in the morning: every one neighs after his neighbor's wife; and there is nothing that can deter or prevent them from this accursed abomination, neither natural honor, nor Moses, with all his threatenings, neither the prophets, nor Christ, nor the apostles, neither heaven nor the angels; yea, neither hell nor devil; neither life nor death; if they can only satisfy their unchaste, disgraceful lust, then all is well with them.

They are wholly bent upon this; some they seduce with fair words, others by promising gifts, some by giving them wine to drink; by dancing, and songs of levity, some by courteous flattery, by amorous tenderness, and the like artifice; yea some deceive by their affected sighings and weepings, so that they can only accomplish their designs, and gratify their lusts, then all is right, and they rejoice. But they do thereby incense almighty God, transgress his holy word. disgrace their neighbor, do violence to the law of love, defile the marriage bed, deflour virgins, have illegitimate children and destroy their souls eternally; about all this they care nothing. They say, this is our portion and our lot and nothing else. (Wis. 2.)

I, therefore, say with Moses: Cursed be they of God, who do works of iniquity; and all the people shall say, Amen, (Deut. 27,) And with Job: That hell will consume them, as drought and heat consume the snow-waters; (Job 24)—with Paul: That God will judge them; (Heb. 13)—and with John: Their part is in the lake which burneth with fire and brimstone, which is the second death. (Rev. 21.) Ah! that these poor people would take heed, awaken and believe the words of the Lord, and observe it.

In the second place, I write this; that every one might awaken, sincerely repent, and weep over his past disgraceful conduct before God, lest he cast him off eternally; but be gracious to him for the sake of the blood of his Son; and no more defile the bed of his neighbor, nor deflour virgins, but live in all honesty, each with his own wife. And that the unmarried keep free from lechery, and if he cannot restrain himself, let him seek a pious wife in the fear of God; and he that has transgressed, and has not taken another, that he honor the disgraced one, and according to christian love and word of God, extricate her from her degraded state. And thus teaching their children, and children's children, from generation to generation, even as Tobias did his Son, saying: Beware of all whoredom, my son, and take not a strange women, but keep to your own wife. (Tob. 4.)

Know ye not, says Paul, that your bodies are the members of Christ? Shall I then take the members of Christ and make them the members of an harlot? God forbid. (1 Cor. 6.) **Again,** he says: For this is the will of God, even your sanctification, that you should abstain from fornication; that every one of you should know how to possess his vessel (body) in sanctification and honor; not in the lust of concupiscence, even as the gentiles which know not God—For God has not called us unto uncleanness, but unto holiness. (1 Thes. 4.) Yes, good reader, true believers have to lead an honorable and chaste life; that not as much as adultery, lechery, and an unchastity be privately or openly mentioned among them; if any one among them, only mention it, it is an abomination for thus it becomes the saints, to live. (Eph. 4.)

We find many wicked men who shamefully seduce poor simple hearts; so on the other hand we find impudent women and girls, who are often the first cause that such disgrace is put on them. And though many are not guilty of the deed, nevertheless they are not guiltless, that they make so free with other men and associates in open triflings, singing, dancing, drinking healths, kissing, courting, in splendor and gorgeousness, and the like vanity and abominations, whereby they kindled the fires of base passions, which continue till consumed, as may be seen.

How properly Sirach admonishes us, when he says: Meet not with an harlot, lest thou fall into her snares: use not much the company of a woman that is a singer, lest thou be taken with her attempts: gaze not upon a maid, that thou fall not by those things that are precious in her: give not thy soul unto harlots, that thou lose not thine inheritance; look not round about thee in the streets of the city, neither wander thou in the solitary places thereof: turn away thine eye from a beautiful woman, and look not upon another's beauty; for many have been deceived by the beauty of a woman; for herewith love is kindled as a fire: set not at all with another man's wife, nor set down with her in thy arms, and spend not thy money with her at the wine; lest thy heart incline unto her, and so through thy desire, thou fall into destruction. (Sir. 9.)

Were it now so, that the aforementioned married and unmarried women were true believers, even as was the sinful woman, they would then also fear the Lord, they would abandon all vanity and ungodly actions, and lay snares for none, nor give any occasion to evil; yea, would walk honorably and modestly, and avoid all manner of pride and superfluity, and make, or desire no other clothes than those necessary and convenient; for they would not frequent the idolatrous temple and idle banquets, where generally such pomp and superfluity are displayed.

The sinful woman (when converted) adorned herself inwardly,

and not outwardly, for she believed; but these dress their bodies, and not their souls, for they believe not.

The sinful woman sighed and wept, was afraid of the wrath and judgment of the Lord, for she saw that she had done wrong and sinned; but these laugh and sing, dance and prance about, and do not see their enormous mis-deeds, and great sins, and therefore, they do not fear the Lord's wrath and judgment.

The sinful woman was compassionate and merciful, anointed the head and the feet of the Lord, and found the true service; but these are unmerciful and shameless, and know of no other service, than to go the chapel to receive holy water, to offer lights and tapers to blind blocks and images, to hear masses and vespers, to call upon the departed saints for help, to confess once or twice a year to their idolatrous, drunken, lascivious priests, to receive their bread of abomination and absolution, and the like superstitions and delusions.

The sinful woman sought the company of the righteous; but these seek the company of the unrighteous, do all manner of folly, defame their neighbors, backbite and slander, speak disgracefully of one another, speak of costly furniture, houses, goods and handsome companions, customs and fashions. In short, their works openly show that they have not the faith of the sinful woman, and belong not to the community of the righteous.

The sinful woman sat at the feet of Jesus and heard his holy word; but these hear teachers, who can tickle their ears, and preach to please them. In short, why need I say much; it is, O God! so corrupted, that we find the whole world filled with folly. I mean spiritual folly, deaf ears, unreasonable hearts, the blind are leading the blind, they will all fall into the abyss of death (unless they receive their sight again;) if we believe it to be true what the mouth of the Lord teaches, for their doctrine is altogether false, as well as their sacraments, and worship unbelief, and sensuality prevail every where.

Behold, reader, here take notice, how vastly this sinful woman, after conversion, in her faith and conducts, differs from the faith and conduct of the world. They are like the sinful woman before her conversion, and not after conversion. Whether such are believers, I will let the sensible reader reflect upon with the spirit and word of the Lord.

I certainly know that a proud, haughty man is no christian, that an avaricious, selfish man is no christian—an unchaste, lecherous man is no christian—a wrankling and envious man is no christian—a disobedient, idolatrous man is no christian—a false, lying man is no christian—an unfaithful, thievish man is no christian—a defaming and backbiting man is no christian, neither are the blood-thirsty, the unmerciful and revengeful men christians—though they were baptized one hundred times, and attend the Lord's supper daily ; for it is not the sacraments, or the signs, such as *baptism* and the *Lord's supper*, but a sincere, christian faith, with its unblamable, pious fruits, represented by the sacraments, that has the promise of life. (Matt. 28 ; Mark 16 ; John 1, 3, 6, 7,) and in other passages.

Here, neither masses, nor holy water, neither holy days, nor rosaries, neither auricular confession nor absolution, avail. Here only a believing, contrite and broken heart, spirit and mind, a penitent, a changed, a new heart, a pious life dead to sin, avail —This was the confession and repentence of the sinful woman, and she also heard immediately : *Thy sins are forgiven, thy faith hath made thee whole, go in peace.*

But the abominable auricular confession which is so highly esteemed by the world, is nothing but hypocrisy, human righteousness and superstition, open delusion of unbelievers, a false hope of the sinner, and a subtle invention of gain by the priests, whereby they set aside true confession and repentance and comfort and encourage the world in their rude, ungodly life.

But if you would rightly confess and repent, to receive true absolution of God, then approach him with a believing, penitent and changed heart, with a sorrowing, broken distressed mind, leave off sinning, do justice to your neighbor, love, aid, serve, reprove and comfort him, and if you have sinned against him, or overreached him, acknowledge it to him and reconcile him. Behold, this is the only true confession and penance, which is taught in the word of God. The Lord grant that you may rightly understand, and perform this confession and repentance.

I, therefore, entreat and desire all women, through the mercy of the Lord, to take this grieved, sinful woman as a pattern and follow her faith, humble yourselves before the Lord, and reprove your avarice, pride, obscenity and all manner of evil. Let all your thoughts be pure, and let your words be circumspect and seasoned. And whatsoever you do, do it in the name and fear of the Lord Jesus, and do not adorn yourselves with gold, silver, pearls, broidered hair or costly array, but dress yourselves in such apparel, which becomes women professing godliness, and which is serviceable. Be obedient to your husbands in all reasonable things, so that those who do not believe may be gained by your good conversation without the word, Peter says, (Col. 3, 4 ; 1 Tim 2 ; 1 Pet. 3 ; Eph 5.)

Remain within your houses and gates, except you have something of importance to do, such as attending to your temporal concerns—to administer to the needy—to hear the word of the

Lord, or to attend upon his holy sacraments, &c. Attend faithfully to your charge, to your children, house and domestics, and walk in all things like the sinful woman did after her conversion ; that you may be true daughters of Sarah, believing women, sisters of Christ, and joint heirs of a future life; (1 Pet. 3 ;) you shall hear the gracious words : *Your sins are forgiven, your faith hath made you whole, go in peace.*

OF THE FAITH OF THE WOMAN OF CANAAN.

MATTHEW informs us that Jesus went out of the land of Genesareth, and came into the coasts of Tyre and Sidon : and behold, a woman of Canaan came out of the same coasts, and cried unto him, saying : Have mercy on me, O Lord, thou son of David ; my daughter is grievously vexed with a devil. But he answered her not a word. And his disciples came and besought him, saying : Send her away, for she crieth after us. But he answered and said : I am not sent but unto the lost sheep of the house of Israel. But she came and worshipped him, saying : Lord do help me. But he answered and said : It is not meet to take the children's bread and cast it to the dogs. And she said : Truth, Lord ; yet the dogs eat of the crumbs which fall from their master's table. (Matt. 15 ; Mark 7 ; Luke 11.) Then Jesus answered and said to her : *O woman, great is thy faith ; be it to thee even as thou wilt.* And her daughter was whole from that very hour.

Here you again have a fine example and pattern of a sincere christian faith ; for when this woman perceived how powerfully Jesus preached grace, and hearing, besides, that he could do what he desired, showed love and mercy, and that he sent none away comfortless, she unhesitatingly approached him, not doubting his grace, mercy, love and power, though she was not heard on the first and second request. She was importunate both in her faith and prayer, with such a desire that she might but eat of the spiritual crumbs of his mercy, and obtain relief for her daughter. Yea, she manifested such a faith, constancy and piety, that the Lord said to her : *O woman, great is thy faith; be it unto thee even as thou wilt.*

Faithful reader, observe ; were we with spiritual eyes rightly to look upon this woman's faith and fruits, we would be aptly taught of her, especially in two particulars.

For, I say, as soon as she heard that the Lord taught pure mercy and grace, repentance and reformation, preached the kingdom of God, raised the dead, made the blind see, the deaf hear, the cripples walk, the leprous clean, healed the sick, and cast out unclean spirits; that he reproved the Scribes, Pharisees and the common people, for their unbelief, perverseness, blind hypocrisy and sensual life; and testified that he was the prophet and Messiah, promised in the law and the prophets, whereby his fame spread abroad through all Judea and the adjacent countries,—hearing all this, the woman's heart was encouraged to go to him, not at all doubting his mercy, power, goodness and grace, she drew nigh to him, through assured faith, and in full confidence entreated him humbly not to deny to her her request, but that he would graciously grant it; and she obtained what she desired.

She heard and believed; she saw and confessed. But these insane people imagine that they are christians, but are, according to my understanding, greater disbelievers, blinder, more hardened and worse than Turks, Tartars, or any of the heathens. Their works testify that I write the truth. And they cannot, by any means, be moved to hear, or be obedient to truth, neither by doctrine nor exhortation, neither by the unblamable lives nor the innocent blood of saints, which is daily shed, as we mentioned, when treating of the *faith of the* THIEF.

The above mentioned doctrine of the holy divine word, we have had in Germany for some years, and have it yet daily more abundantly, in such power and clearness, that they may plainly see it is the finger and work of the Lord. For the haughty are humbled, the avaricious are made kind, the drunkards become sober, the unchaste made pure, &c. and are not allowed to indulge in a single thought, word or act contrary to the will, word and spirit of the Lord, and they receive it with such an affection, that they do not fear to forsake father and mother, man, woman, children, possessions, nay willingly suffer death on account of it. For many of them are burnt, many are drowned, many are apprehended,—are exiled, their property confiscated; nevertheless they are indifferent, If it is but reported, he was an anabaptist, that is sufficient, and the enquiry is never made, what his conduct and life were, whether he injured any one, or not. Neither do they reflect, that it is a special power and work which restrains one wholly from drunkenness, lasciviousness, pomp and pride, full of all vanity, abominable lying, sensual life and from all idolatry; and constrains one to all sobriety, chastity, meekness, piety, truth, and the true worship, on account of which, we have to hear all manner of disgrace, beyond measure, and to endure persecution and misery, and so often have to endure the loss of life, as you may see.

If a thief is led to the gallows or a murderer is broken upon the wheel, or if a malefactor is severely punished every one enquires what he has done. And he is not sentenced by the judges as long as they do not understand fully the ground and truth of his evil deed. But if an innocent christian, (whom the gracious Lord rescued from the ways of sin, and placed in the way of his peace,) is accused by the priests and preachers, and placed before the judges they deem him unworthy of an impartial examination, in relation to what reasons or writings move him that he will not hear his priests and preachers, nor have his children baptized, nor attend their service, nor longer eat and drink with them, and serve the devil. Nor do they desire to know why he reformed his life and received the baptism of Christ, or what urges him that he willingly suffers or even would die for his faith. They only ask: *Is he baptized?* If he answers in affirmative, the sentence is fixed, that he must die.

And all, who see or hear such miracles of almighty God that such poor, unlearned men, (yea, sometimes, poor, feeble women,) are so fortified in God that they fear neither judge nor executioner; that neither fire nor water, neither halter nor sword, neither life nor death can deter them from their faith. These persecutors do not enquire what they did, whether they are traitors of their country or city, whether they have stolen the property of others, or disgraced some one's daughter or wife. Or whether they did any thing not in accordance with the word of God and with common honesty and natural probity. O no! So much discretion and love we find not; if they only have the word of the Lord, and believe the commands and ordinances thereof, and are obedient thereto, and desirous to regulate their poor, weak life by truth; they must be adjudged as seditious and heretical, and that they are guilty of severe punishment and of death. Behold, thus has the murdering, blood-thirsty devil deceived the whole world, through his priests and preachers; yea, that, I fear, scarcely one is to be found among a hundred thousand, who will lay to heart such a strong faith, obedience, frankness, power great suffering and ignominious death, so that he would once reflect upon his abominable unbelief, disgraceful wickedness and presumptuous carnal life, or call in question the doctrine of his teachers, sacraments, their lives and worship. How truly did the prophet say; The righteous perisheth and no man layeth it to heart. (Isa. 57.) There cannot be found beneath the wide canopy of heaven, more hardened unbelief, more perverse, scornful, obdurate wickedness, more accursed madness, more execrated ungodliness, or a worse state of things than that which is related.

If there is a report of war the whole land is in dismay, great and small, citizens and peasants, defensive arms are provided;

they watch and make ready for defence as much as possible. Or if they hear of famine or pestilence, then all fear and tremble, who have come to years of understanding. And, if on the contrary, there is a time of tranquillity and peace, of prosperity and weal, then all who hear it, rejoice. But *now*, the Lord Jesus Christ's trumpets are blowing, and the drums are beating, warning us to tender love, through all his apostles and prophets, to flee satan's crafty wiles and subtle assaults, and that all who follow and are obedient to him, must die. However, but few there are who put on the armor of God, are guarding against satan's secret encroachment, and preparing to resist him. They all run voluntarily into his hands, both men and women, and eagerly to do the things which delight him. And those who do not, have to await great tribulation and much misery. (Eph. 6 ; Thess. 5.)

Besides, it is manifest that the abominable pestilence of false doctrine will destroy the whole world, and the bread of life, which is provided for all the spiritual hungry, is very scarce, in consequence of the envious callings and serpentine preachers. And, alas, there are few who weep and sigh for the bread of life.

The eternal grace, mercy, favour, glory, kingdom and joy of Christ are offered to us. But our ears have waxed dull, our hearts become hardened, and our perverted wickedness desire them not. But this pious woman did not so, but she heard and believed, saw his miracles and confessed his power ; and therefore, prayed with confidence and obtained what she desired. for she believed Christ with all her heart and doubted not his grace.

In the second place, she admonishes all pious parents, that they should be solicitous for the salvation of their children, because she so faithfully entreated for her demoniac daughter, not desisting till she was heard. For it cannot be otherwise, that if I am a true christian, all my work before God and my neighbor, are works of love, for God (by whose word a christian is born) says John, *is love*. And that the Father and those who are born of him, are alike, of one mind and heart, is as clear as day-light.

If I seek the Lord's praise with all my heart, and desire the salvation of my neighbors, many of whom I have never seen ; how much more should I desire the salvation of my children, whom God gave me, who are out of my loins, and are naturally my flesh and bone ? So that the mighty Lord may be praised and be eternally honored by them.

What I write, I consider unquestionably true—I write it from a true witness of my own conscience, as before almighty God, before whom I am, that all true believing parents are thus minded towards their children, that they would far sooner see them set in a dungeon for the sake of the word of the Lord and his testimony, than be with the deceiving priests, in their idolatrous churches, or with drunken erroneous interpreters in taverns, or in company with scorners, who despise the name of the Lord, and hate his holy word.

Sooner far would they see them bound hands and feet, and dragged about for the sake of the Lord, before lords and princes, than be married to rich persons, who fear not God and walk not in the ways of the Lord, but pass away time in splendor, with music, in excessive drinking, dancing and singing, sooner far would they see them scourged from the head to the feet, for the sake of the Lord's glory and holy name, than see them adorn themselves with silks and velvets, with gold and silver, and with costly attire, and the like vanity, pomp and pride. Yea, far sooner would they see them exiled, burnt at the stake, drowned in the water, or placed on the wheel, for righteousness' sake, than see them live out of God, in all earthly and sensual lusts, be emperor and kings, and then be damned.

Wo to those, yea, wo to those, who are not solicitous for their children's salvation. Is it reasonable that we love their bodies, and connive at their sins, and not reprove the transgressions of the young with the rod, and of the aged with words, not teach them the way of the Lord, and not set them an unblamable example, direct them by day and by night to Christ, his word, ordinances, commands and example, and not seek their salvation with all the soul, if not, we will not escape unpunished. For their souls and blood, are required at our hands and their damnation and death will be laid to our charge as dumb and blind watchmen, in the day of the Lord.

Christianity plainly teaches us that all christian parents should be a salt, a shining light, and as unblamable, faithful teachers in their houses. The high priest Eli was punished because he did not zealously reprove his children. (1 Sam. 2, 5.)

If I see my neighbor's ox or ass go astray, I must bring him to the owner, or keep him safe, as Moses teaches. (Deut. 22.) If it becomes me thus to do with another's animal, how much more solicitous should I be for the souls of my children, who are so readily misled by the youthful flesh, in which no good dwells.

If I see my neighbor's ox or ass, fallen in a pit, or meet him on the way lying under the weight of a burden, I must not leave him till he is extricated, (Exod. 23 ; Deut. 22,) how much more should I be solicitous for my children, whom I have before me, that they lie not under the burden of their sins ; and if they are not earnestly reproved and instructed in grace, they will fall into the infernal abyss of the second death.

Again, if I see my neighbor's house on fire, and goods perishing, it is reasonable that I exert myself to put out the fire, and if possible, to save the goods; but it is much more reasonable, that I extinguish the fire of base desires in my child, with the water of the divine word, and preserve, as much as is in my power, the heavenly goods.

The holy scriptures teach, that God purifies the heart by faith, —that faith comes by hearing; and by faith we are justified. (Acts 1, 5; Rom. 3, 5, 10.) Therefore, let every one take heed, if he does love his children indeed, that he teach and instruct them in the way of the Lord, that they may fear, honor, and serve him, so that the depravity of sin may not rule in them, lest eternal disgrace ruin them.

Moses taught Israel saying: And these words, which I command thee this day, shall be in thine heart, and thou shalt bind them for a sign unto thy hand, and they shall be as frontlets between thy eyes, and thou shalt teach them diligently unto thy children, and shalt talk of them when thou sittest in thine house, when thou walkest by the way, when thou liest down, and when thou risest up, and thou shalt write them upon the posts of thy house and on thy gates; that ye may prolong your days in the land which the LORD swore unto your fathers to give unto them and their seed. (Deut. 6, 11.)

In another place he says: And if thy children ask thee in time to come, saying, what is this? that thou shalt say unto them: By strength of hand, the LORD brought us out from Egypt; from the house of bondage. (Exod. 12, 13.)

Joshua commanded Israel, according to the word of the Lord, and said unto the twelve men: Pass over before the ark of the LORD your God into the midst of Jordan, and take ye up every man of you a stone upon his shoulder, according unto the numbers of the tribes of the children of Israel: that this may be a sign among you, that when your children ask their fathers in time to come, saying: What mean ye by these stones? Then, ye shall answer them, that the waters of Jordan were cut off before the ark of the covenant of the LORD, when Israel passed over Jordan, the waters of Jordan were cut off, and these stones shall be a memorial unto the children of Israel forever. (Jos. 4.)

Behold, dear reader, thus the Israelites were obliged to teach their children from their youth, and to acquaint them with all the mercies and miracles of the Lord, which they and their fathers experienced, so that they might fear, love and serve the Lord all their days, and thus receive blessings, and escape cursings which were connected with the law. (Lev. 26; Deut. 28.)

In like manner, if we rightly confess Christ, we believe his word, and we and our children desire to obtain the happy fields and pleasant land, and eternally to inherit the grace which he promised his children; therefore, let us not neglect it, but lay it well to heart, that we teach our children rightly in the word, and instruct them in relation to his righteous judgments, so that they will learn to fear the Lord with all their heart, and turn from evil.

And also, rightly to set forth his unbounded mercy, love and service of his grace, so that they may love him and walk in his statutes—have correct views and just conceptions of Jesus Christ our Lord and Saviour, with his spirit, word and life, so that they may rightly know him and walk in his footsteps. Thus set them an example in all wisdom, righteousness and truth—with a pious and virtuous life, so that they may be instructed thereby, and be taught and trained for the kingdom of heaven, and for every good work.

For all who have such a faith as this woman had, and see that the end of sin is death, will not cease to sigh and lament to God, that he would in mercy assist their children to resist the evil spirit, lest he ruin their poor souls and lead them captive at his will.

But that they may, in their youth, rightly learn how to know the immortal, eternal God the Father, through Jesus Christ his Son, and in truth submit to his cross. And recount all the mighty works and wonders of the Lord our God, the great mercy, grace, favor and love of the almighty Father, his blessed word, will, ordinance and life, with all the merits, power and fruit of the death and blood of Christ his Son; also the munificence, wisdom, truth and the gifts of his eternal and Holy Ghost, this to their children, and children's children, and all their descendants, till the Lord Jesus come in the glorious majesty of his heavenly Father in the clouds of heaven, to the final judging, and where every one will be rewarded according to his works, be they good or evil. (Matt. 25; Rom. 2; 2 Cor. 5.)

Behold, dear reader, thus it behooves true christians to teach, to admonish, to reprove, and to correct their children, to set them an example in all righteousness, raise them in the fear of the Lord, be solicitous for their poor souls, lest they depart from the true path, die in their sins and finally perish in their unbelief.

The Lord spoke of Abraham and said: Shall I hide from Abraham that thing which I do; seeing that he shall surely become a great and mighty nation, and all the nations of the earth shall be blessed in him? *For I know him, that he will command his children and his household after him, and they*

20*

shall keep the way of the Lord to do justice and judgment. (Gen. 18.)

Pious Tobit taught his son and said : My son, obey thy father, serve the Lord in truth and be just, and this teach to thy children, that they give alms, always fear God, and love him, and confide in him with all your heart. (Tob. 14.)

And when they attain the age of maturity, and have not the power to refrain (but he that has, him I would advise with Paul, that he use it to the Lord) let them not marry to those out of Christ and his community, such as the noble, rich, or handsome, as do the proud and unchaste ; but let them marry such as fear, love, honor and follow the Lord with the whole heart ;—be they noble or ignoble, rich or poor, comely or uncomely, for they are holy and children of saints, and therefore, it is of, and must be done in the name of the Lord. (Job 8 ; 1 Cor. 7.)

Let every one beware and do right, lest the wrath and judgments of God be inflicted upon him on account of his lewdness, even as the judgments in the days of Noah and Lot, were inflicted. (Gen. 6, 8, 19.)

But, alas ! how few who take this to heart, and cordially seek their children's salvation. If they can but provide for them temporally, then they have their desires ; their faith is priests' ordinances and church services ; hope is their salvation, and they neither seek nor know another.

All their doings are contrary to the word of Christ, for as soon as they are born, they are brought to idolatrous and false baptism, the holy name of the Lord is pronounced over them, they are raised in all manner of vanity and blindness, in pomp, splendor and excess, in open idolatry and false service, and the dumb, earthly life of this world.

In and out of their houses they hear and see nothing but unrighteousness and malice, lying, defrauding, cursing and swearing, infidelity, avarice, hatred, drinking and eating to excess and all manner of disgrace. They never learn to know Christ and his word, but they hate the truth and persecute righteousness. In short, they show by their actions that they are full of the evil, unclean spirit, and are led by it, as may be seen.

For as your spirit is, so must also your fruits be. Is the spirit of Christ in you, which is holy and pure, then are also your whole life and fruit pure and holy. Again, if the spirit of the evil one is in you, then all your ways and fruits will be evil and impure ;—this is incontrovertible.

Therefore, says Paul : For as many as are led by the spirit of God, they are the sons of God. Again, these are led by the spirit of an evil one, are the sons of the devil. Dear reader, reflect well upon this. Yea, if these poor people had but a spark of the Lord's spirit, they would a thousand times sooner be seethed in boiling oil, and burned with fire, than hear and see such foolishness, ungodliness and wantonness in their children, much less would they teach them or set them an example in such things. For it is incontrovertible, according to the scriptures, if they do not be partakers of Christ, that their end will be eternal death. (Mark 16 ; John 3.)

Hither, all you who fear the Lord : love your children with love divine, seek their salvation with all your heart, even like Abraham, Tobit, and the Maccabean mother did. (Gen. 22 ; Job. 4 ; 2 Macc. 7.) If they transgress, reprove them sharply ; if they err, exhort them parentally ; if they are child-like, bear them patiently ; if they are of good understanding, instruct them christian-like ; dedicate them to the Lord in their youth ; watch over their souls as long as they are under your care ; so that you will not lose your salvation on their account, pray without ceasing, like this pious woman did, that the Lord may grant them his grace, that they may resist the devil, subdue their natural depravity by the spirit and help of the Lord, and walk from their youth up before God and his community, in all righteousness, truth and wisdom, in a firm and sure faith, in unfeigned love and living hope, in an honorable and holy life, unblamable and without offence, abound in the fruits of faith, to eternal life. Amen.

The attentive reader may also add to the aforementioned examples, the faith of the virgin Mary ; the faith of Matthew ; of aged Simeon and Hannah : and that of the blind man, (Luke 1 ; Matt. 9 ; Luke 2, 5, 18 ; Mark 10,) and such like more, to seriously reflect on with a pious mind, I trust he will, by the aid and grace of the Lord, fully understand the nature of true Christian faith, that it is unostentatious, without hypocrisy, fears God, righteous, long-suffering, ardent, peaceable, joyful, merciful, amiable, helpful, kind, meek, zealous, unblamable and pious, ever fruitful inwardly in power to God, outwardly towards fellow men ; even as a good tree brings forth good fruit of its own, so must also a true christian faith bring forth. For it cannot be otherwise, the righteous must live by faith. (Hab 2 ; Rom. 1 ; Gal. 3 ; Heb. 10.)

If Abraham, Isaac and Jacob, Moses, Joshua and Samuel, with all the patriarchs and prophets believed the word of the Lord, which was declared to them by angels, or were found so faithful therein ; how much more should we believe the word, and be faithful to that word which the prince of angels, God's only begotten Son, the true witness and teacher of righteousness, Christ Jesus, who came from the high heavens from his Father's bosom, brought down and taught on this earth. (John 7, 14.)

It will not suffice to say: That Jesus Christ is the Son of God, that he fulfilled the law for us, that he paid for our sins with his blood, and made reconciliation with the Father, by his offering and death: neither will it suffice to only believe that his gospel is true, his word is right, the wages of sin is death, and that grace is eternal life; but the heart must rightly comprehend it, and the mind must be resolved upon it, or it will not otherwise justify. Paul says: With the heart we believe unto righteousness. (Rom. 10.)

But all who believe with their whole hearts, that Christ Jesus is the righteous branch of David; the true promised prophet; the right way and truth, and our only propitiator, intercessor, mediator and high priest. (Jer. 22; Deut. 18; Rom. 3; 2 John 2; Heb. 5, 13.) They also believe that all his words are immutable and true; and his offering sufficient and perfect; they, therefore, obey his word, walk in his commands, bow to his sceptre and pacify their consciences by his grace, reconciliation, merits, offering, promises, death and blood, believe and acknowledge, if they neglect his will and word, and presumptuously transgress his will, and live according to the flesh, that God would require such at their hands, and would eternally punish them, through his righteous judgment, with the fire of his wrath; for those who with impunity transgressed the law of Moses, had to die without mercy, through two or three witnesses: and how much sorer punishment are they worthy, who tread under foot the law of God, and count the blood of the covenant, whereby they are sanctified, an unholy thing, and have done despite unto the spirit of grace? (Deut. 17; Heb. 10.)

Yes, kind reader, if we truly believe it, and rightly understand it in our souls, it moves and influences our hearts so with the fear and love of the Lord, that although all the tyrants that ever were, would rise with all their dread tyranny, torture, pain and blood shedding, and stand before us, they should not in the least deter or hinder us from the Lord's word and way. Besides, all our impure, sensual thoughts, unseasoned words, and our useless, ungodly works would soon die, as Sirach says: The fear of the Lord dispels sin; and it is impossible, without the fear of the Lord, to become right. (Sirach 1.)

Seeing then, it is more than clear, that a sincere christian faith in God, knows God in his righteousness, and therefore fears his judgment, and thus through fear buries sin and dies to it, (as more than once related,) and nevertheless, you live in all avarice, unchastity, drunkenness, wrath, lewdness, blindness, idolatry, and all manner of wickedness; say, beloved, where are your faith and word of God of which you boast so much? Do you not know that it is written: If you live after the flesh you shall die? Or do you think that you can trifle with God as with a man? Be not deceived, says Paul, for God will not be mocked. (Gal. 6.)

Ah! reader, beware, I tell you the truth in Christ; take care of yourself; if you do not repent with all your heart and seek God through Christ, do hear, believe and fear him, but remain earthly and sensual, and walk after the lusts of your flesh, your sentence already pronounced, will be *death.* (Rom. 1, 6; 1 Cor. 6; Gal. 5; Eph. 5; Rev. 21, 22.) As Christ himself says: I judge no man, but the word that I have spoken, the same shall judge him in the last day. (John 12.)

I, therefore, faithfully admonish you, as before God, even as I do my own soul, divest yourselves immediately of false doctrine, of all unbelief, idolatry and earthly, disgraceful lives, in which, alas! you have hitherto walked, lest the wrath of God overtake you in the sleep of your sins.

Awaken! He is still merciful, seek and receive the true doctrine, true faith, true sacraments, the true service, and lead a godly life, as the scriptures teach: Then shall your light break forth as the morning, and your health shall spring forth speedily, and your righteousness shall go before you and the glory of the LORD shall be your reward. (Isa. 58.)

Further, I say: If you truly believe and rightly understand that you became, in and through Adam's disobedience, children of the devil, of wrath, and of eternal death, subjected to God's righteous curse and judgment; but every obstacle and all your sins are taken away through the precious blood of Christ, and you are reconciled; and are called from wrath into grace, from cursings to blessings, and out of death to life, (not to mention the favors which are daily shown you;) to believe this your hearts would sprout forth as the sweet-scented blooming violet, full of pure love: yea, flow as the living fountain, from which flow forth the refreshing sweet waters of righteousness, and you would, with holy Paul, say, from the bottom of your soul: Who should separate us from the love of God? (Rom. 8.) Since it can never be if I am in bonds of perfection with him, and love him with a pure heart, good conscience and unfeigned faith, that nothing then can turn us away or separate us from him. (1 Tim. 1.) For it is my own desire and highest joy, that I hear and speak of his word, and in my weakness, walk as he commanded and taught through his Son, should it even cost money and possessions, flesh or blood, his will be done.

Behold, dear reader, since then it is more than clear in the Holy Scriptures, that the true Christian faith through the fear of God, dies to sin, and through love does the things of righteousness, (though in weakness,) I let you judge whether those believe from the heart, who with the mouth say, that the blood of Christ is the propitiatory sacrifice of their sin; and nevertheless seek and follow up all kinds of idolatry, such as infant baptism, holy water, absolution, auricular confession, masses, gold, silver, and wooden images, wafers, stone churches, and the drunken whoredom of the priests. Ah! how well it would be for them that they would reflect.

. I say: As true as the Lord lives, there will eternally be found no other remedy for our sins, whether in heaven or upon earth, neither works, merits nor sacraments (though they are used according to the scriptures,) neither cross nor tribulation, neither holy angels nor men, nor any other means will avail, but alone the crimson, immaculate blood of the lamb, Christ, which was out of pure grace, mercy and love, shed and spilt for the remission of our sins. (Isa. 53; Matt. 26; Mark 14; Luke 22; Rom. 3; Col. 1; 1 Pet. 1; 1 John 1; Rev. 1, 7.)

Therefore, it is incontrovertible, that all those who use such strange idolatrous means for sin, belong not to the grateful community of Christ. Hence, I will present you with a few passages from the gospel and writings of the apostles, and hang them before your eyes as a clear mirror, in which you may view yourselves, and see whether you are believing Christians.

Thus teaches the word of the Lord: *Verily, verily, I say unto you, except a man be born again, he cannot see the kingdom of God.* (John 3.) And again: *Of a truth I say unto you, except ye be converted and become as little children, ye cannot enter the kingdom of heaven.* (Matt. 18.)

Prove yourselves, if you are born of the pure seed of the holy word, for the nature of the seed must be in you; and have you in malice, become like children, then there are no more pride, unchastity, avarice, hatred and envy in you; for innocent children know nothing of such sins. But if you are yet in Adam and not in Christ, and walk after the desires of your own depraved flesh, then you show indeed that you are not born of God, and have not his faith.

The Lord's word teaches again: *Go and preach the gospel to every creature; he that believeth and is baptized shall be saved.* (Mark 16.) Here, prove yourselves again. He that believes and is rightly baptized, truly repents, circumcises his heart, dies to sin, rises in Christ to a new life, &c. But if you remain impenitent, your hearts uncircumcised, not dead to sin, but live out of Christ and his word, then is the deed your witness, that you are disbelievers and have not the baptism of Christ. Again does the word of the Lord teach: *If thou wouldst enter life keep the commandments.* (Matt. 19) For in Christ, says Paul, neither circumcision nor uncircumcision avail.

eth, but the keeping of the commands of God. (1 Cor. 7.) And this is his command: That you shall love the Lord thy God with all your heart, with all your soul, with all your strength, and your neighbor as yourself. (Matt. 22; Deut. 6; Mark 12; Luke 20; Lev. 19; Rom. 13; Gal. 5.)

Hereby, prove yourselves again: If you love God, you will keep his commandments. (John, 14, 15; 1 John 5.) And you will do to your neighbor as you would have him do to you. If you refuse his word, and live not up to, and walk after his ordinances, doctrine, baptism, supper and separation, and also belie defraud, betray your neighbor and deprive him of life, disgrace his wife, daughter, or maid; deal treacherously with him; deceive the poor, blind souls and lead them off from the truth, way and obedience of the Lord (either by false doctrine or persecution) and rob them of the eternal kingdom and lead them to hell; then it is more than clear, that you hate the command of the Lord and have not his faith.

Again, the word of the Lord teaches: *Enter ye in at the strait gate; for wide is the gate, and broad is the way, that leadeth to destruction, and many there be which go in thereat; because strait is the gate, and narrow is the way, which leadeth unto life; and few there be that find it.* (Matt. 7; Luke 13.) At another place it is written: *If any man will come after me, let him deny himself, and take up his cross and follow me.—He that loves father and mother, man or wife, son or daughter, more than me, is not worthy of me.* (Matt. 10, 16; Luke 14.)

Here prove yourselves. Have you such a spirit, such frankness and faith, that you are ready to suffer on account of the word of God and for his testimony's sake; to forsake in time of need, father, mother and all, take upon you the cross of Christ, deny yourselves, enter with Christ upon the path of misery, and with the little flock enter in at the strait gate. The Lord strengthen you. But if you live unto yourselves, reject the cross of Christ, and love father, mother, wife, children, property or life more than Christ, walk on the broad way with the multitude and enter the wide gate, then the Lord's own mouth gives testimony that you are disbelievers and that your end is damnation.

Again, says the word of the Lord: *And they that are Christ's have crucified the flesh with the affections and lusts.* (Gal. 5.) For those who live after the flesh, such as adulterers, whoremongers, incontinent persons, drunkards, avaricious, gamblers, thieves, the haughty, the hateful, defamers, blood-thirsty, idolaters, shall die. (Rom 1; 1 Cor 6; Gal. 5; Eph. 5.)

Prove yourselves again: Do your lusts reign in you, and do

you walk in such like works as I related to you, or do you subdue your lust through faith, then thank God, fight faithfully,
watch and pray. But if you do, and live in the lusts of your
flesh, then reform ; for it is evident that you are not penitent,
believing Christians, but impenitent sensual heathens.

Again ; the word of the Lord teaches : *Therefore, take no
thought, saying, What shall we eat ? or what shall we drink ?
or, wherewithal shall we be clothed ? For after all these things
do the gentiles seek : But seek ye first the kingdom of God, and
his righteousness ; and all these things shall be added unto
you.* (Matt. 6.)

Here ask yourself again : If you believe that the strong and
mighty God, who nourished Israel for forty years with bread
from heaven and with water from the rock, and kept their
clothes from being worn out, (Exod. 26 ; Deut. 29 ;) and fed
Elias by a raven, (1 Sam. 17,) will not forsake you in your distress, but will provide for you by his grace, this is a true evidence that you have the word of the Lord. But if through your
cares, you are induced or constrained, that you neglect the kingdom of God and his righteousness, seek temporal, more than
eternal things, and are so much concerned as if God had more
concern for the flowers and fowls than for you and your children, boast not that you believe the promise and the word of the
Lord.

Again, the word of the Lord teaches : *For God so loved the
world, that he gave his only begotten Son, that whosoever believeth in him should not perish, but have everlasting life. For
God sent not his Son into the world to condemn the world, but
that the world through him might be saved. He that believeth
on him is not condemned ; but he that believeth not is condemned already, because he hath not believed in the name of
the only begotten Son of God.* (John 3.)

Here prove yourselves for the seventh time. If you believe
these words of Christ with the whole heart, that the almighty,
eternal Father had such love to give you and the whole human
family, that he sent his incomprehensible, almighty and eternal
Ward, Wisdom, Truth and Son, by whom he created the heavens and the earth and the fulness thereof, and his eternal glory,
into this vale of misery ; let him become poor, grieved, miserable man—let him hunger, thirst, and to be slandered, apprehended, scourged, crowned with thorns and crucified, hence it
is impossible for your carnal heart not to become spiritual, your
thoughts must be chaste and pure, your words discreet and
well seasoned, and your whole life, pious and unblamable.

Instantly you should awaken, walk in the right way, keep
aloof from all abomination and idolatry, forsake false prophets,

preachers and priests; and seek for the right doctrine, sacraments and divine service; for a true, sincere, Christian faith cannot be idle; but it changes, renews, purifies, sanctifies and justifies more and more, it makes joyous and glad, for by faith he knows that hell, devil, sin and death, are conquered through Christ, and that grace, mercy, and redemption from sin, and eternal life, are acquired through him. In full confidence, he approaches the Father, in the name of Christ, receives the Holy Ghost, becomes partaker of the divine nature, and is renewed after the image of him, who created him, lives by the virtue of Christ, which is in him, all his ways are righteousness, godliness, honesty, chastity, truth, wisdom, goodness, benevolence, light, love and joy. (Rom. 8; Gal. 4; Eph. 2, 3; 2 Pet. 1; Eph. 4; Col. 3; Gal. 2.)

He sanctifies his body and heart as a habitation and temple of Christ and his Holy Ghost : hates all that is against God and his word, honors, praises and thanks God with a sincere heart; and there is nothing to deter him, neither judgment nor wrath; neither hell nor devil; neither sin nor eternal death. For he knows that Christ is his intercessor, mediator and propitiator. He knows with holy Paul : There is, therefore, now no condemnation to them which are in Christ Jesus, who walk not after the flesh, but after the spirit. (Rom. 8.) The Lord's spirit assures him, that he is a child of God and a joint heir of Christ, he, therefore, wholly dedicates himself to his Lord and Saviour Jesus Christ, who called him through grace, drawed him by his spirit, enlightened him by his word, and purchased him by his blood.

Behold, this is the nature of true faith, which has such an urgent, cogent power, spirit, fear, energy and life ; which avails with God and has the promise in the scriptures. Happy he who has such a faith and will salutarily retain it to the end. I repeat it : prove yourselves, whether you are in the faith ; in Christ or out of Christ ; penitent or impenitent. For in the mirror presented, you may view the whole face of your conscience and life ; if you but believe that your Lord's word is true and right.—Here notice how, that the true christian faith, (in grace, which is a flowing fountain, whence is not only a penitent, new life, but also the obedience to the evangelical ceremonies, such as baptism and the Lord's supper,) will have to come and follow, not as those compelled through the law ; the rod of the oppressor is broken, (Isa. 9,) but voluntarily, through the free will ; and submissive spirit of love, which is of a christian nature, is ready to all good works and obedience of the holy divine word.

For all the truly regenerated and spiritual conform in all

21

things to the word and ordinances of the Lord; not because they think to merit the propitiation of their sins and eternal life, by no means. In this matter they depend upon nothing except the true promise of the merciful Father, graciously given to all believers, through the blood and merits of Christ which blood (I again say) is, and ever will be the only eternal medium of our reconciliation, and not works, baptism or Lord's supper as above related.

For if our reconciliation depended upon works and ceremonies, then it would not be grace, and the merits and fruits of the blood of Christ would be void. O no! it is grace and will be grace to all eternity—all what the merciful Father is doing or has done for us grievous sinners, through his Son and Holy Ghost, is grace. But therefore, it happens that they hear the voice of the Lord, believe his word, and set forth the representation of both signs, under water, bread and wine, in obedience (though in weakness) observe and do it. For a truly believing christian is thus minded, that he will not do otherwise than what the word of the Lord enjoins and teaches; for he knows, that all presumption and disobedience, are like sins of witchcraft, and the end thereof is death. (1 Sam. 15; Num. 15; Heb. 10.)

Yes, good reader, the true christian belief as the scriptures require, is so lively, active, strong and powerful with all those, who have rightly received it through the grace of the Lord, that they do not fear to forsake father, mother, wife and children, money and possessions for the Lord's word and testimony sake, to suffer all manner of scorn and disgrace, fatigue, hardship and prison, and finally be burnt at the stake, as may abundantly be seen in the pious children and witnesses of Christ, especially in these our Netherlands.

Alas! how many did I know before, and know the greater part of them now, both men and women, men and maid servants, and virgins (would to God that they be increased to many hundred thousands) who, from the inmost of their souls, seek Christ and his word, and lead, in all meekness, a pious and unblamable life before God and man; sincere and holy in doctrine, full of the fear and love of God, ready to help one another, merciful, compassionate, meek, sober, chaste, neither refractory nor seditious; but quiet and peaceable, obedient to the magistracy in all things not contrary to God; and who have, nevertheless, for a number of years, not slept in their beds, and even do not now; for they are so much hated by the world, that they have been persecuted, betrayed, taken, exiled and slain like highwaymen, thieves and murderers, and that without mercy; and for no other reason, only because they out of true fear of

God, dare not take part in the abominable, sensual life, and with the accursed, disgraceful idolatry of this blind world: neither dare they hear nor acknowledge the unchaste, drunken, lecherous priests and deceiving blind preachers, as the true apostles and teachers of God; and dare not receive the bread with the avaricious, envious, proud, drunkards, whores and rogues, at their hands; and carry their children to anti-christian washing and baptism, but seek preachers and teachers, and also such a baptism, supper, church and life, which are in accordance with the scriptures, and may stand according to the word of the Lord.

Behold, before God, I write the truth, indeed they are such a people, if I otherwise know them rightly (hypocrites excepted,) who weep more than they laugh, who sorrow more than they are joyful, give more than they receive, who are ready not only to sacrifice possessions, and their all, but also body and life for the praise of the Lord, and to the necessary service of their neighbor, as much as in them is. And no matter how much the poor children are harassed, they are still so much strengthened in God, that they can neither be moved nor deterred. They possess their souls with patience, waiting for the joy promised. Truly said Christ: Ye will be hated of all men for my sake. (Matt. 24.)

Since then it is evident from all this, that the true evangelical faith is of such a nature, as said, and is the only means and tree which through the grace of God, bears and propagates all manner of good fruit, therefore, it is considered, in scripture, the most precious, and greatest work, (John 6,) and all things are ascribed to faith, such as miracles, and the power to become the children of God, and be justified; be blessed and saved; purified and sanctified; and have eternal life, as we have related when treating of the Malefactor's faith. (Matt. 14; Mark 16; Luke 17; 1 Cor. 13; Rom. 3, 5, 18; Gal. 3; 1 Pet. 1; Acts 15; John 3, 7, 11.)

Not, dear reader, that we believe that faith merits this on account of its worth; by no means; but because God's pleasure, through his word, is connected with true faith, (Matt. 14; Mark 16; John 3, 7, 11, 21,) then it must also by virtue of that word, follow faith. For the scriptures plainly teach, that all things, visible and invisible, have to hear, yield, serve and follow God's powerful word, as when he said: Let there be heaven and earth. Heaven and earth sprang into existence at these words. (Gen. 1.) For his word, says Esdras, is his perfect work. (4 Esd. 6.) God also says to Israel: If thou shalt hearken unto the voice of the LORD thy God, all these blessings shall come on thee; but if thou wilt not hearken, the curse shall be upon thee; (Lev. 26; Deut. 28) and it also happened, as it was told Israel: For God, says Balaam, is not a man that he should lie; neither the son of man, that he should repent. (Num. 23.) For these reasons the promise must follow true faith, else God who is a God of truth, must be untrue and faithless, cannot be denied. O no! all that he wills must be done, what he promises must be fulfilled, and not otherwise than he has promised, for he alone is true, and we are all liars. (Ps. 31; Rom. 3.) Paul says: If we believe not, yet he abideth faithful: he cannot deny himself. (2 Tim. 2.)

Since then faith so firmly knows that God cannot break his promise, but must keep it, because he is the truth and cannot lie, therefore, does he make his children joyful, and glad in spirit; though they are confined in prisons, bonds, and have to endure water and fire, or are in chains and at the stake; for they are assured in the spirit through faith, that God will fulfil his promise made to them; for they believe on Christ, inasmuch as the promises are sealed, and they are assured thereof through his grace, word and will, although they did formerly live ungodly and carnally.

They hope with faithful Abraham, where nothing is to be hoped, and wait for things invisible, as though they saw them; and with full confidence adhere to the assurance, truth, faithfulness and power of the heavenly promise, (Rom. 4; Heb. 11,) which is made to us by the infallible, true mouth of our Lord Jesus Christ, the Son of God, without any previous work or merit, through his merciful Father's gracious choice and will, in his true word. (James 1; Eph. 2; Phil. 1; Rom. 10.) And that your regeneration, justifying, converting, penitent, active and confident faith, which comes from the Father of light, by hearing his holy word, is the only faith that avails with God, and which has the assurance of the promise of grace in the word, through the Holy Ghost; besides this, the scriptures know of no other faith.

Before now, I read in some books, which they have written, there is but *one* good work which saves us, namely, FAITH, and but *one* sin which will damn us, namely, UNBELIEF. This I will leave as it is, and not find fault with it; for where there is a sincere, true *faith*, there is also all manner of sincere, good fruits. And on the other hand, where there is *unbelief*, there is also all manner of evil fruits; therefore, is salvation properly ascribed to *faith*, and damnation to *unbelief*. (Mark 16; John 3.)

Faithful reader, pay attention. Since we plainly see and perceive that the whole world, Papists, Lutherans, Zuinglians, Davidists, libertines, &c., walk the broad road of sin, and lead a sensual life, and do not abide by the pure, salutary, perfect doctrine, sacrament and unblamable, pure example of Christ; they are themselves witnesses, that they reject the corner stone Jesus Christ, and believe not his word and truth, though a few of them write much of faith and speak of the scriptures. (Rom. 6; Col. 2; Matt. 22; 1 Pet. 2.) Say, beloved, did you ever read in the scriptures, or did you ever hear, that a truly believing regenerated christian, after repentance and conversion, was proud, avaricious, incontinent, tyrannical and idolatrous, and lived after the lusts of his flesh? You have to say, *no!* And if you speak of Peter and David, you must observe that they did not delay repentance, and what kind of penance they did. (2 Sam. 11, 12; Luke 22.) Turn yourself to the east, or to the west, to the south or north, you find with all those who boast of faith, ungodly, vain, pompous, foolish actions and conduct, that we have to say with Christ and John: That they are, with few exceptions, of the devil and not of God. (John 8; 1 John 3.) For the devil was from the beginning, proud and haughty, so are they, he was a liar, so are they; he was a falsifier of the word of the Lord, so are they; he was disputatious against God, so are they. In short, he is a revengeful murderer, an abominable, blood-thirsty tyrant, so are many of them. The way in which they use those, who seek Christ sincerely and believe, fear, follow, serve and call on him, has been more than once fully related.

Yea, alas, they are so enraged at them, that they will scarce call them by their right names, but they call them anabaptists, fanatics, rioters, factionists, hedge preachers, deceivers, heretics, new monks, knaves and miscreants, although they do seek the kingdom of God and his righteousness with all their hearts, (which God knows, who tries the reins and hearts of men,) and wish no evil to any one upon earth.

And this they do all through the ignorant, defaming of the envious, inhuman, lying, crying and writing of their learned priests and preachers, who from time to time, which the blasphemous beast of antichrist has raised up in his kingdom and glory, (Rev. 13, 19,) these have always been the true cause why innocent blood which was, and is so tyrannically shed; for they are those who instigate the magistracy to murder, and the plebians to defame and blaspheme, and, I fear, will continue such till the end.

Nevertheless, the chosen are to awaken, repent and to obey the voice of the Lord; for idolatrous, blood-thirsty, confused Babel shall sink, and must be desolated; and fair Jerusalem, the city of peace, shall and will increase, and through the power of almighty God must be built up in glory. Of this all rejoice, who are called to the marriage of the Lamb, and whose names are written in the BOOK of LIFE with God. Here is understanding, wisdom, faith and patience of the saints ; let him that has understanding, observe, that the word of the Lord is true. Blessed are they who are ready to meet the coming of the Lamb.

Behold, such a faithless, impenitent, tyrannical, idolatrous, refractory, disobedient, blind, sensual people they are, who imagine that they are the believing community, and the lawful bride of Christ. Observe that all under the heaven is spoiled, even as the prophet complains ; There is no truth, nor mercy, nor knowledge of God in the land ; by swearing, lying, stealing, killing and committing adultery, they break out, and blood toucheth blood. (Hos. 4 :) The world, says John, lieth in wickedness. (1 John 5.) If we come to the lords and princes, there we find such pride, arrogance, pomp and wantonness, such banqueting, eating and drinking to excess, with some such adultery and whoredom, and such unreasonable, blind idolatry, and with many, such unmerciful, raging tyranny, that they are in truth more like proud Nebuchadnezzar, drunken Belshazzar, and Nabal, and blood thirsty, vain Antioch, Nero and Maximinus, than christian believing lords and kind princes. (Dan. 4, 5 ; 1 Sam. 25 ; Macc. 9.) If we come to the judges and rulers, to each in his station, with some we find only violence and injustice, with some nothing but avarice, astonishing practices, they honorably steal and rob, pass sentence for gain and gifts ; honor the high and despise the poor, do not justice to the poor widow, orphan and the oppressed stranger, execute their office and power with rigor, and not fraternally ; serve princes and not God, as the prophet laments : What the prince desires, the judge does, so that he will again reward him. (Mic. 7.) Alas ! where shall we find one, who loves God with all the heart, hates avarice, seeks the truth, who will defend the godfearing, and do him justice ?

If we come to the monks, there we find such insatiable avarice, that they offer and sell for money, prayers, psalms, matins, vespers, masses, sermons, baptism, Lord's supper, absolution, all their church services, together with their own souls ; take rents and gold from the deceased, will go six or ten miles, from one place to another for a guilder ; where they find the most milk and wool, there they prefer to be among the sheep, like to be flattered and honored by the world, they suffer themselves to be called doctors, lords, masters, abbots, provost, priors, fathers, guardians, presidents, like to wear long garments, seek to be greeted at the market, and take the first seats at the table and in the church, as Christ said of the Scribes and Pharisees. (Mark 12 ; Luke 10.) Besides, the greater part of them live in such whoredom and sodomy that the angels are astonished and blush—they defile one woman after another, also daughters and virgins. Defraud and corrupt the whole world, both temporal and spiritual ; they have all their joy in a temporal, sensual life ; study by day and by night, how they may pamper their proud, idle, lazy flesh ; eating and drinking, saying, as it is written in the prophecy of Isa. 16 : Come let us go for wine and drink till we are drunken and do to-morrow as we did to-day, and much more : betray the pious hearts, who with all powers seek Christ and eternal life : they warn them of the truth and their followers, and cry : Hear us, we are your teachers and pastors, we will pledge our souls for you in the judgment of God. (2 Pet. 2.) And thus encourage the malicious, lest they be converted from their wickedness. Promising liberty to others, and are themselves servants of corruption. (Jer. 28 ; 2 Pet. 2.) I do not know how they could make it worse ; nevertheless, those unblushing, abominable men, who according to the law of Moses, would suffer death, and who (unless they repent,) must be eternally cursed and condemned, alas, are called the pastors and teachers of this poor, rude people. Behold, thus the world is corrupted.

If we come to the preachers, who boast of the word, we will find, that some are open liars, others drunken sots, some usurers, some wanton and gay, some defamers and slanderers, others persecutors and betrayers of the innocent ; you will see how others conduct themselves towards their women, and what kind of woman they have,—all I will commit to the Lord and to themselves. Teaching subtilely, that there are *two sons* in Christ, the Son of God, and the son of Mary, and that he who died for our sins, was not the Son of God. Teach and practice a baptism not commanded in the scriptures ; some of them hold also the supper, where they consider the *bread* the *body*, and the *wine* the *blood* of Christ, they have, and hold no other saw, than the gallows, and the wheel ; lead an easy life, maintain themselves by deceiving, they preach as much as the sensual magistracy desire to hear, promise the poor impenitent peace, though there is no peace. (Jer. 8.)

If we come to the common people, we find such an unbecoming, sensual, blind, uncircumcised horde, that we are astonished, they know neither God nor his word. Their piety consists in any thing but the doctrine and commands of Christ. In short, it has come so far in the world, that we may complain and say with the holy prophet : Run ye to and fro through Jerusalem, and see now, and know, and seek in the broad places thereof, if ye can find a man, if there be any that executeth judgment, that seeketh the truth. (Jer. 5.)

Not one stone has remained upon another, all is desolated

which Christ and his faithful messengers taught us of faith, love, baptism, supper, reconciliation of sin, repentance, regeneration, separation, teachers, deacons and of the true divine service, nevertheless, they are called the community of Christ by their blind priests and preachers, even as if Christ and the Father were to be satisfied with names, bread, wine and water. O no! the chosen of God are the church of Christ—his saints and beloved, who washed their clothes in the blood of the Lamb, who are born of God, influenced by the spirit of Christ, who are in Christ and he in them, who hear and believe his word, who follow him in their weakness, in his commandments, walk in his footsteps with all patience and humility, hate the evil, and love the good, earnestly desiring to apprehend Christ as they are apprehended of him, (Phil. 3.) for all who are in Christ, are new creatures. (2 Cor. 5.) Flesh of his flesh, and bone of his bone. (Eph. 5.) Members of his body. (1 Cor. 12.) As you and the whole world agree, I will therefore, leave you and all reasonable readers, to reflect with the understanding and scripture, upon these things, in the fear of the Lord.

Since, then, all things are desolated through God's righteous judgment; because they delighted in the unrighteousness and lies of the false prophets and ravening wolves, and that nothing salutary has remained according to the true sense and ground of Christ and his holy apostles—we find nothing in the whole world, among all the great sects, but vain boastings, mere names, false doctrine, false sacraments, vain unbelief and an impenitent, sensual life, and this is all to be found under the name and semblance of Christ and his holy community; hence, I am constrained, by true Christian love, to make known the power and ground of the holy scriptures, according to my small gift, given me of God, and through this to show which is the *true Christian faith*, having the promise, the faith which changes man from evil into good, to a divine nature, both inwardly and outwardly, and makes him, as heard, holy, righteous, obedient, new, pious, peaceable and joyful. In order that pious hearts, who desire to walk in the right way, but who are hindered therefrom by their blind priests and preachers, may read or hear this my faithful EXPOSITION and INSTRUCTION, that they may thereby be instructed in the truth; the indifferent and drowsy may be awakened, and all thy hypocrites may be ashamed, and reform, and all those who love God sincerely, might be more instructed and taught in the faith; if they do by any means acknowledge this as the sure FOUNDATION of God, as it is, and will be, eternally. The dear Lord, grant that many may read and understand it, and thus receive and obey it, that they may sincerely repent and be saved. Amen.

And since I do it out of a sincere heart, and labor not with any other view (of which the great God, the searcher of men's hearts and reins, is my witness,) than that I may teach the ignorant, rude world, which knows not Christ, repentance, lead them to Christ and his doctrine, sacraments and example, and that many might be saved, and as we plainly see that there are many profligates who have reformed their sinful, sensual lives, and commenced an upright, penitent, pious life in the fear of the Lord; then it is gross ingratitude, yea, hardened, ungodly tyranny, to hate me and my co-workers so enviously and recompense us so shamefully, who manifest such great fidelity and love towards them in our manifold sufferings and trials.

But thus, they treated, in the beginning, all the prophets and servants of God, who preached to them the Lord's word and will with great fidelity, reproved their sins, sought even till death their salvation with all their powers, with many tears, watchings, prayers, labors, cares and sorrows; therefore, it is nothing strange, and no wonder, that they will treat us so; for Christ says: For they did so to the prophets, who were before you. (Matt. 5; Luke 6.)

I entreat and desire, hereby, through the mercy of our Lord Jesus Christ, all my readers and hearers in general, of whatever name, office, station and condition, that you be pleased neither to defame nor to reject my labor, as long as you have not read it impartially, heard it rightly and understood it. Do, therefore, separate Christ's doctrine, sacraments and life from the doctrine, sacraments and life of the priests and preachers; separate faith and unbelief, spirit and flesh, righteousness and unrighteousness. Seek after the truth, strive zealously for your salvation, believe that God is true, that he will reward the good and punish the evil, that his word is, and will be, truth eternally. Fear his judgment, love his bounties, then you will know by the grace of the Lord that the aforementioned is the true Christian faith, which avails before God, and has the promise in the scriptures, as we have so abundantly testified and shown to you by God's word so abundantly, and with such incontrovertible passages, scriptures and examples, without deceit and fraud, as it were before, in Christ Jesus.

The almighty, eternal, merciful God and Father, through his beloved Son, Jesus Christ, lead you all, one with another, into his holy, divine knowledge and evangelical truth, and make your faith fruitful and active, that you may at all times with sincere, new hearts, patiently submit to his cross in every trial and affliction, unfeigned in love, peaceable and joyful in spirit. as the unblamable, pious children of God, (1 Pet. 1,) may walk before the Lord and his community all the days of your lives, and ultimately obtain the promise of grace, the end of your faith, the salvation of your souls. Amen.

TO THE CHRISTIAN READER.
CONCLUSION.

BELOVED reader, here you have my GROUND AND DOCTRINE OF FAITH, with its *properties, power, operation and fruits.* I, therefore, entreat you all, if you appreciate Christ and your own salvation, suppress your perverted minds, be not enraged and embittered, should you find any thing contrary to the usages of our forefathers, standing usages, or philosophic writings and the calling of the learned; but first prove it rightly, and scrutinize it well with Christ and his holy apostles' word, spirit, life and example, whether it is not the true *content, meaning, ground and sense of the whole scriptures;* if so, you will have to give up the unscriptural *usage,* and the deceptive *calling* of the learned, and hold only to the word of the Lord, if you would be saved.   Let, therefore, your heart be impartial, and your judgment sincere and after truth; for almighty God, before whom every knee has to bow and every tongue confess, will not and cannot yield to any of the learned, or to long-standing usages, or customs; for he is Lord, and we are his servants. (Isa. 45; Rom. 14; Phil. 2.) We *must* follow Him, and He *not* us.   Ah! reader! lay it to heart!

Likewise, if you find that we preach our doctrine rightly, respect no man's dignity, fear no man's tyranny, nor yield to the learned, but in true, sincere love, faithfully teach, admonish and reprove every one without respect of person, with the Lord's holy spirit, word, example and ordinance, in all things not right; then, I entreat you again, that you would be pleased not to attribute this to spiritual pride, but to well-meant frankness and Christian simplicity.   I desire that you would all walk rightly, so that you may be saved, on account of which I have to endure not a little tribulation.   I refuse not to become as a fool, so that I may make many wise in Christ, and with the Lord's holy spirit and powerful word lead them to wisdom and to the saints; and I well know that Christ and his apostles, and the prophets, were guilty of the same foolishness, and were of the same mind with me in this matter.

I reprove, they reprove more; I threaten, they do so much more. (Rev. 9.) Were they on account carnal and proud?   Far from it?   Yes, my reader, had not the dark smoke of men-pleasing-preachers, the accursed, false doctrine of the dreadful, abominable locusts out of the abyss, risen up; but had sincere reproving, the true, pure doctrine, the scriptural usage of the sacraments, and the separating of the impenitent, without re-

spect to person, continued in the world; never would the
pleasing sun have lost his splendor, nor would the church have
lapsed into such a dreadful condition; therefore, I esteem it with
Paul, to be unimportant, to be judged of men in this matter. (1
Cor. 4.) For I know that I mean it well, do right and reprove
only with the truth, so that they may be converted.

The true heavenly light, Jesus Christ, eternally blessed, enlighten all dark, benighted hearts with the clear and lucid ray
of his Holy Ghost and eternal truth, in unfeigned, pure faith, to
view the brightness of Christ, to the praise and honor of his
great name, and to the salvation of many souls. Amen.

A FUNDAMENTAL DOCTRINE,

FROM THE WORD OF THE LORD, CONCERN-
ING THE NEW BIRTH.

*Exhorting all of every Christian denomination to the hea-
venly birth and the new creature, without which none, who has
come to the years of maturity, can be a true Christian.*

*In Christ Jesus neither circumcision nor uncircumcision
availeth, but a new creature. Gal. 6.*

*For other foundation can no man lay than that is laid,
which is Jesus Christ. 1 Cor. 3.*

Hear my words, all people, and understand them, all you who
imagine that you are Christians, and presumptuously boast of
the Lord's grace, merits, flesh, blood, cross, kingdom and death,
notwithstanding we find among you neither Christian faith,
brotherly love nor repentance, nor the right use of the sacraments of Christ, nor the pure doctrine, nor the unblamable,
godly life, which is out of God, to which the scriptures admonish
us; neither the true, divine service, nor an evangelical disposition, nor obedience; but throughout nothing else than abominable darkness, unbelief, a lewd, carnal life, false doctrine, false
and self-devised sacraments, a devilish heart and mind, an accursed, heathen idolatry under the name of Christ, blind, blood-
thirsty tyranny, envious and furious revengefulness against all
the children of God; yea, open obstinacy, disobedience and
rejection of the words of Christ and of his Holy Ghost, as may
be very plainly perceived and seen through the world.

In order that you comfort yourselves no longer with lying
and vain hopes, contrary to the scriptures, to your eternal damnation, and not glory in vain, in the afore-mentioned riches and
glory of the children of God, namely of Christ's kingdom, grace,

merits, flesh, blood, cross, death and promises, &c., which do not yet pertain to you, because you are yet altogether earthly, sensually and devilishly minded, reject Christ, and do not keep to his spirit, word and example, without which no one can be a christian; I have undertaken through the merciful grace of the Lord, as much as is in my power, to inform you, briefly, by the infallible, powerful, saving word of the gospel of Christ, and out of the unadulterated, pure doctrine of his apostles, in this my *epistle,* who they are, or who they are not, that are endowed of God, and to whom pertain the aforementioned gifts, merits and promises of Christ.

Tell me, most beloved, where or when did you read in the scriptures, (which is the true witness of the Holy Ghost and the only line of our consciences,) that the unbelieving, disobedient, sensual adulterer, whoremonger, drunkard, avaricious, idolatrous or pompous and arrogant, had a single promise of the kingdom of Christ and community, nay, part or communion in his merits, death and blood? I tell you the truth, nowhere do we read it in the scriptures, nor ever will we: but thus it is written in Paul's writings: *For if ye live after the flesh ye shall die. Adulterers, whoremongers, buggerers, effeminate, unclean, idolators, drunkards, proud, avaricious, betrayers of the innocent, and bloodshedders, thieves, murderers, backbiters, perjurers, sorcers, liars, unmerciful, the disobedient to God and Christ,* (if they repent not,) *will not inherit the kingdom of God, yea, their portion will be in the fiery lake which burns with fire and brimstone, which is the second death.* (Rom. 8; 1 Cor. 6; Gal. 5; Eph. 5; Gen. 38; Rev. 21, 22.)

Behold, worthy reader, this is God's irrevocable sentence, upon all who live after the flesh, whoever they be, emperor or king, duke or earl, knight or squire, noble or ignoble, priest or monk, learned or unlearned, rich or poor, male or female, bond or free. All, who live after the flesh, must forever remain under God's just sentence and eternal wrath, else the whole scriptures are untrue and false. (Acts 10; 1 Cor. 6; Gal. 5; Eph. 5; James 2.)

And, therefore, are the poor, ignorant people comforted in vain with masses, matins, vespers, confession, pilgrimage and holy water, and what is more, with Christ's grace, death and blood. The word stands firm: *For if ye live after the flesh ye shall die; for to be carnally minded is death.* (Rom. 8.) Therefore, I advise and entreat you all in general, do hear Christ Jesus, who is sent to us as a witness of the truth from heaven; for thus says he: *Verily I say unto you except ye be converted and become like little children, ye cannot enter into the kingdom of heaven.* (Matt. 18.) At another place: *Verily, verily, I say unto you except ye be born from above ye cannot enter the kingdom of heaven.* Again: *Verily, verily, I say unto you, except a man be born of water and the spirit, &c.* (John 3.)

Faithful reader, take heed : these words are not invented or instituted of man ; nor are they the resolution of any council ; but they are the infallible, precious words, which the Son of God, Christ Jesus, brought to us from the mouth of his Father, and declared unto pious Nicodemus, the scribe, with a double asseveration. That word is powerful and clear, and has not only reference to Nicodemus, but to all the children of Adam, who have come to the years of maturity. But alas, it is so obscured by the abominable, offensive, leavenous mire of human commands, statutes and glossaries, that scarcely one or two are found of a thousand, who have the true sense and understanding of the heavenly birth, much less have they the active power, properties and fruits of it. Yea, they have brought it so far through their philosophy, wisdom and self-chosen holiness, that the eternal Wisdom of God, Christ Jesus, eternally blessed, is banished as a poor senseless fool, out of the house of his honor, (which is his community,) with his Holy Ghost, word, baptism, supper, divine service, separation and unblamable example ; and the man of sin, the son of perdition, is placed in his stead, (2 Thess. 2,) with his abominable doctrine, idolatrous infant baptism and supper, with his unclean purifications and promises, with his churches, cloisters, priests, monks, masses, mattins, vespers, holy water, images, pilgrimages, purgatory, vigils, confession, absolution, &c. : all of which in short, are nothing but the doctrines and commands of men, raised up contrary to the scriptures, an accursed idolatry and abomination, an open denial and blasphemy of the Lord's death and offering, a despising of the New Testament, or of the covenant which was sealed by the innocent blood of the Lamb, a destroying and desolation of the saving ordinances of Christ, of *doctrine, baptism, supper, life and separation,* abundantly testified in the scriptures, which ordinance he taught in this world with incontrovertible clearness and power according to the command of his Father, and left it to his children in his word ; and none other can be established eternally that will stand before him.

In short, writers and the learned have corrupted every thing so much through their councils, decrees and statutes, with all the tyranny and power of the great, that there is scarcely an article entire of all which Christ and his holy apostles taught. All the afore-mentioned abominations, together with the ungodly, sensual life of the world, I call on as witnesses ; nevertheless they would be called the holy christian church. And he that admonishes them in sincere, pure love, with the Lord's spirit and word, must be an accursed anabaptist and heretic. I tell you again: They want to be the christian church, and it is evident from all their actions, that they are not christians; but sensual, proud, avaricious, lascivious, lewd, drunken and idolatrous blind heathens. And what is worse, some of them are unmerciful, murdering, ferocious, revengeful and blood-thirsty fiends; for many of their works are done according to the devil's will. (John 8.) We may with propriety complain of this matter; for the righteous judgment is come upon them, that they are unconvertible and that little of a salutary kind remains with them.

O! how miserably is the fair vineyard desolated, and how lamentably are its branches withered, its walls are broken down, the destroying foxes have destroyed the grapes, the clouds are dry and give no rain, (Isa. 5; Jer. 2, 12;) there is neither pruner nor knife at hand; and if there is one he must be devoured out of the dragon, or slain by the apocalyptical woman, drunk with blood. O merciful, gracious Father, how long will this great misery endure? Our rulers are like voracious lions and bears. Our fathers are our betrayers. Our leaders our deceivers. And those who feign to be our pastors are thieves and murderers of our souls. (Luke 23; 2 Thess. 2.) Well may we sigh and complain from the inmost of our hearts: *Our house is left us desolate.* For that which was before Christ's church and kingdom, is now, alas! antichrist's church and house, and for no other reason than because they ungratefully rejected the word of grace, and will not have the ruling Lord Jesus Christ, to rule over them, with the righteous sceptre of his holy word and spirit, (Luke 19:) nevertheless, this poor blind people hope to obtain God's grace and promises through their infant baptism, masses, confession and the like superstitious ceremonies and idolatries, which they call the true divine service, and use it as a remedy for their sins. Ah! no, most beloved, no; for the hope of the ungodly is like thistle-down, says Solomon, that is blown away with the wind. I have said it once, and repeat it, and that from the mouth of the Lord, who can neither lie nor deceive: *Except ye be converted, and become as little children, ye shall not enter into the kingdom of heaven.—And if ye are not born from above, ye shall not see the kingdom of God.* (Matt. 18; John 3.)

My beloved reader, do take heed to the word of the Lord, and do once learn to know the true God. I warn you faithfully take heed, he will not save you, nor pardon your sins, nor show you his grace, except according to his word, namely: *If you repent, if you believe, if you are born of him, if you do what he has commanded, and walk even as he walked.* (Matt. 4; Mark 1, 16;

Luke 13; 2 John 3, 15; 1 John 2.) For if he could save unjustified, sensual man, without regeneration, faith and repentance, he did not teach us the truth; but he is the truth, and there is no lie in him. Therefore, I tell you again, that you cannot be reconciled with all your masses, matins, vespers, ceremonies, sacraments, councils, statutes and commands under the whole heavens, together with all the popes and their adherents from the beginning; for I warn you, they are abominations and not propitiations. Christ says: In vain do they honor me, because they teach commandments of men. But if you, by any means, be saved, your sensual, ungodly life, must be reformed; for the scriptures teach nothing but true repentance and reformation and present to us admonitions, threatenings, reprovings, miracles, examples, ceremonies and sacraments; and if you do not repent, there is nothing in heaven or on earth that can save you; for without true repentance, we are comforted in vain. The prophet says: O my people, they which lead thee cause thee to err, and destroy the way of thy paths. (Isa. 3.) We must be born from above, (John 3,) must be changed and renewed in our hearts, transplanted from Adam's unrighteous and evil nature, into the true and good nature of Christ; or we can eternally not be saved by any means, whether human or divine. (Matt. 18.) For wherever true repentance and new creature are not (I speak of adults,) man must be eternally lost—this is incontrovertibly clear. This every one may confidently rely upon, who does not wish to deceive his soul.

That regeneration of which we write, from which comes the penitent pious life having the promise, comes alone from the word of the Lord, if it be rightly taught, and if rightly understood and received in the heart by faith through the Holy Ghost. (Rom. 10; 1 Cor. 4; 1 Pet. 1; James 1.) The first birth of man is out of the first earthly Adam, and therefore its nature is earthly and Adamic, that is, the carnal mind, unbelief, disobedience, in divine things, blindness, deafness and folly, whose end, if not renewed by the word, will be damnation and eternal death. Would you, therefore, have your inbred, evil nature reformed, and be free from eternal death and damnation, so that you may obtain with all true christians, what is promised them, you must be born again. For the regenerated are in grace, and have the promise, as you have heard. They do, therefore, lead a penitent and new life, for they are renewed in Christ, and have received a new heart and spirit. Before, they were earthly-minded, but now heavenly; before, carnally, now spiritually; before, unrighteous, now righteous; before, evil, now good. And live no longer after the old depraved nature of the first earthly Adam but after the new, sincere nature of the new and heavenly Adam

Christ Jesus; as Paul says: I live no more, but Christ lives in me. (Gal. 2.) Their poor weak life they renew daily more and more, and that after the image of him who created them, (Col. 3,) their minds are after the mind of Christ, (Phil. 2,) and they gladly walk as he walked, (1 John 2,) they crucify and mortify their flesh with its evil lusts, (Gal. 5,) they bury their sin with baptism in the Lord's death, and rise with him to a new life, (Rom. 6,) they circumcise their hearts with the word of the Lord, (Col. 2,) and are baptized with the Holy Ghost in the spotless, holy body of Christ, as obedient members and fellow-heirs of his community, according to the true ordinance and according to the word of the Lord. They put on Christ and manifest the power of his spirit in all their fruits, (1 Cor. 12; Gal. 2, 3,) they fear God with all the heart, and seek in all their thoughts, words and works, nothing but the praise of God and the salvation of their brethren. They know not hatred and vengeance, for they love those who hate them, they do good to those who despitefully use them, and pray for those who persecute them: (Matt. 5; Rom. 12,) they hate and resist avarice, pride, lewdness, drunkenness, hatred, envy, backbiting, lying, defrauding, quarrelling, blood-shedding, idolatry; in short, all unclean and carnal works, and deny the world with its lusts, (Gal. 6,) they meditate upon the law of the Lord by day and by night; (Ps. 1,) they rejoice at the good and are grieved at the evil, (Rom. 10,) evil they do not repay with evil, but with good; they seek not *self*, nor their own, but what is good for their neighbors, both as to body and soul; they feed the hungry, and give drink to the thirsty, (Matt. 25,) they entertain the needy, release prisoners, visit the sick, comfort the faint-hearted, admonish the erring, and are ready after their master's example, to give their lives for their brethren. Again, their thoughts are pure and chaste, their words are true and seasoned with salt; with them is *yea*, what is *yea*, and *nay*, what is *nay*, and their works are done in the fear of the Lord; their hearts are heavenly and new; their minds peaceful and joyful; they seek righteousness with all their powers. In short, they are so assured in their faith through God's spirit and word, (Rom. 12, 15; James 1, 5; 2 John 3; Col. 4; Matt. 5,) that they will valiantly overcome, by virtue of their faith, all blood-thirsty, cruel tyrants, with all their tortures, punishment, exiling, plunder, stocks and stakes, executioners, tormentors and counsel; and out of a pure zeal, with an innocent pure heart, and with a simple *yea* and *nay* are willing to die. Christ's glory, the sweetness of the word, and the salvation of souls are dearer to them than any thing under heaven.

Behold, worthy reader: " All those who are born of God with

Christ, thus conform their weak life after the gospel, are thus converted, and follow the example of Christ, hear and believe his holy word, follow his commands, which he left and commanded us in the holy scriptures, form the holy christian church which has the promise; the true children of God, brothers and sisters of Christ; for they are born with him of one Father, (John 1; Heb. 2,) the new Eve, the pure chaste bride. (Heb. 12; 2 Cor. 6.) Flesh of Christ's flesh, and bone of his bone, (Eph 5,) the spiritual house of Israel, the spiritual city, Jerusalem, temple and Mount Zion, (Heb. 9) the spiritual ark of the Lord, in which are hidden the true bread of heaven, Christ Jesus; and his blessed word, the green blossoming rod of faith, and spiritual tables of stone, with the commands of the Lord written thereon; they are the spiritual seed of Abraham, children of the promise, confederates of God's covenant, partakers of the heavenly blessings."

These regenerated have a spiritual king over them, who rules them by the unbroken sceptre of his mouth, namely, with his Holy Spirit and word, he clothes them with the garment of righteousness, of pure white silk; he refreshes them with the living water of his Holy Spirit, and feeds them with the bread of life. His name is Christ Jesus. They are the children of peace, who have beaten their swords into plough-shares, and their spears into pruning hooks, and know of no war; and give to Cæsar the things that are Cæsar's, and to God the things that are God's. (Isa. 2; Mich. 4; Matt. 22.) Their sword is the sword of the spirit, which they hold in a good conscience through the Holy Ghost. Their marriage is that of one man and one woman, according to God's ordinance. Their kingdom is the kingdom of grace, here in hope, and after this is eternal life. (Eph. 6; Heb. 4; Rev. 2, 19; 2 Esp. 13; Gen. 1; Matt. 19, 25; 1 Cor. 7; 1 Tim. 3; Tit. 1; Luke 12, 13; Rom. 8.)

Their citizenship is in heaven; and they use the creatures below, such as eating, drinking, clothing and dwelling with thanksgiving, and that to the necessary wants of their own lives, and to the service of their neighbor, according to the word of the Lord. (Isa. 58; Tob. 4, 14; Matt. 25; Luke 6; Rom. 12.) Their doctrine is the unadulterated word of God, testified through Moses and the prophets, through Christ and the apostles, upon which they built their faith, and save their souls, (James 1) and every thing that is contrary thereto, they consider accursed. (Gal. 1.) They use and administer their baptism on believing, according to the command of the Lord, and according to the doctrines and usages of the apostles. (Matt. 28; Mark 16; Acts 2, 8, 10, 16, 19, &c.

Their Lord's supper they celebrate in remembrance of the

Lord's favors and his death, (Matt. 26 ; Mark 14 ; Luke 22 ; 1 Cor. 11,) and in reminding one another of true and brotherly love. (1 Cor. 10.)

The *ban* and *separation* extend to all the proud scorners, great and small, rich and poor, without any respect to person, who heard and obeyed the word for a season, but fell off again and in the house of the Lord, teach or live offensively, till they again sincerely repent. (Rom. 16 ; Tit. 3 ; 1 Cor. 5 ; 2 Thes. 2.)

They daily sigh and lament over their poor displeasing, evil flesh, over the manifold errors and faults of their weak lives. They war inwardly and outwardly without ceasing. They sigh and call to the Most High ; fight and struggle against the devil, world and flesh during their lives, press on towards the prize of the high calling that they may obtain it. (Phil. 3,) And they prove by their actions that they believe the word of the Lord, that they know and have Christ in power, that they are born of God and have God as their Father. (John 1 ; Eph. 2.)

Behold, worthy reader, as I said before, so say I again. These are the christians who have the promise and are assured by the spirit of God, to whom are given and bestowed Christ Jesus, with all his merits, righteousness, intercessions, word, cross, suffering, flesh, blood, death, resurrection, kingdom, and all his possessions, and this all without merit, out of pure grace from God. But what kind of doctrine, faith, life, regeneration, baptism, supper, ban and divine service, sectarian churches have, of whatever name ; and what kind of reward is promised them in the scriptures, I will let the reasonable meditate on, with the aid of the Lord's spirit and word.

Here I would call on all the high and mighty lords, princes and rulers, all under the canopy of heaven, also on all the popes, cardinals and bishops, together with all the wise and learned, who from the beginning perverted and darkened the scriptures, to show us one single word in the whole Bible, I say in the Bible ; (for we do not regard human fables and lies) that an unbelieving, refractory, sensual man, without true repentance and regeneration, was *ever* or ever *will* be saved, simply because he boasts of faith and the death of Christ, or heard the masses and service of the priests, as the whole world does ; if so, they shall have gained the point. But this *never was* and *never will* be ; for if such vile men could be saved without repentance and regeneration, by hearing masses, and confessing, as they, poor children, without the warrant of the scripture, hope ; then we might of a truth say, that the aforementioned means were stronger, (though they are idolatrous) than the word of the Lord. For the word knows no mass, but says : That the impenitent shall die in their sins. (Luke 13.) Then would also Moses and the prophets, Christ and his apostles, have been false witnesses, and have miserably deceived us, because they directed us upon such a narrow path.

Ah no! friends, no! Beware, I tell you, God will not deceive you. For he says through the prophet Malachi 3 : For I am the LORD, I change not. All that he has testified us in his holy word through his prophets, through Christ and his apostles, is his eternal, immutable will ; on this we may all rely if we wish not to deceive our souls. In short, all is in vain to counsel and advise. True repentance and the birth from above, must take place ; we must believe Christ and his word, and we must abide by his word, spirit, ordinance and example, or eternal misery must be our portion—this is incontrovertible.

Therefore, I admonish and entreat you, as those whom my soul loves, repent! repent!! I say, and delay not ; for the axe is already laid to the root of the trees, and that which does not bring forth fruit, is cut off and cast into the fire. (Matt. 3.) Watch over your poor souls, being bought with a precious price, and be no longer comforted with open lies, nor be fed upon chaff ; for behold, I tell you, there is nothing under heaven that can, or will eternally stand before God, but the new creature, (Luke 15 ; Gal. 6,) and *faith which works by love*, (Gal. 5,) and the *keeping of the commandments.* (1 Cor. 7.)

My faithful reader, do not only believe me, but believe the word, to which, by the grace of God, I directed you with my small talents ; for as true as the Lord liveth: All who teach otherwise than we have shown from the word of the Lord, whoever they be, are prophets, who deceive you, who place pillows under your arms, and cushions under your heads ; who whitewash the wall with delusions, and speak peace to the wicked, but not out of the mouth of the Lord, (Jer. 14, 23 ; Ezek. 13.) For as certain as it is that the penitent and regenerated are the true christians, who have obtained God's truth, the true light, pardon of their sins, and the sure promise of eternal life, so certain also is it, that the sensual and impenitent are false christians, and have serpentine lies, darkness, propensity for sin, and the certain promise of eternal death. This will eternally be found to be true ; of this his word is to me a true witness ; and of this I am confidently assured through his grace.

Now, perhaps, some may answer us : Our belief is, that Christ is the Son of God, that his word is truth, and that he purchased us with his death and blood, and that we were regenerated in baptism and received the Holy Ghost, and therefore, we are the true church and community of Christ.

We reply : If your faith is as you say, why do you not the

things which he has commanded you in his word? His command is: REFORM—BE YE CONVERTED—KEEP THE COMMANDMENTS. (Matt. 18, 19; Mark 1.) And it is evident that you are becoming worse daily; that *unrighteousness* is your father, and *wickedness* your mother, and the expressed command of the Lord is foolishness and derision to you. Since you will not do as he commands, or would have you do, but you act as you choose, it proves sufficiently that you do not believe that Jesus Christ is the Son of God, though you say so. Nor do you believe that his word is truth; for faith and its fruits are inseparable, this you have all to confess by the grace of God. O, you poor, blind men! be silent and blush—let Christ Jesus with his spirit and word be your teacher and example—your way and your mirror. Do you think it will do to only acknowledge Christ according to the flesh? Or if you but say that you believe on him and are baptized—that you are christians, and you that are purchased with Christ's death and blood? Ah no! I told you often, and tell you again, you must be born of God—in your life you must be so converted and changed that you become new creatures in Christ, that Christ be in you, and you in Christ, or you can never be christians; For he that is in Christ is a new creature. (2 Cor. 5.)

If you believe rightly in Christ, as you boast, then manifest it by your lives that you believe; For the righteous live by faith, as the scriptures say. (Hab. 2; Rom. 1; Gal. 3; Heb. 10.) And that this is all true has been fully testified and shown by the works of Abel, Enoch and Noah, Abraham, Isaac, Jacob and Joseph, Moses, Joshua, Caleb, Samuel, David, Matthias, Zaccheus, Magdalene and Paul, and all the pious children of God, who were from the beginning and to this day. But as you conduct yourselves in your faith, and as you are minded, may be more than plainly seen by your prevalent lies, fraud, avarice, hoarding up, cursing, swearing, pride and wantonness; for your hearts burn in unrighteousness; you fear neither God nor his word; nevertheless, you boast that you believe on Christ, have his word, and that you are christians, &c. I repeat it: *Reform*, or hold your peace and be ashamed.

Further, you imagine that you were regenerated in your baptism and received the Holy Ghost. Faithful reader, remember, if it even had been so, as you say, still you have to acknowledge that your regeneration then took place without hearing the word, without the faith and knowledge of Christ, and without knowledge and understanding; and besides, that the aforementioned birth and the received spirit are altogether without operation, wisdom, power or fruit; yea, are vain and dead in you; for that you live neither after the spirit nor in the power of the new birth, is evident from your gross avarice, drunkenness, pride, wantonness, and the idolatrous, sensual lives, of which those baptized among you are my witnesses. Yea, my friends, if you were born of God in your baptism, and had received the Holy Ghost, as your comforters persuade and assure you, then it could not be otherwise than that the new spiritual life and its fruits would also be manifest, as it was the case with the saints from the beginning, and is yet ; for it is more than clear, that the regenerated do not presumptuously live in sin, but through faith, in true repentance, by baptism, are buried into the death of Christ, and also arise with him to a new life, (Rom. 6,) and those who have the spirit of the Lord, bring forth also the fruits of the spirit. (Gal. 5.) But that you do not bury your sins, but serve them in full power, and also bring not forth the fruits of the spirit, is daily testified by your vain, sensual, abominable life. My friends, out of true love I warn you to awaken and observe what the word of the Lord teaches ; for the spirit of the Lord will not dwell in a wicked soul, nor in a body subjected to sin. (Wis. 1.)

In the second place, I tell you : If you are rightly baptized according to the word of the Lord, as you imagine, then you have put on Christ, (Gal. 3,) and live no longer after Adam's inbred evil nature, but after Christ's regenerated good nature, &c. But since this is not the case with you, but you are yet altogether sensual and earthly, as is evident from all your fruits, hence it is clear that you are not regenerated, baptized christians, but impenitent, sensual pagans, for your works are chiefly done after a heathen will, as we may see and hear. Once more, I say : awaken and hear what the word of the Lord says : *For if you have put on Christ, that is, if Christ be in you, the body is dead because of sin : but the spirit is life because of righteousness.* (Rom. 8.)

In the third place, I tell you : if you are rightly baptized according to the word of the Lord, then you are members and joint heirs of the body of Christ, (1 Cor. 12,) and have the evidence of a good conscience before God. (1 Pet. 3.) Inasmuch as a body is never divided in itself, nor hates its members, or does them harm, but one member serves and assists another ; and since it is evident, and is indeed found to be so with you, that you unmercifully persecute, murder and exterminate the chosen members of Christ, who are of your own flesh and blood, whom he purchased by his death, regenerated by his word, endowed with his spirit, and has chosen as his own people ; and besides they seek no help nor comfort of human institutions, but solely adhere with a pure faith to the Lord's grace, righteousness, prayer, merits, death and blood; and you depend upon and comfort yourselves with the priest's and monk's masses, confession, absolution, holy water, bread, wine, oil and vigils; so the works themselves testify that you are not serviceable members of the aforementioned body, but are much more destroyers and defilers. That you have not a firm, joyful, peaceable and good conscience, but a wavering, damning, restless and evil conscience before God; for all unrighteousness is esteemed as abomination by the consciences of the pious; but we see that it is to your conscience great consolation, because you neither have nor know Christ. My friends, beware, you are miserably deceived by your comforters. The spirit of prophesy says: And unto the angel of the church in Smyrna write: These things say the first and the last, which was dead and is alive—I know the blasphemy of them which say they are Jews, and are not: but are of the synagogue of satan. (Rev. 2.) Well may it be said at the present time to all the great and specious sects: I know the great defamations, and see the wicked lives of those who say they are regenerated, baptized christians, and are not, but are satan's synagogue; for I know not how they could do worse.

But if we come to the chief and mighty rulers, there we find pride and wantonness, dancing, whoring, chasing, stabbing, breaking, fighting, destroying of cities and countries—living after the lusts of their hearts.

If we come to the subordinate officers, there we find insatiable avarice, treachery and roguery, cunning devices to defraud the helpless God-fearing, (the good and pious I do not mean,) they take gifts and presents; the right of the righteous they pervert and willingly accept of gifts to shed innocent blood; they persecute the truth; they reject what is right and good; the fear of God is not before their eyes.

If we come to the divines whether preachers, priests or monks, there we find such an idle, lazy, wanton and sensual life, such a corrupted, anti-christian doctrine, and understanding of the scriptures; such hatred, envy, defaming, betraying, lying and uproar against all the pious, that I would be ashamed to mention it before the virtuous.—The common people run, as a frantic heifer, as the prophet laments. (Hos. 4.) They lie and cheat, curse and swear by the Lord's wounds and sacraments, by his judgment, hand, power, might, suffering, death and blood. I am ashamed and astonished that I have to think of these scandalous abominations. They gamble, drink and wrestle, wrangle and quarrel. In short, their prevalent, horrible, cruel and wicked lives are not to be related, and their great folly cannot be prevented; yet it must be said; that the mentioned lords, judges, learned and common people, are the truly regenerated church and baptized community of Christ. May the merciful Lord graciously preserve all his chosen children from such a regeneration, baptism and community. Amen.

I testify to you the truth in Christ Jesus, take heed, if you please : Jesus Christ did not endure from the beginning such openly impenitent, sensual sinners in his holy city, kingdom and community, and he will never endure them—believe this to be true.

O Almighty God and Lord, how miserably thy holy and paternal will and thy adorably great name are derided, and how little is thy saving, precious word esteemed : yea, what an abominable, idolatrous, sensual, revengeful and blood-thirsty devil is made of thy beloved Son ; for they cover all their abominations, sins and disgraces with his blessed, holy name, word, death and blood.

Be ashamed, O you heedless, perverted men, be ashamed, I say, before God and his angels that you are so rebellious and refractory ; that you live so rudely. But yet you say that you are the rightly regenerated community and baptized church of Christ. Oft have I told you, and tell you again ; all who are born of God, rightly baptized with the spirit, fire and water, as the scriptures teach, are of a heavenly and divine mind ; their sins they bury, lead a penitent, pious life according to the Lord's word. They show the nature and power of Christ which dwells in them by word and work; they bring forth the fruits of the spirit, and subdue the works of the flesh ; they are useful members of the body of Christ, and labor according to the gift received. In short, they are fruitful branches of the true vine, and their fruits abide to eternal life. (John 15.)

But since it is manifest in you, that you show the reverse in all your fruits, and we do see in your whole lives, that it is but word and flesh with you, hence it is more than clear, that your boasting of the new birth, spirit, baptism, community and church, is not the truth ; but lies and falsehood.

The holy scriptures and our common belief, teach us that the holy christian church is an assembly of the righteous, and a community of saints ; and he that can see but partially into the scriptures, must confess that your church and assembly are a church and assembly of the unrighteous, of the lascivious, of the impenitent and sensual ; yea, of the blood-thirsty wolves, lions, bears, basalisks, serpents, and fiery, flying dragons.

Ah ! friends, lift your heads, and open your eyes ? O ye bewitched ! look over the whole world, what life they lead who have received the same baptism with you ; who practise like ordinances and worships, who indulge in the same boasting of the Lord's death and blood, and say that they are the church

and people of Christ.   For it is clearer than mid-day, that many
of you are so insane, so influenced by the spirit of the devil, that
you hate, envy, bite and devour one another ; so that you wholly
destroy principalities, cities, castles and citadels with your accursed fightings and uproar ; human blood you shed like water ;
deprive the poor citizen and peasant (those of your own faith)
of body and possessions by burning, robbing, plundering, catch-
ing, imposition, torturing, nay even those who have never harmed
you, or given you a rash word.   In truth, I know not, how the
infernal Behemoth could be more devilish and cruel than you or
your members, who imagine that they are the church of Christ.
God preserve us !   You disgrace families, you persecute the
righteous ; you encourage open brothels, tippling houses, boxing
schools, gaming boards, and the like disgraces, idolatrous houses
and images, with all false service and the like, without measure
and bounds.   I will not touch your intolerable, scandalous
cursing and swearing, drunkenness, wantonness, &c.   I cannot
say much, I tremble ; for it strikes me that none is to be found
under the canopy of heaven, who can minutely relate your belief, and baptized persons' great abominations, wicked acts, mis-
usages, gross scandals ; a righteous person must be astounded,
and terror stricken at those great sins.   O dear Lord strengthen
us !   Yea, he that does not rightly understand that you are not
born from above, but are baptized contrary to all scripture, and
that all your boasting of the forgiveness of sins, Christ's mercy,
grace, merits, flesh, blood, cross, death, community, kingdom
and eternal promise, is vain, and without the scriptures, he must
be, we may say, an irrational man.

Ah, readers ! How little you think upon the word of the Lord,
which is so highly recommended to you ; and how little you regard your poor souls, which are bought with such a precious
price, and are eternally to live with God in heaven, or eternally
to be dying with the devil in hell.   Think you, my friends, that
the Lord is a dreamer, or his word is false ?   Ah, no, not a
letter will fall to the ground of all that be spoke.   It is high
time that you would reflect that God's promise and grace are not
to the unregenerated and impenitent, but to the regenerated
and penitent.   Let every one take warning and trust no longer
in lies, believing that he is baptized and regenerated, nor trust
to long standing usages, nor upon papistic decretals, nor imperial mandates, nor upon the wisdom and glossaries of the
learned, nor upon the opinion of any man, council, institution
and wisdom.   God says through the prophet : My counsel shall
stand, and I will do all my pleasure.   God's word is eternal.
Neither princes, nor power, nor the commands of men with all
their imperial edicts can save a single soul. (Isa. 29, 40, 46 ; 1

Pet. 1; Matt. 25.) Only the heavenly counsel we must hear and follow—that which Jesus Christ, God's true and only begotten Son himself brought from heaven, and taught from the mouth of his Father, and confirmed by signs and wonders, and finally sealed it with his crimson blood. This counsel stands, I say, and can never be changed or prevailed against by the gates of hell. By this counsel we are in common taught, that we must hear Christ—believe on him—follow his footsteps—that we must repent—be born from above—become like little children, not in understanding, but in malice—be of the same mind with Christ—that we have to walk as he did—deny ourselves, take up his cross and follow him—that if we love father and mother, children or life more than him, we are not worthy of him, nor are we his disciples. Again, that adulterers, whoremongers, drunkards, murderers, idolaters and the like, shall not inherit the kingdom of God. That we love not the world and the things therein—nor conform to the world—that we through faith are to die unto our evil flesh, and conquer the devil—that we are to lead an upright, unblamable, pious life through faith in all things, act according to the will of the Lord. Again, that we are to baptize upon faith and not without it—celebrate the Lord's supper in a sincerely penitent communion, I mean so far as man can judge. That we practise exclusion or the ban according to the scriptures. That we are to fear and serve the Lord with all the heart, and walk in his commands—and that we are to assist and serve our neighbor as much as in us is, and the like doctrine and instruction. (John 3, 8, 13; Matt. 5. 7, 10, 11, 16, 19, 22, 28; 1 John 1, 2, 5; Luke 13, 14, 18, 22, 24; 1 Cor. 5, 6, 11; Gal. 5; Rom. 12, 16; 1 Pet. 2, 3, 5; Phil. 12; Mark 16, 24; Tit. 3; 2 Thes. 3; Deut. 5, 10; John 14; Isa. 28; Lev. 19.)

Behold, worthy reader, here you have in part the immutable, eternal council of God, which was sealed in the councils of his Majesty, and besides this, he recognizes no other. Blessed are they who receive this with a firm faith, and conform thereto according to their abilities, in all weakness; that is, live according to Christ's spirit, word, ordinance, command, prohibition and unblamable example. On the contrary, cursed are they who despise, reject, curse, hate, defame, mock and persecute it, and comfort themselves with human power, institutions and fables. For they deny the Lord who bought them, and reject the gospel of peace; and do not believe that Jesus Christ is their Messiah, Saviour, High Priest and Prophet. (2 Pet. 2.) Ah! how well for them if they had never been born. The Lord mercifully grant them converted and renewed hearts, that they may repent and be eternally saved, if it is possible.

I will now close the matter and direct the well-meaning reader

23

to the scriptures; since the whole word, with few exceptions, is built upon human doctrine, lies, invented fables, perverted glossaries, vain idolatry and false service, by which the people of the world comfort themselves and boast of what they neither have nor are; therefore did I very briefly show in this epistle according to my ability, who the truly regenerated and baptized christians are who have the promise, or who are not such; so that all who truly hunger and thirst, who are zealous for God, may be rightly satisfied with the truth unto eternal salvation; and no longer follow deceit to their eternal condemnation. Yea, that all may be benefitted, become whole and be saved—all who now stand so miserably poor and wretched before the eyes of the Lord. The Lord strengthen you—believe God's infallible word—reform your sinful lives, pray with confidence and be obedient to the gospel of Christ, that you may receive the eternal promise to your eternal joy and salvation, which God the Father promised to all his beloved children through Christ. Grace be with all who seek Christ and eternal life with all the heart. Amen. If you will suffer Jesus Christ, with his eternal spirit and word to be judge, then you will learn that the *sure Foundation of Truth* has been shown.

AN EXHORTATION

TO THE DISPERSED AND UNKNOWN CHILDREN OF GOD.

To all the chosen children of God, dispersed here and there, to the sanctified in Christ Jesus, unknown to me, my beloved brethren and fellow believers to you be the kingdom and portion of Christ's grace and peace.

CORDIALLY beloved brethren and sisters in Christ Jesus, I inform you with great joy that some brethren have written and informed me how the merciful, faithful Father endowed you with the heavenly gift of his divine knowledge, and enlightened you with his Holy Spirit, that your faith works by love, your hope is lively, and your union among each other, is christian-like, and that your peace is pleasant, and that the community of the Lord is increased and extended daily in great power and glory, through the grace of God. For this I thank his paternal kindness with joyful heart, and I pray his grace inasmuch as he has called you to the fellowship of his beloved Son, and to the imperishable, eternal kingdom of his glory through his holy gospel that He may now and henceforth preserve you with the strong power of his divine arm, in your faith, love, doctrine, understanding, truth and life, without any offence till the end. Faithful is he who has called you, (1 Thes. 5) and he will undoubtedly do it, if you only continue to be zealous in prayer, and unwavering in your undertaking, never become sleepy nor slothful, nor at last return again, as did refractory and disobedient Israel to the flesh pots of Egypt. (Num. 11.) May the Lord eternally and graciously preserve us. Since, you are then called to such a high and glorious grace, as related, and we undoubtedly know our weak flesh, and the sinful nature which we possess from Adam which makes our whole heart and life unclean, and besides we learn from the scriptures, that our opponent, the devil goes about like a roaring lion, having rest neither day nor night, but always seeking that he might devour us. (1 Pet. 5.)

I do, therefore, exhort you as my fellow-combatants, against evil flesh, and the tents of death, that you may strictly watch over yourselves, that you circumcise, teach and sanctify your hearts with the spirit of God, (Deut. 10, 30;) exhort and reprove one another, curb your thoughts, subdue and extinguish your impure evil lusts, in the fear of the Lord; for blessed are the pure in heart. Walk worthy of the Lord and his gospel to which you have come. Whatever God has commanded do it without murmuring; (Jer. 4; Rom. 2; Eccl. 23; Matt. 5; Phil. 1;) act so that none of a truth may complain of you, be sincere children of God, unblamable in this crooked and perverse generation, and shine as lights in the midst of a dark night in this present evil world. (Phil. 1, 2,)

Take the Lord Jesus Christ as an example, and follow his footsteps; walk as he walked, therefore did Moses and all the prophets preach, (Matt. 11; John 13; 1 Pet. 2; 1 John 2;) to that end did the Son of God come down from heaven, sent out the holy apostles, and instituted baptism and the Lord's supper as the mouth of the Lord commanded, that we may thereby be admonished to awaken, to repent and lead an unblamable pious life in all righteousness. Be ye holy, for I am holy, says the Lord; Peter says: But ye are a chosen generation, a royal priesthood, an holy nation, a peculiar people; that ye should show forth the praises of him who hath called you out of darkness into his marvellous light. (Lev. 19; Exod. 19; 1 Pet. 2; 2 Pet. 1; John 3.) You are guests called to the Lord's table, and have come to the marriage of the Lord; ye are his chosen friends and bride, therefore hear his voice willingly, (Rev. 19,) and whatever is pleasing to him do cheerfully. Adorn yourself with the shining garment of white linen, (Rev. 2,) be faithful unto death, and beware of all strange gods, (Ezek. 16,) dedicate yourselves wholly unto the Lord; that he may teach, reprove, govern and lead you with his spirit and word, and have his perfect work in you, for you are in his grace, and through his grace you are espoused unto him, bought with his blood, reconciled to the Fataer, sanctified as priests and kings, and made heirs of his eternal kingdom. (1 Cor. 6; Col. 1; Rev. 1, 5.) Therefore it is proper and right that we should be grateful to such a kind Lord, for such gifts; hear him, lay his word to heart and do what is well pleasing to him.

Beloved children: Fear not, but be joyful; for he is such a faithful, pious king, to whom you have sworn and bowed your knees, not the least of his promises shall fail you, he will be our shield and great reward, (Gen. 15,) therefore, doubt and stagger not; for it is but a small thing that we endure the heat of the sun, tribulation, fear, sorrow, temptation, robbing, persecution, prison and death for a time. The messenger is now at the door. who says to us: Come ye blessed of my Father, enter the joys of the Lord, (Matt. 25,) then will our short-lived pain be changed into ceaseless exultation; these bloody tyrants, with their bloody mandates, will come to an end, and all our persecutors, avengers, executioners and torturers will cease; we will follow the Lamb, adorned in white garments, (Rev. 7; Esd. 2,) with palms in our hands and crowns upon our head; neither torment nor pain, nor pangs of death will harm us, (Wis. 3;) but we will serve him who sits upon the throne, and praise and adore the Lamb eternally.

Behold, my little children, all the truly believing pious hearts, comfort themselves with the approaching change, that they may possess their souls with patience; well knowing that great is their reward in heaven, (Luke 21; Matt. 5,) and that, on the other hand all the ungodly shall have their portion in the eternal, unchangeable fire, under the intolerable and dreadful sentence of God, in the abyss of hell, if they do not be converted and repent with all their hearts. Wo! wo!! to these wretched people! for it was an evil day in which they were born!!—My little children be cheerful in Christ, and despair not, (Luke 21; Matt. 5,) for so long as we love God sincerely, seek and fear him; and with a pure zeal walk in the truth. (Rev. 21, 22,) neither world nor flesh, neither tyranny nor devil, neither sin, hell, nor death shall hinder us; but we will have for our aid, the victory, by the grace of God, gained by a firm faith in the blood of Christ, and this through the spirit of Christ which dwells in us. David says: By my God I can leap over a wall. (Ps. 18.) Paul says: I can do all things through Christ, who strengthens me. (Phil. 4.) Christ says: Be of good cheer I have overcome the world; (John 16,) and thus will they overcome, who will abide in Christ, as we may not only see in the prophets and apostles. but also in many pious hearts at the present day, in great power and clearness.

I have nothing particular any more, to write, therefore, beware that you walk wisely and circumspectly, (Eph. 2; Matt. 22, 25,) preserve your wedding garment, have oil at all times in your lamp, lest the Lord meet you in an undue time, find you unprepared and in nudity, and close the door on you, or thrust you into deep darkness.

With unfeigned, true, brotherly love, and out of a pure heart, love each other cordially, as those who are regenerated not of corrupt but of incorruptible seed, out of the word of the living God, which abides to eternity. (1 Pet. 1.) For love is of God and of a divine nature; (1 John 4;) love does right before God and man; it is long-suffering, compassionate and peaceable. (1 Cor. 13; Rom. 13.) In short, love is unblamable and brings forth christian fruit; it is the spiritual girdle of Aaron and his sons; the girdle of perfection and the fair bond of peace. (Lev. 28; Col. 3; Eph. 4.) O how completely happy is he, who is girded with this bond, for he is born of God, and God is in him; yea, where this love is, there we find the true, sincere and pious christian. Therefore, take care of this bond, (1 John 1,) for if you loose this, you will lose Christ Jesus and eternal life.

Beware of false doctrine, of all discord, strife and dissention, and without wavering, adhere to Christ's spirit, word and example, if you would not be deceived; for every spirit which is not satisfied with Christ's spirit, word and example, and will not conform thereto, in his weakness, he is not out of God, but he is the spirit of antichrist, who would rob you again and all the pious of the precious light of revealed truth, (which graciously appeared to us, poor children, in these abominable days,) and would again lead you on the crooked paths of death, under the semblance of the scriptures.

My little children in Christ, be you warned, out of true, brotherly love, I write to you; the merciful, gracious God grant that you may read, hear, and understand it, that it may bring much fruit among you, and that you may abide in eternal life. Pray for your unknown brother, who loves you, in truth. He that continues to be perfect to the end, shall be saved. The saving power and fruits of the crimson blood of Christ, be with you, and with all my chosen brothers and sisters to eternity. Amen.

23*

A

CONSOLING ADMONITION

CONCERNING THE

SUFFERINGS, OPPRESSIONS

AND

PERSECUTIONS OF THE SAINTS,

FOR THE

WORD OF GOD AND HIS TESTIMONY.

———————

Blessed are ye when men shall revile you, and persecute you, and shall say all manner of evil against you, falsely, for my sake. Rejoice and be exceeding glad, for great is your reward in heaven: for so persecuted they the prophets which were before you.—(MATT 5.) Yea, and all that will live godly in Christ Jesus, must suffer persecution. —(2 TIM. 3.)

For other foundation can no man lay than that it is laid, which is Jesus Christ.— 1 COR. 3.

PREFACE.

I, MENNO SIMON, desire sincerely that all the true children of God may obtain grace, peace, frankness of heart, a perfect mind, in all temptations, from God our heavenly Father, through his dear son, our Lord Jesus Christ, in the power of his holy spirit, to his eternal praise and glory, and to our edification and salvation. Amen.

Beloved brethren and sisters in the Lord, the all-merciful God and Father, through his boundless grace and goodness, has again, in these last times of unbelief, abominations and idolatry, in this terrible, wanton, ruthless, perverted and blood-thirsty world, revealed before the eyes of the consciences of some, his blessed, only, and eternal Son, Jesus Christ, who was unknown for so many centuries. He has again opened the book of the divine declarations and eternal truth, which had been closed for hundreds of years. (Gal. 3; Rev. 5; 2 Kings, 22, 23.) Some of those who lay dead, not for four days only, as Lazarus did, according to the flesh, but for twenty or thirty years, yea, who all their life-long slumbered in the spiritual death of sin and all ungodliness, have awakened from the foul grave of unbelief and unrighteousness, and have been called to a new unblamable life. And through the preaching of his word, in the power of his holy spirit, he continues to call the poor, miserable, starving sheep out of the hands of the faithless shepherds (Ezek. 34), and out of the clutches of the ravening wolves; he leads them out of the dry, unfruitful pastures of man's doctrine, and commands, to the green, fat pastures upon the mount of Israel, and places them under the power and protection of their only and eternal shepherd, Christ Jesus, who, through his precious, crimson blood has cleansed, purified and taken them for his own. (1 Pet. 1; Eph. 1; 1 Cor. 6; Tit. 2.) Therefore, the gates of hell foam and rage, they erect themselves and show themselves in all their horrors. Herod with the whole city is above measure frightened and enraged, because he has heard of the wise men (those who are taught of God) that the King of the Jews is born. (Matt. 2.) The great dragon, the old crooked serpent, who was cast from heaven, whose head and power has been bruised and broken by the promised seed of the woman, is overcome by the blood of the Lamb, and, on account of the word of his testimony, burns with anger. He knows well that his time is short, and therefore he carries on his works and tyranny, through his children and servants, the unbelievers, with great wrath and fierceness, against those who have been sprinkled with the blood of the Lamb. (Rev. 12; Gen. 3; Eph. 2; Eccl. 12; Matt. 16.) Annas and Caiaphas counsel to slay Christ. Judas and all false apostles and teachers betray and deliver him up. Herod, with all his lords and princes, scorn and mock him. The people cry out, crucify him! crucify him! (Matt. 26.) Pilate, and all those who bear the sword, sentence him to stocks, fire, sword and water. The servants seize, spit upon, scourge, crown and kill him. The centurion opens his side, the others mock, blaspheme and upbraid him. Who is there who does not persecute with heart, word or deed, the poor, innocent, peaceful, defenceless Lamb? Yea, with the ungodly Cain began the bloody tyranny which has manifested itself in oppressing the pious and godly.

Thus the Lamb has been persecuted and belied from the beginning, in his chosen, by the malice of the conquered serpent ; and it appears from the scriptures that such will be the case, as long as the righteous and unrighteous exist upon earth. Particularly in our times it may be seen, that the cross of Christ is renewed in the pious children of God (as was the case with the fathers), who are inwardly born again out of the seed of the word of God. I cannot forbear to admonish with the word of God, my fellow believers and joint sufferers. The crosses and persecutions of the saints were shown in the scriptures to the fathers, both of the old and new testament, and now to the godly witnesses of our times, in order that after their example they may fearlessly and bravely stand the contest, with long-suffering, patience and willingness, through the power of their faith in Christ Jesus, and receive the promised Canaan. (Heb. 12 ; 1 John, 5 ; 2 Tim. 4 ; James, 1.) For this purpose, grant to us, Father of every good and perfect gift, the riches of thy grace in the power of thy Spirit through thy dear son, Jesus Christ, our Lord. Amen.

OF THE CROSS OF CHRIST.

BLESSED are they (said Christ) which are persecuted for right-eousness' sake, for theirs is the kingdom of heaven. (Matt. 5.)

I know well, worthy brethren and sisters in the Lord, that the true laborers and servants of the Lord, have each one planted and watered according to the gifts which they have received. (1 Cor. 3, 4.) They have caused you to be born again of the living word of the holy gospel of Jesus Christ, and to be built upon Christ the firm and immoveable corner stone. They have taught you the word, will and ordinances of God according to his good pleasure. They have united you as a willing, obedient and pure bride to your bridegroom, Christ Jesus. They go before you in all earnestness, in the narrow way—they preach the cross, and point out the pains and costs of this godly build-ing, for it can never be otherwise (as you well know) than that all who would hear and follow Christ, who would enter through the right door, and would walk upon the highway to eternal life in the light of Christ, must first deny themselves, and all they are with the whole heart. They must, in all misery, ignominy and trouble, take upon themselves the pressing cross, and must follow the rejected, outcast, bleeding and crucified Christ, as he himself said: If any man will come after me, let him deny him-self, and take up his cross and follow me. (Matt. 16.) Yes all who do not stand prepared to take up this grievous life of the cross and trouble, and hate not father and mother, son, daughter, husband and wife, houses, land, money, goods and life, cannot be Christ's disciples. (Luke 14.)

My faithful brethren this is a true and sure word; for the eternal truth, Christ Jesus, has in many places of the scriptures, pointed out and testified in great clearness: Behold, he says, I send you forth as sheep in the midst of wolves: be ye therefore, wise as serpents, and harmless as doves. But beware of men for they will deliver you up to the councils, and they will scourge you in their synagogues, and ye shall be brought before gov-ernors and kings for my sake, for a testimony against them and the gentiles.

Again: The brother shall deliver up the brother to death; and the father the child, and the children shall rise up against their parents, and shall cause them to be put to death, and ye shall be hated of all men for my name's sake.

Again: The disciple is not above his master, nor the servant above his lord. It is enough for the disciple that he be as his master and the servant as his lord. If they have called the master of the house, Beelzebub, how much more shall they call them of his household.

Again: He that loveth father or mother more than me, is not worthy of me, and he that loveth son or daughter more than me, is not worthy of me. And he that taketh not his cross and followeth after me, is not worthy of me. He that findeth his life shall lose it, and he that loseth his life for my sake shall find it. (Matt. 10.)

Again: Then shall they deliver you up to be afflicted, and shall kill you: and ye shall be hated of all nations for my name's sake. (Matt. 24.)

Again: They shall put you out of the synagogues: yea, the time cometh that whosoever killeth you, will think' that he doth God service. (John 15, 16; Matt. 16; Mark 8, 13; Luke 9, 14, 21.)

Again: We must through much tribulation enter into the kingdom of God." (Acts 14.) All who live godly in Christ Jesus, must suffer persecutions. (2 Tim. 3.) If we be dead with him, we shall also live with him; if we suffer, we shall also reign with him. (2 Tim. 2.)

Yea, the whole scriptures abound with exhortatious examples, and histories of the troubles sorrows, miseries, proscriptions, upbraidings, rejections, seizures, ignominious death and crosses of the saints.

Since then true righteousness, devotion and piety, are thus miserably hated, persecuted and cast out, as it has been abundantly shewn in the case of the fathers, and as may be seen and found in these last times, (as we have said) I deem it necessary to show from the word of the Lord, to our youthful brethren and sisters, who such persons are, who prosecute us, and inflict upon us this trouble and sorrow; wherefore they do so, wherewith they maintain their bloody deeds for right; what profit we receive from the cross, and what is promised to those, who, through the power of faith, overcome all temptations and extremities, and maintain the conflict through Christ Jesus, in order that they, through such counsels, may be ready and prepared for all trials. That they may put on the breast-plate of righteousness, the helmet of salvation, with the shield of faith, and be girded with the sharp sword of the spirit in all humility and meekness, patience, (Eph. 6; 1 Thes. 5; 1 John 5,) with ardent prayers and sighs to the Lord, in order that when any swift, unseen uproar, shall arise against us, it shall not fall upon us unawares—that an unexpected storm shall not cast down our house—the heat of the sun shall not scorch the growing plant—the heat and power of the fire shall not consume the erected works, (Matt. 7; Matt. 23; Luke 8; 1 Cor. 3,) and that we be not drawn off and frightened to a deadly apostacy by their threats, uproar and tyranny. Therefore, my beloved, so read and understand in all love, for the Lord knows that out of pure love, I have written this for the benefit of my dear brethren, according to my received gifts.

In the first place, dear brethren, I esteem it to be very useful and necessary to all the godly and the strivers under the cross of Christ, who seek for encouragement in their crosses and sufferings, which they endure for the sake of the testimony of God and their consciences, to think carefully and earnestly, upon those who persecute them, of what disposition and nature they are, upon what way they walk, and of what father, according to the spirit, they are born. All who carefully observe them, and try them by the scriptures, will find, according to my opinion, that they are not Christians, but are an unbelieving, fleshly, earthly, wanton, blind, hardened, lying, idolatrous, perverted, malicious, revengeful, unmerciful and murderous people. A people, who by their actions, show that they neither know Christ nor his Father, although they so highly praise his holy name with the mouth, and extol it with their lips. A people, who tread in slippery, crooked and perverted paths. A people who display not Christian love and peace, (John 16; Isa. 59; Rom. 3,) who bathe their hearts and hands in blood,—their disposition is to seize and kill. (2 Pet. 2.) They are children and co-partners of him, who from the beginning was a murderer and a liar, (John 8,) of whom the whole scriptures testify, that they shall bear forever, the intolerable curse and malediction of the righteous judgment of God, and the devouring flames of hell, except they awake from the deep sleep of their sins, cordially repent, believe the joyous Gospel of Jesus Christ, and put on Christ, and thus show by their whole lives and actions, that they seek their God with all their might, and fear and love him, be they emperors or kings, doctors or licentiates, citizen or peasant, man or wife: For with God, says Paul, there is no respect of persons, but whoever committeth sin, he shall bear the sin. (Col. 3.)

Worthy and faithful brethren in the Lord, observe what a poor miserable and unwise people, in divine things it is, who so bitterly persecute and destroy you on account of your faith. Therefore, it becomes all the true and chosen children of God, how severely soever they may be dealt with, and belied by these people, not to be angry with them, but cordially to pity them, and sigh sorely over their poor souls, and with all meekness and ardency, after the example of Christ and Stephen, to pray for their raging, cursed folly and blindness, for they know not what

24

they do. Who knows but that God may give them eyes and
hearts, that they may see and know their blindness and unbelief, what an impure life they lead, what kind of people they
persecute, and whom they have pierced.

O dear brethren! observe and think well upon your own former life, we have all in former times served one Lord, were
attired in the same habit, as has been said. But what we now
are, we are not of ourselves, but of God, by grace, through
Christ Jesus. The mighty God, who, according to his great
mercy, has called us out of our accursed darkness into his marvellous light, (2 Pet. 2,) lives forever, his ears are not stopped,
nor his hand shortened, (Isa. 59,) he can undoubtedly hear and
help them as he helped us. And if they never repent, but continue with impenitent perverted hearts, in all ungodliness, blood,
wantonness and tyranny, we know what the scriptures testify
concerning them; that they shall not inherit the kingdom of
heaven, (Rom. 1; 2 Cor. 6; Gal. 5; Eph. 5; but their part
will be in the fiery lake which burns with fire and brimstone,
(Rev. 21,) and the fire will be everlasting, (Matt. 25.)

Each one, who reflects that his persecutors are so wholly
blind and destitute of understanding, concerning what the
Spirit directs, as above said, and that their lot shall be like that
of the angels of the bottomless pit—the intolerable wrath of
God, death and hell, which shall last forever, and also that
the sufferings which we have to endure from them for the testimony of Jesus, are but momentary, will through grace, by this
means, preserve his heart pure from all wrath, malice and retal-
iation, and will ardently pray for them; he will commend his
affairs to God in all humility, long-suffering, and peace, will preserve his spirit unbroken, amid prisons, fire and water.

Again, I deem it a soft and mild salve, and a cooling to our
miseries and grief, if we but reflect upon the only reason why our
persecutors so malevolently hate us, and so relentlessly destroy
our name, property, reputation, welfare and lives, which is, because the grace of God, through Christ, has enlightened us, (1
Pet. 4,) because we have believed the preached Gospel, and
have ceased from our blind, ruthless life and deadly works, because we desire, in our weakness, to follow in the fear and love
of God, after the righteousness of faith which is required by
God, and in obedience to the holy word, because we acknowledge the ever blessed Jesus alone for our redeemer, mediator,
intercessor, spiritual king, example, shepherd, infallible teacher
and master, (Matt. 18, 20; 1 John 2; Rom. 8; 1 Tim. 2;
Heb. 6, 7; 1 Tim. 6; Matt. 11; John 13; Matt. 13;) because we, as far as concerns spirit and faith, try and prove all
spirits, doctrines, councils, ordinances, statutes and ceremonies

of Christ, and esteem, with the scriptures, the commands and ceremonies of men, which make void the commands and ceremonies of God, as not only useless, but accursed and idolatrous, because we regard and honor God more than man, we hold in exaltation his high, holy, true and precious word ; because we according to the scriptures, listen not to the unclean, unsound, idolatrous, deceiving and blood-thirsty preachers, Matt. 10 ; Jer. 13 ; Matt. 7, 15 ; John 10 ; Rom. 16 ; 2 John 1 ;) because we admonish and set an example in all love, as far as we are able, to the whole world, with the word and sacraments of God, and with humble, meek lives, (though in weakness,) according to our abilities ; and we rebuke and shame, (though always for their good,) their deceiving doctrine, idolatrous sacrament and their wanton. earthly, fleshly life.   (Wis. 5.)   In short, we set forth to them, the sure and infallible truth of God, and the way of eternal life, and warn and alarm them, with doctrine and life, with eternal death and the wrath of God.

Behold my faithful brethren, it is for these reasons here enumerated ; the world lies, writes, calls, preaches and so malicious are the persecutors against all the pious, they burn with such inhuman rage, that the ravening fierce wolves (John 8,) and roaring lions, when compared with them, cease to be wolves and lions, but seem to be lambs.   For they are so moved by the inflamed, blood-thirsty spirit of their father, that they regard neither the law of God and Christ, (which is love) nor reason and discretion, nor the inwardly written law of nature, by which one honest man should reasonably, according to the good pleasure of God, meet, bear, admonish and serve another in all love.   Yea, oft times the natural father delivers the son up to death, and the son his father ; the mother the daughter, and the daughter her mother ; and one brother another on account of their faith, as said.   (Matt. 10.)

Behold thus haughty and malicious, they assume, without any awe or fear, the umpire of God and the office of the Ghost. They-banish Christ Jesus, the head of all princes and powers, who has all might in heaven and upon earth, from the throne of his divine majesty, (Eph. 1 ; Col. 2 ; Matt. 28 ;) and judge also, with their iron sword, after their own blind opinions, the chosen, godfearing, pious hearts, enlightened in God, through Jesus Christ, over whom no literal sword may ever judge, for they are spiritual, and from their inmost soul are zealous for God and his holy word, even till death.

Behold, so malicious and haughty, (I say,) is human reason and so revengeful and envious is satanic hatred, that they fear not to strive against the Most High, and pierce Christ with their murderous, deadly sword, and persecute with all their power, God's holy spirit, gifts, word, truth and all that he commands and will have us do.

O that God would grant that the blind watchmen (Ezek. 33) of this world, I mean the preachers and theologians, may sound their horns to a right tone and at a proper time, or that they would let them hang on the walls, in order that they may not therewith, tyrannically call out the deadly, murder cry, nor longer deceive the sensual, blind world, nor instigate the rulers and magistracy to the destruction and murdering of the saints like hounds pursuing the roe, nor cause the poor common people to be alarmed on account of their leaven and husks, their spiritual theft and murder, (Matt. 15 ; Luke 15 ; John 10 ;) also that all rulers and magistrates would tear the bridle from their mouths, and cast their instigators from their backs, and not suffer themselves to be thus driven like dumb beasts, and then, according (to my opinion,) it will be well for their poor souls before God. Still, I fear that the lying, murderous serpent, will continue its envious bitings, and the striving woman— the new Eve and her children, must endure to the end, in all patience and long-suffering, its daily bites and stings in the heel.

Since I have here pointed out to you, in a few words, the spirit and nature of those who destroy you and seek your property and your life, and the reasons which impel them to do so ; I will now present some histories and examples from the holy scriptures, for the comfort and encouragement of all miserable, afflicted, and the troubled hearts who suffer for righteousness sake, and in these examples all will be perceived with clearness.

First, the two sons of Adam and Eve were Cain and Abel. Abel was a shepherd and Cain a farmer. In process of time it happened (says Moses) that Cain brought an offering to the Lord from the fruits of the field, and Abel brought one from the first of his flock. And the Lord regarded Abel and his sacrifice but he looked not upon Cain and his gift, therefore, Cain became very angry, and his countenance was distorted through great wrath, even as the ungodly always do, because the Lord regards the pious and their gifts. Cain spoke deceitfully to Abel, who knew not the malicious bloody heart of his brother, saying, "Let us go out" and when they were in the field, Cain's hot, envious spirit could not longer be restrained, and his blood-thirsty, revengeful spirit could not be hid. That which lays concealed in the heart must break out in the actions ; he arose against his brother and in anger murdered him, because Cain was of the evil one and his works were evil, and his brother's works were righteous. (1 John 3.)

It seems to me, dear brethren, that this is a fair example and a good admonition; for the righteous always have been off-scourings and preys to the ûnrighteous, and so will they continue to be as the scriptures sufficiently testify, and as daily experience plainly teaches.

Again : God blessed the patriarch Isaac, and gave him two sons. The elder was Esau, and the younger, Jacob. Esau was a farmer and hunter, and had great pleasure in the chase. Once as he came home much fatigued, he sold his birthright to Jacob his brother, for some food, (Gen. 15.)

After this it happened, that Jacob through the artifice and craft of his mother, obtained the blessing of his father Isaac, by assuming the name and appearance of Esau. (Róm. 9.) This was God's intention and will to remember the literal synagogue and the church of Christ, according to his word to Rebecca ; namely, two nations are in thy womb, and two manner of people shall be separated from thy bowels, and the one people shall be stronger than the other, and the elder shall serve the younger.

When Esau was now aware of this, he wept bitterly and said : Rightly is he called Jacob, for he has supplanted me twice. Esau sought the blessing, but did not obtain it, for God willed it otherwise, as said above.

Esau became very angry with his brother Jacob, on account of the blessing with which his father had blessed him. His malicious, bitter fierceness broke forth, and he said . The time will soon come, that my father will repent, for I will slay my brother. Then had the blessed Jacob to fly from his dear father and mother before his wrathful brother. He flew to a distant country, and became a servant for twenty years in the house of Laban, who did not deal with him according to equity and love. He dared not again enter the land of his birth, till the Lord said to him : Go again to thy native land and 1 will be with thee. (Gen. 31.)

My dear brethren, observe ; for like as the patriarch Jacob, on account of his external birthright and blessing, was hated and persecuted by his sensual fierce brother Esau, thus also it is at the present day, with all those who after the spirit are called after the name of Jacob, (namely, true Christians,) who, in the power of the Holy Ghost, through the medium of faith, tread upon the devil, world, flesh, and blood, they obtain the birthrights which are written in heaven, and are blessed through our true Isaac, Christ Jesus, with spiritual blessings in heavenly things, to eternal glory. (Heb. 12 ; Eph. 1.) They are maliciously hated and persecuted to death by their carnal and licentious brethren, they must flee from one land to another, from one city to another, (Matt. 10,) with great misery, hunger and

24*

distress, in prison and in bonds, with stripes, water, fire and sword, all the days of their lives. (Heb. 11.)

Thus tyranizes the fleshly Esau over the spiritual Jacob, on account of the spiritual birthright and blessing, although they both are born of the same father Adam, from one mother Eve, and are created after the image of God.

Saul, the first king of Israel, on account of his thoughts and disobedience, was rejected by the Lord (1 Sam. 15,) and David the son of Jesse the Bethlehemite, was according to the command of God, taken from the sheep, and anointed by Samuel in his stead, yet he did not assume the government during the life of Saul. The Lord was with David, and strengthened his hands. He did great works in the name of the Lord; he released the stolen sheep out of the mouth of the lion and bear; he slew the terrible great Goliah; he subdued two hundred of the uncircumcised of the Philistines. He acted in all things prudently, right and valiantly; for the Lord was with him. (1 Sam. 17, 18.) It happened when Saul returned from the slaughter of the Philistines, and the women of all the cities of Isreal came to meet the king, singing and rejoicing with all manner of stringed instrument and tambours, speaking joyfully one to another, Saul hath slain his thousands, but David his tens of thousands. This enraged Saul more, and displeased him. He said: They have given David ten thousand and me but a thousand! what else does he want but the kingdom. And from that day forth David had no favour with Saul, for Saul sought for his life secretly and openly, with great assiduity and craft, though Saul well knew the godly David and that the Lord was with him; still his heart burned with such ill-will, envy, revenge and blood thirst, that when David had escaped, the good Abimelech and the Lord's priests with the whole city Nob must die and be laid in ruins for David's sake. (2 Sam. 22.)

He regarded neither the piety nor kindness, fidelity nor well-doing of David towards him and towards all Israel, nor the grace, works and will of God, but became unmindful and drunken in his wrath and envy, so that the enemies and betrayers of David (1 Sam. 23) as Doeg, the Indiumean and the Ziphites were highly regarded and honored by him, but the peace makers and those who advised for good, as his son Jonathan were hated by him, and held as suspicious (1 Kings 20) In short, David must take to flight, and for some years fly from one land to another, from one wilderness to another (1 Sam. 22, 24, 25, 28,) till Saul was overcome by the Philistines upon Mount Gilboa, when through vain despair and impatience he thrust the sword, which he had borne against the righteous and innocent, into his heart, and thus took his own life. (Sam. 31.)

Thus the almighty Lord and potentate of all things, punishes the haughty, blood-thirsty tyrants, each one in his time, who bear the sword of their office against God and his chosen, as may be seen here of Saul and elsewhere of Pharaoh, of Antiochus, of Ahab, of Jezebel, of Herod and others. (Ec. 24; 2 Mar. 6; 1 Kings 22; 2 Kings 9; Acts 12.) On the other hand he can guard his chosen, and help them out of all difficulties, how hard so ever they may be pressed. This he has shown in the deliverance of Israel when he led them through the Red Sea, and in preserving David, Helia, Heliseo, Daniel in the Lion's den, and the three young men in the fiery furnace (Exod. 14; 1 Sam. 23; 2 Sam. 17, 19; 2 Kings 6; Dan. 3, 6,) and in many other instances.

Here we have again a clear example in Saul's conduct towards David, of the proud self-willed and carnal princes (although they wish to be called christian princes, and gracious Lords) who with vengeance go forth against the true David, Christ Jesus, and against all his saints, whom he has anointed with the Holy Ghost. Who have power with him from high to overcome the terrible infernal bears, lions and Goliahs, hell, sin, death, the devil, malediction and the wrath of God, yet they receive no peace from the perfidious Saul, no matter how innocent and pious they may be. With the princes no piety, innocence, prayers, tears, word or Christ, avail. But as Saul did with David, they prevent and construe all to the worst. This has ever been the case, and according to my opinion, will ever so continue.

Still my brethern, fear ye not, for all your persecutors and enemies become old like a garment (Ps. 102; Isa. 51,) how mighty, glorious and great they may be esteemed, for all flesh is as grass, and all the glory of the flesh is as the flower of the grass. (Ira. 40; 1 Pet 2.) But ye shall flourish and increase in God, and your fruit shall never more decay, for the kingdom of Jerusulem is given to you, and the glorious Lord will have honor in you (though Saul rages) and will give to you the eternal kingdom, which he prepared and set apart everlastingly for you, and all the chosen.

Again: Jeremiah, the son of Hilkiah, (Jer. 2) a priest of the priests of Anathoth, was sanctified from his mother's womb, and was chosen of God to be a prophet and a seer from his youth. (Jer. 3, 4, 5, 6, 7, 8.) He rebuked Judah and Benjamin on account of their disobedience, stubbornness, idolatry and bloodshed. He taught repentance and reformation: he prophesied of the promised Messiah, whom he called the Branch and Plant of David, (Jer. 23, 33.) He preached the coming punishment and wrath of God, namely, the captivity and destruction of the kings, the wasting of the city and temple, and the captivity of the people for seven years. (Jer. 22, 23, 32.)

And these, his prophesies, faithful warnings, visions and rebukes from the Lord's mouth, became to him as sharp, piercing thorns, for they cast his word and admonitions aside, and would not hear them. The pious prophets and true servants of God must be regarded as betrayers, factionists and heretics. The Lord's word was to him as a daily mockery. He was oft-times imprisoned and scourged, and thrown into a foul pit. They counselled concerning his death. (Jer. 26, 37, 12, 20, 26, 37, 38, 11, 18.) He was so pressed with the cross, that he once resolved in his heart, to preach no more in the name of the Lord, yea, he cursed the day of his birth, and the man who brought the message to his father, that a man child was born. (Jer. 20.) He had to yield his ear to all reproaches, and his back to scourging, till the floods of trouble burst upon the hardened rebellious people, but alas! they saw too late, that Jeremiah was a right messenger, and a true prophet of God.

My dear brethren in the Lord, here will I end the narratives from the Old Testament, for time will not suffice to relate all. The pious Joseph was grievously hated by his brethren, and by them was cast into a pit and again drawn out, and sold to the Ishmaelites, and was complained against as a perfidious adulterer, by the unchaste wife of his lord. Though he was innocent, yet must he suffer his lord's wrath, imprisonment and bonds. The high renowned evangelical prophet Isaiah, under the tyranny of the bloody and idolatrous Manaseh, was sawed asunder with a wooden saw, as the historian mentions. The spiritual prophet Ezekiel, was stoned by those who remained of Dan and Gad. Urias of Kirjatharinn, was slain with the sword by Jehoiakim the king of Judah. Zacharias the son of Barachias, was stoned between the temple and the altar. The great wonder-doing prophet Elijah, must retreat before the blood-thirsty and idolatrous Jezebel, the three youths, Shadrach, Meshach and Abednego, were cast into the glowing furnace, and Daniel into the lion's den, (1 Sam. 12; Dan. 3, 6.) The venerable, pious, old Eleazær, (2 Mac. 6, 7,) and his worthy, pious wife, with their seven sons, were so inhumanly and barbarously treated by the terrible Antiochus—they were murdered, martyred and destroyed.

Brethren, each christian must consider that this is the only reward and crown of this world, with which they reward all true servants of God, who present to them in pure love, the kingdom, word, and will of God; who call to repentance and reformation; direct to salvation, righteousness, truth, piety and love; (Gen. 37,) who are the golden candlesticks in the tabernacle of the Lord, and flourish and blossom as the fruitful olive tree in the house of God. (Ps. 51.) All who reflect on these and similar histories and narratives of the pious men of God, will undoubtedly not despond, but in all their miseries, crosses and sufferings, stand through the grace of God, and abide unwavering till the end.

Since I have now presented some histories out of the holy scriptures, by which it will be seen that righteous have suffered and been persecuted, both before the law and during the law, I will now, through the grace of God, present some examples out of the New Testament, by which all may learn, and acknowledge with Paul: That all who live godly in Christ Jesus must suffer persecution. (2 Tim. 3.)

First. John the Baptist, (John 1,) a man sent of God, as the Evangelist testifies; a burning and shining light as Christ says, and of whom Isaiah had prophesied a long time before, saying: The voice of one crying in the wilderness, prepare the way of the Lord and make his paths straight, (Isaiah 40; Matt. 3,) whom Malachi called the messenger of the Lord, (Matt. 3.) His birth, greatness, holiness, office, doctrines and works were made known to Zacharias, his father, by Gabriel, the heavenly messenger. John was filled with the Holy Ghost from his mother's womb. (John 1.) He preached repentance to all Judea. He pointed out Christ, the Savior of the world, and said: Behold the Lamb of God, who taketh away the sins of the whole world; (Matt 11; Luke 7,) of whom the son of God himself gave testimony, that he was no wavering reed, that he was not clothed in soft raiment, that he was greater than a prophet, that he was the promised Elias, that he came in the way of righteousness, and among all that were born of women, there had not arisen a greater than he; he was also held by the people as a prophet, (Matt. 11, 21,) yet did they say: He hath a devil, yea, Herod, the king, cast him forth as a profligate vagrant, and after some days, the head of this holy man of God was cut off by the executioner, as a shameful transgressor, on account of his rebuking Herod's incest, (Matt. 14; Mark 6.) and besides, it was given as a present to an idle, proud, dancing maid, and an unchaste adulterous woman.

O Lord! how lamentably and grievously the righteous are destroyed on account of their piety, by this bloody, murderous world, and no one takes it to heart. Yea, they are so dealt with, that it appears before the eyes of the unwise as if the godly were an offence and an abomination, and were outlawed and cursed of God, and that they might neither hope for nor find, to all eternity, comfort or grace from God. O no! the Lord be blessed; although their lives may appear to the foolish world to

be but idle phrensy, and their end to be without honor, yet do
we know that they are the people and children of the Lord,
and the apple of his eye, that their blood and death are dear to
him, (1 Cor. 4; Wis. 5; Zach. 2; Ps. 113; Wis. 3; Matt. 5,)
that after a little suffering and trouble they shall be recom-
pensed with good; that theirs is the kingdom of heaven; that
they will not be touched with the pains of ths second death.
(Wis. 3,) but their precious souls shall be in eternal rest and
peace. Yes, my brethren, every christian may trust and rejoice
in the Lord in all his trials and in all his need.

Again, Stephen, the crowned of God, a man full of faith,
power and the Holy Ghost, who did great signs and wonders
among the people, as Luke writes, and was endowed of God with
such wisdom and spirit, according to the promises of Christ,
(Luke 21,) that also his enemies, namely, the Libertines, Cyre-
nians and Alexandrians were silent, and stood abashed before
him. (Acts 6.) As they saw this, the spirit of their fathers displayed itself as it had done from the beginning, consuming envy
must use its artifices; Stephen must lead the way: they have
rejected justice and equity; the men of Belial they employed to
belie the pious Stephen, and say: We have heard him speak
blasphemous words against Moses and against God; and we
have heard him say, that this Jesus of Nazareth shall destroy
this place, and shall change the customs which Moses delivered
us; thus the serpents lies overcome justice. They counsel to
exterminate and root out the saints. His own enemies saw his
countenance, as the countenance of an angel. (Acts 6.) He
spake the Lord's word without fear; he rebuked the false trust
in the law and the temple; he testified of Jesus Christ in great
power, of whom Moses and all the prophets prophesied. At
length he grew very warm and ardent in his speech to the multitude, because they had ungratefully rejected the merciful visitation of God in his proffered race. Oh ye stiff-necked! he said,
and you uncircumcised in heart and ears, ye do always resist the
Holy Ghost: as your fathers did, so also do ye. Which of the
prophets have not your fathers persecuted? And they have
slain them which shewed before of the coming of the just One;
of whom you have been now the betrayers and murderers; who
have received the law through the dispositions of angels, and
have not kept it. And when they heard these things, they were
cut to the heart, and gnashed on him with their teeth. But
Stephen being full of the Holy Ghost, looked up steadfastly
into heaven and saw the glory of God, and Jesus standing on
the right hand of God, and said: I see the heaven opened and
the Son of man standing on the right hand of God. (Acts 7.)
Then they called aloud and stopped their ears, and as if they

could not longer endure the blasphemous words with which the wicked heretic (as they considered him) boasted, and with which he gave such honor to Christ; they rushed upon him with one accord and with great vehemence and wrath, cast him out of the city, and stoned him; and Saul kept the witnesses' clothing. Stephen called out, Lord Jesus receive my spirit. He kneeled down and cried with a loud voice (after the example of his master on the cross,) Lord lay not this sin to their charge; for they know not what they do, (Luke 23.) And thus the pious martyr fell asleep in the Lord, and received the crown of life which God promised to all those who fear him from the heart, with all sincerity, and love and seek him. (James 1; 2 Tim. 4.)

O! god-fearing reader, observe and learn to know by such examples, that all those who believe the word of the Lord with true hearts, who become partakers of the Holy Ghost, who are clothed with power from on high, (Tit. 1; Acts 9,) out of whose mouth flow grace and wisdom, who shame the world and rebuke sin, (Acts 14; 1 Tit. 2; 2 Tim. 1; Gal. 1,) they must, with Stephen, be cast out of the city and stoned with stones.

Dear brethren, pray ardently and prepare yourselves, (1 Cor. 2,) through much misery and trouble must you enter into the kingdom of heaven. (Acts 14.) Here is the patience and faith of the saints, (Rev. 13,) O my brethren, observe.

Again, Paul, a servant of God, and an apostle of Jesus Christ, a chosen vessel, a champion of the holy word, an apostle and teacher of the Gentiles, who was not called by men, but of God himself, from heaven, to the service of the gospel, was powerful and zealous in his teaching, and unblamable in his life. He labored more than all the other apostles. (Acts 16, 20.) He cast out devils in the Lord's name, awakened the dead Eutychus again to life, restored health to the sick, he shook off the serpent without receiving injury. (Acts 28; 2 Tim. 4, 3.) As a true prophet, he foretold many things which were to come to pass in the last times; was taken up into the third heaven and to the paradise of God, and saw such vision as no man might with propriety speak of. (2 Cor. 12.) He was an infallible leader in all righteousness, holiness, piety and virtue, (1 Cor. 12,) who sought and loved not himself, but God and his neighbor from the whole heart, (Phil. 3, 4; 2 Thes. 3,) he had nothing by which to justify himself, he regarded all gain as loss, that he might win Christ alone, (1 Cor. 4,) yes, he dare not speak of any thing, but what Christ had wrought through him, (Phil. 3; Rom. 15.) It availed not how holy, how unblamable, how zealous, how high called, how powerful or how devout he was, yet must he, with Simon, the Cyrenian, help to bear the cross of Christ. (Matt. 27; Acts 9.) For as soon as he was called from heaven, taught and baptized by Ananias, and had left off his tyranny, and had preached Christ in Damascus, he had to be let down over the wall in a basket to escape the snares of the blood-thirsty.

He was often imprisoned; thrice scourged with rods, stoned once, (2 Cor. 11,) in Ephesus he was cast to wild beasts, (1 Cor. 15,) and at last, after inconceivable and innumerable pains and journeys from one land to another, after enduring much from nakedness, cold, heat, thirst, hunger, labor, watchings, dangers and anguish, he was seized by the Jews at Jerusalem. (Acts 21,) they accursed him before the judges, swore to take his life, secured him in Ceasarea, and after his appeal to Cæsar, he arrived with much danger and shipwreck at Rome, (Acts 23, 27, 28;) he stood before the emperor, and at last, under Nero, (the most blood-thirsty of tyrants,) was put to death by the sword. He offered up his soul and surrendered his life.

In like manner were the apostles imprisoned and scourged in Jerusalem; the church was dispersed and persecuted, and James was put to death under Herod. (Acts 5, 8, 12.) All who desire to become acquainted with other narratives besides those here noticed, from the holy scriptures, can read Eusebius's church history, there will they find similar inhuman abomina-tions, tyranny, unmercifulness and falsehood against the inno-cent. Besides such new invented sins to punish, martyr, root out and murder the Christians, that even a natural man, I say, not a spiritual, must fear and be astonished, as one may see at the end of this *Treatise*.

My most beloved brethren in Christ Jesus, trust ye in the Lord, you who willingly submit to the cross of Christ. For you may see and observe from the scriptures, in the above ex-amples from the Old and New Testaments, how all pious men and children of God, all the righteous and prophets, all apostles and true witnesses of Christ, yea, Christ himself, (as we shall yet hear,) have gone through this lonesome wilderness, through this narrow, ignominious and bloody way of misery, crosses and sufferings, to the true promised land, and to eternal glory. (Matt. 7.)

Yea, this is the only narrow and straight way, and door through which we all must enter, neither can we ever desire in any other way to enter with the saints into eternal life, rest and peace, as Christ himself said. (Matt. 16.) Whosoever will fol-low after me must deny himself, take up his cross, and follow me. Therefore, dear brethren, you who have sought, feared and loved the Lord, must suffer and bear much from this wicked and idolatrous race. (Matt. 10; Luke 12.) Fear not those who take from you your earthly goods; for Christ and heaven they cannot take from you, or those who kill the body, for they cannot kill your soul, but fear him who has power to cast your soul and body eternally into hell. (Matt. 10.) Yes, my brethren, would you be the Lord's people and disciples, so must you also bear the cross of Christ. This is, without doubt, the truth.

We have set forth to the reader several excellent histories out of the scriptures, in which are represented the tyrannical mind, the envious heart, the wolfish rage, the murdering deeds of this miserable, brutal, murderous and blood-thirsty world, against the righteous. We shall now, through the grace of God, notice, for a short time, not only how the servants, of whom we have spoken, suffered, but also how the Lord and Prince himself had to endure much, and again enter into his glory. (Luke 14.)

The apostles testify abundantly how that the Lamb of God, Christ Jesus, the true head of all true believers, (Rev. 13,) had not only suffered from the beginning, as above said, but that he must suffer in these last times. although he was the conqueror of the servant, was promised to Adam and Eve; a blessing and benediction to all people, the true Shiloh, Messiah and Emanuel, the true plant of David, the Lord who justifies us, the Prince of Peace, and the true Son of the living God, whom all the true prophets desired. (Gen. 46, 16; Isa. 7, 9; Jer. 23, 33; Matt. 16.)

When he had now become man, according to the promise of the fathers, he preached repentance and regeneration in the full power of the spirit, in all love, righteousness, peace, humility and obedience; the rigid, terrible judgment of God over the impenitent; and also the eternal kingdom, eternal grace and mercy, the cordial favor and love of his heavenly father over the penitent. (Rom. 9; John 13; Matt. 12.) He himself was that Word, fulfilling all righteousness, blessed of God forever, the infallible Example, the eternal Wisdom, Love and Truth, the brightness of the divine glory, the express image of his Father, (John 14; Heb. 1,) after whom Adam was created according to the inner man, the eternal power of God, the almighty Word of God, through whom all things were created, (Gen. 1,) and are governed, and in whom all things stand. He knew no sin, neither was deceit found in his mouth; he is the true light of eternal life, (John 1; Col. 1; 1 Pet. 2; John 1, 3, 8, 12,) and by the darkness, which is the world, he is hated, blasphemed, rejected and despised, as the most degraded of men. (Isa. 53.) The king of kings, the Lord of lords, became poorer than the foxes or the birds; for he had not where to rest his blessed head. (Matt. 8; Luke 9.) On the day of his birth, he found no place in the inn—the manger was his couch. Even shortly after his birth, his parents had to fly with him to the land of Egypt. (Matt. 2.)

And although in the time of his ministry he made the blind see, and the deaf hear, the dumb speak, the leprous he cleansed, the palsied and feeble he made sound, he cast out devils, restored the dead, twice he fed thousands with a few loaves and fishes, (Matt. 8, 10, 12, 14, 15; Luke 11, 18,) and showed to them the works and service of pure love.   None would rebuke him in his word or his life, (John 6, 10,) yet, their bloody, envious hearts burned towards him, so that they desired that the wicked murderer, Barabbas, (Luke 23) who was adjudged to death by the law, should live, and that the eternal Life itself—the Creator and Upholder of all creatures, should die.   His pure, heavenly body, the seat of all virtue, is scourged and abused, the glorious countenance and head of all honor is disfigured with blood, spit and thorns. (Mark 15; John 14; 1 John 5.) They also mocked him with a ludicrous garment, so that even the heathen judge, Pilate, pitying, said: "Behold the man!" (John 19.)   Yea, worthy brethren, it avails nothing, no pain nor torture, no misery was enough: they would not be satisfied, till he was taken away and condemned to the most shameful death, and extended upon the cross, and his hands and feet were nailed to the wood, and his side was pierced with a spear.   He was crucified as a prince and leader of the vicious, and reckoned among murderers.   Thus they requited him for his incomprehensibly great love and beneficence, and in his great bitter thirst in the last hour of his sufferings, he could not obtain a drop of cold water, but they gave him vinegar and gall.   In short, they treated him so that he cried with a loud voice to his Father: My God! my God! why hast thou forsaken me? (Matt. 27.) He also laments through the prophet: I am a worm and no man, a disgrace among men, a reprobate among the people. He might well sigh and lament with Jeremiah or Jerusalem: O all ye who pass over, see if there be any sorrow like my sorrow. (Sam. 1.)   Thus he, who was eternally rich, for our sakes became poor; (2 Cor. 3; Phil. 2,) the eternal glory was dishonored, the eternal righteousness was persecuted, the eternal truth was blasphemed, the eternal happiness was rejected, the eternal blessing was cursed, and the eternal life was made to suffer a shameful death. (Gal. 3.)

Most beloved brethren in the Lord, observe well, the laborers have not spared their Lord's Son, but have cast him out of the vineyard and have slain him, how much more shall they destroy the servants. (Matt. 21.)   For they have called the master of the house, Beelzebub, how much more shall they call them of his household. (Matt. 10.)   Christ said, if they have persecuted me, so will they also persecute you. And further, if the world hate you, then shall ye also know that it also hated me before; for the disciple is not greater than his master, nor the servant than his lord; but it is enough for the disciple to be like his master, and the servant to be like his lord. (John 15; Matt. 10; John 13.)

I hope, worthy brethren, that here, from these examples, the pious may learn what kind of a people it is, from what father they are born, and by what spirit they are moved—who from the beginning till the present day, have rejected and persecuted Christ, the holy Lamb of God and his people: and according to my understanding of the scriptures, this tyranny shall not cease till the rejected, murdered and crucified Jesus, as an almighty potentate, conqueror and glorious king, with all his saints, shall appear in the clouds before all the tribes and people on the last judgment. (John 8; Rev. 13.)

Since then the terrible tyranny of this blind world, has always thus, in blindness, been laid upon the necks of the children of God, and so will continue to be laid to the end. Besides, there is no other way to life, than this narrow, rough and thorny way of the cross. I mean according to the flesh, for after the spirit it is broad and easy. (Matt. 7.) The scriptures say: Have your feet shod with the gospel of peace, with the precious promises of God, with the pure knowledge of Christ, with the denial of yourselves, with the patience and faith of the saints, and with the sure hope upon the kingdom of God. (Eph. 6; Rev. 13; Rom. 8.) Let not the hard, sharpened thorns of persecutions, with which all the pious are persecuted, terrify you so as to drive you to the soft broad way of the flesh. (Heb. 12; Rom. 13.) Lay aside all things which hinder you—the besetting sin, the cursed works of darkness, useless cares, avarice, pride, haughtiness, and all that is perishable, all drunkenness and luxury, all idolatry and idleness, all uncircumcised fleshly words, and all manner of wickedness, in order that you may not be overcome, and turned aside from the narrow way to the way of death, as alas, is too frequently the case in these days.

Therefore, my dear brethren and sisters in the Lord, take the crucified Jesus as your example and also all the servants of God,—the apostles and prophets, and learn to know of them;— they entered this narrow path and left all behind. For they prepared their hearts and were endowed and drawn of God, that they knew nothing, sought nothing, loved nothing, and desired nothing else than eternal and heavenly blessings, the unchangeable things—God and eternal life. Thus they were grounded in ardent love, and became firm and immovable, so that they could not be affrighted from the love of Christ, neither by life nor death, neither by angel, prince nor potentate, neither by hunger nor sword, neither by martyrdom, pain nor ease. (Rom. 8.) Their thoughts and words, their acts and sufferings, their life and death, were Christ's. (John 19.) They sought not their kingdom and rest upon earth, for they were spiritual and heavenly-minded. All their fruit was righteousness, light and truth. Their whole lives were pure love, charity, chastity, humility, obedience and peace. The changeable wicked world with all its evil works, was to them an offence and abomination. They loved their God with all their soul and, therefore, they rebuked all that was against his glory, will and holy word. They loved their neighbors as themselves, and therefore, they admonished and rebuked them in love, served them, pointed out and taught them God's pure will, word and truth, and sought their salvation with all their power, with great loss of life and reputation, therefore has the foolish, envious unthankful world, which swims in blood so grievously hated them and rewarded them with death. (Matt. 5; I Cor. 4.)

My dear brethren, it was not only the prophets, apostles and those of former times, to whom these things happened, which the scriptures relate, but we, ourselves, may in these times witness the like with our own eyes. How many pious children of God have we known in the space of a few years, and we yet know some, (the Lord be praised,) who sought Jesus Christ and the eternal unchangeable life, and continue so to seek, who fear God from their inmost soul, their hearts burn with the word and love of the Lord, out of their mouths flowed power, spirit and wisdom. Their whole life was repentance and piety—they hated, shunned and rebuked all ungodliness. None could reprove their conduct with the word of God; they were opposed to the world's idle, fleshly, ungodly life, as they yet are, and by the grace of God will continue to be. They listen not to the deceiving prophets. (Jer. 23.) They confide not their precious souls to the care of the spiritual thieves and murderers. (John 10.) They serve not the wooden, stone and silver gods. They do not use the unscriptural, earthly sacraments, &c. In short, because they heard, believed, feared, served and loved the true living God, therefore, did the lying serpent open its mouth and spew out so many false, inhuman lies into the face of the pious, and depict them in such horrible colors, through their blind disciples, that the whole world fears them as abominable; yes, every one, who can slander and defame the christian, is the world's favorite preacher and esteemed teacher.

No lie is so gross and disgraceful, that they dare not bring it against the godly. At one time they accuse and upbraid us, as though we wished to invade cities and countries; they say: that we will injure the whole world—now we are adulterers—again, thieves and murderers; now, say they, we say there is no repentance left to the sinner; again, we have rejected Christ and the Testament. In short, whosoever does not defame and upbraid the godly, is not considered by the world as a christian! O Lord, how pure and free are all the saints in heart and conscience before God of all these lies and slanders.

And these unchristian lies are not enough for the world, but they who know Christ, and would gladly live after his word, must endure something harder; they must meet with severer persecution, as we may witness with our own eyes, for how many pious children of God, have they in a few years deprived of their possessions, and caused their goods to be confiscated, for the testimony of God and their conscience sake. How many have they betrayed, how many have they driven out of city and country, and put them to the stocks and torture; the poor orphans and children are left naked in the streets; some have they hanged, some they punished with inhuman tyranny, they afterwards choked them with cords on stocks and pillars; some they roasted and burned alive; some with their own reeking bowels in their hands, powerfully confessed the word of God. Some they slew with the sword and gave them as food to the fowls of the air; some they cast forth to the wild beasts, some have their houses torn down, some have been cast into the muddy bogs, some have had their feet cut off, one of whom I have seen and conversed with. Others wander about here and there, in hunger and affliction, in mountains, holes and caves of the earth, as Paul says: They must fly with their small children and their wives, from one country to another, from one city to another. (Matt. 10.) They are hated, upbraided and belied by all men, and spoken against in the pulpit and the councils, (Matt. 5;) they have deprived them of food—have driven them forth in the cold winter, and point at them with the finger of scorn, yea, whoever can slander a poor oppressed christian, supposes he has done God some service, as Christ said. (John 16.)

Observe, dear brethren, how far the whole world is from God and his word, how swift their feet are to shed blood, how maliciously they hate the light, (Isa. 52; Rom. 3; John 3,) and how bitterly they persecute the eternal truth—the immaculate gospel of Jesus Christ, the pious godly life of the saints. This is not only done by the papists and Turks, but by those who boast of the holy word, who preached much concerning faith, that faith was the gift of God, (Eph. 2,) that it must not be forced with the iron sword, but with the word, into the hearts of men, for it is a willing assent of the heart.

But the learned, within the last few years, have suppressed

25*

this doctrine, and as it appears to me, have effaced it from their books, for lately they draw unto their sensual doctrine, lords, princes, cities and countries; they have preached the contrary from what they did formerly, as is evident from their writings. By their seditious writings and preachings they deliver into the hands of executioners, many pious hearts, who gainsay, reprove and admonish them, by the clear word of God and the gospel, and point out to them the true ground of the gospel, which is powerful, active faith, which works by love, a penitent new life, obedience to God and Christ, and the true evangelical ordinances of baptism, Lord's supper and *Separation*, as Christ himself instituted and commanded, and his holy apostles practiced and taught. (Gal. 5; Matt. 26, 28; Mark 14, 16; Luke 22; 1 Cor. 5, 10; 2 Thess. 3.)

Yea, all who do this out of pure love, must be accursed as anabaptists, factionists, deceivers and heretics, all the pious may expect this, nevertheless, they still want to be called the christian community, and be esteemed the holy church, whether lords or princes, preachers or theologians. The common people, whether papists, Lutherans and Zuinglians, never take notice of their gross, ungodly, lazy and impenitent lives, that they are altogether earthly, sensual, and contrary to the word of God. There are some, from whose hands trickle the blood of christians, and all their doings are diametrically opposed to the spirit, word, and example of Christ. O! that these, blind, hardened ones would lay this well to heart, and examine well the true nature and spirit of christianity! They would be ashamed before God, and cordially lament that they so miserably abuse his glorious name, his blessed word, his divine grace, his crimson, precious blood, of which they vainly boast, and thus make the name of Christ as a cover to all their wickedness and disgrace.

For a truly believing christian is one that is born of God according to the spirit, has become a new creature in Christ, crucified his flesh with its lusts, and cordially hates the old, sinful life. (John 1; 2 Cor. 5; Gal. 5, 6; Rom. 12.) All his fruits are righteousness, patience, truth, obedience, humility, chastity, love, grace and peace; he is influenced by the spirit of the Lord, and his delight is in the law of the Lord, he meditates thereon by day and by night, all his words are seasoned by grace, he strives for the life which is from God. He fears God with all his soul. (Rome. 8; Ps. 1; Col. 4; Phil. 2.) In short, according to the grace received, he is of one mind with Christ.

Could these only see that a christian is thus minded, as related, that he is such an amiable person and child of God; and if they had the grace, they also would be thus minded. They would then hate none, but would be hated; they would belie none, but they would be belied; they would prejudge none, but would be prejudged; they would betray none, but be betrayed; they would rob none, but be robbed; they would not murder, but be murdered; they would not devour the lamb, but be torn of wolves; not ensnare the dove, but be taken by the falconer and devoured.

Are our persecutors christians, as they imagine? Why are they then not of God and born of his word? Why are they yet the old accursed creature, and live according to the lusts of the flesh? Why are they influenced by the spirit of the devil? And why have they fixed their thoughts and affections upon perishable and temporal things, and are concerned therewith day and night? Why are they guilty of talking of all manner of unchastity, vanity, lying, cursing and swearing? Why do they not fear God and his word? Why are they like the old deceitful serpent, and obedient to him? And why are they still like terrible, ravenous beasts and birds of prey, instead of innocent lambs and doves, as the scriptures teach?

Ah! dear brethren, let them boast as they will, Christ Jesus does not know such wicked and blood-thirsty christians. (Rom. 8.) He only knows those having his spirit, who cordially believe and who are obedient to him; who are flesh of his flesh, and bone of his bone, (Matt. 5; Mark 8,) who are meek, humble, pious, holy and pure of heart, who confess Christ Jesus, in word and deed before this wicked world, who deny themselves and take up the cross and follow him. (Matt. 16.) Who say with holy Paul. (Rom. 8.) Who shall separate us from the love of God? They glory in nothing but in the cross of our Lord Jesus Christ, by which they are dead to the world and the world unto them. (Gal. 6.) All who are thus minded, are the anointed of God and Christ, and not the impenitent, sensual, blood-thirsty boasters. Every one may be mindful of us, that this is true, else the whole scriptures are false.

It appears to me, dear brethren, that the pious reader may fully understand from what has been said, what kind of people these are, who so shamefully tread you with their feet, strike you, belie you, and deprive you of life and property. Why do they so? It is on account of your testimony of God and your consciences. Even as all from the beginning, who sought, feared and loved the Lord, and reproved the world, were esteemed as off-scourings and heretics.

We will now proceed in the name of the Lord, and show with few words, what a feeble and unbecoming excuse our persecutors advance, (which before God is as stubble before fire,) whereby they think to excuse themselves, that they are doing right to slander and abuse the pious; for all sinners seek some excuse; and no matter how disgracefully soever any one conduct himself, he wishes not to be considered as wicked, but as a true christian!

In the first place, our persecutors accuse us as seditious, even as those of Munster are, that we are not subject to the magistracy.

To which we reply, in the first place: That the Munsterites were seditious, and in many things acted contrary to the word of God. But we *do not* agree with them. For we are wholly opposed to, and disapprove of these seditious abominations, such as resisting the king, seeking for a kingdom, taking hold of the sword, polygamy, acting the hypocrite with the world and the like guilt; we neither eat nor drink, nor have any communion with those who do such things, according to the doctrine of Christ and Paul, unless they cordially renounce their errors and become sound in the saving doctrine of Christ. (Matt. 28; 1 Cor. 5; 2 John 1.)

As the Papists and Lutherans are not a little divided, so we are more divided in our views, from the Munsterites and other sects which sprung from them. That this is the truth, we have shown by our writings, life, and oral testimony, before lords, princes and the whole world; and it has been testified by the blood of many pious christians, which flowed like water, in many countries, for many years, to the present time.

But we cannot help that the world will not believe this. Nevertheless, we testify that our hearts and consciences are pure and free before God, of all sedition, hatred, vengeance and thirst for blood; and we strive earnestly to live as much as possible, in peace with all men, according to the doctrine of Paul, (Rom. 12,) and if it is not possible for us to keep peace with them, still we do not desire to avenge ourselves, but we will commit it to him, who says: To me belongeth vengeance and recompense. (Deut. 34.) And we commit to him alone all our concerns, as Jeremiah and all the pious did from the beginning. (Jer. 11.)

In the second place, we reply: Why do they so indiscreetly accuse us of such sedition, since we are wholly innocent and clear, and they pay no attention to their own bloody, murdering uproar, which they, alas! commit without bounds? O Lord! how many principalities, cities and countries, have they destroyed and desolated! how many houses have they fired; how many hundred thousand have they murdered! how many a poor innocent man have they robbed of his possessions and destroyed! how many women and virgins did they disgrace; what brutal and inhuman tyranny did they do and continue daily to practice

—all this they do not notice—it must be said; all is right and well done. Ah!! how well does this accord with the doctrine, nature and spirit of Christ!! (Matt. 28; 1 Cor. 14.) How badly this accords with the disposition of innocent children, whom christians must resemble in malice; or defenceless lambs and innocent doves, to which the scriptures direct us. If the temporal magistracy have not the disposition and spirit of Christ, then must all acknowledge that they are not christians.

I am well aware, that these tyrants, who boast themselves christians, justify their abominable warring, uproar and shedding of blood, by referring us to Moses, Joshua, &c. And do not reflect that Moses and his successors have served their day, and that Christ has *now* given us a *new command and given us another sword*. (Matt. 10; John 3; Eph. 6; Rom. 13.) I do not speak of the sword of the judge, for that is quite different; but I speak respecting war and sedition. (2 Pet. 2.) And they do not reflect, that they bear the sword of war, contrary to the gospel, and that they bear it against their own brethren, namely, against their brethren of the faith, who have received the same baptism with them, and break the same bread with them, and are thus members of the same body.—Again, what strange, bloody uproar the Lutherans made for several years, to introduce their doctrine; yet have we, although innocently, to be called *the seditious heretics* and they, pious, peaceable christians! Behold, thus lamentably is their understanding of the work darkened. Well then! let them deal with us as they think proper, the merciful, gracious Father will preserve us from such abominable disturbances as the Munsterites have caused, and which, alas! are yet in vogue among the supposed christians; for we have, by the grace of God, beaten our swords into plough shares, and our spears into pruning hooks; (Isa. 2; Mich. 4;) and we shall sit under the true vine, Christ, under the prince of eternal peace, and will never take part in bloody wars.

In the third place, we reply: That we know and use no other sword than that which Christ himself brought down from heaven, (Matt. 10,) and which the apostles used with power and spirit; which proceeds from the mouth of the Lord—the sword of the spirit, (Eph. 6,) which is sharper than any sword, having two edges, (Rev. 1,) piercing even to the dividing asunder of soul and spirit, and of the joints and marrow, and is a discerner of the thoughts and intents of the heart. With this; and with no other sword, do we desire to destroy the kingdom of the devil, to reprove all wickedness, and to preach righteousness, to raise the father against the son, the son against the father; the mother against the daughter, and the daughter against the mother, &c. (Matt. 10.) In such a way, even as Jesus Christ, the holy apostles and the prophets did in the world. I do not here mean the prophets Elias and Samuel, (1 Kings 18 ; 1 Sam. 15,) understand me rightly, who also used the sword ; but I mean the prophets Isaiah, Jeremiah, Zecharias, Amos, &c., who only reproved with doctrine, and not otherwise.

That is the sword we bear; and we will lay it down for none, neither for emperor, nor king, nor other authorities. For Peter says : We ought to obey God rather than men. (Acts 5.) He that committed us, we must serve, whether we chance to live or die, as it may please God.

That the world is now ascribing to us this uproar for the pure love which we manifested toward them we must endure, as did our forefathers. Art thou not he, said Ahab to Elijah, that troubleth Israel ? The prophet answered : I have not troubled Israel ; but thou and thy father's house. Jeremiah, on account of his faithful warning and salutary admonition, was regarded by them as a mutineer, rebel and heretic. Paul and the apostles were cast into prison as deceivers and rebellious, and finally had to suffer martyrdom. If the world could pass a true sentence, they would well perceive, that Christ and his followers were not tumultuous towards the world, but the world towards them. And so also we, who are not tumultuous towards any one, but all are against us, they tyrannize and rave as may be seen.

Again, that we are opposed to the magistracy in the things to which they are ordained of God, *is not true*, understand me in lawful things ; as giving of toll, tribute, and paying taxes, &c. (Rom. 13 ; 1 Pet. 2.) But that they are to rule and lord over our consciences, contrary to the spirit of Christ, as they please, to *this* we *do not consent*, but we will sacrifice, possessions and life, rather than sin against Jesus Christ and his holy word for any man's sake, whether he be emperor or king.

That we are not wrong, but right in this respect, the scrip-' tures abundantly testify; and therefore, with pious Susan, we wish rather to obey God than man, (Dan. 13,) and thus fall into the hands of men, rather than into the hands of God. May the gracious Father, through his blessed Son Jesus Christ, grant to this deaf, blind world ears to hear, and eyes to see, that they may be converted and be eternally saved.

In the third place we are without cause, accused hard : That we are stubborn, selfish and unconverted persons, who will by no means suffer ourselves to be taught or instructed.

To which we reply, first : If this accusation even were true, it is still very unbecoming for our persecutors, to exterminate or harm us, because they would be, or boast themselves chris- tians, for the punishment of the wicked will be eternal, as the scriptures testify. (Mark 16 ; John 3.)

All men, says Paul, have not faith, but it is a gift of God. (2 Thes. 1 ; chap. 3.) Now if it is a gift, it may not be enforced by worldly power, nor sword, but it must by means of the pure doctrine of the holy scripture, in conjunction with the ardent prayer of humility, be apprehended, by the grace of God, through the influence of the Holy Spirit. (Rom. 10 ; Matt. 13.) Moreover, it is not the will of the householder, that the tares be rooted up, until the time of harvest ; as is clearly evinced in the parable.

Now, if our persecutors were christians, as they suppose, and if they considered the Lord's word as true, why do they not hear, and follow, the word and commandment of Christ? Why do they root up the tares before the time ? Why are they not afraid, lest they root up the good wheat, and not the tares ? (Matt. 12,) why do they arrogate to themselves the duty of the angels, who, at the proper time, shall bind the tares in bundles, and cast them into the furnace of everlasting fire ?

Since, by our belief or unbelief, (unbelief it must ever be, if their assertions are true,) we injure no man upon earth ; justice demands, that they should commit us with our belief or unbelief to the Lord alone, and his judgment, who, in the fullness of time, will judge all things in righteousness, and that they should not, like savage pagans, pursue us with the sword of destruction. The true disposition of a pious and sincere christian, is to lead poor, wandering sinners to repentance, and not to destroy them, as these men do. (Matt. 9.) In regard to all those who evidence a contrary spirit, it is an easy matter for any intelligent christian, to show from the scriptures what father they are children of.

Again, we reply, that we are prepared, in every way, even unto death, for the reception of all sound doctrine, admonition, instruction, and chastening, in righteousness ; we spare no labor, pains, nor expense, if we can only obtain faithful stewards to dispense bread to us in proper season ; for our souls hunger after the living bread, and our spirits thirst for the living water. (Matt. 24 ; John 6.) All who are qualified, rightly to break the former, and pour out the latter ; we desire to hear with devotedness of heart, and to live in obedience to their doctrine. (John 4, 7.)

But the leaven of the Pharisees and Sadducees, the lies and deceivings of false prophets, the stealing and outrages of thieves and murderers, we will have nothing to do with, let what may happen by divine permission. Thank God, we have tasted the heavenly bread, (John 10,) hence, we have become heartily tired of the leaven and husks of the learned ; we drink the pure water, the impure we leave for them ; we received the truth and rejected lies ; the light hath shined upon us, there is no more place for darkness. (Luke 15 ; Ezek. 34 ; John 1.) In short, we have found Christ, the true Messiah, his saving word, his pure ordinance, and his holy, and unblamable life, (according to the gift of grace within us,) and as a consequence, have turned away from antichrist, with the confident hope, that we will never more observe, or make use of, his ordinance of infant baptism, and idolatrous supper, nor ever be reconciled to his odious, carnal, and ungodly life.

If in this matter, we do wrong and transgress, in the presence of God, and before his community, as they imagine : then must the fathers, and the scriptures have miserably betrayed us. But no ; the word of God is truth ; and the truth shall abide forever, even though the whole world be offended. (John 17.)

And because we dare not again take part in their false doctrine, pretended sacraments, idolatry, false worship, and in their shameful, wicked, and ungodly life ; because by the spirit of God, by the evidence of the scriptures, and by the witness of our own consciences we have turned away from such ; therefore, must we be called stubborn, selfish and obstinate, and, alas ! must be to all men heretics, spoils, and derision.

I hope, beloved brethren, that such absurd accusations may never dismay the hearts of the pious, nor render them faint, inasmuch as, they are entirely destitute of foundation ; while, we on the contrary have, the whole scripture, together with prophets, apostles, saints, nay, Christ Jesus himself ; all of whom in truth and righteousness, remained steadfast and immovable, even unto death, in their opposition—to all false doctrine, torture, and tyranny, and did not, in a single point, agree with, or consent to, their ungodly deeds, neither in heart, speech, nor behavior.

Ought we then to reject the heavenly light, and embrace the darkness of condemnation? Forsake eternal truth, and everlasting life ? Follow after lies, and pursue death, for the sake of a little perishable wealth, and a half hour's enjoyment of temporal life ? If so, it would be better for us that we had never been born. From a contingency so dreadful, it is our firm hope, that God, by his boundless love, will ever preserve and protect us.

In the third place we answer : That we sincerely detest and abhor such teaching and conversion, as our persecutors would make use of, in order to instruct and convert us ; for their end is death, according to the testimony of the whole scriptures ; the reason is, that their doctrine is false and deceptive, their sacraments are idolatrous, and contrary to the word of God ; their worship is sheer idolatry, and their whole life is earthly, sensual, and contrary to the word of God ; as may be seen,

(James 3,) yea, they are a people of whom we may justly testify as they do of us, namely: This is a stiff-necked, seditious, unconverted people, whose hearts are harder than diamond, a people who know not their God, as the prophet speaks of Israel, saying: The ox knoweth his owner, and the ass his master's crib; but Israel doth not know, my people doth not consider. (Isa. 1.)

Ah, sinful nation, a people laden with iniquity, a seed of evildoers, children that are corrupters! they have forsaken the Lord, they have provoked the Holy One of Israel unto anger, they are gone away backward; they hold fast to deceit, says Jeremiah, they refuse to return. I hearkened and heard, says he, but they spake not aught: no man repenteth him of his wickedness, saying: What have I done? Every one turned to his course, as the horse rusheth into battle. Yea, the stork in the heavens knoweth her appointed times; and the turtle, and the crane, and the swallow, observe the time of their coming: but my people know not the judgment of the Lord. (Jer. 8.) And more passages of a similar nature.

Like John the Baptist, one might well rebuke them, and say: Bring forth fruits meet for repentance: and say not that you are christians; as the Pharisees said they had Abraham for their father; for such perverse, sensual christians, God knoweth not: the axe is laid unto the root of the tree, (Matt. 3,) therefore, every tree that bringeth not forth good fruit is hewn down and cast into the fire. Drunkards, says Paul, (Rom. 1; 1 Cor. 6; Gal. 5; Eph. 5,) covetous, envious, proud, idolaters, adulterers and fornicators, shall not inherit the kingdom of God; hence, in the spirit of commiseration, we may aptly say to our persecutors, who are still such: Reform, for, alas! princes, rulers, learned, unlearned, citizens, countrymen, husband and wife, all, on every hand, have become degenerate, walking in the accursed fruits of profanity and ungodliness; they reject God and his word; they grieve the Holy Spirit; they persecute the righteous and pious; the fear and love of God are an abomination to them; yet to such as walk in the way of truth, die unto unto flesh and blood, are heavenly and spiritually minded, with sincerity of heart seek Christ Jesus and the imperishable everlasting life, they say: Reform; be instructed; with similar expressions,—just as if we had the lies, and they the truth; though according to the gift imparted to us, we love and seek the Lord cordially; but what they do, I leave it to any intelligent christian to decide.

Moreover, even they themselves demonstrate, that the fruits and ardent charity of our members, far exceed and surpass that of theirs, (Deut. 4, 43) nevertheless, we have to be looked upon,

26

as deceived, selfish, obstinate, and unconverted heretics, while they are considered the real, spiritually anointed christians, the truly legitimate children of God.

Now, dear brethren, judge by this how puerile and nonsensical is the excuse of the world, with regard to their tyrannical proceedings, and how indiscreetly and childishly, we are accused by them. O! it is our heart's desire, that all our predecessors may receive from the Lord grace unto repentance. For it is high time that they awake, and turn to the Lord.

Again, our persecutors bring in an excuse, saying it is right that we should be persecuted; because by us many men are deplorably misled, and brought to destruction.

To this we reply: That if the case is examined, and sentence passed upon it, according to the flesh, it does appear, that many are miserably deceived by us, for all those who follow our doctrine, faith, life, and confession, in obedience and power, must bring into jeopardy all which they have received from God, character, reputation, land, house, gold, silver, father, mother, sister, brother, husband, wife, son, daughter, yea, life itself. The finger of scorn will generally be pointed at them; they shall be trampled under feet, hated of all men, slandered and calumniated, betrayed, and delivered up unto death; gallows, racks, offensive pools, stocks and swords, as also hunger, thirst, want, toil, affliction, distress, anxiety, nakedness, tribulation, sorrow, buffeting, bonds and imprisonment, must be their portion and recompense here upon earth; no man may administer unto, or befriend them, but at the risk of person and property; the father may not receive and assist the son, nor the son the father. In short, they are looked upon by the world as too unworthy to be in heaven, or upon earth; moreover, they shew all pomp and parade, rioting, drunkenness, sensuality, &c., towards which the whole world is inclined, all men, to the extent of their power, deriving from such practices, the greatest self-gratification. They, on the contrary, take delight in humility, sobriety, an indigent, blameless, and rejected life in the fear of the Lord, which is an abomination to the whole world. It is, therefore, no wonder, in my opinion, that the erring, blind world who have not, neither know the Holy Spirit, as Christ says, (John 14,) who seek, understand, and judge earthly things alone, should regard, consider, and detest such a life, as the result of imposture and deception.

But those, who are taught of God, who have risen with Christ to newness of life, are made partakers of the Holy Spirit, are spiritually-minded, look upon, and judge all things by the Spirit, such do not consider it as imposture and deception, but they esteem it above all gold and silver, all knowledge and wisdom, all riches and honor, all parade and ostentation; nay, above all that is named under heaven; for they know from their hearts, that this is the only doctrine that leadeth to immortality and eternal life; they look not at the things which are transitory, but at things which are imperishable. They provide and prepare a treasure and inheritance that abideth in heaven, but earthly treasure they esteem not. (2 Cor. 4.) they seek the wisdom which is eternal, being, therefore, regarded by the whole world as fools, (Matt. 6,) they adorn themselves with the inner garment of righteousness, despising the outer moth-eaten garment of pride; (1 Cor. 3;) they strive for that kingdom and crown of glory which will abide forever; the earthly kingdom with its glory, they leave to such as take delight in them.

Hence, dearly beloved, it is absolutely necessary to judge all things spiritually,; for the world is come to such a state that the pure doctrine of Jesus Christ and his apostles, is esteemed heresy; to preach Christ Jesus, his spirit and life, his unadulterable word, will and ordinance, to turn the people from ungodliness to piety, is considered as imposition and deception. Behold, how blind and ignorant, in divine things, are our persecutors who so miserably oppress, persecute and destroy us for the truth's sake! Yea, my brethren, here is the patience, and the faith of the saints; (Rev. 13;) all, who in their hearts experience this, (as here related) will possess their souls in patience, let the opposition be ever so great, and will pray for their enemies with all the ardor of the power that is in them.

In the fourth place, our persecutors accuse us with great bitterness, because we separate ourselves from their doctrine, sacraments, church service, and from a carnal and sensual life, and in such things dare have nothing to do with them; they say that, in this thing, we condemn them, and banish them to hell.

To this we reply, in the first place: The reason why we can never, by word or deed, consent to, nor allow of, their preachers, sacraments, church service, and impure sensual life, is, that they are openly opposed to God and his word; the preachers serve when they are not sent, (Jer. 23,) their doctrine is false, deceptive and contrary to the saving doctrine of truth, their life is in every respect, blamable; they preach for filthy lucre's sake; they act the hypocrite for the world, to flatter the desires thereof; the foundation of their faith and religion, is emperor, king, princes and men of power; what they command, that teach they; and what they forbid, that leave they untouched. Their infant baptism is unfounded in scripture; their supper is idolatrous and impure, and by the impure administered and received; their church-service is contrary to the doctrine of the apostles; and for the most part so sensual and ungodly is the ordinary tenor of their life, that every child of God must be exceedingly amazed and astonished at it.

Seeing then that their doctrine, sacrament, church service and life, are in fact, so palpably opposed to the word of God, how could we again intermingle and enter into familiarity, with them in such heinous abominations? That we separate ourselves from them, is the express word and will of God : For says Paul, (2 Cor. 6 :) What communion hath light with darkness? what concord hath Christ with Belial? what fellowship hath righteousness with unrighteousness? or what part hath he that believeth with the infidel? and what agreement hath the temple of God with idols? for ye are the temple of the living God ; as God hath said : I will dwell in them, and walk in them; and I will be their God and they shall be my people. Wherefore come out from among them, and be ye separate, saith the Lord, and touch not the unclean thing ; and I will receive you and will be a Father unto you, and ye shall be my sons and daughters, saith the Lord Almighty. (Lev. 26 ; Isa. 52.)

These words of Paul are plain and intelligible : It is, therefore, utterly impossible, that those who have, through the beneficence of God, received from on high, the true light, Christ Jesus, unfeigned righteousness, pure effective faith, have become a fit and worthy temple of the Lord, are under the influence of the Holy Spirit, are chosen and adopted as the children of God; that such should again have fellowship with darkness, Belial, unrighteousness, infidels and idolators ; for, knowing, by the grace of God, that their doctrine, sacraments, service and life, are truly and fundamentally false and erroneous ; if you have a true zeal for God, count all things but dross, that with Paul, you may win Christ ; according to scripture abhor that which is evil, and cleave to that which is good ; have washed your robes in the blood of the Lamb, (Phil. 2 ; Rom. 12 ; Rev. 7,) and conform in all your thoughts, words and actions, to the touchstone of the word, and the example of Christ ; how can you again have communion with them, and say amen to their abominations? (Matt. 6 ; 1 Cor. 10;) we cannot serve two masters at once; we cannot hold communion with Christ, and at the same time fellowship with the devil ; we cannot be the children and servants of God, and also the children and servants of satan ; if we love that which is good, we must abhor that which is evil ; if we embrace the truth, we must forsake lies, &c., &c.

Now, forasmuch as we thus separate ourselves from them, and testify by word and deed, even unto death, that their works are evil ; therefore they are filled with the most inhuman rancor and indignation, and say from the heart, as all the ungodly have done from the beginning : Let us lie in wait for the right-eous ; because he is not for our turn, and he is clearly contrary to our doings : he upbraideth us with our offending the law, and objecteth to our infamy, the transgressions of our education, &c. He exposeth our secret designs and cunning devices. He is grievous unto us even to behold ; for his life is not like other men's, his ways are of another fashion. We are esteemed of him as counterfeits : he abstaineth from our ways as from filthiness : he pronounceth unto us the end of the righteous, &c. Let us, therefore, condemn him with a shameful death. (Wisd. 2.)

Here, my dearly beloved brethren, the Holy Spirit has given a faithful delineation of our persecutors ; for our actual confession, that is to say, our separation from them is the sole reason why the blind, blood-thirsty world, frantic with rage, tyrannizes over us with so much cruelty ; and why we must bear and suffer so much ; as Peter also says. (1 Pet. 4.) They think the stranger that you run not with them to the same excess of riot, speaking evil of you. Nay, for this reason, Isaiah, Jeremiah, Zachariah, Shadrach, Meshach, and Abednego, Daniel, Eleazar, the mother with the seven sons, and Christ Jesus, had to die and bear the cross ; because they earnestly reproved the world in its doctrine, ceremonies and conduct.

This is, even unto this day, the only and principal reason, and in reality there is no other, notwithstanding our persecutors allege many, (as we have shown,) why we must be considered by the word as ana-baptists, heretics, knaves, deceivers and movers of sedition, and be regarded as fit subjects for persecution. But, thank God, we know the reason of our suffering ; we know also that he who called us to this grace, and in whom we put our trust, will successfully plead our cause, and will faithfully stand by and deliver his poor oppressed children, in every time of need, to the advancement of his eternal praise and everlasting glory.

Though our persecutors assert that our separation from them is the result of pure obstinacy and caprice, yet their declaration is false and unjust, in the presence of God who knoweth the hearts of all men ; because our separation has no other foundation nor design than this, that we desired, in our weakness, to observe with all our heart the word of God, and keep his commandments ; and that we might, in real charity, and in fact, show to the whole world that they lie in wickedness, and are strangers to God and his word, to the end that they may, in due time, awake and turn from iniquity. For how can they in truth, teach others generosity, chastity, humility, and every virtue, if they themselves are abandoned to avarice, lewdness and pride,

26*

and addicted to every vice? It would be the height of folly for a person to point out the right way to others, warning them o. robbers and murderers, while he himself would take a winding, unfrequented road and voluntarily offer himself an easy prey to thieves and robbers. My brethren may reflect upon what I mean.

It is not sufficient for a sincere christian merely to speak the truth; but he must also demonstrate in power and in deed, that which he speaks, conforming himself thereunto, or he shall hear, with the Pharisees: You say, and do not; (Matt. 23,) and also as Paul, in writing to the Romans, says of the Jews: You that teach a man should not steal, do you steal? You that say a man should not commit adultery, do you commit adultery? You that abhor idols, do you commit sacrilege? You that boast of the law, do you, through breaking the law, dishonor God? (Rom. 2.)

In short, a christian teaches and acts; he professes and practices; he believes and obeys; he directs and advances; his heart, word and deed are in unison; if not he is a hypocrite, and no christian; as, alas! there are numbers in our day, who boast highly of knowledge and wisdom, though in power they are vain and unfruitful.

Again, we reply: That our persecutors do violently and unjustly accuse us of condemning and banishing them to hell. Ah no! far be it from us to condemn any man under heaven before his time, let him be ever so wicked. For we are well aware that the scriptures say: Condemn not, that you be not condemned. (1 Cor. 4; Matt. 7; Luke 6.) There is one who, in the fulness of time, will judge all men, every man according to his works, namely, he to whom the Father has committed all judgment; (2 Cor. 5,) whosoever usurps his judgment shall not go unpunished. Moreover, we know not the measure of grace, the sinner may be made partaker of before death, in order that, in condemning others, we might be innocent in the sight of the Lord. Nevertheless, we are permitted to judge and speak by the word of God, as follows: If a miser does not abandon his avaricious principles; a whoremonger his lewdness; a drunkard his strong drink; an idolator his worshipping of strange gods; and by a pious, penitent life, turn to the true and living God with sorrow and anguish of heart, in the operative faith of Jesus Christ, he is no christian, nor shall he inherit the kingdom of God: (Rom. 1; 1 Cor. 6,) if sentence is thus passed, it is not we that judge, but the scriptures; as Christ says: He that rejecteth me, and receiveth not my words, hath one that judgeth him: the word that I have spoken, the same shall judge him in the last day. We are well assured that God does, and can save no man contrary to his word; (Gal. 5; John 12,) for he is truth, and cannot lie. Where there is no faith, no newness of mind, there is no repentance, nor sorrow of heart, &c., (John 14; Tit. 1,) upon such, alas! Christ has already passed sentence, saying: If ye believe not that I am he, ye shall die in your sins; if ye repent not, ye shall all perish; and more similar expressions. (John 8; Luke 13.)

Brethren, we therefore judge no man with our word before the time, as you well know; but we commit that unto Jesus Christ and his word, who will judge them in due season; we do not condemn them by our separation, as they complain; but we teach and admonish them by word and work, with all diligence and threatening, that they cease from evil, follow that which is good, do righteousness, seek and fear God in a good conscience, lest they die in sin and unbelief, and abide forever the wrath and judgment of God. (Ps. 33; Pet. 3.) Nevertheless, the pure charity and faithful service of the pious are ascribed to bad motives, and construed to their disgrace.

In the fifth place, many cover their tyranny and shedding of blood with a thin fig-leaf, and say: We judge you not, but the emperor's mandate judges you.

We reply: If our persecutors are christians, and have the knowledge of Christ, as they suppose, we earnestly desire in the spirit of humanity, for God's sake, that they would draw a comparison between the emperor and Christ, and observe with attention, whether the emperor and Christ are of one spirit; whether he walks as Christ taught his disciples: also, that they would compare the emperor's mandate with the gospel of Christ. If they discover that the emperor does not agree with Christ in spirit and in life; and that his mandate, in accordance with which they frame their conduct, is contrary to the gospel, then they must acknowledge that the emperor is no christian, and that his mandate is proscribed and accursed in the presence of God.

It is the most lamentable blindness that they fear and honor the poor, earthly emperor more than Christ Jesus, and pay more respect to his blood-thirsty, malicious mandate, than to the gospel of love. Yet they desire to be considered christians. O! that the emperor and his subjects were christians! This is our most earnest desire. Then would be spared a great deal of innocent blood, which is now spilt like water, contrary to all scripture and charity.

Say now, all who are guilty of innocent blood, and who palliate your conduct with the emperor's mandate; where have you read a single passage in the whole life of Christ, which authorizes men to shed blood and punish with the sword for opinion's sake? Where have the apostles once taught or countenanced such a practice? Should not the cause of the Spirit (understand faith,) be reserved unto the judgment of the Spirit? Why do you and the emperor place yourselves in God's stead, judging things which you understand not, neither are they commanded you? Do you not consider what befel Pharaoh, Antiochus, Herod, and many others, because they feared not the Most High, and vented their wrath against his people? (Eph. 1.) Consider, O you tyrants and blood-thirsty! that the emperor is not the head of Christ, but that Christ is the head of the emperor; that the emperor shall not judge and govern Christ, but Christ the emperor. (Col. 2; Heb. 2.) Dear men, how can you be so arrogant and so rebellious against him who created you? Do you consider the scriptures as mockery and as destitute of truth? Or do you hope that your glass will remain forever, and that it will never run out? Stand in awe of Him who locks up the heavens and the earth in the palm of his hand, who sends forth the lightning, gives wings to the tempest, and shakes the foundations of the mountains, who rules all things with the word of his power, at whose name every knee shall bow, of things in heaven and things in earth, and things under the earth, and to whom every tongue shall confess that he is the Lord, (Deut. 32; Phil. 2;) as soon as he calls, you must appear at his tribunal, (his summons is peremptory) no matter who you are, where you be, or what your pretensions; there will be no equivocation, no counsel, no excuse; when he calls, you must be there to give an account; you may be no longer steward, (Luke 16;) yet a little while, and the wicked shall not be; though his throne is exalted unto heaven, and his dominion extends to the ends of the earth, yet in a short time, he shall be sought for, and shall not be found. (Ps. 37; 2 Mac. 2.)

Therefore, beloved brethren and children in the Lord, be of sincere minds, and full of consolation in Christ Jesus; for all who persecute you shall be as grass; and all their power and glory as the flower of the field; (Isa. 40; 1 Pet. 2,) therefore, be not afraid of perishable, mortal man, but fear the Lord who has chosen you; for all the children of men shall wither as the grass, vanish as a mist, and wax old as a garment; but you shall abide forever, (as the scripture testifies,) and your souls shall enjoy everlasting life. (Isa. 51; 1 John 2.)

Yes, dearly beloved, the longed-for day of your visitation is at hand, in which you shall stand up with great power against those who have troubled you, (Wis. 3, 5.) and exacted your sweat and toil, nay, your blood and life, (Matt. 4;) then shall our persecutors be as ashes under the soles of our feet; and know, but too late, that emperor, king, duke, prince, crown, sceptre, majesty, power, sword and mandate, are but earth, dust, wind and smoke.

Against this day, all afflicted and oppressed Christians, who now labor under the cross of Christ, console themselves, in the firm hope of a future life, and commit all tyrants with their heathenish mandates unto God and his judgments; they remain firmly attached unto Christ Jesus and his holy word, and conform thereunto, their whole doctrine, faith, sacraments and life, never paying respect to any other doctrine or mandate; even as the Father commanded from heaven, (Matt. 17,) and as Christ Jesus with his holy apostles taught in all clearness, leaving it as a legacy unto all pious, god-fearing children.

I suppose, beloved brethren, it is sufficiently evident that the apology of tyrants, (in which they aver the justice and right of the outrageous murders,) is perfectly futile and barbarous; and that their accusation against us has no foundation in truth, is diametrically opposed to Christ and his word, nay, contrary to the principles of love, justice and equity. May the Father of mercies grant unto all, who suffer for his truth's sake, a sound understanding of his word and truth, and a freedom of mind in all temptations. Amen.

We will now, by the grace of God, show, in few words, how greatly it serves for our good, that our flesh is afflicted and tempted with many crosses and tribulations here upon earth.

Beloved brethen, when we consider the weakness of our sinful nature, (Gen. 6,) and how prone we all are to evil from our youth; that in our flesh dwelleth no good thing, (Rom. 7,) and that we drunk iniquity and ungodliness like water: as Eliphas, the Temanite, said to Job. And have, at all times, (though we seek and fear God,) an affection for the things of time and sense, (Job 15,) the gracious God and Father, who, through his eternal love, is always greatly concerned for his children, has prepared, and left in his house, an excellent remedy therefor, namely, the oppressive cross of Christ; so that we, who, in unbounded, mercy are received, through Christ Jesus, to the glory of the Father, believing in pureness of heart on Christ Jesus, and love him in our weakness, may, through the aforesaid cross, that is, through much affliction, forsake all the transitory delights and enjoyments of earth, die unto the world and the flesh, love God alone, set our affection on things above, where Christ sitteth on the right hand of God, (Col. 3;) as Peter also says: Forasmuch, then, says he, as Christ hath suffered for us in the flesh, arm yourselves likewise with the same mind; for he that hath suffered in the flesh, hath ceased from sin; that he no longer should live the rest of his time in the flesh, to the lusts of men, but to the will of God. (1 Pet. 4.)

It appears to me utterly impossible, beloved brethren, that they, who voluntarily submit to the word and will of God, who are willing and prepared to support the word in all things, being for this reason constantly persecuted and afflicted, slandered, imprisoned, robbed and put to death, should turn again and set their affection upon sensual pleasures, and the vain and sinful desires of the world. For, of what value are money and possessions, if we but believe, that we have in heaven a better and an enduring substance, that temporal riches can neither render us happy, nor afford us relief, (Matt. 6 ; Heb. 10,) and that we know not how soon they may be taken from us by robbers ? Or, why should we gratify the lusts of the flesh, when we look for, and expect nothing else every instant, than to be apprehended by the officers, and be treated by the executioners after this manner, be racked, tortured, drowned, burned and assassinated ? Moreover, how can the world afford us any enjoyment, seeing we are looked upon by the whole world as deceivers, heretics, scorners and fools ?

Forasmuch as eternal Wisdom recognizes an extreme weakness, and sincere earthly toil, peace, and felicity have so great a tendency to ruin and undo us before our God, and to render us careless, refractory, lukewarm and drowsy, he has appointed his cross as an awakening rod for the use of all his followers, by which, as a faithful Father, he restrains, awakes and excites the children of his love; as Solomon says, (Prov. 3, 12.) My son, despise not the chastening of the Lord; neither be weary of his correction ; for whom the Lord loveth he correcteth ; ho chasteneth every son in whom he delighteth. (Rev. 3.) If ye endure chastening, God dealeth with you as with sons ; for what son is he whom the father chasteneth not ? But if ye be without chastisement, whereof all are partakers, then are ye bastards, and not sons. (Heb. 12.) Furthermore, we have had fathers of our flesh which corrected us, and we gave them reverence : Shall we not much rather be in subjection unto the Father of spirits, and live ? For they verily, for a few days, chastened us after their own pleasure; but he, for our profit, that we might be partakers of his holiness. (Heb. 7, 10.)

Behold, brethren, these words of the apostle are, beyond measure, gracious, and replete with consolation unto all those who have to bear the cross of Christ; for, as a strict and faithful father who loves his children, desiring to teach and instruct them that which is best, does, sometimes, out of pure paternal love, admonish, chasten and punish them with stripes for the edification and promotion of his dear children, not regarding the pain inflicted in the flesh, in order that they may not despise their father's will, command and voice, but that they may fear and obey with all their heart, learn and practice modesty, piety and docility; so does our heavenly Father ofttimes chasten his elect children with his paternal rod, that they may hear and obey him in his holy word, will and commandment, practice piety and every moral virtue, fear God with sincerity of heart, unite not, nor familiarize themselves with the world, live no longer unto flesh and blood; and hereby, as obedient and chastened children of God, be finally made partakers of the promised kingdom and inheritance.

But if they refuse the rod of chastisement, reject the cross of Christ, and become, in consequence of their Father's kind chastening, the longer, the more abandoned and refractory, despising their Father's will and word, dealing and acting according to their own inclination, they must at last be cast off and be considered as infamous bastards.

Therefore, holy brethren, refuse not the rod and correction of your kind Father, for its tendency is extremely beneficial, namely, that you lay aside every weight and the sins which so easily beset you, and in all things, without exception, fear, love, and obey your Father. Thus, is this rod of the cross of Christ pure love and benevolence, and not indignation and wrath: as may be perceived and evinced by the spirit of God, and not by the dictates of the flesh.

For a similar reason did God ofttimes permit his people Israel to be chastized by the Philistines, Assyrians, Chaldeans, &c., when they forgot and rebelled against their God, in order that, by such scourges and punishments, they might again seek their God, hear his law, cease from evil, and act uprightly in all things. Notwithstanding, the paternal punishment was for the most part lost upon Israel; as the Prophet says. He hath often reproved, but what did it avail? The rod amendeth not the wicked children, saith the Lord God. (Ezek. 31.)

Behold, also, famine and plague, tribulation and anguish, are sent as scourges for amendment. But for all these things they shall not turn from their wickedness, nor be always mindful of the scourges. (2 Esdras. 16, 19, 20.)

Again: Thou hast stricken them, but they have not grieved; thou hast punished them for amendment, but they refused to receive correction: They have made their faces harder than a rock; they have refused to return. (Jer. 5.)

The above cited words of the prophet show plainly why the Israelites were so often punished and stricken of the Lord, namely, that they might turn themselves from iniquity. Yet all in vain, as the prophets complain and declare in the above words.

Beloved brethren, let this serve you as an admonition, that

you be not like circumstanced with disobedient and hard-hearted Israel, but that you willingly submit yourselves to the chastening and correction of your merciful Father, reflecting upon that which is written: When we are judged, we are chastened of the Lord, that we should not be condemned with the world. (1 Cor. 11, 32.)

Therefore, dearly beloved brethren and sisters in the Lord, reject not the chastening and instruction of your affectionate Father, but receive, with abundant joy, the exhortation of his sincere affection, giving thanks, that through his paternal favor he has chosen you in Christ Jesus, as the children of his love, taught you and called you by the word of his power, (Eph. 1.) enlightened you with the Holy Spirit, that through the salutary influence of the cross of Christ you may restore to health your poor, weak, mortal flesh, which is obnoxious to so many loath-some infectious diseases of concupiscence, and wean it entirely from the pleasures and enjoyments of the world, that you may be made partakers of the cross of Christ, and rendered conform-able unto his death, (Phil. 3,) and, by this means, attain unto the resurrection of the dead; as Paul, in a certain place in-structs, saying: We are troubled on every side, yet not dis-tressed; we are perplexed, but not in despair; persecuted, but not forsaken; cast down, but not destroyed; always bearing about in the body of the dying of the Lord Jesus, that the life also of Jesus might be made manifest in our body. (2 Cor. 4, 8, 9, 10.) But we who live, surrender ourselves daily unto death for Jesus' sake, that the life also of Jesus might be made manifest in our mortal flesh.

Behold, for this cause, he teaches, admonishes, threatens, chas-tens, and rebukes, that we should deny ungodliness and worldly lusts, die entirely unto the world, flesh and the devil, seek our trea-sure, portion and inheritance in heaven, alone love and believe the only true, living and eternal God, looking in patience for that blessed hope, and the glorious appearing of the great God, and our Saviour Jesus Christ, who gave himself for us, that he might redeem us from all iniquity, and purify unto himself a peculiar people, serving him in righteousness and godliness all the days of our life. (Tit. 2.)

And for the same reason James says: (James 1.) My brethren, count it all joy when ye fall into diverse temptations; knowing this, that the trying of your faith worketh patience. But let patience have her perfect work, that ye may be perfect and entire, wanting nothing; for as gold in passing through the fire is severed from the dross, and becomes more and more re-fined; so, the susceptible man of God is subdued, purified, and refined, in the fiery furnace of affliction, that he may enhance the everlasting praise, and glory of Christ and the Father, and may out of a pure heart, without hindrance, fear, love, honor, thank, and serve the same eternal God.

And this is the word that is written in the book of Wisdom, namely : Having been a little chastised, they shall be greatly rewarded : For God proved them, and found them worthy for himself. As gold in the furnace hath he tried them, and received them as a burnt-offering. And in the time of their visitation. they shall shine, and run to and fro like sparks among the stubble. They shall judge the nations, and have dominion over the people, and their Lord shall reign forever. (Wis. 3.)

Beloved brethren, be you, therefore, full of consolation in the Lord, and bear willingly your tribulation as pious soldiers of Christ, that you may please him who hath called and chosen you as soldiers : For, says Paul, (2 Tim. 2) if a man also strive for masteries, yet is not crowned, except he strive lawfully. Conduct yourselves, therefore, valiantly in the strife, and you shall gain favor in the eyes of your King ; but if you become intimidated, throw down your arms, and forsake the combat, you shall receive no crown ; for he that endureth unto the end says Christ, shall be saved. (Matt. 10.)

I fear that some may be found among our young and inexperienced brethren, who suffer themselves to be perplexed by the fleeting thought. Wherefore doth the way of the wicked and ungodly prosper ? And why do the righteous suffer much tribulation ? (Jer. 12 ; Ps. 73.) Yea, it appears in the eyes of the imprudent as if the ungodly were born to prosper ; for they grow and increase like a blossoming branch. They marry and are given in marriage ; they sow, plant, and gather the grain into barns ; they hoard up money in their chests ; their dwellings are magnificent and filled with costly things ; they deck themselves with gold and silver, with silk and velvet : they nourish their hearts as in a day of slaughter. (James 4.) Their fields and meadows flourish luxuriantly ; their cattle are healthy and prolific ; their children are merry, gay and vigorous in their sight ; they play upon the organ and the tambour, the viol and the lute ; they sing and leap for joy, and say to their souls : Rejoice, and be gay while life endures.

Their preachers confirm and console them, and their worship is a pleasure exceeding all pleasures. In short, it would appear as if they were loved and blessed of God with a peculiar love, and that the righteous are accursed and hated of God with a peculiar hatred ; for they are like a slender shrub in a barren soil ; like a poor frighted owl that is persecuted by all other birds ; like a pelican of the wilderness ; and as a sparrow alone under the roof. (Isa. 53 ; Ps. 102.) All who look upon them,

27

mock them ; all who know them, despise them. There is no kingdom, principality, city, nor country, large enough to endure and tolerate a poor, rejected Christian. All who abuse, slander, and injure them, think they do God service.

Brethren, were we to speak, or judge after the manner of men, we would doubtless complain with holy Jeremiah, and say, (Jer. 12.) Righteous art thou, O Lord, when I plead with thee : yet, let me talk with thee of thy judgments. Wherefore doth the way of the wicked prosper? Wherefore are all they happy that deal very treacherously? Again : (Heb. 1.) Wherefore lookest thou upon them that deal treacherously, and holdest thy tongue when the wicked devoureth the man that is more righteous than he? and Esdras, (2 Esd. 3:) Are they of Babylon better than they of Sion? Asaph's feet were almost gone, his steps had well nigh slipped, when he saw the prosperity of the wicked, and observed the opposition and tribulation of the righteous. (Ps. 73.)

I counsel and admonish all who have to contend with such thoughts, that they direct their hearts and eyes unto the Lord's word, and observe with attention that which is written concerning the end and issue of both : and first of the ungodly. They spend their days in wealth, says Job, (Chap. 21,) and in a moment they go down to the grave. Again : Fret not, thyself, says David, because of evil doers, neither be thou envious against the workers of iniquity ; for they shall soon be cut down like the grass, and wither as the green herb. Again, If ye live after the flesh, says Paul : Ye shall die ; to be carnally minded is death, (Ps. 37 ; Rom. 8, and many similar passages.)

But respecting the end of the righteous, it is written : The souls of the righteous are in the hand of God, and there shall no torment touch them. In the sight of the unwise they seemed to die : and their departure is taken for misery, and their going from us to be utter destruction ; but they are in peace. (Wis. 3, 1, 2, 3.) Many are the afflictions of the righteous, but the Lord delivereth him out of them all. (Ps. 34.) Again : Blessed are ye when men shall revile and persecute you, and say all manner of evil against you, falsely, for my sake. Rejoice and be exceeding glad ; for great is your reward in heaven. (Matt. 5.) Again ; seeing, says Paul : It is a righteous thing with God, to recompense tribulation to them that trouble you ; and to you who are troubled rest with us, when the Lord Jesus shall be revealed from heaven with his mighty angels in flaming fire, taking vengeance on them that know not God, and that obey not the Gospel of our Lord Jesus Christ : who shall be punished with everlasting destruction from the presence of the Lord, and from the glory of his power. (2 Thess. 1,) when he shall come to be glorified in his saints, and to be admired in them that believe ; yea, all who truly read, believe, and understand, the scriptures, and have a correct perception of the vast dissimilarity in end and issue of both, will not envy them their short-lived prosperity, joy, and felicity, and will, by the grace of God, be prepared for, and find consolation in, their own cross, tribulation and affliction.

Moreover, brethren, we are well aware that the cross appears to the flesh as grievous, harsh, and severe, and is not, in this life, looked upon as productive of joy, but much rather of sorrow ; as Paul says. (Heb. 11.)   Yet, since it contains within itself, a source of profit and delight, in that it adds to the piety of the pious, separates them from the world and the flesh, makes them revere God and his word, as mentioned above ; and that it is also the Father's holy will that by it the sincere be approved, and the pretender exposed in his hypocrisy ; therefore, all the true children of God are prepared through love, to do the will of the Father, rejoicing in it ; as Paul says, (Gal. 6.) God forbid that I should glory, save in the cross of the Lord Jesus Christ, by whom the world is crucified unto me, and I unto the world.   Again : The apostles departed from the presence of the council, rejoicing that they were counted worthy to suffer shame for his name.   (Acts 5, 41.)

Forasmuch as we are well convinced that our weak flesh, is very intimately united with us, and is a source of vexation as we find in the case of Job, Jeremiah, Elijah, and many others, as also of our Lord himself who earnestly desired that, if it were possible, the cup might be removed from him, nay, in excess of agony he trembled, quaked, and sweat as it were great drops of blood, so that an angel appeared unto him from heaven strengthening him, (Luke 22,) therefore our best counsel is, that in faith and humility of heart, we fly for refuge to our God, as all sincere bearers of the cross have done from the beginning : and seek, in full confidence, his grace, aid, assistance, and consolation ; for whom does he forsake that trusts in him ? and who hath called upon him, that he did not hear ? he is our God and Father ; he is our Lord and King ; our helper and protector ; our strength and fortress ; our consolation and refuge in the time of need ; he is the horn of our salvation and our shadow at noonday.   By my God, says David, have I leaped over a wall.   (Ps. 18 ; Isa. 4.)   If God is for us who can be against us ? We can do all things through Christ, who strengthens us.   To him commit thy cause ; he worketh in his saints that which is pleasing in his sight.   Some he has rescued from the hands of tyrants, some he has preserved in the midst of fire ; for others he has stopped the mouths of fierce and ravening lions; (Dan. 3, 6,) he has released some from prison and confinement, others have trampled the fear of death under their feet, and through the strength of their faith, have triumphantly and victoriously conquered hunger, thirst, shame, derision, nakedness, stripes, imprisonment, anguish, and, in addition, the gallows, rack, massacre, torture, water, fire, life and death, &c. (Jer. 26; Acts 5, 12, 6;) they were actuated by the constraining effective influence of divine love, which converts the bitter into sweet, and the horrible into that which is greatly to be desired.   Love, says Solomon, is strong as death; many waters cannot quench it, neither can the floods drown it; all who possess it, ought to say with Paul : Who shall separate us from the love of God? shall tribulation, or distress, or persecution, or famine, or nakedness, or peril, or sword? (Rom. 8.)   As it is written : For thy sake we are killed all the day long; we are accounted as sheep for the slaughter.   (Ps. 43.)   Nay, in all these things we are more than conquerors through him that loved us :   For I am persuaded, that neither death, nor life, &c., shall separate us from the love of God, which is in Christ Jesus our Lord.

Therefore, beloved brethren, bearers of the cross of the Lord, know you God, fear and love him, believe and confide in him, love and serve him, and that in the fulness of pureness of heart, according to the example of all saints, and of Christ Jesus : and the Father of mercies and of truth, in the excellency of his love, will not forsake you, but will care for you as the apple of his eye, will support you, with all the faithful, in every misfortune and extremity, will extend his hand, and guard and preserve you, in life or in death, as is pleasing in his sight, to the enhancement of his glory, and to the salvation of your own souls, for he is so kind and faithful, that he will not suffer you to be tempted above that you are able, but will in his boundless mercy, make a way for you to escape if you only remain steadfast in the belief of his word, and consider him as your faithful Father.   (1 Cor. 10.)

Dear brethren, if, in your trials and temptations, you exhibit such evidence as here related; drinking with patience the cup of the Lord; bearing witness of Christ Jesus and his holy, inestimable word, in action, and conversation; suffering yourselves, in perfect constancy, to be led as meek lambs to the slaughter, for his testimony's sake; then will the name of the Lord be sanctified, and exalted with praise and abundant glory; the hope of the righteous shall be revealed; the kingdom of heaven, spread abroad; the word of God acknowledged; and your poor weak brethren and companions in the Lord, edified and confirmed by this your plain dealing.

Yea, my brethren, in the manner here related, we are informed and instructed, even unto this day, by the offering and blood of Abel; by the faith and obedience of Abraham, Isaac, and Jacob; the chastity of Joseph; the patience of Job and of Tobit; the excellent and manly confession of Eleazer; the mother and her seven sons, (Heb, 11, 12; Rom. 4; Gen. 39; Job 2; Tob. 2; 2 Macc. 6, 7;) the candor, constancy, and piety of all the pious before us; the pure, unspotted love, (Heb. 11,) humility, peace, righteousness, and pure voluntary offering of Jesus Christ, who, according to divine promise, was sent from heaven, in everlasting love, by God our heavenly Father, and descended upon earth as an infallible teacher, and as an eternal example of all good. (Matt. 23; John 13; Chap. 3; 1 John. 4.)

My dearly beloved brethren and sisters in Christ Jesus, dispersed abroad in every land, for whom, out of pure, christian love and duty, I have composed and written this exhortation: I will now draw to a conclusion, and I do entreat you, in all humility, that you consider well, in the first place, the nature of the people who so malevolently persecute you, spoiling your property, and destroying your lives.

Secondly, why they persecute and injure you. Thirdly, that all saints, as also Christ Jesus himself, have suffered and all the pious must suffer persecution; as may be seen. Fourthly, how futile all their arguments are, with which they try to excuse themselves of their bloody deeds, accusing us, as though they did right, and we merited every kind of punishment and disgrace.

Fifthly, how profitable and advantageous to us is the cross of Christ, which, for sake of the Lord's word, we must take up and bear daily, since it is our desire to hear, believe and obey Christ Jesus. Now, if you consider with discretion, according to the scriptures, and reflect, in purity of heart, upon these five points, I have not the least doubt that this exercise will afford you invincible strength, and an invulnerable armor and shield against all tribulation, persecution and distress.

Finally, I beseech and exhort you to consider with earnest diligence that which is promised to all the conquering soldiers of Christ Jesus in the world to come, namely, the eternal, incorruptible kingdom, the crown of glory, and the life unending and immortal. (1 Pet. 1; Heb. 10; 2 Tim. 4.) Therefore, O thou people of God! equip thyself and make ready for battle, not with external weapons and armor, as the blood-thirsty barbarous world, but with the firmness of confidence, the tranquillity of patience, and the vehement ardor of prayer. There is no alternative, the combat of the cross must be maintained, and the wine-press of affliction must be trodden. O thou bride and sister of Christ, prepare thyself; the thorny crown must pierce thy head; and the nails transfix thy hands and feet; thy person must be scourged, and thy face spit upon. Gird thyself round about, and be prepared; for thou must go forth with thy Lord and Bridegroom without the city, bearing his reproach. (Heb. 13.) On Golgotha thou must offer up thy sacrifice. Awake and pray, for thy enemies are more numerous than the hairs of thy head, more innumerable than the sand of the sea. (Esd. 16; Tob. 7.) Though their hearts, hands, feet, and swords are exceedingly red, and stained with blood, be not dismayed; for God is thy leader. Thy life on earth is an incessant warfare. Strive valiantly, and thou shalt receive the promised crown.

To him that overcometh will I give to eat of the tree of life, which is in the midst of the paradise of God, and of the hidden and heavenly manna. (Rev. 1.)

Him that overcometh will God make a pillar in his temple, and will write upon him his name and the name of the new Jerusalem.

He that overcometh shall not be hurt by the second death. He that overcometh, the same shall be clothed in white raiment; and his name shall not be blotted out of the book of life, but Christ Jesus will confess his name before his heavenly Father, and before his angels. (Rev. 3.)

He that overcometh shall sit with Christ in his throne, even as Christ overcome, and has sat down with his Father on his throne.

O thou soldier of God, prepare thyself and fear not! The wine-press thou must tread; thou must go the narrow way. and enter in through the strait gate unto eternal life. (Matt 7.)

The Lord is thy strength, thy refuge and consolation; he flies with thee to foreign lands; he is with thee in fire and in water; he will never leave thee, nor forsake thee; yea, he will come quickly, and his great reward shall be with him.

Blessed are they which are persecuted for righteousness' sake; for theirs is the kingdom of heaven. (Matt. 5.)

Be not grieved that thou are black; (Cant. 1) thou art still comely and pleasing to the King.

As a rose thou must grow among thorns, and be stung with the prickles. (Ps. 44.) Rejoice for the King delighteth in thy comeliness.

Though in his first appearance he was offered as an innocent Lamb, and opened not his mouth, yet the time shall come when he will appear in judgment as a triumphant Prince and a victorious King. (Isa. 53; Chap. 42.) Then will our persecutors look upon him whom they pierced. (Rev. 1,) then will they cry aloud and exclaim: Ye mountains fall upon us, hide us ye hills, (Rev. 6.) But you shall leap and dance in excessive joy like calves of the stall. (Matt. 4.) Joy and exultation will never forsake you; for your King, Bridegroom and Redeemer, Christ Jesus, will remain with you forever; there shall be no more death, neither sorrow, nor crying, neither shall there be any more pain; and all tears shall be wiped away from your eyes. (Rev. 21.)

Praise, thanksgiving, and glory to God, shall flow from your mouth in an eternal stream. I repeat it, strive, the crown of glory is prepared,—shrink not, neither draw back; for yet a little while, and he that shall come, will come, and will not tarry. The just shall live by faith: but if you draw back the Lord's soul shall have no pleasure in you. (Hab. 2; Heb. 10.)

Take heed and watch, lest the fire of the cross consume you as wood, hay and stubble, (2 Cor. 3; Matt. 7) and the rains and storms of persecution overthrow the house. (Matt. 13.) Let not the heat of the sun wither the cross, lest like the dog you turn again to that which you have ejected. (2 Pet. 2.) Let not your garments and your feet, which you have washed, become unclean, lest seven worse spirits enter you, and so the last error be worse than the first. (Luke 12.)

Therefore, beloved brethren and sisters in the Lord, fear God with all your heart, and with all your souls, and seek him with all your powers. Watch night and day; knock before the throne of his mercy, that with his paternal hand he may support you under every affliction, succor you in trouble and distress, and faithfully preserve you in his way, word and truth, (Ps. 91,) that you may not dash your feet against a stone, and so failing in your profession and your life, be overcome and disgraced; but that you may preserve the treasure, intrusted to your care, pure and untarnished against that day, and thus obtain, with all saints, the promised land, inheritance, kingdom, life and crown. May the Father of mercies and of love, grant this unto you and us through his blessed son, Jesus Christ, in the power of his eternal Holy Spirit, to his praise, and everlasting glory. Amen and Amen.

Here according to promise, (page 288) the christian reader is presented with an account of the unheard of, newly invented, dreadful martyrdom of the christians and believers. An extract from Eusebius and others, &c., &c. The author appended this with the hope that it would be well received—"Concerning HUMILITY AND MEEKNESS OF THE BELIEVING MARTYRS OF THAT DAY." (Eus. B. V. C. 3.) *Presented as a mirror for the present time.*

They followed Christ Jesus in all humility, although they were oft made martyrs.

However they did not call themselves *martyrs* nor consented that others should call them such; but when even one of us called them *martys* they reproved us severely, saying: That this name properly belonged to Christ, who alone was the true and faithful Martyr and witness of the truth, the first born of the dead and the Restorer of eternal life. Or that this name could only appropriately be given to those, who after laying off a testimony had departed this life and gone to God. But we, (say they,) as humble poor people, wish alone to adhere undeviatingly to the confession, and therefore, they entreated the other brethren with tears, that they would pray to God that they might obtain the witness of a *martyr;* (full confession) and they were so humble, though in truth they were *martyrs*, still they avoided the honor of the name. But among the heathens they acted with all constancy, showed great magnanimity, by scorning the offered insults, and through patience suffered. For among the brethren they were meek, among persecutors brave, a terror to the refractory, subject to Christ, opposing the devil; they humble themselves under the mighty hand of God, by which they are now exalted; they favored all, they accused none, relieve all, bound none; prayed for those who persecuted them, as did Stephen, saying; Lord, lay not this sin to their charge. The devil opposed them powerfully, because they out of great love, in Christ Jesus, restored the fallen, whom the devil would fain have devoured. They entreated God to give them grace and constancy, lest they might depart from the church and become a prey to the devil.

They preferred peace before every thing else, and commanded us to maintain peace. They were martyred without cause and were conscious that they made no discord among the brethren and no grief to the church; but they admonished assiduously, that we should by all means maintain and preserve peace, and cherish love, which is the bond of union.

These things we mentioned for the benefit of the reader, because they have been recommended by worthy and beloved men. And on account of those who deal so haughty with the brethren—and when the pious err through weakness, they have no compassion upon them, as if Christ should have no mercy on them. We will further relate what we found in the aforementioned book. There was one among the number apprehended for Christ's sake, called Alcibiades, he led a strict, zealous life, he would use no sustenance except bread and water. And as he was determined to live thus abstemious in prison, it was made known to Allalas, that Alcibiades did wrong, because he would not rightly use the creatures of God, lest he might cause others to take offence thereat. But when Alcibiades was informed of the matter, he then enjoyed all things with thanksgiving, for there was a spirit which taught him and persuaded him to obey, &c.

Afterwards, Montanus, Alcibiades and Theodotius were regarded by many in the land of Phrygia as prophets, for in those days many favors were granted to some of the churches through the gift of the Holy Ghost, so they believed that there was imparted the gift of prophecy. And when great contention rose among the brethren, the churches in France again issued their sentence, with all discipline, reverence and the true exposition of the faith, and brought forward the epistles of the martyrs, who among them ended their lives, which they wrote in their prisons to the brethren in Asia and Phrygia, &c.

The whole Bible, especially the 11th chapter of the epistle to the Hebrews, speaks of the great crosses, tribulation, the martyrdom and deaths of the believers. Here we read of inhuman, cruel torturings, such as was not heard before nor since. Boiling water and oil were poured upon their naked bodies—they were placed upon red hot gridirons and roasted there; their members were pierced through with sharp pointed instruments —they were scourged, and red hot irons were applied to their limbs—sharp thorns were thrust into their posterior and privates —other indignities were offered not to be mentioned—hot pitch was thrown into their faces—their eyes were bored out with pointed irons, —they were beaten from head to foot with clubs— they were dragged through the streets by their feet—they were suspended and their flesh torn from them with pincers, that their bodies were all raw, then vinegar, salt and lime were mixed and poured upon them, they were then rolled about upon thorns, potsherds, broken glass and other sharp instruments, and then placed the tortured body upon a gridiron, and roasted them lingeringly to protract the pain—rolling the mangled body backward and forward upon the gridiron till the ghost was given up.

They were cast before beasts of prey, such as lions, bears, and leopards; and before infuriated bulls—and after repeated tortures, were again cast into prison, and after a short time tortured them anew, which was repeated often, as we read of Maturo, Sanato, Allalo and others; and above all the amiable Blandina, whom they tortured six different ways—she may properly be called the pattern of martyrs. Others died in prison on account of their excruciating pains; some were starved to death —some women they hung up by the feet and suffocated with offensive smoke—flayed them, led them about on camels, and tore them to pieces with tongs;—cast them into privies—their bones were broken, and they were cast into clefts of rocks; their heads were bruised so much till the brain ran down upon the earth—cut off their sinews and veins then thrust them down precipices—they were first severely tortured, butchered like swine and then cast into the sea—their abdomen was cut open and barley strewn in, and in this condition let hogs devour them—yea, some of the tyrants, for fierce anger ate pieces of their livers—they watched day and night, lest their remains would be taken and buried!—they were smeared over with honey and lard, and suspended in baskets in the air for the flies, wasps and bees to eat them—women and virgins were stripped stark naked, and while thus exposed, they suspended them by one leg, forcing the head down and leaving them in this position for one day—they cut off their breasts—horrible! horrible to relate!!—melted lead they poured into their secrets—forced red hot spears in!—applied red hot iron—sturdy trees they bent down and tied a leg fast to two trees and then let them spring up again, and thus tore the women—took sharp splinters of pine wood, forced them under the nails of their hands, and then set them on fire—melted lead they poured down their backs. Twenty sharp pointed pieces were forced under the nails of one Benjamin of Persia, this was not enough, they forced a sharp rugged tube into his urethra—and this was repeatedly done—after this a rod full of thorns was taken and forced into his posteriors, till the valiant man gave up the ghost.—It is impossible, nay, incredible, with a few words to describe the unheard of cruelties and tortures which were practiced—besides these other modes of torturing were invented, and he that succeeded in inventing the most cruel mode was highly honored: The number that were slain, like beasts, was so great that even the executioners became fatigued and their swords became dull.

One king in Persia, as history relates, had sixteen thousand slain. But the more the christians were opposed the more their number increased, so powerfully did Christ reign in them, that the heathens themselves said: *The christian blood is a true seed, &c.*

A

PLEASING MEDITATION

AND

DEVOUT CONTEMPLATION,

TOGETHER WITH

CHRISTIAN DOCTRINES FOR A TROUBLED AND ANXIOUS CONSCIENCE, WHICH IS OPPOSED BY THE WORLD, FLESH, HELL, DEATH AND THE DEVIL.

ON THE TWENTY-FIFTH PSALM,

CALLED IN LATIN

Ad te lebabi animam meam,

EXPLAINED BY WAY OF SUPPLICATION.

In my distress I cried unto the Lord, and he heard me. Deliver my soul, O Lord, from lying lips, and from a deceitful tongue.—PSALM cxx. 1, 2.

For other foundation can no man lay than that is laid, which is Jesus Christ.—1 COR. iii. 11.

PREFACE.

DEAR READER, it is evident, that I am charged behind my back with many slanders and lies of the envious, hence I have sought briefly to express the feelings of my whole *heart, ground, spirit, faith, doctrine, seeking, &c.*, in short prayers on the twenty-fifth psalm; not with words of human wisdom, nor logically or rhetorically; for these I possess not; but in a simple narration of my heart, to show the different dispositions of a true and false Christian, with the whole ground and hope of my faith, what I maintain concerning Christ Jesus, of his doctrine, *baptism, supper, ordinance, command and prohibition.* Again: How I am disposed towards lords and princes, and towards all who yet sit in the darkness of their unbelief, and know not the light of truth; and that I seek nothing else upon earth, nor shall seek by the grace of God, than the pure word of our Lord Jesus Christ, and that according to the contents of the scriptures.

If I do err, which I hope, by the grace of God, is not the case, I do pray every one, for the Lord's sake, that I may not be put to shame; if any one has more powerful writings and convincing truth, that he through brotherly exhortation and instruction would assist me, I desire with my heart to accept of it, if he is right. Deal with me as Christ's spirit and word teach; if any one can convince me of an error, by the scriptures, and if I will not renounce it, but continue obstinate to the word of God and brotherly admonition, then practice upon me the tyranny of Nero, Diocletian, or Maxeritius, as an obdurate and ungodly heretic; for this I stand prepared, although this *would* be contrary to the usages and doctrines of the first church; for it is evident, that they persecuted not on account of faith, much less did they kill them, but the erring and heretical they faithfully admonished, and those who would not return were then excommunicated. (Tit. 3.)

Afterwards, in the time of Arius, they exiled them. Ultimately antichrist's bloody tyranny generally prevailed. All had to suffer who did not agree with the Pope in his abominations. It is yet the case, which alas! may be plainly seen in many places.

Many who have neither seen nor heard me, called me a deceiving heretic. This must be all endured. I am not better than the pious fathers, who had to hear and suffer; nevertheless, I feel disposed to give my life, if it would induce the world rightly to understand my seeking, faith and doctrine; for I assuredly know that I have the word of God. My reader, pervert not what I write. I desire nothing else, before God, who created me, than to deal plainly, with a living voice, before every one, as one willing to be overcome by the spirit of Christ, or to overcome; for my desire is that I and many with me be saved; hence, it is unnecessary to use the sword against me; if I have not the truth, I desire with all my heart to be instructed in it;

but if I have, you then do not persecute me, but him, who is the truth, Christ Jesus.

Again, I say, with Christ's spirit and word I desire to overcome, or to be overcome; in this I appeal to all the world. But it is in vain— the truth they will reject, and maintain and defend lies with the sword; for it is the true disposition and manner of antichrist to defame, slander, apprehend, torture, burn and murder, contrary to the spirit and word of God. But the Lord will see and judge it. (2 Chron. 14.)

I would, therefore, faithfully admonish the reader, that he would zealously and earnestly strive after the kingdom of God, and examine this *Psalm* with assiduity,—every word of it, with a submissive, humble heart; I hope he will find, by the grace of God, in the examination, and see clearly, the true difference between a believer and an unbeliever.

May God, the Father of our Lord Jesus Christ, grant the reader a zealous, ardent heart, a sincere, active faith, unfeigned christian love, and obedience to his holy word, through Christ Jesus, his beloved Son our Lord, to him be everlasting praise. Amen.

THE TWENTY-FIFTH PSALM
EXPLAINED BY WAY OF SUPPLICATION.

UNTO THEE, O LORD, *do I lift up my soul, O my God, I trust in thee ; let me not be ashamed.*

O Lord, thou that bearest rule, Lord of heaven and earth, I call·thee Lord, though I am not worthy to be called thy servant ; from my youth I did not serve thee, but thy enemy, the devil ; him I served diligently, nevertheless, I do not doubt thy grace ; for I find in the word of thy truth that thou art a bountiful, rich Lord to all those who call upon thee. Therefore, I call unto thee : O Lord hear me, hear me, O Lord ! (Matt. 11 ; Joel 1 ; Rom. 10.) With full confidence and assurance, I lift up, not my head or my hands as the hypocrites do in the synagogues, but my soul. (Matt. 6.) I lifted up my heart, not to Abraham, for he never knew us, nor to Israel, for he never had knowledge of us, but alone to thee, for thou art our Lord and Father, thou art our Redeemer, this is thy name of days of yore, as the prophet says. (Isa. 64.) Hence it is, dear Lord, that I trust in thee, for I truly know that thou art a faithful God over all who trust in thee. (Isa. 43.) If I am in darkness, thou art my light ; am I in prison, thou art with me ; am I forsaken, thou art my comfort ; am I in death, thou art my life ; if they curse me, thou dost bless ; if they grieve me, thou dost comfort ; (Ps. 9,) if they wilt slay me, thou wilt raise me up ; and if I walk in the dark valley, thou wilt ever be with me. (Ps. 9.) It is right, O Lord, that I lift up my grieved and miserable soul to thee, trust in thy promise, and am not ashamed. (Ps. 23.)

Let not mine enemies triumph over me ; yea, let none that wait on thee be ashamed.

O Lord of hosts, Lord of lords, I am weak, miserable and in great distress ; nevertheless, I fear not the sensual scoffing of my enemies ; but I fear greatly, lest I deny thy adorable and revered name, and depart from thy truth, and that they rejoice over my weakness and the transgression of thy will, and mock me and say : Where is thy God now? Where is thy Christ? And that thine divine honor be thus reproached through me. O Lord, preserve me ; keep me, O Lord ! for my enemies are strong and many ; yea, more numerous than the hairs of my head, and the spires of grass in the fields ; my unclean flesh is never at rest; satan encompasseth me as a roaring lion, that he may devour me; (Rom. 7; 1 Pet. 3,) the blood-thirsty, revengeful world is determined upon my life; they also hate, persecute, burn and murder those who seek thy praise. Wretched man, I know not whither to go, misery, tribulation, fear and dread are on every side; strife within, and persecution without. I say with king Josaphat: If I know not whither to go, I lift my eyes unto thee, and depend only on thy grace and mercy, as Abraham in Gerar, Jacob in Mesopotamia, Joseph in Egypt, Moses in Median, Israel in the wilderness, David in the mountains, Hezekiah in Jerusalem, the young men in the fiery furnace, Daniel in the lion's den; yea, all the pious fathers trusted in thee, and were not made ashamed. (2 Chron. 23; Gen. 20, 28, 37; Exod. 2, 15, 17; Isa. 36: 1 Sam. 26; Dan. 3, 6; Ps. 11.)

Let them be ashamed which transgress without a cause.

O Lord, thou that bearest rule, even as thy merciful grace is over all who fear thee, so also is thy fierce ire over all who despise thee, (Exod. 34,) who walk after their lusts, and dare to say with all fools: There is no God; we have made a covenant with death, and with hell an agreement; God knoweth not what we do, thick clouds are a covering to him that he seeth not the works of men; we will eat and drink, to-morrow we will die; (Ps. 13; Isa. 28,) for our life is short and full of trouble, and there is no consolation when we have gone hence; we will live in affluence and use the creatures as we desire; (Job. 22; 2 Cor. 18,) we will oppress the poor, defraud the righteous, we will condemn him with the most disgraceful death. (Wisd. 2.) O, dear Lord, thus does the world err, and live every where in the lusts of the flesh, lust of the eyes, and in the pride of life; (1 John 2,) in vain deceit, unrighteousness and tyranny, wherever we turn. Few are they who fear thy name. Paul says: To be carnally minded is death; sentence is already passed, if we live according to the flesh we must die, so teach the scriptures; if we do not repent there is nothing more certain than fierce anger. Therefore, dear Lord, threaten thou, reprove, admonish and teach, perhaps they may sometime repent, know the truth and be saved; they are the works of thy hands, created after thy image, dearly bought, let them not be confounded like Cain, Sodom, Pharaoh and Antiochus with all those who have transgressed without a cause. (2 Tim. 1; Gen. 1, 2, 4, 19; 1 Cor. 7; 1 Pet. 1; Exod. 14; 2 Macc. 9.)

Shew me thy ways, O Lord; teach me thy paths.

O Lord of hosts, I know through the word of thy grace that there is but one way which leadeth to life, which is strait and narrow for the flesh, (Matt. 7; 2 Esd. 7,) beset with thorns and dangers all around, and is found by few, and still fewer walk therein, it is like a treasure hid in a field which none can find but he to whom it is shown by the spirit. (Matt. 13.) Dear Lord, there is no way but thou alone, all who walk through thee will find the gates of life. (John 14.) There is another way which seems very pleasant to the flesh, which appears, soft, smooth and broad, strewed with roses, pleasant and agreeable to the eye, but its end leads to death. On this way the whole world walks, unconcerned and without fear, and prefers things perishable to imperishable, evil to good, and darkness to the light of the world. They all walk on the perverse, broad and crooked way; they become faint in the way of unrighteousness, and know not the way of the Lord. (Wis. 5.) It is true, the way of error seems right in the eyes of fools, but I know through thy spirit and word that it is the certain road to the abyss of hell. Therefore, I entreat thee, dear Lord, be merciful to me a poor sinner, show me thy path, and teach me thy way; for thy way is the right way, godly and pleasant, humble, chaste, full of peace and of all good, and will lead my soul to eternal life.

Lead me in thy truth and teach me : for thou art the God of my salvation ; on thee do I wait all the day.

O Lord! Lord! My tears, says David, have been my meat day and night. (Ps. 42.) My heart within me quakes, my strength forsakes me, and the light of my eyes is dim, and this on account of the innumerable dangers and snares which beset my soul. I am in constant fear lest I be led from the way of truth by misapprehension or through the deceit of satan. O Lord, the subtlety of the learned is great; satan uses his wiles artfully, some teach but the doctrine and commandments of men which are fruitless and corrupt trees. (2 Cor. 11 ; Job. 4 ; Judges 1.) Some cry only grace, spirit and Christ, and daily trample on grace, grieve the Holy Ghost, and crucify the Son with their vain, sensual life, as is evident. Some who had before escaped Babylon, Egypt and Sodom, and taken upon them the yoke and cross of Christ, are again devoured by satan, and so deceived by the false prophets, as if they had never known thy word and will. (Ps. 90.) Yea, seven spirits, alas ! worse than the former, entered them, (Luke 11,) although they cloak themselves under thy word, ordinances, and pretend that it was thy pleasure, word and will, although thou never didst think upon, much less didst thou desire it; on account of which I am more grieved, full of sorrow of heart, well knowing that thy true word is no deceiving lie, as they teach, but it is the truth which thy infallible mouth taught here upon earth and in this grievous world.

28*

All who are of the truth hear thy voice, as the voice of their own shepherd, (John 17,) and the true bridegroom, but the voice of a stranger they flee, (John 10,) always fearing lest they might be deceived. O Lord, remember thy afflicted and poor servant; thou art a searcher of all hearts, thou knowest me that I seek nothing but thy will. (Jer. 8, 17.)   Therefore, dear Lord, direct me to thy truth, and teach me; for thou art the God of my salvation; besides thee I acknowledge none other; thou art my hope, my comfort, shield, defence and fortress upon which I depend with confidence, and wait upon it in fear, misery, tribulation and need. (Isa. 43.)

Remember, O LORD, thy tender mercies, and thy loving kindness, for they have been ever of old.

O Lord of hosts, when I am buoyed up in the waters of thy grace, I find that I cannot fathom or measure them, for thy mercies are greater than all thy works.   Who is it, Lord, that ever came to thee with a pious heart that thou didst reject? Who ever sought thee and found thee not? Who did ever desire help of thee and did not obtain it? Who ever prayed for thy grace and did not receive it? And who ever called upon thee that thou didst not hear? Yea, dear Lord, how many didst thou accept in grace, who, according to thy strict justice, merited otherwise.   Adam departed from thee and believed the counsel of the serpent, (Tit. 3; Gen. 3,) he broke thy covenant and was found a child of death before thee, thy paternal kindness did not reject him, but thou didst seek him graciously, thou didst call and reprove him, and his nudity thou didst cover with coats of skin, and so graciously comforted him with the promised seed. Paul, thy chosen vessel, raved like a roaring lion and a devouring wolf in thy holy mountain, nevertheless, thy grace shone around him in his blindness and illuminated him, thou calledst him from heaven, and didst choose him as an holy apostle and as servant of thy house.   I also, dear Lord, the greatest of all sinners, and the least among all the saints, am called thy child or servant, for I have sinned against heaven and before thee, (Luke 15,) although I did resist thy precious word and thy holy will, with all my powers, before this with open eyes, and with full understanding I disputed, taught and lived after the ease of the flesh, and sought my own praise more than thy righteousness, honor, word and truth; nevertheless, thy paternal grace did not forsake me, a wretched sinner; but received me in love, converted me to another mind, led me with thy right hand and taught by thy Holy Ghost, till I voluntarily fought against the world, flesh and the devil, renounced all my pleasure, peace, glory, lust and the ease of the flesh, and willingly submitted to the pressing cross of our Lord Christ Jesus, that I may inherit the promised kingdom with all the valiant of God and the disciples of Christ. Again, I say: thy mercies are greater than all thy works; therefore, dear Lord assist me, stand by me, comfort me, a poor sinner, my soul is in great distress, and the dangers of hell surround me; help Lord, and preserve me, and be not angry; remember, O Lord, thy great mercies, of which all are made partakers who have graciously waited upon thy holy name, and remember, O LORD, thy tender mercies, and thy loving kindness, for they have been of old.

Remember not the sins of my youth, nor my transgressions; according to thy mercy remember thou me, for thy goodness' sake, O LORD.

O Lord, thou that bearest rule, I was shapen in iniquity and in sin did my mother conceive me, (Ps. 51,) I am of sinful flesh, through Adam's seed has been sown on my heart, where so much misery has grown up. I miserable sinner did not know my infirmities, so long as they were not manifested to me by the spirit. I thought I was a christian; but when I saw rightly, I found myself without thy word, altogether earthly, and sensual; my light was darkness; my truth was lies; my righteousness sin; my worship open idolatry; my life certain death. O dear LORD, I knew myself not till I viewed myself in thy word, (James 1,) then I learned to know with Paul, my blindness, nakedness, uncleanness, my depraved nature, (Rom. 7; Gal. 3,) that nothing good dwelt in my flesh, I was full of wounds, and bruises' and putrifying sores from the sole of the foot even to the head. (Isa. I.) Ah, alas, my gold was dross: my wheat chaff, all my services were deceit and lies, I followed before thee the things of the flesh, my thoughts were sensual, my words and works without the fear of God; my watching and sleeping were unclean; my prayer hypocrisy. In short, I did nothing without sin. O Lord, remember not the sins of my youth, those committed knowingly and unknowingly, which were so numerously committed, nor my daily transgressions, which I am guilty of in my great weakness, but remember me according to thy great goodness, I am blind, enlighten thou me; naked I am, clothe thou me; I am wounded, heal thou me; dead I am, raise me up. I know of no shelter, light, medicine, or life except thee, accept of me graciously, grant me thy mercy, favor and faith, fullness, and thy good will, O Lord. (Ecc. 7; Gen. 3; John 8, 11; Ezek. 16; Wis. 16; Matt. 9; John 11.)

Good and upright is the Lord; therefore, will he teach sinners in the way.

O Lord of hosts, although I walk so unrighteously before thee from my youth, that I am ashamed to lift my eyes to thee in heaven, nevertheless, I appear at thy throne of grace; for I know that thou art merciful and kind, and desirest not the death of the sinner, (Ezek. 18,) but that he repent and live.   Thou didst send forth thy faithful servant Moses, who gave Israel the law by the disposition of angels, (Exod. 19, 20; Acts 7,) also thy servants and prophets who preached the way of repentance, and broke the bread of life for the people, (Deut. 5; Gal. 3,) sin they reproved earnestly; proclaimed thy grace far abroad, and taught the truth, thy sharp piercing word was in their mouth, their light shone as the golden lights, they were as flowering olive trees, (Heb. 4; Exod. 25; Eccl. 50,) as a sweet smell of an apothecary, yea, as the fair mountain strewed with roses and lilies, (2 Esd. 1,) nevertheless, they did not desire them, but thrust them out furiously, derided, persecuted, and delivered them unto death, still the wells of thy mercy flowed, thou didst send thy beloved Son, the dear pledge of thy grace, who preached thy word, fulfilled thy righteousness, accomplished thy will, bore our sins, blotted them out by his word and brought about reconciliation, conquered the devil, hell, sin and death; and obtained grace, mercy, favor and peace for all, who truly believe on him, (John 3, 12; 1 John 4; 2 John 1; Rev. 1,) his command is eternal life, he sent out his messengers and ministers of peace, his apostles. who spread this grace abroad through the whole world, (Matt. 28; Mark 16,) who shone as bright burning torches before all, that they might lead me and all erring sinners into the true way.   O Lord, not unto me, but unto thee be praise and honor, (Ps. 115,) their words I love, their usages I observe, thy Son Christ Jesus whom they preached to me, I believe, I seek his will and way, thy abundant, great love I know, not through me, but through thee, for thou art good, and I am evil, thou art true, and I am deceitful; thou art righteous, and I am unrighteous; instruct me, dear Lord; teach me in the right way, foster me for I am of thy pasture, take me into thy tabernacle, under the shadow of thy wings, protect me; for I am greatly tormented, I am poor and wretched, and am grieved unto death.

The meek will he guide in judgment, and the meek he will teach his way.

O Lord, thou that bearest rule, thy divine grace has shone around me, thy word has taught me, thy Holy Spirit has influenced me till I forsook the course of the ungodly, the way of sinners, the seat of scorners, (Ps. 1,) I was ungodly, and carried the standard of unrighteousness for many years; I was a chief one in all manner of folly; idle words, vanity, gambling, drinking, eating to excess were my pastime; the fear of God was not before my eyes, besides, I was a lord and a prince in Babel, every one sought me, the world loved me and had my affections, I had the first place at feasts and in synagogues; I had the preference among all men, I was respected of the aged, every one revered me; when I spoke, they were silent; when I nodded, they came; when I bid them depart, they went; what I desired, they did; my words prevailed in all things; the desire of my heart was granted; but as soon as I, with Solomon, saw that all was vanity, and with Paul, esteemed all as nothing, (Phil. 3; Ezek. 1, 2, 10,) renounced the ungodliness of this world, sought thee and thy kingdom which will abide in eternity, I have found everywhere the counterpart and reverse; before I was honored, now I am dishonored; before all was love, now hatred; before I had friends, now they are my enemies; before I was considered wise, now a fool; before pious, now wicked; before a christian, now a heretic; yea, I have become an abomination and evil-doer to all. O Lord, comfort me, preserve thy troubled servant; for I am exceedingly poor and wretched, my sins rise up against me, the whole world hates and mocks me; lords and princes persecute me; the learned curse and slander me; my dearest friends forsake me, and those who were near me, stand aloof; who will have mercy on me and receive me? Miserable am I, dear Lord, have mercy on me and receive me with honor; for there is none that can preserve me, but thou; therefore, I entreat the Lord, vouchsafe thine ear to supplication, lead me by the right hand, lead me in the right way lest I stumble upon the dark mountains. (Jer. 13.) I see that the children of men do neither teach nor do right; deceit and hypocrisy are in all flesh, (Rom. 3;) the deceiving sects are great and many; every one avers his as if it were built upon a rock, yet they have not thy truth. Therefore, dear Lord, teach me thy truth and cast me not off from thy presence, for I am miserable, I am in the midst of lions and bears, which seek to destroy my soul, and thrust me from the way of truth. O Lord, strengthen me, keep me in thy way for I assuredly know that it is infallible truth and the sure way of peace.

ALL *the paths of the* LORD *are mercy and truth unto such as keep his covenant and his testimonies.*

O Lord of hosts, they all boast of thy grace and favor, although they, in all their works, prove themselves children of wrath; they lie and cheat, eat and drink, are guilty of adultery and fornication, they covet and hoard up, curse and swear without bounds, and all this they cloak with thy grace and the blood of Christ: every one sings lustily: The mercy of the Lord is great

—Christ died for our sins—our doings are unjust, sinful and fruitless. It is true, dear Lord, in the true sense of the word, that they have no lot in thee, and their hope is vain, their labor is without fruit, and their works useless; yea, their hope is like thistle-down before the winds, (Wis. 4, 5; 1 Cor. 6; Gal. 5; Eph. 5; Ps. 103,) they will have no part in thy kingdom; for they are still impenitent, and believe not thy truth. Alas! they know not that thy mercy is forever over those who fear thee and keep thy covenant. (Ps. 34.) Thy goodness, says David, is extended to the saints, thine eyes are upon the righteous, and thy ears are open to their cries, but thy face is against them that do evil, to cut off the remembrance of them from the earth. (1 Pet. 3.) I am thy friend if I do what thou didst command. (John 15.) It is true, dear Lord, that Christ was bestowed to us, and died for us, but not in such a way that we are to live according to our wicked lusts, and sinful will, but according to thy good will, word and command. Lord, I know that thou art no less righteous than good, thou hatest the evil, and lovest the good, (Prov. 18,) for to the good thou art kind, but to the wicked thou wilt in due time appear as a righteous Judge. What did the pure blood of the eternal covenant demand of Cain and Judah, because they despised thy grace and excluded themselves from the merits of thy Son? (1 Cor. 1.) What does it profit Pilate, Herod, Annas, and Caiaphas to have seen thy fountain of grace, Jesus Christ—nay, touched him, and yet condemned to the accursed death of the cross, the immaculate Lamb, the King of glory! But they, who, like Abel, Enoch, Noah, Abraham, Isaac and Jacob, did, keep thy covenant and preserve thy testimony, to them thy ways are peace and joy; yea, altogether mercy, kindness and truth. (Lev. 22; Gal. 3.)

For thy name's sake, O LORD, *pardon mine iniquity; for it is great.*

O Lord, Lord! I pray thee with holy David, (Ps. 3, 6,) rebuke me not in thine anger, neither chasten me in thy hot displeasure; for my loins are filled with a loathsome disease, and there is no soundness in my flesh; my sins have borne me down; there is no peace in my bones. From the bottom of my heart I humble myself with beloved Daniel. (Dan. 9.) O dear Lord! O thou great and terrible God! I have sinned, and done unjustly before thee I have been ungodly, I wandered from thee and walked not in thy commands and statutes, they preferred grace, I rejected; thy holy word I thrust from me; thy beloved Lord I crucified, I grieved thy Holy Spirit, I acted unjustly in all my doings. O Lord, the multitude of my sins frighten me, there is no evil but what I am guilty of. I was as envious as Cain ; proud and unchaste as Sodom ; unmerciful as Pharaoh ; refractory as Korah ; lascivious as Simri ; disobedient as Saul ; idolatrous as Jeroboam ; hypocritical as Joab ; haughty as Nebuchadnezzar ; covetous as Balaam ; drunken as Nabal ; insolent as Sanacherib ; blasphemous as Rabsaces ; bloodthirsty as Herod ; lying as Annanias. (Gen. 4, 18 ; Exod. 14 ; Num. 16, 34, 25 ; 1 Sam. 15 ; 1 King 13 ; Dan. 4 ; Isa. 36, 37 ; Acts 5, 11.) Yea, I say with king Manasseh : That my sins are more numerous than the sands of the sea shore and the stars in the heavens ; they trouble by day and by night ; nothing good dwells in my flesh. (Rom. 7.) All that I seek is unrighteousness and sin ; that which I would not that I seek and do ; I miserable man know not whither to go ; if I go into myself, I find great faults, impure desires, a vessel of sins ; if I go to my neighbor, he has nothing to give me, but here nothing else avails, but thy word only. (Wis. 16.) The wages of sin, says Paul, is death ; but thy grace is eternal life. This grace I seek and desire ; for this is the only ointment which can heal my soul. This is what the sinful woman availed herself of, (Luke 7,) as soon as she was sensible of her wants. This is what wounded David availed himself of when he disgraced Bathsheba the wife of Uriah, and slew him. (2 Sam. 12.) Great was his distress, he saw his wickedness and said : I have sinned against the Lord. He desired balm ; O God ! said he, according to the multitude of thy tender mercies blot out my transgressions, wash me thoroughly from mine iniquity, and cleanse me from my sin. (Ps. 51.) In the same hour he heard the gracious word of the prophet : Thy sins are forgiven thee. His troubled heart was quieted—he praised his name, proclaimed his mercy, and exalted his grace above all his works. O Lord ! O dear Lord ! I a grieved sinner, have the same disease, I desire the same balm, and I do desire help from them ; I seek only comfort with thee, O Lord, for thy holy name's sake. Help me, that I may eternally praise thee. Wash me from all my sins, and be merciful to me in all my transgressions, for they are great.

What man is he that feareth the LORD? *Him he shall teach in the way that he shall choose.*

O Lord, thou that bearest rule, thy path is the path of peace blessed is he that walketh therein ; for we find mercy, love, righteousness, humility, obedience and patience in her ways. She clothes the naked, feeds the hungry, she gives drink to the thirsty, entertains the needy, she reproves, threatens, comforts and admonishes ; she is temperate, honest and chaste, upright in all her ways ; none takes offence at her, her goings forth are to eternal life, but few there are that find her. I fear dear Lord, that there are scarce ten of a thousand that find her, scarce five who cherish her; it continues as it was from the beginning, when there were but four upon earth of whom the scriptures testify that two of them were disobedient, and a third one slew his brother. There were eight righteous when the world was drowned, one of them mocked his father. In Sodom and Gomorrah, with the adjacent country, there were four righteous persons, one looked back and was changed into a pillar of salt. (Gen. 3, 9.) More than six hundred thousand valiant men left Egypt, of whom but two entered the promised land, (Num. 22, 26, 14,) not, dear Lord, that all were damned who died on the way, but they did not on account of their unbelief inherit the promised Canaan. (Heb. 3, 4.) Thus also, dear Lord, is the eternal land promised us, if we otherwise walk the way which thou hast chosen for us. (Prov. 16.) But now they walk the crooked way of death, and even as those did not inherit the temporal, so will also these not inherit the eternal Canaan. O Lord, well may I sigh and say: Where is he who fears the Lord? Where is he, who has understanding? Where is he, who seeks after God? They are all gone out of the way, they are together become unprofitable : there is none that doeth good, no, not one! Their throats are as an open sepulchre, with their tongues they have used deceit : The poison of asps is under their lips, their feet are swift to shed blood. Destruction and misery are in their ways. The way of peace they have not known ; thy fear is not before their eyes; all that is among them is infidelity and lies, they despise thy righteousness yet they sing and speak much of thy truth, and glory in thy great name although there is not one ripe grape on their vine, nor any good fruit to be found with them. But those who fear thee, O Lord, depart from all iniquity; For thy fear (says Sirach, Chap. 2) dispels sin and is the beginning of wisdom. Thine eyes are upon those who fear thee, thy Holy Spirit leads them, thy gracious hand preserves them, they will fear not nor tremble ; for thou art their protector and shelter against intense heat, thou didst pardon their sins ; rescue them, thou dost enlighten them, makest glad their souls, givest them grace, blessing and peace. (Ecc. 34.) He that fears thee, walks upright in all his ways, for thou teachest him in the way that he shall choose.

His soul shall dwell at ease ; and his seed shall inherit the earth.

O Lord, thou Lord of hosts! those who know thee shall be blessed in the paradise of their God, upon Mount Zion, in the heavenly Jerusalem, in the church of the living God—in the assembly of the righteous whose names are written in heaven. They are released from hell, sin, the devil and death, and they serve before thee in peace and joy of heart through life. They repose without fear, for thou art their strength and shield. They rest under the shadow of thy wings, (Lev. 26,) for they are thine. They freeze-not, for thou warmest them with the beams of thy love—they hunger not, for thou feedest them with the bread of life ; (John 6;) they thirst not, for thou givest them to drink of the waters of the Holy Ghost ; they want not, for thou art their treasure and their wealth. They dwell in the house of thy peace, in the tabernacles of righteousness, and in sure peace. (Isa. 52 ; Ps. 1.) They have pleasure in thy law, and speak of thy word day and night, with all the people. They wash their souls in the clear waters of thy truth. (Wis. 7.) They view their consciences in the clear mirror of thy wisdom —their thoughts are upright, their words are words of grace, seasoned with salt. (James 1 ; Matt. 5.) Their words are faithful and true. The light of their piety shines around them, what they seek they find, what they desire they obtain, their souls dwell in the fulness of thy goodness ; the dew of thy grace has sprinkled them ; the soil of their consciences bear wine and oil without measure, and although they must endure in their flesh, for a time, much misery and suffering and trouble, yet they know well that the way of the cross is the way of life. They are not ashamed of the way of the cross and the weapons of the Lord. (Acts 14.) They patiently go with Christ to the conflict, and contend valiantly, till they have reached the boundary of life. and have received the crown. (Heb. 12 ; 2 Tim. 2 ; Phil. 3.) Nothing can hinder them, since they have become partakers of thy spirit, and have tasted of thy sweetness. They neither waver nor turn aside ; their house stands firmly upon a rock, (Matt. 7,) they are as the pillars of the holy temple, they have eaten of thy hidden manna. (Rev. 3, 5.) O Lord, to thee be praise ! Thy fear abides continually before their eyes. They walk in thy way, therefore, shall their souls be blessed, and their seed, if born of the Holy Spirit and word, will enjoy the land of everlasting life. (Ps. 142,) wherein thou, and thy chosen shall reign in endless glory.

The secret of the Lord is with them that fear him, and he will show them his covenant.

Oh Lord, Lord, the thoughts of my heart terrify me, and my heart trembles within me ; because, with Ezra, (1 Ezra 7,) I perceive so many born in vain. What shall I say, dear Lord ? Shall I say that thou hast ordained the wicked to wickedness, as some have said? Be that far from me; I know, O Lord, that thou art eternally good, and that nothing wicked can be found in thee. We are the works of thy hand, created in Christ Jesus to good works, that we should walk therein. (Eph. 5.) Water and fire. life and death, hast thou left to our choice. (Gal. 15.) Thou willest not the death of the sinner, but that he would repent and live. (Ezek. 18.) Thou art the eternal light, therefore hatest thou all darkness; (1 John 1,) thou desirest not that any should perish, but that all repent, come to the knowledge of thy truth, and be happy. (2 Pet. 3; 2 Tim. 2.) O dear Lord, how grievously have they blasphemed thine unspeakably great goodness, thy eternal mercy, and thy almighty Majesty, that they, O God, the Creator of all things, and God of all grace, have made thee to be as the devil, by saying that thou art the source of all evil, but thou art the Father of days and of lights. It is plain that evil cannot flow from good, nor light from darkness, nor life from death; yet must their stubborn hearts and fleshly minds be attributed to thy will, in order that they may continue upon the broad way, and have a cover for their sins. They neither know thy divine goodness, nor their own inbred wickedness. O Lord, thou hast loved us with an eternal love, thou hast chosen us before the foundation of the world, (Jer. 31,) that we should be unblamable, and holy before thee in love, not regarding what we find written by the faithful Paul concerning Esau, Pharaoh and Israel; (Eph. 1; Rom. 9,) he hath done all for us, for the best, in order that we should give the honor to thy name, and not to ourselves. What have we miserable sinners of which we may boast? (Ps. 114.) What have we that we have not received? All that we have is of thy fulness. (1 Cor. 4; John 1.) For this, all who know thy word thank thee. O dear Lord, the mystery of thy holy word is not revealed to the rich, the honorable, or the wise, but to the poor simple children. (1 Cor. 2.) Yea, Father, said Christ, such was thy good pleasure. (Matt. 11; Luke 11.) Isaiah says: (Chap. 66) Thou wilt look upon the miserable, and those who are of a broken spirit, and who fear thy word. Then, dear Lord, lead us in thy truth; teach us thy mysteries; enable us rightly to know the power of thy covenant, that thou art ours, and we are thine—that covenant which thou hast made with us in Christ, without any merit on our part. (Tit. 3.) For thy mystery will be found with those who fear thee and those to whom thou hast made known thy covenant.

Mine eyes are ever towards the Lord, for he shall pluck my feet out of the net.

O Lord! thou who bearest rule! If thou shouldst mark iniquity, who could stand? (Ps. 130.) I, a miserable, great sinner, have, with the full lust of my heart, turned to all folly, to gold and silver, to pride and haughtiness, to strange and forbidden flesh. I have turned mine eyes to open idolatry, to wood and stone, and have served them many years, upon high mountains and under green trees, as the prophet said: (Isa. 66.) My idolatry was according to the number of my days. I have bowed my knee before the graven and molten image, and said: Save me, for thou art my God. I sought sight from the blind, life from the dead, and help from those who could not preserve themselves from dust, corruption, thieves and worms. (Bar. 6.) Yes, I have said to a weak, perishable creature, that grew out of the earth, was broken in a mill, baked by the fire, chewed with my teeth, and consumed by my stomach—to a mouthful of bread: Thou hast released me; as Israel said to the golden calf: Rejoice, Israel! these be thy gods, which have led thee forth from Egypt. O God! thus have I, a miserable sinner, courted the whore of Babylon for many years, for I supposed that she was modest, honest and chaste—a queen of righteousness, who was glorious, holy and acceptable before thine eyes, for I saw her adorned with purple and scarlet, with gold and precious stones, and pearls, a golden cup in her hand, powerful over all kings upon earth. Therefore, I knew not that she was so very loathsome and polluted; that there was in such a splendid cup so much abomination, that she was such an unblushing, impudent whore and murderess; that deceived the world, persecuted the chosen, and drank the blood of the saints. But now I have seen her abominations, and I quake, because I left thee so long, the living well, and comforted myself with useless pools, that can give no water, (Jer. 2,) that I gave thy honor to images and other creatures, and worshipped the creature more than the Creator, who is blessed forever. (Rom. 1.) This happened, in part, through the deceitfulness of my eyes, because I was bewitched in my heart, by the goodly appearance of the woman. But now, dear Lord, my eyes are directed unto thee, till thou hearest me, they are directed to thy mercy seat, till I obtain grace and mercy from thee, (Heb. 1,) for thou alone art he, who can help me in the time of my temptation, and pluck my feet out of the net of sin.

Turn thee unto me, and have mercy upon me; for I am desolate and afflicted.

O Lord of hosts, my sins and transgressions I do not hide from thee, but unreservedly acknowledge that I spent my former days after the will of the heathens, and walked with them in all manner of ungodly lusts, pride, wantonness, in eating and drink-

ing, and in abominable, blind idolatry. (1 Pet. 4.)   I did all that
pleased my wicked flesh, I was a child of wrath, (Eph. 2,) even
as others ; thy holy name I held in derision ; thy word was as a
fable to me ; in reliance upon thy grace, I did all manner of
evil ; I was as a white-washed sepulchre, outwardly in behavior,
chaste and mild ; there was none that reproved my conduct, but
within I was full of dead men's bones, stench and worms, (Matt.
23 ;) my platter was clean on the outside, but within full of
rapine and lust.   What I did privately is a scandal to mention,
all my thoughts were unclean, vain, proud, ambitious and ungodly, (Eph. 5 ;) my heart was full of disaffection, hatred, envy,
vengeance and dislike ; my thoughts were bent upon all manner
of wickedness ; I sinned without bounds ; I neither feared God
nor the devil, neither law nor gospel, heaven nor hell ; there
was nothing that could deter me, I neither regarded thee nor
thy word, my course was onward to all wickedness, I sought
nothing but the friendship and love of this world,—I was guilty
of adultery and fornication, and the like, this I did secretly, not
on account of thy fear, but for fear of the world, lest I might
lose the favor of men and my good name, and besides all my
idle trifling, my drunkenness and merriness, my pride and im-
morality, and my idolatry were called the true worship ; yea,
all my transactions, private and public, were not concealed before thy eyes.   Thus did I, a grieved sinner, spend my days, and
did not, O God of grace, acknowledge thee as my God, Creator
and Redeemer, till thy Holy Ghost taught me, through thy word,
made known to me thy will, and gave me a partial knowledge
of thy mysteries ; now I know how dishonorably I walked before
thee, not otherwise than if I had spit in thy face, treated thee
with indignity and derided thee as foolish.   O Lord, have
mercy upon me ; for I am desolate and afflicted ; my sins are
great and many, my conscience troubles me, my thoughts cause
me to quake, my heart laments and sighs, because I sin so
heinously before thee, my sins have separated me from thee,
hid thy countenance from me, and excited thy wrath.   I have
become a prey and brand of the burning, (Isa. 59,) though the
longer, the more I was grieved, the more I was consoled by thy
word, for it teaches me corncerning thy mercy, grace and favor,
and the remission of my sins, through Christ, thy beloved Son,
our Lord, not regarding that, I neither knew nor feared thee.
This promise pacifies me ; this promise gladdens me, it leads
me with the sinful woman to thy blessed feet, (Luke 7, 10.) with
full confidence and clear conscience, well knowing that thou wilt
not cast off from thee thy returning son, although I spent thy
paternal inheritance and possessions dishonorably, with harlots
and rogues, in a strange country, devoured it in my unrighteous-

ness. My God, turn the pleasing countenance of thy peace unto me, I have sinned before heaven and in thy sight, (Luke 15,) lay thy hand of grace upon me, have mercy upon me ; for I am desolate and afflicted.

The troubles of my heart are enlarged ; O bring thou me out of my distress.

O Lord, Lord, my heart weeps and sighs, my conscience quakes and trembles, my soul is as a grieved mother deprived of her only child and cannot be comforted, since I, an ungodly sinner sought not thy divine love and paternal good for many years. I have lived more disgracefully than an irrational creature, which in eating, drinking and other things, goes not beyond nature, not transgressing the law which is prescribed to it. But I lived in all unrighteousness against the imbred law of nature according to the lusts of my flesh. I did in part know that the desires of my flesh worked death. (Rom. 8.) Thy spirit warned me often of all wickedness, nevertheless all was suppressed, through my flesh. I was in all things a servant of sin, and had sworn unto unrighteousness. I drank down sin as water ; my delight was in all manner of folly and vileness ; (John 8 ; Rom. 6 ; 2 Pet. 2 ; Prov. 1) the outstretched arm of thy grace, I saw not ; thy calling voice. I heard not ; thy inviting love I regarded not. In short, I hated thy knowledge, and thy fear I cast behind me ; and this is not all, dear Lord, that I acted so wickedly and lamentably in my ignorance, but I daily find, that my righteousness is as filthy rags ; (Isa. 64 ;) when I think that I am going, I feel that I stand, I am down, and that I am something, I am nothing. Therefore, O Lord, preserve me, for the fear of my heart is very great ; yea, greater than I can express it ; I often am as a woman in travail, my countenance is changed pale ; (Jer. 30 ;) my hands are upon my loins on account of the trouble of my heart ; the dangers of hell surround me, the fatness and marrow of my bones are dried up ; for here neither money nor possessions, neither flesh nor blood avail, but my soul is at stake, eternal life or eternal death is the issue ; I, therefore, pray : Forsake me not, dear Lord, but open the eyes of thy mercy and behold my great burden, stand by me and deliver me from all my distress.

Look upon mine affliction and my pain ; and forgive all my sins.

O Lord, thou that bearest rule, if the righteous call upon thee, thou receivest them ; (Ps. 34 ;) thou art nigh to those who are of a broken heart ; thou dost comfort those who are of a contrite spirit ; the offering acceptable to thee is a contrite spirit ; a broken heart thou dost not despise. (Ps. 51.) Thou didst send forth thy beloved Son, anointed with the Holy Ghost, to preach the gospel to the poor, to heal the broken hearted, to preach deliverance to the captives, and recovery of sight to the blind; to set at liberty them that are bruised, to proclaim the acceptable year of the Lord, (Luke 4,) to comfort all that mourn; to appoint unto them that mourn in Zion, to give unto them beauty for ashes; the oil of joy for mourning; the garment of praise for the spirit of heaviness. He preached ransom to all who are heavy laden, and with faithful hearts come to him; he invites all to the waters of life, (John 7; 2 Pet. 2,) he bore all our sins upon the cross, in his own body, and our debt he blotted out by his blood, even as Moses did afore through types and shadows. when he sprinkled unclean Israel with the blood of oxen and rams, and with the ashes of the heifer; under the law nearly all things were purified by the shedding of blood. (Exod. 14; Num. 19; Heb. 9.) Had the figurative blood such virtue, that it could purify the flesh to sanctification, how much more shall the blood of the beloved Son, who offered himself unspotted through the eternal spirit, purify our consciences from dead works, (Eph. 2.) O ever living God, through the merits of thy Son, and through the riches of thy grace, we receive the remission of our sins; yea, through his blood thou didst reconcile all upon earth and in heaven above. (Col. 2.) I, therefore, dear Lord, confess that I have or know of no remedy for my sins, neither works nor merits, neither baptism nor the Lord's supper, (although all sincere christians use both as signs of thy word, and hold them in respect;) but alone the precious blood of thy beloved Son, who is bestowed upon me, and who has redeemed me, a poor sinner, through mere grace and love, from my former walk; therefore, O God of truth, with whom there is no lie, remember the words of the prophet, which he spoke in thy name; namely: But if the wicked will turn from his sins, that he hath committed, and keepeth all my statutes, and do that which is lawful and right, he shall surely live, he shall not die; all his transgressions that he hath committed, they shall not be mentioned unto him. (Ezek. 18.) O my God, look not upon me, but upon the eternal Melchisideck, Christ Jesus, whom thou hast appointed high priest over thy house, upon the blessed king of thy righteousness, who has no beginning nor end of days, and is a high priest for ever, who did not honor himself, but is ordained of thee, as Aaron, who in the days of his flesh, offered up prayer and supplications, with strong crying and tears, unto him that was able to save him from death, and was heard in that he feared; for his sake hear me, for his sake accept me, for his sake be merciful to me, console thy afflicted servant. I have no comfort neither in heaven above nor upon earth, but in thee alone, have mercy upon me in my great distress; my unclean, sinful flesh afflicts me; my wicked nature wages war against me, and besides for thy word's sake, I have become an abomination, an outcast and a fable to all men. (1 Cor. 4.) All who hear of me shake their heads at me; without and within I have no peace. I say again, my sins combat me, my soul is in tribulation and pain; therefore, dear Lord, I pray thee not for gold and silver, for it can profit me nothing in the day of vengeance, (Ezek. 7,) neither for long life, for it is always perverse, but this I desire alone of thee, from my whole heart, that thou wouldst look upon me, a miserable sinner, with the eyes of thy mercy, in my affliction and pain, comfort me with thy holy spirit, and forgive all my sins.

Consider mine enemies, for they are many and they hate me WITH CRUEL *hatred.*

O Lord of hosts, when I was of the world, I spake and did as the world, and the world hated me not, but as soon as I had eaten the book that was shown me, although it was in my mouth sweet as honey, yet it made my belly bitter, for there were written therein lamentations, and mourning, and wo, (Ezek. 2; 2 Chap. 3; Rev. 10, 10.) While I served the world I received my reward; all men spake well of me, even as the fathers did to the false prophets. (Matt. 5; Luke 6.) But now, that I love the world with a godly love, have sought from my heart their welfare and happiness, rebuked, admonished, and instructed them with the word of God, pointing out to them Jesus Christ and him crucified, they have become unto me as a grievous cross, and as the gall of bitterness: so fiendlike is their hatred, that not only I myself, but all those who loved me, showing me favor and mercy, must, in some place or other look for imprisonment and death. O blessed Lord! I am more despicable in their eyes than a notorious thief and murder; I am like a lost sheep in the wilderness of the world, chased, tormented, and pursued unto death by ravenous wolves. Am I not like a person without hope, forsaken and comfortless like a ship in the depth of the ocean, destitute of mast, sail, and helm, tossed about by every wave and every tempest. My flesh had almost said, I am betrayed because I find the unrighteous, froward nation enjoying riches, honor and prosperity, and reposing in quietness and peace, (Ps. 73,) while the godly must endure so much hunger, thirst, affliction, and violence; their habitation is insecure, they must toil and labor for their bread; they are defamed, reviled, persecuted and hated of all men, as the filth of the world, and as an abomination. (1 Cor. 4.) O blessed Lord! mine enemies are many and great, their heart roars like the furious lion, their words are as deadly arrows, their tongues are always against me; at one time I am reviled by them as a false seducer, at another reproached as an accursed heretic, though by thy grace I possess nought but unyielding truth. (Gal. 4.) Thus am I their mortal enemy, because I instruct them in the way of righteousness. O Lord! I am not ashamed of my doctrine before thee and thy angels, much less before this rebellious world; for I know assuredly that I teach thy word; I have taught, throughout, a true repentance, a dying unto our sinful flesh, and the new life that cometh from God. I have taught a true sincere faith in thee and in thy beloved Son, that it might be made powerful through love. (1 Cor. 2.) I have taught Jesus Christ and him crucified, very God and very man, who, in an incomprehensible, inexpressible, and indescribable manner, was born of thee from all eternity, thy eternal Truth and Wisdom, the brightness of thy glory, and the express image of thy person, and that in fulness of time, through the power of thy Holy Sprit; he became in the womb of the virgin Mary, real flesh and blood, a visible, tangible, and mortal man, (John 1; Col. 2; Heb. 1; Matt. 1; Luke 1; John 1,) like unto Adam and his posterity in all things, sin excepted; born of the seed or lineage of Abraham and David, dead and buried, arose again, ascended into heaven, and thus became before thee our only, and eternal advocate, mediator, intercessor, and redeemer, (Rom. 1, 10; chap. 8; 1 Tim. 2; 1 John 2.) If all the prophets, apostles, and evangelists have not taught with the greatest clearness from the beginning, I will gladly bear my shame and reproof. I have taught no other baptism, no other supper, no other ordinance than that sanctioned by the unerring word of our Lord Jesus Christ, and the declared example and usages of his holy apostles, to say nothing of the superabundant evidence of the historians and learned of both the primitive and the present church. Since then, I substantiate my doctrine by the evidence of thy plain, ineffable word, and by the ordinance of thy Son, who can reprove me, and show with the argument of truth that I am an imposter? Does not the whole scripture teach, that Christ is the truth, and shall abide forever? (John 14.) Is not the apostolic church, the true church? We know that all human doctrines are chaff and froth, (Isa. 1; Jer. 23,) and that antichrist has spoiled and corrupted the doctrine of Christ; why then do they hate me because out of pure zeal I teach and propound the doctrine of Christ and his apostles unadulterated? No one however, hates the opposers of antichrist but such as are his members. Had I not the word of Christ, how cheerfully would I be taught it, for I seek it with fear and trembling; in this I can not be deceived. I have by grace, through the influence of thy Holy Spirit, believed and accepted thy holy truth as the sure word of thy pleasure ; it will, also, never deceive me. Let them write and vociferate, threaten, and dispute, boast, vapor and insult, extirpate, persecute and destroy, as they please, still thy word will triumph and the Lamb will gain the victory. (Rev. 17.) Yea, I rest assured, that with this my doctrine, I shall, at the coming of Christ, judge and condemn, not only men, but also angels. (2 Cor. 6.) And though I and my beloved brethren were totally extirpated, and taken from the earth, yet thy word would remain eternal truth. (Isa. 40 ; 2 Peter 1.) We are no better than our co-workers who preceded us. Yet the time will arrive when they shall exalt thy power, and look, perhaps too late, upon him whom they have pierced. (Rev. 20 ; Acts 20.) O Lord ! with what cruel hatred they hate me ! whom have I slandered in a single expression ? whose gold, silver, cattle, have I courted ? I have loved them with a pure love, even unto death ; thy word and will have I taught them, and with earnest diligence have I shown them, by thy grace, the way that leadeth to felicity, therefore my enemies are many, and hate me with cruel hatred.

O keep my soul, and deliver me ; let me not be ashamed, for I put my trust in thee.

O Lord. Lord ! the word of Paul fills me with terror, where he says : Let him that standeth take heed lest he fall ; for if a man thinks himself to be something when he is nothing, he deceiveth himself, (1 Cor. 10 ; Gal 6,) for the flesh, destitute of thy Spirit, is perfectly blind in divine things, ignorant, entirely false and unjust, nay, sin and death, as I have remarked publicly in speaking of David and Peter, for though David was a great prophet, a man after thy own heart, faithful in all thy ways, yet when thy Spirit departed from him, where were his chastity, love, humility, and the fear of his God ? did he not become an open adulterer, murderer, and boaster of his own glory ? (2 Sam. 11, 24,) until thy Spirit again enlightened him by the word of the prophet, and he acknowledged the deadly sin he had committed and how foolishly he had acted before thee, (2 Sam. 12,) in like manner as regards Peter. He acknowledged Christ thy beloved Son not by flesh and blood, but by the Spirit of thy grace, was called by Christ a stone and a rock, (Matt. 16,) was ready to go with Christ into into person and to death ; the trial came, thy Spirit forsook him for a season, he could not bear a trifling expression of a maid, he denied Christ, and swore that he knew him not, (Matt. 26 ; Luke 22,) but as soon as Christ looked upon him, and thy spirit returned, he acknowledged his fall, wept bitterly, and afterwards publicly preached the name of Christ among all nations, (Acts 2,) paying no regard to his having been strictly forbidden .to do so, by imprisonment, stripes and menacing words, he frankly answered : We ought to obey God rather than men. I beseech thee, therefore, blessed Lord, that thou wilt keep my soul, which is bought with so dear a price, lest I turn from thy truth ; for though I may now think with Peter, that I could give my life for thee, and with Paul, that neither tribulation, nor distress, nor persecution, nor famine, nor nakedness, nor peril, nor sword, nor life, nor death, nor any other creature, shall be able to separate me from thy love, yet I do not sufficiently know myself. (Rom. 8.) All my trust is in thee ; I have not yet resisted unto blood, (Heb. 12,) though I have drank a little of the cup of thy affliction, yet I have not tasted the dregs ; for when prisons and bonds are suffered, when life and death, fire and sword are threatened, then will the gold be separated from the wood, silver from the straw, and pearls from the stubble. Forsake me not, therefore, gracious Lord, for trees of deepest root are torn up from the earth by the violence of the storm, and the lofty immoveable mountains are rent asunder by the force of the earthquake. Had not Job and Jeremiah, men of thy love, well nigh lost all patience in temptation, and murmured against thy will ? Suffer me not, therefore, gracious Lord, to be tempted above what I am able to bear, for thou art true and faithful, lest my soul be ashamed. (Job. 1 ; Jer. 20 ; 1 Cor. 10.) I pray not for my flesh, (Gen. 3 ; Heb. 9,) being well aware that I must once suffer and die ; but this alone I desire, that thou strengthen me in my warfare, assist and preserve me, make me a way to escape in temptation, deliver me, and let me not be ashamed ; for I put my trust in thee.

Let integrity and uprightness preserve me ; for I wait on thee.

O LORD of hosts ! O God, when the householder had sown good seed in his field, his enemy came while he slept and sowed tares among the wheat, (Matt. 13) for when the sons of God presented themselves before the Lord, satan came also among them ; (Job 1 ;) wherever Christ is, there will the devil be found near at hand, as alas, I have fully observed in a few short years; thy saving word, thy gracious gospel, which is the proper food of my soul, imparting to it the power of eternal life, which has been trampled upon for so many years by antichrist as an idle tale, and a useless fabrication, is again received, believed, and acknowledged, in power, by some through the influence of thy compassionate favor, the hellish lion or behemoth roars now in excessive rage, walks about seeking to devour them, has no rest, nor repose, knowing well that his kingdom and dominion must decline and be destroyed thereby, makes use of all his cunning and subtlety, transforms himself into an angel of light, (1 Pet. 5 ; 2 Cor. 11) those he lost through thy word he has allured again by false doctrine into his snare and net, and has changed the pure, salutary sense of the scriptures, by means of false prophets and unskilful teachers, into a meaning entirely sensual, and completely calculated to mislead, has authorized the sword and destructive weapons, and excited a vindictive spirit against the whole world, moreover he has instituted open adultery with the custom of the Jewish fathers, also established a literal king and kingdom, together with many other abuses, at which a sincere christian is astonished and confounded. But all which thou hast not planted shall come to nought. (Matt. 15.) O Lord I preserve me pure and upright in thy truth, that I may neither believe, nor teach anything that is not in conformity with thy holy will and word, with true faith, sincere love, real baptism and supper, a blameless life, a scriptural separation from such as cause offence in doctrine and in life. Preserve me, gracious Lord, from all error and heresy, preserve me as thou hast done heretofore in thy mercy ; grant that I and my beloved brethren may seek, love, and fear thee with all our hearts, render obedience to the magistrate in all things not contrary to the word of God ; for this, says Paul, is good, and acceptable in thy sight ; preserve us from the wiles of the devil who would fain teach us another king, after the spirit, beside the true king of Zion, Jesus Christ, who rules over thy holy mountain with the iron sceptre of thy word, is King of kings and Lord of lords, is set at thy own right hand in the heavenly places, far above all principality and power, and might, and dominion, and every name that is named, not only in this world, but also in that which is to come ; under whose feet all things are put, who hath all power in heaven and on earth, before whom every knee must bow, and every tongue confess, that he is Lord, to the glory of thy great name. (Eph. 1 ; Matt. 28 ; Phil. 2.) O gracious Lord, let integrity and uprightness preserve me under thy cross, that I may not deny thee, and thy holy word, in the time of temptation, nor conceal thy divine truth and will under the mask of hypocrisy, lies, and obscure equivocal expressions, so that at the appearance of thy dear Son, my Lord Jesus Christ, I may receive with all saints, the promised kingdom, inheritance, and reward which, with firm assurance and perfect confidence, we daily hope, and expect, as the consequence of thy gracious promise.

Redeem Israel, O God, out of all his troubles.

O LORD of hosts, now, that I have confessed my sins before thee, prayed for my transgressions, praised thy mercy, and desired thy grace. (Matt. 10; Mark 6.) I must, with David, beseech thee, in behalf of my brethren; for I observe Israel scattered abroad and going astray, like sheep without a shepherd, and the pleasant vineyard of the Lord is laid waste, and trodden down of all men, (Isa. 5; Jer. 12;) the chosen seed of Abraham, the house of Jacob, has again become a proper slave or bond servant in the grievous service of Pharaoh in Egypt, the royal line of Judah is carried away into Babylon, together with the holy vessels, which are so lamentably abused by Belshazzar, his lords and concubines: Jerusalem, the personification of peace, which was likened to a dove, is changed into a barbarous gormandizer of innocent blood, and a rapacious lioness; she that was princess among the nations, the city of the great king is become destitute of kings, citizens and walls, waste and solitary; the temple of the Lord, the house of prayer, in which the true worship ought to be performed, has become a notorious nest of robbers, a den of lions, bears, wolves, basilisks dragons and serpents, a house of all idolators; nay, the unchaste bed of the adulteress Jezebel. The bride of Christ, the glorious, who was clothed in variegated raiment, and decked *with* divine ornaments, in honor of the king, is changed completely into a disgraceful harlot. (Mic. 2; Isa. 56; Jer. 7; Matt. 9; Rev. 6; Ps. 45; Ezek. 16.) The ark of the Lord, the glory of Israel, is seized by the Philistines, and taken into the temple of Dagon, (1 Kings 5;) Why make a long lamentation? Judea is changed to Babylon, Canaan to Egypt, and Palestine to Sodom, and the king of glory, Christ Jesus, blessed forever, is daily esteemed as a simpleton, and despised as a fool; his holy apostles, the beloved witnesses of thy truth, must as liars give way with their doctrine unto all men, his knit or wrought garment, which the scriptures were unwilling should be rent or divided, is torn into four or five pieces; antichrist exercises authority and dominion in all countries by the preaching of lies; and with violence, is thy word proscribed and rejected; if I travel east, west, north or south, I find in all places, nothing but vain obstinacy, perversion, blindness, avarice, pride, wantonness, rioting, drunkenness, pomp and splendor, strife, envying and ungodliness. I find, (I repeat,) violence, false doctrine and an impure, deceptive employment of thy sacraments, throughout the world I find tyrants triumphing in might, power, influence and wantonness, in the courts of all princes, I find that the learned speak like the beast, covetous of honor, desirous of wealth, gluttonous, earthly and carnally minded, and teach according to the lusts and desires of men; there is scarcely any that inquires for the truth, or if there is any one who asks for, or finds it, he must bear thy cross; therefore are my cheeks wet with tears day and night, my soul findeth no comfort, neither bread nor drink is sweet to my taste. Like the prophet Micah, I may well go stripped and naked, make a wailing like the dragons, and a mourning as the owls; for the wound of Israel is incurable. In sorrow, I may well lament with Esdras, and say: Our sanctuary is laid waste, our altar broken down, our temple destroyed; our psaltery is laid on the ground, our song is put to silence, our rejoicing is at an end, the light of our candlestick is put out, the ark of the covenant is spoiled, our holy things are defiled, and the name that is called upon us is almost profaned: our children are put to shame, our priests are burnt, our people are gone into captivity, our virgins are defiled, and our wives ravished; our righteous men carried away, our little ones destroyed, our young men are brought in bondage. and our strong men are become weak; and which is the greatest of all, the seat of Sion hath now lost her honor; for she is delivered into the hands of them that hate us. (2 Esd. 10.) Redeem Israel, O God, out of his troubles! look with the eye of thy mercy, upon our great misery and distress, release us from the iron furnance of Egypt, bring us out of the land of the Chaldees, let the holy city be builded again upon her own heap, (Jer. 30,) having walls and gates, repair and rebuild thy fallen temple, the stones of which are trampled upon in every street. (Sam. 4.) Gather together thy wandering sheep, receive thy returning bride. who has behaved so perversely with strange lovers. O God of Israel, effect in us a pure heart, that longeth for thy blessed word and will. Send forth faithful laborers into thy harvest, (Ps. 3; John 4,) who cut and gather the grain in due season, perfect the builders who lay for us a good foundation, that in the last days thy house may be established, and appear above all the hills, that many people may go thither and say: Come ye, and let us go up to the mountain of the Lord, to the house of the God of Jacob; and he will teach us of his ways, and we will walk in his paths, (Isa. 2; Mic. 4;) that we may walk before thee, in peace and liberty of conscience, all the days of our life, under a good government and blameless teachers, with a christian baptism, true supper, godly life, and a just separation, that thou mayest in power be eternally honored and praised in us, as in thy beloved children, through thy dear Son, Jesus Christ, our Lord, to whom with thee, O Father, and thy Holy Spirit, be praise and everlasting dominion. Amen! Amen! Amen! Even so, come quickly, Lord Jesus.

30

A PLAIN INSTRUCTION

FROM THE WORD OF GOD, CONCERNING THE SPIRITUAL RESURRECTION, AND NEW OR HEAVENLY BIRTH.

Blessed and holy is he that hath part in the first resurrection: on such the second death has no power. Rev. 20.

For other foundation can no man lay than that which is laid, which is Christ Jesus. 1 Cor. 3.

AWAKE thou that sleepest and arise from the dead, and Christ shall give thee light. (Eph. 5, 14.)

The scriptures point out to us two resurrections: namely, a bodily resurrection from the dead at the last day, and a spiritual resurrection from sin and death, to a new life and a change of heart.

That a man should die spiritually unto sin, be spiritually buried and rise again to a life of righteousness in God, is plainly taught in various parts of the scriptures.

Paul also exhorted to the same effect: (Eph. 4, 22 : Rom. 6 ;) Put off, concerning the former conversation, the old man, which is corrupt according to the deceitful lusts ; and be renewed in the spirit of your mind, and that ye put on the new man, which, after God, is created in righteousness and true holiness. (Col. 3, 9.) Put off the old man with his deeds, and put on the new man which is renewed in knowledge, after the image of him that created him. (Col. 32.) Mortify your earthly, &c., &c. Before a resurrection from the dead can take place, the death of the body is necessary, and before death, sickness, pain and tribulation must precede, which have a tendency to make death still more bitter to the flesh : Likewise in a spiritual sense, there can be no resurrection from sin and death, unless this body of sin be first destroyed and buried, and has sensibly endured pain and the burden of sin.—That is sorrowfulness of heart, remorse and a sincere repentance on account of sin, as is evidently shown in the scriptures. David says, (Ps. 38 : O Lord, rebuke me not in thy wrath ; neither chasten me in thy hot displeasure. For thine arrows stick fast in me, and thy hand presseth me sore. There is no soundness in my flesh, because of thine anger : neither is there any rest in my bones, because of my sin. For mine iniquities are gone over my head ; as an heavy burden they are too heavy for me. My wounds stink and are corrupt, because of my foolishness. I am troubled, I am bowed down greatly : I go mourning all the day long. For my

loins are filled with a loathsome disease, and there is no soundness in my flesh. I am feeble and sore broken ; I have roared
by reason of the disquietness of my heart. O Lord, all my desire is before thee ; and my groaning is not hid from thee. My
heart panteth ; my strength faileth me ; as for the light of mine
eyes it has departed.

Endure sorrow and distress : according to James 4, 9. Be
afflicted and mourn and weep : Let your laughter be turned to
mourning, and your joy to heaviness. Paul says, (2 Cor. 7, 9 :)
Ye were made sorry after a godly manner to repentance : For
godly sorrow worketh repentance to salvation, not to be repented of ; but the sorrow of the world worketh death : seeing
that ye sorrowed after a godly sort, what carefulness it wrought
in you, what clearing of yourselves, yea what indignation, what
fear, vehement desire, revenge, &c.

Behold, thus we have to die with Christ unto sin, if we would
be made alive with him ; (1 Tim. 2,) for none can rejoice with
Christ, unless he first suffer with him ; for this is a sure word,
says Paul : If we died with him, we shall also live with him, if
we suffer with him, we shall also reign with him.

This resurrection includes the new creature, the spiritual
birth, sanctification, without which none shall see the Lord,
(Heb. 12,) this Paul testifies in a few words, saying : In Christ
Jesus neither circumcision nor uncircumcision availeth, but a
new creature. Again : If any one is in Christ Jesus he is a new
creature—old things have passed away, all things have become
new, &c. (Gal. 6 ; 2 Cor. 5,) and this is the first resurrection ;
for if we have been planted together in the likeness of his death,
(Rom. 6,) that is through mortifying the sinful nature of earthly
Adam, (Col. 3,) with all his members or wicked lusts, we then
shall also be made partakers of his resurrection, (Rom. 6,) and
know that our old man is crucified with him, that the sinful
body is destroyed, (Col. 2,) and keep the true sabbath in Christ,
by putting off the sinful body in the flesh, circumcised with the
circumcision of Christ, which is done without hands, (Gal. 5,)
buried through baptism, in which we have also risen with him
through faith, which is the operation of God, (Col. 2,) we cease
from all works of the flesh, (Rom. 6 ; 1 Pet. 4,) are led by the
spirit, bring forth the fruits of the spirit, henceforth, not serve
sin ; let it suffice that we spent our former days after the manner of the heathens, when we walked in vanity, wantonness,
drunkenness, eating and drinking, and in abominable idolatry,
and that we spend the remainder of our days not after the lusts
of men, but live according to the will of God, that we may say
with Paul : I am crucified with Christ ; nevertheless, I live !
yet not I, but Christ liveth in me ; and the life which I now

live in the flesh, I live by the faith of the son of God, who loved me and gave himself for me, (Gal. 2,) therefore, died he for all, so that those who live, should not live unto themselves, but unto him who died for them, and rose again. (2 Cor. 5.)

To have a more correct knowledge of this resurrection and regeneration, we must bear in mind that all creatures, (1 Gen. 1,) bring forth *after their kind*, and every creature partakes of the properties, propensities and dispositions of that which *brought it forth*, as Christ says: That which is born of flesh, is flesh, and cannot see eternal life; and that which is born of spirit, is spirit, life and peace, which is eternal life, (John 3; Rom. 8,) that which is born of flesh, out of the earth through corruptible seed, is carnally-minded, that is, earthly, and speaks of earthly things, is desirous after costly and perishable things; all the thoughts, the whole seeking, all the desires are directed towards earthly temporal, or visible things, such things as those of which it is born, or from which it proceeds. That which is born of flesh and blood, is flesh and blood, and is carnally-minded; but the carnal mind is enmity against God, for it is not subject to the law of God, neither indeed can be. (Rom. 8.) Therefore, those who are carnal cannot please God; for such are altogether deaf, blind and ignorant in divine things. For a carnal man cannot apprehend or comprehend divine things, for by nature he has not that discernment; but on the contrary his mind is depraved—God is not in his mind. A carnal man cannot understand spiritual things, for he is by nature a child of the devil, and is not spiritually-minded, (Rom. 8; 1 Cor. 2,) hence, he comprehends nothing spiritual; for by nature he is a stranger to God; has nothing of a divine nature dwelling in him, nor has communion with God, but is much rather at enmity with God; he is unmerciful, unjust, unclean, not peaceable, impatient, without understanding and unhappy, &c. So are all men by nature according to their birth and origin after the flesh. This is the first or old Adam, and is called in the scriptures ungodly, that is, without God, a stranger and destitute of the divine nature. (Rom. 5; Eph. 2; Col. 1.)

This is the nature and property of the earthly and devilish seed; for as the seed is, so is the fruit; for what a man sows, he shall also reap. For he that sows to the flesh, shall of the flesh reap corruption, (Gal. 6, and bring forth fruit unto death: he sins like his father, of whom and through whose seed he is born, for he is the father of lies and sinned from the beginning, and did not abide in the truth, (Rom. 8; Wis. 2; John 8; Gen. 8,) he, therefore, that sins is of the devil, for sin is not of God, but of the devil, and he that sins has not seen God, nor knew him; and we know that the son of God was made manifest to take away sins and destroy the works of the devil, (1 John 3,) and through his death deprive Him of power who had the power of death, that is the devil, (Heb. 2,) and deliver them, who through fear of death were all their life-time subject to bondage, (Rom. 5; John 8,) for by the sin of one man all were made sinners. He that sins is the servant of sin; and does the will and works of him whose servant he is, and whose spirit leads him; for every one is a servant to him whom he serves, whether of sin unto death, or of obedience unto righteousness; (Rom. 6,) for he that does unjustly shall receive according to his works. To them Paul speaks, that they should awaken from the sleep of sin and death, so that the second death shall have no power over them; saying: *Awake thou that sleepest, and arise from the dead, and Christ shall give thee light.* (Eph. 5, 14.)

On the other hand, all those who are born from above out of God, through the living word, (John 1; James 1; Pet. 1,) and are renewed, they are also minded, and have a disposition and propensity for good, as he has who has begotten them and of whom they are born. And what the nature and disposition of God and Christ are, we may readily perceive through the instruction of the sacred scriptures; for Christ has expressly set forth *himself* in his word: namely, after his human nature, that we are to know, apprehend, and follow him, and shall be like him: not according to his divine nature; for he is the true image of the invisible God, the brightness of his glory, and the express image of his person, who dwells in ineffable light whom none can approach or see, (Col. 1; Heb. 1; 1 Tim. 3; Exod. 33; John 1,) but after his walk and life here upon earth, as he testified and showed among men in words, deed and example, for us to follow and conform thereto, in order that we may become partakers of his nature in the spirit. (Matt. 11; Ps. 54, 85.) Christ is every where in the scriptures represented to us as being humble, meek, merciful, just, holy, wise, spiritual, long suffering, patient, peaceable, salvation, love, obedience and good, as the perfection of all things; for in him there is sincerity. (Acts 3; Heb. 7; 1 Pet. 1; 1 Cor. 1; John 4; Matt. 5; Col. 3; 2 Cor. 4.) Behold, this is the image of God, or Christ in the spirit, whose example we shall follow till we become like it in nature, and evidence it by our lives, all the regenerated children of God are thus minded, for they take after him of whom they are begotten; and those are like the others, comprised in one word, namely, godly, or godly persons, as those who have communion with him are one mind and disposition, and who have the image of God in them, as the scriptures, both of the Old and New Testament, abundantly show, especially in the epistle to the Collossians, in the 3d *Chap.* where he says : *Put off the old man with his deeds, and put on the new man which is renewed in knowledge after the image of him who created him ; Put on, therefore, as the elect of God, holy and beloved, bowels of mercies, kindness, humbleness of mind, meekness, long suffering, forbearing one another, and forgiving one another, if any man have a quarrel against any, even as Christ forgave you, so also do ye ; and above all things put on charity, which is the bond of perfectness ; and let the peace of God rule in your hearts to the which ye are called in one body : and be ye thankful, &c.* (Gal. 4 ; Phil. 2.) *My little children, of whom I travail in birth again until Christ be formed in you. Let this mind be in you which was also in Christ Jesus, for Christ is the image of God to whom we must conform.* (Heb. 1.) *For whom he did foreknow, he did also predestinate to be conformed to the image of his Son.* (Rom. 8.) Those, therefore, who have conformed to the image of Christ Jesus, they are the truly regenerated children of God, and have put off the old man, and put on the new which is created after God, in true righteousness and holiness.

These, when they have conformed to the image of God, and and have been born of God, and afterwards continue in God, will not commit sin, for the seed of God remains in them; and they have overcome the world, (Gal. 6 ; 1 John 3,) they are crucified to the world, and the world unto them ; (Rom. 6,) have mortified their flesh, and buried their sinful body with Christ in baptism, with all their lusts and desires, and no longer serve sin unto unrighteousness, but much more righteousness unto salvation ; for they have put on Christ, and are purified through the Holy Ghost, in their consciences, from dead works to serve the living God ; bringing forth through the spirit the fruits of the spirit, whose end is eternal life. (Gal. 5 ; Heb. 9.) When these (as above said) have renounced the devil, flesh, and world and the service of sin, no more to serve sin, they have voluntarily obligated themselves with David, as faithful servants of God, and henceforth live according to his blessed will all their days. (Ps. 118.) And on the other hand the devil with his adherents, is mightily enraged, is waging war against them ; because they are deadly enemies ; (Rev. 12 ;) and they are enemies to sin and the devil, and have enlisted under the banner of the red cross of their prince, and have taken the field against all their enemies —they are armed with the armor of God, and surrounded with angels of the Lord, (Acts 3 ; Heb. 12 ; Ps. 33,) always watching with great solicitude, lest they be overcome by their enemies, who do not slumber, but are always going about like roaring lions seeking whom they may devour, and although they receive occasionally a wound, and are overtaken by their enemies, still their souls remain uninjured, and this wound is not unto death; for they have the unction of God, (1 John 5,) the true Samaritan and the true physician with them, who binds up and heals their wounds; for he has compassion over our weakness and sickness. Through his stripes and wounds we are made whole. (Luke 10; Isa. 16, 53; Rom. 6.) Nor are they so overcome that they will cast from them their weapons, and thus surrender, again to become servants of sin. (Eph. 6; Phil. 4,) which should again acquire the ascendency over them and rule them; but they are encouraged anew of the Lord, and in the strength of his power, they persevere valiantly in battle, till they, through him, by whom they can do all things, have conquered their enemy, and gloriously say to their enemy: O death, where is thy sting? O grave, where is thy victory? (1 Cor. 15,) thanking God with Paul: But thanks be to God. who giveth us the victory, through our Lord Jesus Christ. The Lord, says Jeremiah, (Jer. 20,) is with me as a mighty, terrible one, therefore shall my persecutors stumble, and they shall not prevail, &c., and say with David: Blessed be the LORD, my strength, who teaches my hands to war and my fingers to fight; (Ps. 144,) and they are not moved till they have broken their enemies to pieces: Blessed be the Lord that he has not given us as a prey in their teeth; our souls have escaped, like a bird from the fowler's snare; the cord is rent, and we are ransomed from our enemies, and out of the hand of those who hate us, &c. (Luke 1.) The Lord is a rewarder of them that diligently seek, love and serve him; (Heb. 11,) as it written: Behold the Lord cometh, and his reward is with him; (Rev. 22,) yea, his reward and the gift of God are eternal life through Jesus Christ our Lord. For, if you serve the Lord Jesus Christ, you will receive the reward of your inheritance, the crown of life, which God has promised those who love him. (Rom. 6; Col. 3; James 1; 2 Tim. 4.)

As stated above, that every creature has the nature and disposition of him of whom it is born, therefore, we will speak a few words concerning the nature, properties and effects of the seed of the divine word, whereby we are begotten in the image of God; for where this seed is sown upon good ground, into the heart of man, there it grows and produces its like in nature and property, it changes and renews the whole man, from the carnal into the spiritual, the earthly into the heavenly, it transforms from death unto life, from unbelief to belief, and makes man happy, (John 3; Rom. 8; John 1; Gal. 3,) for through this seed all nations upon earth are blessed. (Gen. 22.) Therefore, says James: Wherefore lay apart all filthiness and superfluity of naughtiness, and receive with meekness the engrafted word which is able to save your souls. (1 Cor. 3.) It is also the pure, unadulterable milk, whereby the young and new born children of God are nurtured, till they attain to a perfect man, unto the measure of the stature of the fullness of Christ, (Eph. 4,) it is also strong food for the perfect and aged in Christ Jesus. (Heb. 5.) In short, this seed of the divine word is spiritual food whereby the whole inner man is ascertained, (1 Pet. 1,) so that he perish and faint not in this wilderness and desolate world, as all have to starve and faint who do not daily gather the bread of the divine word to satisfy their starving souls, (Deut. 8 ; Matt. 4,) for man lives not by bread alone, but by every word which proceeds from the mouth of God. Therefore, is he blessed who hungers after this heavenly bread, and receives the ingrafted word ; for it will bring forth after its nature, in due time, one hundred fold. (Matt. 13.) For, says the Lord, as the rain cometh down, and the snow from heaven, and returneth not thither, but watereth the earth, and maketh it bring forth and bud, that it may give seed to the sower and bread to the eater, so shall my word be that goeth forth out of my mouth ; it shall not return unto me void, but it shall accomplish that which I please. (Isa. 55.)

Behold, this is the nature, property and effects of the seed of the word of God, by which men are renewed, regenerated, sanctified and saved through this incorruptible seed, (namely, the living word of God which abides to eternity,) (1 Pet. 1.) and are clothed with the same power from above, are filled with the Holy Ghost, (Luke 24.) and are thus united to God, that they become partakers of the divine nature, and be made conformable to the image of his Son, who is the first of the regenerated, (2 Pet. 1 ; Rom. 8 ; 2 Cor. 3 ; Col. 1,) and those who rose with him from the sleep and death of sin, henceforth serve him not in the oldness of the letter, but in the newness of the spirit. (Rev. 1 ; Rom. 7.)

He that is truly sincere, and has this principle and disposition in his heart, has put on Christ Jesus, is become like unto Christ, and has the image of God in his heart, and is spiritually minded, is led by the Spirit in his spirit, from whose spiritual body, spiritual fruits are brought forth, as a well springing up unto eternal life. (John 4, 7.) For they are regenerated through the word which was sown in their hearts, begotten of God, and born anew to bring forth fruit of eternal life ; they, therefore, as children born of God, are the same as the father, of one mind and disposition, have the divine nature of their Father, who has begotten them ; whose thoughts are heavenly, whose words are truth, well seasoned, whose good works are holy, acceptable to God and man ; for they are holy vessels of honor, useful and ready to every good work. (Col. 3, 4 ; 2 Tim. 2.)

Even as Paul (Rom. 6) exhorts those who are born of the corruptible seed of flesh and blood, who are earthly, sensual, without understanding and blind in divine things; yea, children of wrath, that they should die unto sin, mortify and bury the lusts and desires of the flesh, and then rise by virtue of the heavenly seed from the sleep and death of sin and be regenerated, and walk in newness of life, which is the first resurrection, saying: *Awake thou that sleepest, and arise from the dead, and Christ shall give thee light.* (Eph. 5.) So does he also admonish all regenerated children of God, who have been changed in mind and disposition through the eternal saving seed of God, who have been regenerated and are risen, that they should be godly, spiritually and heavenly minded, and strive for and desire heavenly, incorruptible things; and that their heart (1 Pet. 1) should be where their treasure is, (Luke 12 ; Eph. 1, 2,) and their conversation in heaven, as fellow saints of the house of God, telling them: *If then ye be risen with Christ, seek those things which are above, where Christ sitteth on the right hand of God ; set your affections on things above, not on things on the earth ; for ye are dead, and your life is hid with Christ in God, when Christ, who is our life, shall appear, then shall ye also appear with him in glory.* (Col. 3.) Here we have an account how the regenerated children of God have risen with Christ from the dead, and now live with him, converse upon heavenly things. and appear to the world as not living, for their life is hid in God, as St. John says : Now we are the sons of God, and it doth not yet appear what we shall be ; but we know that, when he shall appear, we shall be like him ; for we shall see him as he is. (1 John 3.)

With these and the like words the scriptures admonish the truly regenerated and those who have arisen, that they should take heed to their calling, and continue perfect in a new, godly walk, (Heb. 3,) for if they have been made partakers of Christ, they should persevere to the end, lest they again depart from the living God through the deceitfulness of sin and an evil heart of unbelief; and they should remain steadfast and perfect, as the children of God, and inherit the kingdom of their Father, and reign in eternity and rule over sin, death, devil and hell, and all the enemies of the kingdom, whom they overcome with Christ as valiant men ; therefore, will they also sit with Christ at the table of the Lord, (Luke 13,) eat the bread and drink the wine of the kingdom of heaven ; even as Christ overcame, and sitteth with his Father in his kingdom which is prepared for them ; as a fortified city ; (Rev. 3 ; 2 Esq. 7, 8;) free from all care of their enemies; in full rest, full of life and joy ; for they eat of the tree of life which is in the midst of Paradise ; which pleasure garden is ever close to the unregenerated, who are still earthly and sensually minded, who still have by nature the vail and partition wall of sin before their hearts.

These are they, who died with Christ unto sin, and have truly risen, (Rom. 6 ; John I,) these are the new born, to whom the power is given to become the sons of God, these were redeemed out of all nations, (Rev. 5, 7, 19,) these have on the wedding garments against the marriage of the Lamb, these have received the sign TAU in their foreheads by which the servants of God are designated, (Ez. 9 ; Rev. 7,) these are the spiritual bride of Christ, his holy community, his spiritual body, flesh of his flesh, and bone of his bone, (Eph. 5,) these have come to the heavenly Jerusalem, the city of the living God, which came down from heaven, (Rev. 21,) these have come to an innumerable company of angels, to the general assembly of the church of the first born which are written in heaven, (Heb. 12,) and to Jesus, the mediator of the new covenant ; they are fellow citizens in the household of God who have put off the corruptible garment, (Eph. 2, 4 ; Esd. 3,) and put on the incorruptible, have acknowledged the name of God, and kept his commandments, (Rev. 14,) and the faith of Jesus ; the true sheep of Christ, who hear his voice, and follow no other ; (John 10 ;) the first fruits of his creatures, have the spirit and mind of Christ, therefore, knowing what the will of the Lord is ; (James 1 ; Rom. 8 ;) yea, the chosen generation, the spiritual and royal priesthood, a holy nation, a peculiar people ; (Eph. 5 ; 1 Pet. 2 ;) who in times past were not a people, but now the people of God, for God had compassion on them ; these are the souls who were slain, under the altar, for the word of God. (Rev. 6.)

In short, with them old things have passed away ; *behold all things have become new ; but this is all of God, who has reconciled us unto himself through Jesus Christ ;* these are they who stand before the throne of God, with palms in their hands, and clothed in white, saying : Blessing, and glory, wisdom, thanksgiving, honor, power and might be unto our God forever and ever, Amen. (2 Esd. 2 ; Rev. 7.)

This is a short instruction concerning the spiritual resurrection and the new birth, and the difference between the natural and spiritual ; between the earthly and the heavenly ; and how every one is disposed, inclined, and of what mind he is, according to his birth or origin, and that he is of the same disposition, of the same mind, and of such a nature as that is of which he is born, that which generated him ; for the natural man is not spiritual, neither is that which is born of flesh and blood, the spiritual birth of God from heaven ; but *like produces like.* (John 4.) As the natural man is, so are they, who are naturally born.

Such as God is, who is a Spirit and in heaven, such are also they who are spiritually born from heaven, who far exceed those naturally born of flesh.

Here, as in a mirror, one may view and examine himself, and judge of what birth, mind, disposition, nature, life and conduct he is; for here a man, by taking a little pains, can judge and prove himself. A man's walk, word and actions, and the thoughts of his heart, all show what he is; (1 Cor, 2,) for man knows himself best, and no one knows what is in man, but the spirit which is in man.

Again: as many therefore, who after having proved themselves, find that they are not renewed and regenerated after their first birth, according to the flesh, in their mind, understanding, spirit and disposition, but are yet altogether sensual, earthly, worldly and devilishly minded; and from their depraved, inbred nature, are prone and willing to do all manner of evil, they will humble themselves before God, with Jeremiah, (Jer. 3,) saying: Let us examine and prove our ways, and let us turn unto the Lord, let us lift our hands and hearts to God in heaven, and say, we have sinned before heaven and in thy sight, and have excited thy wrath: Let us weep and let our eyes run over with water; and say with David: Come let us worship and bow down; let us kneel before the Lord our Maker, and entreat him that he would make glad the work of his hands, and renew us whom he created—let us humbly entreat him for his spirit, which is the great cause of all this, and say: Lord send forth thy spirit, and they will be created, and thou wilt renew the face of the earth, (1 Cor. 12; Ps. 95, 103;) and thus they continue in prayer and in their desires to God, till they are clothed with the power of the spirit from on high, converted and renewed in the spirit of their mind; and with astonishment say: This is the change wrought by the right hand of God the most High. (Ps. 76.)

Also, those who on examining themselves, find that they are born from above by the grace of God, that they are new in Christ, and have become a temple of God, and that they take heed to themselves according to the counsel of the scriptures, in order that, since they are washed, purified, regenerated and sanctified, they do not again defile themselves, and pollute the temple of God; if any man defile the temple of God, him shall God destroy, (1 Cor. 3;) they pray in the spirit with assured confidence, to God, their Father, with David: O God strengthen us and confirm in us that which thou didst cause in us! (Ps. 17.) He will then hear in his holy temple, according to his promise; for he is faithful who has begun the good work in you, he will also perform it until the day of Jesus Christ. (Phil. 1.)

Peter says: Give all diligence add to your faith virtue; and to virtue knowledge; and to knowledge temperance; and to temperance patience; and to patience godliness; and to godliness brotherly kindness; and to brotherly kindness charity; for if these be in you, and abound, they make you that ye shall neither be barren nor unfruitful in the knowledge of our Lord Jesus Christ; but he that lacketh these things, is blind and cannot see afar off, and hath forgotten that he was purged from his old sins; wherefore, the rather, brethren give diligence, to make your calling and election sure; for if ye do these things, he shall never fail; for so an entrance shall be ministered unto you abundantly, into the everlasting kingdom of our Lord and Saviour, Jesus Christ. (2 Pet. I,)

May the God of all grace, who will gather all his chosen in the last resurrection, into his kingdom, grant us such hearts, minds and dispositions, that we through true faith, may die unto yourselves, deny and renounce ourselves, that we may have part in the first resurrection spoken of, which resurrection does not take place in the bodily resurrection from the dead, as will be the case in the other resurrection, at the last day, but this resurrection consists alone in dying unto, mortifying and burying the sinful body through putting off, and dying unto the old life, and to rise and be received into a new, divine conduct and pious life. May Jesus Christ help us in all this, who is blessed forever, Amen.

CONCLUSION.

HERE, kind reader, you have a brief instruction of the *Spiritual Resurrection from death or the sleep of sin*, some inducements to awaken and arise, and henceforth to live a godly, pious, unblamable life, according to the example of Jesus Christ, as the scriptures abundantly instruct us, and as is partially related here; for the Father himself, in heaven directs us to Christ, and says: *This is my beloved Son, in whom I am well pleased, hear ye him.* He says: *Ye shall hear him.* Moses also testifies of him, and says: *The Lord, thy God, will raise unto thee a prophet from the midst of thy brethren, like unto me, unto him ye shall hearken, and every soul which will not hear that Prophet, shall be destroyed from among the people.* (Acts 3.)

Thus we counsel and admonish all in general, of whatever name, city and condition, that they would be pleased to take good heed to the word of the Lord, which we have here briefly presented, according to my limited gift; I hope by the grace of God, that you will find nothing in it but the infallible truth of Christ, (Matt. 15,) for we have not directed you to men, nor to the doctrine nor commands of men, (John 19,) but alone to Jesus Christ, and to his holy word which he taught and left upon earth, and sealed it with his blood and death, and afterwards had it promulgated throughout the world, by his faithful witnesses and holy apostles. (Mark 16.)

Besides, we say, that all doctrines, which do not agree with the doctrine of Jesus Christ and his apostles, if ever so fair in appearance, they are accursed. (Gal. 1.) For his word is the truth, and his command is eternal life, (John 12, 17;) therefore, we kindly entreat you, from our inmost souls, that you be pleased to accept and read with an understanding heart, this our *Instruction concerning the Spiritual Resurrection and New Creature*, and compare and prove it with the doctrines of the apostles; if it does not agree with theirs, let it be accursed, for no man can lay any other foundation than that which is laid, which is Christ Jesus. (1 Cor. 3) To him be praises forever and ever, Amen.

A

FUNDAMENTAL DOCTRINE,

OR AN ACCOUNT OF

EXCOMMUNICATION, BAN, EXCLUSION,

OR

SEPARATION FROM THE CHURCH OF CHRIST;

ITS NATURE, POWERS, TO WHOM IT EXTENDS;
ITS REASONS, OBJECTS AND DESIGN, &c —WHY IT WAS TAUGHT AND
PRACTICED BY THE APOSTLES,
AND COMMANDED THAT WE SHOULD PRACTICE IT.
FAITHFULLY COMPILED FROM THE SACRED SCRIPTURES, FOR THE USE
OF ALL LOVERS OF THE DOCTRINE OF ETERNAL TRUTH,
TO PROMOTE CHRISTIAN PEACE WITHOUT
RESPECT TO PARTY.

Be of one mind—let nothing be done through strife or vain glory.—PHIL. 2.

Other foundation can no man lay than that which is laid, which is Christ
Jesus.—1 COR. 3.

PREFACE.

BRETHREN and sisters in Christ, it is known and evident to all the true children of God, who are enlightened by his spirit, that human reason is so depraved in Adam that it possesses but little light which can lead to godliness; yea, it has become so unfit, haughty, dumb and blind that it would even attempt presumptuously to alter, bend, break, gainsay, judge and find fault with the word of the Lord God, it will not yield to any spirit or gift and persists that it is right, and that all it does or says is to be called God's word, whereby the saving truth, and blessed love and peace have often to endure and suffer much detriment and infamy.

In the second place, it is evident that also the enchanting spirit of antichrist has made the whole world so drunk with the cup of his abominations, (Rev. 17,) has so rejected the doctrine of Christ and his holy apostles, his sacraments, spirit, life, ordinance, usages, example and the true worship, that but little of a salutary nature is left among men, and hence it is difficult to restore what has been destroyed to its true order and proper usage, to which the Lord had ordained it.

In the third place, it is evident that the old master, satan, the arch enemy of God and souls, is always about us, as a roaring lion, and seeks whom he may devour, as Peter says: (1 Pet. 5) he assails us in diverse ways; now with the unclean wicked nature of our depraved flesh, and anon with some enchanting false doctrine and fair words, and again, by persecution, cross and fears, then with liberty and worldly life of the flesh; now with riches and abundance, then again with defects, wants and poverty. In short, he shoots his fiery darts constantly, they fly by day and by night, in secret and in public. He that does not zealously abide in the fear of God cannot withstand the manifold assaults of his temptations. Yea, we may at times imagine all is gained, then we are assaulted most violently, he raised up some under semblance of truth, whom Paul calls: Men of corrupt minds, destitute of truth, who dispute and wrangle, they are envious persons, malicious slanderers, unclean perverted minds, they are guilty of a lamentable destruction of the holy peace of God, a grievous denial of christian love, a hindrance of the saving doctrine, they sustain factious sects, and make paths to reprobation as we have abundantly seen in the days of the open truth. (1 Tim. 6.)

Alas! brethren, take warning; again I say, beware and watch; for James says that such wisdom is not from above, but it is earthly, sensual and devilish; for the wisdom which is from above, is first pure, then peaceable, gentle and easy to be entreated, full of mercy and good fruits, without partiality and without hypocrisy. (James 3.) Yea, my brethren, where there is no peaceable, friendly, saving and impartial wisdom, there is nothing but forced appearance of good, powerless, impure and sinful prayer, an unsteady, wavering mind, a restless and troubled conscience, full of strife and dissension, no

31*

matter how much we may boast of the truth. The Lord grant that we may see this.

In the fourth place, it is evident that the community or church cannot continue in the saving doctrine, unblamable and pious life without the proper use of the *Excommunication* or *Ban;* even as a city without a good police, or laws and regulations, or a field without any inclosure, and a house without walls and doors, so is also a community which has not the true apostolic *Exclusion* or *Ban,* for without it there would be an opening for all deceiving spirits, for all abominations, and for proud scorners, for all idolatrous and wantonly, perverted sinners : yea, for all lewd debauchees, sodomites, adulterers, as is the case with all the great sects of the world, which call themselves, though improperly, the church of Christ ; according to my opinion it is the distinguished usage, honor and prosperity of sincere community, if they with christian discretion teach the true apostolic *Separation,* and observe it carefully in love, according to the ordinance of the holy divine scriptures ; it is more than evident, if we had not with due zeal insisted upon it, that we would be esteemed and called, by every one, the members of the sect of Munzter and all other perverted sects. But (thank God) since, in consequence of the proper use of Excommunication, it is well known, among several thousand honorable, sincere persons, in different principalities, cities, and countries, that we are guiltless of, and free from all ungodly abominations, and preverted sects, and that we also do make this known, unreservedly, to the whole world, not only by our doctrines, but with our possessions and blood.

Having observed, and laid this to heart, that now the bright light of the holy gospel of Christ shines again in refulgent splendor in these vexatious times of all antichristian abominations ; God's own and first begotten Son, Christ Jesus, is gloriously revealed, his good will and pleasure and holy word concerning faith, regeneration, repentance, baptism, the Lord's supper, and the whole saving doctrine, life and ordinance, have again come to light through much seeking, prayer, reading, teaching and writing, that now all things (God be praised for his grace) proceed according to the true apostolic rule in the community, whereby the kingdom of Christ rises in honor, and the kingdom of antichrist is sinking. For this reason the arch enemy of our souls violently opposes, uses his old wiles and arts most subtlely against it. He appears under the cloak of a christian, (understand me rightly) boasts of faith proudly, upbraids ; yea, rejects all the Babylonian deeds, is baptized, seats himself with the saints at the Lord's supper, praises the lives of the pious, hears exhortations, gives alms, receives the poor, washes the saints' feet, says that Christ is the son of God. In short, in appearance he is an unblamable, regenerated, penitent and true christian. But in the mean time, he watches where he may assail us most easily and injure us the most, slily enters our depraved and enchanted understanding, some of whom, as is evident, as yet know little what the nature and mind of the Holy Ghost are, he presses them closely, for he knows how skillfully to defend his cause with the letter of the scriptures, he speaks gently ; whatever he does, he does as though out of pure fear of God, and love to the community, with the word and truth of the Lord. Through his influence some, as it were, out of great distress and anxiety of conscience, wrangle and dispute, principally concerning the separation which he can so little tolerate and endure; here and there they raise pernicious questions and answers whereby those who are of a perverted and enchanted understanding, begin to be inflamed at each other, so that some of them when they find that they cannot stand before the power of the truth, leave, out of mere party spirit, the pleasant Jerusalem and return again to unclean, blind Babel; or build up a sect of their own, as I have with much sorrow seen it to be the case two or three times. Behold, this is the pearl which the old deceiver seeks with his ire and wrangling; for whether we stay away from the idolatrous church or not, be baptized or not, it is immaterial to him; if he can only inflame our hearts with hatred and envy one towards another, corrupt our minds, mar our love, destroy our peace, if he can but sow discord, defamation, hatred, lies, enmity and backbiting, which generally arise from such disputes; if he can but do this, then he has accomplished what he sought. Ah! dear brethren, beware, for it is more than clear, that all those who have not the meek, friendly, peaceable spirit of Christ, but are contentious, are not of God. Be this known to you.

Seeing then we know, that he did from the beginning of the expounded gospel, to the present moment, cause us much pain and sorrow of heart, with his cunning, unfruitful question of contention, and other pernicious disputations, I do most affectionately and cordially entreat all who would desire to walk peaceably and quietly in the fear of God with a good conscience, before the Lord and his community, that they would all before God, in Christ Jesus, lay this sincerely to heart, how faithfully the Holy Spirit of Christ warns us concerning our unprofitable, foolish questions, answers, disputations, and quarrels, (1 Tim. 6; 2 Tim. 2; Tit. 3,) for the spirit of Christ is the spirit of love and peace, and therefore, teaches all his children love and peace, and writes it upon the tablets of our hearts with his gracious finger. Ah! do reflect upon what we teach; and that his holy kingdom and word are a word and kingdom of peace, and not of strife, his messengers and servants, are messengers and servants of peace, (Isa. 2, 52; Mich. 4; Nah. 1; Rom. 10,) in order that you, who call yourselves after his holy name, who alone has graciously called you into his kingdom of peace, (Isa. 9; Heb. 7,) through the word of his peace may escape the snares of the devil, and that you may so conduct yourselves in all your ways after Christ's will and pleasure, towards all men, and observe his holy word and ordinance, and defend it; that you may promote that true righteousness required of God, such as faith, love, repentance, regeneration, piety and peace with all other fruits of the Holy Ghost; gladden the hearts of all the sorrowful of heart and the young and tender in Christ Jesus, and console and encourage them in all their trials, need, temptations, tribulation and fear, so that the most holy city may again be rebuilt, which lay desolated for so many centuries, and restore all its usages, ordinances and services to primitive order. Yea, that the saving light of the true gospel of Christ may be spread among all nations, kindred and tongues, in its full splendor, and that the accursed, lying and anti-christian darkness may be dispelled.

Then observe that the Lord's powerful word is more and more miraculously breaking forth and that, therefore, all true hearts would gladly see and have unanimity in this part of the BAN (whereby they are sometimes so greatly troubled and perplexed, as related,) that they might all orderly proceed observing one rule, according to the scriptures as it becomes christians ; and I an unworthy person, the weakest of all the saints, have been tried severely in this part by many different spirits for twenty-two years, and have endured many an attack, whereby others are not only taught of me, but I am also taught of others, (the giver of all good gifts be praised for all this.] And also after some considerable time through many adventitious circumstances, examining into and reflecting upon some of the things connected with this, I was through experience, induced to yield to the solicitations and prayers of the brethren who were desirous of seeing good in all respects, that before the close of my life, I would examine and revise the *Ground and meaning of the true apostolic Ban or Separation*, arrange it formally and present it for examination to the elders and ministers of the community, to all desiring peace, so that if any one, after my departure, (as I am now an old feeble man) might cause any trouble, strife or dissention among the quiet and peaceable, under pretence that he heard this or that from me at any time, or might infer wrong views from some of my writings which have not as yet been so fully explained by me *concerning man and wife*, and of open, offensive sensual sinners, (as it is done here,) in order that the brethren may refer them to my *conclusive ground*, after I shall have fallen asleep in God, and made my exit hence. Besides, that the pious doubtful conscience may thereby be relieved, so that they may attain an assurance of confidence in their minds. Which I have undertaken with great diffidence (although it was quite christian like and good before) and did it especially, because I knew that they were not all brethren and sisters in truth and power who should read, hear or see this. And where the mind is not pure, and love is not genuine, there the understanding is generally partial and the construction perverse, this I have learned to be the case myself of some towards me. Ah ! that some of them would obtain grace. Besides I know, that the opinions, judgments, affections and minds are different ; and that the all-prevailing truth and the fear, spirit and unction of the Lord, are not possessed by every one in their fulness ; therefore, I fear that all will not receive and follow this doctrine as the *True Ground of Truth*. O that we all had the eyes of the understanding, those of us who think we see, it would, according to my opinion, soon gain a strong hold with some.

I have full confidence in those, who in the true fear of God seek union and peace with sincerity among all the pious, and are anxious for the truth ; they will receive my brotherly work, to promote holy peace, and to explain eternal truth, with christian fidelity ; they will not despise it, but gladly receive it, and thank the Lord for his grace ; for it appears to me, almost impossible to hit upon a surer and more certain way according to truth, in which we may stand, before God and man, and that which I have impartially, and according to my limited talents, pointed out and explained as before God in Christ Jesus, and which is according to the sacred scriptures.

I do not serve the stiff-necked, haughty and perverse scorners, neither immovable bigots and wranglers, but those I serve, who are

of an impartial, new christian mind who suffer themselves to be instructed, and are under the guidance of the Holy Ghost, and live in
the fear of God and in pure love, who have received the Lord's holy
word and truth in a pure mind, follow it through the received unction
implicitly, and are free from all bitter party spirit, vain horror,
hatred and envy; for with such we find the amiable spirit of peace,
sincere and pious disposition, an unleavened, pure heart and conversation, and, therefore,.also an upright and pure understanding, and
an incorrupt, saving ground and exposition, and they live no more
with their selfish flesh, but unto Christ and their neighbors, resist
none, are humble, are opposed to all unscriptural contention and
strife, readily acknowledge their short comings wherein they have
erred; reconcile their neighbors whom they had grieved, regarding
neither honor nor dishonor; heap fiery coals upon the heads of their
adversaries; walk unblamably, in order that they may awaken them
again unto truth with love, lead them from the way of error, bring
them unto Christ, and save them eternally. Behold these are they,
I say, whom I serve with my writings; for they have Christ in power
with his spirit, word and love, and thus with him, and in him they
have TRUE CHRISTIANITY, which will stand before God—which is
a useful, cheering, peaceable and joyful thing. Ah, children, be
admonished; learn rightly to know the subtlety of the devil, and
beware of discord. May the merciful Father grant us all the wisdom
of Christ, Amen.

EXPLANATION

OF THE TRUE APOSTOLIC SEPARATION OR EXCOMMUNICATION.

I. *What is meant by Separation or Excommunication?*

CORDIALLY faithful children of the Lord, whom I love in truth. Since I have, but of paternal fidelity, undertaken this very critical task, for the benefit of you all, and the pious generally, (I say a critical task, for I am well aware that it causes much grief among the simple for some time; and I fear that all is not over yet,) I therefore entreat you all in general, both the afflicted and unafflicted, by the bloody wounds of Jesus, all of you, who with me bow your knees before the almighty, great God, I exhort you by the righteous judgment, which he will hold at his future coming in the clouds of heaven, in flaming fire with his mighty angels, that you would be pleased to judge this my work impartially, and with a pure heart of peace—read article after article, nay, every word, with sincere Christian discretion, in true love, according to the rule and ground of truth; and, in the first place, well observe what *Excommunication* of the church of Christ is in power, which was left and taught us by the Lord's holy apostles, "so that you despise none ignorantly, nor say with scorners: Let them freely excommunicate, their excommunication is not dangerous:" and similar unguarded expressions. I tell the truth in Christ, and lie not, that I would sooner suffer myself to be cut into pieces, till the day of judgment, if it were possible, than to suffer myself to be excommunicated, according to the scriptures, by the servants of the Lord, and from his community. Brethren, beware!

All that was cursed in Israel according to the ordinances, of the law whether man or beast, had to die, and the accursed goods had to be burnt with fire. (Num. 21; Deut. 7, 13; Jos. 6, 7, 8, 19; 1 Sam. 15.) This was a dreadful and severe curse (anathema.) But in Christ's kingdom and government, (if we rightly view it in its true character, if repentance follow not,) it is still more dreadful; it is not now a bodily extermination or the death of our flesh, as Moses' curse, (anathema, or excommunication,) was, nor is it an exclusion from a temple or synagogue, even as is the excommunication of the Jews or of the world; but it is a true declaration of the eternal death of the soul, made through the sincere servants of Christ, against all offending, sensual sinners, (1 Cor. 5; 2 Cor. 13,) and stubborn wranglers, (Rom. 16; Tim. 3,) a delivering over to satan, (1 Cor. 5; 1 Tim. 1,) yea, a common renouncing, excommunicating or separating from the community, church, body and kingdom of Christ, and that in the name of Christ, with the binding efficacy of his Holy Ghost and powerful word. (1 Cor. 5.)

Since, then, this is such a dreadful and severe Anathema, as related, then may every one see well to it, that he walk and conduct himself so before God and his church, as not to be eternally smitten with such a curse, either of Christ or his community, that he must be such an excommunicant out of the holy community, body, city, temple, church, kingdom and house of Christ. For all who are out of Christ's community and church, must be in anti-christ's; this is incontrovertible. And what the award of such will be, if they will not repent, may be plainly read in Rom. 1, 6 : 1 Cor. 6; Gal. 5; Eph. 5; 1 Thes. 1; Rev. 21, 22. Ah! children, beware – be careful with all your powers; watch assiduously; pray fervently and be prepared; for God's judgments are terrible—It is a fearful thing to fall into the hands of the living God. (Heb. 10.)

II. *Over whom this Apostolic Excommunication is to be used.*

We find in many places of the holy scriptures, that the truly believing community is the spiritual body, bride, camp, city and temple of Jesus Christ, our only spiritual head, bridegroom, king and high priest, prefigured by the literal Eve, Rebecca, and the camp, city and temple of Israel. (Eph. 1, 5; Rev. 19; Heb. 12; 1 Cor. 1, 6; 2 Cor. 6.) (In the political dominion of Israel no leper, none that had an issue nor those who were defiled by the dead, were suffered to come into camp as long as they were not healed and purified according to the law; (Num. 5,) none were allowed to ease themselves within the camp, (Deut. 23,) neither an uncircumcised, nor an unclean person, was allowed to eat of the passover, (Exod. 12; Num. 9.) all those (here observe well Israel's Ban) had to die without mercy, on the testimony of two or three witnesses, who despised the word of the Lord and set aside his commandments, (Num. 15,) those who were guilty of abomination in Israel, and served strange gods. (Deut. 13, 17; Heb. 10.) For, says Moses, they were to be a holy people to the Lord. (Exod. 19.))

And thus it is in the Christian dispensation; for his community is a communion of saints, or an assembly of the righteous, even as the Nicean fathers some centuries ago did confess with us; and, as Adam had but one Eve, who was flesh of his flesh and bone of his bone. (Gen. 2.) Isaac had one Rebecca, who was of his own family, (Gen. 24,) and Christ had one body, which was heavenly and from heaven, and was perfect and holy in all its members: (1 Cor. 15,) thus has he also, spiritually, but one new Rebecca, who is his spiritual body, spouse, community, church and bride, namely, the believers, regenerated, meek, merciful, dead to sin, peaceable, amiable and obedient children in his kingdom or house of peace; pure, chaste virgins in the spirit, holy souls, who are of his divine family, flesh of his flesh and bone of his bone. (Eph. 5.)

From which, according to the doctrine of the holy apostles, it is evident that the obstinate disturber or sectary who causes, contrary to the doctrine of godliness, offence and discord, (Rom. 16; 1 Tim. 6; 2 Tim. 2; Tit. 3,) and those who do not abide in the doctrine of Christ, (2 John 1,) who lead an offensive life, (1 Cor. 5; 2 Cor. 13,) or the over-curious, inquisitive and lazy, who live at the expense of others, (2 Thess. 3,) shall not be suffered in Christ's holy house, camp, city, temple, church and body; which is the community, but they, with one accord, are excluded, and, according to scriptures, we are to avoid and shun them, to save our own souls; and to the reformation of their own. Faithful children, be you warned: terrible is the word which John utters: Whosoever transgresseth, and abideth not in the doctrine of Christ, hath not God. (2 John 1.) And in another place: He that committeth sin, is of the devil. (1 John 3.)

III. *The reason why this Excommunication is commanded in the scriptures.*

John teaches and says: That God is love. (1 John 4.) Since, then, as God is love, so does he also manifest the nature, of that of what he is, namely, love. That this is the truth, may be readily perceived from the creation and preservation of all his creatures, the restoration of Adam and Eve, the preservation of Noah and his sons from the flood with an ark; in blessing Abraham, Isaac and Jacob; in ransoming Israel from Egypt; in sending Moses and the prophets; (Gen. 1, 3, 6, 7, 8, 12, 26; 28; Exod. 3, 14; Zech. 7; 2 Esd. 1,) and more especially in the holy incarnation of our Lord Jesus Christ, the Son of God; in his gracious, efficacious doctrine, miracles, prayers, weeping, cross, blood and death; also, in the effusion of his Holy Ghost, and sending forth of his holy apostles. (John 3; Rom. 8.)

Since, then, it is evident that God is love, and will be, eternally, and in the beginning manifested the glorious fruit of love towards his children, and thus does he likewise by this his *exclusion or separation*, although it is terrible and severe, and that it has such a terrible consequence with the stubborn and unconverted sinner, as heard. For, since he is the wise and omniscient God, who with his flaming eyes sees into the inmost recesses of the hearts and reins of men, judges their ways, and knows us best, who are his feeble creatures and workmanship, what weak vessels we are; yea, that some of us can scarce withstand a gentle breeze of deception; but suffer ourselves to be led away immediately, or we are soon polluted with the pernicious, abominable life; for that reason he has, through his paternal love and great mercy, given us, his poor, weak children, this means of *Separation*, approved it by the Holy Ghost and word in the beginning, and commanded it to that end, that we should exclude the restless, stubborn wranglers and schismatists, together with the offensive, sensual and lewd, from his holy community, church and house of peace, and, according to the scriptures, avoid and shun them till they repent, in order that they shake us not in the confident hope we have in the truth of Christ, with their fair words; for their false doctrine eats as a canker, Paul says; (2 Tim. 2,) nor that the abominable with their impure, sensual life pervert us, nor make us as a bad name among those without, (1 Cor. 5,) and, behold, this is the *first reason* why the spirit of the Lord so earnestly commanded and taught Excommunication in his holy word. Whether this *reason* is not a special work of the love of Christ, which is of great usefulness, service, power and fruit to all the pious, I will let all the faithful reflect upon in the fear of God.

The other *reason* is, that all those who again forsake the holy word and true way and go astray in the world, despise the holy covenant, make void their received baptism and the promise of righteousness, again hear the false prophets, love the world, walk the broad way of the flesh, or cause contention, schisms and sects and perverse things among the pious, &c. They are deterred by means of this excommunication, and brought to repentance, seek union and peace, and thus be set free before the Lord and his community from the satanic snares of their strife, or from their ungodly life. (1 Cor. 5.) Behold, this is the other reason why the spirit of the Lord so earnestly recommended and taught excommunication in his holy word. And whether this reason is not a special work of his love and of like power, usefulness, service and fruit to the impious, if they will by any means observe it in fear, as the first is to the pious: upon this all the faithful may reflect in the fear of God. Yea, whoever can rightly know and see the aforementioned *reasons*, according to the scriptures, has already found the true ground of the holy excommunication, according to my opinion.

Since we know, then, that this our excommunication and separation are commanded us in the scriptures, for two such highly important reasons, as related, hence we have reason enough, if we rightly boast of the Christian name, regularly to teach the evident and direct command, doctrine and ordinance of the Lord and his holy apostles, (Matt. 18; 1 Cor. 5; Tit. 3,) as a highly useful and good work of great love; and obediently to follow it; and besides, it is also more than evident, that those sin heinously against the word of the holy apostles, and their great love, and the fidelity and love of the community, and especially against their own soul, who call this useful, divine ordinance, in the perverseness of their sinful flesh, a contentious work of the devil, and thus trample it so shamefully under the unhallowed feet of their impious calamity, into the mire—haughty is that man who would rebuke his God, or gainsay and censure his word. Reflect upon that in which we have instructed you.

IV. *The true Apostolic Excommunication has no respect to persons.*

Undoubtedly, it is well known to us all, dear brethren, that it is so strongly and earnestly commanded in the scriptures, nay, it is one of the chief commands, that we are to honor father and mother, and that all had to die according to the law of Moses, who cursed and disobeyed them. (Matt. 15; Mark 7; Eph. 6; Col. 3; Exod. 20; Deut. 5, 21; Lev. 20.) And also, that the bond of undefiled matrimony is so unchangeably bound in the kingdom and government of Christ, that neither a man nor woman can forsake one the other, and take another, (understand rightly what Christ says,) except for fornication's sake. (Matt. 19; Luke 16.) And Paul also holds the same doctrine, that they shall be bound to each other, and that they are to live in union; that the man has not power over his own body, nor the woman over hers. (1 Cor. 7.)

Both these rules, the first in relation to parents, and the second in relation to wedlock, stand fast and unbroken, and can never be altered or infringed by any man, so far as we can, in God and with God, in a good conscience, observe and keep them, as the aforementioned rules require, without transgressing the holy word; but if this cannot be done thus, the spiritual must not, in that case, yield to the carnal, but the carnal must yield to the spiritual—this is incontrovertibly true.

I, therefore, entreat all the pious, for the Lord's sake who, with us, are sanctified to Christ Jesus, through the Spirit of peace, that they may, with God-fearing, understanding hearts, view impartially, with spiritual eyes, the *Six* following *Reasons*, which urgently engage our minds, that we would gladly teach this *Ground* to all our fellow-believers, whose lot it might be, or whom it might concern (may the Lord ever preserve them from it) to teach it with christian deliberation, and to the saving of their souls, without giving offence to the young and tender minds, and propound it in true love. All who fear God, I will let judge what we teach.

The *First Reason* is, that we do truly know through God's Spirit and word, that the heavenly espousal between Christ and our souls, is made through his innocent death and precious blood by faith, (Hos. 2; Rev. 19,) and must be voluntarily kept up unbroken, in obedience to the only and eternal bridegroom, and that, therefrom, a man shall not, neither for the sake of father, mother, son, daughter, husband nor wife, in life or death, be disobedient to his word, in the smallest matter, or yield any the least; for God, the Lord will, shall and must alone be the God of our conscience, and be the only Lord of our souls; and not our father, mother, husband or wife, as we may plainly see from Deut. 13, 33; Matt. 10; Luke 14.

The *Second Reason* is, that the faithful apostles, John and Paul, teach us so; that in the first place, we are to avoid the apostates, lest they contaminate us with the impure, deceiving doctrine, and with ungodly, sensual lives; nor that we partake with them of their unfruitful works, (1 Cor. 5; 2 John 1,) and for the reasons above assigned; and since we plainly see, that none can sooner contaminate and pollute us, than our own fathers, mothers, husband, wife or children, if they are corrupted, and especially on account of the daily intercourse with and love for them, which is existing among them; and moreover, since man and wife are one flesh, I scarce know, if they, in this respect, do not especially observe the Lord's holy word and counsel, how they will escape the snares of death; for now they pray and sigh, and anon they rage and quarrel. Now they slander and defame, then they weep and lament. Ah! children, take warning. Their tears are crocodile's tears, and their tongues are set on fire from hell, as James says. I forbear to mention in detail, that some of them run after false prophets, revile Christ's holy word, sacraments and ordinances; and highly recommend antichrist's abominations, and besides, the conduct of some of them is nothing but sheer avarice, pride, wantonness, eating and drinking to excess, &c., and how scandalously some of them live with their poor women; especially when they are intoxicated. I let the Lord judge. (James 3.) And that any one could live in the midst of such wanton, sensual, ungodly abominations, and not be hurt in his faith, love and unction, and have intercourse with such abominable unclean, adhesive pitch vessels, and not be polluted in his conscience. I will let all, with the unction of their spirit, reflect, who have an understanding of the holy word.

The *Third Reason* is, because Paul teaches us that we are

also to avoid the apostate, that they should thereby be brought to reflect, and thus be led to repent of their wicked life, or of their schismatic doctrine. Seeing we know this, that it is the *Ground and Intention* of the Holy Ghost, with Excommunication, as related: then it is also proper, and according to the scriptures, that we, in this matter, implicitly follow his divine counsel, love, doctrine, good will and earnest commands, and obediently follow him and observe *it*, in true love, towards our most beloved father, mother, husband, wife and children, rather than towards others, because, I say, they are our dearest friends; yea, our own flesh and bone, and we cannot by any other salutary means, lead them off from evil, and again lead them on the way of the saints. Reflect upon what we teach you.

The *Fourth Reason* is, because we certainly know that there is but one Exclusion or Excommunication in the scriptures, which does not only extend to the spiritual communion, such as to the Lord's supper, hand and kiss of peace; but it extends also to the bodily communion, such as eating, drinking, daily actions and conduct, (1 Cor. 5,) and that if the father is to avoid the son, or the son the father, the husband his wife, or the wife the husband, only in the spiritual communion, and not in civil community, in that event there would be two kinds of Excommunications in the scriptures; the one would only extend to the spiritual communion, and the other, both to the spiritual and civil communions; this is clear as daylight. Again, reflect upon what we teach you.

The *Fifth Reason* is, because pious parents, as well as the community, consent and approve of the excommunication of the apostate children; and the pious children consent that the apostate parents should be excommunicated; and the husband consents that the apostate wife should be excommunicated, and the pious wife that the apostate husband be excommunicated, and that they be severally dealt with according to the scriptures; and if they would then afterwards avoid them only in the spiritual community, they would make void their own sentence, which they in common with the church pronounced, and thus they would not seek the salvation of their dearest friends with that spiritual love and zeal as the Lord's word and spirit command them, and still be in great danger of perdition. In order, unmolestedly to escape it, their excommunication has been commanded, taught and left on record in the word of the Lord, to every man, woman and child, without exception. Again, I say, reflect upon what we teach you.

The *Sixth Reason* is, because I know no less than three hundred married persons in my time who did not observe the ordinance, counsel, doctrine, will and command of the Lord and

32*

his apostles concerning *avoiding*, and thus run together into perdition. Ah! Lord, we stand in deliberation and dismay, that not a similar evil has befallen us on account of our silence; we would, therefore, gladly, hereafter, observe it, since the care of the community is entrusted to us, that we might the better prevent, according to the apostolic doctrine and counsel, all corruption and apostacy, and freely, purely and fully teach and maintain the regulation of Excommunication, as well between parents and children, man and wife, as among others—to all our brethren, (if circumstances require it,) in order that we, in the first place, clear our own souls, and thus stand acquitted before God and his saints in the great day of Christ; and secondly: So that none can excuse himself and say, "It was never told to me."

Behold, brethren in the Lord, *these* are the important articles and principal *Reasons* which urge us most that we willingly teach this *Ground*, and put it into practice. Is there now a single individual under the canopy of heaven, learned or unlearned, young or old, without or among us, man or woman, who can teach us the truth, that the espousals of the spirit made with Christ through faith, should yield to human wedlock?

Or that a man cannot deceive or corrupt his wife, or a woman her husband? Or that a pious man is not bound according to the scriptures, to promote the salvation of his unconverted wife, or the woman of her unconverted husband? Or that there are two Excommunications in the scriptures; that the one only extends to the spiritual community, and the other both to the spiritual and temporary. Or that the pious husband dare not vote with the communion against his unconverted wife, or the wife against the husband in excluding her. Or that there is an exception in the whole scriptures of man or wife, parents or children, in this respect. Or that spiritual love has to yield to conjugal love, &c. If so, then we desire with all the heart to abandon this our ground, and acknowledge our error, and with great zeal teach the contrary before the whole world, as is christian and right; for we regard neither slander, nor praise, honor, nor disgrace; but we have only regard for the honor of God and Christ, and the eternal salvation of your souls; on account of which, we are esteemed as detestable,—such offscourings, filth and offence to many, as may be seen.

But if this cannot be done, (as it never can be done) then in the first place, my cordial prayer, and fraternal admonition, are to all who might have erroneous views of this matter, that they would not improperly meddle through impure and perverted minds, by slandering the chief stone and the builders; nor that they would persude any to disobey the word, or keep them in the dangers of apostacy and perdition, lest they make themselves guilty of other men's sins; but that they would give the Lord's good will and ordinance, due praise in this respect, pluck out the offending eye of their misunderstanding, and pass a sound judgment according to truth, avert sin from the community, and thus observe the Lord's incontrovertibly clear word, counsel and command, with all the pious, and assist with all deliberation to maintain it.

Secondly: I entreat all who might have any concern for the irrational slanders, that they would view the matter impartially in a divine light, that not only Excommunication is hated, but also all the doings of Christ, such as the true evangelical baptism, Lord's supper, life and the whole divine service, &c. All this is hated by the whole world, and considered as abomination, scandal and disgrace, so that they, out of pure hatred to the truth, are not ashamed to call all the pious by such names as accursed heretics, anabaptists, ringleaders, whores and rogues; and in many places deprive them of possessions and life, as may be seen; although the pious are so much honored of God, that he acknowledges and adopts them as his chosen children, as his sons and daughters, as the apple of his eye, as his bride and spouse; and endows them with the gift of eternal life. (Eph. 1; Heb. 2; 2 Cor. 6; Zach. 2; Matt. 5: Luke 6; 2 Tim. 2; Rev. 19.) For there is nothing that they love more than their God, as they fully testify and make known by their actions to the whole world. And thus it is in this matter. For how can there be a greater love for God, and how can there be found a more praise-worthy confession, than where one is willing and ready, not only to give up his temporal goods, ease, honor and happiness; but also avoid their dearest friends upon earth, out of sincere regard to Christ, in obedience to his eternal and holy truth? No abominable vice nor disgrace does become God's pure knowledge together with the unfeigned obedience of his most holy word.

Thirdly: I entreat all dear brethren in general, that they would always think with wise and sober minds, to what end they bent their shoulders under the pleasing yoke of the living and almighty God, so that they may act and walk in a becoming manner, in the most holy covenant of grace, before Him and all mankind, and live and walk with their consorts in such piety, love, union and peace, with such fidelity and care, observe that hereafter in eternity we have not to hear of Excommunication or Exclusion; but of sincere christian piety, delight and divine joy. Reflect upon these things which we teach you.

Fourthly: I entreat all, if they should at any time feel themselves aggrieved by this part of our doctrine, that they would thus wisely examine this matter in the pure fear of God, that they do not seek the solicitous selfish, lazy and idle flesh above Christ, nor cover it with fig-leaves, lest the warmth, of the Lord who hates all lies, hypocrisy and subtle roguery, punish them with blindness and perversion, and assign them their portion with hypocrites; (Matt. 24,) but that they might, by virtue of true faith in Christ Jesus, valiantly overcome themselves, and obediently and fully observe what the Holy Spirit of the love of Christ has commanded and taught by his holy word in this part. Ah! let us reflect upon this.

Finally: I entreat elders, teachers, ministers and deacons, in the love of Christ, that they would not teach this whole matter carelessly and irrationally; but teach and inculcate in full fear of God, and with christian deliberation and paternal solicitude, in an apostolic manner, not too hastily, nor too slowly; not too rigidly nor too leniently; lest they seethe a kid in its mother's milk; (Exod. 23, 34: Deut. 14,) but that they take of the first green ears of their land, dry them by the heavenly fire of pure and unfeigned love, and beat them into pieces in the mortar of the holy word, and pour upon it the oil of the Holy Ghost, which makes us willingly obedient unto Christ, pour upon it the sweet smelling frankincense of a sincere and firm faith from which all must result, to be a sweet savor to the Lord; and thus bring Him an acceptable meat-offering in his holy temple. Lay to heart, in true love, the ground of my admonition.

V. *That we are to put away from the community the openly offensive, sensual sinner, and excommunicated of God, and thus direct them to true repentance with the scriptures.*

BEFORE I proceed to explain this article, I would earnestly admonish the reader, that about eighteen years ago, I published an admonition, in which I made no distinction of sin: but through my inexperience, directed them without discrimination, to three different admonitions. I say inexperience; for to the best of my knowledge, I neither heard nor knew at that time, any thing of fornication, adultery, &c., among the brethren; and it appeared to me impossible, that those who entered with us upon the paths of righteousness, should have any desire or will to such gross abominations, and therefore, did not earnestly reflect upon the matter. See before God it is the truth which I write.

I likewise wrote a book in 1549, in reply to those who would only extend excommunication to the spiritual communion, and charged us on all sides with slanderous words, that we practiced a rigid, cruel, unmerciful and Pharisaic Excommunication.

Finally, I wrote a few words against G. F. And to this day have made no particular distinction thereof in my writings, nor could I have made it, this I acknowedge openly, for my information of it was too limited, so long as the matter was not disputed and again come to me for re-consideration. But now having heard the ground of dispute, and having carefully weighed all the circumstances connected with it, in the balance of the holy, divine word, the following six reasons have given me such a powerful assurance in the matter, (the helper of all distressed souls be praised for his grace) that we are to exclude from the Lord's holy community, all offensively sensual sinners, such as fornicators, adulterers, drunkards, &c.; these all ought to be put to open shame and reproof, with their ungodly works, and that without previously admonishing them, by virtue of the holy divine word, and thus direct them to repentance, (1 Cor. 5; 2 Cor. 13,) I say by virtue of the word, for, in the first place, it is evident, as Paul teaches : That neither fornicators nor idolators, nor adulterers, nor effeminate, nor abusers of themselves with mankind, nor thieves, nor covetous, nor drunkards, nor revilers, nor extortioners, shall inherit the kingdom of God, (Rom. 1 ; 1 Cor. 6,) but that their portion will be eternal death in the lake of fire. (Gal. 5 ; Eph. 5 ; 2 Thes. 1 ; Rev. 21, 22.)

Seeing then, it is more than clear, that their condemning sentence is already passed, whereby they are already judged of God through his eternal Spirit and powerful word, both in heaven and upon the earth ; that they exclude themselves, and by their ungodly works forsake the community, that they are not as they were before, flesh of Christ's flesh, and members of his holy body ; because they are so sensual and devilish ; yea, make themselves dogs and swine, and servants of sin; (2 Pet. 2 ; John 8; Rom. 6,) and that we should hold them as our dear brethren and salute them with the peace of the Lord, who, are already, I say, the children of the devil, and that we are to exhort without any evidence of true repentance, would in fact be nothing less than that we would be for making void and of none effect, the righteous judgment of almighty God, uttered by his holy apostles against such offensive, abominable defilers? and esteem such a gross wretch as a child of God and joint heir of Christ. But how such a great despising of Christ and his righteous judgment, could stand according to the scriptures, I would, that we might all impartially and in the fear of God, reflect upon it.

In the second place, it is evident that all those who are envious of us, are assiduously bent upon finding but a *mote* in us, (because they so despitefully hate us for truth's sake) in order to magnify it into a *beam* and defame us grossly ; and we then yet should retain such offensive, infamous and abominable sinners, accursed of God, as our brethren upon a slight confession, yet without the least satisfactory evidence of repentance, which is, perhaps, more the result of shame, fear or feigned hypocrisy, than through the fear of God, and that we should break with them the peaceable and blessed bread of the Lord's holy supper, and thus by actions show that as if they were joint members of our community; and were we to do so, we would then undoubtedly, in that case, expose the fair bride of the honor of Christ to all the ungodly as infamous, and make her a scoff to all our enemies. May the gracious Lord preserve us from this, that we may never think of it, much less do so. Take notice of this.

In the third place, it is evident, that with those three admonitions concerning such gross, offensive abominations, we would make many great hypocrites; since I hear that there were some within a few years, who carried on their horrible roguery and infamy in secret, till time and circumstances could no longer conceal them; yea, as I have understood, if some of them had not been detected by great wisdom, they would, I fear, have continued in their old course; but as soon as it was disclosed they began to wail and weep. Who could ever have been so blinded, if a man has disgraced his neighbor's wife, daughter or maid, or robbed him of his moneys, &c., and being seized, spoken to and admonished, that he would not say : " I am sorry that I did so." Seeing then that experience teaches us the longer, the more, so it is also proper and consistent with the scriptures, that we should not at all countenance such a gross, shameless sinner, much less are we to cherish him in his ungodly actions and wicked career with false prophets. but direct them where the Holy Ghost directs them with the scriptures, namely, out of the community, (Deut. 23; Ezek. 13,) lest we derogate from the Lord's sentence pronounced in his word, against such people, that the community of grace, the unleavened lump of Christ, the anointed, King and Priest of God, may continue to be agreeable and dignified; and also, that the transgressors may be brought sincerely to repent before God and his community, and may again present their offering and gift with a clean, pure, new conscience, as the truly sanctified saints of Christ, to the altar of reconciliation in his holy temple. Ah! reflect upon what we teach.

In the fourth place, it is evident that Paul teaches us how we are to avoid a heretic, after we have admonished him once and again, if he will not amend. (Tit. 3.) Since then we are not urged by the Holy Ghost to reprove a man more than once or twice, some of whom are outwardly yet quite pious, and perhaps some of them know no better, but suppose they are in the right, say beloved, how should we then admonish these thrice, who are not ashamed to sin, not only against God's powerful word, but also against the law of nature; being bent upon disgracing a neighbor's wife, daughter or maiden; to frequent public taverns and houses of infamy; in selling and buying, practice fraud, &c. In short, all these are sentenced to eternal death, by the spirit and word of the Lord, if they will not repent as heard.

It would, according to my opinion, be very unbecoming, if we rightly reflect upon it, that we should run after those who are already condemned, to admonish them thrice before separation should take place; and though they regard not the first and second admonition, that we should still hold them as brethren in the community, till the third time; if they would even then evince that they were sorry, they should remain brethren, if not, then it should be told them before the community, out of the word of God, that they had no more fellowship with Christ, but are accursed according to the scriptures. All who are taught of God, I will let judge how such doctrine and conduct could stand the test of the Lord's justice and word.

In the fifth place, it is evident, so far as I am able to judge, that holy Paul wrote his first epistle to the Corinthians with such a view, as related; for he says: that they shall neither eat nor keep company with any that is a fornicator, or covetous, an idolator or drunkard, &c., he does not even mention one admonition, much less two or three; but he says: A little leaven leaventh the whole lump; which is undoubtedly true; for facts have more than satisfactorily proven how often the pious, on their account, are considered rather as an offensive savor, who should otherwise be a sweet savor, were it not for those shameful members.

In the sixth place, it is evident, that Paul did not only thus teach this ground; but also showed it by an open example to the unclean Corinthian who sat with his step-mother in a very unbecoming manner; for without any previous admonition he judged him according to his ungodly works, and put him, by the word and spirit of the Lord, out of the community, and delivered him unto satan, into whose hands he had already fallen through his unnatural, detestable incontinency, in order that through this severe sentence and open shame, he might mortify and bury his unclean, shameful flesh, with its sensual lusts, and that his soul might be saved in the day of the Lord, (1 Cor. 5,) and was not received again before the term of a year or longer, as history informs, till they saw that he sincerely repented, and might have been swallowed up with ever much sorrow. (2 Cor. 2.)

And it would, according to my opinion, be proper that we should not so soon again admit such sensual persons, who have beyond measure defamed the holy word, and brought such great tribulation upon the pious with their abominable disgrace, though they may seemingly lament and promise much; but examine more closely the fruits of their repentance for some time; for it is not repentance though they say: "We have sinned!" but repentance is a converted, changed, pious and new heart, a broken and contrite spirit, from which flow the tears of sincerity, a candid confession, a true desire to depart from the evil in which a person was. A sincere and cordial hatred to sin, and an unblamable, pious Christian life—this is repentance which will stand before God. I entreat you learn rightly to know both repentance and sin. Take heed thereto.

Behold, faithful brethren, here you have my most important writings, discourses and reasons which moved me more deeply to reflect upon this matter in the fear of God. Again I say, as I said above, in speaking of the separation of man and wife. Is there one under the canopy of heaven, whoever he be, that can instruct me, by divine truth, that a secret or open fornicator, adulterer, drunkard, &c., can be a member of the Lord's holy body, till he is admonished two or three times; observe this well. Or that the sentence of the Holy Ghost pronounced by Paul, (in all the scriptures) against such deadly abominations, depends upon the condition of two or three admonitions. In the second place, observe: Whether we have not cause to fear that the pious will be derided when we have no other evidence of reformation than a mere promise; or that we may, by the power of the keys, retain those which God has already excluded by the word of his truth; or that the community should judge uncertainties by Christ's holy spirit and word, (I mean without evidently true repentance) and, in such a case by permission of the scriptures, esteem hypocrites as well as the truly penitent, and greet them as brethren. Or that the community may also proclaim the grace, mercy and peace of God and eternal life by virtue and truth of scripture to those though they are under His displeasure, curse, wrath and punishment of eternal death, on account of their bloody and wicked deeds. Or that the abominations or sins committed, do not bring the sinner to death as soon as exclusion from the community. Or that the spirit of grace with a sincere faith and true repentance, which avail with God, does not assure the transgressor of the promise of life, more than the outward conversation in the community, &c. If he can convince us of all this, we desire then cordially to follow him, and change and renounce our our views.

But if this cannot be done, as it never can be, I therefore entreat all who are concerned, that they would not liken themselves unto vain comforts and false prophets, (Jer. 23,) who strengthen the hands of the wicked, and daub the wall with untempered mortar, (Ezek. 13,) and teach peace, peace, where there is no peace, (Jer. 8,) but that they would leave the sentence of the Lord which proceeded from his divine righteousness, unbroken ; and tear the deceptive bolsters and pillows from under the heads of the ungodly, and keep clean and pure Christ's holy community as much as in them lies, that they may build upon a sure foundation, and direct the impenitent, sensual sinners to repentance, as heard. Deal faithfully, reflect upon these things and learn wisdom.

VI. *Of secret sinners, who are again inwardly admonished of the Holy Ghost and are sincerely and truly converted.*

The full desire of my heart is, that each one would so fear and know God as to say in spirit and truth with David : Whither shall I go from thy Spirit ? Or whither shall I flee from thy presence ? If I ascend up into heaven, thou art there ; if I make my bed in hell, behold, thou art there ; if I take the wings of the morning, and dwell in the uttermost parts of the sea, even there shall thy hand lead me, and thy right hand shall hold me ; if I say : Surely the darkness shall cover me ; even the night shall be light about me ; yea, the darkness hideth not from thee ; but the night shineth as the day ; the darkness and the light are both alike unto thee ; for thou hast possessed my reins ; thou hast covered me in my mother's womb. (Ps. 139.) And with Isaiah : Wo unto them that seek deep to hide their counsel from the Lord, and their works are in the dark, and they say : Who seeth us ? And who knoweth us ? (Isa. 29.) Observe this denunciation, " Wo to them," &c.

Chosen brethren, take heed ; none under the canopy of heaven, can so conceal himself that he cannot be seen by the flaming eyes of the Lord, or not be found by the avenging hand of His wrath in his wickedness. Yea, the least thought is not concealed in our hearts which is not open to the eyes of the Lord. (Heb. 4.) I, therefore, warn every one in general, that you with all your powers watch against sin, whether secret or open ; if sin is not sincerely repented of, your portion will be eternal death. Let all the impenitent and heedless sinners reflect upon this, (Rom. 1 ; 1 Cor. 6 ; Rev. 21.)

This I write to all beloved brethren as a christian warning, that you may fear the Lord's sentence, both openly and privately, and dread sin. Though we may not be reproved or seen of men here, still we cannot escape the eyes and punishment of God ! Ah ! that we all understood this.

However, should it ever happen that any one should sin against God in private, (from which may all his power preserve us,) and should the spirit of grace, which works repentance, again operate upon his heart, and cause genuine repentance, of which we have not to judge; for it is a matter between him and God. And since it is evident that we do not seek our righteousness and salvation, the remission of our sins, satisfaction, reconciliation and eternal life in or through Excommunication, but alone in Christ's righteousness, intercession, merits, death and blood. There are but two objects and ends why the Ban is commanded in the scriptures, which can have no reference to such an one. Because, in the first place, his sins are private; hence no offence can follow. And secondly, because he is in deep contrition and is penitent in life. Therefore, he has no need then of being brought to repentance. Nor are we any where commanded of Christ to put him to open shame before the community. Reflect upon these things.

VII. *What is the true sense of the passage in Matthew* xviii. *where Christ says : If thy brother shall trespass against thee, &c.*

Our only and eternal high priest, Jesus Christ, undoubtedly knew our weak and feeble nature, (that if we are not watchful) we would often fall into errors towards our neighbor, and therefore does he teach and say : *If thy brother trespass against thee, go and tell him his fault between thee and him alone : If he shall hear thee, thou hast gained thy brother ; but if he will not hear thee, then take with thee one or two more, that in the mouth of two or three witnesses every word may be established ; and if he will neglect to hear them, tell it unto the church, but if he neglect to hear the church, let him be to thee as an heathen and a publican, -&c.* Whereupon Peter asked him : How oft shall my brother sin against me, and I forgive him— till seven times ? Christ answered : *I say not unto thee, until seven times ; but, until seventy times seven.* (Matt. 18 ; Luke 17.)

It is evident that these words of Christ teach, in the first place, that if any one should err or sin against his brother through negligence, infirmity, inconsiderateness, inexperience, or ignorance, that he should not, therefore, hate him in his heart ; nor conceal or connive at his transgression ; but out of true brotherly love admonish and reprove him, lest his brother fall into greater errors and perish ; but by this means reclaim him, and, as Moses says, not make himself guilty or his sins. (Lev. 19.) It is the nature and disposition of Christians not to hate any on account of his infirmities, but they seek with all their heart how they may lead such an one in the true way of love by instructing him ; for a true Christian knows nothing of hatred. (James 3, 4.)

In the second place ; those words teach us that he who has transgressed should receive the admonition of his brother in love and be again cordially reconciled; as he teaches at another place, and says : *Therefore, if thou bring thy gift to the altar, and there rememberest that thy brother hath aught against thee ; leave there thy gift before the altar, and go thy way ; first be reconciled to thy brother.* (Matt. 5.) Here it is also the nature and disposition of the anointed, those who are born of the holy seed of divine love, that if they trespass against a brother, they have neither peace nor rest of conscience till they are again fully reconciled in Christ Jesus, and that without hypocrisy. For they are a seed and generation of peace, children of love, who manifest their Christianity in full power ; and testify it by deeds that they know God. But those who do not so, have Christ's word to judge them. Although the first transgression may at times not be of itself a sin unto death ; but will after some time make him sensual if he has no peculiar regard to love, that he will have to endure severe punishment on account of his wickedness. For it is more than clear that he, who despises his brother, rejects the affectionate admonition, acts against Christian charity, despises the community of God, rejects the word of the Lord, and that he would rather continue unreproved in his transgression, through his immoveable stubbornness, rather walk in the crooked paths of the unrighteous ; yea, sooner forsake Christ's kingdom and people, than subdue his stubborn, proud flesh, and again be reconciled in love, according to the word of the Lord, with his brother against whom he transgressed. Paul rightly observes : That to be carnally minded is death. (Rom. 8.) Observe this.

In the third place ; if the transgressing brother will sincerely receive, in love the brotherly admonition of his offended brother, and is humbly reconciled, and afterwards ceases transgressing, then in that case he will no more remember, but cordially forgive him, although he may have often sinned against him. Even as God for Jesus' sake, forgives all our sins ; so must we also forgive our neighbor all his transgressions in Christ, which he has committed against us. (Col. 3 ; Eph. 4.) And we dare not under any circumstances indulge in hatred or vengeance against him, though he should never reform. We have a true example in Christ, and Stephen his witness. (Luke 23 ; Acts 7.) And it is also the nature and disposition of all anointed, who are born of God that they possess their souls in peace and patience, they keep pure and uncorrupted their conscience ;

their prayer unhindered; their love perfect sound and true; their minds firm and unwavering, no matter how we behave towards them.

From all of which it is more than clear that these three several admonitions of which Christ speaks, are to take place first between him and you alone; secondly before witnesses and then, thirdly, before the church, and do not extend to all offensive sensual sinners, over whom the eternal sentence of death is already pronounced; but it has reference only to the shortcomings between brother and brother, and that for the following seven *Reasons.*

First, he says; *If thy brother trespass against* THEE, observe what he says: AGAINST THEE—not: AGAINST GOD. For all the sins he commits *against you,* you may forgive him, so far as respects *you;* but not as it respects *God.* (1 Sam. 2.)

Secondly, he says: *Tell him his fault between* THEE *and* HIM *alone.* Observe *between* THEE *and* HIM *alone.* (1 Cor. 5; 2 Cor. 13.) And I trust that all who understand the holy word will assent that an open transgression or sin, requires no private admonition, but is to be publicly reproved.

Thirdly, he says: *That in the mouth of two or three witnesses every word may be established.* Observe, that he says: *Two* or *three.* And that an open transgression requires no witness, but is itself its own accuser and witness, is clear as the meridian sun.

Fourthly, he says: *Then tell it unto the church,* Observe, *unto the church.* And for us to tell an open, well known disgrace to them, which is already known, is quite useless—to this all must assent who have understanding.

Fifthly, he also says in Luke 17: *And if he trespass against thee seven times in a day.* Observe, he says: *Against thee.* And that any one should sin seven times a day, much less seventy times seven a day, against his brother, (which no true Christian will do) much less against God.

Sixthly, that he says: *And seven times in a day, turn again to thee saying, I repent.* Observe, he says: *Turn to thee seven times in a day.* And my opinion is that if any one were to come to us; but two or three times in a year, much less daily, whenever he rumaged our chest, stole our purse, or disgraced our wife, daughter or maid; and say. "*Ah, brother I repent!*" How soon would he not hear that he is a desperate rogue and an ungodly knave. Again, I say, observe this.

Seventhly, that he says: THOU *shalt forgive* HIM. Observe, he says: THOU *shalt forgive* HIM. And the scriptures plainly teach that none can forgive sins (these are the ten thousand talents which were owing to the king), but God alone. (Matt 9;

Mark 2; Luke 5, 7.) And that we alone can pay the hundred pence which we owe our brother, as the Lord teaches in the parable with all plainness. (Matt. 18.)

Behold, in this sense the holy scriptures are salutary to us, and proceed in its order and thus direct to deal when one brother trespass against another to admonish him three times. (Matt. 18.) And that we are to admonish a heretic once or twice, (Tit. 3.) And an open offensive sensual sinner, who is already condemned by the word, is not all to be admonished. (1 Cor. 5; 2 Cor. 13.)

Do impartially reflect upon what the scriptures say, without hypocrisy and in love.

VIII. *That we are not to pervert the truth with David's sin, repentance and remission ; but have to understand it rightly according to scripture.*

It is evident that abominable, sensual sins, such as fornication and adultery and the like, generally arise from blindness of heart; that they are committed presumptuously, are the result of unclean, inflamed passions and sensual lusts ; notwithstanding the beginning of them may have taken their rise apparently from infirmity. Of this we have a true case in David, although he was a man after God's own heart, (1 Sam. 17,) and by virtue of his faith slew the giant Goliah, (whom all Israel dreaded,) and rescued the lamb from the jaws of lions and bears, still he was so led captive in his flesh by the sight of his eyes that he sinned greatly ; for as soon as he consented sin was committed, and his heart (which was before a temple of the Holy Ghost,) was so blinded and bewitched, that he, without any dread, fell into one deadly sin and wickedness after 'another ; yea, as appears, he never thought of the Lord who saved him from so many dangers, and called him to such distinguished honor, and endowed him with such a precious spirit. For when it was told him of Bathsheba, that she was with child to him, he sought to hide this flagrant act ; had Urias called from the field and pretended as if he wished to consult him in relation to the war, admonished him twice ; that he should go into his house : why he did so is well understood. Afterwards he invited him to feast, pretending as if he was sincere, so that he might make him drunk, and go in unto his wife and cover David's shame. But when he failed in all this, he gave this truly valiant man an ungodly, treacherous letter, that Joab should place him in such a point where the danger of being killed was greatest, so that he might be slain.

Behold, thus you see how one wicked act engendered another when he consented to the lusts of the eyes, and gave place to sin. He was blinded to such a degree in his inflamed flesh, and was so deeply involved in sin, that, according to the rigor of the law, (had he not himself wielded the sceptre,) he would have been two-fold guilty of the Ban or curse of death; first, because he was an adulterer; secondly, because he was guilty of innocent blood.

He continued in such abominations till the prophet came to him, and through a parable, so wisely reproved him that he pronounced his own sentence as worthy of death. When he heard the word of the prophet who appealed powerfully to his heart, he was moved, sought for grace, and without delay turned to God with a broken heart, and bitterly wept over his great sin, and confessed to the Lord that he had sinned: prayed and sighed painfully. O God! said he, be merciful unto me according to thy loving kindness, according to the multitude of thy tender mercies, blot out my transgressions; wash me thoroughly from mine iniquity, and cleanse me from sin. Create in me a clean heart, O God, and renew a right spirit within me: cast me not away from thy presence; and take not thy Holy Spirit from me, &c. (Ps. 51.) On account of which he was again comforted of the prophet, who told him: The Lord hath put away thy sin; thou shalt not die. Nevertheless, he had to endure a severe punishment on account of it: For, said Nathan, therefore, shall the sword never depart from thy house; because thou hast despised me—the Lord said, behold, I will raise up evil against thee out of thine own house, and I will take thy wives before thine eyes, and give them unto thy neighbor, and he shall lie with thy wives in the sight of this sun; because thou didst despise me. Observe, he says: *Because thou didst despise me.* (2 Sam. 12.)

And behold, thus David's wantonness resulted in greatly despising God, and it was a grievous sin unto him. True are the words of James: *Then when lust hath conceived, it bringeth forth sin, and sin when it hath finished, bringeth forth death.* (James 1.)

Thus it is in the new state of things in Christ, for since we are not to punish the abominable, sensual transgressors with fire, stone or sword as Israel did of old, but only by excommunication, as is well known to all who are taught of God; and thus it behooves us to consign those with their wicked deeds, where the scriptures direct them, namely, into death, and to the wrath of God, as holy Nathan did blood-guilty and adulterous David. And they will then, under such a dread, severe sentence, (which, according to the scripture is pronounced upon them by exclusion in true love) by the grace of God, go within their hearts, and are provoked, like penitent David, to true repentance ; yea, that we may evidently see by all their words, works, and whole life in truth, that the gracious Father has again received and endowed them with his spirit, and pardoned their sins ; then, and not till then, (understand well what I say,) have we the same word of promise whereby we can again comfort them and proclaim to them the grace of the Lord, namely : *The Lord hath put away thy sin, thou shalt not die, thy sins are pardoned, go and sin no more ;* and the like consolation.

And thus it becomes us rightly to divide the scriptures, that we do not make David's sin, repentance and remission as an example of encouragement to the blind world, that we do not esteem them our brethren who are accursed of God, without giving full evidence of their repentance and reformation, so that the community may be fully satisfied. For we must not build upon uncertainties, and comfort in vain, but like Nathan comfort when we see true repentance, if we would not wish to flatter sinners with lies, and derogate from the judgment of God as heard.

IX. *Of Peter's inconsiderate backsliding, and immediate recovery.*

Dearly beloved brethren, beware, even as we have shown and explained to you, that the abominable, sensual sins generally arise from the inflamed passions of the flesh ; and so it can happen that sins may be committed through infirmities. Of this we have a true example in Peter ; for when the Lord said to him : Simon, Simon, behold satan hath desired to have thee, that he may sift thee as wheat : but I have prayed for thee, that thy faith fail not ; and when thou art converted, strengthen thy brethren. To which he replied with much assurance : If all will leave thee, I will not, Lord, I am ready to go with thee, both into prison and to death. (Matt. 26 ; Mark 14 ; Luke 22.)

Peter was for venturing all with his master, as he said ; but as soon as he stood alone, he could not endure a single question put to him by a maid ; he openly denied Christ, though the evening previous he said that he would die with him. Yea, he was so alarmed and frightened that he began to curse, and swore that he did not know Christ ; (Matt. 26 ; Mark 14 ; Luke 22 ; John 18.)

O God ! there lay the upright, bold Peter, the firm rock, broken. Although he had been taught of the heavenly Father and honored by Christ, the beloved son of God, with the promise of the keys of the kingdom of heaven, (Matt. 16,) nevertheless, he could not endure but such a faint blow. Behold, thus man is nothing, poor, miserable, sick and impotent, (especially in so great need,) if he is not strengthened by the spirit of God. But what was it? Peter had to learn to know what that man is, who depends upon his own strength, and not in the full fear of God, upon Christ and his grace. Besides he learned how to be compassionate and merciful towards his poor, fallen brother, who would again be heartily converted and rise without hypocrisy from his fall.

It appears to me that this may justly be called an unexpectedly precipitate error in Peter. For he entertained not a single thought before, that he would deny his Lord and Savior. And he also rose in the very hour, went out and wept bitterly, (Luke 22,) and on the third day he was again comforted with the gospel by the holy angels of the Lord, (Mark 16.)

Observe, brethren, how Paul teaches : Brethren, if a man be *overtaken*, (observe, he says overtaken) in a fault, ye which are *spiritual*, restore such an one in the *spirit of meekness;* considering *thyself*, lest *thou be also tempted.* (Gal. 6.)

Chosen brethren in the Lord, I would then most affectionately entreat you by the words of Paul and the fall of Peter, and admonish you faithfully in Christ Jesus, that you would by all means, discriminate, by the spirit of wisdom, between simple backsliding and continuing in *that state.* For if any one continues in a sin (upon which eternal death depends) he is already condemned by the scriptures, (Rom. 1 ; Gal. 5 ; Eph. 5 ; 2 Thess. 1 ; Rev. 21.) But if any one falls into it unwarily, of him the prophet says : Shall they fall and not arise ? (Jer. 8.) And as Paul says : Restore such an one. It is, therefore, just and right that we are truly circumspect ; that we do not depress too much a poor, broken-hearted sinner, who would willingly be restored and rescued from his deplorable condition ; but we must, in christian meekness, tender him the hand of charity, lift up and help him to bear his burden as much as in us is, and as far as our conscience and the word of God permit. Ah ! do take heed, be not too rash in such a case, lest you may also be tempted or overcome, as Paul says. Let holy Peter be an admonition to you, in order that you will not lose yourselves in your proud minds. For if a man thinks himself to be something when he is nothing, he deceiveth himself. (Gal. 6.) In short : Let him that thinketh he standeth, take heed lest he fall. (1 Cor. 10.) For the snares are more numerous than we are aware ; those who would wish to escape them must be dead to sin, regenerated and true christians, be constant in prayer, be circumspect, watch assiduously, and must be led and influenced by the Holy Ghost, else they will soon be in the snare of death. Ah ! let us reflect upon this.

Let every one examine himself fully, whether he has not sinned before God since his conversion, and became a faulty vessel. He that may think he is free, let him cast the first stone. But he that does not find himself altogether free, let him with Peter, strengthen his weak brother, who, perhaps, has not sinned half so heinously.

Since then, it is manifest, that to *fall*, and to *continue* in that condition, and presumptuously to sin, are different; therefore, will I leave such sins, on account of which the people of the Lord are grieved, (if such should be the case) to the spirit, unction, deliberation, fear of God and love of the community, to look into with wisdom and understanding. If they deem it deserving excommunication, let them judge as the scriptures teach. If they consider it not in that light, but only as a sin, unwarily committed, that they then restore the sinner or transgressor, with a spirit of meekness and love. This is my admonition with all the faithful apostles, fathers, teachers and our predecessor, the apostle Paul, to all the pious. These words are full of power and spirit: *Considering thyself, lest thou also be tempted.* (Gal. 6.)

X. *How we should understand, according to the scriptures, the saying of James: If any of you do err from the truth, &c.* (James 5.)

In the first place, the rational law of nature teaches us, that if one sees his neighbor's house or goods on fire, or sees his neighbor sick, or his body, his wife, his children or his cattle needing assistance, he must willingly render him aid, and extend his hand to his neighbor, in time of need.

Again, Moses says: When one sees his brother's ox or his sheep go astray, he shall not hide himself from them, but shall bring them again to him. (Exod. 23; Deut. 22.)

Thirdly, Christ says: What man of you have a hundred sheep, if he loose one of them, doth not leave the ninety and nine in the wilderness, and go after that which is lost till he find it. (Matt. 18; Luke 15.)

Observe then, how the law of nature, of Moses and of Christ, teaches us such great love and discretion not towards men alone, but towards our temporal goods, and to our creatures, so it is proper that we, who are born of the holy seed of love, should seek for the souls of our neighbor, whose feet we see upon the way of sin, which leads to death. Thus James says: Brethren, if any of you do err from the truth and one convert him, let him know that he which converteth a sinner from the error of his way, shall save a soul from death and shall hide a multitude of sins. (James 5.)

Here we would entreat all pious hearts, for Jesus' sake, that they would make a distinction between those who ignorantly err, and those who willingly go in the way of death, in order that the word of James be not expounded so as to become a false comfort and support, to wanton and benighted sinners; for it is clear, that they are already judged to death by the scriptures, as we frequently have observed; but when any of our Father's little ones, Christ's sheep (Matt. 18) err, and begin to turn their ears to false doctrine, which is adorned with fair words, who suffer themselves to be led from the truth, and begin to set their feet upon the broad way, and bow their hearts, again to covetousness, pride, haughtiness, &c. entertain inordinate affections for the property of their neighbors, become cold and weak in their faith, dislike the truth and err grievously; yet suppose that they go upon the right way—such erring ones, we should not suffer to be lost, but should seek them with all our power and might, not with one or two admonitions only, as is done with heretics, (Tit. 3) nor but three times, as is the case with a dissension between brother and brother, (Matt. 18) but as often as the Lord gives spirit and grace, till they again conform in all things to the truth, depart from their errors, and enter upon the right way, or till they become as ravening, biting dogs or unclean swine. Yes, my brethren, whoever follows a poor, erring sinner, with the truth, and turns him from the way of error, and brings him back to Christ's fold rescues his soul from death, and covers a multitude of sins. From whom are they covered? From me nor from God? Not from men, but from God; for it is impossible to hide from men that which they see, and which happens before them; as open adultery, murder, idolatry, drunkenness, &c. Aaron's idolatry with the golden calf, David's misconduct with Uriah and Bathsheba, and Peter's denial are examples. For though they repented, and their sins were covered from the sight of God, yet were they set forth to the whole world as admonitions and warnings, and as examples of his grace over all who truly repent; (Exod. 32; Deut. 9; 2 Sam. 11, 12; Matt. 26; Mark 14; Luke 22; John 18) of this covering of sin David spake: Blessed is he whose transgression is forgiven, whose sin is covered. Blessed is the man to whom the Lord imputeth not iniquity. (Ps. 32.)

I will now leave to the godly for reflection, whether or not these words of James as here expounded, are not salutary; for those worthy of exclusion would be excluded, the erring be sought, love would exert its full power, the penitent would be rescued from death. Both their open and secret sins would be covered before God, and all would proceed according to the scriptures. In true love observe what is the mind of the holy word.

XI. *How the latter part of the twelfth, and the beginning*

of the thirteenth chapter of the second epistle to the Corinthians, are to be understood.

We find by Paul's epistle to the Corinthians, that there were many parties and sects among that people. Some boasted that they were of Cephas, others of Paul, and others again, of Apollo. On this account, Paul reproved them in love, and admonished them to be one in Christ. (1 Cor. 1, 3.) He writes also in the eleventh chapter of the same epistle: When ye come together in the church, I hear that there be divisions among you, and I partly believe it, for there must be also heresies among you, that they which are approved may be made manifest among you. There were also some among you who said there was no resurrection, (1 Cor. 15,) therefore, he also feared (2 Cor. 12) if he came, that he would not find them as he desired, lest more dissension than union, more malice than love, more wrath than meekness, more strife than peace, more whispering than rebuking of wickedness, more pride than humility, more tumult than quiet, should be found among many. Such is commonly the condition where the high and proud of heart, who neither know nor love the peaceful, humble spirit of Christ, move in high esteem, and attain authority over the plain, simple people. They regard the adornment of words more than spirit and power. This I write in upright, undissembled love, without regard to party. God grant us grace to enable us to perceive it.

Again, we find that the impenitent, self-seekers, covetous and contentious, (1 Cor. 6) incontinent, unchaste, &c. (2 Cor. 12) were among them. Therefore he feared that when he came, he should have great sorrow on account of those who repented not of their iniquity. For it is manifest that lewdness at that time among the gentiles, was so common that the holy apostles admonished and counselled the brethren among the heathen, in a common counsel: as may be seen from Acts 15; Rom. 1; 1 Cor. 5, 6, 7; Gal. 5; Eph. 5; Col. 3; 1 Thes. 4.

Some so lightly regarded the lewdness and dissensions of the time, that they looked not upon apostolic doctrine of excommunication as sincere. This may be seen from Paul's own words, to wit: Ye are puffed up, &c. (1 Cor. 5.)

Through their heedless disobedience, they permitted the good and evil to exist among them, so that the faithful man of God upbraided them sharply, saying: This is the third time I am coming to you. In the mouth of two or three witnesses shall all things be established. I told you before, and foretell you as if I were present, the second time; and being absent now, I write to them which heretofore have sinned, and to all others, that if I come again, I will not spare. (2 Cor. 13.) These hard words of Paul testify clearly that in that time, although such wicked persons were held in communion, yet they did not regard his writings concerning the Ban; for it is plain if the historian rightly testifies, that some years had passed away before Paul made his last journey to them, and it is against all scripture and reason to suppose that they, in the mean time, admitted these persons with Paul's consent. It is plain and manifest that he rebuked all iniquity both with word and writing, (Cor. 5,) and directed to the Ban, as had been related, yet the foul leaven which was against the holy divine word, and which disgraced the church, they did not put away. He wrote and expressed his meaning by these words, that all those who oftentimes had sinned and had not repented, and those who sinned more recently, that if he would come the second time, that if he should find one or the other, testified to by two or three witnesses that they have been guilty of ungodliness, that he would not then spare him. (2 Cor. 13.) Observe this.

It is also manifest that he did not write this rebuke privately to this one or that one, but he wrote openly to a whole church, in a common epistle, that the disobedient might be rebuked, as we ourselves (unworthy) at times write, and teach the word of the Lord. There is not a syllable which tells us to admonish such one twice or thrice, but to reprove them in round terms, that if he came, that he would make known to them their merited punishment. His words are firm and immovable: That we shall not eat, or have fellowship with fornicators, &c. O! reflect upon what the scriptures say. (1 Cor. 5.)

XII. *It is our duty to pass Christ's sentence and judgment without blame according to the scriptures, and to make use of his keys in a proper manner.* •

Chosen brethren in the Lord, forasmuch, then, as I have seen in my day much ignorance and misapprehension displayed by many in regard to this point, some of whom, (in my humble opinion) were too rigorous and severe, while others were too lenient and remiss, in consequence of which some of our members have been affected, alas! with no little sorrow. And as I have now faithfully explained the true apostolic Excommunication in pure, unadulterated love without partiality, therefore, I am further impelled by the same love to offer a few remarks upon the keys and their appertinent use, (inasmuch as they pertain to the excommunication) so that no one, misled by ignorance, may with anti-christ presumptuously place himself in Christ's seat, nor follow and execute his own judgment, design and resolution, but those of Christ, his Lord, and the doctrine, ordinance and commandment of the holy apostles, without any regard to the flesh, party, or self-wisdom, lest he should reject him whom God saves by his grace, and retain him whom he in his righteousness rejects; for, to him alone pertains the right of binding and loosing, as we shall hear more fully in the sequel. Therefore, consider our advice.

It is to be observed, in the first place, that there are two heavenly keys, namely, the key of binding, and the key of loosing; even as the Lord said to Peter: *I will give thee the key of the kingdom of heaven: and whatsoever thou shalt bind on earth, shall be bound in heaven; and whatsoever thou shalt loose on earth, shall be loosed in heaven.* (Matt. 16.) At another time, and after his resurrection from the dead, he spoke in a similar manner to his disciples: *Rejoice ye the Holy Ghost. Whosoever sins ye remit, they are remitted unto them; and whosoever sins ye retain, they are retained.* (John 20.)

In the second place, we must observe that the key of binding is nothing else than the word of God's righteousness, the directing, demanding, constraining, terrifying and condemning law of the Lord, by and through which all are locked up under the curse, sin, death and the wrath of God, who do not by faith receive Christ, the only and eternal means of grace, hear his voice, and follow and obey his will. (Acts 4; Mark 16; John 3.)

Again: On the other hand, the key of loosing is the abundantly cheering and delightful word of grace, the pardoning, consoling and unbinding gospel of peace, by and through which all those are delivered from the curse, sin, death and the wrath of God, who, with regenerated, new, converted, voluntary, rejoicing and believing hearts, receive Christ in power and with a firm confidence in his innocent blood and death, fear, love, hear, follow and obey him, (Deut. 18; Acts 3, 7; Mark 16; John 3, 6, 7,) and many other chapters.

In the third place, it is to be observed that this binding key of Christ is given to his ministers and people for this purpose, namely, that by and through it they shall, in the power of the Spirit, represent unto all earthly, carnal, obdurate and impenitent persons, their great sins, unrighteousness, blindness and wickedness, together with God's righteous wrath, judgment, punishment, hell and everlasting death, and thus render them contrite, dismayed, humble, broken, penitent, dejected and sorrowful of heart before God, and little in their own eyes. Wherefore, it is compared in its power and virtues to the rod of the oppressor, (Isa. 9,) a hard hammer, (Jer. 23,) the north wind, (Cant. 4,) a sorrowful singing, (Matt. 1,) and sharp detergent wine. (Luke 10.)

Again: On the contrary, the key of loosing is given to the

end that with it the ministers and people of God may direct such contrite, troubled, dejected, sorrowful and broken hearts, as aforementioned, which are enabled, by the first key, to feel and see the deep, mortal wounds, their great defects and the profound fascination in which they were held, to the spiritual, brazen serpent, (Num. 21; John 3,) to the throne of grace, (Rom. 3,) to the open fountain of David, (Zach. 13,) to the merciful, compassionate high priest, our only and eternal offering of reconciliation, Christ Jesus, (Heb. 4, 5, 6, 7, 8, 9, 10, 12,) and thus heal their dangerous, malignant and deadly abscesses, stripes and the venomous wound of the infernal serpent. It is, therefore, likened in strength and virtues to the cheering olive-branch of Noah's dove, (Gen. 8,) the balm of Gilead, (Jer. 8,) the voice of truth, (Cant. 3,) the south wind, (Cant. 4,) the joyful pipe, (Matt. 11,) and sweet, soothing oil. (Luke 10; James 5.)

In the fourth place, it must be observed that these keys are given us from heaven, by him who created heaven, earth and the sea with the fulness thereof, the Almighty Father's eternal power, word and wisdom, (John 1; Col. 1; Heb. 1,) the King of all glory, our only and eternal Redeemer, Intercessor, Bridegroom, Prophet and Teacher, Christ Jesus. (Matt. 16; John 20.) We may, therefore, with the greatest propriety, take heed in this part of the Ban, with fear and trembling, that we do not conduct ourselves in it as if under the influence of flesh and blood, hatred or love, favor or disfavor, enmity or friendship, strife, dissension or partiality; but that with a good and upright conscience, without respect of persons, we execute it aright in the perfect fear of God as the proper, earnest, and heavenly command, word, and will of our Saviour. For without doubt they are precious keys since they are given us from heaven, as a present from so illustrious a friend. Ah! suffer yourselves to be told.

In the fifth place, it is to be observed that these keys are given to, and bestowed upon none but those who are anointed of the Holy Ghost, even as Christ says: Receive ye the Holy Ghost, &c. (John 20.) From this it is more than evident that they must be a believing, true, penitent, sober, chaste, humble, upright, friendly, obedient, devout, peaceful, and spiritual people; (observe) a people dead unto sin, a regenerated people, who sit with the apostles in the seat of righteousness, (Matt. 19) and pronounce with them the Lord's righteous judgment against all stiff-necked, ungodly sinners, and teach, admonish, chastise, punish, and, in real power, judge or bind with the Lord's word and spirit, the unbelieving, impenitent, earthly-minded, drunken, adulterous, lecherous, unchaste, proud, haughty unrighteous, perverse, disobedient, quarrelsome, sensual sinners. For it is more than evident that a carnal man cannot understand the things of the spirit of God; but they that are spiritual examine all things aright, judge all things aright, yet they themselves are judged of no man. (1 Cor. 2.) Yes, my brethren, it is utterly impossible for one carnal-minded man, or for one quarrelsome person, to teach, instruct or chasten another rightly through the spirit of Christ, or in the power of his word rightly to separate him from his community according to the will of God. For their fruits plainly testify that they are both one as well as the other, impenitent, destitute of the spirit, nature, and disposition of Christ, and subject to death and the curse.

Therefore, fear God, and know how or what you judge. If a man was to put the law in force against a person obnoxious to excommunication, as a whoremonger, drunkard, or one guilty of any other carnal abominations, while he himself was full of hatred, avaricious, proud, haughty, uplifted, ambitious, choleric, unchaste, lying quarrelsome, impure, envious or false hearted, secretly committing evil, he does nothing else according to Pauls doctrine, than pass judgment upon his own soul, for he says: Thou art inexcusable, *O man whosoever thou art that judgest: for wherein thou judgest another thou condemnest thyself.* (Rom. 2.)

I therefore, counsel and admonish all the pious generally, who sit in judgment upon a sinner that is to be excommunicated, that they previously examine well their own conscience, heart and mind, and see whether or not they have the spirit of Christ, whether or not they sit in the apostles' seat, and also whether they do it out of pure fear of God, in obedience to his word, and out of sincere love to the brethren or out of flesh and blood through the hypocrisy, to the will of men. For if they have not the spirit of Christ, do not sit in the apostles' seat and carry the keys of heaven, their judgment can not be of God, and will tear down more than build up. It is even in reality nothing but a sore judgment against their own souls. But if they have the spirit of Christ, sit in the apostles' seat and make use of the keys of heaven, their judgment will doubtless be righteous, will agree as the judgment of Christ, and they will by no means make themselves guilty in passing judgment against the transgressor. Those who are born of Christ, may judge what I advance.

In the sixth place, it is to be observed that these keys must not be made use of except in the name of Him who committed them to us, and by his power, that is with his spirit and word, (1 Cor. 5,) for He alone is the king and prince of his community, the shepherd, teacher and master of our souls, before whose sceptre we must all bow, and hear his voice. (Deut. 18; Acts 3, 7; John 3, 10,) if we would wish to be saved, as has been heard.

Since then he is both the ruler and the giver of this, and both the binding and loosing are in his hand, and must therefore be done in his name with his spirit and word alone, as related, we may well take heed lest through our profaneness, inclination or foolish purpose, we loose those whom he himself has bound in heaven, or bind those whom he himself has loosed in heaven even as the sin of perdition and the man of sin together with all his deceiving and impure prophets have done for thousands of years, O God!

As far as concerns the key of binding of this evangelic Ban, it is more than clear that when an open fornicator or adulterer is convinced by two or three witnesses, (2 Cor, 13,) or an abuser of himself with mankind, or an idolator, or a drunkard, or envied, or a perverse self-willed disputer, or an impenitent, froward, lazy, a fastidious idle, glutton, or a blasphemer, thief, robber or murderer, &c., is brought before the community, they have the judging word of the scriptures, by which they may separate and exclude him, and announce to him by the spirit of Christ, that he is no longer a member of Christ's body, has no more promise, but that he shall endure everlasting death, and fail of the kingdom of grace: In short that his final part and lot (unless he sincerly repents) shall be the burning lake of fire, hell and the devil. (Matt. 3, 25; Rom. 1; 1 Cor. 6; Gal. 5; Eph. 5; 2 Thess. 1; Rev. 21, 22.) For his works show plainly that he is of the wicked one. (John 8; 1 John 3.)

Behold, such are those over whom the first key has power. For God's righteous judgment and his firm binding, take hold of them, since they again forsake Christ, despise his holy word and covenant, live according to the flesh, stir up strife and dissension, break the bond of love, separate the pious, disquiet those of a gentle, peaceable disposition, introduce and establish offences and slanderers, as the evident fact has frequently taught and as is known to many others, alas! as well as to myself. Ah me! what a severe stroke he receives who is bound by God's people with this dreadful key and punished by his righteous spirit with this dreadful curse. O Father grant them thy grace.

The same thing applies to the key of loosing in this use of the Ban. For if a poor, proscribed sinner humble himself again before his God, heart broken and penitent, groans and weeps bitterly, experiences heartfelt sorrow for his sins and an earnest longing for the truth, hates perverse paths of the ungodly and walks again in the path of the pious. In short, conducts himself so in his whole life, that we cannot perceive any thing in him but that the Lord's spirit has again anointed him, and received him into his grace, and would have him included in the number of the Lord's people; they have then the cheering word of promise, by which they may again bring him to the altar of the Lord, sprinkle him with the spiritual keys of God, announce to him Christ's grace, and receive him again as a beloved brother in Christ Jesus and greet him with the salutation of his holy peace. For, says the prophet: the Lord has no pleasure in the death of the sinner, but that he repent and live. (Ezek. 8.)

Forasmuch as it is manifest and established that Jesus Christ alone has the key of David (Isa. 22; Rev. 3) who unlocks heaven for the true penitent, unties the knot of unrighteousness loosen and forgives and remits their sins. And again, it is he who closes heaven against the impenitent, carnal sinners, binds them under his judgment and retains their sins, and we are nothing more than heralds, ministers and messengers in his name, and can make it neither longer nor shorter, narrower nor wider than taught us by his spirit, and commanded us in his word, as heard. Lo also is it thereby more than evident, that they greatly err, who in the pride of their ignorance suffer themselves to think that they have power to retain or remit any man's sins, or who with perverse, inconsiderate minds dare separate or excommunicate any one out of carnal motives, hatred or bitterness, and not purely and solely through the spirit and word of Christ; or on the other hand, retain him through natural affection, friendship or partiality, contrary to the word of God and comfort him at a venture in his sins, winking at them; for with such after the example of the false prophets, they strengthen the hands of the ungodly since they retain them, appear to adjudge their life, though without true repentance they shall not live. (Ezek. 13.) Ah! brethren beware.

I would, therefore, brethren and sisters, in the love of Christ, have you all faithfully admonished in God, that no one attempt in this weighty, important and spiritual matter, to act higher or lower, severer or milder than the word and spirit require, whether it be with the binding of the first key in righteousness unto eternal death, or with the loosing of the second key in grace unto eternal life; lest, by passing an unscriptural judgment, he offend against God and his neighbor, and so be constrained to undergo the punishment of this pride, along with the angel of the bottomless pit. Observe this!

Ah! most beloved brethren, to what an amazing extent in my opinion is that man taught of God, who is able in this thing so to keep the true royal highway, that he can properly employ the intrusted keys in devout, heavenly wisdom, and correctly pass and impose his Lord's judgment with a sure, sealed conscience in true apostolic measure, to the edification of all the pious. Let all who are born of God, who are impartial and pure in heart, reflect, with the unction of their spirit, upon the grounds of my writing and admonition.

CONCLUSION AND EXHORTATION TO ALL THE PIOUS.

BELOVED brethren, with much trouble, pains and anxiety, I have now, in the infirmity of my declining years, added another small gift to the Lord's treasury, not of the price of a dog, nor of the hire of a harlot, which was forbidden to Israel; but of the abundant benediction of my God, namely, from the settled principles of his truth. Though it is not to be compared in value or worth with the gold, silver, metal, silk, or precious stones of the offering, yet, if it be reckoned with the rams' skins, goats' hair, and shittim wood, I have attained my wish. For my prayer and desire before God and his community, is, that the living building of the heavenly tabernacles may advance with the greatest speed to the attainment of their intended splendor and magnificence. For this cause, I have suffered not a little hardship, affliction, sadness, poverty and reproach, so that I hope I may boast in my weakness with all the pious of God, apostles and prophets, nay, with Christ Jesus himself, that the zeal of the Lord's house hath eaten me up. (Ps. 69; John 2.)

I would, therefore, earnestly desire all the pious (who, with a pure, unadulterated conscience, have drunk the water of love at the foundation of God,) that they do not despise this gift, but that, with candid and discerning minds, they examine, as in the presence of God in Christ Jesus, the nature, principles, vigor, cogency and virtuous tendency; and having thus passed a sound, impartial judgment upon it, that you leave it unbroken in all its parts. For it is my valedictory which I now offer, as I take my leave of you all in this part of the Ban, and retire to rest.

In this I have not sought the acquirement of human favor or honor, the indulgence of the flesh, or the promotion of party purposes, but I have illustrated the principles of truth, confirmed the holy ordinance of the apostles, rendered due praise to the justice and mercy of God, assigning to each its part, have added nothing new, nor varied in the least from its principles of my plan, except that in consequence of much conversation with the pious and meditation upon certain writings, as also on account of great dangers, actual occurrences and heinous abominations, and in order to put a stop in some measure to all offensive, disgraceful actions; I have more deeply considered the excluding sentence of the flagrant, sensual sinner, and, in this way, placed it upon a more certain basis, as may be seen.

We are well convinced that the depth of satan is to some but impartially known and manifest, and as a consequence that he does great injury, by means of his subtle, pernicious wrangling and disputation, as may be seen: therefore, my first earnest request unto all, who are named after the name of Christ, is, that they would reflect soberly, judiciously and discreetly upon the nature, character, heart, mind, spirit and disposition of Christ, and consider that all which he has commanded, left and taught his followers, is nothing but pure righteousness, truth, patience, love and peace. Also, that they bow their knees before him, and have received the token of his most holy covenant, that they should bury their former sinful life in his death, circumcise their hearts with his sharp word and spirit, follow him, walk in all his ways, and be one with him in both the inward and the outward man, as taught in scripture, (Rom. 6; Col. 2,) also that they reflect upon the high promise, and follow his word and will, in power and in truth. For he is such a God, that he does not take pleasure in outward shadows, ceremonies, types, bread, wine, water, nominal service, but in spirit, deed and truth. (2 Cor. 1; Eph. 4; Col. 2.)

My second request is, that they would on the other hand, consider the nature, character, heart, spirit, mind, and work of satan, that he is from the beginning a shrewd, cunning, deceiver, an impudent, wanton liar, and a revengeful murderer, (John 8,) a malicious envier of God's honor and truth; a falsifier of his holy word, and a deadly enemy of pious souls, seditious, factious, unruly, schismatic, envious, perverse, and destitute of love, incapable of conceiving and bringing forth any thing but hatred, backbiting, lies, deception, jealousy, impure hearts, vice and shame, and all in semblance of the truth. In semblance of the truth, I repeat, for although he is the infernal satan, Beelzebub, Belial, Behemoth, Leviathan, the Angel of the bottomless pit, the Prince of darkness, the old Serpent, and the very devil himself, yet it is manifest notwithstanding, that he has the power of transforming himself into an angel of light, as Paul informs us. (2 Cor. 11.)

There is nothing of an external nature oppressive or vexatious to him, if he can only gain possession of the citadel of our heart, and expel therefrom, Christ's nature, disposition, spirit and power; if he can do this he has already won the prize of his craftiness, yea, if a man was even baptized by Peter or Paul himself, had received the bread of the holy supper from the Lord's own hand, would nevermore take part in papistic idolatry, yet if he retained but one of the fruits of the devil, whether hatred, or party spirit, envy or bitterness, avarice or revengefulness, pride or incontinence, or any other vice, we must declare with the scripture that his spirit is devilish, and his life hypocrisy. (Gal. 5 ; 1 John 3.) For it is more than evident that the whole man must be regenerated, sincere, unsophisticated, spiritually minded, godly, holy, devout, united and subject to Christ ; as James says: Whosoever shall keep the whole law and yet offend in one point, he is guilty of all. (James 2.)

Yes, worthy brethren, they who are so far taught of God, that they are able, well and truly to distinguish between Christ and the devil, in relation to their nature, disposition, doctrine, and works, and thereby perceive that Christ's disposition is productive of life, the devil's disposition productive of death, shall, and will undoubtedly, separate and depart entirely, from all vain and unprofitable disputation, schism, separation, division, contention, dissension, sedition, and sectarianism, and also from all deadly abominations, sins, and shameful actions : of this I am fully convinced by the grace of God.

My third request is, that they would all with candor and sincerity of heart, meditate upon the glorious and illustrious names with which they are honored in the scriptures, namely : Children of God, saints and beloved of God, chosen of God, regenerated seed and children of Abraham, seed of peace, plants and scions of righteousness, fruitful grafts of Christ, members of Christ's body, his flesh and bone, Christ's mothers, sisters, brothers, disciples, guests, friends, sons, daughters, maiden, virgin, bride and spouse, His holy vineyard, camp, city, Jerusalem, temple, ark, house, abode, chosen people, citizens of heaven, living stones, companions of the saints, apostles and prophets, household of God, kings and priests, doves, sheep. The light of the world and the salt of the earth, &c. (John 1 ; Col. 3 ; 1 John 3 ; Rom. 9 ; Gal. 3 ; Job 15 ; Eph. 5 ; Matt. 12 ; Mark 3 ; Luke 8 ; Matt. 22 ; Luke 14 ; Rev. 19 ; Isa. 5 ; Rev. 21 ; 1 Pet. 2 ; Eph. 2 ; Matt. 5, 10.) To the end that by such meditation, their conduct inwardly and outwardly, privately and publicly, may be such in all their ways, words, and works, before God, in the presence of the church, and before the whole world that they may by grace, with all the pious, walk worthy of all such glorious names, in all love, peace and harmony, and by his paternal bounty forever escape the severe curse of excommunication, aforementioned, and not hear the stern sentence : Depart from me, ye cursed with the goats to the left hand, (Matt. 25,) but the cheering words : Come ye blessed, with the sheep to the right hand, and so not be numbered in eternity with those, who being bound by the Ban of the word in the power from God, and styled in scripture, a cursed, ungodly race, cursed children, children of wrath, children of the devil, servants of sin, servants of perdition, mockers, revilers, wicked, carnal, perverse, unrighteous, ungodly, stiff-necked sinners, dogs and swine, for whom are reserved the eternal wo, death, fire, lake and torment of hell. (2 Pet. 2 ; Eph. 1 ; John 8 ; Matt. 25 ; 1 Cor. 6 ; Gal. 5 ; Rev. 22.)

My fourth request is, to all those to whom the charge of the Lord's word is committed, who are fellow laborers with me in the ministry, that in all their actions, they so conduct and approve themselves before God and his community, (2 Cor. 6,) that no man can in truth censure or speak evil of them, sincere ministers of Christ, faithful and sound in all things, men full of the Holy Ghost, born of the incorruptible seed of God, encompassed with heavenly light, transplanted into the good disposition of Christ, partakers of his grace, taught and anointed of God, having their minds upon eternal things, hating their own fame, vainglory and impure carnal lusts ; lowly and little in their own eyes, of a meek and gentle spirit, compassionate, merciful, paternal, long-suffering, friendly, humble, chaste, given to hospitality, submissive, (1 Tim. 3, 4 ; Tit. 3,) mild, courteous and peaceful, well versed in the sound doctrine ; seek and act in accordance with the good nature, disposition, character, heart, mind and example of Christ, confirmed in spirit, blameless shepherds, taking oversight of the flock of God, not by constraint, but willingly, not for filthy lucre's sake, nor for the sake of their own bellies, but of a ready mind, (1 Pet. 5,) neither as being lords or rulers, but being examples to the community of Christ, that in consequence of their faithful ministry they may run in fulness of joy upon the mountain of the Lord without fear or shame, and escape unharmed the mouths of fierce and ravenous wolves.

Yes, my brethren, if we could all proceed according to this rule in unity of spirit, unaccompanied by the destructive foxes, how soon would the lamb's bride shine forth in costly and variegated apparel, adorned in white and glittering robes, splendid bracelets, ear-rings and neck-laces, (understand the beauty and ornament of her virtues,) and with the brilliancy of her appearance, excite the admiration of the whole world ; whereas, now, in consequence of deceitful workers, cunning wranglers and sewers of dissension, she must sit, at times, in rags and tatters, and, oh God ! be the scorn and derision of multitudes.

The anguish of my soul is oft times so great that I am unable to write; God omnipotent, strengthen me. And this, because I see that the house of the Lord has to endure so many offences, not only from without, but, alas! from within also. O men! men! arm yourselves! for the words of Paul are true, that the ministry of the New Testament is not a ministry of the letter, but of the spirit. (2 Cor. 3.) Its duties, cannot, therefore, be truly discharged to the glory of God, by the proud, the arrogant, the ambitious, or the self-willed, who wish to perform every thing after their own mind, humor and inclination, but always pull down more than they build up, and do more injury than they do good. This is a necessary consequence, inasmuch as according to the tenor of Paul's doctrine, this ministration is not the depth of wisdom or eloquence, or a dead letter, (with which they are generally replete) but it is God, spirit, truth, power and life, of which they are entirely destitute. O take heed.

Arm yourselves, I repeat; for true teachers are called in scripture, the angels of the Lord and valiant soldiers; be therefore manly, keep the commandment of God; hold fast and waver not. (Ps. 103.) They are called watchmen and trumpeters. Blow your trumpet to the right sound. Watch over the city of God, watch wisely, I say, and neither slumber nor sleep. (Ezek. 33.) Spiritual pillars they are styled. O be steadfast in the truth; bear your burden willingly, waver not, neither be faint. (Exod. 26, 27.) Messengers of peace they are called. Ah, brethren live up to, and justify your name, walk in peace, maintain and break it not. (Isa. 52; Nah. 1.) They are called bishops and overseers. O take great care of the flock of Christ; take great care of them, I say, and see that you neither destroy nor neglect them. (1 Tim. 3; Tit. 1.) Shepherds they are called. O keep and feed the lambs of Christ, and leave them not to pine away. (Eph. 4; Acts 20; 1 Pet. 5.) They are styled teachers. Make known the word and truth of Christ, publish it abroad and conceal it not. (Eph. 4.) They are styled spiritual nurses and fathers. O nourish and cherish your young children; vex them not, neither cast them away. (1 Thess. 2.) They should be as the parent bird to her young. Gather together the young and tender ones in Christ, and scatter them not, nor hurt them. (Matt. 23.) They are called the stewards of God. O perfect the mystery of the name, abuse it not, nor disgrace it. (2 Cor. 4.) They are called the light of the world. Shine and glitter in full glory, and conceal not the brightness of your virtue. (Matt. 5.) They are called the salt of the earth. O let the salt penetrate through and through, and be not ill savored. (Matt. 5, Mark 9; Luke

14.) Ministers in Christ's stead. Ah, brethren serve, but rule not. Let no man glory in any gift, I beseech you. We are receivers, not givers of grace, not of ourselves, observe, servants, and not lords. (1 Cor. 4.) Ah, bow down and submit. My chosen in love and truth, the joy and delight of my soul, so long as you stand fast in the Lord, abide in the way of peace and are faithful to your brethren. (Eph. 4.) Walk worthy of the vocation wherewith you are called; fear your God with all your heart; love the brethren; discharge faithfully the duties of your ministry; rich is he who will reward you. Watch and pray. (1 Pet. 2; 2 Tim. 4; Matt. 26.) Pray, I say, and that with confidence, and so the giver of every good and perfect gift, will not withdraw from you his grace, spirit, love and wisdom., (James 1.) Doubt not, neither be afraid. Let the glorious typified breastplate of Aaron, (Exod. 28,) Christ Jesus, decorated with its beautiful colors, its twelve pearls, its Urim and Thummim, be bound fast to the breast of your conscience, with the two golden chains of the two testaments, and with the two blue laces of pure faith and unadulterated love; wash the feet of your affections, purify them in the spiritual laver, Christ Jesus, with the living water of his eternal and Holy Spirit, take of the blood of his unspotted offering, and in a true spirit, put it on the tip of your right ear, in order rightly to understand his word, and upon the thumb of your right hand, and upon the great toe of your right foot, in order to act and walk uprightly before him, and in the presence of his community. (Exod. 29, 30.) Have your spiritual mitres, girdles and garments made for glory and for beauty, that like verdant olive trees and luxuriant vines, and as burning torches and brilliant luminaries, in the firmament of the holy word, you may serve in fullness of glory, with all the faithful servants of Christ, day and night in his holy temple, to the glory of God and to the reformation of Israel, bring forth abundance of fruit, and when he shall appear with all his chosen saints, apostles and prophets, you shall receive in everlasting joy the promised reward. *Sweet gracious and full of consolation is the word which the Lord utters: Well done, thou good and faithful servant; thou hast been faithful over a few things, I will make thee ruler over many; enter thou into the joy of thy Lord.* (Matt. 25.) *Ah brethren, from our hearts, let us be admonished, that we be faithful to Christ and his community.*

Brethren and sisters, I will now in the peace of Christ, commit you all with one accord into the hand of the King of peace, and I do with Paul entreat you from my heart. (Phil. 2.) If there be any consolation in Christ, if any comfort of love, if any fellowship of the spirit, if any bowels of mercies, fulfil my joy, that you be like minded in the truth, having the same love, being of one accord, of one mind, let nothing be done through strife or vain glory; but in lowliness of mind, let each esteem others better than himself. For you well know by whom and whereunto we are called. Reflect upon this. So that no one may lose himself, on account of other's shameful actions, and abominations, nor destroy the good works of Christ, disturb the peaceable, grieve the pious, offend the weak, give excuse to the wanton, drive the wavering again to the world, bring reproach upon the word of the Lord and his community, bring revilers into repute, and encourage the blood-thirsty; but that we be careful in all things to finish with joy, our course in Christ Jesus, and magnify his holy name, refresh one another in the peace of Christ, strengthen our sick, weak members, and young brethren, reprove the disorderly, publish abroad the truth of the Lord, and show unto all men, a blameless, christian example. To this end may the eternal God of omnipotence, grant us all, collectively and individually, the active spirit of his grace, with perfect obedience and love in Christ Jesus, our Lord. Amen. Ah chosen children, God knows, this is my final adieu to you all. Love the brethren, and beware of dissension.

A PLEASING AND EARNEST

INSTRUCTION AND DOCTRINE HOW ALL PIOUS PARENTS ARE TO GOVERN, DIRECT AND EDUCATE THEIR CHILDREN IN A PIOUS, VIRTUOUS AND GODLY LIFE.

THE wise man says: *Withhold not correction from thy child; for if thou beatest him with the rod, he shall not die. Thou shalt beat him with the rod, and shalt deliver his soul from hell*. (Prov. 23.)

Correct and instruct thy son, and he shall give thee rest; for the rod and reproof give wisdom; but a child left to himself, bringeth his mother to shame. (Prov. 29.)

Chasten thy son while there is hope, &c. (Prov. 19.)

Other foundation can no man lay than that which is laid, which is Christ Jesus. (1 Cor. 3.)

PREFACE. To the elders, in all churches, and chosen of God in Christ Jesus, my beloved brethren in the Lord, unto you be grace, peace and mercy from God, our Father, (Rom. 1; 1 Cor. 1; Gal. 1; Eph. 1; Col. 1; 1 Thes. 1; 2 Thes. 1; 1 Tim. 1; 2 Tim. 1; 1 Pet. 1,) through the merits of our Lord Jesus

Christ, in the power and operation of the Holy Spirit, (Tit. 3,) which he shed on us abundantly, through Jesus Christ, our Saviour; that being justified by his grace, we should be made heirs according to the hope of eternal life. To whom be praise forever and ever. Amen. (Acts 15; Eph. 2; Tit. 3; 2 Tim. 4.)

My dearly beloved brethren in the Lord, we thank the Lord always for you in all our prayers, 2 (Tim. 1,) and pray without ceasing, unto our kind Father, (Luke 18,) that he would strengten you with the gift of his Holy Spirit, that you may be filled with all knowledge, (Eph. 6; Col. 4; 1 Thes. 5; 2 Tim. 1; 1 Eph. 6; Col. 4; 2 Thes. 3,) wisdom, discretion and power necessary rightly to oversee the community of Christ, and to dispense the word of God to sincere, pious souls, according to your gift and calling, and that you may walk worthy of the vocation wherewith you are called and chosen of God and his holy community, as shepherds and teachers, to the end that the saints may be kept firmly united by the common service, to the edification of the body of Christ. Take diligent care of your charge, and display a sincere concern for your flock, at all times earnestly exhort them to love, to good works, (like Paul,) to the pure fear and love of the Lord, to a godly, unblamable conversation, in all humility, righteousness, love, peace, harmony, mercy, and obedience to the whole word of God. Caution them against all false doctrine, and against the sword of evil tongues; for if a man bridle not his tongue, nor restrain it, his worship is vain and unprofitable. Also, that they take heed in their whole walk and conversation, circumcise their hearts, season their words, and do and perform all their actions in the fear of the Lord, that they may procure a good name for the gospel of Christ and his holy community, comply with his word and will, and thus attain unto salvation. Beware of all innovaters and strange doctrines not contained in the word of Christ and his apostles, nor conformable thereunto. Show forth, at all times, Christ and his word. If any man introduce a doctrine differing from that taught by Christ and his word, let him be excommunicated. *For other foundation can no man lay than that which is laid, which is CHRIST JESUS.* (Gen. 17; Phil. 1; 2 Thes. 2; John 5; 1 Cor. 3, 7, 10, 12; Rom. 2, 12; 1 Eph. 1, 4, 5; Prov. 27; 1 Thes. 5; 2 Tim. 4; Tit. 2, 3; Heb. 3; Acts 11, 14, 20, 27; Phil. 1; Ps. 34, 118; 1 Tim. 3; 1 Pet. 3; James 2, 3; Deut. 10; Jer. 4; Phil. 3; Col. 2, 3, 4; Jer. 23, 27, 29; Matt. 22, 24; 1 John 4; Gal. 1; Isa. 28; Mark 12.) He is the precious corner-stone in Zion, which shall abide forever. (Luke 20.) Hear him, believe him, trust in him, follow him, hope and abide in' him, (Rom. 9,) press diligently after him, conforming yourselves unto his spirit, word and life, and you shall neither

35

deceive nor be deceived. (1 Pet. 2; Deut. 18; Matt. 17; 2 Chron. 20: Eccl. 2; Matt. 10; Mark 8; Luke 9, 14.) My dearly beloved brethren in the Lord, I beseech and admonish you, neglect not the ministration of your brotherly love, but attend faithfully thereto. Take heed unto yourselves and to all the flock over which the Holy Ghost has made you overseers, to feed the church of God which he hath purchased with his own blood. (John 10; Ps. 37; Eccl. 2; Rom. 12; 1 Eph. 1, 4; 1 Pet. 1; Heb. 9, 13; Col. 1; 1 Pet. 1; Rev. 5.) Again, all the elders I exhort with Peter, who am also an elder: Feed the flock of God which is among you, taking the oversight thereof, not by contraint, but willingly. (1 Pet. 5.) You who teach obedience, be yourselves obedient to the church of Christ in all things, which are good and expedient, as examples to the flock. (Tit. 2.) As Paul directed Titus, saying: In all things show thyself a pattern of good works; in doctrine, showing uncorruptness, gravity, sincerity, sound speech that cannot be condemned; that he that is of the contrary part may be ashamed, having no evil thing to say of you. Also watch thou in all things, endure affliction, do the work of an evangelist. (2 Tim. 4.) Make full proof of your ministry, do all in the fear of the Lord faithfully, and with obedient and perfect hearts, (2 Chron. 19,) for you are made keepers of the charge of the house, for all the service thereof, and for all that shall be done therein. (Ezek. 44.) Study, therefore, to show yourselves approved unto God, workmen, obedient, blameless, that need not be ashamed, rightly dividing the word of truth. (2 Tim. 2; Tit. 3.) My wish and desire therefore is, that you be earnest in this, so that they who believe in God, may be made zealous to excel in good works, which is good and profitable unto all men, (2 Tim. 4,) instruct, reprove, rebuke, exhort and console, as occasion may require; and forsake not the fraternal assembling of yourselves together, the meeting and ordinance of the Lord. (Heb. 10.) Strengthen one another kindly with the word of the Lord, that you may increase in faith, love and righteousness, and come unto a perfect man, unto the measure of the stature of the fulness of Christ. (Col. 1; Eph. 4.)

With this, dear brethren, I will commit you to almighty God, with the earnest desire that you propound unto all the brethren this brief admonition concerning the Education of children, in order that every one may observe and comply with the same in the full sense, in the bringing up, teaching and instructing his children. The Lord Jesus Christ be with my beloved, yea, dearly beloved brethren throughout eternity. Amen.

ON THE EDUCATION OF CHILDREN.

Unto all elders and joint-heirs in the faith of Christ, grace be to you and peace from God, our heavenly Father, through his beloved Son, Christ Jesus, our Lord and Saviour, (Rom. 1; 1 Cor. 1; 2 Cor. 1; Gal. 19; Col. 1; 1 Thes. 1; 2 Thes. 1; 1 Tim. 1; 2 Tim. 1; 1 Pet 1,) by the power and co-operation of His holy spirit, to his overlasting praise and glory, and to our edification and salvation. Amen.

You are aware, beloved brethren and sisters in Christ Jesus, that we all, without exception, inherit from Adam an ill-disposed, evil and sinful flesh; (Gen. 6, 8; Job 29; Ps. 51,) nay, that all our desires from our youth are evil continually, as Moses writes; also, we find nothing in ourselves, as the proper treasure of our first birth, but perfect blindness, unrighteousness, sin and death. If now the power of this innate disposition is to be diminished, suppressed and destroyed, it must be accomplished by the pure fear of the Lord, which proceeds from a true faith through the word of the Lord, and out of a clear perception of the righteous judgment and terrible wrath of God, which will burn forever against all impenitent sinners. For the fear of the Lord is the beginning of wisdom : it drives out sin and makes upright, pious children, as Jesus Sirach says. (Job 28; Ps. 111; Prov. 1, 9, 19; Eccl. 1; Sirach 12.)

Since, then, the merciful Father of our Lord, Jesus Christ, the great, almighty Lord, has encompassed us with the light of his grace, and through faith in Jesus Christ, has weakened us from iniquity and ungodliness to a life of righteousness; therefore, let us diligenily follow the glorious example of the true love of Matthew, the publican, who was not satisfied with enjoying the heavenly calling and grace himself, but went and invited other publicans and sinners, that they might also be saved and obtain like spirit, grace and mercy from the Lord, for such is the nature and disposition of Christ. (Matt. 9; Mark 2; Luke 5, 19.)

Trade, therefore, among yourselves with the talent (Matt. 25; Mark 13; Luke 19) given you from on high, and cordially compassionate your unbelieving, blind parents, brothers and sisters, husbands, wives, servants and neighbors; do not conceal from them God's gift, grace, word and will; (2 Tim. 2;) for their feet are in the way of death. Perhaps they may, at some time or other, extricate themselves from the snares of unrighteousness in which they are bound and entangled, and turn themselves to the Lord with all their hearts. (2 Chron. 20; Matt. 11, 18; Luke 20.) My dear brethren, understand this as regards men of sense and discretion. Brethren in Christ, if we saw any such in danger of being drowned or burned, or in any danger that threatened his life, and there was a prospect that we could render them assistance, would not our inmost souls be moved with compassion towards them, if haply we might afford them relief? Undoubtedly. And now we see with our own eyes, (if we but believe the Lord's word) that they are walking in the shadow of eternal death, already committed to the grave of hell, and liable to be devoured forever and ever by the eternal, unquenchable fire, unless from their hearts they turn unto Christ and his word, repent, and become regenerated, as the scriptures teach. (2 Chron. 30; Matt. 8, 11; Luke 10; Matt. 3; Mark 1.) Therefore, consider seriously the heart-rending misery and wretchedness of their poor souls which must live forever, either in heaven or in hell, and strive diligently and faithfully whether they may not yet, in some way, by your faithful ministry of pure love, and by the direction and instruction of the divine word, be rescued and delivered from everlasting destruction, and be made partakers of eternal salvation. (Acts 2; John 3; Rom. 6; Eph. 4; Col. 3; Heb. 12; 1 Pet. 2; Rom. 12.) For genuine charity is of such a nature that it is constantly hungering and thirsting after the glory of God and the salvation of all men, even of those who are strangers to us according to the flesh.

Beloved brethren and sisters in Christ Jesus, forasmuch as we are now constrained by saving charity with benevolence and sympathy, and know by the unction of the spirit and word of God, that the nature of man is completely corrupted in Adam, and is opposed from youth to the word of the Lord, (1 John 2; Gen. 6, 8; John 25: Ps. 51) as aforesaid; let us, therefore, be particularly vigilant and solicitous with regard to our own children, displaying unto them a greater degree of spiritual love than towards others; for they are the offspring of our nature, of our flesh and blood, a serious and precious charge committed by God to our especial care. Be, therefore, particularly mindful, that you instruct them from their youth in the way of the Lord, that they fear and love God, walk in all modesty and submission; be genteel, well-disposed, discreet, honor and obey their father and mother, using reasonable discourse, not lying, nor clamorous, not stubborn nor self-willed; for such is not becoming the children of the saints. (Deut. 6, 16; Ex. 20; Eccl. 3, 7; Tob. 4; Eph. 6.) The world desire for their children that which is earthly and perishable, money, honor, fame, wealth. From infancy they train them up to vice, pride, haughtiness and idolatry. But with you, who are born of God, this is not the case; (John 1, 3) for it behooves you to seek something else for your children; namely, that which is heavenly and eternal, and hence it is your duty to bring them up in the nurture and admonition of the Lord, as Paul teaches. (Eph. 6.) Moses commanded Israel to teach their children the law and commandments of the Lord, to talk of them when they sat down in their houses, and when they walked by the way, and when they lay down, and when they rose up. Now, since we are a chosen generation, a royal priesthood, a holy nation, a peculiar people; that we should show forth the praises of him who hath called us out of darkness into his marvellous light, (Exod. 19; 1 Pet. 2; Rev. 1, 5; Deut. 7,) it greatly behooves us to show ourselves patterns and examples (Isa. 4, 3; 1 Pet. 2) in all righteousness and blamelessness, and to appear unto the whole world as we are thereunto called; for if we do not keep a strict eye upon our own children, but permit them to follow the inclination of their evil, corrupted nature and disposition, not correcting and chastising them according to the word of the Lord, we may with the greatest propriety lay our hand upon our mouth, and remain silent and speechless. (Rom. 12; 1 Thess 4; 1 Pet. 1, 5; 1 Tim. 4; Tit. 2; Eccl. 7; Prov. 13.) For why should we teach those not of our household, when we take no pains to preserve our own families in the love and fear of God? For, says Paul, (1 Tim. 3, 5) if a man provide not for his own house, he hath denied the faith and is worse than an infidel.

My dearly beloved brethren and sisters in Christ Jesus, take heed that you do not ruin your children through carnal love, by giving offence, and training them up in vice lest in the day of judgment their souls be required at your hands, and it happen unto you, on account of your children, as it did unto Eli, the high priest, by the chastening hand of the Almighty, on account of his sons; (1 Sam. 4;) but diligently imitate the testimony declared by the angel of the Lord respecting pious Abraham: I know, says he, that Abraham will command his children and his household after him, and they shall keep the way of the Lord, to do justice and judgment. (Gen. 18.) For this is the chief and most important care of the godly that their children may fear God, do good, and be saved; even as the God-fearing Tobias admonished his son's children, saying: My son hearken unto thy father, serve the Lord in truth, and cleave unto him in equity; be mindful of him, and let not thy will be set to sin or to transgress his commandments; teach this to thy children that they give alms, fear God all their days, and trust in him with their whole hearts. (Deut. 6; Jos. 24; 1 Sam. 7; Tob. 14, 4; 2 Chron. 20; Sirach 2.)

My beloved brethren and sisters in Christ, who, from your hearts, love the word of the Lord, thus instruct your children from youth up, and daily admonish them with the word of the Lord, setting a good example. (Eph. 6.) Teach and admonish them, I say, in proportion to the development of their understanding; constrain and correct them with discretion and moderation, without anger or bitterness, (Col. 3,) lest they be discouraged; spare not the rod, if reason and necessity require it, reflecting upon what is written. (Prov. 13, 19, 23, 29.) He that loveth his son causeth him oft to feel the rod that he may have joy of him in the end. He that chastiseth his son shall have joy in him. (Sirach 7, 30.) He that maketh too much of his son shall bind up his wounds, and his bowels will be troubled at every cry. A horse unbroken becometh headstrong: and a child left to himself will be wilful. Give him no liberty in his youth, and wink not at his follies. Bow down his neck while he is young, (observe,) lest he wax stubborn, and be disobedient to thee, and so bring sorrow to thine heart. (Heb. 12; Deut. 6; Prov. 29; Sirach 30.) Correct thy son, and keep him from idleness, lest thou be made ashamed on his account. (Sirach 22; Prov. 29.)

Dearly beloved brethren and sisters in the Lord, if all parents, (who glory in the name of the Lord,) would deeply impress the words of Sirach upon their hearts, and inscribe them on the tablet of their souls, O how virtuous, pious and devout would many children be raised, who now, alas! run wild and unrestrained, honoring neither their parents, nor the community and gospel of Christ. An evil-nurtured son, (says Sirach, chap. 22,) is the dishonor of his father; again, says he: (chap. 16,) Rejoice not that thou hast a multitude of children, except the fear of God be with them; for one that is just, is better than a thousand ungodly; and better it is to die without children, than to have them that are ungodly. (Sir. 16.)

Beloved brethren, consider these words well, and revolve them in your minds. Necessity impels me to write; for some, alas! live such lives with their children, that one is constrained to write and reprove. I write and admonish you again: Take heed, lest the blood and condemnation of your children come upon you. If you love your children with a godly love, teach them, admonish and instruct them in God, (Prov. 13, 29; Eccl. 30,) lest the Lord's word, blood and death be made unto them of no effect, and his name and community be blasphemed by the unwise, through them. (Rom. 2.)

Beloved brethren in Christ, if you rightly know God and his word, and believe that the end of the righteous is everlasting life, and the end of the wicked eternal death, endeavor to the utmost of your power, to conduct your children in the way of life, and divert them from the way of death, as far as in you lies. Pray almighty God for the gift of his grace, that in his great mercy, he may guide and preserve them in the right path, through the directing influence of his Holy Spirit. Watch over their salvation as for your own souls. Teach, instruct, admonish, threaten, correct and chastise them, as circumstances require. Keep them away from naughty, wicked children, among whom they hear and learn nothing but lying, cursing, swearing, fighting and knavery. Have them instructed in reading and writing, bring them up to habits of industry, and let them learn such trades as are suitable, expedient and adapted to their age and constitution. If you do this, you shall live to see much honor and joy of your children. (Sirach 30.) But if you do it not, heaviness of heart shall consume you at last. (Jer. 22.) For a child left to himself, without reproof, is not only the shame of his father, but he bringeth his mother to shame. (Prov. 29.)

This brief admonition I have written to my beloved, from motives of sincere love, and not without a reason ; for in the course of my ministry, I have too frequently observed, how disorderly, improperly, nay, heathenlike, many parents conduct themselves towards their children. The absurd, senseless love of the flesh, has such an influence over some, and they are so blinded by the natural affection for their children, (O observe,) that they can neither see, perceive nor observe any evil, error or defect in them, notwithstanding they frequently abound in idle tricks and wantonness, are disobedient to father and mother, murmur at them, collect and carry abroad lies, quarrel and fight with other children, and mock people as they pass by, crying and calling after them.

Brethren in Christ, to connive, by reason of a blind, carnal love, at these and similar disgraceful tricks of children, is a love not to be applauded, but much rather to be shunned and avoided ; for it is earthly, sensual, devilish. And forasmuch, as we ought to be the salt of the earth, the light of the world, the holy nation, the chosen generation, yea, the bride of Christ, it by no means becomes us, to have, or to bear such sensual love or preposterous affection, in any circumstances, towards our children ; but it is our duty, as far as in us lies, diligently and earnestly to instruct and govern our children and household, as well as ourselves, in conformity to the sincerity of godliness, a life of virtue, and the word of God. (Matt. 5 ; Mark 9 ; Luke 14 ; Prov. 4 ; Wis. 2 ; Mark 4 ; Luke 8 ; Phil. 2 ; 1 Pet. 2 ; Deut. 7 ; Exod. 19 ; 2 Cor. 11 ; Eph. 5 ; Rev. 19, 28 ; Acts 20.)

With this, I will have delivered and preserved my soul in the presence of the Lord and his community, and I do desire, for the Lord's sake, that this epistle may be taken in good part, and be read by the elders, in the hearing of all the brethren, to the end that the innocent may take heed, and be circumspect, and those who are guilty of these mis-steps, errors and failings, may reform, and that without considering me as being officious, in regulating the concerns of their household. Ah no ! in the presence of God, I desire nothing in this, but that in all things, you conform yourselves to the scriptures, and to christian gravity, and that all the concerns of the Lord's community, may be conducted according to the divine will and ordinance. (1 Cor. 14.) The searcher of hearts and reins knows that I lie not. I would, therefore, that you also accept and receive it in love; for in sincerity have I written it. (1 Sam. 16; 1 Chron. 29; Ps. 7; Jer. 17; Acts 1; Rev. 2.)

And now, beloved brethren and sisters, I commend you to God, and to the word of his grace, which is able to build you up, and to give you an inheritance among all them which are sanctified. (Acts 20.)

The very God of peace sanctify you wholly, that your whole spirit, and soul, and body be preserved without spot, and blameless, unto the coming of our Lord Jesus Christ. (1 Thess. 5.) Faithful is he who called you. May the merciful Father, through his beloved Son, Jesus Christ, our Lord, strengthen you all with the precious gift of his Holy Spirit. Amen.

LETTER TO THE BRETHREN IN AMSTERDAM.

Jesus said to Martha : *I am the resurrection, and the life, he that believeth in me, though he were dead, yet shall he live ; and whosoever liveth and believeth in me shall never die.* (John xi. 25, 26.)

Chosen Brethren and Sisters in the Lord :—Since I hear that the fire of the pestilence is spreading itself among you, I am constrained by love, which I bear towards you and all the pious ; because I know that all flesh is afraid of death, and the death of our friends is grievous to us) to visit you with a letter of consolation, who are encompassed by the heavenly light, and are called to the communion of Christ ; so that you might watch now, and at all times, for the coming of the Lord ; prepare yourselves in all things to meet death. For Paul says : *It is appointed unto men once to die, but after this judgment.* (Heb. ix. 27.) And Sirach says : *All flesh waxeth old as a garment, for the covenant from the beginning is :* THOU SHALT DIE. (Sirach xiv. 17.)

If we then adhere closely to Christ with a regenerated and penitent soul ; and truly believe his word, and faithfully follow his footsteps ; and are governed by his Holy Ghost . . . . . Then shall we live in, with and through him eternally ; *and we shall not be hurt of the second death.* (Rev. ii. 11.) Though we were, in times past even as others, dead in sin, full of avarice, unchastity, pride, hatred, envy, idolatry and all manner of wickedness, children of hell and of the devil. (Eph. ii. 3, 12.) For all things are forgiven to the penitent and believing through the death of Christ, and satisfied with his blood, and reconciled by the only peace-offering of his innocent and painful death. So that Paul says: *There is therefore, now no condemnation to them which are in Christ Jesus, who walk not after the flesh, but after the spirit; for the law of the spirit of life in Christ Jesus hath made me free from the law of sin and death.* (Rom. viii. 1, 2.) Therefore, be of good cheer, and be grateful; praise Him who has redeemed you by the power of his word, from the dominion of sin and death; and called you through the spirit of his grace to the inheritance of his glory. Again, I say, laud him, and that with a pious and pure conscience, with an unblamable and holy life by faith . . . . So that when the true householder, the king and bridegroom of our souls comes, he may not find you sleeping, and cast you unprepared into eternal darkness, close the door upon you and give you a portion with the Gentiles. Therefore: *Be sober, vigilant!* (1 Pet. v. 8.) *Wake while you have the light, lest darkness come upon you.* (John xii. 25.)

Faithful brethren! be strong in the Lord, be of good cheer, for all your doings, life and death are in the hands of the Lord. Yea, *the hairs of your head are all numbered.* (Matt. x. 30.) And without his will, not one can fall from your head. The number of your days are before him; yea, the time of your life is measured as to a hand-breadth. Therefore, fear not; but willingly assist and serve each other in time of distress. Be not slow to visit the sick; for that shall make you beloved, as Sirach says. (Sir. vii. 35) And you ought out of unfeigned love, as John says: *To lay down your lives for the brethren.* (1 John iii. 16.)

For this you know, that a virtuous son, servant, or bride, fears not the coming of the father, lord or bridegroom, but that there is nothing but desire and hope, as long as they have not yet arrived. For John says: *There is no fear in love; but perfect love casteth out fear.* (1 John iv. 18.)

You also know, that a wearied laborer is delirous of rest, and a drooping soul of consolation. And I doubt not, nor you, my dear children, that you are assured of a quiet conscience in God, that he is your Father; and that Jesus Christ is your Lord, and you his servants; that he is your bridegroom, and you his spouse. Why you must endure so much misery, toil, anguish of mind, shame and disgrace, from a perverse, idle generation, for his blessed and holy name's sake—whom you ought to make known to the whole world, without hypocrisy, in order that they may turn to God as true penitents.

Therefore, we must not fear death so greatly, which is but a rest from sin, an entrance to a better life; nor must we be grieved so much on account of our friends, who fell asleep in the Lord; as those who do not expect the reward of the saints.

But, let us, therefore, lift our heads with joy, gird the loins of our minds with truth, and prepare for the heavenly Canaan, that we may inherit the only and eternal Joshua, Christ Jesus, the inheritance and kingdom, which are appointed to us; and thus be released from the arduous and tedious way of our pilgrimage, which we have to make through this untrodden wilderness. Then we shall rest in eternal joys.

O chosen brethren and sisters! How highly and gloriously they are endowed of God, who are here, through grace, freed from the body of sin, redeemed from the vanity of perishable things, received into the holy tabernacles of peace, called to the eternal, great and holy sabbath! There the crooked, old serpent will no more sting them in their heels, neither pain nor misery shall touch them; and the last enemy, death, shall be overcome and swallowed up. Then their tears will be wiped off, and their souls will enjoy a true rest and peace, in Paradise and the pleasure garden of grace, in Abraham's bosom, under the altar of God. (Rev. vi. 9.) They came out of great tribulations, they stand upon Mount Sion, in white robes, worshipping before the throne of GOD and the LAMB; and rest for a little season, till the number of their fellow-servants be fulfilled. (Rev. vi. 11.) And then be together changed into the glory of Christ; (Phil. iii. 21.) to shine as the sun. (Matt. xiii. 43.) And thus come to the eternal festivity, the eternal joys, prepared for all the chosen in heaven through Christ's blood and death.

O! how holy and happy are they who are called of Christ to his holy day, and come to it dressed in clean garments? Come, sing the pleasing and joyful hallelujah, in your hearts, and thank him, who has ordered all this toward them, by the spirit of his love, through grace, and has chosen you with them to the same. Reflect upon this, and be comforted.

Nothing more; but fear your God, with all your hearts; serve him in truth; maintain union, love and peace among you; watch and pray; be patient in your conflicts; seek that which is best; follow after that which is good; be friendly towards one another; willingly obey your teachers, and remember them and me in your prayers. May the God of peace, our merciful Father, through his blessed Son, Jesus Christ, bless you now and forever, to abound more in righteousness and perfect love.

MENNO SIMON,
Your fellow brother, and lover of your souls in truth.

FOR OTHER FOUNDATION CAN NO MAN LAY THAN THAT IS LAID, WHICH IS JESUS CHRIST. (Cor. iii. 11.)

INDEX.

CPSIA information can be obtained
at www.ICGtesting.com
Printed in the USA
BVHW091453260819
556817BV00019B/2641/P

9 780371 058114